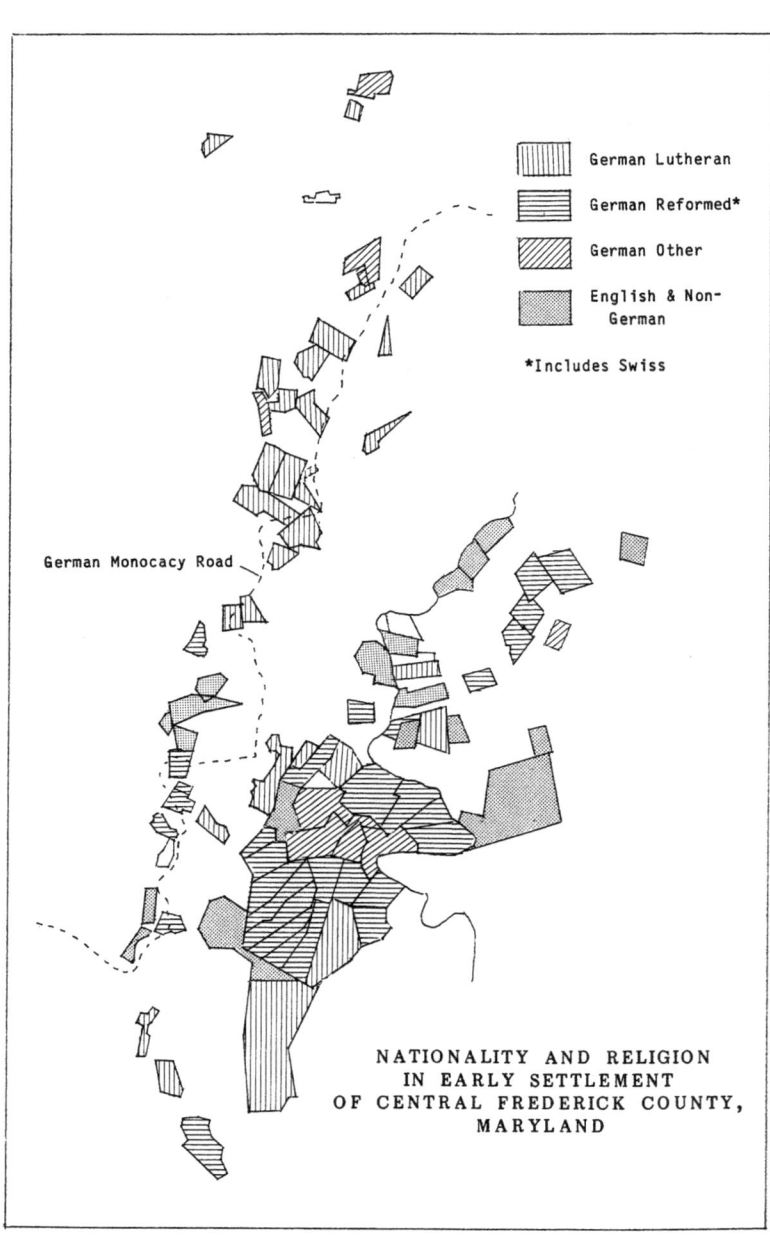

PIONEERS OF OLD MONOCACY

The Early Settlement of Frederick County, Maryland

1721-1743

By
Grace L. Tracey
and
John P. Dern

CLEARFIELD

Copyright © 1987 by the
Historical Society of Carroll County [Maryland]
All Rights Reserved
Published by Genealogical Publishing Co., Inc.
Baltimore, Maryland
Second Printing, 1989
Library of Congress Catalogue Card Number 86-83226
International Standard Book Number 0-8063-1183-5
Made in the United States of America

Reprinted for
Clearfield Company, Inc. by
Genealogical Publishing Co., Inc.
Baltimore, Maryland
1998, 2000, 2001, 2002

ADDENDA & CORRIGENDA

pp. 84, 96: John Beall was the son of John Beall (Beals) and Mary Clayton, not of Robert Beall.

pp. 106, 315: Recent research in Chester County (Penna.) tax lists by Peter S. Craig has fairly well established that brothers Joseph Hedges (d 1732) and Charles Hedges (1673e-1743) were sons of William Hedges who died in New Castle County in 1678. The William Hedges who acquired "Hedge Hogg" after 1740 (see p. 112) was a son of Charles Hedges and so a nephew of Joseph Hedges, the land's original patentee.

pp. 109, 114, 309: John BIGGS's second wife Mary Stilly or Stell was not the widow of Jacob Stilley, who died after John Biggs.

pp. 155, 171, 365, 367, 372: For Thomas House read John House.

p. 272: Third paragraph should read: Joseph Brunner lived another five years, signing a deed to his son on January 17, 1753. Because no wife signed off her dower rights, she presumably died before him.

p. 272: Sellers as the maiden name for Henry Brunner's wife Maria Magdalena should be omitted.

p. 296: Samuel Fleming cannot be substantiated as a son-in-law of Daniel Dulany the Younger.

p. 336, last line: In 1767 title to "The Disappointment" passed from Edward Diggs to Jacob and David Martin.

p. 428: Add to the Index, Renn, Bernard 201.

CONTENTS

Introduction	1
Early Explorers and Traders	7
Land Investors and Speculators	23
The Monocacy Area and Its Roads	45
Point of Rocks	59
Carroll Creek	69
The Quakers at "Monoquesey"	79
Sugar Loaf's Shadow	89
Upper Potomac	94
Upper Linganore	99
The Hedges Family	106
"Dulany's Lot"	115
Arrival of the Germans	130
Lower German Settlement	154
Upper German Settlement	185
Catoctin Valley	222
New Market Area	228
Flat Run (Emmitsburg)	237
Middletown Area	243
The Catholic Settlement	247
"Tasker's Chance"	257
Monocacy Manor	302
Rocky Ridge	324
Mid-Monocacy	337
All Saints' Parish	348
Epilogue	356
Appendix	359
Bibliography	381
Index	390

MAPS AND TABLES

Nationality and Religion in Early Settlement	ii
Franz Michel's Map of 1707	8
Christoph von Graffenried's 1712 Map	11
Philemon Lloyd's 1721 "Potowmack" Map	12
Major Investor Surveys	24
The Carroll Family	26
Carrollton	29
Relationship of Early Maryland Families	32
Landholdings East of the Monocacy River	34
Merryland Tract, 1762	38
Monocacy Rivers and Creeks	46
First Surveys in Creagerstown Area	49
Probable Routes of Early Monocacy Roads	51
Key to Settlement Maps	58
Point of Rocks Settlement	60
Carroll Creek Settlement	70
Quaker Settlement	80
Sugar Loaf Settlement	90
Upper Potomac Settlement	95
Upper Linganore and Beaver Dam Area	100
Hedges Family Land	107
"Dulanys Lot"	116
Lower German Settlement	155
Upper German Settlement	186
Catoctin Valley Settlement	223
New Market Area	229
Flat Run Settlement	238
Middletown Area	244
Catholic Settlement	248
"Taskers Chance"	259
Monocacy Manor Lessees, 1741-1743	304
Monocacy Manor, 1757	307
Monocacy Manor, 1781	322
Rocky Ridge Area	325
Mid-Monocacy Area	338

INTRODUCTION

In the early 1930s Dr. Arthur G. Tracey of Hampstead, Maryland turned his avocational interests to the subject of early land grants in the western portion of his state. Maryland's Land Office, which had been formed in Colonial days long before, was still in existence. But its function of governing and regulating initial grants of land to first-time owners had become almost a thing of the past. No longer was there land remaining which had not already been passed to private ownership. The Office had become little more than an anachronism, a sinecure with scant interest in the accumulated records and virtually no concern for the proper archival maintenance of those records.

To retrieve anything of historical importance involved therefore a process of digging one's own way through much unorganized material. This Dr. Tracey did by directing his attention to the accumulation of thousands of certificates prepared by surveyors at the time land was first granted. Each survey included a drawing accompanied by a description of the metes and bounds of the parcel or lot. By tracing onto tissue paper what these surveyors had drafted, Dr. Tracey was able to accumulate from out of countless envelopes and folders a huge file of material showing in one series and in one place a picture of what Maryland's initial individual land grants had actually been.

Next came the process of discovering from reference clues in the surveys themselves where the land had lain and how the location of the various individual parcels related to such natural features as mountains, streams and roads, and how they all fitted together one parcel in relation to the others. Not to be forgotten, either, was the problem of careful referencing of all such diagrams to the original records at the Land Office itself as well as the construction of a system of map coordinates from which tissue tracings, card files and maps could be related to each other.

To appeciate the immensity of the study, one should view this material personally. One should likewise visualize the nature of the work at the time it was performed. Xerox copying machines or other economical means of photoreproduction did not then exist. Mathematical multiplications were made by painstaking use of logarithms. Trigonometrical functions were found in tables instead of hand-held calculators. To reduce a surveyor's scale of 100 perches or rods per inch to a more workable scale of an inch to the mile required the use of a large desk-top pantograph. In sum, it was not easy. Fortunately, however, Dr. Tracey had the help of his daughter, Dr. Grace L. Tracey, who worked with him and continued the work after his death in 1960.

For further understanding of the Tracey material we would do well to review the methods by which early settlers acquired their land. Maryland, it will be remembered, was granted to the Lords Baltimore almost as a feudal fiefdom. The land was theirs to do with almost as they pleased. They were able to govern its use and, in the absence of mines or other special resources, on its use their income depended. Land had value only if it were cleared and worked by settlers. Therefore at first the land was granted to individuals in exchange for their settling a given number of people on that land. By about 1683, however, actual settlement had progressed well enough that such "rights" based on settlement gave way to actual purchase of the land, with settlers paying "caution money" to the Proprietor as the price of land acquisition. This amounted at first to 200 pounds of tobacco per hundred acres, but increased inexorably over time.

The method of obtaining land involved the following. An individual applied for a **warrant** for a given number of acres where he had found vacant, unoccupied land. Beginning with the restoration of Proprietary rights in 1715,[1] his application, accompanied by a purchase payment, or **caution money**, was directed to the Colony's Land Office, headed by a Judge and Register. He in turn issued the warrant, directing the Surveyor General to designate a deputy surveyor in the County concerned who was to lay out the land, marking and describing its location, its point of beginning, nearby geographic features, often the names of adjoining parcels or owners and, most importantly, the courses and distances necessary to describe the size and shape of the parcel. The surveyor then prepared a **certificate of survey** which summarized this information and included a plat diagram of the proposed parcel. The certificate was returned to the Land Office where it was checked for conflicts through encroachments or overlaps on existing land grants. These certificates are kept today at the Maryland Archives Hall of Records, filed by the Counties which existed at the time of the survey.

If all was in order, the survey information was then recorded in bound volumes and a **patent** was issued granting title in fee simple to the person for whom the survey had been made or, in some cases, to the individual to whom the certificate of survey may have been assigned. From this point on, the land was owned by the individual, who was then free to do with it as he wished. It was subject only to a small annual quitrent and to escheat[2]. After 1733, for example, quitrents amounted to four shillings per hundred acres, in effect a property tax on the land. Ownership was also subject to an alienation fine assessed at each subsequent transfer of title to a new owner. These two sources of revenue together with the original "caution money" made up the major portion of revenue received by the Proprietor from his Maryland lands.[3] By far the most important of

---

[1] From 1689, following the "Glorious Revolution" against the threat of Catholicism, until 1715 at the end of Queen Anne's reign, Maryland was governed as a crown colony.

[2] Land could revert to the Proprietor in the absence of heirs or in case of non-payment of the quitrent.

[3] A fourth source of revenue from the land came from Manors, large parcels of a thousand acres or more, which were leased to tenants, rather than granted outright. This practice, employed by

these were the quitrents, which brought a greater total return than did the sale of the land itself.

It was the task of the Land Office to record all patents and certificates of survey, as well as assignments if such occurred. These were copied into a series of bound volumes which comprise the so-called "Patent Series" portion of the Maryland Land Office Records. Generally patents were kept in one volume, certificates of survey and assignments in another, but by itself the Liber number does not indicate whether the volume contains patents or certificates of survey. The periods covered by the two types of records were not contemporaneous, nor was each type segregated according to specific time periods. Dates also overlapped between given volumes. Thus Liber EI 2 contains patents from 1734-1739, EI 4 1734-1740 and EI 6 1737-1744, while Liber EI 3 includes certificates and assignments 1730-1737, EI 5 1734-1741, etc. The Liber designation consisted of letter initials and numbers. These varied over time as new series were begun, thereby resulting in what more aptly could be termed a "series of series." The Liber EI series, for example, consisted of six volumes, EI 1 through EI 6 (1730-1744). Liber BT & BY 3 represented a single volume following PT 1 and PT 2. The last series, which terminated with the end of the Colonial period, ran from BC & GS 1 through BC & GS 51 (1751-1777).

All of these volumes and series have now been placed in a single "Patent Series" numbering from Liber 0 to Liber 132, housed currently with the Maryland State Archives at the Hall of Records in Annapolis. Since the current arrangement was made after the Traceys began their work, it would be manifestly impossible to alter the thousands of tracings, indexes and cross-references in the Tracey files to reflect this change. Therefore their collection as well as related references in this work remain based on the old "series of series." Fortunately, because the Hall of Records Indexes were also based on the old series, personnel there today likewise use the old groupings! For ease of conversion, however, one may readily consult the excellent treatise by Elisabeth Hartsook correlating the two systems.[4] In addition, an appendix has been included with this work converting the two arrangements for the period covered by this study. In the pages which follow, certificates of survey in the "Patent Series" are referred to in footnote citations by the abbreviation "C/S." References to Patents are not abbreviated.

Also important in a study of land records are the **Rent Rolls**

---

large landholders as well as the Proprietor himself, is discussed further in the Chapter on "Monocacy Manor," pp. 302-323.

[4] Elizabeth Hartsook and Gust Skordas, *Land Office and Prerogative Court Records of Colonial Maryland* (Maryland Hall of Records Commission, 1946), pp. 13-77. The revised arrangement singles out into a separate series those 42 volumes pertaining solely to warrants. But in the remaining series it does not segregate patents from certificates of survey, nor does it alter the confused overlapping of time periods between given volumes. Proposed computerization, though possibly imminent, still remains at this writing a problem -- or an opportunity -- for the future.

and **Debt Books.** Here, however, a distinction must be drawn between the public nature of surveys and patents described above and the private nature of purely revenue records kept more or less as account books for the Proprietor. In the beginning, all land records were considered private Proprietary matters. With the growing emphasis on the public nature of Land Office transactions, however, a fuzziness developed in the distinction between the public and private nature of the two. It might have been more consistent for the revenue records to have been kept separately in the Receiver General's Office. But the connection with Land Office operations was so close that for practical purposes both public and private records were left together. And there, for the most part, they remained after the Proprietorship ceased to exist at the time of independence from England.

Quitrent was due the Proprietor on all land which had been granted to individuals. To assure this, Rent Roll keepers were appointed for each Shore. They in turn worked through quitrent farmers, or deputy sheriffs, whose duty it was to make the semi-annual collections in their respective areas and to remit the revenue to the Proprietor's Rent Roll Keeper. Kept by Counties, Rent Rolls showed what had been paid and what was yet due. These Rolls listed, under the name of each parcel, the names of the individual to whom the land had originally been granted and who then owned it, together with the acreage and the amount of quitrent due. They also showed alienations or subsequent sales and leases. Debt Books, on the other hand, listed the same information in reverse, being arranged by name of the individual owning the land. This was a later development and a much more effective arrangement. Debt Books were compiled annually. But since those for Prince George's[5] and Frederick County were not begun until 1753, they are not of great importance in this study.

In theory the keeping of Rent Rolls was of sound economic necessity. But during the royal period (1689-1715) the actual maintenance of the Rent Rolls grew very lax. Moreover, shortly after the restoration of Proprietary Government, quitrents were temporarily abolished in favor of a tobacco tax instituted in their place. Such factors led to a highly unsatisfactory current set of Rent Rolls. Especially on the Western Shore, they were irregular, haphazardly kept and confusing. It was therefore difficult, if not virtually impossible even after 1733, to continue such rolls. Efforts were made to compile new Rent Rolls every few years, basing them as best one could on such unsatisfactory old ones. But their very incompleteness has often led to confusion and misinterpretation, wherein even this study may err.

This brings us to the pages which follow. As Dr. Grace L. Tracey gradually took over the work of her father, it became apparent to her that perhaps an important next step, after satisfactorily locating and describing the land of the early settlers, was to know something more of those settlers themselves. Without becoming

---

[5] Prince George's County was the parent County of Frederick County. The latter was formed in 1748, actually after the period covered by this work.

enmeshed in the creation or utilization of countless genealogical studies, she nevertheless set out to assemble what she and others could bring together concerning those first inhabitants. From the outset she sought to concentrate on primary material coming from the records themselves. So doing, she began a review of County deeds, wills and inventories, court judgment records and rent rolls, together with gleanings from the Calvert Papers and the Archives of Maryland. This emphasis on primary source material will account for the detailed use of footnotes in the following pages. They are designed to offer springboards to the researcher who wishes to dig deeper and pursue more directly a particular subject. Our apologies are tendered to the more casual reader who feels encumbered by them!

Because of the sheer scope of the undertaking, Dr. Tracey found it necessary to set both geographic and time limitations on her first studies. She therefore directed her initial attention to the Monocacy Valley and the mountainous country to the west, the area which eventually became Frederick County.[6] Here the significant beginnings of the first settlements away from Maryland's tidewater area occurred and here much of subsequent history was based. Approximately two decades encompassed the period of isolated settlements scattered throughout this geographical area. During that time the way was paved toward consolidation of settlements throughout the entire area and foundations were laid for the beginnings of villages and towns. The story of these subsequent periods remains for further historical treatises. The material in the Tracey land records is vast enough to provide excellent springboards for such studies.

Thus these pages concentrate primarily on settlers and the land they had obtained through the year 1743. While some history of the land and its people is included after that date, the subject matter is for the most part restricted to that land which had been granted up to 1743. The period is an important one, for it precedes even the beginning of church records, ordinarily the first detailed sources relating to early individuals. One cannot, however, overemphasize how small a portion of the total Tracey land records, in scope of both area and time, is therefore covered here. Also omitted is the story of those settlers who were present either as squatters or as residents living with others but who did not own land themselves. Their numbers and importance can only be guessed.

It was my pleasure, because of common historical interests, to have worked for a number of years with Dr. Tracey in this endeavor. She was able to put together a rough draft manuscript which she

---

[6] Frederick County, which initially encompassed all of western Maryland, was split away from Prince George's County in 1748. The area west of today's Frederick County, separated by the ridge known as South Mountain, subsequently evolved into three other counties, beginning with Washington County in 1776. In 1837 Carroll County was formed out of eastern Frederick County and western Baltimore County. Its border with Frederick County now follows Sam's, Little Pipe and Double Pipe Creeks until they join the Monocacy River west of Detour, Maryland.

titled "Notes from the Records of Old Monocacy." It was more or less a preliminary cut-and-try typescript effort, which made it obvious to us both that innumerable corrections and considerable research yet remained, not to mention an adequate polishing of the material already at hand. As long as she lived, we were able to pursue these matters together. But after she died in 1972, it became apparent that henceforth the Tracey material was only as valuable and as available as the calibre and interest of the personnel associated with its custody.

Physical safe keeping was guaranteed by the Historical Society of Carroll County in Westminster, Maryland, where the files and material now remain. But only recently has the Society found a person with the dedication, perseverence and intelligence necessary to bring these Tracey holdings back to life. That person is Joanne Scandling Manwaring. Although the observation may be tritely overworked, it is nevertheless fundamentally true that the final publication of these pages would have been completely impossible without her help. We have also had immeasurable assistance and counsel from Millard M. Rice, who over the years has contributed an incredible amount in the way of knowledge and interest in the Tracey work.

Our attention to original source records has an admitted limitation in that the research has been based primarily in Maryland records. While attention has been directed to material located elsewhere, much work remains before all the available records affecting the story of Maryland settlement may be considered fully explored. This is especially true in Pennsylvania where additional material covering the earlier history of Germans before they became Maryland settlers should be sifted. Church records there have not been read in the original as they have been in Maryland, and Pennsylvania land records themselves await as thorough a treatment as given by the Traceys to their Maryland counterparts.

A caveat should be entered concerning the maps included in this work. They are suggestive, rather than precisely conclusive as to both configuration and location of the land itself. Since there was often a difference between where the land actually lay and where the surveyors said it lay, our reliance on the original surveys themselves will not always portray what was intended or what is established today. For precise locations one must still work a complete title search, platting descriptions as he goes, from the earliest surveys to present deeds.

A final word may also be in order concerning what may seem to be needless repetition of material previously published. During the nearly thirty years that this manuscript has been in preparation, various historians and genealogists have quoted from its preliminary draft. For the record it seems only fair that what originally came from the Tracey manuscript should appear in its final form. With such inclusion it is our hope that the work may be considered, as it was originally intended, a source book from the Records of Old Monocacy.

John P. Dern
950 Palomar Drive
Redwood City, Calif.

EARLY EXPLORERS AND TRADERS

Years before there was even a dream that a Maryland town would nestle along the Monocacy River in the shadow of Catoctin Mountain, Indians, explorers, adventurers and traders made their way through the wooded hills and along the plentiful springs and streams in the area that is now Frederick County. The River which flows southward through this once forested valley was called Cheneoowquoque by the Seneca Indians. Early white visitors named it Quattaro or Coturki. Then, by what seemed to be general consent, the Shawnee name Monnockkesey was adopted in simplified form, and both River and surrounding area became known as **MONOCACY**.

The Monocacy region has always been a picturesque one. To the River's east lies a gently rolling countryside of rich farmland through which a series of streams wind their way to join the Monocacy. To the west the hills rise much more rapidly, forming a succession of elevated ranges which parallel the Monocacy River from north to south. The first of these is Catoctin Mountain, and beyond it, separated by the the valley of Catoctin Creek, lies South Mountain, now the boundary between Frederick and Washington Counties. These heights rise to nearly two thousand feet. In silhouette they remind one, not without significance in the history of settlements which were to follow, of the Palatinate hills in southwestern Germany. All these natural features of the Monocacy area — the Monocacy River itself, the creeks and the mountains — stretch southward until they ultimately meet the broad Potomac River, and there the Monocacy area ends.

In early days when the first English arrived in Maryland, the Conoy Indians, an Algonquian tribe, were settled at Piscataway Indian village on Piscataway Creek. Harassed by other tribes, they abandoned their villages and moved up the Potomac to make a temporary home, first about 1697, in the Opequon valley of today's West Virginia and shortly afterwards on and near what is now Heaters Island in the Potomac, just below present-day Point of Rocks. The spring on the Maryland side from which they carried their drinking water was surrounded by jetting rocks, magnolias and other deep foliage. It can still be seen near Rock Hall. When representatives from the Governor of Virginia visited the Conoys in 1699, they found the tribe to be without canoes but in the process of building a fifty foot square fort on the upper end of their island.[1]

An early visitor to the Monocacy region was **Franz Louis Michel**, a Swiss explorer supposedly questing for land and for possible silver mines. Beginning in 1702 he made several trips to this

---
[1] William B. Marye, "Patowmeck Above Ye Inhabitants, A Commentary on the Subject of an Old Map," *Maryland Historical Magazine*, 30:5, 115-116.

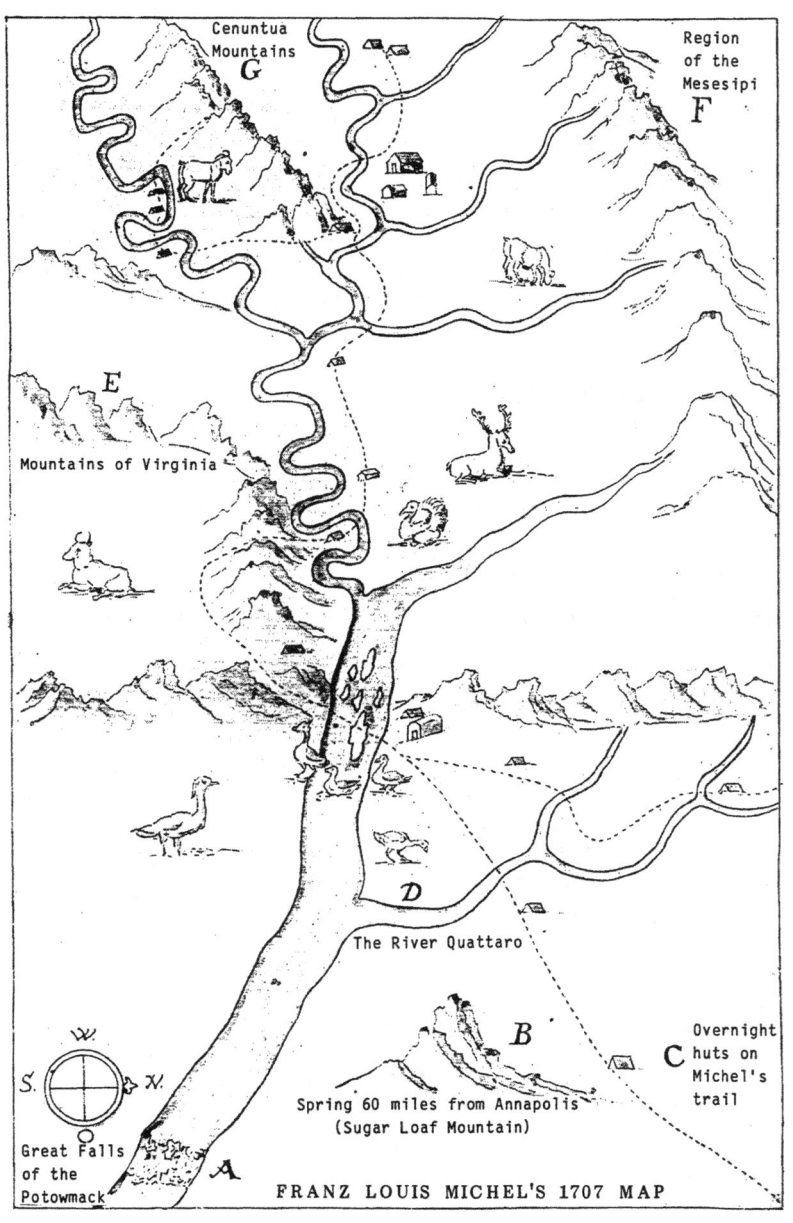

country, which were described in manuscripts later housed in the Library at Berne in Switzerland as well as the British Library in London.[2] In 1707 he drew a map charting a journey probably made in the previous year to and from the upper reaches of the Potomac River. In this exploration he approached the region from the east, passing north of Sugar Loaf Mountain near the southeastern border of present-day Frederick County. He crossed the Monocacy River, quite possibly at today's Hughes Ford just east of the present-day city of Frederick, and continued southward to cross the Potomac at Conoy [Heaters] Island. He then followed up the Virginia side of the Potomac to the west. On his return journey he once more crossed the Potomac at Heaters Island, but then worked his way northward on the west side of the Monocacy, crossing Fishing and Hunting Creeks and following in general what was to become known as the German Monocacy Road.

His map, reproduced on the preceding page, is picturesquely illustrated with examples of wild life of the region. The map shows virtually no habitation and none at the mouth of the Monocacy, which he labeled "a river called Quattaro." Letters on the map are keyed to a succeeding page which lists in French the equivalent of the Great Falls of the Potomac about 15 miles above present-day Washington, D.C., a spring on the side of Sugar Loaf Mountain 60 miles from Annapolis, a series of hutments where Michel stayed overnight along the trail, the Quattaro, the mountains of Virginia, the Mesesipi country (Mississippi, the region beyond the Alleghenies) and the mountains of Cenuntua, the Massanutten range between the North and South Forks of the Shenandoah River.

Michel returned to Switzerland in 1708 and there met Baron **Christoph von Graffenried,** a 47-year old native of Berne, who was finishing his term as Bailiff of Yverdon in Neuchatel. The war in Europe and strife between the Catholic and Protestant cantons in Switzerland had become particularly distasteful to Graffenried, who at the same time had become financially encumbered at Yverdon -- so much so that he found himself particularly susceptible to Michel's descriptions of silver mines and other potentials in America.

The two joined forces with George Ritter, also of Berne, who for some time past had been seeking help from Queen Anne of England in a proposed Swiss colonization scheme in America. They went to London to submit appropriate petitions and plead their case. While there, their path crossed that of the 1709 mass exodus of Germans from the Palatinate,[3] some of whom the eight proprietors of Carolina were seeking to bring to their domain. Graffenried joined their project and crossed the Atlantic with these Swiss and Germans

---

[2] William J. Hinke, transl., "Report of the Journey of Francis Louis Michel from Berne, Switzerland October 2, 1701-December 1, 1702," *Virginia Magazine of History and Biography,* 24:1-43, 113-141, 275-303. Board of Trade Papers, CO/5/1316, Public Record Office, Kew, England. See also Charles E. Kemper, "Documents Relating to Early Projected Swiss Colonies in the Valley of Virginia," *The Virginia Magazine of History and Biography,* 29:1.

[3] See below, p. 130.

in 1710, settling on the Neuse estuary in North Carolina.

Though they fared well at first, lack of support from both Berne and London, coupled with a factional dispute over the Governership of Carolina and a disastrous attack by the Tuscarora Indians, led Graffenried to seek a new haven for his settlers. In 1712 he journeyed northward across Virginia and into the Monocacy area. Since navigation of the Potomac was impossible above the Great Falls, his route took him overland. From the home of M. Rosier just below the Falls he passed through the vicinity of present-day Poolesville and Beallsville, then around the southeast side of Sugar Loaf Mountain to the mouth of the Monocacy. He called the latter the River Coturki and found settled there the French trader Martin Charetier from Canada and his Indian wife.

Graffenried, Charetier and the Indians climbed to the top of Sugar Loaf Mountain from where he claimed to be able to see Pennsylvania, Maryland, Virginia and Carolina. At a little distance three mountain ranges were observed, each one higher than the other, with very beautiful little valleys in between. The first of these was the Catoctin range, beyond which Catoctin Creek flowed south, paralleling the Monocacy River, to join the Potomac between today's Point of Rocks and Brunswick. Farther west rose South Mountain. All this he depicted on a map reproduced on page 11.[4] The map also shows the Conoy Indian village which he visited and which he called Canavest. But the detail of his map does not carry much beyond this village. There was apprehension concerning the feelings of more distant natives following the hostilities in North Carolina. Hence Graffenried himself did not travel as far as the Shenandoah River, which he called Senantona, beyond which he felt Michel's silver mines must lie.

Later Graffenried wrote, "I believe there are hardly any places in the world more beautiful and better situated than this of the Potomac and Canavest." He contemplated dividing the region for two little colonies, one just below the Potomac Falls, the other near Canavest. Michel was scheduled to bring the settlers and point out the silver mines, which Graffenried and several investors from Pennsylvania had been unable to locate on this trip. But Michel failed to appear and the question of the mines grew ever more vague. Back in Carolina, Graffenried found his debts were mounting, and he was at last forced to avoid his creditors by deserting what was left of his colony in North Carolina and to return, disheartened, to England and Switzerland.[5] Thus what might have been the first white settlement in this interior part of Maryland failed to materialize.

Meanwhile the Tuscarora Indians, among whom Graffenried had

---

[4] This map appeared in the *Virginia Magazine of History and Biography*, 24:303. In 1916 the original was in the possession of Professor W. C. von Mülinen at the City Library in Berne.

[5] Baron Christoph von Graffenried, ...*Christoph von Graffenried's Account of the Founding of New Bern*, edited with historical introduction and an English translation by Vincent H. Todd .... in cooperation with Julius Goebel .... (Raleigh: Edwards and Broughton Printing Co., State Printers, 1920), pp. 43-52, 88-91, 142-150, 246-254, 347-350.

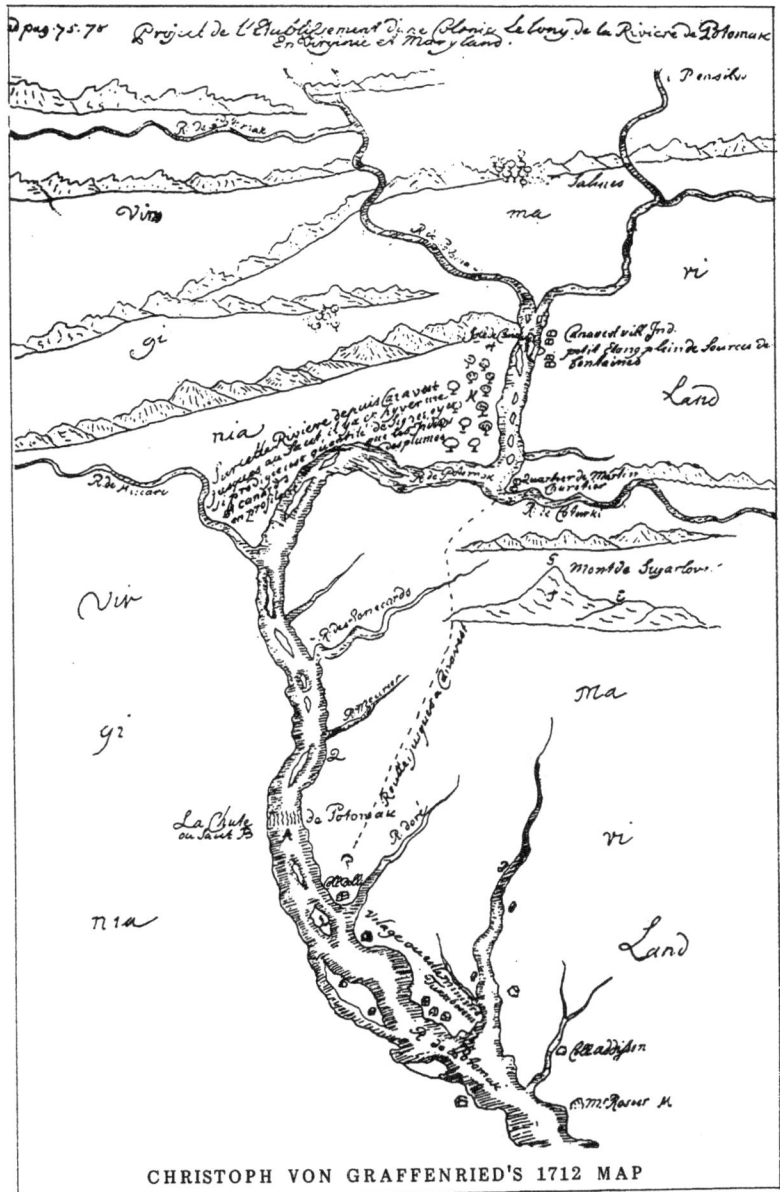

CHRISTOPH VON GRAFFENRIED'S 1712 MAP

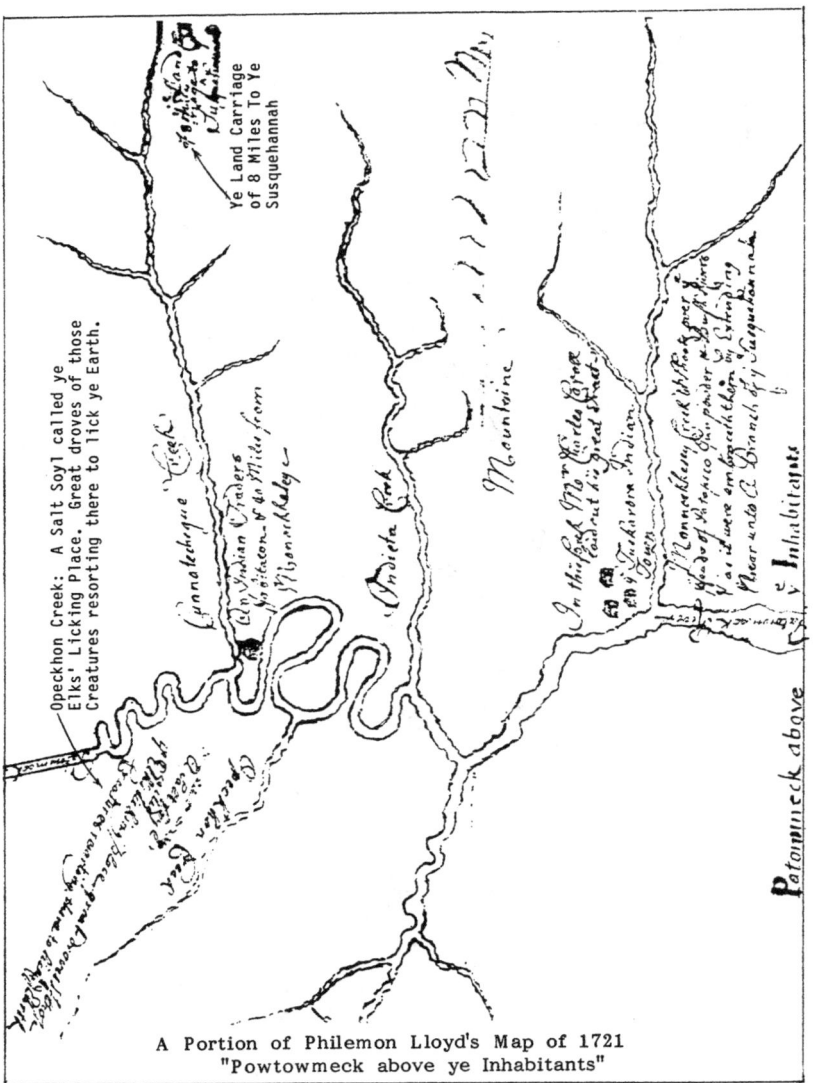

A Portion of Philemon Lloyd's Map of 1721
"Powtowmeck above ye Inhabitants"

lived in North Carolina, suffered badly at the hands of the Carolinians and withdrew to the north. They tarried in the Monocacy area, roaming the hills and crossing the streams. Two of the latter were named for them, and Election District No. 21, northwest of Frederick, is known today as Tuscarora District. The name thus survives.

Charles Carroll the Settler "purchased from ye Indians a Lycence to take up his tract of land in ye Fork of Patowmeck and Monockkascey."[6] When in 1721 Philemon Lloyd drew his map "Patowmeck above ye Inhabitants," he identified "Monnockkesey Creek which shoots over ye Heads of Patapsco, Gunpowder and Bush Rivers and as it were embraceth them by extending near unto a branch of ye Susquehannah." At the confluence with the Patowmeck Lloyd depicted Tuskarora Indian Town and added the notation, "In this fork Mr. Charles Carroll laid out his Great Tract."[7] Even as late as 1728 a beginning point for the survey "Broken Island" (today's Nolands Island) was identified as "a little above the Indian Town landing."[8]

Eventually the Conoys and Tuscarora Indians began a gradual migration northward to more permanent homes in Pennsylvania and New York. The Conoys probably left their island in the Potomac about 1711-1712, and were certainly gone by February 18, 1724 when Arthur Nelson had Heaters Island surveyed into a parcel called "Nelson's Island."[9] The Tuscaroras had pressed on in 1713 to join the Five Nations Indians in New York, and together they afterwards became known as the Six Nations.

Gradually white traders appeared. Two of the few Quakers who embarked in Indian trade were **John** and **Edmund Cartledge** from the Conestoga area of present Lancaster County, Pennsylvania. They traveled down Little Owens and Owens Creeks to what is now Stulls Ford of the Monocacy River, a route which eventually became known as "Cartledges Old Road."[10] In the course of their travels they worked as intermediaries between the Indians and the Pennsylvania authorities in efforts to maintain friendly and peaceable relations with Indian tribes and to govern white encroachments. Unfortunately in early February of 1721/22 while trading rum for skins with a Seneca warrior named Sawantaeny, who was hunting on "the Manakassy," an altercation arose as a result of the liquor, and Sawantaeny was killed.[11] Reverberations were inevitable.

---

[6] Philemon Lloyd to Co-Partners, July 28, 1722, Calvert Papers, MS. 174, Document 1079, Maryland Historical Society. Carroll's land was eventually defined as "Carrollton" which was surveyed April 20, 1723 (C/S: IL A:405). See below, pp. 28-29.

[7] Only a portion of Lloyd's map is illustrated on p. 12. The entire original may be found in the Calvert Papers, MS. 174, No. 1035, Maryland Historical Society and as a copy in Marye, "Patowmeck," loc. cit., 30:1-11, 114-137, who offers a commentary on this map.

[8] C/S: AM 1:27, 45 acres surveyed November 10, 1728 for Arthur Nelson.

[9] C/S: IL B:132.

[10] C/S: BY & GS 1:303.

[11] Charles P. Keith, *Chronicles of Pennsylvania from the English Revolution to the Peace of Aix-la-Chapelle, 1688-1748* (Philadelphia,

John Cartledge died in 1726. Edmund lived on to become a taxable in "Monocasie Hundred" in 1733[12] and at the age of forty-six appeared before the November Court of 1734. In 1737 he established a trading post known as "Hickory Tavern" located where Sharpsburg in Washington County stands today. In 1748 he had land at "Antietam Level," now the site of Fort Ritchie.

William Wilkins was another early trader. He carried his business from Pennsylvania into the Shenandoah and Cumberland Valleys and had been in the company of the Cartledges on their eventful trip in 1722. Wilkins died in 1734.

One of the first documented uses of the name Monocacy occurs in an October 3, 1724 reference to the trader **John Hance Steelman** "of Menawkos in Prince George's County."[13] As late as January 12, 1721/22 he had been in Cecil County, but by 1724 he had established a trading post at the confluence of Roop's Branch and Little Pipe Creek, midway between today's New Windsor and Union Bridge on Route 75 in Carroll County. Later still he moved on to a point three miles northwest of Emmitsburg in the border area under dispute with Pennsylvania. He died in Lancaster, Pennsylvania in 1749.[14] On November 29, 1740 Daniel Dulany had "Deeps" surveyed where Steelman's Carroll County cabin once stood. On the patent is the notation that this was land "whereupon a certain William Kersey has seated and made improvements without making rights to us."[15]

Another contemporary trader, **Charles Anderson,** lived in western Maryland where in 1722 he acted as intermediary seeking a meeting at Annapolis between the Indians from Shawan Town and Governor Charles Calvert with some of his Council. The Indians did not appear, and a second meeting was attempted on August 5, 1725 at Anderson's Cabin "near the Monacacy River." The Governor came, but again the Indians did not.[16] The November Court of 1725 allowed Anderson 1200 pounds of tobacco for keeping John Fowler, an orphan. In 1732 the August Court ordered Anderson to pay a debt of 57 pounds, 15 shillings which he owed to Richard Bennett. This suggests

---

1917), 2:612; Charles Augustus Hanna, *The Wilderness Trail* (New York, 1911), 1:173.

[12] *Maryland State Papers, No. 1, The Black Books* (Hall of Records Commission, 1943), para. 272 in the Calendar.

[13] New Castle County (Delaware) Land Records, G 1:161, 372.

[14] Courtland B. and Ruth L. Springer, "Communicant Records, 1713-1756, Holy Trinity (Old Swedes) Church, *Delaware History,* 5:275n. References to Steelman's locale appear in C/S for "Gabriel's Choice" (LG E:164), "Cross Lot" (LG E:415), "Level Bottom" (BY & GS 15:491) and "Lane's Bottom and Hills" (BY & GS 5:18).

[15] C/S: BY & GS 1:201; Patent: BY & GS 2:304, November 13, 1747. Because of cultivation, Dulany thought a common warrant might not be effective and so sought a special warrant for this survey. The survey was assigned to Erhart Appler, who received the patent.

[16] Proceedings of the Council of Maryland, 1698-1731, *Archives of Maryland,* 25:394, 443, 451. Shawan Town was also known as Shuano Town, todays' Oldtown on the Potomac River in Allegany County. See also Marye, "Patowmeck," *loc. cit.,* 30:132.

that Anderson may have lived on Bennett's land, called "Hope," at the mouth of Bennett Creek.[17] Like Edmund Cartledge, Anderson removed to what is now Washington County.

Where present-day Brunswick now stands, **Abraham Pennington,** an Indian trader[18] from Cecil County, built his cabin.[19] The waterfalls in the Potomac near his cabin were called "Abraham's Falls" and were so mentioned on the certificate of survey for the "Merryland" tract.[20] The creek we now know as Catoctin Creek, curving its way between Catoctin Mountain and South Mountain, appears to have been Pennington's special hunting ground. On a host of surveys located along its banks, some dating as late as 1739-1753, it is recorded as "Abraham's Creek."[21]

Of all the celebrated traders to exchange their wares with the Monocacy and Catoctin Valley Indians, **John van Metre** was the first to acquire a title to the land on which he lived. He is believed to have discovered prior to 1725 the fine country of the Wappotomack, the South Branch of the Potomac River. There he became well acquainted with the Delawares and once accompanied a war party marching to invade the Catawbas. Near present-day Franklin, West Virginia, they met the enemy, suffered defeat, but managed to return to their homes.

On one of his several trips between New York and Virginia, John van Metre had 300 acres surveyed for himself "on Metre branch," which enters the Monocacy River where the present county road crosses from Frederick to Reel's Mill. The survey, dated April 21, 1724, was the sixth survey to be made within the present confines of Frederick County.[22] John called the tract "Metre," and with it he began Frederick County's Second Settlement, described in more detail below.[23]

The most active of all traders in western Maryland was **Thomas Cresap.** His influence was felt from 1737 until after the Revolutionary War. He was born at Skipton in Yorkshire, England and came to this country at a relative young age. In the spring of 1730, he settled in what is now Pennsylvania in the region of Conojohela Creek, known today as Canadochly Creek,[24] immediately south of the 40th parallel below today's Wrightsville but west of the Susquehanna

---

[17] See below, p. 25.
[18] Through the courtesy of Lee R. Pennington of Chevy Chase, Maryland, we learn that Abraham Pennington and his wife Mary made several purchases of land in Cecil County in 1714 and 1719. On one of these conveyances he identified himself as an Indian trader.
[19] C/S: AM 1:303. See also below, "Coxson's Rest", pp. 94-95.
[20] C/S: IL B:453. See below, pp. 37-38.
[21] "Ram's Horn," "Abenton's Cabin," "Cooperton," "Burnt House," "Green Meadow," "German Plains," "Maple Bottom," "Friendship," "Batchelor's Hall," "Mason's Folly," "Johnson's Level," "Misery" and "Lamar's Generosity."
[22] C/S: IL B:18.
[23] See pp. 69 et seq.
[24] Pastor Johann Caspar Stöver (see below, pp. 133-134) usually called the area Canashochele.

River. This was disputed territory, argued over by William Penn, Lord Baltimore and their descendants for almost ninety years. The contention hinged initially on the unknown exact location of the 40th parallel which was intended as the boundary between Maryland and Pennsylvania. It was further complicated by Penn's efforts to achieve access, much farther south, to Delaware Bay and the sea. The significance of the argument becomes even clearer if it is remembered that Philadelphia as initially settled was itself south of the 40th parallel.[25] Thus, had boundaries been kept as originally granted, Philadelphia would today be the largest city in Maryland.[26]

As settlers moved westward, each proprietor made surveys and land grants while attempting to collect quitrents, all in the same disputed territory. In early 1737 Stephen Onion listed a number of specific examples of parcels which had been laid off (i.e., surveyed) on warrants out of the Maryland Land Office. These were located in the vicinity of Conojohela Creek. Onion himself had "Pleasant Garden" surveyed in 1729 on the west side of the Susquehanna. This he transferred to Thomas Cresap, who built his home there. The 81-acre "Bulford" was surveyed in 1729 for Jacob Herrington who in that year settled a mile and a quarter west of Cresap. In 1730 "Bond's Mannour" was laid out as 460 acres for Thomas Bond, and on it William Cannon and John Lowe made their homes. For himself, on a warrant dated December 17, 1729, Onion surveyed "Conhodah" as 600 acres on June 2, 1730, and he settled there in February of 1732. On September 26, 1731 he surveyed "Smith's Choice," 290 acres which he sold to William Smith. All these lands, he testified, were deemed to have been in Baltimore County. The settlers considered themselves inhabitants of Maryland and paid their taxes to Maryland. No others were in the area before them "except for the cabin of a white man who was driven away by the Indians."[27]

Rachel Evans, wife of Edward Evans, testified about the same time that she and her husband lived a half mile from Cresap and had for the past five years. Robert Cannon had lived a mile and a half from Cresap for three years, and William Smith had lived two miles to the west for four years. She also swore that no demands for taxes had been made by any Pennsylvanian, nor had these settlers ever been required to provide any service or duty to Pennsylvania.[28]

Conflict between the settlers was inevitable. It was suggested that Cresap was actually an agent for the Maryland authorities. His house became something of a fortress as both Pennsylvanians and

---

[25] For a good summary of the legal ramifications of the boundary dispute, see Dudley Lunt, "The Bounds of Delaware," *Delaware History*, 2:1-40.

[26] And Pittsburgh, which lies west of the meridian passing through the headwaters of the Potomac River (the intended western boundary of Maryland and Pennsylvania with Virginia), would be the largest city in West Virginia. Cf. below, p. 22.

[27] "Attack on Cresap's Home: A Relation of the Case of Thomas Cresap of Baltimore County, Maryland," *Maryland Historical Magazine*, 3/48-49. Testimony by Stephen Onion, age 40, January 12, 1736/37.

[28] Ibid., 3:50-51.

Marylanders attempted to prevail. Each side claimed the right to arrest the other, and the resulting altercations have sometimes been called the "Conojohelar War." It is a significant part of Maryland history because so many of the participants later settled in the Monocacy area.

In a statement made June 14, 1732, Charles Carroll reported that together with John Ross of Annapolis and John Tredane he had gone to Susquehanna, a short distance from Cresap's home, where they were detained by a warrant from Justice [John] Wright of Pennsylvania for the arrest of "John Tredane of the Province of Maryland, resident of Monochasie."[29] John Tredane lived on "Kilfadda" where Union Bridge is now situated.[30]

In the dead of night on November 26, 1732, according to depositions by John Lowe, age 40, and Thomas Cresap, age 30, both "Baltimore County planters," the former was arrested by a posse under James Pattison and after a struggle, which left him with but one shoe, he was forced to cross the Susquehanna on ice. There he appeared before Wright and Justice Samuel Blunston on charges relating to comments made by Lowe's son which were deemed hostile to Pennsylvania's sovereignty. Maryland retaliated by ordering the Sheriff of Cecil County to apprehend "the Pennsylvanians."[31]

Lowe, who lived a half mile from Cresap, was at the latter's house on the night of January 29, 1733, when a group of some fifty men led by John Hendrick pried open Cresap's barricaded door and another melee ensued. William Boring, William Smith and Lowe's son aided in the resistance. Hendrick had taken issue with Cresap's "advice" concerning land held under Lord Baltimore and was seeking to imprison anyone taking up land under Maryland rights. In this struggle Cresap fired a gun, wounding or killing one of the assailants.[32]

In 1734, eight of Cresap's helpers, including Michael Reisner and Anthony Bancuff,[33] were arrested by a Pennsylvania Sheriff, but were immediately released. On another occasion Cresap as a Captain of the Maryland Militia stood guard while Joseph Ogle[34] made surveys for Lord Baltimore. Ogle, along with the German Philipp Ernst Grüber,[35] was a sponsor on July 21, 1735 when the German pastor Johann Caspar Stöver baptized four of Cresap's children.

Admittedly one-sided testimony was given by Jacob Lochman, who lived two miles south of Little Codorus Creek, within a hundred yards of the main wagon road. He claimed that on October 18, 1735 Robert Buchanan, Sheriff of Lancaster County, his brother Archibald

---

[29] John Gibson, *History of York County, Pennsylvania* (Chicago, 1886), p. 49.
[30] C/S: AM 1:52, June 10, 1729, 200 acres.
[31] *Proceedings of Council, 1732-1753, Archives of Maryland, op. cit.,* 28:18-24.
[32] *Ibid.,* 28:60-64. See also Lawrence C. Wroth, "The Story of Thomas Cresap, a Maryland Pioneer," *Maryland Historical Magazine,* 9:8.
[33] See below, p. 168.
[34] *Ibid.,* p. 324.
[35] *Ibid.,* p. 198.

Buchanan and a third man broke open the door of Lochman's house, beat him and his wife, then departed for the [Susquehanna] River, taking Lochman to the Lancaster gaol as a prisoner. Three miles off, they met a group of five "Dutchmen," provoked a fight in which Lochmann joined his countrymen and was knocked unconscious. The Germans pursued the fleeing Sheriff, captured him and took him to Captain Cresap's house.[36] By name, the five Germans were Barnett Weymour,[37] Michael Risenar,[38] Feltie Craw, Leonard Feeroar [Firor or Vieruhr],[39] and Francis Clapsaddle.

Henry Munday,[40] then of London Grove Township, Chester County, Pennsylvania, was in effect another of Lord Baltimore's land agents associated with Cresap. On November 15, 1736 he was arrested and taken to Philadelphia. State papers and letters to him from Maryland's Governor Samuel Ogle were found in Munday's home and on his person. Also found were thirty applications for land from settlers who wished to live along the Susquehanna under Maryland's protection. Seven of these applications were from members of the Charlton family, which later settled in Maryland's Washington County and, after it was formed, in the town of Frederick itself. Charles Higginbotham, another subsequent settler in Washington County, was also associated with this group.

A short time later, during a night raid against Cresap's home, one assailant received a shot wound which caused his death. Maryland officers exonerated Cresap from all blame. But Pennsylvania authorities demanded the arrest of the "Maryland Monster" on a charge of murder. Early on the morning of November 24, 1736 the Sheriff of Lancaster County surrounded Cresap's home with a posse. After a day-long siege they succeeded in driving Cresap, his family and his friends out of their cabin by setting fire to it and burning it to the ground. Cresap was shot, clubbed and captured, as was his servant Loughlin Malone, who died as a result of his wounds. The protesting Cresap, along with Michael Reisner, Miles Foy (stepfather of Cresap's wife),[41] John George Bare[42] and Jacob Matthias Manshaw[43] were then carried across the Susquehanna River and subsequently imprisoned in the jail at Philadelphia.[44]

Joseph Ogle,[45] then age 29, was admonished by the posse to stay his distance. He did so, but observed the proceedings from that

---

[36] Proceedings of Council, 1732-1753, *Archives of Maryland*, op. cit., 28:82-84. The name is spelled Loughman in this record. See below, p. 191n.

[37] See below, p. 191.

[38] Ibid., pp. 193-196.

[39] Ibid., pp. 211-212.

[40] Ibid., p. 332.

[41] Ibid., p. 224.

[42] Ibid., p. 193.

[43] Ibid., p. 190.

[44] Cf. *Minutes of the Provincial Council of Pennsylvania* (Harrisburg, 1881), 4:109-112. The Pennsylvanians claimed Reisner shot Malone by mistake.

[45] Ibid., p. 324.

distance. Five days later he was able to give testimony to the Maryland authorities. Also testifying were the other participants and observers including Cresap, Reisner, Manshaw, Foy, his wife Frances, Rachel Evans, Sophia Cannon and Henry White.[46]

Soon after Cresap and his fellow prisoners were lodged in prison, the guards were anxious to be rid of them. No doubt they were not the most considerate of guests. Maryland's Provincial Secretary Edmund Jennings and attorney Daniel Dulany on December 7, 1736 delivered to Philadelphia an open letter from the Governor of Maryland demanding the release from Philadelphia jails of all Marylanders. They succeeded in getting Cresap released from his chains, but not from captivity until, on a direct appeal from the Maryland Council dated February 18, 1736/37,[47] it was so ordered by the King. Reputedly, Cresap had refused his release until that order.

By March 20, 1738/39, Cresap and his family had removed to "Long Meadow" in today's Washington County. This location became his base for business ventures as an Indian trader in western Maryland. But his financial dealings were not always successful. It may have been as a mortgage that he transferred "Long Meadow" to James Wardrop in 1743, but he had possession again before Mar. 25, 1746 when he conveyed the property to Daniel Dulany. He was not bankrupt, for at that time he held several other valuable tracts.[48]

In 1738 Cresap qualified as a Justice for the Court of Prince George's County, which then included present-day Montgomery County, parts of Carroll County, Frederick County and all the rest of Maryland to the west. Notwithstanding his serving as Justice for many years thereafter, his rambunctious ways continued. He was fined by the November Court of 1742 for detaining Edward Nicholas, a Pennsylvanian, in the Cresap house for a day and a night against Nicholas' will.

As Deputy Surveyor for the Province, Thomas Cresap's survey work interests us most. He made single surveys in each year from 1739 to 1742.[49] But between 1743 and 1748 he alone made 37 of the total 143 surveys in present-day Washington County and 61 of 186 surveys in the area which is now Frederick County.[50] As percentages

---

[46] *Maryland Historical Magazine, loc. cit.*, 3:33-51; Proceedings of Council, 1732-1753, *Archives of Maryland, op. cit.*, 28:111-114.

[47] Proceedings of Council, 1732-1753, Archives of Maryland, op. cit., 28:110.

[48] "Forest of Needwood," "Anderson's Delight," "Skie Thorn," "Skipton on Craven," "Linton" and "Barrens."

[49] "Lafforty's Lot" (1739) and "Baker's Lookout" (1740) in present Washington County, "Cooper's Point" (1741) and "Wooden Platter" (1742) in present Frederick County.

[50] The 61 in Frederick County included "Cooper's Point," "Wooden Platter," "Longatepaugh," "Bush Creek Hill," "Chancey," "Creager's Delight," "John and Priscilla," "David's Choice," "Ballenger's Endeavor," "Virgin's Delight," "Battleham," "Brown's Choice," "Small Hope," "New Germany," "Allamangle," "Addition to Saint Elizabeth," "Watson's Welfare," "Chevy Chase," "Horseshoe," "Beauty," "Four Springs," "Addition to Wolf Pit," "Wilbersign," "Fatt Oxen," "Stoney

these figures are even more impressive: 26% in Washington County, 33% in Frederick County. More significant still is the refutation of the claim by Daniel Dulany's biographers[51] that Cresap was working as Dulany's land agent. In the decade 1739-1748, Dulany had 110 tracts surveyed for himself in the area of today's two counties. Cresap surveyed only nine of them.[52]

In 1746 Thomas Cresap took himself farther west into today's Allegany County, to "Indian Seat" at Oldtown, the abandoned Shunto town where several years earlier he had built a shelter in connection with his Indian trading. At his home there he fed the many Indians who passed his way[53] and welcomed the Moravian missionaries from Bethlehem[54] as well as George Washington in his travels.[55] Ever the crusty independent, Cresap was seeking compensation in 1751 for damage done him by the Indians over the previous five months. But, he added, if necessary he'd take his own revenge.[56]

In 1749 the first Ohio Company was organized as a commercial project for trade with the Indians and as a means of wresting control of the Ohio Valley from the French. Joining Thomas Cresap and his son Daniel as principals were Thomas Lee of Virginia, George Fairfax, Lawrence and Augustine Washington, brothers of George Washington, John Hanbury from London, James Wardrop, Thomas Nelson and others.[57] Reports were made both to the Maryland Assembly and to Lieutenant Governor Robert Dinwiddie of Virginia.[58] With his Indian

---

Hill," "Deep Run," "Middle Choice," "Parson's Delight," "Taylor's Shears," "Addition to New Germany," "Good Luck," "Trura," "Friendship," "Harveysburough," "Carpouch," "Peace and Plenty," "Martin's Field," "Malchersfield," "Turkey Thicket," "Round Meadow," "Addition to Beaver Dam Level," "Locust Level," "Harris' Delight," "Batchelor's Hall," "Spring Garden," "Addition to Carrollton," "Martin's Intent," "Fry's Habitation," "Burgess' Choice," "John and Sarah," "Gift," "Davis' Delight," "Andrew's Folly and Discontent," "Uncle's Gift," "Cocold's Horn," "Exchange," "Kingsteinstead," "Harry's Grove," "Rich Thicket," "Dickson's Struggle" and "Bailey's Purchase."

[51] Cf. Aubrey C. Land, *The Dulanys of Maryland* (Baltimore, 1955), pp. 172-175.

[52] "Lafforty's Lot," "Davis' Bargin," "Wolf's Purchase," "Chevy Chase," "Watson's Welfare," "Round Meadow," "Wolf's Lot," "Gift" and "Locust Level."

[53] Cresap wrote to the Maryland Assembly, "These Indians stayed at my house for days and complained of hunger. I gave them at their first coming two buschels of meal..."

[54] See, for example, below, p. 147.

[55] John C. Fitzpatrick, *George Washington, Colonial Traveler, 1732-1775* (Indianapolis, 1927), pp. 10-11, 272.

[56] *Maryland State Papers, No. 1, The Black Books*, 5:83 (para. 687 in the Calendar).

[57] F. B. Kegley, *Kegley's Virginia Frontier* (Roanoke, 1938), p. 132n.

[58] *The Official Records of Robert Dinwiddie, Lieutenant Governor of the Colony of Virginia, 1751-1758*, with Notes by R. A. Brock (Richmond, 1884), 1:10, 106, 185.

friend Nemacolin, Thomas Cresap blazed the trail which afterwards became the passage between the Potomac and Ohio Rivers. It was variously known, through the years, as Cresap's Road, Nemacolin's Road, Gist's Trace, Washington's Road, Braddock's Road, the National Pike and U.S. Highway 40.

Life had its unusual moments for Hannah Cresap, too. In 1756 she reported that "a gang of horses came up to the door of the dwelling house of the said Thomas Cresap and a certain Michael Cresap, son of Daniel Cresap, aged four years or thereabouts, going out of the house of the aforesaid Thomas in order to go to another house, a small stallion came in amongst the gang [of horses] and got to fighting and the said stallion ran and catch'd ahold of the lower part of the ear of the said Michael in his teeth and bit it entirely off to the great damage of the said Michael..."[59]

As head of the western division of the Maryland Militia, Thomas Cresap from Fredericktown on August 20, 1749 sent to Annapolis a list of Military Commissions.[60] During the French and Indian War, Cresap's role was primarily that of supplies commissary, recruiting officer and advisor on frontier conditions. Throughout the early years of the War he was a confidant of Governor Horatio Sharpe. On one occasion, in June of 1755, he advised Sharpe that "A party of Indians fell upon some of the inhabitants of Frederick County of whom they killed three with the loss of only one of their own party and carried away eight prisoners."[61] By September he had moved back to "Conegogeck" where one of his sons lived.[62]

Following a Royal Order in 1738, Maryland and Pennsylvania agreed to reduce border tensions by establishing a "temporary line." It was Thomas Cresap who was called upon fifteen years later to determine whether that line cut through a northern bend of the Potomac, thus depriving Maryland of its western territories.[63] His "Plan and Certificate" was sent to Lord Baltimore by Governor Horatio Sharpe, but it was many years before he was paid for his work.[64]

In 1758 and for some years thereafter, Cresap represented Frederick County in the Maryland Assembly. But in late 1766 he was

---

[59] Frederick County Land Records, F:84.

[60] Majors Pyle and Munday, Captains Thomas Prather, Meadon, Charleton, Robert Debutts, William Griffith, Wickham, Crabb, White, George Be[a]ll, Hugh Parker and Joseph Wood. *Maryland State Papers, No. 1, The Black Books*, 4:180; para. 591 in the *Calendar*.

[61] Correspondence of Governor Horatio Sharpe, 1753-1757, *Archives of Maryland*, 6:232. At about the same time Governor Sharpe was writing to his brother John, "As the inhabitants of Fredericktown did not shew more forewardness here than in Virginia to serve troops with their own waggons and horses, we were obliged to press [commandeer] and take all we could find." (*Ibid.*, 6:211)

[62] *Ibid.*, 6:287.

[63] *Ibid.*, 6:5, 91, 130.

[64] *Maryland State Papers, No. 1, The Black Books*, 11:26; para. 788 in the Calendar. Cresap's map is reproduced in Correspondence of Gov. Sharpe, *Archives of Maryland, op. cit.*, 6: opposite p. 72. The final, or Mason and Dixon, line was not surveyed until 1763-1767.

marked as a leader in a threatened rebellion against the Assembly whose two Houses were divided concerning the Journal. Governor Sharpe addressed the Assembly thus: "....Between three and four hundred men, many of them armed with guns and tomahawks, were assembled on Fryday last at Fredericktown, Frederick County, and about to chuse Officers intending to march hither .... their proceedings were supposed to be owing to Colonel Cresap...."[65] Subsequently both Cresap's participation and the bearing of arms were proved false: the men were merely in their cups at the home of Arthur Charlton.[66]

Old age was never a problem for Thomas Cresap. In 1770 at the age of 80 he was surveying the meridian or north-south line (Maryland's western boundary) from the "fountain" [source] of the Potomac River.[67] He was also receiving visits again from George Washington.[68] In 1774 Cresap served as a judge in the trial of William Vermillion, who was accused of stealing a horse and was sentenced to hang. In June of that year he was chosen as one of the delegates for the Provincial Convention which governed Maryland immediately before and during the Revolutionary War. During that War he raised $1,300 in Frederick County for arms and supplies.[69] And when his son's army commission papers arrived but his son was away from home, "the brave old Colonel Cresop, now ninety-two years of age, took the command."[70]

A vivid picture of the man who knew the Monocacy valley in its formative years has been left us by General Andrew Ellicott, the Nation's first Surveyor General who laid out Washington, D.C. according to the plan of Major Pierre Charles L'Enfant. On May 17, 1785 he wrote, "This evening I spent with the celebrated Colonel Cresap. He is now more than a hundred years old. He lost his eyesight about eighteen months past, but his other faculties are yet unimpaired, his sense strong and manly, and his ideas flow with ease."

For all his activities, Thomas Cresap had but one tract of land surveyed for himself in the area of today's Frederick County. That was "Mount Olivet," 364 acres, located south of present Sabillasville. The date was November 6, 1750.[71] Nevertheless, as we shall see in succeeding pages, his influence and his assistance to the early settlers of Frederick County was immense.

---

[65] Proceedings of Council, 1761-1770, *Archives of Maryland*, op. cit., 32:110-114.
[66] Ibid., 32:172.
[67] Ibid., 32:470.
[68] Fitzpatrick, op. cit., p. 272.
[69] *Calendar of Virginia State Papers and other Manuscripts*, William P. Fuller, ed. (Richmond, 1893), 11:625.
[70] Letter from Silas Deane to his wife Elizabeth, June 29, 1775, *The Deane Papers*, New-York Historical Society, p. 65.
[71] C/S: BY & GS 5:621. Very shortly title to this parcel went to Caspar Schmidt, for whom it was resurveyed on October 8, 1751 (C/S: GS 1:94). The Rent Roll (Calvert, Prince George's Frederick No. 1), 3:147 says nothing about this Resurvey or a few acres going to George Harbaugh.

LAND INVESTORS AND SPECULATORS

Gradually Maryland's back country began to change. Traders who followed the initial explorers and adventurers were a less mobile crowd. They needed bases for their operations, and tenatively at least they began to put down their roots. As we have seen in the story of Thomas Cresap, however, they didn't always remain long in any one place. Whether attracted by what lay beyond or merely desirous of avoiding the press of others following in their footsteps, they tended to push ever farther into the wilderness. There was no thought nor even need to own the land on which they stayed. Instead, they squatted where they pleased in varying degrees of permanence.

How widespread this squatting was we have no way of knowing. But as more and more settlers came into the area, men of means at Annapolis and along the Eastern Shore began to recognize that a market for land was developing. Income, they discovered, could be made from rentals and sales of the land farther to the west. But if there was to be wealth in the land, they had best stake their claims by nailing down title to that land. This was naturally also of great benefit to Lord Baltimore, for his own recompense lay largely in the recurring annual quitrents payable to him once title to the land had passed to individuals. So began an era when speculators or land investors surveyed rather large tracts of land, not with the intention of living on that land, but with the hope of sizable subsequent profit from others settling there.

Both the size and the location of the tracts held by these early land investors proved significant. Representative surveys made for such absentee land owners are depicted on the map on page 24. Ten of the parcels shown there, all surveyed before 1732, i.e., within the first decade of land activity in today's Frederick County area, averaged in size just over 5,000 acres each, nearly eight square miles in area. More significantly these parcels were all located reasonably close along either the Potomac or the Monocacy Rivers. Taken collectively, they thus "usurped" most of what was to prove the choicest land. "Free" and accessible land available to the small settler thus proved limited and difficult to come by. It was a different story, however, in the back country of Virginia where large landowners had not yet turned their attention. In the succeeding decade when the push of settlers with limited means reached the back country, it was Virginia and not Maryland where the majority headed.

Large acreages, however, were not destined to end as large plantations similar to those in eastern Maryland and Virginia. On the contrary, many of the large parcels were subsequently divided into smaller lots and, through rentals and resale, the land was gradually made available to settlers of relative modest means, not unlike the holdings of those later settlers who had their own land surveyed

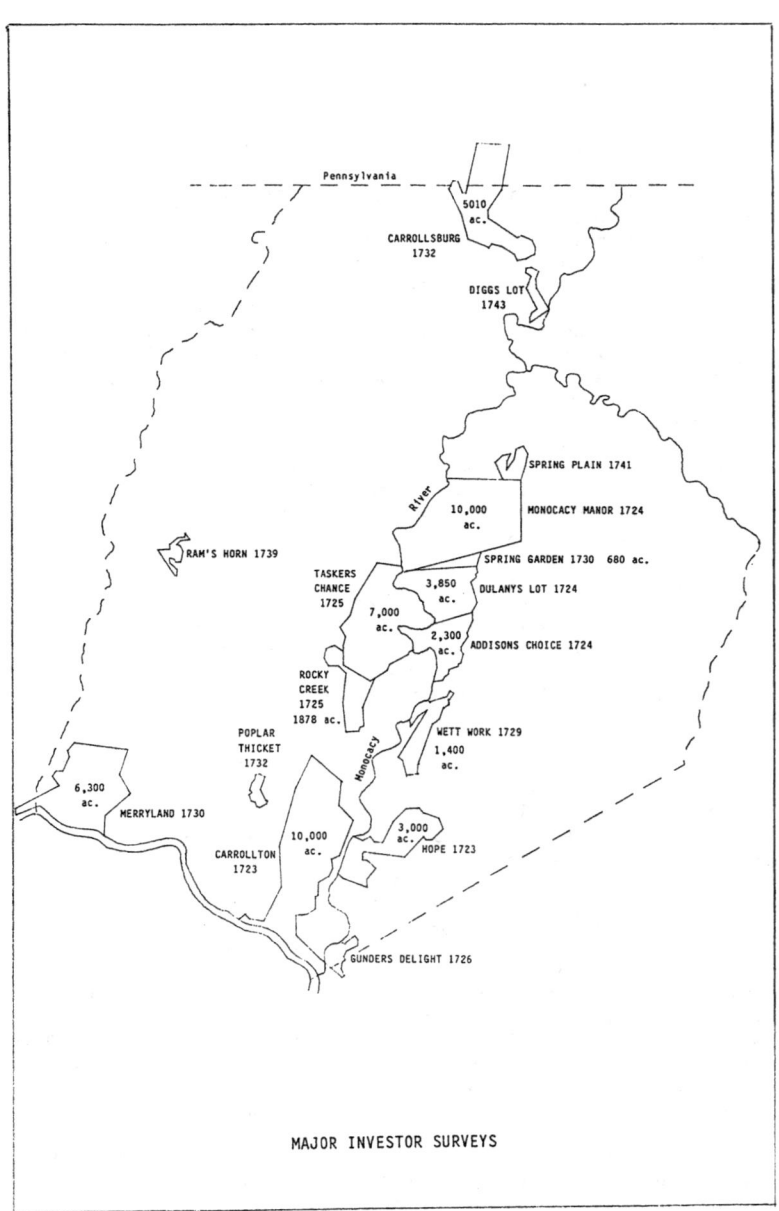

MAJOR INVESTOR SURVEYS

directly. The significant observation is that this "subdivision" process was delayed until individual settlement could occur elsewhere.

As noted in our Introduction, the process of establishing title to a given piece of land involved first the issuance of a warrant authorizing a survey of the land. The actual survey was then made on the land itself with a certificate of survey filed at the Land Office showing the metes and bounds of the parcel and a platting to scale of its outlines. Finally, after review, a patent was issued granting ownership. From that point on, one could deed or lease the property to whom he pleased or develop it himself, for title had now been established. A study of the surveys made for these investors and speculators, the average size of their holdings and the dates at which the surveys were made proves enlightening. What the records show concerning all these individual landowners during the first two decades of Frederick County's history is the subject of our pages which follow.

The first survey within the confines of today's Frederick County was made on November 10, 1721 for **William Fitzredmond,** a nephew of Charles Carroll and a business associate of Daniel Dulany, both of whom we shall meet shortly. The tract was called "Hope" and was located in the southern part of today's Frederick County east of the Monocacy River, some five miles north of its mouth.[1] The parcel included present-day Lilypons at the mouth of Bennett Creek and totaled 2,800 acres. As an example of how paper rather than land itself could be negotiated, the certificate of survey on this parcel was assigned to **Richard Bennett,** who in turn received the actual patent. Bennett lived on the Eastern Shore and was thought by many to be his Majesty's richest American subject.[2] On November 20, 1723 Bennett had the tract reshaped and resurveyed as 3,000 acres.[3] He held ownership until 1738 when he assigned 216 acres "out of love and affection" to Dorothy and Francis Hall,[4] and in 1747 he conveyed another 823 acres to John and Mary Darnall.[5]

"Carrollton," the second survey of record, was surveyed on April 20, 1723 for the young children of Charles Carroll who earlier had purchased the land from the Indians.[6] To distinguish the father from a host of other Charles Carrolls, he is usually identified as **Charles Carroll the Settler.** Some such appellation was found necessary to distinguish among the several Charles Carrolls even during their own lifetimes, and to this day the blood relationships of all the Charles Carrolls cannot be vouched with certainty.[7] The tract

---
[1] C/S: FF 7:406; Patent: PL 4:445.
[2] Cf. Land, *op. cit.*, p. 150.
[3] C/S: IL B:1.
[4] Prince George's County Land Records, T:665.
[5] *Ibid.*, BB:328.
[6] C/S: IL A:405. See also above, p. 13.
[7] The ancestors of Charles Carroll the Doctor (1691-1755) and his son Charles Carroll the Barrister (1723-1783), for example, lived in the same part of Ireland as did the forebears of Charles Carroll of Annapolis. The two families called each other cousins, but their nearest connection went back some fifteen generations. For the land

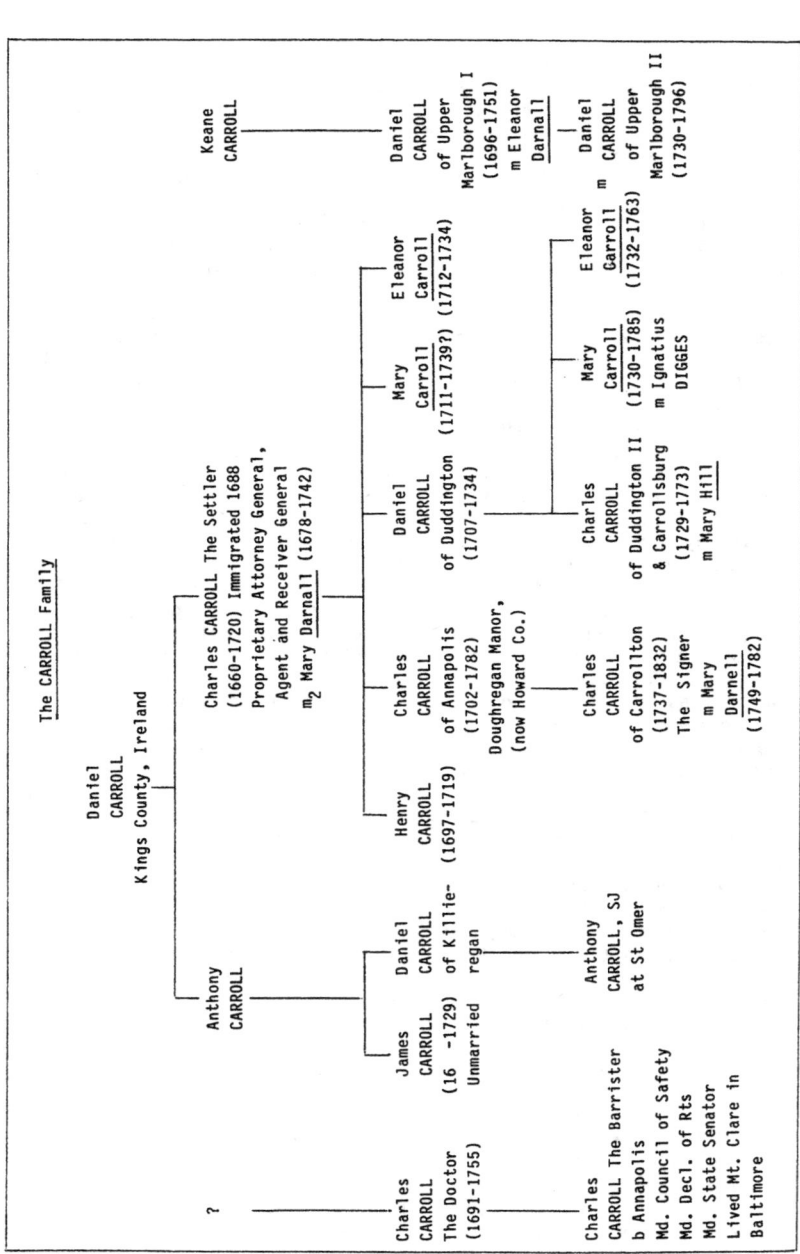

"Carrollton" is best remembered today because Charles Carroll of Carrollton (1737-1832), a son of one of the original patentees, used the tract's name from 1765 onwards to establish his identity, and with that designation he signed the Declaration of American Independence in 1776.[8]

Charles Carroll the Settler (1660-1720), also known as the Attorney General, was the Signer's grandfather. He served as legal advisor to Charles Calvert, Third Lord Baltimore, who in 1688 appointed him his Attorney General in Maryland. But Carroll arrived in Maryland just as the ground swell from the Glorious Revolution against Catholicism in England was abolishing the Proprietary form of government in Maryland. He continued as Proprietary Attorney General during the succeeding period of Royal Government while Col. George Plater and others served as Attorney General for the Crown. Carroll also served as Clerk of the Land Office from 1694 to 1711, no doubt appointed to that position by his father-in-law, Henry Darnall. He also began acting as Surveyor-General for both Shores. Throughout this period he gave close attention to his own acquisition of Maryland land.

When Darnall died in 1711, Charles Carroll the Settler succeeded him as Proprietary Agent and Receiver General. The Royal Government continued until 1715 when Benedict Leonard Calvert, Fourth Lord Baltimore, succeeded his father. By conforming to the Church of England, Benedict achieved the return of his lands to Proprietary status. But his tenure was short-lived: He died in the same year. Charles Carroll, who had been in England settling the estate of Benedict's father, was thereupon recommissioned as Proprietor's Agent and Receiver General for young Charles Calvert, the new Fifth Lord Baltimore. He returned to Maryland, but anti-Catholic sentiment there, especially from Governor John Hart, remained so high that early in 1717 his appointment was revoked. He retired from public life and concentrated his energies once again on land acquisition and the profits to be made from money lending.[9]

In his lifetime Charles Carroll the Settler had thus amassed considerable wealth through such acquisition of land. But it was after

---

interests in Frederick County of these other Carrolls, see below, p. 215n.

[8] Charles Carroll of Carrollton outlived all the other signers and died in Baltimore fifty-six years after the Declaration. He had been a member of both the Continental Congress and the United States Senate.

[9] Mrs. Eleanor S. Darcy, Assistant Editor with the Papers of Charles Carroll of Carrollton, Department of History, University of Maryland, has been of generous help with the history of the early Carroll Family. See also Donnell MacClure Owings, *His Lordship's Patronage; Offices of Profit in Colonial Maryland* (Baltimore: Maryland Historical Society, 1953), Thomas O'Brien Hanley, *Charles Carroll of Carrollton, The Making of a Revolutionary Gentleman* (Loyola University Press, Chicago, 1982) and *"Anywhere So Long As There Be Freedom," Charles Carroll of Carrollton, His Family and His Maryland* (Baltimore Museum of Art, 1975).

his death in 1720 that his four surviving children by his second wife, Mary Darnall, began to acquire land in what was eventually to become Frederick County. These children, Charles Carroll of Annapolis (the Signer's father), Daniel, Mary and Eleanor Carroll, were all still in their minority but under the legal guardianship of their older, unmarried cousin, James Carroll.[10] Their "Carrollton" land lay on the west side of the Monocacy River. From its beginning point at the mouth of the Monocacy its 10,000 acres extended four miles west along the Potomac and north a distance of nine and a half miles. Today's New Design Road may be considered the backbone of "Carrollton," for almost all of its length lies wholly within the land surveyed in 1723, stretching through its middle from one end to the other.

The courses and distances of the "Carrollton" survey are platted on the following page. Like all succeeding plats or maps in this work, it is drawn to a scale of 1/62,500 or roughly one mile to an inch. This permits direct comparison with United States Geological Survey and County road maps.[11] Parenthetically a caveat should be entered here against too literal interpretation of such plats. One should not assume that the knowledge of natural features or the precision of 18th Century instruments equated with those of the present day. Hence reference to modern locations (shown in parentheses on these maps) cannot be as precise as we might like or expect. An illustrative example of such vagaries and inexactitudes occurs in the mapping of "Addison's Choice," p. 34.

In 1734 John Nelson was made overseer of "Carrollton"[12] and on March 25th of that year Charles Carroll of Annapolis leased portions of the whole to William Griffith, William and George Matthews, James Wright, Richard Touchstone and John Powell.[13] On August 29th he leased a lot to Thomas Prather.[14] Then in 1744 and 1746 he leased still other lots to Thomas Richards, Thomas Matthews, Thomas Jacobs, Thomas Wilson, Henry Hill, John Adams, Daniel Pearle, John Johnson, Jacob Duckett, Robert Pearle and John Burgess.[15] Some of these names will be recognized among those who petitioned in 1742 for the creation of All Saints' Parish.[16]

---

[10] Henry Carroll, an older brother, had died at sea in 1719. Daniel died in 1734, and Eleanor presumably in 1739. Eleanor was still unmarried, though Daniel left a small family consisting of a son Charles Carroll of Duddington II (1729-1773) who became the father of Charles Carroll of Belle Vue (1767-1823), and two daughters, again named Mary (1730-1785) and Eleanor (1732-1763).

[11] See for example State of Maryland, Department of Natural Resources, Maryland Geological Survey, "Topographic Map of Frederick County," compiled from 7.5 minute topographic quadrangles of the U. S. Geological Survey" (1982). See also Maryland Department of Transportation, State Highway Administration, "General Highway Map of Frederick County, Maryland" (1984).

[12] Prince George's County Land Records, T:172.
[13] Ibid., T:161-164, 167-172.
[14] Ibid., T:166.
[15] Ibid., BB 1:179-180, 182, 185-189, 196, 264-265.
[16] See below, p. 371.

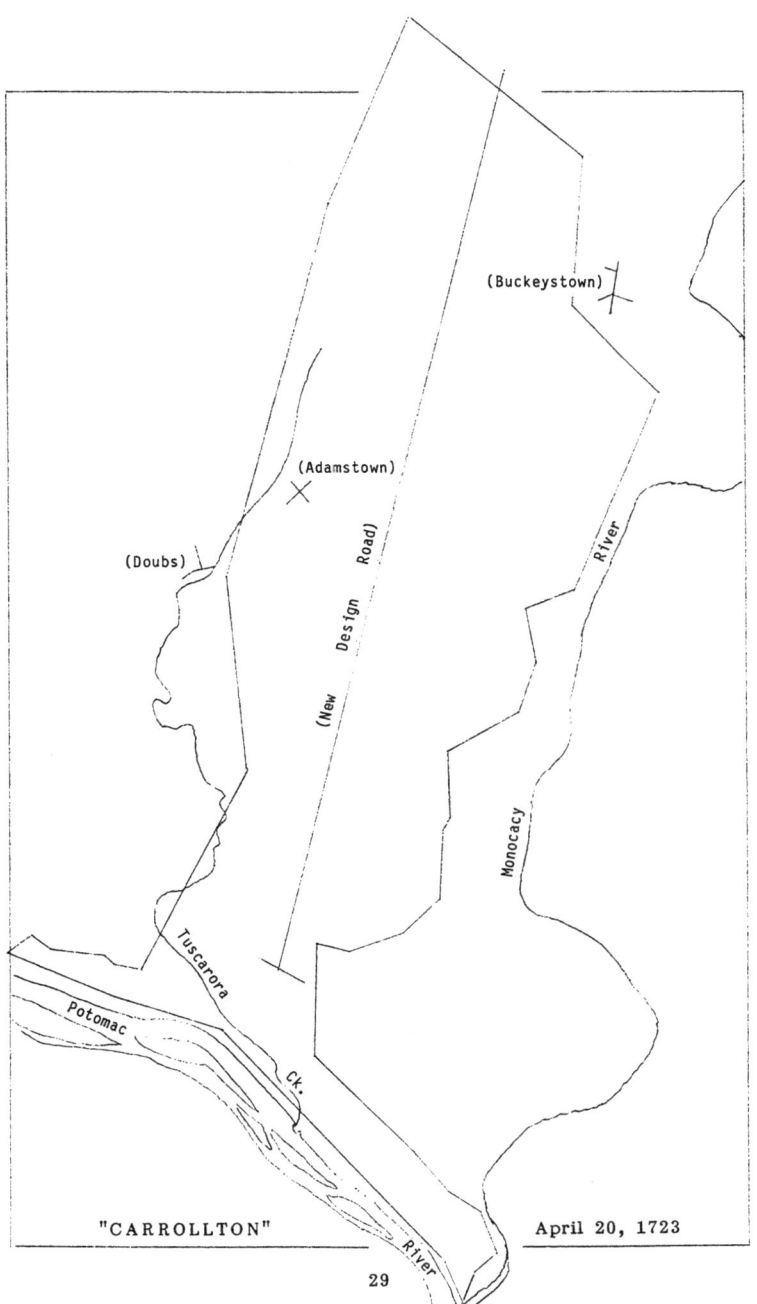

There were two large tracts called "Carrollsburg." One, surveyed on November 10, 1724 for 10,000 acres for Charles, Daniel, Mary and Eleanor Carroll, had its beginning "on the high point of a great rock on the eastward side of a branch called Linganore Creek which falls into Monocacy at the lower end of Oliccin Land."[17] But this tract was never patented.

The other "Carrollsburg," surveyed on September 2, 1732, was located in present-day Emmitsburg District.[18] It contained 5,010 acres, a large part of which lay in Pennsylvania as the boundary between the two states was eventually set. The survey's beginning was "at a rocky point near the creek, 19 perches above where the creek divides," which in today's terms was a little west of the old Tom's Creek Chapel near Four Points Bridge across Tom's Creek. Mary Carroll of Annapolis, in exchange for 5,000 acres assigned to her on "Carrollton," conveyed her interest in "Carrollsburg" in 1734 to her brothers Charles and Daniel.[19] Before a patent could issue, however, Daniel died and title to the parcel went instead to his children in the following year.[20] On May 6, 1757, Charles Carroll sold 2,750 acres of "Carrollsburg," most of which eventually would lie in Pennsylvania, to William Cochran.[21] The remaining 2,260 acres went to Samuel Emmit. Disposition of the latter's portion of "Carrollsburg," and of his son's tract "Silver Fancy," originally surveyed on October 15, 1744 for Daniel Dulany, is described in a separate chapter.[22]

The third survey within the limits of today's Frederick County was made on November 20, 1723 for **Philemon Lloyd** (1672-1732), Lord Baltimore's resident Secretary of State. Its 10,790 acres lay on Linganore Creek. The tract was called "Clovin," but it was never patented.[23] Philemon Lloyd's daughter, Henrietta Maria, was married first to Samuel Chew, a wealthy merchant and planter, and second to Daniel Dulany, Sr., as the latter's third wife. Her daughter Ann Mary Chew married William Paca (1740-1799), another signer of the Declaration of Independence, later Governor of Maryland (1782-1785) and a Judge appointed by President Washington.

"Black Acre" was surveyed next on May 1, 1724 for **William Black**, a London merchant. The land's 437 acres were located on the east side of the Monocacy between the River and Sugar Loaf Mountain."[24] In addition, "Happy Choice," 1,186 acres on the present Frederick-Montgomery County line, was surveyed on May 20, 1724, also for Black,[25] who conveyed it on September 28, 1739 to Edward Sprigg.[26] The latter had petitioned the Court in March 1736 for a ferry over the mouth of the Monocacy River.

---
[17] C/S: IL A:755. For Oliccin Land, see p. 36n.
[18] C/S: EI 5:89. See maps, pp. 24, 238.
[19] Ibid.
[20] Patent: EI 4:323.
[21] Frederick County Land Records, F:239.
[22] See pp. 239-242.
[23] C/S: LG C:43.
[24] C/S: IL A:464. For Sugar Loaf Mountain, see pp. 10, 89.
[25] Ibid.
[26] Prince George's County Land Records, Y:92. See pp. 225-226.

The beautiful and productive land on the east side of the Monocacy River, crossed by what is now known as the Linganore Road and the Gas House Pike, was surveyed on May 27, 1724 for 2,300 acres as "Addison's Choice," in the name of Colonel **Thomas Addison**.[27] In 1734 John Addison, possibly the Colonel's son acting then as caretaker of the property, and John van Metre were constables of Monocacy Hundred. At the Colonel's death in 1727 the land passed to his sons Thomas, Henry and Anthony Addison.[28] In 1759 the Reverend Henry Addison paid its taxes, and on January 4, 1771 Ann and Eleanor Addison sold a large part of the tract to Colonel Joseph Sim for 2,000 pounds. After the Revolutionary War the State of Maryland confiscated property belonging to Loyalist sympathizers. Included therein was the remainder of the Addison property, which was then also sold to Joseph Sim.[29] The 1873 Atlas[30] shows on this choice land the homes of David F. Kolb, A. Marriot, Robert I. Dutrow, P[hilemon] Cromwell Dudrear, Mrs. Catherine A. Schell, John Diffendal and J. L. and H. Routzahn.

On May 28, 1724, one day after the Addison parcel was surveyed, "Dulany's Lot," adjoining it on the north, was surveyed for **Daniel Dulany** (1685-1753).[31] More than any other individual, Dulany is inextricably tied to the history of land dealings in Frederick County. Born in Ireland, he had come to Maryland on indentured passage, but by 1724 had managed a successful and remunerative career as an Annapolis attorney. He subsequently served as Attorney General, Justice of the Prerogative Court, and member of the Maryland Assembly. Significantly, much of his early wealth came in the form of remuneration for his legal work, rather than from inherited land. The resulting liquidity gave him later a leveraged advantage over some of his fellow land investors. His marriages were likewise fortuitous. A second wife, Rebecca Smith (1696-1737), was the daughter of Walter Smith and Rachel Hall. Her sisters Eleanor and Lucy married, respectively, Thomas Addison and Thomas Brooke. Dulany's third wife, Henrietta Maria Chew, was the daughter of Philemon Lloyd and the niece of Richard Bennett.[32]

"Dulany's Lot" with its 3,850 acres lay along the east side of the Monocacy in present-day Mount Pleasant District. It extended from Addison Run northward past the mouth of Israel Creek to the mouth of Glade Creek near Biggs' Ford Bridge and extended some three miles to the east of the River. A thousand of these acres were destined for purchase by Susanna Beatty of New York. Subsequently both sales and leases were made to settlers, although for some of

---

[27] C/S: IL B:104. See map, p. 34.
[28] Jane Baldwin and Roberta B. Henry, *Maryland Calendar of Wills, 1635-1743* (Baltimore, 1904-1928), 6:30: Dated April 9, 1722, probated June 28, 1727.
[29] Frederick County Land Records, WR 7:341.
[30] D. J. Lake, *Atlas of Frederick County, Maryland* (C. O. Titus & Company, Philadelphia, 1873), p. 33.
[31] C/S: EI 5:244.
[32] See chart, p. 32. For a biography of Daniel Dulany and that of his son Daniel Dulany the Younger (1722-1797), see Land, *op. cit.*

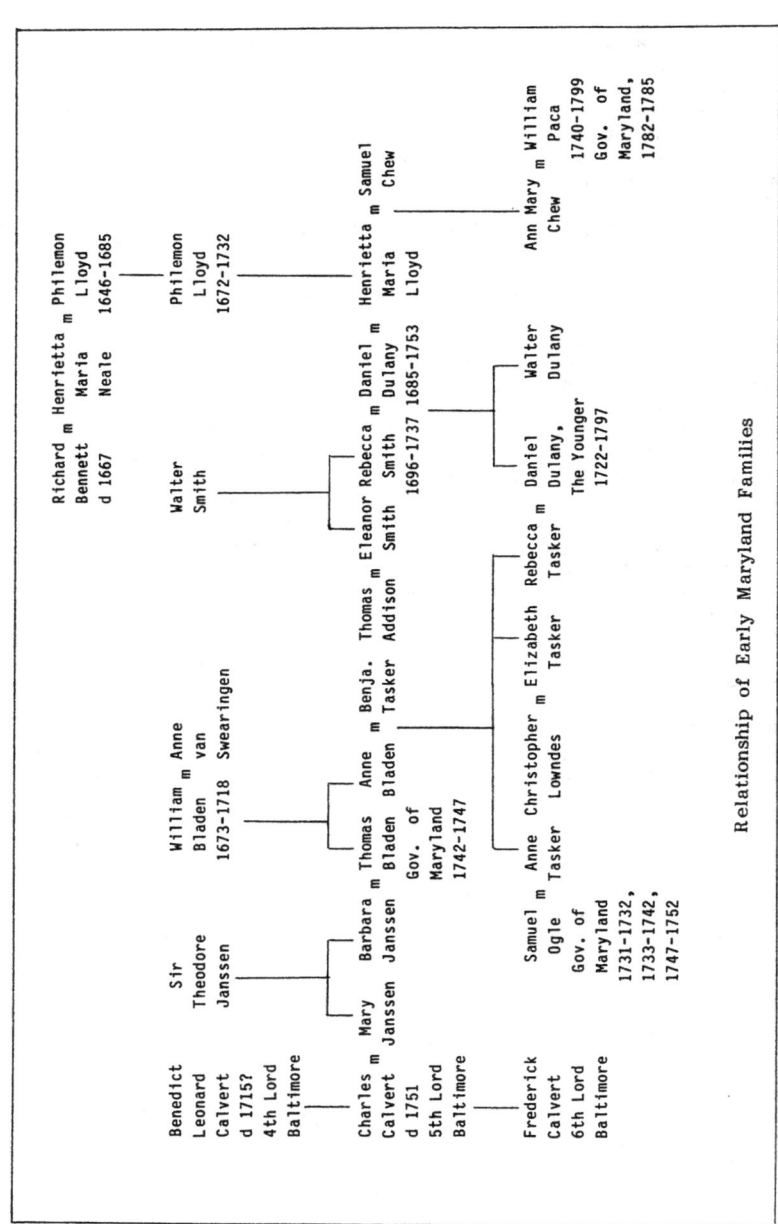

Relationship of Early Maryland Families

them title to the property was not forthcoming until they received deeds from Daniel Dulany the Younger (1722-1797), long after Daniel Sr. had died.[33] The settlement on "Dulany's Lot," which was begun about 1732, is treated in a separate chapter.

"Dulany's Lot" was only the first of many land transactions involving the senior Dulany. His next largest tract was "Ram's Horn," 494 acres surveyed Mar. 10, 1739 and located along Catoctin Creek in present-day Jackson District, one mile south of Myersville.[34] Patented to Dulany on October 3, 1744, it passed subsequently to John George Arnold. He in turn deeded 102 acres of it on February 9, 1749 to Henry Rod (Rhodes), who called his land "Rod's Purchase" and who later, on March 18, 1750, deeded it to Jacob Keller [Koller]. The balance (392 acres) went to Daniel Arnold on October 3, 1752[35] and to Captain Peter Bainbridge on November 1, 1756.[36]

Unlike the large, single land investments made by most of his contemporaries, Dulany spread his acquisitions widely in a large number of smaller surveys. By 1743, for example, in the area of today's Frederick County alone, Dulany had had 26 surveys made. Except for the two tracts mentioned above and "Mankine," surveyed November 28, 1741 for 231 acres,[37] each of the others was smaller than 150 acres. Dulany himself or his sons received the patents for nine[38] of the 26 surveys. The remaining 17[39] were leased or sold to

---

[33] The younger Dulany married Benjamin Tasker's daughter Rebecca. When their son Benjamin Tasker Dulany married Elizabeth French in 1773, her guardian, George Washington, gave her away in the ceremony. William B. Dulany, an attorney in Westminster, Maryland and former President of the Historical Society of Carroll County, is currently engaged in some interesting historical research relating to the career of their son Colonel William Washington Dulany, a leader in the Seminole Wars, who established Fort Dulany (near present Fort Myers) in Florida and led one of the charges at Chapultepec, now memorialized in the Marine Corps hymn as the "Halls of Montezuma."

[34] C/S: PT 2:225. See map, p. 24.

[35] Frederick County Land Records, E:61.

[36] *Ibid.*, F:86. For further history of "Ram's Horn" see Millard M. Rice, *New Facts and Old Families* (Redwood City, Calif., 1976), *passim* but especially p. 114.

[37] C/S: BC & GS 23:363.

[38] "Dulany's Lot," "Ram's Horn," "Saint Elizabeth," "Cooperton," "Exchange," "Burnt House," "Green Meadow," "Christian's Choyce" and "Addition."

[39] Jacob Staley ("Switzerland" and "Otersum"), Jacob Staley the Younger ("Craime's Quietness"), George Schweinhardt ("Lost Spring"), Adam Stull ("Chestnut"), Caspar Devilbiss ("Hunting Lot"), Jacob Bonnett ("Wine Garden"), Hardman Vertries ("Blue Spring"), Martin Wetzel ("Bonnett's Resolution"), Daniel Leatherman ("German Plains"), Henry Six ("Piney Neck"), Philipp Kens ("Shoemaker's Choice"), Melchior Staley ("Masswander"), Martin Shoup ("Mankine"), John George Arnold ("Hog Yard"), Robert Marks ("Shettle") and Frederick Woodapple ("Abenton's Cabin"). Christian Getzendanner later owned the "Resurvey on Christian's Choyce."

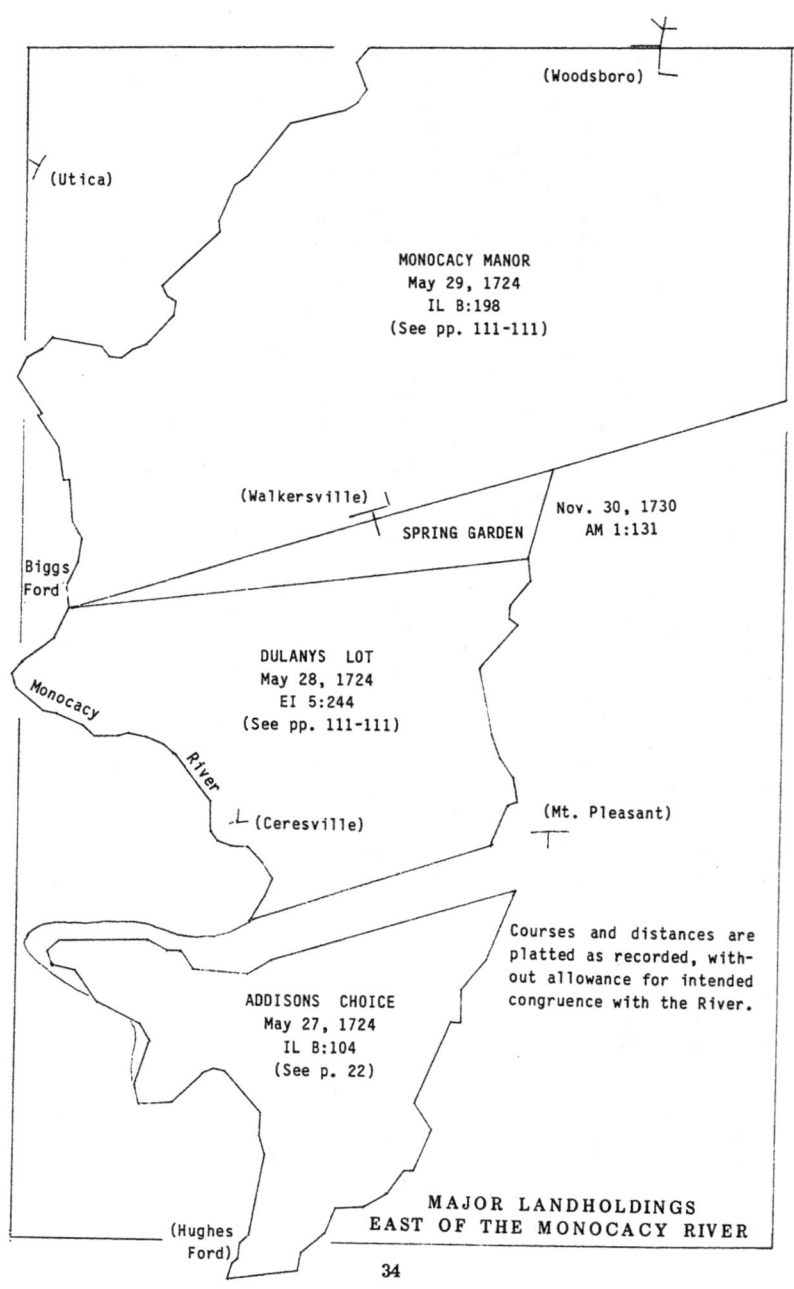

individual settlers who received the patents. Although we lack the accounts to show it, undoubtedly in many instances Dulany sold the land "on time," in effect advancing credit in the interim. This conclusion is drawn from an analysis of the sometimes lengthy span of time which elapsed between survey dates and the dates when Dulany finally "assigned" the survey to the individual who then received the patent. Typical of this arrangement was "German Plains," located northeast of Ellerton on a branch of Catoctin Creek above Myersville. It was surveyed February 10, 1743[40] but not assigned to Daniel Leatherman, leader of the Church of the German Baptist Brethren, until May 21, 1762. A note in the survey book, signed by Lord Baltimore's Agent and Receiver General Edward Lloyd, states, "I have received the sum of three pounds and four shillings for sixteen years [quit]rent of the within land to March 1759."

It has been said that Daniel Dulany's intelligence was surpassed by few and his integrity by none. We have no quarrel with this report. But, from his land records in western Maryland, we cannot conclude that his transactions were wholly magnanimous or undertaken for much other than his own personal gain. The Lord Proprietary had made an effort to induce settlers into western Maryland by offering them in a proclamation of March 2, 1732/33 two hundred acres in fee simple for their settling on "vacant back lands on the northern or western boundaries of the Province between the Potomac and Susquehanna." The usual caution money (40 shillings per 100 acres) and quitrents (4 shillings per 100 acres) were not to be due for three years after the land's first settlement.[41] Since each colony had its own laws pertaining to the ownership of land, many settlers, even some English newly arrived in Maryland, were ignorant of the "gift of land" offered them. Most of all it was the poor, hard-pressed Germans to whom this lack of understanding was most costly.[42] While the likes of Thomas Cresap helped some of them with their surveys and claims, Dulany had the land surveyed for himself and then sold or leased it to the newcomers at his own profit.

The Lord Proprietary, absolute Lord and owner of the soil, assumed the right of reserving for his own use such tracts or quantities of land as he thought proper. One such was known as "Monocacy Manor," whose survey on May 29, 1724[43] was undoubtedly

---

[40] C/S: BC & GS 14:711.

[41] Proceedings of Council, 1732-1753, *Archives of Maryland*, op. cit., 28:25. See also John Kilty, The Landholder's Assistant, and Land-Office Guide (Baltimore, 1808), p. 230.

[42] Illustrative of the scant heed paid to this proclamation initially, only six surveys were recorded in the area of today's Frederick County in the ensuing five years, none of them for a German. This compares with a total of 31 surveys in the two years, 1738-1739. In late 1749 with the arrival of a group of "Foreign Protestants" on the ship *Eastern Branch*, Lord Baltimore had Benjamin Tasker restate the policy, granting like acreages with freedom from quitrents for three years and from caution money for five years. (Executive Papers Portfolio 43, No. 14, Hall of Records.)

[43] C/S: IL B:198.

arranged for **Lord Baltimore [Charles Calvert II]** by Dulany just one day after he had taken care of his own "Dulany's Lot." The survey began "on the east side of a branch of the Potomac River called the Monocacy River and at the mouth of a branch that proceeds from a great spring on land called 'Olacin'[44] and at the boundary of 'Dulany's Lot'." The branch referred to was Glade Creek which enters the Monocacy near an important road junction at what was later known as Biggs' Ford.[45] On November 21, 1724 Lord Baltimore wrote Philemon Lloyd, "Whereas you have located for me a new Manor upon Potomack containing 10,000 acres, I am well pleased therewith and would have you do everything accessary to complete the same..."[46]

Over a period of time, the 10,000 acres of "Monocacy Manor" were divided into 85 small parcels, each averaging slightly less than 120 acres. These were then leased to individuals for varying periods of time, often for the lessee's lifetime or that of members of his immediate family. But because the individual component parcels were leased and not surveyed and patented, ownership remained with the Proprietor and it is impossible to judge in full detail who lived on this land, when and exactly where. Even from subsequent lease information, we have no knowledge of inhabitants actually settled on "Monocacy Manor" before 1741, fully 17 years after its survey. It is quite probable that in representing Baltimore's interests, men like Dulany took care of their own interests first.

In 1781 Maryland moved to confiscate the property of Loyalists and British subjects. "Monocacy Manor" was included in the proceedings, and with its confiscation the chains of title finally began. Until that time, i.e., over a period of at least forty years, its individual parcels had been merely "tenanted," but not owned.

In order to effect the subdivision of "Monocacy Manor," it was necessary to survey the component parcels. From survey notes made at the time of the 1781 confiscation, John P. Dern was able to plot 85 individual lots, then assemble them as one would solve a jig-saw puzzle. The composite results match the original survey's overall outlines and enable us to determine who tenanted these lots and where they were located.[47]

Another early investor in the lands of western Maryland was

---

[44] Hamill T. Kenny, The Origin and Meaning of the Indian Place Names of Maryland (Baltimore: Waverly Press, 1961), p. 7, identifies "Olicin" as an Indian name left by the Shawnees during their temporary (1697-1707) stay in Maryland on their way from the Savannah River in South Carolina to Pequea Creek, Pennsylvania. Although some sixty miles east of their Shawnee Town (Old Town in Allegany County), the region appears to have been near the Monocacy River between Glade and Linganore Creeks. See also William B. Marye, "The Old Indian Road," *Maryland Historical Magazine*, 15:369.

[45] See below, p. 52. The roads involved here were the Manor Monocacy Road, a branch from the German Monocacy Road, the Monocacy-Annapolis Road, and the road from the Manor to Henry Ballenger's branch.

[46] The Calvert Papers, Maryland Historical Society.

[47] See below, pp. 302-323.

Benjamin Tasker. A wealthy early mayor of Annapolis, he had married Anne Bladen, the sister of Thomas Bladen (subsequently Governor of Maryland, 1742-1747), who in England had married Barbara Janssen, sister of Mary, Lady Baltimore.[48] Tasker became a member of the Proprietary circle and was a friend and business associate of Daniel Dulany, with whom he served as joint Commissary General. His daughter Rebecca later married Daniel Dulany, Jr.

"Tasker's Chance" was surveyed for Tasker on April 15, 1725.[49] It consisted of approximately 7,000 acres located on the west bank of the Monocacy River where the city of Frederick stands today. A number of Germans had settled there in the 1730s, and on June 11, 1737 in consideration of a down payment of 200 pounds, Tasker assigned the land to six of them, subject to their raising the full purchase price of 2,000 pounds. This they could not accomplish and on January 13, 1744 they entered into an agreement with Daniel Dulany that the total area "shall be conveyed by the said Benjamin Tasker to the said Daniel Dulany." Thereafter Dulany gave deeds to individual settlers at whatever time they were able to pay him. The subsequent history of "Tasker's Chance" is described in more detail in a separate Chapter.[50]

The well-known "Merryland" tract was surveyed as 5,000 acres for Benjamin Tasker on November 14, 1730.[51] Petersville, Weverton, Brunswick and Knoxville have since been built, in whole or in part, on "Merryland" which thus represents the most southwesterly tract in Frederick County. Tasker assigned the certificate of survey to Captain John Coville who was trading in the Potomac with his own ships about the year 1730. Coville had the tract enlarged to 6,300 acres by a resurvey on February 14, 1732[52] and seemingly intended to divide the total into lots for men named Lee, West, Magruder, Garrett and Philpot. The actual transaction was not recorded and the whole was ultimately conveyed intact on January 23, 1772 to Adam Stewart, Thomas Montgomery and Cumberland Wilson.[53] The grantors in the deed were Francis Colville, George Washington and John West, Jr., executors for the estate of Thomas Colville, who left the bulk of his estate to his son-in-law, the Earl of Tankerville.

"Rocky Creek," 1,878[sic] acres located below "Tasker's Chance" and immediately south of the future town of Frederick, was surveyed on November 22, 1725 for **Thomas Bordley**, another investor from Annapolis.[54] Bordley, who had immigrated to Maryland from Yorkshire, had developed a highly successful and remunerative legal career. Although he was a keen rival of Daniel Dulany in the

---
[48] Christopher Johnson, "Bladen Family," *Maryland Historical Magazine*, 6:297-299. See chart, p. 32.
[49] C/S: IL A:738.
[50] See below, pp. 257-301.
[51] C/S: IL B:453. See plat, p. 38.
[52] C/S: AM 1:345.
[53] Maryland Rent Rolls (Frederick No. 1), 32:43, not always to be trusted, dates this June 23, 1772.
[54] C/S: IL B:108; see also original Patented Certificate of Survey, Prince George's County, No. 1886.

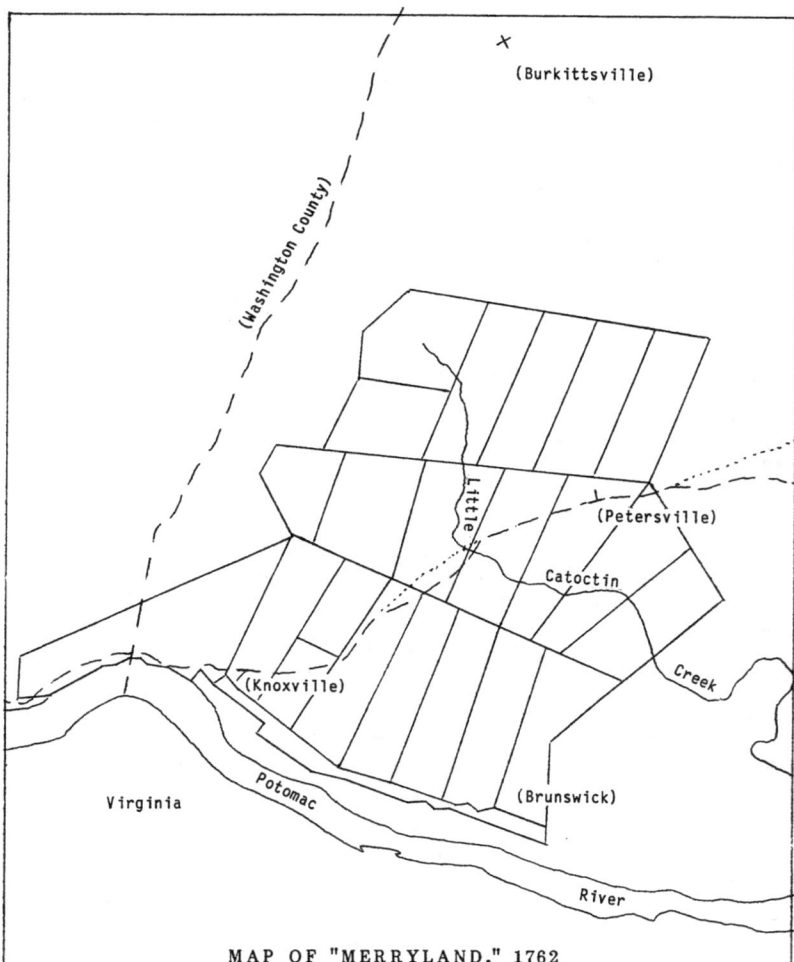

MAP OF "MERRYLAND," 1762

Surveyed initially on November 14, 1730 for Benjamin Tasker as 5,000 acres (C/S: IL B:453). Resurveyed on February 14, 1732 as 6,300 acres for Captain John Coville (C/S: AM 1:345). Note slight extension into today's Washington County. Map of 1762 by Charles Beatty showed subdivisions of the whole into 22 lots, averaging 286 acres. Also shown was the road from Harper's Ferry to Frederick Town. The latter coincides remarkably (see dotted variations) with today's State Route 180. Reference: Patented Certificate of Survey, Prince George's County #1446.

practice of law, both men played prominent roles in the very early struggle for popular rights as opposed to proprietary prerogative. Bordley did serve as Attorney General and Commissary General until dismissed in 1721 because of his independence. Subsequently elected to the Lower House of the Assembly, he was instrumental in establishing William Parks as public printer, thereby opening to public review the hitherto closed doors of Assembly debate.

Bordley died in 1726[55] before "Rocky Creek" could be patented. He had, however, assigned the Certificate shortly before his death to James Stoddert who had made the original survey, and from the latter ownership passed to Captain John Stoddert.[56] It was he who opened the way for eventual settlement when he divided the land into equal halves, conveying an upper 929 acres on May 21, 1733 to Susanna Beatty[57] and a like 929 acres farther south on March 29, 1738 to Jacob Fout.[58] On May 28, 1725 "Backland" was surveyed for Thomas Bordley. Not to be confused with "The Back Land" which became Arnold Livers' land near Thurmont,[59] Bordley's parcel of 2,542 acres was located some three miles east of Sugar Loaf Mountain on today's Montgomery County line. It was not patented, but on October 26, 1747 its area was resurveyed as 632 acres for Elizabeth Bordley and was then called "Remainder."[60]

Four years passed after the 1725 surveys for Bordley before the next survey was made for purely investment purposes as distinguished from intended direct settlement. On November 3, 1729 **John Abington** had "Wett Work" surveyed.[61] Its 1,400 acres were located along the east side of the Monocacy River, crossed today by U.S. Interstate Highway I-270 between State Routes 80 and 355. Abington devised his share of "Wett Work," which he had taken up in partnership with surveyor George Noble, to his son Andrew and the remainder to Noble's heirs. In 1759 a large portion was conveyed to James Marshall,[62] who had a resurvey made on January 1, 1797.[63] There he built his brick mansion which is still standing. By his 1799 will Marshall directed that his lands be sold and recommended that his "esteemed friends, Norman Bruce and his son Upton Bruce" assist the executors. John McPherson's 1832 "Araby" of 111 acres was a further resurvey,[64] and on a part of this land the Civil War Battle of Monocacy was fought.

---
[55] Original Wills, Maryland Hall of Records, Prince George's County, Box B, Folder 72. Bordley indicated that he was the youngest son of the Rev. Stephen Bordley, late Prebendary of St. Paul's and Rector of St. Mary Newington in London. He also noted that he was about to make a voyage to London. The will was dated June 29, 1726 and was probated January 14, 1726/27.
[56] Patent: PL 7:60.
[57] Prince George's County Land Records, Q:661. See below, p. 118.
[58] *Ibid.*, T:576. See below, p. 161.
[59] See below, p. 249.
[60] C/S: TI 1:410.
[61] C/S: AM 1:311.
[62] Frederick County Land Records, F:654.
[63] C/S: IC 4:206.
[64] C/S: GGB 2:388.

Abington had two other surveys. One of these was "Pains Delight," 100 acres located "between the first and second ledges of mountain on the bank of the Potomac a little below Colonial [Colonel!] Island" where Knoxville is situated today. The parcel was surveyed on November 2, 1730 and patented to Abington on July 31, 1732.[65] It was later conveyed to the Payne family,[66] a name still well known in nearby Brunswick, Maryland. Abington's other tract, "Spring Garden," evidently caught a 680-acre surveyor's error which had left a long triangular wedge of vacant land between "Dulany's Lot" and "Monocacy Manor." It was surveyed on November 14, 1730 for Abington and George Noble, again in partnership,[67] and then sold, along with "Addition to Spring Garden," to Daniel Dulany on June 9, 1738. "Spring Garden" is discussed in more detail below, p. 123. John Abington wrote his will on December 8, 1738 and died before June 15, 1739, its date of probate.[68]

A number of other early tracts should be mentioned which were acquired by investors who did not live on their land. Compared to those listed above, most were relatively small in size. **John Radford,** for example, had "Henry" (385 acres) and "Albin's Choice" (300 acres) surveyed on November 23, 1724.[69] "Gunder's Delight" with 200 acres was surveyed March 5, 1725/26 for **Gunder Erickson**[70] and later conveyed to John Harding, Richard Snowden and Sarah Davis.[71] On April 1, 1728 **Thomas Wilcoxson** had "Coxson's Rest" surveyed.[72] **John Magruder** on January 4, 1731 had "Kettankin Bottom" surveyed near the mouth of Catoctin Creek[73] and gave part of it to his friend James Hook. He also had "Forrest" surveyed for himself on April 9, 1733.[74]

The survey for "Poplar Thicket" made for **John Beal, Jr.** and **Dr. Thomas Creary** on September 5, 1732[75] gave rise in the court records of 1744 to the term "Mr. Bel's Gap" as a way over Catoctin Mountain. In his will Beall devised half of the 470-acre tract, which he said was "near Monoquasy River" to his son Basil and requested the other half be sold to pay debts.[76] Actually the land lay four and a half miles from the River near today's Mountville. On August 22, 1754, 326 acres of the land were conveyed to Gabriel Thomas, who on January 19, 1756 assigned portions of it to John and Valentine

---

[65] C/S: AM 1:30; Patent PL 8:514; Original Patented Certificate of Survey, Prince George's County, No. 1594. See map, p. 95.
[66] Prince George's County Land Records, T:243.
[67] C/S: AM 1:31; Patent PL 8:8.
[68] *Maryland Calendar of Wills*, op. cit., 8:31.
[69] C/S: IL B:16, 17.
[70] C/S: IL A:732.
[71] Maryland Rent Rolls (Frederick No. 1), 32:26.
[72] C/S: AM 1:303.
[73] C/S: EI 2:48. See also below, p. 65.
[74] C/S: AM 1:365. This "Forrest" tract, located west of where Middletown was later built, should not be confused with Sprigg's 1734 "Forest" in Locust Valley, C/S: AM 1:375. See p. 225.
[75] Pat'd. July 17, 1733 per Orig. Pr. George's Co. Certif. of Survey No. 1735; but svyd. Jan. 10, 1731, pat'd. Sept 5, 1732 per AM 1:321.
[76] *Maryland Calendar of Wills*, op. cit., 8:173.

Thomas.[77] Gabriel, John and Valentine Thomas married sisters, daughters of George Riemensberger [Remsberg], an immigrant from Walldorf, Germany. Part of "Remsberg's Lot" was a resurvey on a portion of "Poplar Thicket."[78] Gabriel Thomas, Valentine Thomas [Valentint Tamas] and George Remsburg [Riemensberger] are buried on this land.[79]

At least in connotation there may be differences in interpretation between an investor and a speculator. No doubt nearer to the latter was **John Digges**.[80] A wealthy Catholic resident of then Prince George's County in Maryland, he concentrated his land interests in the area west of the Susquehanna, directly in the contested area between Maryland and Pennsylvania. As early as October 14, 1727, he received from Maryland a "right" or warrant[81] for 10,000 acres which in part he used for the survey of "Digges' Choice," a 6,822 acre tract on which Conewago Chapel and present-day Hanover, Pennsylvania were located. It included parts of today's Conewago and Germany Townships in Adams County and Heidelberg Township in York County.[82]

There followed a vigorous campaign to interest Germans east of the Susquehanna in settling on "Digges' Choice." The first to do so was Adam Forney, who had arrived from Wachenheim, Germany in 1721. Forney settled where the business section of Hanover now stands. He was followed by numerous other Germans including, in 1734, Andreas Schreiber from Alsenborn, an ancestor of Admiral Winfield Scott Schley.[83]

But title to the lands purchased from Digges proved vague and conflicting. It gradually became apparent that John Digges was a man of somewhat doubtful honor. When he refused the settlers' requests for more specific deeds, the Germans sent Martin Updegraf to Annapolis to investigate. It was discovered that Digges had indeed sold land he didn't possess. His efforts to rectify matters in Philadel-

---
[77] Maryland Rent Rolls (Frederick County No. 1), 32:42.
[78] C/S: BC & GS 50:177.
[79] Jacob Mehrling Holdcraft, *Names in Stone, 75,000 Cemetery Inscriptions from Frederick County, Maryland* (Ann Arbor, 1966, 1972; Baltimore, 1985), 2:926, 1140, 1145.
[80] John Digges was the son of Colonel William Digges and Elizabeth Sewall Wharton, grandson of Governor Edward Digges of Virginia and great grandson of Sir Dudley Digges of Kent, England. About 1680 John's father established himself at Warburton Manor by the mouth of Piscataway Creek. The manor is now the site of Fort Washington, opposite Mount Vernon. John's mother was the stepdaughter of Charles Calvert, 3rd Lord Baltimore. Effie Gwynn Bowie, *Across the Years in Prince George's County* (Richmond, 1947), pp. 248-252. Gibson, *op. cit.*, p. 78, called Digges "a petty nobleman."
[81] A warrant gave the holder the "right" to survey and then patent new land. See above, p. 2.
[82] C/S: EI 3:433; Patent: EI 4:332. "Digges' Choice" was surveyed by Philip Jones, its subsequent Resurvey (C/S: LG E:421) by Thomas Cresap.
[83] Dieter Cunz, *The Maryland Germans* (Princeton, N.J., 1948), pp. 53-54.

phia failed, but at Annapolis in 1745 he succeeded in getting a grant of 3,679 acres of new land, this despite the prohibition against the sale of new land in the disputed area after the establishment of the temporary line in 1739. Worse, the 1745 grant covered land of fourteen Germans whose title came from Pennsylvania.[84]

Digges apparently assumed his rights to land entitled him to most of northern and western Maryland. George Noble, deputy surveyor, told the Maryland Assembly in 1732 that Digges claimed all the vacant land on Monocacy and its branches as well as the branches of the Susquehanna. Noble also told the Assembly that he had seen a letter written by Digges to Joseph Hedges demanding "satisfaction" for the land upon which Hedges had settled.[85] That land was located west of Biggs Ford, some sixteen miles south of the present Pennsylvania-Maryland boundary and nearly half the distance to the Potomac River!

Court records exist in both Maryland and Pennsylvania Archives covering suits over "Digges' Choice." Even after the death of John Digges, his sons William, Henry, Edward and Dudley were involved in further legal tangles, and in 1752 Dudley Digges was killed in a battle between contesting groups.

Fifty years after the first settlers came to Conewago, Hannah Farquhar Owings, formerly of Pipe Creek and widow of Robert Owings, testified in Court that "she heard John Digges tell her father Allen Farquhar at Pipe Creek in the year 1730 that the survey (of "Digges' Choice") was defective....that at Christmas time in the same year she intermarried with Robert Owings....that in the following year....Edward Stevens or Stevenson came to survey this land and there were two hundred and seventy-two courses. When Stevenson saw the figure of the plat he was very angry and fretted and swore at the number of angles and courses, and cut them off....the next day he went away and carried the plat with him, but left the field notes which last remained in her (Hannah Owings') possession in a small box for ten years or upward, that then she delivered them at her house to John Digges, in the presence of old Prather."[86]

Of more concern to us, however, are the surveys for John Digges of land located on the Maryland side of the border. These were widespread and may be summarized with their present-day locations as follows:

"The Back Land"	Aug. 14, 1732	2,578ac	Northeast of Thurmont[87]
"Justice's Delight"	July 3, 1741	250ac	Betw. Oak Orchard & McKinstry's Mill[88]
"Richards Hunting Ground"	July 3, 1741	366ac	Libertytown District[89]

---

[84] *Ibid.*

[85] Proceedings and Acts of the General Assembly of Maryland, 1730-1732, *Archives of Maryland*, 37:506.

[86] "Old Prather" was Thomas Prather of the Point of Rocks settlement. See p. 63.

[87] C/S: EI 3:348. See also p. 249. Not to be confused with "Backland," p. 39.

[88] C/S: LG E:61. See p. 101.

[89] C/S: LG E:64. See map, p. 100.

"Spring Plain"	July 3, 1741	848ac	Near Woodsboro[90]
"Williams Intention"	July 3, 1741	46ac	Johnsville District near Beaver Dam Creek[91]
"Hazel Valley"	July 7, 1741		Union Bridge[92]
"Papan [Paw Paw] Bottom"	July 7, 1741	160ac	Northwest of Woodsboro at mouth of Hunting Creek[93]
"Rich Level"	July 7, 1741	352ac	Mumma Ford, just east of the Monocacy River, Carroll Co.[94]
"Disappointment"	May 3, 1742	182ac	Thurmont District,[95]
"Digges Lot"	June 3, 1743	547ac	Emmitsburg District[96]
"Brother's Agreement"	Apr. 14, 1744	60ac	Taneytown, Carroll Co.[97]
"Brother Try All"	Apr. 14, 1744	30ac	Near Taneytown, Carroll Co.[98]
"Buck Lodge"	Apr. 18, 1744	200ac	Carroll County[99]
"Cedar Cliffs"	Apr. 18, 1744	290ac	Johnsville District[100]
"Chittam Castle"	Sept 16, 1740	218ac	Near Oak Orchard; surveyed for John Digges' nephews, Nicholas and Ignatius Digges[101]

Finally, surveys made for a few miscellaneous land investors should be noted. Among them was a 200-acre tract known as "Two Brothers" whose beginning point was "near the head of a glade of a branch of the Potomac called Lick Branch." This parcel was surveyed for **Thomas** and **John Fletcher** on March 26, 1734. They conveyed 100 acres of it to Richard Powell in 1755.[102] "Forest," located "on the north side of the Conegechiany[103] Road" was surveyed for **Osborn Sprigg** in 1734 and conveyed to Josiah and Absalom Wilson in 1745.[104] **Thomas Wilson** had "Delight" surveyed on April 1, 1740 in the Catoctin Valley.[105] On May 24, 1740 he added "Prevention," located "at the mouth of Mill Run [now known as Little Catoctin Creek] that falls into Catoctin Creek."[106] In his will of March 30, 1744 Wilson directed his widow Priscilla to convey his 100-acre "Prevention" to Thomas Whitaker.[107]

---

[90] *Ibid.*
[91] C/S: LG E:59. See p. 100.
[92] C/S: LG E:62.
[93] C/S: LG E:62; Patent: B:481. See pp. 49, 339-340.
[94] C/S: LG E:63.
[95] C/S: LG E:196. See map, p. 325.
[96] C/S: LG E:197, 528.
[97] C/S: LG E:342.
[98] C/S: LG E:343.
[99] C/S: LG E:528.
[100] C/S: LG E:361.
[101] C/S: LG C:183. See p. 100.
[102] C/S: EI 5:291.
[103] The Conocacheague settlement was located along the Creek of that name which flows south from Pennsylvania, passing a few miles west of Hagerstown and emptying into the Potomac at Williamsport.
[104] C/S: AM 1:375; Patent: EI 1:483. See p. 225.
[105] C/S: EI 5:495. See p. 243.
[106] C/S: EI 5:492. See p. 243.
[107] *Maryland Calendar of Wills, op. cit.,* 8:266.

"Dispatch"[108] and "Kemp's Delight"[109] were surveyed for **Dr. George Stewart** [Steuart], who assigned the certificate of survey to Christian Kemp. **Richard Davis** of Anne Arundel County had "Dear Bought" surveyed May 23, 1741 with its beginning point "between Linganore Creek and the mouth of a run called Dolernides [Dollyhyde].[110] Davis conveyed it to Daniel Dulany, who sold it to Andrew Smith.[111] The 1873 Atlas showed the property (and mill) to be in the possession of Z[achariah] Myers and John Snider.[112]

James Wardrop was a wealthy merchant originally from Virginia who lived at Marlborough in lower Prince George's County, Maryland. He began his land investments in western Maryland on March 2, 1742 when his friend Thomas Cresap surveyed "Wooden Platter" for him near present-day Middletown.[113] His other surveys included "John's Delight," "Bloomsbury," "Brentford" and "Oxford." In 1744 he received the patent for Thomas Gittings' 1742 "Resurvey of Partnership" near the mouth of the Monocacy. With Lawrence and Augustine Washington, Thomas Lee and others, he was a participant in the Ohio Company. Although "of Upper Marlboro," Wardrop wrote his will in New York City. It was probated in Prince George's County in 1760, and in it he named his wife Lettice and his brother-in-law Alexander Symmer as executors. He devised to a nephew houses belonging to his father in Edinburgh, Scotland and to his wife all his real estate in America.[114]

The **Alexander Beall** who had "Joviall Ramble" surveyed on March 15, 1742[115] appears to have been a land speculator from southern Maryland rather than the Alexander Beall who settled in Frederick County after it was formed in 1748. One Alexander Beall purchased "Jacob's Cow Pen" on July 17, 1755 from William Williams, Sr., planter,[116] who had the original survey made on June 18, 1743.[117]

By way of summary concerning these early landowners, we calculate that during roughly the first two decades of land patents in present-day Frederick County, i.e., in the period up to the end of the year 1743, a total of 109,326 acres of land had been surveyed. Only 20,653 of these acres were surveyed directly for settlers themselves. The balance, over 80% of the land which had thus been patented up to that date, was therefore possessed initially by or through these investors.

---

[108] C/S: LG E:271.
[109] C/S: LG E:273.
[110] C/S: LG C:184. See map, p. 100.
[111] Frederick County Land Records, B:142.
[112] Lake, op. cit., p. 23.
[113] C/S: TI 1:486.
[114] Prince George's County Wills, 1:520, probated August 20, 1760.
[115] C/S: LG E:186.
[116] Frederick County Land Records, E:747.
[117] C/S: LG E:278.

THE MONOCACY AREA AND ITS ROADS

Before we come to the story of the actual settlers, the people who lived on the land at Monocacy, it might be well to sweep away the misconception that the term "Monocacy" once upon a time referred to a village, a ghost village which somehow existed and then disappeared without a trace. The misconception no doubt arose from modern minds unaccustomed to distinguishing between place names which refer to a given area and those naming a specific town or village. One must visualize that before any village could evolve from so large a region previously inhabited only by Indians, families had to clear the forest wilderness and begin earning their livelihood through farming on their separate parcels of ground. They lived nearby one another, of course, but distant enough to allow for the acreage required for each one's self-sufficiency. Thus Monocacy represented a rather extensive *area* of beginning agriculture, not an isolated urban *village* in the midst of a wide wilderness.

The records show this to be true: John Hanse Steelman, a trader "of Menawkos in Prince George's County" in 1724 located his trading post midway between today's New Windsor and Union Bridge in Carroll County.[1] In 1726 the "Monoquesey" Quaker Meeting began at the home of Josiah Ballenger.[2] He lived near present-day Buckeystown. John Tredane "of Monachasie," whom we have met in our description of the Pennsylvania border unrest, was living in 1732 where today's Union Bridge in Carroll County now stands.[3] Joseph Hedges, Sr. of "Manaquicy"[4] in 1732 took up land near Biggs Ford in the neighborhood of present-day Hansonville.[5] His sons initially lived near Yellow Springs. Susanna Beatty settled near today's Mt. Pleasant but held land as far west as Ceresville. In her will she identified that locale as "Monocksey."[6] Cornelius Carmack lived near present-day Libertytown[7] and in his 1746 will stated that he was of "Monocksey."[8] Peter Hoffman from "Tasker's Chance" near today's city of Frederick wrote his 1748 will at "Manakesen.[9] Joseph Hedges, Jr., who was located on leased "Monocacy Manor" land, declared in his 1753 will

---

[1] See p. 14.
[2] *Ibid.*, p. 82.
[3] C/S: A M 1:52.
[4] *Maryland Calendar of Wills, op. cit.,* 6:236.
[5] C/S: A M 1:44.
[6] Frederick County Wills, A1:12. This, the first Will Book after Frederick County was formed in 1748, was originally numbered "A1," but when rebound in modern times, the "1" was dropped, and the spine is now marked simply as Vol. A.
[7] Prince George's County Land Records, Y:92.
[8] Frederick County Will Records, A1:27.
[9] Frederick County Will Records, A1, after f. 14. See p. 279.

45

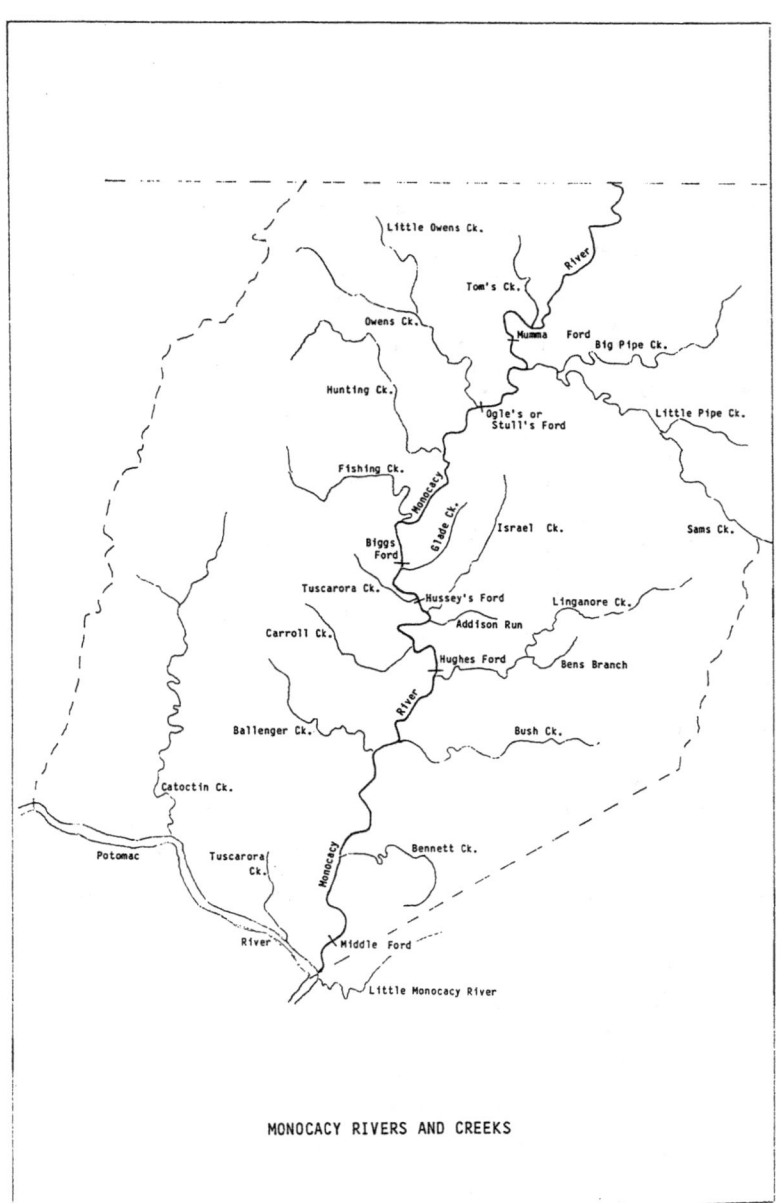

MONOCACY RIVERS AND CREEKS

that he was "of Monocacy."[10] Frederick Unselt lived on "Beauty" west of Fredericktown[11] and wrote his will in 1755 from "Monksey."[12] Arnold Livers' farm, in the forks of Owen's Creek near present-day Thurmont, was described to the Maryland Assembly as being "at Monococy."[13] And perhaps most significant was the agreement of March 28, 1746 between the Reverend Joseph Jennings, Clerk rector of "All Saints Parish in Monocksesy," with Robert Debutts and Kennedy Farrell.[14]

Thus in the early history of Frederick County, the Monocacy River's entire watershed *area* was known as **MONOCACY**. It was not a single German village as claimed by Pastor George A. Whitmore,[15] Edward T. Schultz,[16] Daniel W. Nead,[17] Folger McKinsey,[18] James A. Boyd[19] and others. Most assuredly it was not a forerunner of Creagerstown, where a small monument on the Creagerstown-Woodsboro Road about three-quarters of mile from the town center, attests to the misconception. Nor was it at a location nearby at the mouth of Hunting Creek. Both are still too often claimed as sites of the Germans' "Old Monocacy Log Church in the village" of the same name.[20] Our factual knowledge concerning the site of that Lutheran Church is discussed in more detail below.[21]

The Creagerstown claims can be effectively refuted by reference to the land records. These show that until after 1759 only three persons, none of them German and none a Lutheran, owned land between today's Creagerstown and the Monocacy River.

---

[10] *Ibid.*, A 1:85.
[11] C/S: Y & S 7:115. See p. 184.
[12] Frederick County Will Record, A1:102.
[13] Proceedings of the Assembly, 1745-1747, *Archives of Maryland, op. cit.*, 44:692.
[14] Prince George's County Land Records, BB:14. See below, p. 351.
[15] Reformed Pastor at Thurmont, whose charge included the congregation at Creagerstown.
[16] Edward T. Schultz, "First Settlements of Germans in Maryland" (Frederick, 1896; reprinted in 1976).
[17] Daniel Wunderlich Nead, *The Pennsylvania German in the Settlement of Maryland* (Lancaster, Penna., 1914), p. 93.
[18] *Baltimore Sun*, July 7, 8, 9, 1941.
[19] Boyd varied from the others in attempting to place Monocacy "village" in the Ceresville area (Frederick *News*, May 28, 1953), where he "discovered" the remains of the well-known Cock-Grahame cemetery, identified by J. M. Holdcraft, *op. cit.*, 1:19. See below, p. 128n.
[20] A recent propagation of this error occurred with the "250th Anniversary" celebration by the St. John's Evangelical Lutheran Church of Creagerstown (Frederick *News*, Oct. 2, 1982). The first Lutheran church in the Monocacy Valley probably dates from about 1742 (see p. 142). But historians can establish no direct tie to St. John's in Creagerstown, which most likely actually dates from the late 1780s. See also Charles H. Glatfelter, *Pastors and People: German Lutheran and Reformed Churches in the Pennsylvania Field, 1717-1793* (The Pennsylvania German Society, Breinigsville, 1980), 1:187-188, 193.
[21] See pp. 138-139.

On July 7, 1741 "Papan Bottom" was laid out for John Digges on the east side of the Monocacy River, but its 160 acres extended across the River to include the mouth of Hunting Creek.[22] He assigned the certificate of survey to Nathaniel Wickham, Jr., and patent was issued to the latter on August 7, 1742. Digges was a Roman Catholic and Wickham belonged to the Church of England. On June 6, 1749 Wickham increased the parcel's area to 710 acres by his "Resurvey on Paw Paw Bottom." His land then included the area where the Creagerstown-Woodsboro Road now crosses the Monocacy.[23]

On April 12, 1759 Richard Lilly, a Roman Catholic, had 50 acres surveyed for himself which he called "Lilly's Lot." His parcel began "on the west side of the Monocacy River near the mouth of Hunting Creek."[24] On September 7th of that year he had the area increased to 300 acres. This "Resurvey on Lilly's Lot" adjoined Wickham's "Resurvey on Paw Paw Bottom," and it, too, was crossed by the present road.[25]

Earlier, on October 25, 1754, Reverdy Ghiselin had 710 acres north of Lilly's land surveyed as "Third Addition to the Resurvey of Fountain Low." Many years after that, in 1786, Thomas Beatty had a further survey made of this land, which he then called "Town Tract."[26] It was on "Town Tract" that Creagerstown itself was then finally built, a half century after the Germans supposedly erected their so-called "Monocacy" Church.

For taxation purposes, it was required that certificates of survey include notations describing all improvements on the land being surveyed. Some of these descriptions give a good insight concerning the development and uses of the land up to the time of the surveys. Thus we may read such notations as, "On this land is a large log house and one old one and two large wheat fields well fenced."[27] Or: "On this land is a good dwelling house 24 x 18 with a stone chiminy and a stove, covered with shingles, two old log cabins 14 x 10, each covered with puncheon and a very good roof."[28]

But for the surveys at Creagerstown the comments report only a bare minimum of development. On none of the original surveys is there a notation concerning houses or structures. And on only one resurvey is even a single building mentioned. That was on Richard Lilly's Resurvey of 1759 where we read, "On this land is about four acres of cultivated land inclosed by a fence and one log house 20 x 16 feet." The description hardly typifies the *village* of Monocacy in whose existence tradition would have us believe.

---

[22] C/S: LG E:62.
[23] C/S: BC & GS 41:15. This certificate was assigned to Daniel Dulany in return for Dulany's discharging of Wickham's £69/19/6 debt to Osborn Sprigg. In 1761 Dulany's son Walter assigned the Resurvey to Christopher Stouder. It was finally patented on April 9, 1770!
[24] C/S: BC & GS 12:520.
[25] C/S: BC & GS 14:42.
[26] C/S: IC B:674.
[27] C/S: LG E:385 for "Chestnut," November 28, 1741.
[28] C/S: BC & GS 1:163 for "Resurvey on Teernoch," May 15, 1753.

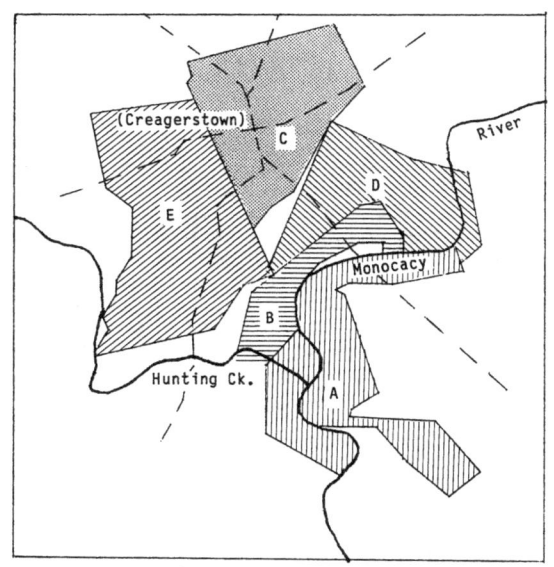

APPROXIMATE LOCATION OF FIRST SURVEYS
IN THE CREAGERSTOWN AREA

A "Papan Bottom" July 7, 1741, John Digges, assigned to Nathaniel Wickham, 160 acres. "Resurvey on Paw Paw Bottom" June 6, 1749, Nathaniel Wickham.

B "Lilly's Lot" April 12, 1759, Richard Lilly, 50 acres. "Resurvey on Lilley's Lot" September 7, 1759, 300 acres.

C "Third Addition to Resurvey on Fountain Low" April 23, 1763, Charles Carroll, 510 acres.

D "Fourth Dividend," April 23, 1763, Charles Carroll, 510 acres.

E "Friendship," September 20, 1749, William Murdock and Henry Addison, 1,000 acres.

For a more complete refutation of the claims concerning the village of Monocacy, with special emphasis on the original Lutheran Church's location, the reader's attention is also invited to Millard M. Rice's essay, "Three Lost Towns."[29]

As the overall Monocacy region developed, paths used by the Indians and early traders became the roads used by settlers. Most of these roads in turn remain as antecedents of roads we know today. But to define and identify the early roads from out of the web of present roads and highways, one must turn to the early records of yesteryear.

In general there were two principal directions pursued by the first inhabitants. From the tidewater area, either along the Potomac or from points farther north, routes headed toward the backwoods country of the West. Simultaneously early settlers were moving south from Pennsylvania's back country to Virginia. In both directions, Frederick County itself, as we know it today, was not the initial destination. Instead, the first routes were headed elsewhere and were only of necessity passing *through* the area of our study.

Unlike other streams and rivers, the Monocacy River, which flows in a general southerly direction through the heart of Frederick County, was not itself a route of travel. Instead, it was a River to be crossed. This in turn led to the practice of referring to all roads leading toward the Monocacy River or its general region as *the* "Monocacy Road."

There was, in other words, no one Monocacy Road. A survey, for example, of June 10, 1732 for "Strawberry Plains," located near present-day Westminster in Carroll County, had its beginning point "by the Monocacy Road."[30] The tract called "Ludwig's New Mill," surveyed May 10, 1734 and located near present-day Hanover, Pennsylvania, began at a point "on the waggon road leading from Connewago to Monocacy."[31] A survey of November 26, 1741 for "Jack of the Green" in today's Montgomery County, Maryland, started "on the north side of a nole [sic] on the south side of the old Monocacy Road."[32] And Prince George's County Court of August 1744 received a petition for clearing the road "from the foot of Shenandoah Mountain [South Mountain] where the old Monocacy Road crosses [now Crampton Gap] and from thence via Richard Touchstone's."

Because the Monocacy River had to be crossed, the general directions of paths and the roads which succeeded them often were determined by where the Monocacy could be forded. The first mention of one of these fords in early records occurs in a 1725 Act of the Maryland Assembly describing the backwoods as lying "northwestward of Monocacy River from the mouth thereof, up the same River to the

---

[29] Rice, *New Facts, op. cit.*, pp. 161-187.
[30] C/S: EI 5:222.
[31] C/S: EI 3:442. Conewago was an area of early German settlement in the extreme southern portions of today's Adams and York Counties, Pennsylvania. It extended roughly between Littlestown and Hanover.
[32] CS: LG E:99; Original Patented Certificate of Survey, Prince George's County No. 1159.

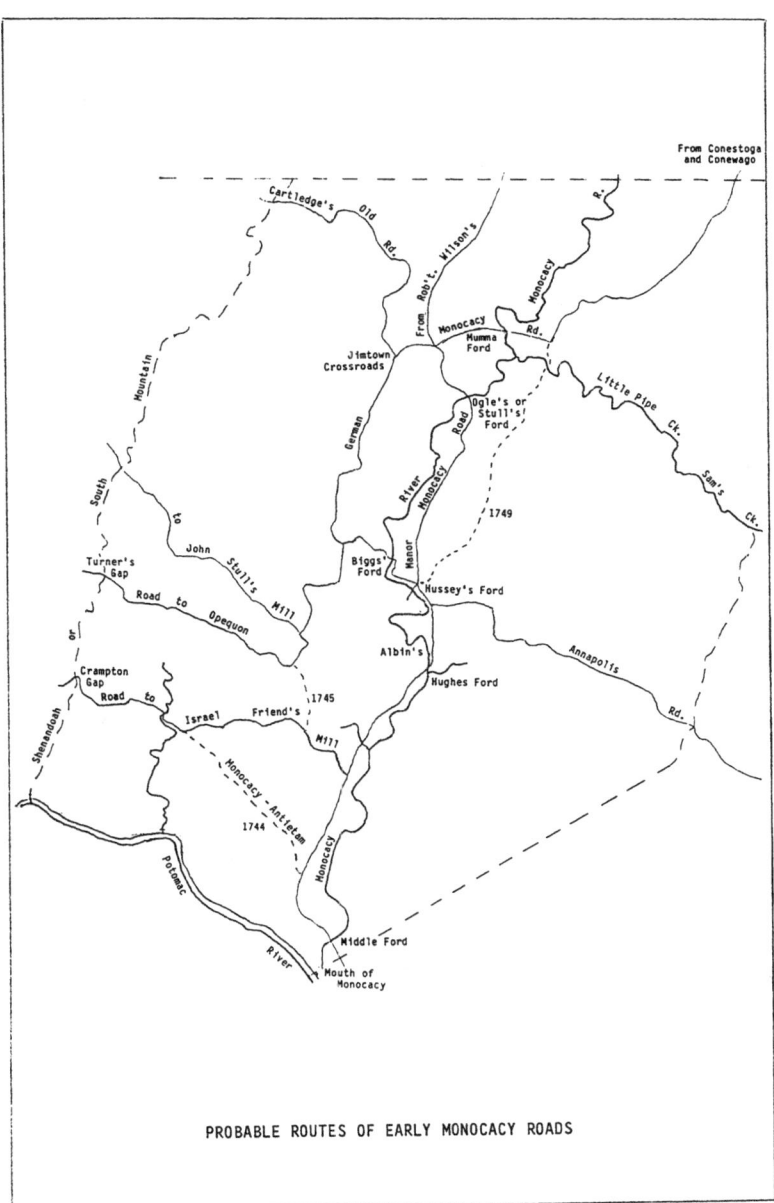

PROBABLE ROUTES OF EARLY MONOCACY ROADS

fording place where the Conestoga Path crosses the same, near one Albine's plantation, and then to the northwestward of the said Conestoga Path until it meet the Susquehanna River..."[33] The fording place to which this record referred was near the mouth of Linganore Creek and is known today as Hughes Ford.

In addition to this crossing, five other important fords across the Monocacy River were mentioned in early records: (1) At the mouth of the River where it joins the Potomac,[34] (2) Middle Ford where today's State Route #28 crosses the River,[35] 3) At His Lordship's Manor, now marked by Biggs Ford Bridge west of Walkersville, (4) Ogle's Ford, today's Stull's Ford west of LeGore Bridge,[36] and (5) Ogle's Wagon Road Ford, today's Mumma's Ford.[37] These fords are described in more detail below.

The two earliest north-south Monocacy Roads through present Frederick County might well be designated as the "German Monocacy Road" and the "Manor Monocacy Road." Their common beginning was at Conestoga, an area of German settlement extending some 15 to 20 miles along Conestoga Creek, north and east of Lancaster, Pennsylvania. The route to Monocacy passed through the Conewago area of today's York and Adams Counties in Pennsylvania to present Taneytown, Maryland. A little south of today's Keysville, the road turned west[38] and at Ogle's Wagon Road Ford it crossed the Monocacy River into today's Frederick County. It continued its way via what is now Appold Road to a junction near Loys Station. Here the road divided. The German Monocacy Road continued its way west through Graceham, then south through Jimtown crossroads, Lewistown, Bethel and on to today's junction of Butterfly Lane and Mount Phillip Road.[39]

From Loys Station another road turned south, recrossed the Monocacy at Ogle's (now Stull's) Ford and then followed along the east side of the River. This was the so-called Manor Monocacy Road. From Leonard Schnell's 1743 Diary[40] it is clear that a road, or at least a path, also worked its way south from Keysville, staying exclusively on the east side of the Monocacy until it met the road

---

[33] Proceedings of the Assembly, 1727-1729, *Archives of Maryland, op. cit.*, 36:583-585: An Act to encourage Takers up of run-away slaves. See also Marye, "Indian Road," *loc. cit.*, 15:367. Marye could not locate Albin's Plantation. It is described below, pp. 70-75.

[34] Mentioned in 1728 in C/S: AM 1:27 for "Broken Island."

[35] C/S: IL A:732 for "Gunder's Delight," 1726. Known as Furnace Ford today.

[36] See below, pp. 237, 326, 328.

[37] See also below, pp. 250, 328.

[38] "Dispatch," for example, which George Steuart conveyed to Daniel Dulany in 1744, had its point of beginning "on the east side of Big Pipe Creek on the south side of the wagon road from Pipe Creek to Conewagoe." Prince George's County Land Records, BB 1:133.

[39] See below, p. 166. This junction was formerly known as Fulmer's Station, one of the stops on the old electric railroad from Frederick to Braddock Heights.

[40] See below, pp. 142, 281.

from Ogle's Ford. But from that point the Manor Road continued all the way to the ford at Thomas Albin's plantation. His land "Albin's Choice" was located on the west side and in a bend of the Monocacy River, "being a place called Oleakin,"[41] where a portion of the Frederick Airport is situated today.[42] The fording place, later known as Hughes Ford, was just above the mouth of Linganore Creek at the south end of "Albin's Choice," east of today's Airport and about three-quarters of a mile north of where U.S. Highway 40 crosses the River. The November 1739 Court of Prince George's County identified this crossing as the "Monocacy Wagon Road Ford near Thomas Beatty's." It appears to be the same crossing used by Michel in 1707.[43] From this ford the Manor Monocacy Road continued along the west side of the River almost to the River's mouth where it empties into the Potomac. The November Court of 1753 referred to this latter stretch as coming "from Monocacy Ferry to Ballenger's Branch."

The German Monocacy Road is so named because it was traversed by the many Germans bound for the backwoods area of Virginia, especially after 1731. Not all of them, however, ended in Virginia. Many Germans stopped along the way, satisfied to establish themselves in the Monocacy Valley. Between May 10, 1738 and December 10, 1743, for example, 33 of the 36 land surveys made along the German Monocacy Road between present-day Jimtown crossroads and Butterfly Lane were made for German settlers.[44] Their settlement of this area is discussed in detail in separate chapters below.

A portion of the German Monocacy Road appears to have coincided with one of the routes taken by Michel in 1707. On the 1733 survey for John Magruder the western end of "Forrest" (today's Middletown) was described as the road from "Connestoga to Opeckon."[45] Daniel Dulany's survey in 1741 for "Mankine" referred to the German Monocacy Road as the "main road."[46]

---

[41] For Oleakin, Olicin, see above, p. 36n.
[42] C/S: IL B:17; Frederick County Land Records, B:218. See also below, p. 75, map p. 70.
[43] See above, p. 9.
[44] Including one or more surveys for Jacob Matthias Mansser, Jacob Weller, George Baer, Michael Reisner, John Vertries, Jacob Staley, Melchior Staley, Martin Wetzel, Philip Kens, Tetur Laney, Jacob Bonnett, Hardman Vertries, Isaac Miller, George Honig, John House, Pastor David Candler, Bernard Weymore, George Swinehart, Adam Spough, Philip Grüber, Peter Shaver, Christian Getzendanner, Hendrick Six, Adam Stull, Henry Bachdold, Conrad Kemp, Martin Shoup and Isaac Lehnert. We exclude only Charles Hedges, Peter Stilley and Chidley Matthews.
[45] C/S: AM 1:365. The German Opequon settlement was situated south of today's Winchester, Virginia. The Creek of that name flows from Frederick County, Virginia, north through Berkeley County, West Virginia, paralleling the Shenandoah River and emptying into the Potomac below Williamsport.
[46] C/S: BC & GS 23:363.

Initially the German Monocacy Road did not reach southward all the way to that part of the Potomac River which marks the southern boundary of today's Frederick County opposite Virginia. Instead the route turned west and slightly north again at today's junction of Butterfly Lane and Mt. Phillip Road. It then headed through present-day Middletown and on over South Mountain into today's Washington County, continuing westerly to cross the Potomac (which here flows in a southerly direction) and thus reach Virginia.

The connection between the German Monocacy Road and the mouth of the Monocacy River was made following a March 1745 petition which asked for a road from "the main road above Isaac Leonard's along to Baltis Fout's so as to come into the main Minoccaccee Road by the Quaker Meeting House" and then continue with that road to the mouth of the "Minoccoccee."[47] This road was laid out by Baltis Fout, William Griffith and Robert Debutts. Baltis Fout then became the initial overseer of the road. Leonard's parcel lay just south of the junction of Butterfly Lane and Mt. Phillip Road. This junction was also the fork referred to in John Smith's August 16, 1745 certificate of survey for "Addition to New Germany." The latter had its beginning point "on the east side of Kitoctin Mountain near where the roads fork, one to the mouth of Minorcocee and the other to Abram Miller's" at present-day Lewistown.[48]

By contrast and with few exceptions until after the end of 1743 it was the large land investors, e.g., Thomas Addison, Daniel Dulany and Lord Baltimore himself, who had surveys made along the Manor Monocacy Road on the eastern side of the River. Leonard Schnell reported in 1743 walking 25 miles from Conewago without seeing a house.[49] When "Papan Bottom" was surveyed on July 7, 1741, a part of the Manor Monocacy Road was described as the road from "Robert Wilson's to His Lordship's Manor."[50] Since Robert Wilson lived near present-day Emmitsburg on "Wilson's Fancy,"[51] this portion of the road presumably forded the Monocacy at Ogles or Stull's Ford, described above. As more and more people came into the region, the northern part of these roads gave way in importance to the subsequent traditional Monocacy Manor Road from Keysville through present-day Woodsboro and Walkersville, in essence coinciding with much of today's Maryland Route 194. Joseph Wood had petitioned to the Court of 1745 for this road and did so again to the March Court of 1748/49[52] so that its inception occurred after our period of the first two decades of earliest Monocacy settlement. The November Court of 1753 seems to have indicated that both routes were then in use, for road overseers were appointed for the road from Ogle's Ford to Biggs' Ford and from Hussey's Ford via Smith's Branch [at today's Woodsboro] to Great Pipe Creek.

The first roads of present-day Frederick County to be made

---
[47] See below, pp. 82, 181.
[48] C/S: LG E:567. For Miller, see below, pp. 283-287.
[49] See p. 142.
[50] Patent: LG E:62. See Maps pp. 41, 238.
[51] C/S: BY & GS 1:152. For Wilson, see below, p. 237.
[52] Frederick County Court Judgment Records, A:18.

"public roads" were identified in Prince George's County Court of November 1733. John Nelson was appointed overseer of the road from the "mouth of Monocacy to the first Mountain." Most of this road later became the route of the Chesapeake and Ohio Canal. William Matthews was likewise appointed overseer of the road from "Monocacy to Henry Ballenger's Branch." This represented the lower part of the Manor Road. And Henry Ballenger was appointed overseer for the road "from Mill Branch[53] to the Manor" near Biggs Ford, a mid-part of the Manor Road.

The records show various references to the principal east-west road on the west side of the Monocacy River. It bore various names, but ultimately came to be known as the Monocacy-Antietam Road. From the lower Monocacy region it proceeded west toward South Mountain, crossing it at Crampton Gap on the present boundary between Frederick and Washington Counties. On May 28, 1734 Osborn Sprigg had 285 acres surveyed for himself on the north side of what he called the "Conechigany Road near the Shenandoah Mountain."[54] In present-day terms, his land lay about one half mile north of Burkittsville. One month later, on June 30, 1734, Richard Sprigg had his survey of 366 acres located along part of this same road, i.e., about a mile directly north of today's Jefferson on the Roy Remsburg Road. He described his beginning point as near "Israel Friend's Mill Road[55] and near where the said road crosses a hill called Katoctin."[56]

The Prince George's County Court of November 1738 referred to this road from "Monocacy to Antietam" and made it a public road with Flayl Payne as overseer. A petition from 68 individuals living in what is now Washington County[57] was presented to the August Court of 1744 requesting that the road be better located and designated to go from the foot of Shenandoah Mountain where old Monocacy Road crosses and from thence via Richard Touchstone's to Mr. Bel's Gap[58] on Cottacken Mountain." The Court appointed John Hawkins, Captain William Griffith and Joseph Chapline to lay out this revised route which would then continue by Edward Mobley's into the wagon road by John Pyburn's.[59] The latter represented the southern portion of the Manor Road described above.

The road from Monocacy to John Stull's mill was made a public

---

[53] Also called and now known as Ballenger's Branch.
[54] C/S: AM 1:425 for "Forest." Shenandoah was an early name for South Mountain.
[55] Prior to 1736 Israel Friend operated a mill at the mouth of Antietam Creek in today's Washington County. But Benjamin Winslow's "Plan of the Upper Part of Patomack River called Cohongorooto, surveyed in the year 1736" (original at Enoch Pratt Library, Baltimore) shows Israel Friend living in that year west of the Potomac nearly four miles south of the mouth of "Undietum" Creek. See John P. Dern, "The Upper Potomac in 1736," *Western Maryland Genealogist*, 2:86-87.
[56] C/S: EI 3:425, "Pile Hall."
[57] Formed from Frederick County in 1776.
[58] Cf. above, p. 40.
[59] Prince George's County Court Records, CC:505.

road by the November Court of 1739. John Stull had built his mill on "Whiskey," located where the Hagerstown power plant now stands. The road divided off from the German Monocacy Road at today's village of Shookstown. It then ran through Hawbottom, Harmony and Myersville, crossing the mountain where U.S. Highways 40 and I-70 also cross today. The surveys for "Barren Hill," "Termstool," "Gaming Alley," "Little Meadow,"[60] and others refer to this important artery of transportation.

In the extreme southern part of today's Frederick County a road followed the Potomac River westward. It came from the vicinity of present-day Beallsville, site of the "English Church" mentioned in a 1740 road petition. Until 1744, however, there was no bridge across the mouth of Catoctin Creek, and it was only then that a petition was submitted for such a bridge and for "a main road to be laid out from Tuscarora Creek to the mouth of Katoctin and from thence to Antietam Creek" in present-day Washington County.[61] This road was known as the road from Monocacy to Shenandoah Mountain and for the most part proceeded along the route later made famous by the Chesapeake and Ohio Canal and the Baltimore and Ohio Railroad.

The so-called Annapolis Road was another east-west road, which ran through the eastern part of the Monocacy region. Court records described it as "the road from Monocacy near James Beatty's [i.e., Biggs'] Ford to Poplar Springs." From the Monocacy Ford near James Beatty's it ran south and east to cross Israel Creek and pass the home of William Beatty. At what is now the town of Mt. Pleasant it turned southward toward present-day McKaig, before continuing on to New London, Mount Airy, and then another three and a half miles further to Poplar Springs. It thus traversed a route somewhat south of what is popularly known today as the Old Annapolis Road. Robert Kendrick's 50-acre survey of "Kendrick's Hap" made on August 22, 1739 began "within a quarter of a mile of the wagon road that goes from Monocacy to Annapolis."[62] Certificates of survey for "Patrick's Colt," "Mackey's Delight," "Pretty Sally" and others mention this important transportation route. John James was appointed overseer by the November Court of 1740.

In the northern part of the County a road ran from "Kitoctin Mountain near William Elder's to the wagon road near Little Pipe Creek." It was made public by the November Court of 1741 with William Elder as overseer. At that date Elder lived on "Slate Ridge," located on Little Owen's Creek about a mile southwest of present

---

[60] C/S: GS 1:57, GS 1:126, Y & S 7:103, BC & GS 5:163.
[61] Signing this petition were Thomas Payne, Benjamin Shacklett, George Fee, Richard Ancrum, Robert Jones, Cornelius Hortsey, Thomas Fee, Andrew Cox, Richard Touchstone, Jonathan Prather, William Nicholas, Isaac Wells, Nathaniel Wood, William Griffith, John Poole, H. Frigs, Edward and Thomas Williams, Notley Thomas, Flayle Payne, William Thomas, Henry Dickeson, Joseph Mowes, William Tucker, John Tucker, William Tanneyhill, Henry Touchstone, James and John Hook, John Hawkins, James Aris, Thomas Morris and John Booth.
[62] C/S: LG C:54.

Saint Anthony's Church on the road now known as Kelbaugh Road.[63] Originally this road was a part of Cartledge's Old Road (see p. 13).

At the end of 1743 there were five important road junctions in the area that is now Frederick County: (1) near present-day Loys at what is today the intersection of State Routes 72 and 77, (2) at Biggs Ford Bridge where the Manor Monocacy Road, a branch from the German Monocacy Road, the Monocacy-Annapolis Road and the Road from the Manor to Henry Ballenger's Branch all met, (3) where the village of Shookstown now stands, the junction of the German Monocacy Road and the road to Stull's mill, (4) today's junction of Mount Phillip Road and Butterfly Lane, originally the junction of the German Monocacy and Monocacy-Antietam Roads, and (5) the present-day junction of Buckeystown Pike and the Greenfield-Mountville Road.

Baltis Fout in 1743 was overseer of the road "from the top of Katoctin Mountain to the ford of the Monocacy Wagon Road near Thomas Beatty's." If we locate the latter ford as today's Hughes Ford, we are undoubtedly foretelling the beginnings of a tie between the two principal north-south roads, 1) the German Monocacy road which paralleled the River well to its west until it reached the approximate latitude of today's city of Frederick, then headed farther west away from the River toward today's Washington County and 2) the Manor Monocacy Road which paralleled the River on its east side until it crossed over, also at the latitude of today's Frederick, from where it paralleled the river on its west side southward toward its mouth. Below the mouth of the Monocacy, now in Montgomery County, was Cornelius Elting's mill, frequently referred to in various road petitions.

We turn now to the history of the first individual settlements in the region known as Monocacy. Initial habitation was widely scattered throughout the area we have described. It began first along the Potomac River, then leap-frogged here and there along the Monocacy River. Subsequent settlement occurred at ever greater distances away from both Rivers. Each settlement began with a single survey or two and gradually expanded outward until one settlement became almost contiguous with another or even infiltrated into its neighbor's midst.

Within about twenty years these settlements had fairly well covered all of present-day Frederick County with the sole exception of the mountainous area in the extreme northwest and some of the southeastern region along the boundary with today's Montgomery County. Rather arbitrarily we have grouped the initial settlements as some twenty-odd distinct areas. While it is perhaps presumptious to separate them into such distinct packages, we do so for the matter of convenience. Each "settlement" is described in a separate chapter which follows, showing who settled where, together with something of the nature of their surveys as well as the origins of the settlers before they came to Monocacy. A special map has been prepared for each settlement, whose location within the whole may be found by means of the key map on the following page.

---

[63] C/S: EI 5:500.

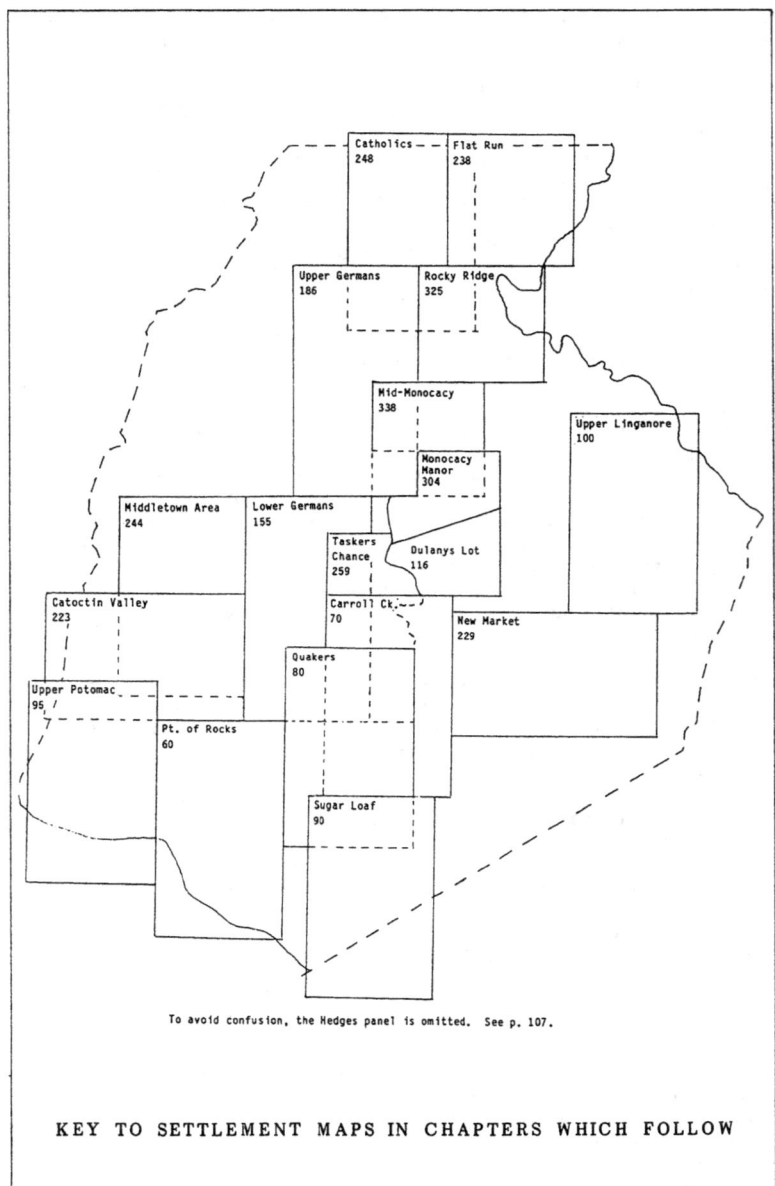

To avoid confusion, the Hedges panel is omitted. See p. 107.

KEY TO SETTLEMENT MAPS IN CHAPTERS WHICH FOLLOW

POINT OF ROCKS

In the great marble corridors of the Department of Justice Building in Washington once hung the portrait of John Nelson, Attorney General of the United States from 1843 to 1845. A former Congressman, Nelson had also served as Chargé d'Affaires to the Kingdom of the Two Sicilies in 1831-32 and very briefly finished out the remaining week of President John Tyler's term as Secretary of State ad interim after the death of Secretary Abel P. Upshur.[1]

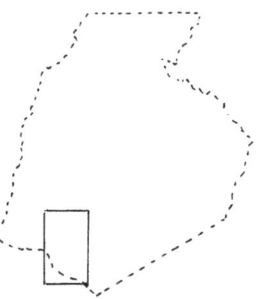

More impressive, at least as concerns this study, John Nelson was the great grandson of **Arthur Nelson**, in turn the first settler to have land surveyed for his own home residence in present-day Frederick County. Nelson located in the area along the Potomac River known subsequently as Point of Rocks, Rock Hall and the route of the Chesapeake and Ohio Canal.

The Nelsons came from England about 1694[2] and in 1718 owned land which is now part of Washington, D.C. On February 18, 1724 "Nelson's Island," then known as Conoy Island but now called Heaters Island, the largest of several islands in the Potomac, was surveyed for Arthur Nelson.[3] A year later, on March 2, 1725, he had "Hobson's Choice" surveyed on the land to the northeast, and here he lived with his sons Arthur, Jr. and John, Sr. and his grandsons John, Jr. and [General] Roger Nelson.[4] In 1728 he added "Broken Island."[5] John Nelson, Sr. enlarged his portion of "Hobson's Choice" by a Resurvey dated October 20, 1739.[6]

Isaiah Bonnett [Bennett], an indentured servant of Arthur Nelson, charged Nelson with "barbarus" treatment. The November Court of 1724 found Nelson guilty and fined him 500 pounds of tobacco. In November 1733 Arthur Nelson was again in Court, petitioning that he

---

[1] John Nelson (1794-1860) was born in the town of Frederick and lived in the fine white house at 112 West Church Street.
[2] Colonial Dames of America, *Ancestral Records and Portraits* (Chicago: Grafton Press, 1910).
[3] C/S: IL B:132.
[4] Frederick County Will Records, A1:140 and GM 2:419. Charles Varlé, "A Map of Frederick and Washington Counties, State of Maryland" (1808) shows General Roger Nelson's home directly north of Mason Island, not far from present-day Camp Kanawha.
[5] C/S: AM 1:27. Today's Nolands Island.
[6] C/S: IL B:131 for original survey, LG E:183 for Resurvey.

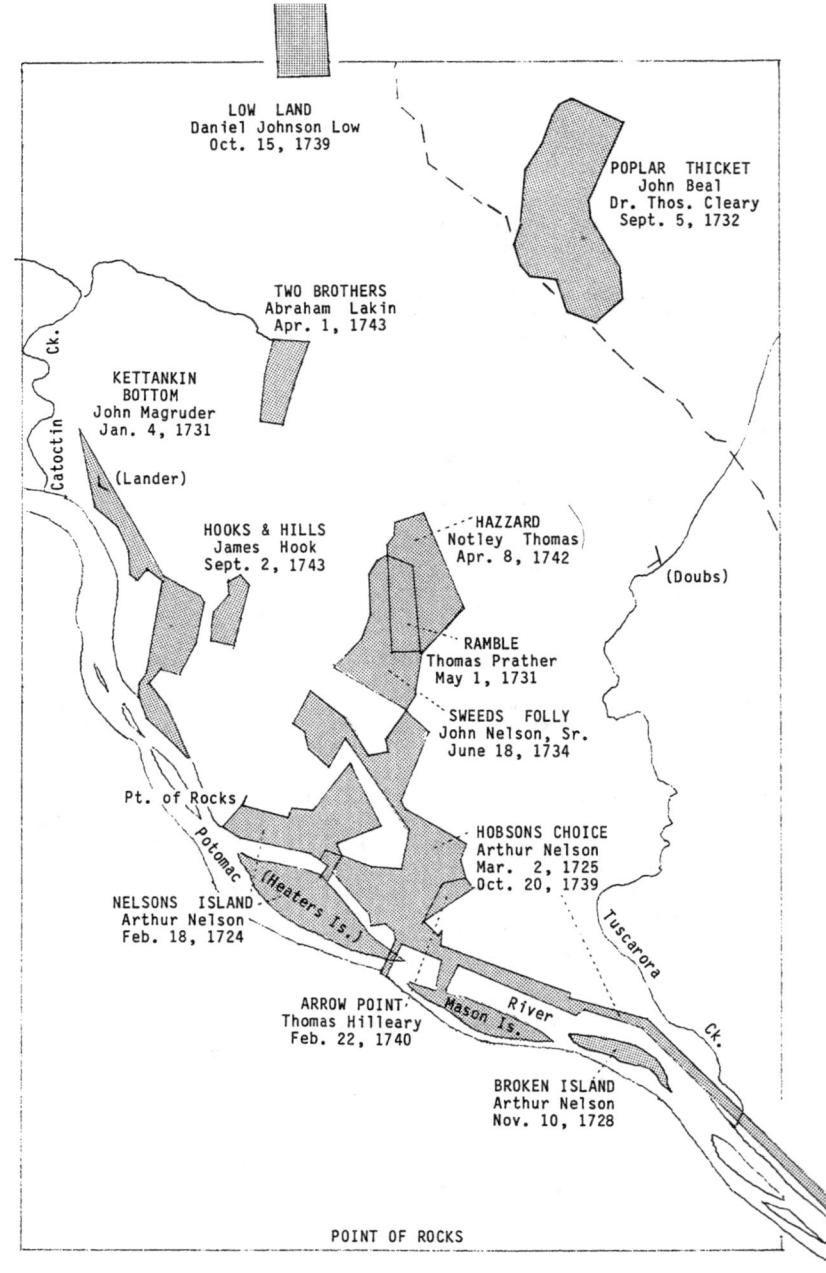

is "now near 70 years of age and hath a very infirm wife and hath not anybody to assist him in giting anything for his or her support but is oblidged to do it by his own labour." He "....humbly prayed that for the future he be not levied [taxed]." The Court rejected the petition. In March of 1742 Arthur Nelson, Sr. again made his appeal to the Court for relief from taxes, he then "being nearly eighty years of age and crippled." Again the request was rejected. Finally we have word of his death, with Arthur Nelson, Jr. administering his estate in 1754.[7] Apparently Valentine Nelson, wife of Arthur Nelson, Sr. had predeceased him.[8]

On June 18, 1734 "Sweed's Folly" was surveyed for John Nelson, Sr., to whom it was patented on November 26, 1737.[9] The certificate located the parcel on "a branch called Dry Branch which falls into the Potomac" near the tract "Arthur's Island." This was a little north of present-day Point of Rocks, where the 1873 Atlas shows the homes of O[tho] W[ilson] Trundle and J[acob] Wirtz.[10] In 1743 Nelson and his wife Jane divided the parcel's 200 acres equally between their sons-in-law Elias Delashmutt, husband of Elizabeth Nelson, and John Delashmutt, husband of Sarah Nelson. John Nelson called them his beloved sons.[11] Elias Delashmutt had several surveys made for himself, and he purchased other land between today's Point of Rocks and Jefferson. One of these purchases represented a part of "Children's Chance"[12] which later became the home of his son Elias Delashmutt, Jr.[13] This land, at the west end of Jefferson, is crossed today by U.S. Highway 340 which has undoubtedly evolved out of what was first known as the "Touchstone Road."[14] According to the elder Delashmutt's will, he and his wife Elizabeth also had as children: Elias, Jr., Basil, Linsey, Ann Warfield, Rachael Lemaster, Elizabeth Bolter (wife of Edward Bolter) and a daughter who married a Mr. Noland.[15] Elias Delashmutt, Sr. was a Captain during the French and Indian War. His Company's 1757 muster roll, reproduced on page 379, lists friends and neighbors who undoubtedly lived nearby.[16]

In 1733 the November Court appointed John Nelson, Sr., Constable of Monocacy Hundred. One of his duties was to provide the Court with a list of those persons who had not burned their tobacco according to law. Such condemnation of tobacco was undertaken in order to protect the general price level of the crop.

---
[7] Frederick County Administrative Accounts, A1:64.
[8] She was named in Prince George's County Land Records, M:36, when on June 30, 1726 Arthur Nelson conveyed land to Joseph Belt.
[9] C/S: EI 5:294.
[10] Lake, op. cit., p. 7.
[11] Prince George's County Land Records, BB 1:37, 39.
[12] Frederick County Land Records, H:429, 454.
[13] Frederick County Wills, GM 1:37.
[14] See below, pp. 222-223. Cf. also Rice, New Facts, op. cit., pp. 45-48, 55-59, etc.
[15] Frederick County Wills, A1:79, December 2, 1752.
[16] "French and Indian War -- Rolls Taken from a 109-page manuscript with the Society," *Maryland Historical Magazine*, 9:262-264. Delashmutt's roll is dated August 13, 1757.

For the August Court of 1734, Nelson produced just such a list. It included the names of 84 individuals. A most valuable list, it is almost the equivalent of a "census" of early Monocacy settlers. When combined with a tax list from the previous year, John Nelson's tobacco list of planters represented fully 70% of all propertied inhabitants in Monocacy Hundred.[17] The notable absence of German names suggests that either the Germans had not yet arrived in any significant numbers, or their unfamiliarity with tobacco kept them from planting it. The former explanation is the more probable. Moreover, as the 1757 muster roll indicates, the Germans seem not to have settled to any great extent in the Point of Rocks area even in the succeeding quarter century.

In 1734 John Nelson, Sr. and John Pyburn were appointed tobacco burners for Monocacy Hundred.[18] Nelson was also selected as overseer of the road from "Monocacy to the First Mountain." This meant that he was responsible for the maintenance of the road which ran from the mouth of the Monocacy west along the Potomac River as far as today's Point of Rocks, where the north-south range of the Catoctin Mountain has been cut through by the River.[19] The June Court of 1735 appointed Thomas Prather as tobacco burner, replacing John Nelson who was excused because of illness in his family. John Nelson's home was mentioned in a road petition of November 1740 seeking a connection between "John Nelson's and John Pyburn's for the benefit of our mill and church."[20] The road referred to was to run from the mouth of the Monocacy beside a part of Little Monocacy River in today's Montgomery County, past Elting's Mill to present-day Beallsville. In June of 1741 John Nelson was appointed Deputy Ranger under Meredith Davis. The records of the June Court of 1748 (still Prince George's County) show Thomas Cresap suing John Nelson for a five pound debt for one year's rent of a ferry. William Marshall "of Monockasey" and Elias Delashmutt assumed the debt for Nelson. In 1748 four Nelsons, John Sr. and John, Jr., Arthur Sr. and Arthur, Jr., all signed a road petition seeking construction of a road from Nelson's Ferry to Fredericktown.[21] This became the Ballenger Creek Pike, a portion of which is now State Route 78.

---

[17] See Appendix, pp. 368-369. The combined total of both lists numbered 117, of whom 11 appeared only on the tobacco list.
[18] Prince George's County Court Records, V:302.
[19] See above, p. 56.
[20] The 1740 petition was signed by Henry and Richard Touchstone, Richard Touchstone, Jr., John Nelson, George Murdock, John Beals Abington, George Colvin, Thomas Prather, Baltis Fout, Robert Jones, James Hook, Isaac Wells, Joseph Ogle, John Middaugh, Chidley Matthews, Robert Debutts, John Pyburn, John Martin, Henry Ballenger, George Matthews, John Wright, Michael Reisner, Bernard Weymore, Martin Wetzel, Patrick Holagon, Phillimon Plummer, James Orrick, Thomas Fee and others.
[21] Others who signed this 1748 petition were Elias and John Delashmutt, Notley Thomas, James Dickson, James and John Hook, John Jacobs, Christian Kemp, Thomas Morris, John Crampton, Benjamin Pyburn and Samuel Davis.

Arthur Nelson, Jr. served as clerk in his brother-in-law's military company during the French and Indian War. He married Lucy Waters, and they had as issue: Roger, John (who married Louisa Fairfax from Virginia), Jane (who married a Mr. Watson from Georgetown) and Sally (wife of Col. William Luckett).[22]

During the Revolution Roger Nelson served with Augustine Washington in the defense of the city of Charleston, South Carolina, where he was taken prisoner by the British. After his release he rejoined the Maryland line and marched into the battle of Camden where he was severely injured and left on the battlefield for dead. He recovered and was with General George Washington at the surrender of Lord Cornwallis at Yorktown. General Nelson served several terms in the Maryland House of Delegates and was a member of the U.S. Congress. In 1810 he was Associate Judge of the Circuit Court for the Sixth Judicial District. He was twice married, first to a Miss Simms and second to Betsy Harrison, daughter of John Harrison and Catherine Contee. His son John Nelson was the Attorney General. A daughter Emily Catherine Contee Nelson married Colonel William Pinkney Maulsby, who lived a portion of his life in Frederick's well-known mansion, "Prospect Hall."[23] Their daughter Betsy Harrison Maulsby married Judge John Ritchie.

The first Luckett to appear in Frederick County land records was William Luckett, who contracted to keep a ferry at the mouth of the Monocacy in 1758. According to the tax rolls, he then lived on the land of Meredith Davis at the mouth of the Monocacy. In 1755 he had "Luckett's Merry Midnight" surveyed near the Nelson land, and the tract still carries his name. It may be located on the 1866 map by Bond as the home of J. C. Luckett and in the 1873 Atlas as the home of D. Himes.[24] William Luckett became a Captain during the French and Indian War, and his son, William Luckett, Jr., served as a Colonel during the Revolutionary War. The latter was the husband of Sally Nelson, General Roger Nelson's sister. Their son William Arthur Nelson Luckett is mentioned in his grandfather's will.

By 1743 in the area north of Point of Rocks where the Nelsons had settled, there were new neighbors, including Thomas Prather, Notley Thomas, James and John Hook, the Lakins and the Fees.

Thomas Prather, Jr. was one of the most active men in the business affairs of western Maryland. His grandfather Jonathan Prather had arrived in Maryland from England in 1658. Thomas Prather, Sr., his father, had married Martha Sprigg, daughter of Thomas Sprigg, Sheriff of Calvert County.[25] He himself came to the area north of the Nelson Family settlement shortly after May 1, 1731 when the parcel called "Ramble" was surveyed.[26] It lay along the northeastern line of "Sweed's Folly" and contained 100 acres. In 1734

---

[22] Frederick County Wills, GM 2:419.

[23] Prospect Hall was built on "Dickson's Struggle," surveyed in 1748 for James Dickson, son-in-law of John Darnall. Dickson deeded it to Stephen West who in 1767 assigned it to Daniel Dulany the Younger.

[24] Lake, op. cit., p. 35. For Bond, see p. 97n.

[25] Ancestral Records and Portraits, op. cit.

[26] C/S: AM 1:49.

Thomas Prather, Jr. leased another 100 acres of land, a part of "Carrollton."[27]

Colonel Thomas Prather, as he became known in western Maryland, was a surveyor, Constable of Lower Monocacy Hundred in 1738, a Justice of the County Court, an officer with the Maryland Militia and a member of the vestry of All Saint's Church. A few years after 1738 he removed to present-day Washington County, where he built the Prather homestead near Big Pool, Maryland.[28] In 1760 his home on "Ramble" was in the possession of Elias Delashmutt, who in 1778 devised both it and "Sweed's Folly" to his son Basil with the condition that "during his natural life, he shall not dispose of or even lease it during his life except to one of his brethren or one by the name of Delashmutt."[29]

On his 1748 journey to western Maryland and Virginia, the Moravian missionary Matthias Gottlieb Gottschalk[30] was hospitably received by Thomas Prather, who then lived some ten miles beyond Jonathan Hager. Prather hosted him overnight, provided him with a passport for entry into Virginia and loaned him his horse to travel the 70 miles farther west to Colonel Cresap's.[31]

The **Hook Family** also settled in the area north and west of Point of Rocks. They were English and descended from Thomas Hook, a taxable freeman in Maryland in 1677. He lived not far from present-day Laurel, near the Patuxent River, midway between Washington, D.C. and Baltimore. His son James married Margaret Thrasher and had as children Mary (wife of Thomas Fee), Arabella (wife of John Giles), Rachel (wife of Robert Owings), Stephen (husband of Dorothy Barkett), Samuel, Sarah (wife of Abraham Lakin), James Jr., and John.[32] The latter two are of interest here.

Although we have no land record for them until 1740, John Hook was in the area by 1734 when he was fined for not burning his tobacco as required by law and James in 1739 was appointed overseer of the road from "Monocacy to Shenandoah Mountain."[33] In 1740 James Hook was among those who signed the petition for the road "from John Pyburn's to John Nelson's.[34] In 1742, six years before Frederick County was actually formed, both James Hook and John Hook signed a petition seeking division of Prince George's Parish and the creation of a new Parish that same year.[35]

---

[27] Prince George's County Land Records, T:166.
[28] Maryland Rent Rolls (Frederick No. 1).
[29] Frederick County Will Records, GM 1:37.
[30] See below, p. 147.
[31] William J. Hinke and Charles E. Kemper, "Moravian Diaries of Travels through Virginia," *Virginia Magazine of History and Biography*, 12:62-76.
[32] Family information through the courtesy of James William Hook of New Haven, Connecticut. See especially his *Captain James Hook of Greene County, Pennsylvania* (Ann Arbor, 1952).
[33] As was Richard Touchstone, 1740-1742 and 1745-1749, and Isaac Wells, 1742-1743. See below, pp. 86 and 222.
[34] See above, p. 62.
[35] See below pp. 68, 371.

On August 26, 1740 James Hook received from his good friend John Magruder a "deed of gift" for 150 acres of "Kettankin Bottoms"[36] on the west side of Catoctin Mountain, extending from the mouth of Catoctin Creek south along the Potomac River as far as (and including) Paton Island.[37] Magruder had originally had this land surveyed nine years before. On November 26, 1740 James Hook gave his brother John 50 of these acres,[38] and on this land the two brothers appear to have built their homes.

James Hook built his mansion, called Potomac Hills, overlooking the Potomac River and the countryside beyond. It was constructed of Catoctin Mountain stone with some stucco and brick. A kitchen in the basement was connected by a hung stairway to the dining room immediately above. All rooms had high ceilings and one of them was set aside as a chapel for worship. Also known as the old McGill home or the Abram Hemp farm, the house at Potomac Hills is still standing, having been extensively restored in 1957 by Mr. and Mrs. Thomas M. Hoffmeister.[39]

Apparently James Hook was unfamiliar with the boundary lines of his own land, for he did not use them to determine a starting point for a new parcel adjacent to his "Kettankin Bottoms." Instead, the starting point for his survey "Hooks and Hills," laid off on September 2, 1743, was marked as "150 yards west of Thomas Fee's spring."[40] Fee was Hook's brother-in-law and seems to have owned no land of his own. In 1763 James Hook received a special warrant for a resurvey on the original land plus adjoining vacant land, but omitted paying the caution money. Thomas French discovered the oversight, paid the fee and received title for the land upon which Hook had been living for over thirty years. Hook then purchased title from French and called his 1,265 acres "Hook's Neglect Recovered by a Hard Struggle."[41] Still having trouble with his boundaries, Hook once more in 1788 had his land, including "Kettankin Bottoms," resurveyed, this time naming the tract more succinctly and perhaps hopefully, "Hook's Conclusion."[42]

James Hook's children were James Samuel (who made his home at Potomac Hills), Stephen (married Sarah Thrasher) and Daniel (married Sarah Burgess). Daniel Hook's daughter Mary was the wife of Patrick McGill, Jr., who purchased Potomac Hills. His son Dr. Daniel Hook, Jr., was Mayor of Augusta, Georgia, 1840-1843.

John Hook and his wife Sarah Snowden removed from "Kettankin Bottoms" to a parcel they called "John and Sarah," surveyed for them October 15, 1747. The beginning point was "on the

---

[36] C/S: AM 1:364. The name was also spelled Kittoctin or, as today, Catoctin.
[37] Prince George's County Land Records, Y:195.
[38] *Ibid.*, Y:244.
[39] Rice, *New Facts, op. cit.*, pp. 44-45, has speculated that St. Alban's Masonic Lodge No. 65 was first convened in James Hook's home in 1819.
[40] C/S: LG E:408.
[41] C/S: BC & GS 51:240.
[42] C/S: IC D:663; Patent: IC C:696.

side of a draft of Prick Run, just below Teley's Cabin on the west side of Katectin Mountain."[43] Prick Run was a tributary of Catoctin Creek. Teley apparently owned no land of his own and may have been a trader. From the original "John and Sarah" and its subsequent Resurvey of 1750[44] one has a wide view of the countryside, to Harper's Ferry on the west and the Potomac River on the south. In making their move to this location, John returned to his brother James the latter's 50-acre gift of "Kettankin Bottoms." The Prince George's County Court of June 1748 excused John Hook from jury duty when he explained, "I came part of the way but my horse being taken lam was forst two retorn hom."

John and Sarah Hook had two sons, James and John Snowden Hook. James Hook was born about 1749 and married the niece of Abraham Lakin and Sarah Hook. He spent a part of his life with his Uncle James at Potomac Hills, but after his marriage made his home on "John and Sarah" and its 388-acre Resurvey of 1750. Later James Hook and his wife moved to Greene County, Pennsylvania, where he died in 1824. John Snowden Hook, born about 1752, married Elizabeth Ward and moved to Cumberland, Maryland about 1786.

John Hook, Sr., and Sarah deeded 113 acres of their "Resurvey on John and Sarah" to Richard Ancrum, the son of John Ancrum and Martha Wells. Richard's sister Elizabeth Ancrum married John Lakin and another sister, Sarah, married Thomas Beall. A copy of the latter's marriage record, dated "of Prince George's County,[45] Maryland the 12th day of the 9th month, 1741," can be found in the Quaker records of New Garden, North Carolina.

Richard Ancrum used his part of "John and Sarah" in his resurvey of March 6, 1770, which he named "Betsy's Delight."[46] In his will of November 29, 1790, he mentions a wife Elizabeth, daughters Elizabeth Thrasher and Mary Delashmutt, sons Richard, Jr., Jacob and Aaron Ancrum, granddaughters Nancy and Sarah Delashmutt and grandsons Richard and William Ancrum, children of his "deceased" son John.[47] Richard Ancrum (son of Richard Sr. or of John?) had a resurvey made May 26, 1792 on "Betsy's Delight" which was then called "Richard and Elizabeth."[48] This tract, in the vicinity of present-day Lander and Fry Roads, extended northward toward today's town of Jefferson from the old Colonel Hammond home on Catoctin Creek.

Back on the east side of Catoctin Mountain, **Notley Thomas** by means of a survey dated April 8, 1742 located his land "Hazzard" adjacent to and northeast of Thomas Prather's "Ramble."[49] Later Thomas had it enlarged by a Resurvey.[50] In 1753 he received a patent

---

[43] C/S: TI 1:26.
[44] C/S: Y & S 7:146.
[45] Frederick County, it will be remembered, was not created out of Prince George's County until 1748.
[46] C/S: BC & GS 47:169.
[47] Frederick County Wills, GM 2:507.
[48] C/S: IC I:270.
[49] C/S: LG E:192.
[50] C/S: BC & GS 1:399.

for "Leonard's Beginning" and in 1763 had "Gleanings" surveyed for himself next to "Hazzard."[51] All of Thomas' land was located between "Carrollton" and the lands of Hook and Prather.

Notley Thomas does not appear in the records as frequently as the Nelsons, Hooks or Prathers. But in 1744 he did sign a petition for a bridge "to be laid out at the mouth of Katoctin Creek and a main road to be laid out from Tuscarora Creek to the mouth of Katoctin and from thence to Antietam Creek."[52] In 1749 Thomas signed a petition for a road to Fredericktown from Nelson's Ferry,[53] and in 1751-1752 he served as Constable of Lower Monocacy Hundred. Much of Notley Thomas' land was incorporated in 1792 by Samuel Skinner Thomas in his resurvey called "Thomas' Profit."[54]

Abraham Lakin and his wife Martha Lee were the last to join this area of settlement before the end of 1743. Martha was the daughter of William and Ann Lee and had lived on "Cold Spring Manor" west of the Patuxent River. On April 1, 1743 Lakin had a survey made which he called "Two Brothers," located east of Fry Road about midway between Point of Rocks and Jefferson.[55] He divided this land between two of their sons, Abraham Lakin, Jr. and Joseph Lakin.

Like the Nelsons, Hooks and Prathers, the Lakins were English and associated with the Church of England. The Lakin children included Deborah, Elizabeth, Mary, Rachel, Ruth, Sarah Lyeth, Martha Plummer, Benjamin, Joseph and Abraham Lakin, Jr. Sarah Lakin married Robert Lyeth, a planter in Anne Arundel County. Their daughter Mary Lyeth married Capt. James Hook, son of John and Sarah Hook while her brother Abraham Lakin, Jr. married James Hook's aunt, Sarah Hook, a sister of John Hook. Benjamin Lakin married Rachel Fee, Joseph married Elizabeth Fee and Sarah Lyeth, sister-in-law of James Hook, married Thomas Fee.

On January 30, 1752 Abraham Lakin, Jr. had his portion of his father's gift of "Two Brothers" enlarged,[56] and on the original document Abraham and Sarah listed their children's names: Eleanor, Deborah, John, Sarah (married Duckett Wells), Abraham 3rd (married Mary Ungles), Daniel (married Ann Sheckels) and Nancy (married Abraham Deaver).[57] The 1873 Atlas shows the Lakin home as belonging to the heirs of Capt. William Lakin.[58] Some of the land is still in the hands of Lakin descendants. An old family burying ground likewise remains, from which J. M. Holdcraft recorded some 25 inscriptions.[59]

Joseph Lakin and his wife Elizabeth Fee stayed several years on "Two Brothers," then moved on to the Ohio Territory.

There appear to have been two men named **Thomas Fee** in the

---

[51] C/S: BC & GS 1:273.
[52] For a list of other signers, see p. 56n.
[53] Cf. above, p. 62.
[54] C/S: IC N:596.
[55] C/S: LG E:379.
[56] C/S: GS 1:71.
[57] Hook, op. cit., p. 72.
[58] Lake, op. cit., p. 35.
[59] Holdcraft, op. cit., pp. 19, 689-690.

area of this first settlement. In 1733 one Thomas Fee married Mary Margaret Hook, a sister of John Hook. The other married first a Miss Thrasher, had children named George, John, Mary and Ruth, then married as his second wife Sarah Lyeth, as above. A George Fee was listed in 1734 as not burning his tobacco.

In October 1742 nearly 200 residents of today's Frederick County signed the petition seeking division of the Church of England's Prince George's Parish. The resulting Act of Assembly that same year led to the creation of All Saints' Parish which remains in Frederick today. Grouped all together on the list of petitioners[60] were eight Point of Rocks people: Thomas Prather, John Nelson, James Hook, John Hook, John Delashmutt, Elias Delashmutt, Thomas Fee and George Fee.

---
[60] See below, p. 371.

CARROLL CREEK

The second person to settle on Frederick County land which he himself owned did so where the city of Frederick stands today. His survey was dated April 21, 1724, only two months after Arthur Nelson's survey at Point of Rocks on the Potomac. But it was a full twenty-one years or more before the site of this second settlement saw the beginning of today's city of Frederick.

John van Metre (1683-1745) was a trader of Dutch descent, who lived originally in New York and New Jersey. His parents, Joost Jansen van Meeteren[1] and Sarah Dubois lived in the Kingston area along the Hudson River. By 1714 John, together with his mother and his younger brother Isaac, were in Salem County, New Jersey, where they obtained from Colonel Daniel Cox 3,000 acres on Alloway Creek. Two years later this land was divided between them.[2] Isaac stayed on in New Jersey and in 1734 John deeded him his remaining holdings of New Jersey land.[3]

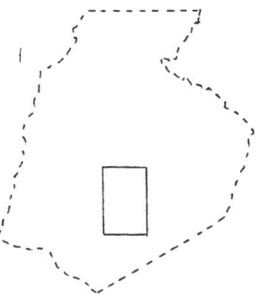

Meanwhile John van Metre had journeyed through Maryland to Virginia. Along the way he discovered land to his liking and by a survey dated April 21, 1724 he acquired some 300 acres in Maryland. This he called "Metre." It was the sixth parcel to be surveyed within the area of present-day Frederick County.[4] Then, a year and a half later on November 18, 1725, John van Metre had another Maryland parcel surveyed and this he called "Meadow."[5] Here he and his family lived until about 1735. Together with its subsequent Resurvey, his land extended along Carroll Creek. It is now the southeastern part of the city of Frederick, stretching from today's intersection of South Market and South Streets eastward through a portion of the Fair Grounds. On it he built what was subsequently described as a "Dutch frame house 18 x 14 feet, clay and white-washed outside with a stone

---

[1] The name Jansen is a patronymic. Joost Jansen came from Meeteren, a small village located a short distance from Buren in Gelderland. He arrived at New Amsterdam on the ship "Fox" in 1662. For a genealogy of this family, see Samuel Gordon Smyth, *Genealogy of the Duke-Shepherd-Van Metre Family* (1909) as well as his *Origin and Descent of an American Van Metre Family* (Lancaster, 1923).
[2] Salem County Deeds, DD:316, at Trenton.
[3] *Ibid.*, E:32.
[4] Prince George's County Patented Survey 1434.
[5] Prince George's County Patented Survey 1450.

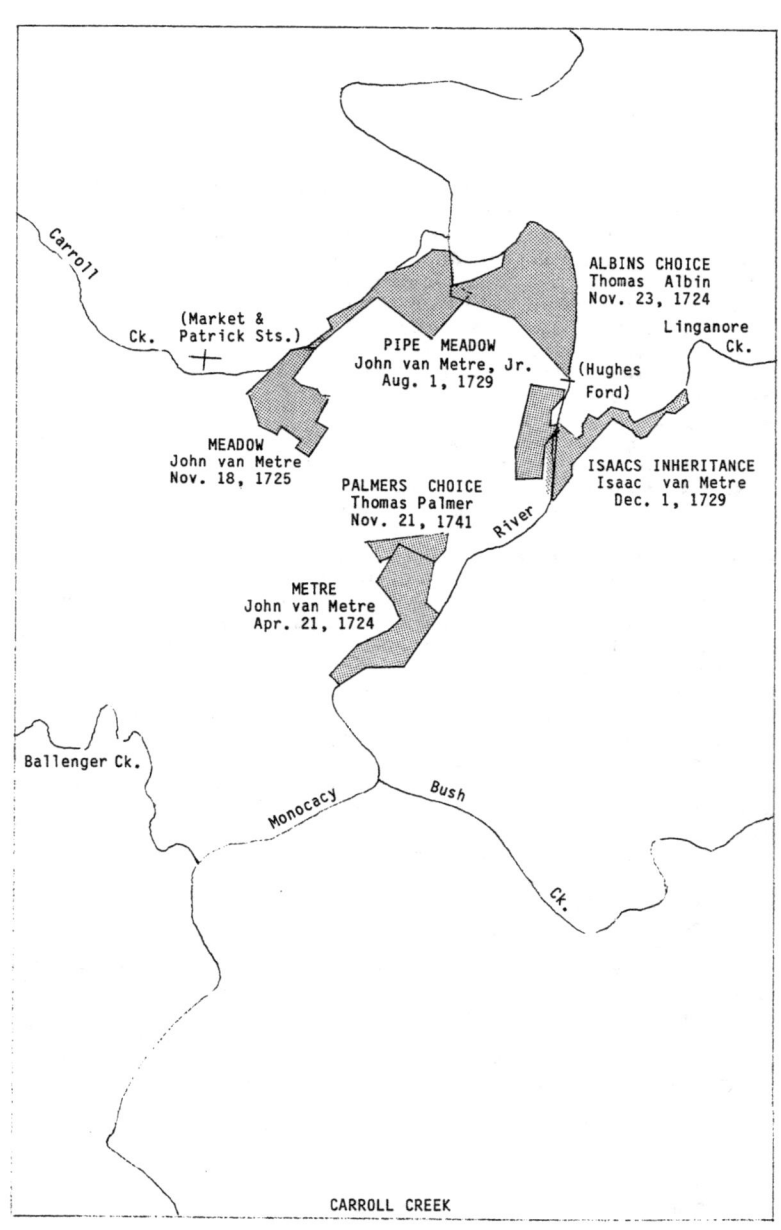

chimney, a log house 20 x 16 feet, a frame house covered with shingles, a house raised four feet from the ground 18 x 14 feet covered with boards."[6]

On February 20, 1725 John Rolfe and Ranier Snowden, Quakers from the town of Salion, Maryland, declared that Adam Strangler was indebted to them. John van Metre stood "pledge and security" for Strangler. After a hearing before the Prince George's County Court of June 1727, Snowden was fined 622 pounds of tobacco for bringing "false clamor" against Strangler. Subsequently, in the June Court of 1728, John van Metre paid a five pound debt of his own to his Lordship.

The Courts of 1729, 1731, 1732 and 1734 appointed John van Metre Constable of Monocacy Hundred, which at the time extended from the mouth of the Monocacy River northward to Pennsylvania, eastward to include a part of today's Carroll County and westward to encompass all the lands of western Maryland as we know them today. It was a vast area and in 1729 the Constable of "Monocoughsin" Hundred reported to the Court that he had received many "abuses in the execution of his office insomuch that he is afraid to comply with the order of the Court and humbly prays for protection." In answer, the Court ordered Joseph Mounts and John Gratharm to join in authority with van Metre.

On June 17, 1730 John van Metre and his brother Isaac each secured from the Governor and Council of Virginia grants of 10,000 acres of Virginia land located in the Shenandoah Valley. An additional 20,000 acres would be granted if twenty families were settled within two years.[7] In the following year on August 5th, the van Metres transfered title, along with the conditions, to Just Hite, a German who had come to New York in the year 1710.

Hans Justus Heyd was born in Bonfeld in the Kraichgau area of Germany in the year 1685, and there in 1704 he married Anna Maria Merckle. With their first-born child, they joined the huge German exodus of 1709, migrating to London and on to New York in the following year.[8] A significant portion of these German settlers moved into Pennsylvania where they were joined by the succeeding waves of German immigrants who followed them throughout the next two decades. In 1730 Hite was living in the Perkiomen region, near today's Schwenksville in Montgomery County, Pennsylvania,[9] an area heavily populated by recent German immigrants.

With his partner Robert McKay from Cecil County, Maryland, Hite sought an additional 100,000 acres in Virginia[10] and set to work

---

[6] C/S: BC & GS 5:51.

[7] *Executive Journals of the Council of Colonial Virginia, 1721-1739*, H. R. McIlwaine, ed. (Richmond, 1930), 4:223, 224.

[8] Henry Z. Jones, Ralph Connor and Klaus Wust, *German Origins of Jost Hite, Virginia Pioneer, 1685-1761* (Edinburg, Virginia, 1979), pp. 10, 12. This work, especially pp. 27-30, factually analyzes and refutes many earlier misconceptions concerning Just Hite and his alleged wife Sarah and/or Anna Maria Dubois.

[9] Ibid., pp. 15-20.

[10] *Executive Journals, Virginia*, op. cit., 4:253.

inducing the Germans to move to the backwoods there. He himself left Pennsylvania in 1731[11] and after him followed the great trek by other Germans traveling via the German Monocacy Road through the Monocacy region, then over South Mountain, across the Potomac from today's Washington County and into Opequon and Shenandoah Valleys. Quite obviously settlers found the enticements offered from Virginia much more advantageous than those from Maryland where, as we have seen, land investors and speculators had acquired so great a control over the available land.

In 1735 John van Metre also joined the move to Virginia. He sold his farm animals[12] and removed himself and his family into Virginia[13] where he died ten years later.[14] On July 18, 1745, just before his death, John Vanmetree of Frederick County, Virginia, appointed his "well-beloved friend Baltis Foutt of Prince George's County" as attorney to effect the sale of "Meadow" to Michael Raymer.[15] Although he had lived in Maryland for only a little over a decade, he left an indelible imprint on the Frederick County area: it was he who had begun actual settlement in this area and, at least indirectly, it was he who had been responsible for the area's discovery by the German element passing through from the north.

John van Metre's children also played important roles in the early settlement of both Maryland and Virginia. His five sons and six daughters were named John Jr., Isaac, Henry, Abraham, Jacob, Magdalena, Rebecca, Elizabeth, Sarah, Rachel and Mary.

John Jr., the eldest son, had 200 acres surveyed on August 1, 1729 "at the mouth of Beaver Run," now Carroll Creek which flows through the city of Frederick. Called "Pipe Meadow," his parcel was contiguous with his father's "Resurvey on Meadow" and extended the joint holdings from present-day downtown Frederick all the way to the Monocacy River.[16] Apparently John Jr. died at Monocacy fairly early, leaving two small children, John III and Johanna, who inherited their father's land.[17] Jonas Hedges, son of Joseph Hedges, Sr.,[18] later took the two children with him to Virginia, where he was appointed their guardian.[19] Johanna later married William Burns from Virginia.

---

[11] Letter from Jost Hite to Lord Fairfax in 1741, Manuscript Division, Library of Congress: See also Charles E. Kemper, "Documents Relating to Early Projected Swiss Colonies in the Valley of Virginia," *Virginia Magazine of History and Biography*, 29:2.
[12] Prince George's County Land Records, Y:102. Johannes van Meter was still in the Monocacy area in May 1734 when he witnessed a bill of sale from George Sweinhart to Baltis Fout (ibid., T:240).
[13] Orange County, Virginia, Land Records (1736-1738), 1:384, 1:449, 2:437.
[14] Frederick County (Virginia) Will Book, 1:52-60; August 13, 1745, probated September 3, 1745.
[15] Prince George's County Land Records, BB 1:491. For Baltis Fout, see below, p. 161.
[16] C/S: AM 1:56.
[17] Frederick County Land Records, F:837, 899.
[18] See below, pp. 108-109.
[19] Frederick County (Virginia) Will Book No. 1.

Interestingly in August 1749 and again in June 1751 Francis Wise had been charged by the Grand Jury with waste and destruction on the land of John Van Metre, an orphan."[20] Earlier, on April 1, 1746, Daniel Dulany had taken out a writ of ad quod damnum on 20 acres on Carroll Creek, part of John Vermitre's "Pipe Meadow." For an annual five shillings sterling this gave Dulany the mill seat mentioned in subsequent Court records.[21]

Isaac van Metre also had 200 acres surveyed in the area of the van Metre Monocacy settlement, though his land, called "Isaac's Inheritance," was situated at the mouth of Linganore Creek. It was surveyed on December 1, 1729,[22] four months after his brother John's land had been similarly surveyed. Isaac's land was located on both sides of the Monocacy River, extending along the south side of Linganore Creek to the east of the Monocacy and along the Monocacy itself on its west side. It thus lay quite some distance east of the other van Metre holdings and touched the southern extremity of "Albin's Choice" near Hughes Ford. In October 1744 Isaac van Metre and his wife Alice conveyed their Monocacy land "with houses, orchards, gardens and pastures" to Jacob Stoner.[23] They had by then moved on to Virginia where Isaac died about 1748.[24]

Henry van Metre, even though he returned to New Jersey, had land interests on the present-day Montgomery County side of the Monocacy. In 1746, for example, Daniel Dulany had agreed to sell to "Henry Vanmetre of West New Jersey, farmer," Fair Island "in the Potomac, a little below the mouth of Monoccasy River." Cornelius Eltinge paid Henry Vanmetre £70 for the land which Dulany then conveyed to Eltinge.[25] Henry van Metre later settled on Patterson Creek Manor in Virginia near Solomon Hedges. The latter had married Henry van Metre's sister Rebecca and was a brother of the Jonas Hedges mentioned above. In 1748 Henry van Metre and Solomon Hedges were visited by the 16-year-old George Washington on his surveying trip with George William Fairfax.[26]

Jacob van Metre, who spent his boyhood in the Monocacy Valley, in later years removed to Kentucky. There a member of his family was killed by an Indian who thrust his spear through Jacob's Bible which she was carrying. The damaged Bible is today in the Iowa State Historical Library in Des Moines.[27]

---
[20] See below, p. 263.
[21] Chancery Records, IR 4:628. Our thanks to John W. McGrain of Towson, Maryland for pointing out this record. For Dulany's Mill, see below, p. 261.
[22] C/S: AM 1:56.
[23] Prince George's County Land Records, BB 1:209. Seemingly Isaac was obligated by his father's will to sell "Isaac's Inheritance" and divide the proceeds in order to inherit his father's land in Virginia. Yet the 1740 sale presumably preceded John's will by five years.
[24] Frederick County (Virginia) Will Book No. 1.
[25] Prince George's County Land Records, EE:91.
[26] Fitzpatrick, op. cit., pp. 12-14.
[27] Rita Goranson and Jo Ann Burgess, "Bible Records from Iowa Libraries and Museums" (typescript, 1977).

Abraham van Metre married Ruth Hedges, a sister of Solomon and Jonas Hedges, and removed from Monocacy Valley to settle in Berkeley County, now West Virgina. Sarah van Metre married James Davis, and they made their home on Tullis' Run, also in Berkeley County. James Davis was killed by Indians in 1752.

Mary van Metre married Robert Jones who had lived at Perkiomen Creek in Pennsylvania in the early 1720s. In 1729 he was appointed, along with John van Metre, as Constable of Monocacy Hundred. His name is found on the 1734 list of persons who had not burned their tobacco according to Maryland law.[28] Later he moved into Virginia with the van Metre and Hite families. He had also signed several road petitions during his stay in the Monocacy area.

Elizabeth van Metre married Thomas Shepherd, also originally from New Jersey. In 1734 they settled on the land where Shepherdstown, West Virginia is now located. Elizabeth inherited her father's "Pell Mell," located in Maryland directly across the river from Shepherdstown. Her sister Rachel married a Lefarge, had one son, but died before her father.

Abraham and Jacob Hite, sons of Just Hite, married sisters Rebecca and Mary van Metre, who appear to be the children of John van Metre's brother Isaac. Presumably about 1736 Isaac made a tomahawk improvement near the later site of Fort Pleasant in Hardy County, West Virginia. This was above the "Trough," a steep-sided syncline valley six miles in length through which the South Branch of the Potomac flows straight as an arrow. Isaac supposedly returned to New Jersey, but came out again to find a man named Coburn settled on his land. He bought out Coburn and again returned to New Jersey. Then, about 1744, he moved his family, undoubtedly by way of Monocacy Valley, into the West Virginia area.

During the bloody battle of the Trough in 1756, it is said that "old Mr. Van Metre mounted his horse, rode to a high range and witnessed the battle." He was killed by Indians in 1757. His will, probated December 12, 1757, shows him as a resident of the South Branch of the Potomac River, living in what was then Frederick County, Virginia. His legatees named in his will were his wife Annah, sons Jacob and Garet, daughters Sarah Hickman, Catherine, Hellita and Rebecca, widow of Abraham Hite.

Rebecca van Metre, a sister of John and Isaac, also figures in the history of early Maryland land holdings. Born in 1686 in the Kingston area of New York, she married there in 1704 Cornelius Elting. The record of their children's baptisms at Kingston extends until 1728, showing that they did not leave New York as early as Rebecca's brothers. Ultimately she and Cornelius settled on the Montgomery County side of the Monocacy River near its mouth, as did their daughters Sarah and Eleanor Elting who married John and Isaac Hite, other sons of Just Hite. Their daughter Jacomyntje Elting married John Thompson, whose will was the second to be recorded after Maryland's new Frederick County was formed in late 1748.[29] The

---
[28] Cf. Appendix, p. 368.
[29] Frederick County Wills, A1:2; dated September 25, 1748, proved March 17, 1750/51.

Elting mill was the mill referred to in the 1740 petition for a road from John Pyburn's to John Nelson's.[30]

On November 9, 1739 John "Vanmatre of Orange County, Virginia" entered into an agreement to transfer title to his first survey, "Metere," on the Menockecy River to **Joseph** and **Thomas Palmer**, who also came from Westchester County, New York to live in the area of the van Metre settlement.[31] They were to pay £80 each December for three years for the 300 acres. Joseph Palmer later sold his interest to his brother Thomas and went back to New York. An additional 58 acres were added by Thomas, who had "Palmer's Choice" surveyed on November 21, 1741. Its beginning point was "near the upper side of the land ["Metre"] he [Palmer] now lives on." In 1752 Thomas Palmer used most of "Metre" for a resurvey which he called "Palmerzaner."[32] This he conveyed to Abraham Crum on May 13, 1754.[33]

In his will of the following February, Edward Beatty claimed to have a third interest in "Metere," "Palmer's Choice" and "Palmerzaner" which he devised to his son Elijah Beatty. He provided, however, that Abram Crum and his brother Gilbert Crum could keep the land if they gave Elijah land of equivalent value.[34] This Crum must have done, for Abraham Crum's son William used portions of "Metere," "Palmer's Choice" and "Palmerzaner" in a resurvey of October 20, 1796 for his "New Barn."[35] Both father and son, Abraham Crum in 1787, and William Crum in 1810, were buried on this property in a small graveyard which remains today, located at the foot of the Grove Lime Company's spoil bank, south of Reich's Ford Road and just east of the Quynn Orchard Road. Prior to the 1873 Atlas this property came into the possession of the Reich family.[36]

The records yield little or no information concerning **Thomas Albin** whose 300 acres of "Albin's Choice" lay close by the van Metre property. His parcel had been surveyed for John Radford on November 23, 1724 and patented to him in 1726. Radford posted a bond for £100 guaranteeing that he would deliver to Albin by May 1, 1727 all 300 acres of "Albin's Choice."[37] After Albin's death his administrators James and Mary Thatcher conveyed the land to Captain Robert Debutts by means of an assignment attached to this bond which was then recorded again on August 3, 1750, this time in Frederick County.[38]

Captain **Robert Debutts** is said to have been a brother of the Rev. Lawrence Debutts of Maryland's Established Church. The latter was licensed to Virginia in 1721 but came to St. Mary's County in

---
[30] See pp. 19, 349.
[31] Prince George's County Deeds, Y:105. John and James Beatty and Robert Debutts witnessed the agreement.
[32] C/S GS 1:47. Orig. Certificate, Prince George's Co. No. 154.
[33] Frederick County Land Records, E:435.
[34] Frederick County Wills, A1:52.
[35] C/S: IC R:530.
[36] Holdcraft, *op. cit.*, pp. 32, 287, 290; Lake, *op. cit.*, p. 11.
[37] This bond was originally recorded in Prince George's County.
[38] Frederick County Land Records, B:218.

Maryland in 1734.[39] Seemingly Robert Debutts was in possession of "Albin's Choice" on March 23, 1746/47 when he wrote: "Whereas in all appearances my wife Anna Debutts is now in a very sick and languished condition and is likely to leave behind my son John Donaldson Debutts, her only child, not three weeks old...to manifest my tender affections to her and her dear child, I hereby voluntarily and freely give unto my said son my dwelling plantation called Albin's Choice containing 300 acres of land with all improvements and everything given and delivered unto his mother, my wife, by his grandfather John Donaldson, after my decease."[40] Subsequently, on October 23, 1751, Debutts mortgaged "Albin's Choice" to Daniel Dulany for £176, and then conveyed it and 264 acres of "Spring Garden" to Dulany three days later for £375.[41] "Spring Garden" lay between "Pipe Meadow" and "Albin's Choice."[42] The names of these parcels were still being used in 1791 when Richard Potts had a resurvey on parts of "Spring Garden," "Albin's Choice," "Pipe Meadow" and "Meadow," surveying them into what he then called "Bellvue."[43] In the 1873 Atlas the home there was still shown with the name of "Bellvue."[44] This parcel was located on what is now a part of the Frederick Airport property.

Elsewhere Robert Debutts had other land holdings. In 1752 "Sun Is Down and Moon Is Up" was surveyed for him in the Middletown Valley.[45] Much earlier still, on March 25, 1741, he had had "Debutts' Hunting Ground" surveyed.[46] It was located near today's village of Middlepoint, northeast of Myersville, and was the first survey in that western area. In 1758 Luke Barnard, stepson of Nathaniel Wickham and son-in-law of Debutts, assigned the Middlepoint property to John Ferguson, in turn the second husband of Debutts' widow Abigail.[47]

Prince George's and Frederick County Land Records show several other exchanges of property in which Debutts was interested, as well as loans of money made by him. The Court records likewise contain frequent references to Debutts.[48] His name appeared, though

---

[39] Rightmyer, Nelson Waite, *Maryland's Established Church* (Baltimore, 1956), p. 179.
[40] Prince George's County Land Records, BB:381. Witnesses were R. Cooke, Baptist Barbar and William Brackenburg. In a Frederick County Court case four years later, Dr. Richard Cooke was suing Debutts for failure as Cooke's "bailiff and receiver" to render proper accounts during the period 1746-1749. Cf. Millard M. Rice, *This Was the Life; Excerpts from the Judgment Records of Frederick County, Maryland, 1748-1765* (Redwood City, Calif. 1979), pp. 81-82.
[41] Frederick County Land Records, B:459, 464.
[42] C/S: BC & GS 3:319.
[43] C/S: IC I:60.
[44] Lake, *op. cit.*, p. 11.
[45] C/S; Y & S 7:207.
[46] C/S: LG E:78.
[47] Frederick County Inventories, A1:100.
[48] See for example, Rice, *The Life, op. cit.*, pp. 69, 71, 81, 82, 90, 93, 96, 98.

for reasons unknown to us, on the Plummer family's first land acquisition in the Linganore Creek area in 1739.[49] In 1740 he signed the petition for a road from John Nelson's to John Pyburn's and on to Beallsville in Montgomery County. In 1742 he joined others in two petitions, one to Governor Bladen to divide Prince George's County,[50] the other to divide Prince George's Parish.[51] In 1743 the Prince George's County November Court appointed Debutts as Constable of Linganore Hundred. In 1745 he worked with Baltis Fout and William Griffith to lay out a road from "above Isaac Leonard's along by Baltis Fout's so as to meet the Main Minoccaccee Road" coming from the ford at "Albin's Choice." In the same year he acquired Jacob Brunner's "Inlett" on Carroll Creek.

On March 28, 1746 Debutts and Kennedy Farrell[52] signed an agreement with Joseph Jennings, the first "clerk rector of All Saints' parish in Monocksesy," guaranteeing the minister's salary,[53] and in 1749 he was the overseer for the inventory of Jennings' estate. As Captain Robert Debutts, his name appeared on the list of Militia officers sent to Annapolis by Thomas Cresap on August 20, 1749.[54] The November Court of 1750 heard his suit against Bernard Weymore on a debt.[55] His name is found on Frederick County juries in 1751, and in the following year he was named foreman of the grand jury. Also in 1751 he sold a slave for £80 to Joseph Mayhew.[56] In late 1751 Debutts sued Joseph and Charles Hedges on a debt owed him as administrator for the estate of Isaac Bloomfield. In the same capacity he was in turn sued by Charles Carroll.[57] The following year Debutts served as security in the administration of Cornelius Carmack's estate.

Another side of Debutts' personality, if not that of another individual with the same name, appears in the Prince George's County Court records of 1736 when the grand jury presented Robert Debutts for: 1) assault on Jacob Lynes, 2) drawing his cutlass on the Constable, 3) making three strokes at Anthony Bancuff, one of which went through Bancuff's "westcot and lining," 4) hitting Tetur Laney on the cheek and occasioning blood to flow, 5) taking by force from Solomon Hedges a horse committed to Solomon's care by Allen Farqhaur, 6) taking a bear skin from Allen Farqhuar, and 7) taking a woolen blanket from Allen Farqhuar. Farquhar, Francis Wise, members of the Hedges family and others appeared against Debutts and he was found guilty on all counts. Unable to pay his fine, he was committed to the care of the Sheriff, but the June Court of 1737

---

[49] For "Debutts' Delight" see p. 234.
[50] *Maryland State Papers No. 1, The Black Books,* 3:9; para. 454 in the *Calendar.* See below, po. 370.
[51] See below, p. 371.
[52] In lieu of a Court House which had not yet been built, Kennedy Farrell's tavern was used as a meeting place in early 1749 for the newly forming Frederick County Court.
[53] Prince George's County Land Records, EE:14-15. See p. 351.
[54] See above, p. 21.
[55] See pp. 191-192.
[56] Frederick County Land Records, B:449.
[57] For Isaac Bloomfield, see p. 110.

discharged him. The November Court of 1739 held Debutts and John Brunner for breaking the Sabbath.

Robert Debutts on April 24, 1749 appointed his "loving friend" Peter Butler as his "true and lawful attorney" to aid him in the collection of debts.[58] But there is no mention of Butler in Debutts' will, drawn up three years later. The will names as daughters Mary-Ann-Christian-Abigal Debutts [sic] and Margaret Barnard, the wife of Luke Barnard. It provided for the division of his land between his son John Donaldson Debutts and the "child with which my wife is now big." This second wife, Abigail, who later married John Ferguson, was named as executrix.[59]

Perhaps the significant observation concerning the Carroll Creek settlement is its transitory nature. The area itself was inhabited early. But its original settlers, the van Metres and Albins, soon passed from the scene leaving only the Palmers and Debutts to carry on. The latters' activities date mostly from the period after our study. Even the town of Frederick, which now occupies the Carroll Creek area, likewise came later. Its origins sprang from nearby "Tasker's Chance" and did not, at least initially, involve these Carroll Creek lands.

---
[58] Frederick County Land Records, B:29.
[59] Frederick County Wills, A1:79; Administrative Accounts A1:161.

THE QUAKERS AT "MONOQUESEY"

The beginnings of a small Quaker settlement in the area near today's Buckeystown paved the way for the organization of the first religious establishment in western Maryland. The resulting "Monoquesey Meeting" of the Society of Friends thus preceded the churches organized by the far more numerous German Lutherans and Reformed, as well as the Established Church of England.

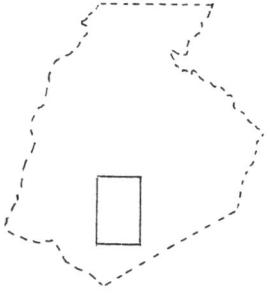

The earliest of these settlers, Henry and **Josiah Ballenger**, were sons of Henry Ballenger, Sr. of Burlington, New Jersey. They came to Maryland sometime before November 4, 1725 when Josiah Ballenger had his first land surveyed. His tract, which he called "Josiah," was located on the Monocacy River northeast of present-day Buckeystown, some five miles south of today's city of Frederick. It was surveyed in the same month as were John van Metre's "Meadow" and Thomas Bordley's "Rocky Creek."[1] The latter, in fact, made reference to its beginning point as "a mile above the plantation of Henry Ballenger."

Also living in this settlement, eventually (on March 23, 1734) renting land on "Carrollton,"[2] was the beloved Quaker leader **James Wright**, whose daughters Hannah and Mary Wright were to marry, respectively, Henry Ballenger in 1726 and Josiah Ballenger in 1727.

James Wright's other children became active participants in the Monocacy Quaker community. James Wright, Jr. and his wife Lucy continued their association with the Meeting until the 1750s when they moved with their children to Virginia. Most of their children -- Ralph, Elizabeth, James, Ann, Susanna, Boyater and Micajah -- were born at Monocacy. John Wright and his wife Rachel Wells, the daughter of Joseph and Margaret Wells of "Boyling Springs," were overseers of the Monocacy Meeting in 1745, though afterwards with their children -- William, Mary, Joseph, Margaret, Charity, Rachel and John Wright, Jr. -- they moved on to North Carolina. Martha Wright Mendenhall became an able Quaker leader and died in Martinsburg, (West) Virginia in 1794 at the age of 82. Elizabeth Wright married George Matthews, son of Oliver Matthews. Oliver Wright moved to what is now Hampstead in Carroll County and Sarah, Lydia and Ann Wright, though apparently born in the Monocacy area, left for Virginia with their parents while they were still children.

Henry Ballenger appeared in the Court records of 1732, being

---
[1] C/S: IL A:727. For "Rocky Creek," cf. above, p. 37.
[2] Prince George's County Land Records, T:168. See p. 369.

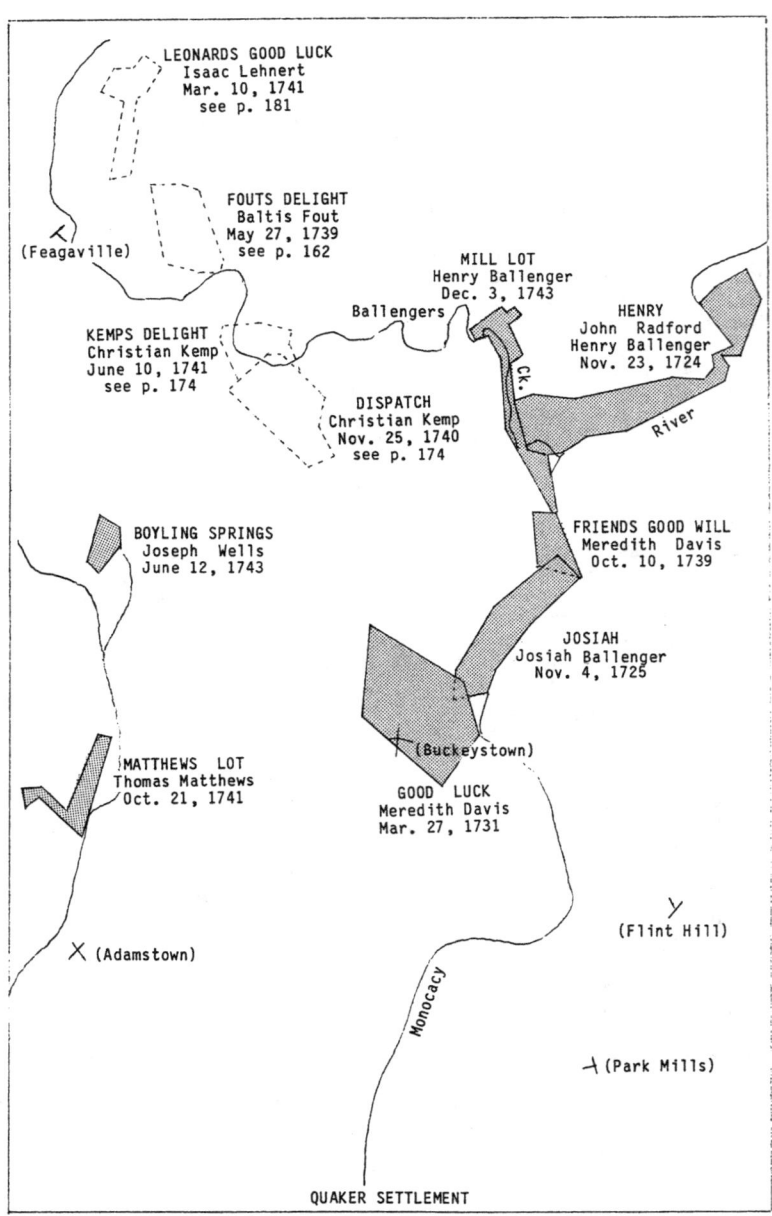

paid a bounty for the heads of three wolves. He was an overseer of roads, appointed by the Courts of 1735, 1742, 1743 and 1747. In March 1749 he contracted with the Court to keep a ferry over the Middle Ford of the Monocacy, where State Route 28 now crosses the River. With his wife Hannah Wright he lived a short distance north of his brother Josiah on a tract called "Henry." Though named for him, the land had been patented to John Radford in late 1724, a year before Josiah got his land. "Henry" straddled a rather sizable creek which empties into the Monocacy midway between today's Frederick and Buckeystown. With its many branches the creek drains a sizable area southwest of Frederick. About a quarter mile from its mouth Henry Ballenger built his mill, the first of record in the area which is now Frederick County. Not surprisingly, therefore, the creek was known initially as Mill Branch, although it is now called Ballenger Creek. By both names it was frequently referred to in old road records. Henry Ballenger leased the land "Henry" until he could purchase it from John Radford on May 1, 1748.[3] He had, however, surveyed for himself in 1743 an adjoining parcel which he called "Mill Lot."[4] This he sold to Mary Fout in 1748.[5] Of Henry Ballenger's children -- Rachel, Mary, William, Henry, Jr., Hannah, Rebecca, Moses, Martha and John Ballenger, all born at Monocacy -- only William, who married Cassandra Plummer, remained in the area.[6]

Meredith Davis, originally from Wales, was destined to become a mainstay of the Monocacy Quaker community. His wife Ursula Burgess, was the daughter of Charles Burgess and granddaughter of Colonel William Burgess who supported early Quakerism in Maryland. In 1726 Davis had 450 acres surveyed at the mouth of the Monocacy River. He called the tract "Meredith's Hunting Quarter"[7] and here, twelve years later, he was appointed by the Prince George's County Court to keep a ferry across the Monocacy "next to his land at the mouth of the river." Seemingly he and his wife maintained a residence both here and on "Westfailure" in lower Prince George's County. On April 10, 1728 he had "Welch's Tract" surveyed beside the Monocacy.[8] Early County Court records indicate that Meredith Davis and Thomas Griffith were the chief rangers for upper Prince George's County. In 1731 Davis became more closely associated with the "Monocacy Quakers" when on March 27th he had "Good Luck" surveyed as 400 acres next to Ballenger's "Josiah." Its first line was on the 17th line of "Carrollton."[9] Eight years later he surveyed 67 acres as "Friend's Good Will," also an adjoining parcel.[10]

In 1726 the New Garden Monthly Meeting, which had been established at Chester, Pennsylvania some eight years earlier, gave

---

[3] Frederick County Land Records, B:30. See also above, p. 40.
[4] C/S: LG E:569.
[5] Prince George's County Land Records, BB:418.
[6] Mary, Rebecca and Moses Ballenger died at Monocacy.
[7] C/S: IL B:451. See map, p. 90.
[8] C/S: IL B:119. See map, p. 90.
[9] Patent: PL 8:649; Maryland Rent Rolls (Frederick No. 1), 32:38. For "Carrollton," see above, pp. 28-29.
[10] C/S: LG E:194.

permission to the Quakers settled along the Monocacy River "to hold religious services on first days in the home of Josiah Ballenger, the Meeting to be called Monoquesey."[11] This authorization that the services be held at Josiah Ballenger's and a reference to the Quaker Meeting House being "near Josiah Ballenger's" led historians for long years to believe that the Meeting House had actually been located on the land "Josiah." The research of Millard M. Rice has shown this to be in error,[12] for on April 27, 1739 Meredith Davis transferred five acres of his "Good Luck" to William Matthews and Henry Ballenger as trustees of the Monocacy Meeting "to build thereon one or more house or houses for a Meeting Place for...the People called Quakers."[13] He may have made this grant after actual construction of the Meeting House had begun, for in late 1738 Allen Farquhar on "Dulany's Lot"[14] was asking in his will that he be buried at the "new Meeting House" and we know of no other in this region at that time. Known as the "Cold Spring Meeting House of Monoquesey,"[15] the building seems to have predated by at least four years Frederick County's first Lutheran log church, which was constructed in 1742 or 1743.[16] The Quaker building was mentioned in a petition to the March 1745 Prince George's County Court from the "back inhabitants" who sought a road from Isaac Leonard's to the mouth "of Minoccoccee," to run "from the main road above Isaac Leonard's along by Baltis Fout's so as to come into the main Minoccaccee Road by the Quaker Meeting House."[17]

Growth of the Maryland Quaker community was slow compared to the rapid influx of Quakers across the Potomac in Virginia. When Jeremiah Brown, William Kirk, Joseph England and John Churchman visited the Friends in 1734, they reported "that those Friends residing at Monoquacy and Oppeckon and thereabouts have and keep a Monthly Meeting for discipline amongst them and that it go under the name as they call it, Hopewell..."[18] Although the Monocacy Quakers established religious services prior to those of the Quakers in Virginia, by 1735 there were so many more Quakers in Virginia than at Monocacy that Virginia's Hopewell was made the business meeting for the combined area.

Between 1736 and 1739, Josiah Ballenger with his wife Mary and children Josiah, Jr., Sarah and James, together with his father-in-law James Wright, joined the Quaker movement to Virginia. His brother Henry Ballenger remained. So also did Meredith Davis who on December 1, 1739 for thirty pounds purchased "Josiah, the houses, yards, gardens, orchards, fences and wood."[19] A few months

---

[11] *Hopewell Friends History, 1734-1934, Frederick County, Virginia* (Strasburg, Virginia, 1936), p. 54.
[12] Rice, *New Facts, op. cit.*, pp. 6-17.
[13] Prince George's County Land Records, Y:21-22.
[14] Maryland Calendar of Wills, op. cit., 8:4. See below, p. 124.
[15] Report of the Fairfax Meeting, William Wade Hinshaw, *Encyclopedia of American Quaker Genealogy* (Ann Arbor, 1950), 6:358-359.
[16] See below, p. 137.
[17] See above, p. 54.
[18] Minutes, Nottingham Monthly Meeting, 1734.
[19] Prince George's County Land Records, Y:117.

earlier, on September 11th, Davis had leased his "Good Luck" to William Matthews, although its designation as the Davis Mill near present-day Buckeystown remained. Catastrophe struck, however, and in 1741 Davis had to have his land resurveyed and repatented to include additional land replacing that which was washed away by the Monocacy River. Illustrative of the inexactitudes of early surveying was the further Resurvey made by Thomas Cresap on November 21, 1745. He found that 6 acres of "Good Luck" lay foul on "Josiah," 80 more acres were on an elder survey called "Carlton" ["Carrollton"] belonging to Charles Carroll, 10 acres of "Friends Good Will" were on "Josiah" and 78 additional neighboring acres could be incorporated in the whole Resurvey, which then would total 649 acres.[20]

In 1742 Meredith Davis signed the petition to divide Prince George's County. After his wife Ursula died, Meredith Davis married Ann Belt, widow of Thomas Claggett. They transferred to John Darnall on June 29, 1751 for 124 pounds 160 acres of "Good Luck." This represented acreage on the west side of the "Great Road that leads from the mouth of Monocacy to Frederick Town." The deed expressly omitted five acres, "where the Quaker Meeting House now stands and already conveyed by the said Meredith Davis for the use of the said Meeting."[21]

Meredith and Ursula Davis had four children, but their two daughters died at an early age. Their sons Meredith Davis, Jr. and Charles made their homes along the Monocacy, although for a short period about 1745 Charles lived between today's Jefferson and Feagaville near what is now U.S. Highway 340.[22] Charles Davis' daughter Ann married William Richardson, who died in 1755, and, as her second husband, Israel Thompson.[23] Meredith Davis, Jr. married his step-sister Sarah Claggett, daughter of Thomas Claggett and Ann Belt,[24] and together they had four children: Thomas and Ursula Davis, both born at Monocacy where they died unmarried in the 1790s, Richard Davis who died as an infant and Ignatius Davis (1759-1828). The latter had another resurvey made on the Davis land on April 13, 1798. He named it "Mount Hope,"[25] the name by which the property is still known at Buckeystown today. Ignatius lived on "Mount Hope" for many years and operated the Davis Mill near Buckeystown. He was

---

[20] C/S: BC & GS 19:469. Meredith Davis, [Jr.,] as executor of his father's estate, submitted accounts on February 23, 1754 and on May 20, 1756. The latter covered costs of other surveys of his father's land made by William Luckett (Frederick County Administrative Accounts, A1:35, 46, 141).

[21] Frederick County Land Records, B:418. See also Rice, *New Facts, op. cit.*, p. 9.

[22] The C/S for "Hazel Thicket" refers to a beginning point "under Catoctin Mountain on the north side of a draft of Ballenger's Creek whereon Charles Davis and Thomas Bails now live."

[23] Frederick County Administrative Accounts, A1:79.

[24] After the death of Meredith Davis, Jr., his widow Sarah married Samuel Perry, whose father Ignatius Perry married Ann Belt after the death of her husband Meredith Davis, Sr.

[25] C/S: IC O:514. Frederick County Surveys THO 1:152.

married four times and was the father of about twenty-three children. One of these was Catherine Lackland Davis, who married Dr. Albert Ritchie.[26]

George Williams, a Welsh Quaker who signed the 1742 petition to divide Prince George's Parish,[27] had no land surveyed or patented in the Frederick County area. He may even have lived a little south of the mouth of the Monocacy River. But he was associating with the Monocacy Quakers when his son Richard Williams was born in their area in 1726. The records of the New Garden Meeting of North Carolina on December 11, 1746 reported the marriage of Richard Williams and Prudence Beals, daughter of John Beals, "of Monoquosy, Prince George's County in Maryland or Virginia."[28]

Geographically, **John Beall** was also not living in the Quaker area, but his religious association linked him there. Not to be confused with the Beall Family of southern Maryland, he was a Pennsylvania Quaker, the son of Robert Beall, and lived on the west side of Catoctin Creek, along the Potomac. His land "Chance" was surveyed on January 12, 1732[/33].[29] It was probably his son Thomas Beall who married Sarah Ancrum. The list of witnesses to this marriage is especially interesting for its identification of a number of the Quakers from Monocacy: Oliver, Thomas, Mary and Elizabeth Matthews, Francis Henley, Amos Jenny [Janney], Evan Thomas, John Wright, Sarah Bealls, Hannah Ballenger, Susanna Moon and Mary Tannyhill.[30]

In the 1733 list of taxables in Monocosie Hundred appeared the names of Chidley, William and George Matthews. **Chidley Matthews** had one year earlier witnessed the will of Joseph Hedges[31] and in November 1736 was appointed Constable by the Prince George's County Court. He lived in the present Braddock area in the forks of U. S. Highways 40 and 40-Alternate, but seemingly owned no land until on August 25, 1739 he had "Chidley's Range" surveyed. Its point of beginning was on "the westernmost draft of Carroll's Creek near the foot of Catocktin Mountain."[32] In October 1742 he signed the petition for division of Prince George's Parish, which led to the formation of All Saints' Parish.[33] Chidley Matthews died in 1762 and was survived by his wife Mary and children Mary, Samuel and John Matthews.[34] His connection, if any, to the Quaker settlement is unknown.

---

[26] See below, p. 123.
[27] See below, p. 371.
[28] Abstracts, New Garden Monthly Meeting, Hinshaw, *Encyclopedia, op. cit.,* Vol. 1. The original records are in the Guilford College Library, Greensboro, North Carolina.
[29] C/S: EI 5:289. His name here is spelled Beal. See map, p. 95.
[30] *Hopewell Friends History, op. cit.,* p. 539.
[31] See below, pp. 106-107.
[32] C/S: EI 5:506. See map, p. 155.
[33] See below, p. 371.
[34] Frederick County Inventories, A1:496; Administrative Accounts, A1:258.

George and William Matthews leased land on "Carrollton" on the same day, March 25, 1734, as did James Wright,[35] whose daughter Elizabeth had married George Matthews sometime before 1731. In the latter year a son Oliver Matthews was born to them. George Matthews represented the Monocacy Quakers at the Chester, Pennsylvania Quarterly Meeting in 1737, 1739 and 1740.[36] He had his own "Good Luck" surveyed on May 27, 1741,[37] located about five miles west of the Quaker nucleus. In 1746 this was enlarged by a resurvey, and in early 1749 George Matthews conveyed 100 acres of it to Charles Davis.[38] In 1755 the remaining 212 acres, with a beginning point on Ballenger Creek, went to Daniel Bailey.[39]

William Matthews and Henry Ballenger were serving as trustees for the Monocacy Quakers when on April 27, 1739 Meredith Davis, Sr. deeded them the five acres of his "Good Luck" for the construction of the Quaker Meeting House. But William Matthews did not long survive. He wrote his will on November 12, 1739, mentioning a daughter-in-law Sarah Ancrum and naming children Elizabeth, Mary, Hannah and William Matthews, Jr. To these children he gave personal property. His land in Calvert County was to be sold to pay debts, and his wife Mary was named as executrix. Henry Ballenger and George Matthews were to be overseers of his estate.[40] It was probably his son William Matthews who had "Widow's Rest" surveyed on October 27, 1746 with its beginning point "about a mile west of Isaac Well's Plantation."[41] In 1755 this land was in the possession of Francis Cost.

Thomas Matthews had "Matthews' Lot" surveyed on October 21, 1741, two and a quarter miles west of "Josiah." Its 100 acres were located where "the elder tract of Mr. Carroll's occasions the irregularity."[42] In 1764 this land was the property of James Dickson, who conveyed it to his father-in-law John Darnall.[43]

Oliver Matthews "of Monocquacy" is mentioned in early Quaker records. He was the son of Thomas Matthews of Baltimore County, who gave him land near present-day Mountville southeast of Jefferson.[44] On February 9, 1749 he had "Chestnut Valley" surveyed for himself, 25 acres beginning "on the north side of a head of a spring of the north fork of Tuscarora Creek that descends into Potowmack River."[45]

Joseph Wells and his wife Margaret came from Chester County in Pennsylvania, settling on "Boyling Springs," a 40-acre tract which had been surveyed on June 12, 1743. Its beginning point was also "on

---
[35] Prince George's County Land Records, T:164, 169, 170.
[36] Minutes, Chester (now Concord) Quarterly Meeting.
[37] C/S: LG E:591.
[38] Frederick County Land Records, B:1.
[39] *Ibid.*, E:794.
[40] Prince George's County Wills, 27:427.
[41] C/S: TI 1:36.
[42] C/S: LG E:65.
[43] Maryland Rent Rolls (Frederick No. 1), 32:84.
[44] Frederick County Land Records, B:297.
[45] C/S: BY & GS 1:678.

a north side branch of the Tuscarora."[46] This land was later conveyed to Baltis Fout. Both Joseph and Isaac Wells signed the October petition seeking to carve All Saints' Parish out of Prince George's Parish.[47] Earlier in 1742 Isaac Wells had been appointed overseer of the road from Monocacy "to Shenandoah," and the November Court of 1743 made him Constable of Monocacy Hundred. On October 27, 1741, Isaac Wells had purchased "Lowland" from Daniel Johnson Low of Prince William County, Virginia, who had had the parcel surveyed for himself on October 15, 1739.[48] Low was apparently a nephew of Thomas Cresap's wife and the grandson of Frances Johnson, wife of Miles Foy. Cresap himself was one of the witnesses to the 1741 transaction.

In 1744 Cresap surveyed "Children's Chance" to the south and west of "Lowland" for Isaac Wells.[49] And on October 27, 1746 "Wells Invention," a 92-acre parcel located east of the other two, was also surveyed for Isaac Wells. Wells had omitted paying caution money, and following his early death in 1747 this last parcel went to John Cholmondley for whom it became the basis for a huge Resurvey of 2,017 acres. Chalmondley died, but willed the land to Robert Lamar, Jr., to whom it was patented on August 10, 1753.[50] "Lowland" passed through several hands to Mrs. Eleanor Medley for whom Leonard Smith in 1774 divided it into town lots to form New Town, the forerunner of today's town of Jefferson.[51] "Children's Chance" was sold by Samuel Wells, brother of Isaac, in two parts, a northern 48 acres to Elias DeLashmutt, Jr. on May 21, 1763, and the remaining 177 acres to the south to Elias DeLashmutt, Sr. on November 8, 1764.[52]

Although Pennsylvania had been created initially as a haven for Quakers, the arrival of numerous immigrants with other religious beliefs provided in time such a shift in emphasis that many Quakers felt compelled to move elsewhere. In the year 1730 the Quaker leaders Alexander Ross and Morgan Bryan appeared before the Governor and Council of Virginia and from them received a grant of 100,000 acres on the Opequon River in Frederick County, Virginia.[53] This encouraged the move of many Quakers who followed them to the back Virginia country. Because these people moved through the Monocacy area of Maryland it may prove interesting to list some who were named in the Virginia State Land Office records.[54]

---

[46] C/S: LG E:290.
[47] See below, p. 371.
[48] C/S: EI 5:498.
[49] Original Patented Certificate of Survey, Prince George's County No. 508. For location, see map, p. 60, and Rice, *New Facts, op. cit.,* pp. 22, 62.
[50] C/S: BC & GS 1:166. This parcel is fully described in Rice, *New Facts, op. cit.,* pp. 60-65.
[51] For a complete study of the land records relating to the town of Jefferson, see Rice, *Ibid.,* pp. 20-65.
[52] Frederick County Land Records, H:454; Frederick County Survey Record THO:299.
[53] *Executive Journals, Virginia 1721-1734, op. cit.,* 4:253.
[54] Book 16, pp. 315-415.

Thomas Curtis and his wife Mary Bryan, daughter of Morgan Bryan, came from Pennsylvania into today's Berkeley County, West Virginia. Isaac Perkins, likewise from Pennsylvania, became a member of the Virginia House of Burgesses and a friend of Lord Fairfax. He devoted his life to the Society of Friends. Thomas Anderson built one of the first mills on Mill Creek in Virginia. John Mills, Sr. described himself in 1743 as a farmer from Prince George's County, Maryland; his son John Mills, Jr. was a cordwainer. John Richards was born in England, was taxed in Chester County, Pennsylvania from 1720-1726 and then moved to Virginia, joining the Hopewell Quakers. Cornelius Cockerine likewise owned property in Chester County, then moved to the mouth of the Opequon. William Hogg was a taxable in East Nottingham Township of Chester County, Pennsylvania from 1718 to 1730 and appeared in the Hopewell Minutes sometimes as Hoge, sometimes as Hogue. John Littler was a business partner of James Wright. He kept a tavern in Chester County, Pennsylvania, 1729-1730, where his records in 1731 show "he is going away." His daughter married Alexander Ross. Thomas Branson in his will of November 21, 1744 identified himself as from Burlington County, New Jersey. He devised his land "on Shannandow River" to his sons who were then living on it. Evan Thomas was a Quaker minister who came from Wales in 1719. His son Evan Thomas, Jr. married the daughter of Alexander Ross. Abraham Hollingworth according to the Minutes of the Nottingham (Pennsylvania) Monthly Meeting in 1729 was "under dealings and absent from home." Family tradition claims he paid first "a cow, a calf and a piece of red cloth to the Shawnee Indians for his land." But on November 23, 1732 he received a survey for 582 acres "within the limits of an order of Council granted to Alexander Ross." John Willson, Nathaniel Thomas, John Haitt, Jr., John Peteate, George Robinson, Robert Luna, Luke Emelen, Francis Pincher, John Frost, George Hobson and John Calvert were other Quakers who moved through Maryland to Pennsylvania.

Richard Beeson and his family moved from Chester County, Pennsylvania in 1735 to settle on a branch of the Opequon near today's Martinsburg, West Virginia. Quaker religious services were held in their home until the Providence Meeting House was built.

Closer even than these Quakers was Amos Janney from Bucks County in Pennsylvania, who in 1733 settled about ten miles south of the Potomac River near today's Waterford in Loudoun County, Virginia.[55] Quaker services were held in his home until 1741, when the Fairfax Meeting House was built nearby. The route between Waterford and today's Buckeystown area was traveled frequently.

In contrast to the growth of Quakerism in Virginia, conditions in the Monocacy area seemed to ebb. On June 28, 1759 the Monocacy Meeting House burned. It was rebuilt by November 29th of the same year, but for reasons not recorded, the Monocacy Friends refused to meet in the new house and on April 28, 1764 the Monocacy Meeting was abandoned.[56] In 1751 Henry Ballenger sold his property to Quaker Richard Richardson and moved to North Carolina. Richardson's

---
[55] See below, p. 235.
[56] Report of the Fairfax Meeting, Hinshaw, op. cit., 6:465.

descendants lived in the Buckeystown area for many years, but organized Quakerism there was at an end.

The five-acre Monocacy Quaker Meeting House site survived until 1805 and the burial ground somewhat longer. In 1792 an attempt was made to reestablish title to the Quaker land. Daniel Ballenger of Frederick County and William Matthews of York County, Pennsylvania, as descendants of the two 1739 trustees who had received the five acres from Meredith Davis, deeded the site to eight new trustees.[57] They in turn, in 1805, deeded the land to Ignatius Davis. But a provision in the latter deed called for Davis to deed back to these trustees a quarter acre described as the Friends Burying Ground.[58] He did so, also in 1805, in a conveyance of 30.25 square perches (0.189 acre), part of a tract called "Good Luck," to Asa Moore of Loudoun County, Virginia, William Stabler of Montgomery County, Maryland, and William Wood of Frederick County, to be held in trust "for the Religious Society of People called Quakers...with power to continue as a burial ground...with leave to pass to and from the same, repair and keep up forever the enclosures thereof..."[59] Subsequent deeds, one as late as 1844, continued to refer to the five acres originally belonging to the Society of Friends and the Quaker graveyard and nearby Quaker spring.[60]

In 1753 a new Quaker group developed. Less than five miles away, the Quakers who had settled on Bush Creek were given permission to hold meetings on first days at the home of Thomas Plummer. Their first Meeting House was built in 1757. In 1756 a third group, called the Pipe Creek Meeting, was organized in the area where Union Bridge in Carroll County now stands. William Farquhar was instrumental in helping to establish that Meeting and in uniting it officially in 1775 with what was left of the Monocacy Meeting. He was the son of Allen Farquhar who in his 1738 will had made reference to the then new Monocacy Meeting House. A resident on Dulany's Lot," the elder Farquhar had earlier purchased "Kilfadda" in the Pipe Creek area from John Tredane, and here his sons William and Allen, Jr. had continued to live.[61]

---

[57] Frederick Land Records, WR 10:685.
[58] Ibid., WR 27:195.
[59] Ibid., WR 27:283.
[60] Ibid., HS 22:409ff. For a meticulously complete summary of the Monocacy Quaker site, see Rice, *New Facts, op. cit.,* pp. 6-17 from which notes and deed citations have been taken.
[61] For Farquhar, see also below, pp. 124-125.

SUGAR LOAF'S SHADOW

Sugar Loaf Mountain, a monadnock located almost at the southern tip of today's Frederick County, rises to a height of 1,282 feet above sea level, nearly a thousand feet above the Monocacy River which flows into the Potomac only four miles to the southwest. It is the highest point in the County east of the Catoctin Range and can be seen for miles around. Christopher von Graffenried climbed the mountain in 1712, and from here he sketched the map which he included in the account of his early visit to Maryland.[1] The Mountain's pink and white quartzite stone was used in the construction of the Chesapeake and Ohio Canal's aqueduct across the Monocacy River. The longest of the Canal's eleven such aqueducts, its 433-foot length consisted of seven arches, each 54 feet in length.

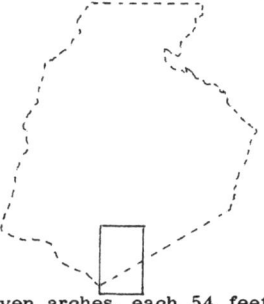

Thirteen years after von Graffenried's visit **Josiah Jones** arrived in the area, settling some four miles north of Sugar Loaf. His survey, the nineteenth to be made in present-day Frederick County, was completed on November 9, 1725. Called "Jones Bottom," it defined 100 acres just south of today's village of Flint Hill[2] and marked the beginning of a predominately English settlement below Sugar Loaf near the mouth of the Monocacy. The area lay to the east of the previously described Point of Rocks settlement and south of the Quaker area. In the 1873 Atlas[3] the home of Josiah Jones is shown as belonging to J[ames] H. Simmons, near the intersection of Park Mills and Peters Roads. We have little information concerning Jones, other than his witnessing the will of William Ray on April 19, 1760[4] and the administration of his own estate by Robert Ferguson and Thomas Richardson on July 4, 1774.[5]

Thomas Hilleary was Jones's nearest neighbor, although he didn't have his tract "Sugar Loaf" surveyed until April 7, 1741. It was located "on a ridge a small distance from a spring that runs into Bennett Creek below the main fork of said creek,"[6] i.e., in the area east of today's Park Mills. Earlier, on February 22, 1740, Thomas Hilleary had had 27 acres surveyed "on the Potomac near the corner

---
[1] See above, pp. 9-11.
[2] C/S: IL A:725.
[3] Lake, op. cit., p. 21.
[4] Frederick County Wills, A1:140.
[5] Frederick County Administrative Accounts, B2:318.
[6] C/S: LG C:181.

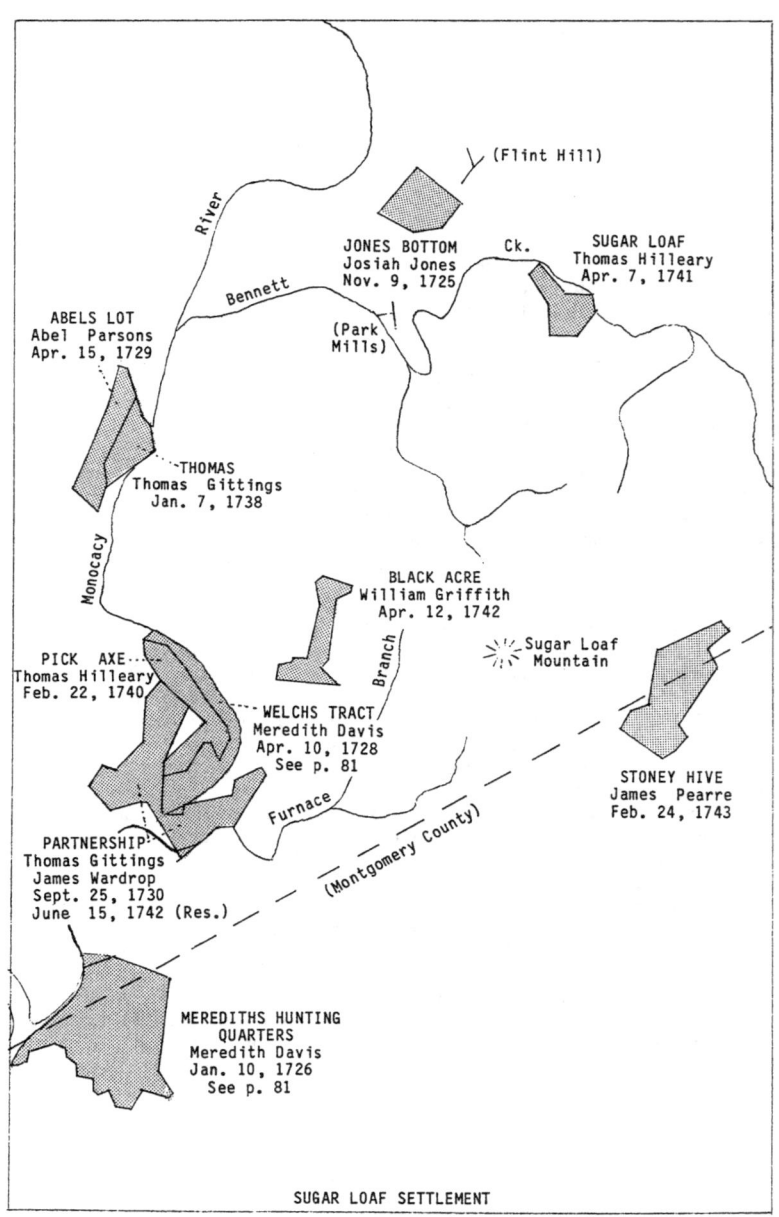

SUGAR LOAF SETTLEMENT

of Arthur Nelson's land." This he called "Arrow Point."[7] On the same day 58 more acres were surveyed for him, also on the west side of the Monocacy River, situated in the large bend of that river between present-day Greenfield and Furnace Ford.[8] This parcel he called "Pick Axe." In 1762 William Hilleary, presumably a brother of Thomas, enlarged the "Sugar Loaf" parcel with a resurvey.[9] Thomas Hilleary is believed to have been the third of that name. His grandfather had come to Maryland from England in 1639. His father, the second Thomas Hilleary, had received a patent for "Three Sisters" located near present-day Hyattsville in Montgomery County. He had married Eleanor Young, but died in early 1729 leaving his widow with six children.[10] Six Hillery households were listed in Frederick County in the 1790 census, three in 1800. The latter census, coupled with Varlé's map of 1808,[11] suggests that some of this family had moved on to the Petersville District of southwestern Frederick County before the end of the 1700s.

William Mears and his wife Elizabeth lived on Dumpling Creek, a fork of Bennett Creek near present-day Urbana. They had 100 acres surveyed there on February 19, 1742 and named their parcel for themselves, "William and Elizabeth."[12] On August 26, 1747 this land was conveyed to Abraham Green for £25.[13].

William Griffith lived immediately south of Jones and Hilleary on "Black Acre" which was surveyed for him on April 12, 1742. It was located off today's Ira Sears Road east of Koontz Chapel and should not be confused with the earlier "Black Acre" surveyed on May 1, 1724 for William Black of London.[14] The first "Black Acre" had two "arms" extending eastward. Between them lay William Griffith's "Black Acre." An earlier William Griffith was settled in Anne Arundel County in 1699 when he devised his dwelling plantation there to his wife Sarah.[15] The younger William Griffith had come to western Maryland by 1734 when he leased two lots on "Carrollton," between "Monoccose and Potowmack."[16] He was appointed Constable for Upper Monocacy Hundred in 1735, and in 1742 signed the petition to divide Prince George's Parish. He also signed the 1744 petition for a road to be laid out from "Tuscarora Creek to Kitoctin Creek." The March Court of 1748 (still Prince George's County) ordered him to alter the road which led to the Ferry at the mouth of the Monocacy River. In 1757 he wrote his will, which was witnessed by Arthur Nelson.[17]

William Griffith's wife was Comfort, the daughter of John

---

[7] C/S: LG C:194.
[8] C/S: LG C:198.
[9] C/S: BC & GS 21:241.
[10] Original Wills, Prince George's County, Box 3, folder 70, Maryland Hall of Records; probated February 14, 1728/29.
[11] Varlé, *loc. cit.*
[12] C/S: LG E:283.
[13] Prince George's County Land Records, EE:281.
[14] See above, p. 30.
[15] *Maryland Calendar of Wills, op. cit.*, 2:185.
[16] Prince George's County Land Records, T:161, 163.
[17] Frederick County Wills, A1:111.

Duvall.[18] Their sons William, Jr. and Orlando lived with them at "Black Acre" until William, Jr. moved into the Catoctin Valley immediately east of today's Broad Run to live on his father's tracts "Nipple" and "Bubby" which had been surveyed in 1749.[19] William Griffith, Jr. is mentioned in the Frederick County Court records in 1749 as an overseer appointed for a portion of the Touchstone Road which ran "by William Griffith's to the top of Katoctin Mountain." A William Griffith died before 1751. Thomas Cresap was administrator for his estate.[20]

Orlando Griffith continued to live on "Black Acre." After his father's death he had the tract enlarged by a 1758 survey to 708 acres, but renamed it "Griffith's Chance."[21] In 1767 he added other surrounding vacant land to increase the total area to 1,002 acres.[22] Two years later a further survey, now called "Chargeable," extended the Griffith holdings all the way to today's Greenfield Mills.[23] The map of 1808[24] identifies the little water falls in the Monocacy there as "Griffith Falls." On May 31, 1774 Orlando Griffith devised his estate to his brothers Henry, Joshua, Benjamin, Charles and Greenbury and to a niece Lydia.[25]

On Feb 24, 1743 "Stoney Hive" was surveyed for **James Pearre.** His land lay about two miles southeast of the Griffiths at the eastern foot of Sugar Loaf Mountain, and it straddled the present Frederick-Montgomery County line.[26] In 1762 Pearre conveyed this land to his daughters Ann Mackey and Mary Buchanan,[27] but the Pearre family left the lower Monocacy area to live near today's Oak Orchard in the Sam's Creek area of extreme eastern Frederick County. They were active in the early 1800s in the newly organized Methodist Church.

Across the Monocacy River from Jones, Hilleary and Griffith, **Abel Parsons** had his "Abel's Lot" surveyed. The survey was dated April 15, 1729,[28] but Parsons' stay there was brief. His certificate of survey was assigned to **Thomas Gittings,** who received the patent in 1734. Gittings came from lower Prince George's County, where he had been a taxable in 1719. In 1730 "Partnership" was surveyed for him on the west side of the River immediately above its mouth.[29] This he enlarged in 1742 by a resurvey which included land on both sides of the River at the mouth of Furnace Branch.[30] He assigned the certificate to James Wardrop,[31] who received the patent. On January 7, 1738

---

[18] Proceedings of the Assembly, 1737-1740, *Archives of Maryland,* op. cit., 40:88.
[19] C/S: BC & GS 1:667, BC & GS 5:594.
[20] Frederick County Administration Records, A1:5.
[21] C/S: BC & GS 40:86.
[22] C/S: BC & GS 37:127.
[23] C/S: BC & GS 41:33.
[24] Varlé, *loc. cit.*
[25] Frederick County Wills, A1:507.
[26] C/S: LG E:381.
[27] Frederick County Land Records, H:22.
[28] C/S: AM 1:370
[29] C/S: AM 1:372
[30] C/S: LG C:654.

Thomas Gittings had a survey made for "Thomas," which lay along the river adjacent to "Abel's Lot."[32] Two years earlier, in 1736, he had served as Constable of Monocacy Hundred. Under the terms of his 1744 will, his land passed to the Sprigg and Berry families into which his daughters had married. To Osborn Sprigg, Thomas Gittings gave "Abel's Lot, and the remainder of his estate went to Philip Berry.[33] Priscilla Sprigg in 1753 had "Abel's Lot" resurveyed into "Father's Gift and Uncle's Good Will."[34] A half century later, in 1806, Elizabeth Dawson resurveyed "Partnership," "Pick Axe," "Griffith's Chance" and Chargeable" into one parcel and called it "Greenfield,"[35] the name by which it is still known today.

---
[31] See above, p. 44.
[32] C/S: LG C:51.
[33] Frederick County Will Records, A1:20.
[34] C/S: BC & GS 19:429.
[35] C/S: IC R:464.

UPPER POTOMAC

The first record of a white man's domicile in the area along the Potomac River between the mouth of Catoctin Creek and the present County border at South Mountain to the west was that of Abraham Pennington. Pennington was an Indian trader living on "Coxson's Rest," surveyed for Thomas Wilcoxson on April 1, 1728.[1] This tract stretched along the Potomac as a thin narrow band nearly three miles long and less than a quarter of a mile deep. Through its length later ran the Baltimore and Ohio Railroad and the Chesapeake and Ohio Canal. The land included a portion of today's town of Brunswick in whose eastern section is the site of Pennington's cabin. "Coxson's Rest" was later included in a resurvey known as "Hawkins' Merry-Peep-O-Day."[2]

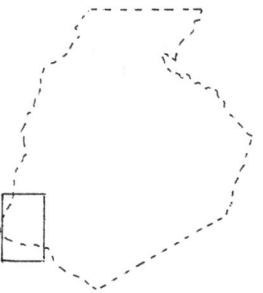

In 1730 **Flayle Payne** joined Pennington as a neighbor to the west of "Coxson's Rest." He presumably was purchasing his land from John Abington whose survey of November 2, 1730 was called "Pain's Delight."[3] On it today lies the town of Knoxville. Payne was granted a reward by the Lower House of the Maryland Assembly on July 28, 1731 for bringing runaway slaves back to their rightful owners. In 1733 he was listed as a taxable in Monocacy Hundred.[4] Payne was appointed overseer of the road from "Monocacy to Antietam" in 1738 and two years later was named Constable of Lower Monocacy Hundred. He witnessed the will of William Diggs of "Mellwood Park" in lower Prince George's County in 1739,[5] and in 1742 his name, as Frail Pain, appeared on the petition to divide Prince George's Parish. In 1744 he was one of the signers of the petition for a road from "Tuscarora Creek to the mouth of Kitoctin Creek and then on to Antietam Creek.[6] Payne added to his land holdings on November 17, 1741 with a survey of "Payne's Industry" on the "north side of the Blue Ridge Mountains about a mile from the Potomac River."[7] Actually this lay *west* of South Mountain in today's Washington County, somewhat above Weverton and Sandy Hook. By his will of October 27, 1764, Payne gave "Payne's Industry" to his son Thomas. The upper

---

[1] See above, pp. 15, 40.
[2] See below, pp. 97-98.
[3] C/S: AM 1:30.
[4] See Appendix, p. 369.
[5] Maryland Provincial Wills, 22:232.
[6] See p. 56.
[7] C/S: LG E:76.

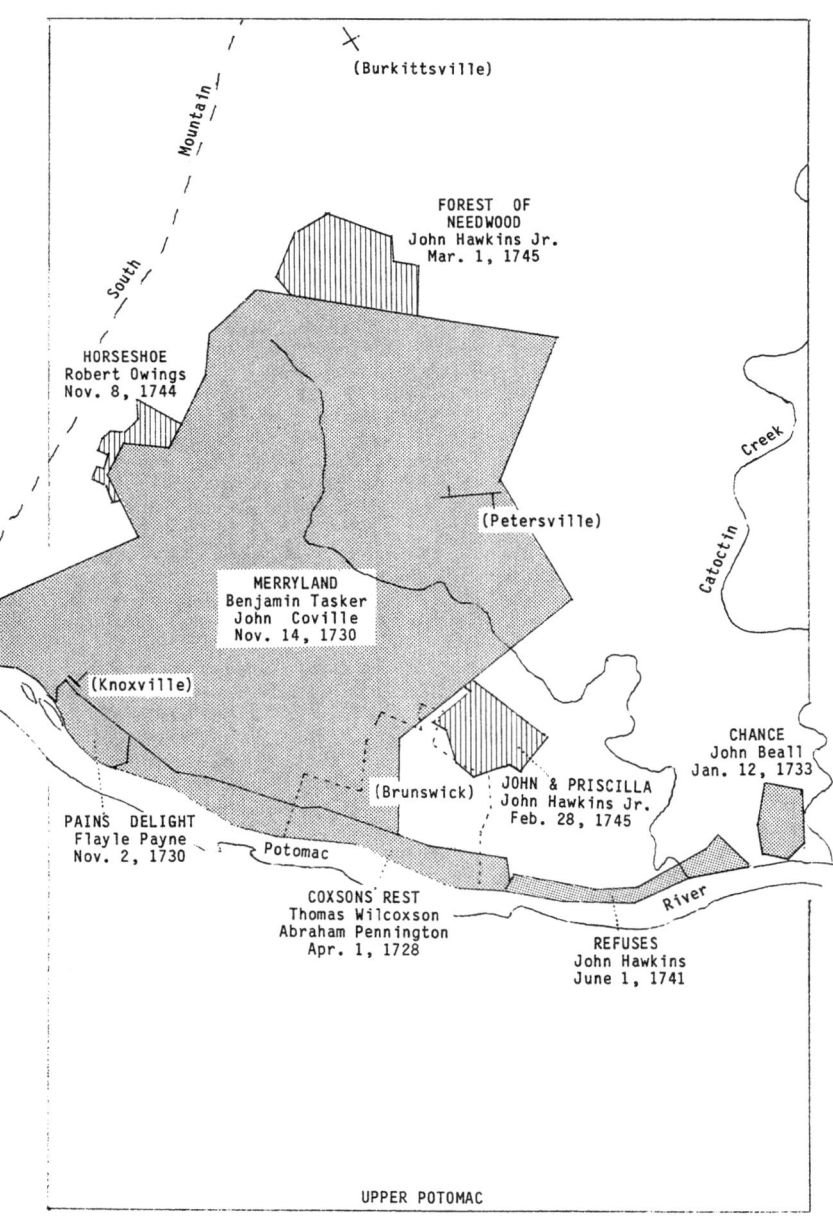

UPPER POTOMAC

part of "Payne's Delight" went to his son John and the lower part to his sons Flayll, Jr. and Peter.[8] The November Court of 1760 appointed Thomas Hogg (in turn succeeded by Jacob Brunner in 1763) as overseer of the road from "Frail [sic] Payns to Harpers Ferry and the new road when laid out from Payns into the main road leading to Conococheague."[9] The former approximates today's Maryland Route 180 west of Knoxville, the latter Maryland Route 17 from Knoxville to Burkittsville.

For historians the curse of a large survey like "Merryland" is that public land records leave very little information concerning the early settlers who, as tenants rather than owners, actually lived there. "Merryland" was laid out for Benjamin Tasker in 1730, but was then assigned to Capt. John Coville, who enlarged its original 5,000 acres to 6,300.[10] Coville seems to have intended dividing this acreage into separate parcels for a number of specified individuals, but of those named only John and Thomas West appeared on the 1733 list of Monocosie Hundred taxables and the 1734 list of those not burning their tobacco according to law.[11] Thus in the early years before 1743 we have no further word of settlers on this large tract. Quite possibly there were few, if any, because so little of the total acreage fronted on the Potomac. And through the backwoods, where the bulk of the tract was located, there was no urgency to construct roads until as late as 1763.[12]

John Beall, son of Robert Beall, has been mentioned in connection with the Quakers with whom he associated,[13] but he, too, lived along the Potomac just west of the mouth of Catoctin Creek. His land there was surveyed on January 12, 1732/33 and was called "Chance."[14]

John Hawkins was the last of the early landowners along the upper reaches of the Potomac whose land bordered the River itself. His land stretched almost two miles westward from the land of John Beall to Abraham Pennington's "Coxson's Rest." His survey, dated June 1, 1741, was called "Refuses" and had its beginning on "the banks of the Potomac near the end of the eighth line of 'Chance'."[15]

An ancestor of the Hawkins family was Thomas Hawkins, who settled in Westmoreland County in Virginia. From there he moved to Maryland about 1650. Two of his sons, Thomas Jr. and John, were prominent in Maryland history. Colonel John Hawkins was a Justice of the Provincial Court in 1698 and presumably the father of Captain John Hawkins, a member of the Lower House of the Assembly in 1722 and for some years thereafter. Still another John Hawkins married Susanna Fraser, the daughter of the Reverend John Fraser, Rector of

---

[8] Frederick County Wills, A1:256.
[9] Frederick County Judgment Records: See Rice, *The Life*, op. cit., pp. 217, 250.
[10] See above, p. 37.
[11] See Appendix, p. 369.
[12] For division of "Merryland" by 1762, see p. 38.
[13] See above, p. 84.
[14] C/S: EI 5:289.
[15] C/S: LG E:314.

Prince George's Parish. He is the one who is presumed to have acquired the large acreage of Hawkins land in western Maryland. Though he continued to maintain a legal residence in lower Prince George's County, he at the same time established "quarters" for himself and his sons along the Potomac.

After 1743 the Hawkins landholdings expanded appreciably. On February 28, 1745 "John and Priscilla" was surveyed for John Hawkins, Jr. by Thomas Cresap, and on it the homes of William Graham and Mrs. L. C. Marshall noted on Bond's map of 1866[16] were built. On March 1, 1744/45 "Forest of Needwood" was surveyed next to "Merryland" for John Hawkins, Jr. This he devised to his son George Fraser Hawkins, who on October 19, 1765 conveyed it to Fielder Gannt, a resident near present-day Feagaville.[17] In 1747 John Hawkins, Jr. had "Haw Bottom"[18] and "Andrew's Folly and Discontent" surveyed. The latter had its beginning point "near the bank of Catoctin Creek, two miles from the mouth of same."[19] In 1752 Hawkins located a survey "Hawkins' Plains"[20] next to "Forest of Needwood." This also was conveyed to Fielder Gannt in 1765.

In spite of these subsequent surveys, the conclusion may be drawn that, up until 1743, settlement in today's Frederick County along the upper reaches of the Potomac River probably did not penetrate far from the River. It was not until March of 1744 that John Hawkins, John Nelson and Moses Chaplain were ordered by the Prince George's County Court to lay out a road from "Tuscarora Creek to the mouth of Katoctin Creek and from thence to the Shenandoah Mountain."[21] This road followed the bank of the Potomac and became known as the River Road. In its entirety it has not survived to this day but was mostly taken up by the Chesapeake and Ohio Canal and by the Baltimore and Ohio Railroad. Indicative of the greater importance attached to the road to the west over Crampton Gap is the notation that the same John Hawkins was ordered by the August Court, also in 1744, to join with William Griffith and Joseph Chaplain in clearing and relocating the "road via Richard Touchstone's to Mr. John Bels Gap on Kitoctin Mountain, thence by Edward Mobberly's into the waggon road by John Pyburn's."[22]

On March 25, 1753 a resurvey was made for John Hawkins on "Coxson's Rest," "Chance," "Refuses," "Haw Bottom" and the vacant land between "Merryland" and Catoctin Creek.[23] The whole

---
[16] Isaac Bond, "Map of Frederick County, Md." (Baltimore: E. Sachse & Co., 1866).
[17] Maryland Rent Rolls (Calvert, Prince George's, Frederick No. 1), 3:64, 211.
[18] C/S: TI 1:431.
[19] C/S: TI 1:439.
[20] CS: GS 1:68.
[21] Shenandoah Mountain is today known as South Mountain, which marks the boundary between Frederick and Washington Counties. Across the River in Virginia the range continues as part of the familiar Blue Ridge Mountains.
[22] See above, p. 11.
[23] C/S: GS 1:102.

became known as "Hawkins' Merry Peep-O-Day." Four years later, John Hawkins, Jr. died. By his will of January 23, 1757 he devised to his wife Priscilla his salt stores and tobacco houses, as well as several tracts of land in lower Prince George's County. She also received his "quarters near the mouth of Kittakin Creek with 1,000 acres adjoining that plantation, being 'Hawkins Merry Peep-O-Day'," which was to go, after his wife's death, to son John Stone Hawkins. The remainder of "Hawkins Merry Peep-O-Day" was to be divided between sons Alexander Thomas Hawkins and John Stone Hawkins. The tract "John and Priscilla" was also to be divided between these two sons "according to the judgment of my good friends Thomas Hawkins, George Fraser and Alexander Magruder."[24] The "friends" made this division in the following year,[25] and in 1766 Fielder Gannt acquired 1,550 acres of the original "Hawkins' Merry Peep-O-Day." Still, in 1808 the home of Thomas Hawkins was located on the original Hawkins land,[26] where the 1873 Atlas shows the home of W. B. Claggett. Fairview, the home of J. T. Frazier, is also shown in this Atlas as on the old Hawkins land.[27]

The November 25, 1763 will of son John Stone Hawkins notes as his brothers and sisters George Fraser Hawkins, Alexander Thomas Hawkins, Elizabeth Laurence Hawkins and Susanna Fraser Hawkins, as well as his uncle George Frazier.[28]

One final resident who arrived in the upper Potomac area before 1743 should be noted. He was **Robert Owings,** who in that year was appointed overseer of the road from "Monocacy to Concocheague," the road over Crampton's Gap. His land "Horseshoe" lay to the west of the "Merryland" tract between that parcel and South Mountain. Its 96 acres were surveyed for him on November 8, 1744.[29] Robert Owings and his wife Rachel Hook[30] were the parents of sons Thomas, Jeremiah, Robert, John, James, Owen, and David Owings and of daughters Margaret Cherk, Lydia Pyles and Rachel Harper. Both Robert and John Owings signed the 1742 petition to divide Prince George's Parish. In his 1760 will, Robert Owings referred to "Horseshoe" as his home plantation. He devised it to his son Thomas. Arthur Nelson, James Hook and John Simpson were witnesses to that will.[31] Thomas Owings died in 1779 and left "Horseshoe," subject to his mother's dower, to his brothers.[32]

---

[24] Prince George's County Wills, 30:337.
[25] Frederick County Land Records, F:604.
[26] Varlé, *loc. cit.*
[27] Lake, *op. cit.*, p. 31.
[28] Prince George's County Wills, 32:76.
[29] C/S: LG E:383.
[30] Cf. above, p. 64.
[31] Frederick County Wills, A1:230.
[32] *Ibid.*, GM 1:115.

UPPER LINGANORE

Early settlement in the eastern portion of present-day Frederick County was by far the most extensive, covering here and there an area extending over some 48 square miles and including today's Libertytown, Unionville, Oak Orchard, Clemsonville, Johnsville and the area of Frederick County opposite Union Bridge.[1] This is a gently rolling countryside extending easterly to the present Carroll County boundary which in part is now delineated by the course of Sam's Creek as it flows north to join Little Pipe Creek.

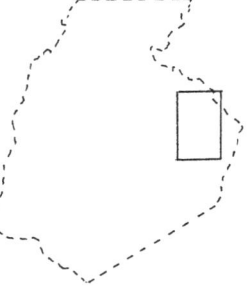

The first to settle in this area was **John Williams** whose survey of "Breeches" was made on September 1, 1729. His land straddled Haines Branch just before it "falls into Sam's Creek"[2] and is now crossed by State Route 75 on its way to Union Bridge and Carroll County. John Tredane[3] was a nearby neighbor who lived just across the creek where Union Bridge now stands. In 1751 Williams resurveyed his land to include vacant land around his original parcel. "Resurvey on Breeches" may be further identified as the home of R. Saylor in the 1873 Atlas.[4] In the late 1800s the Rineharts and McKinstrys were in possession of this land.

Williams attempted to gain more land some two miles to the southwest with a large survey on Beaver Dam Creek, east of today's Johnsville. The survey, called "Ivy Church," was made for Williams on April 9, 1731 and consisted of 1,045 acres. For reasons not explained, however, the tract was patented to Dr. Samuel Stringer of Albany, New York. In 1770 he transferred more than 600 acres of the parcel to Leonard Kitzmiller.[5] There is no basis for inferring from the name of the tract that an existing or intended church was located here even though, almost a century after the survey was made, the Beaver Dam Church of the Brethren was built on this parcel. In 1873 the homes of S. McKinstry, David Stoner, A. Willard and C. Repp were located on "Ivy Church."[6] Ten years after its initial survey and

---
[1] By comparison we estimate the approximate size of the earlier settlements previously described as Point of Rocks 12 square miles, Carroll Creek 16, the Quaker area 7, Sugar Loaf 30 and the Upper Potomac 24 square miles.
[2] C/S: IL B:450.
[3] See above, pp. 17, 45.
[4] Lake, *op. cit.*, p. 41.
[5] C/S: AM 1:238. Frederick County Land Records, N:396.
[6] Lake, *op. cit.*, p. 41.

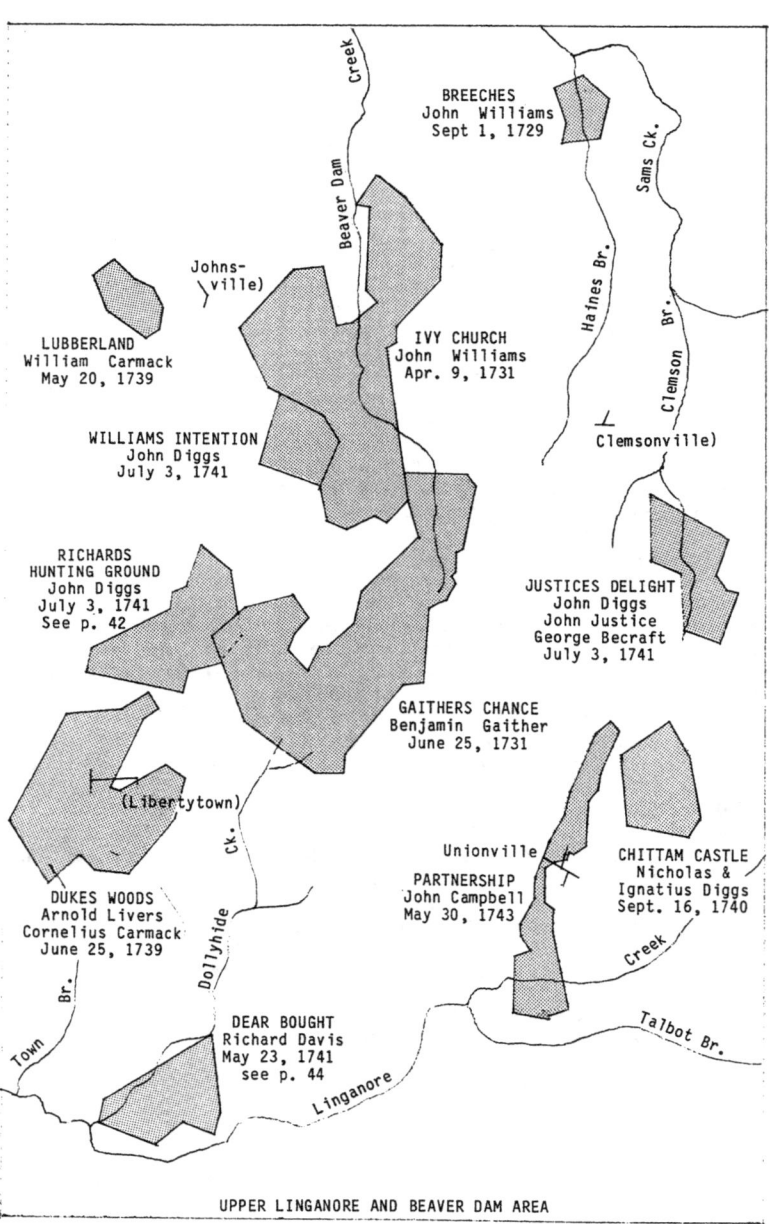

UPPER LINGANORE AND BEAVER DAM AREA

adjoining it on the west, John Diggs on July 3, 1741 had "Williams' Intention" surveyed, obviously hinting at further land interests by John Williams.

John Williams had a large family, including as children Henry, Eleanor, Mary, Margaret, Jean, Esther, Thomas and Martha Williams. At his death in 1764, his wife Mary inherited the home plantation.[7] Their son Captain Henry Williams served during the Revolutionary War and at the battle of Brooklyn Heights took charge of "Game Cock" Company when Capt. Blair, its commander, fell. After the War Captain Williams settled in the Emmitsburg District. His son John H. Williams (1814-1896) was an attorney in Frederick, where he was also editor of the Frederick *Examiner* and for over forty years was associated with the Frederick County National Bank.[8]

South of "Ivy Church" and "Williams' Intention," just two months after the former was surveyed, **Benjamin Gaither** on June 25, 1731 had "Gaither's Chance" surveyed for 1,060 acres.[9] The land lay in the forks of what is now State Route 31 (New Windsor Road) and Coppermine Road and included within its boundaries the head of Beaver Dam Creek. By the terms of Gaither's will the land was divided between his son Henry and his daughters Sarah, Ann, Mary, Cassandra and Elizabeth. Much of it later came into the possession of the Hammonds. The 1873 Atlas shows located on "Gaither's Chance" the homes of Colonel Thomas Hammond (1790-1874), Samuel Urner (1796-1872), Joseph Foutz (1793-1878) and Henry Hyder (1826-1904).[10]

The **Justice family** arrived in this area before July 3, 1741 when John Diggs had "Justice's Delight" surveyed for 250 acres, obviously intended for them. The land lay on the easternmost fork of Clemson Branch between present-day Oak Orchard and McKinstry's Mill,[11] an area very near the divide in drainage which flows north into Sam's Creek and south into Linganore Creek. In 1752 out of the 250 acres for which the parcel was originally surveyed, 100 were in the possession of John Justice. The other 150 acres went to George Becraft in 1759.[12] Before the Frederick Court of August 1750 John Justice, George Becraft and Benjamin Becraft, all farmers of Frederick County, entered into a writing obligatory to insure proper payment by John Justice to the children of John James of their shares in his estate.[13] Before the same Court in November 1758 John Justice petitioned to be made levy-free, since he was then almost 80 years of age and not able "to do anything for the support of his family."[14] That family consisted of his wife Margaret and their children John, Jr., Jacob, Hans, Joseph, William and Elizabeth, wife of Robert Birchfield.

---

[7] Frederick County Wills, A1:211.
[8] Thomas J. C. Williams and Folger McKinsey, *History of Frederick County, Maryland* (1910; reprinted Baltimore, 1967), p. 711.
[9] C/S: AM 1:239.
[10] Lake, op. cit., pp. 23, 41.
[11] C/S: LG E:61.
[12] Maryland Rent Rolls (Frederick No. 1), 32:95. See p. 231.
[13] Rice, *The Life*, op. cit., p. 52.
[14] *Ibid.*, p. 187.

Both John Justice, Sr. and John, Jr. were active in 1749 in the erection of a Chapel "between the drafts of the Linganore and Sam's Creek." Traditionally this is believed to have been a Church of England chapel of ease. It was still known in 1803 when a lot was deeded for the present-day Unionville Methodist Chapel, "adjoining what is commonly called Linganore Chapel."[15] Methodism reputedly came to Frederick County about the time of Robert Strawbridge's preaching in the Sam's Creek area in the early 1760s.[16] Still, the Frederick Court Judgment Records indicate that Strawbridge was present, albeit in another part of the County and under other circumstances, as early as 1753.[17] Methodism thus undoubtedly existed in this area well before 1803 and not long after the "adjoining" chapel was constructed in 1749.

The wording of the 1749 petition "sheweth that there is a great necessity for a road to be cleared from the chapell which the said inhabitants are now building between the drafts of the Linganore and Sam's Creek to the main waggon road from Annapolis to Fredericktown and to fall into said road near Mr. Edward and William Beatty's. Likewise there is a great necessity for a road to be cleared from the said chappell to the road that leadest from Baltimoretown to Digges' copper works and to fall into said road near Burnt House Woods so that we may have a road to our chappell and to travel in and carry our commodities to both Fredericktown and Baltimoretown whereas at this time we do not have any road fit to carry a waggon or any other carriage to either of these towns."[18]

This petition thus marked the beginning of the Liberty Road, Maryland State Route 26, from Mt. Pleasant (Beatty's) to Taylorsville (Burnt House Woods). It also means that before 1749 the settlement

---
[15] Frederick County Land Records, WR 25:380-381. See also below, p. 352.
[16] Williams & McKinsey, *op. cit.*, p. 457, cite 1766 as the year Strawbridge brought Methodism to America, but make no mention of the activities at Unionville in 1749. Others believe Strawbridge could have arrived about 1759-1761, basing their undocumented claim on John Wesley's visits to Ulster in 1756-1758, on known ship movements from Ireland to Annapolis about that time and on the tradition of Strawbridge's baptizing Henry Maynard (born August 12, 1757 according to a Bible record) at the "age of 4 or 5 years." The baptism allegedly occurred at John Maynard's, Strawbridge's "second regular preaching place," five miles west of his home near today's Clemsonville. See Ruthella Mory Bibbins, *How Methodism Came, the Beginnings of Methodism in England and America* (The American Methodist Historical Society of the Baltimore Annual Conference, Baltimore, 1945), pp. 28-35.
[17] Frederick County Court Judgment Records. See Rice, *The Life, op. cit.*, pp. 126, 139. In November of 1753 the grand jury presented Robert Strawbridge "for philonesly (feloniously) stealing of a pig, the property of Elias DeLashmutt." In June 1754 the case was called up after one continuance and was ordered struck off, "defendant being run away."
[18] Frederick County Judgment Records, A:135. See also, p. 352.

on Beaver Dam and Upper Linganore was probably served by a road coming from Carroll County to connect into what is now known as Coppermine Road. Such a road was first identified on the certificate of survey for "Strawberry Plains" in 1732.[19]

Signers of the 1749 petition who had arrived in the area before 1743 included John Justice, Moses Justice, John Justice [Jr.], John Carmack, William Carmack, and Archibald Cambill [Campbell]. Also signing was Darby Ryan who lived along the Monocacy-Annapolis Road.

But the large number of others signing this petition shows how rapidly after 1743 the settlement grew. These included: Joseph Wood of Linganore[20] ("Wood's Lot" 1748[21] a half mile south of present-day Unionville), John Phillips (of "Walnut Bottom" in today's Carroll County), John Howard, son of Gideon, and Philip Howard ("Howard's Range" 1748[22]), Stephen Richards ("Spring Garden" 1749[23] near today's Libertytown), Patrick Holligan ("Patrick's Colt" beginning in 1746 "on the east bank of the Linganore above the waggon road leading from Monocacy to Annapolis"), James Brown ("Brown's Delight" 1750[24] about two miles northeast of Unionville on the farm owned in 1956 by Snader Baker), Matthias Stalcap (who lived on the present Carroll County line east of Unionville), Robert Birchfield (near Stalcop in present-day Carroll County), Solomon Sparks ("Cold Friday" 1750[25] in today's Woodville District), Charles Wood ("Charles' Choice" 1748, beginning "in the forks between Linganore and Comb's Woolpit Branch"[26] one mile east of Unionville), John Brightwell (also on "Charles' Choice"[27]), Richard Combs, Sr., Richard Combs, Jr., and Dennis Ensey (all on "Coomes His Inheritance" 1749[28] one mile east of Unionville), James MacDaniels ("Galloway" 1749[29] on the north side of Talbot Branch) and Daniel Sing and William Lacefield whose locations are unknown.

The most active members of the Upper Linganore settlement were the families of **Cornelius Carmack** (1681?-1748) and his son William Carmack (1716-1776). They had come from Cecil County to the Linganore area after 1733, for on July 2, 1733 William and his wife Jane baptized their daughter Sarah in Cecil County.[30] Once in the

---

[19] C/S: EI 5/222. For John Digges, who assigned the certificate to Enoch Conly of Baltimore County.
[20] Not to be confused with his contemporary, Joseph Wood of Israel's Creek. See below, p. 311.
[21] C/S: TI 1:39. Some of the buildings built by Wood were still standing in 1956 on Wilbur Baker's farm.
[22] C/S: BY & GS 1:656.
[23] C/S: TI 1:502.
[24] C/S: Y & S 7:170.
[25] C/S: Y & S 7:731.
[26] C/S: BY & GS 1:157.
[27] Maryland Rent Rolls (Calvert, Prince George's, Frederick No. 1) 3:122; (Frederick No. 1), 32:201.
[28] C/S: BY & GS 5:622.
[29] C/S: BY & GS 1:213.
[30] St. Mary Anne Parish, Episcopal Church Records, p. 334.

Monocacy area, the family settled where Libertytown stands today. On November 27, 1742, thirty years before the town was first laid out,[31] both father and son purchased land there on a parcel known as "Duke's Woods." Cornelius Carmack acquired 52¼ acres and William Carmack 50 acres, each for a price of 15 pounds, 15 shillings.[32] This land had been surveyed originally for Arnold Livers, whose survey for its 633 acres was dated June 25, 1739.[33] The 1742 deed made reference to Cornelius Carmack's home, indicating that he was there before that date. On May 20, 1739 Arnold Livers also had "Lubberland" surveyed, near where the village of Johnsville now stands. He assigned its 99 acres to William Carmack.[34]

Cornelius Carmack wrote his will from his residence on "Duke's Woods" on May 13, 1746 and in it indicated that he was "of Monocksey" in Prince George's County. The will was probated, however, in Frederick County in 1749, the year after the new County had been established. In his will Cornelius named his wife Guein, sons William and John, and daughters Mary Richards, Catherine Richards, and Elizabeth Evans.[35]

Presumably John Carmack lived initially with his father, for there are no land records for him until in 1753 he acquired "Widow's Lot" (90 acres), "Pleasant Mount" (160 acres) and "Hit or Miss." In 1755 William Carmack conveyed 52¼ acres of "Duke's Woods," presumably their father's, to his brother John.[36] In 1750 Peter Barrick was appointed overseer of the lower part of the Manor Monocacy road to Henry Smith's Branch (a small branch of Israels Creek near Woodsboro) and "from thence to John Carmack's and then with a straight line to Linganore."[37] At the same time William Carmack was made overseer of the road's middle part from Smiths Branch to Great Pipe Creek and from Digges' works (copper mine) to Baltimore County, while John Carmack, along with Joseph Wood and Matthew Stalkup, became overseers of the road from Thomas Beatty's to Baltimore Town. John Carmack served frequently on grand juries and was probably the John Carmack who petitioned the Frederick Court of June 1764 "that as he now keeps a house of entertainment for travellers on the main road that leads from Frederick Town to Baltimore" he asks that the Court "allow the road to be turned through his plantation by his door which will not alter the distance above 40 rods and....will save him the trouble of making gates to pass through the plantation much to his disadvantage."[38] John Carmack

---
[31] Frederick County Land Records, WR 6:381.
[32] Prince George's County Land Records, Y:571, 572.
[33] C/S: LG C:31. See also below, p. 249-250.
[34] C/S: LG C:35; Maryland Rent Rolls (Frederick No. 1), 32:64.
[35] Frederick County Wills, A1:27. Willie Anne [Cary] Turk, *Beatty-Asfordby; the Ancestry of John Beatty and Susanna Asfordby with Some of the Descendants* (New York, F. Allaben, 1909) claimed Cornelius Carmack's daughter Elizabeth married William Beatty, Sr.
[36] Frederick County Land Records, E:768.
[37] This would seem to describe the beginning of the road from Woodsboro to Libertytown, about 1750.
[38] Rice, *The Life, op. cit.*, p. 256.

later left for Tennessee, where in 1779 he entered 300 acres on Big Creek in Hawkins County.

His brother William Carmack stayed on in Frederick County where, sometime shortly after 1748, he signed a petition seeking establishment of a town at Elk Ridge landing to "serve the western parts of Baltimore [County] and all the back land on Potowmack and Monocacy Rivers."[39] William Carmack also served on County grand juries. In November 1753 he was named Constable of Manor Hundred, whose rather extensive outlines are described below.[40] William Carmack died in 1776, leaving a will which named his wife Jane, daughter Sarah Brightwell (wife of John Brightwell), and sons Cornelius, William, Jr., Evan, John, Levy and Aquila.[41] Presumably a son Nathan had died young. John, William, Jr. and Aquila were to divide "Lubberland" and the adjacent "Resurvey on Spring Garden" while "Carmack's Choice" went to Levy. The original "Spring Garden," not to be confused with the parcel north of "Dulany's Lot," had been surveyed for Stephen Richards in 1749. Evan and John C. Carmack married sisters, respectively Mary and Sarah C. Wolfe, daughters of Paul Wolfe. Levi married Susannah Justice and Aquila married Eunice Williams. William Carmack, Jr. is thought to have married Rachel C. Richards. Cornelius and his wife Margery went to Overton, Tennessee.

John Campbell was the last to join the Linganore settlement before the end of 1743. He did so with a survey called "Partnership" dated May 30, 1743. It was a long thin strip of land near today's Unionville, stretching northward from Talbot Branch across the north fork of Linganore Creek for over two miles, but averaging no more than a quarter of a mile in width.[42] In 1789 a portion was included in Andrew Worman's 248-acre "Level Farm."[43] The northern end of "Partnership" lay near "Chittam Castle" which in 1740 had been surveyed between today's Unionville and Oak Orchard for Nicholas and Ignatius Diggs, nephews of John Diggs.[44] In 1766/1768 the latter parcel was in the possession of George Cooper and Philip Bayer.

Northwest of Johnsville, but off the map on page 100, John Chalmers on November 6, 1742 surveyed 100 acres as "Bear Den." But the patent was issued in the following August to Charles Carroll.[45]

---

[39] *Maryland State Papers, No. 1, The Black Books*, 3:108; para. 568 in the *Calendar*.
[40] See below, p. 127.
[41] Frederick County Wills, A 1:575.
[42] C/S: LG E:576.
[43] C/S: IC F:135.
[44] C/S: LG C:183. See above, p. 43.
[45] C/S: LG E:311.

THE HEDGES FAMILY

A number of the early settlers along the Monocacy came originally from the upper reaches of today's New Castle County, Delaware or from neighboring Chester County in Pennsylvania. Typically representative of these was the family of Joseph Hedges.

Joseph Hedges was English, but -- notwithstanding elaborate family claims to the contrary -- no substantiated tie has ever been established to a marriage in England or to his antecedents there. He first appears in American records in a warrant dated September 8, 1702 and its certificate of survey of April 4, 1703 for 100 acres located on Red Clay Creek in Mill Creek Hundred, New Castle County. Some fifteen or twenty years later he and his wife Catherine moved to the London Tract in London Grove Township, Chester County, Pennsylvania. Then, although now well advanced in years and with a family nearly grown, Joseph Hedges on April 22, 1730 sold his Pennsylvania land and moved on to Maryland.

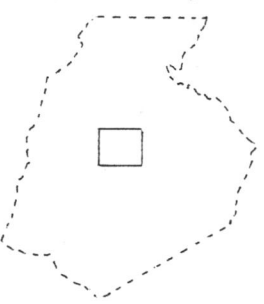

On July 1, 1730 Joseph Hedges had 258 acres surveyed in Maryland on the Monocacy River some five miles north of today's downtown Frederick. The land bordered the River, extending north and west from what was soon to be known as Biggs Ford. It also supposedly bordered the northeastern line of "Tasker's Chance."[1] Hedges named his land "Hedge Hogg," and this has puzzled historians ever since. They are unable to ignore the notation that Hedges' first land in New Castle County was "at the head of a tract formerly taken up on new rent by George Hogg" or that when Hedges and his wife Katherine in Chester County sold the New Castle land on August 17, 1725, George Hogg was one of the witnesses to the deed.[2] Even more mysterious is the question who or what encouraged Hedges to come to Maryland and why he settled where he did.

Although his residence on "Hedge Hogg" proved to be a focal point for nearby parcels of land surveyed or rented by his children, all of whom came to Maryland with him, his own Maryland chapter ended almost as soon as it began. Joseph Hedges received his patent for "Hedge Hogg" on August 25, 1732. Two weeks later, on September 6, 1732, only two years after his arrival and almost exactly 30 years to the day after his initial warrant for land in Delaware, Joseph Hedges "of Manaquicy in Prince George's County" wrote his

---
[1] C/S: AM 1:44. For "Tasker's Chance" see pp. 37, 257-301.
[2] New Castle County Land Records, G 1:524.

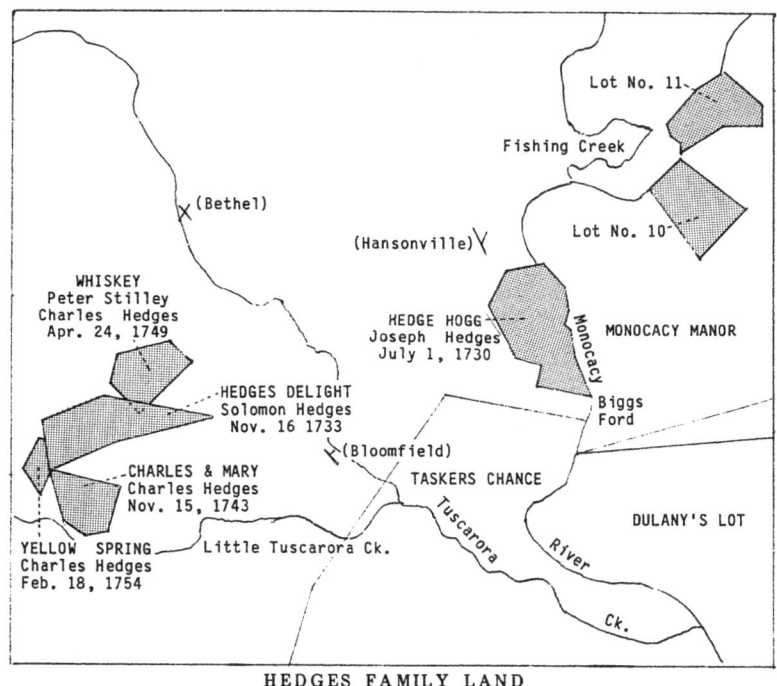

HEDGES FAMILY LAND

will. It was probated on November 29th. In the will he named no wife, though she survived him.[3] His eldest son Solomon Hedges was to inherit "the 258 acres on Manaquicy Creek," while sons Charles and Joshua were each to receive 200 acres at Opeckan in Virginia -- obviously already purchased for them. More significantly, Solomon and Charles as executors, one of whom seemed slated to stay in Maryland while the other was to go to Virginia, were instructed to purchase an additional 400 acres at Opecken to be divided equally between sons Jonas and Joseph. The executors were also directed to purchase 100 acres at Manaquicy for son Samuel. Personalty was to go to daughters Ruth, Cathren and Dorcas and to sons Joseph and Samuel. All nine children and Joseph's wife were to divide the remainder.[4] Chidley Matthews, Thomas Hillard and John Hillard

---

[3] Smyth, *Duke-Shepherd-Van Metre, op. cit.*, p. 43, claimed Joseph Hedges had married Catharine Stalcop, daughter of John Stalcop and Catharine Erickson, early Swedish settlers in Salem County, New Jersey, who later moved to New Castle County. This is not an impossibility, for the presence of Matthias Stalcap has been noted in the Upper Linganore settlement in 1749 (cf. above, p. 103).

[4] Prerogative Court Records, 20:468.

witnessed the will and on February 27, 1733 Robert Jones and Henry Ballenger inventoried the estate.[5]

It would appear that a move to Virginia was contemplated for at least some of the family almost before roots could be established in Maryland. Presumably none of the children was yet married, and Joshua was only seventeen years of age. The purchase of Virginia land, both actual and contemplated, was being made by Joseph Hedges himself for, but not by, his children. Thus the question is posed, how permanent did he view his family's stay in Maryland? Unless we are plagued by positive hindsight which he did not have, why also would he want his family to desert an area where all about him lay good choice land almost theirs for the asking? It was not a wholesale commitment, however. He did provide for two of his children to stay on in Maryland. And so our curiosity turns to how the future actually did unfold.

At first the family seems to have stayed put. In the year after his father died, Solomon Hedges had "Hedges Delight" surveyed — 192 acres near Tuscarora Creek some three miles southwest of "Hedge Hogg" and near the Monocacy road which was soon to carry the bulk of those settlers going to Virginia. In 1733 he was listed as a taxable in Monocacy Hundred, and in the June Court of 1734 Solomon declared that he had paid Robert Jones and John Tredane a debt of 15 pounds for Flower Swift, who had been a Constable for Monocacy Hundred with John van Metre in 1732. Also in 1734 Solomon's name appeared on the list of those not burning their tobacco properly, and in 1735 he himself was named Constable for Monocacy Hundred, replacing Thomas Doudith, possibly a relative, who was incapable of duty.[6] About this time Solomon married John van Metre's daughter Rebecca, and the connection with that family made it only a matter of time before they joined the move to Virginia. This occurred about 1738. They sold their farm animals, which they had purchased from Rebecca's father, to John House and moved to Patterson Creek near present-day Keyser, West Virginia. This area was then a part of Orange County, Virginia, where the November 2, 1739 bill of sale for the livestock showed Solomon Hedges was then residing.[7] George Washington in 1748 at the age of 16 "traveled up ye Creek to Solomon Hedges, Esq., one of his Majesty's Justices of the Peace for ye County of Frederick."[8] The family was still there in 1753 when Hampshire County was formed, but by 1778 had moved on to Buffalo Creek in Ohio County in the [West] Virginia panhandle. There Solomon Hedges is alleged to have lived and died after the turn of the century at an age of over one hundred.

Jonas and Joshua Hedges settled next to each other at

---

[5] Prince George's County Inventories, 17:67-69, Hall of Records. Bonds were still due on the sale of the Chester County land and therefore another Inventory was made in that County December 19, 1734.
[6] Prince George's County Court Records, V:296.
[7] Prince George's County Land Records, Y:102.
[8] Fitzpatrick, op. cit., p. 26. Frederick County, Virginia was formed out of Orange County in 1745.

Hedgesville on Tulisses Branch in today's Berkeley County, West Virginia. Jonas married Agnes Powelson about 1738, and in 1743 Joshua married Elizabeth Chapline. The fate of Samuel Hedges is unknown. Presumably he died shortly after his father, sometime in the 1730s, still in the Monocacy area and probably unmarried. What became of his sister Dorcas is also unknown. But Ruth Hedges married Abraham van Metre, brother of Solomon Hedges' wife and they, too, moved on to [West] Virginia, settling in Berkeley County.

This leaves Charles and Joseph Hedges, both of whom according to their father's will were destined to go to Virginia. Neither did. Nor did their sister Catherine, who stayed on in the Monocacy area with her two husbands, Jacob Julien and Joseph Wood.[9] Joseph Hedges became a tenant on Monocacy Manor,[10] married and had but a single child Rebecca before he died in 1753. His widow Mary, later the wife of John Wilson, and his brother Charles Hedges were Joseph's executors.[11] Joseph's will provided that, should his daughter Rebecca die before coming of age, half his land should go to the children of his brother Charles Hedges. She did not die, but was raised by Charles Hedges and in storybook fashion married her first cousin Charles Hedges, Jr. As a result, they together inherited the 150-acre lease to Lot No. 10 on Monocacy Manor!

So it was that Charles Hedges, alone among the nine children who came to Maryland with their parents, continued the Hedges story in Frederick County. With his brothers Solomon and Joshua, he was listed as a taxable in Monocacy Hundred in 1733. In 1736 he journeyed all the way back to New Castle County where at Old Swedes Church in Wilmington on February 12th he married Mary Stilley, the daughter of Jacob Stilley.[12] In the same year he was appointed by the Prince George's County Court as overseer of the road from Mill Branch[13] to Monocacy Manor. On May 8, 1740 he purchased "Hedges Delight" for fifty pounds from Solomon and Rebecca Hedges,[14] who by then were residents in Virginia. On the same day Solomon and Rebecca transferred title to "Hedge Hogg" to Jacob Nafe (Neff), blacksmith, for £127/10 "for his own use and no other purpose." Charles Hedges witnessed this deed and collected the alienation fine of 10sh 3d.[15] The amount paid for the land at a time when land was free or only a few pennies an acre probably indicates that considerable improvements had been made by the Hedges family after their arrival in Maryland. For a blacksmith, its location must also have been important, suggesting considerable growth in the neighborhood and the importance of the road junctions nearby.

The hypothesis is quite plausible that Catherine Hedges, widow of the original Joseph Hedges and mother of Charles Hedges,

---

[9] See below, pp. 113, 311-312.
[10] See below, p. 322.
[11] Frederick County Administrative Accounts, A1:40, May 11, 1754.
[12] Horace Burr, *The Records of Holy Trinity (Old Swedes), Wilmington, Delaware, 1697-1773* (Wilmington, 1890), p. 364.
[13] Ballenger Creek. See p. 81.
[14] Prince George's County Land Records, Y:170.
[15] *Ibid.*, Y:171.

sometime after Joseph Hedges' death in late 1732 married **Isaac Bloomfield** as her second husband. There are no records of surveys or patents in Frederick County for him, but in 1739 he had been a witness to six of Susannah Beatty's deeds.[16] The November Court of 1743 appointed him Constable of Linganore Hundred. He witnessed the 1740 transfer of "Hedges Delight" and in 1747 he also witnessed the will of Jacob Julien, who three years earlier had married Charles Hedges' sister Catherine. Isaac Bloomfield died shortly before December 27, 1748, the date of his Inventory as presented by Robert Debutts, his administrator. As administrator, Debutts was sued by Charles Carroll.[17] But Debutts in turn sued Joseph and Charles Hedges in November 1751 for a debt of £12/19/8 due from them to Isaac Bloomfield's estate.[18] Catherine Bloomfield died in 1749. Joseph Hedges, Jr. (d 1753) and Joseph Wood signed her Inventory as near of kin. Charles Hedges was her executor and in his administrative account of 1751 accounted for payments to Thomas Douthitt,[19] John Bell, Joseph Wood and Stephen Julien. He also recorded debts due the estate from Allen Farquhar, Daniel Pepinger, Jacob Barton, John Biggs, William Hedges, Jonas Hedges, James Head, Mary Martin and others, all known to have been living in the immediate neighborhood of "Hedge Hogg." In 1751 Thomas Douthitt "swore for Isaac Bloomfield" in the probate of the 1747 will of Jacob Julien.[20]

On November 15, 1743 Charles Hedges had a tract surveyed just south of "Hedges Delight" which he called "Charles and Mary."[21] In 1749 by patent he acquired "Whiskey" which had been surveyed for Peter Stille. Its 100 acres lay adjacent to "Hedges Delight."[22] He then followed this on February 18, 1754 with the survey for "Yellow Springs,"[23] named for those springs traditionally known to the Indians for their great healing power. Though he now owned four parcels of land well west of the Monocacy River, Charles Hedges apparently tenanted, rather than owned, Lot No. 11 on his Lordship's Monocacy Manor directly across the river from "Hedge Hogg."[24] John Biggs was a near neighbor on the Manor and to the two of them in 1754 Robert McPherson and John Beard mortgaged their livestock and household items.[25] In 1759 Charles Hedges was named Constable for Monocacy Hundred.

Charles Hedges' wife died in the mid-1760s. His family was

----
[16] Prince George's County Land Records, Y:148-153.
[17] Frederick County Court Judgment Records, A:33.
[18] *Ibid.*, D:311.
[19] Thomas and Mary Douthitt as near of kin had signed Joseph Hedges' estate inventory in early 1733 (Prince George's County Inventories, 17:67-69, Hall of Records).
[20] Stephen and Jacob Julien were brothers.
[21] C/S: LG E:293
[22] C/S: BY & GS 1:198.
[23] C/S: BC & GS 4:340.
[24] See below, pp 304, 322.
[25] Frederick County Land Records, E:353, 426   John Beard may possibly relate to the John Beard who in 1739 received half of Joseph Hedges' land in Chester County, Pennsylvania (cf. above).

110

nearly grown. Still, a new wife seemed desirable and in April 1769 Charles Hedges married Isabella Wirk. She was at least 35 years his junior and was destined to outlive him by over 30 years. By an antenuptial agreement, in order to bar her rights of dower, Isabella was to receive only one-third of "Yellow Springs."[26] Actually they each received far more, she in property, he in children. To the eight children of his first marriage, six more were added in the second. Altogether they included Jacob, Moses, Joseph, Absalom, Rachel, Susannah, Charles, Shadrack, Isaac, Samuel, Ruth, Margaret, Hannah and Dorcas. Some of these, or their immediate families, moved on to the Middletown Valley, Greene and Washington Counties in Pennsylvania, the West Virginia Panhandle, Belmont and Seneca Counties in Ohio and Bourbon County in Kentucky.

Though he did not die until December 1795, Charles Hedges wrote his will in 1790. His wife Isabella was to get "Hedges Delight," "Yellow Springs" and "Charles and Mary." After her death these tracts were to be divided equally between Isaac and Samuel Hedges, sons of the second marriage. Later surveys, including "Johnson's Level" (150 acres), "Leddy" ("Leeds" 50 acres) and "Hedges Chance" (50 acres), were to go to son Shadrack Hedges after he made compensatory payments to Charles Hedges, Jr. and their four half-sisters from their father's second marriage.[27] The other children had already been provided for, with, for example, the parcel "Whiskey" going to son Jacob Hedges in 1765 before Charles' first wife died.[28]

The subsequent history of the original "Hedge Hogg" is clouded with uncertainty. Although the land was transferred to **Jacob Neff** in the year 1740, there is a question whether he was actually living there when on October 2, 1750 he wrote his will. The language is stilted: Wife Catharina as executrix "is to dispose of this place which I live on and pay my debts now named 'Durnah'[29] and all my goods and chattels." She was to receive 100 acres of land "betwixt mountains which I bought," 50 acres from Daniel Dulany and 50 acres from Nodley Thomas, "for my wife to live on or dispose of."[30] There is no reference to "Hedge Hogg" even though subsequent deeds indicate that the parcel was still known by that name as late as 1809.[31] Yet the

---

[26] Frederick County Land Records, M:192 Throughout the document her name was spelled as "Wirk," although her signature was copied as "Wink."

[27] Frederick County Wills, GM 3:109. The first two parcels had belonged to the Rev. Samuel Hunter in 1754: see below, p. 354.

[28] Frederick County Land Records, J:1282.

[29] A tract with a name spelled thus has not been found in the land records. Nor has "Teernoch" although a "Resurvey of Teernoch" was made on May 15, 1753, i.e., after Neff's 1750 will. The "Resurvey" was patented to Peter Bolsell on November 1, 1753 and was located in today's Gambrill State Park picnic area north of Braddock Heights and west of Yellow Springs. Cf. C/S: BC & GS 1:163. The "Resurvey" may have had a name change and may have been on "Baltzell's Content" as surveyed October 24, 1751.

[30] Frederick County Wills, A1:6.

[31] Frederick County Land Records, WR 35:550.

witnesses to the will, Stephen Julien, Charles Hedges, Adam Stull and John Stoner, all were living near "Hedge Hogg" at this time, and the estate's inventory, made by Charles Hedges and Adam Stull, included blacksmith tools, indicative of Jacob Neff's trade when he purchased "Hedge Hogg" in 1740. Moreover, the inventory shows Notley Thomas as a creditor.[32]

The mystery thickens with the sudden appearance of a **William Hedges** whose relationship to the first Joseph Hedges has not been determined. William wrote his will on August 11, 1742 and died relatively young, before its probate on January 29, 1743. Calling himself a farmer of Prince George's County, he provided that his wife Ann should "live on my estate during life of my son" Joseph, who was to get all the land unless an expected posthumous fourth child was a son, in which case the two sons were to divide the land equally. Ann was to serve as executrix. Robert Jones, Robert Baker and Jacob Neff witnessed the will, but only Robert Baker was present for its probate.[33] Co-sureties on Ann's bond were Charles Hedges and Filip Kinss.[34] The inventory of March 6, 1743, made by John Middah and Robert Jones, was signed by a single creditor, Jacob Neff, and by kin Charles, Joseph and Andrew Hedges.[35] In none of these documents is the land named or otherwise identified. But there are clues to help: Stephen Julien became Ann Hedges' second husband on July 14, 1743[36] and together they prepared the estate accounts. In the account of June 12, 1747 they took credit for a payment to Jacob Neff on a debt owed by William Hedges but paid by Stephen Julien on bond of £22/5/6 plus interest.[37]

The posthumous child referred to above did turn out to be a son. He was given the name of William Hedges, Jr. and, because he was born in late 1742, should have expected to inherit his father's land, whatever it was, when he reached majority in 1763. By then Jacob Neff had died. But our attention is directed to a deed dated March 15, 1763 from his son "Jacob Kneff, heir at law to Jacob Kneff of Prince George's County, deceased," which transferred to Joseph and William Hedges, sons and heirs of William Hedges of Prince George's County, a 258-acre parcel called "Hedge Hogg."[38] The conclusion seems obvious: Whatever his origins and whatever his

---
[32] Frederick County Inventories, 47:60, Hall of Records, April 1, 1751.
[33] Prince George's County Wills, 1738-1742, 22:528, DD 1, Hall of Records.
[34] Prince George's County Bonds, Hall of Records, Box 12, No. 31. For Philip Küntz, see below, p. 169.
[35] Prince George's County Inventories, 30:210, Hall of Records. Joseph and Andrew Hedges were sons of Charles Hedges, in turn believed to have been a brother of the first Joseph Hedges.
[36] Church Book, All Saints Parish, Frederick County: See p. 353. Cf. also Gaius Marcus Brumbaugh, *Maryland Records, Colonial, Revolutionary, County and Church from Original Sources* (Baltimore/Lancaster, 1915/1928), 1:260.
[37] Prince George's County Administrative Accounts, 23:339.
[38] Frederick County Land Records, H:330.

relationship to the other Hedges who preceded him, William Hedges sometime between 1740 and 1742 had begun purchasing "Hedge Hogg" from Jacob Neff. But he had died before the transaction could be concluded and it took until the youngest son reached majority for title finally to be established. As proof of the pudding, it will be noted that Stephen Julien paid taxes on "Hedge Hogg" from 1753 to 1773 and early in that period was shown as "in possession."[39] In 1772 Joseph and William Hedges divided "Hedge Hogg" between them.[40] Five years later they both died, and their wills were probated on the same day, May 6, 1777. Again there were heirs who had not yet reached majority. But the land remained in the Hedges family well into the next century. The 1873 Atlas, for example, shows the home of Eneas Hedges (1800-1873) still on "Hedge Hogg."[41]

No relationship has been found between Jacob Neff and Johann Henry Neff of "Tasker's Chance," p. 296 below. Jacob's widow Catherine Neff wrote her will in 1776, naming her children as John, Jacob, Henry, Francis, Adam, Margaretta and Esther Neff.[42] Peter Bainbridge, Bartholomew Booker and John Arnold were witnesses to the will.[43]

No survey or patent records exist for the brothers **Stephen** and **Jacob Julien,** both of whom were associated through marriage with the Hedges families. They were sons of the immigrant René Julien who had lived in Eastern Maryland early in the eighteenth century and who later went with most of his sons to the Winchester area of Virginia. Only Stephen and Jacob lived in today's Frederick County area, where they first appeared in 1743. Stephen's first wife Allatha, the mother of all his children, was buried April 6, 1743 according to All Saints' Church Records, and, as noted above, he married as his second wife Ann, the widow of William Hedges. There were no children in the second marriage. Stephen died some time after 1760 when he witnessed John Biggs' will.[44]

Jacob Julien married Catharine Hedges, daughter of the first Joseph Hedges, on Feb. 2, 1743/44, but died shortly thereafter. All Saints' Church records note his burial on March 26, 1747, the day after he wrote his will. The will was not probated, however, until August 30, 1751. It had been witnessed by René Julien, Isaac Bloomfield and James Beard, and it divided most of his estate between his wife Catherine and his only child Rachel Julien.[45] Rachel Julien was born June 26, 1746, but did not live long. She was buried April 25, 1751. Catherine Hedges Julien married Joseph Wood as her second husband on September 11, 1747.[46] He died in 1782 and she

---
[39] Maryland Rent Rolls (Frederick No. 1), 32:39.
[40] Frederick County Land Records, P:150.
[41] Lake, op. cit., p. 10.
[42] Esther Neff married Gabriel Swinehart on November 14, 1745. See below, p. 158.
[43] Frederick County Wills, A1:567; or 41:192 at Hall of Records.
[44] Frederick County Wills, A1:152.
[45] Ibid., A1:73; or 28:129 at Hall of Records.
[46] Church Book, All Saints' Parish. For Joseph Wood, see below, p. 311.

survived him.

There was one other tie between the Hedges and Julien families. On June 3, 1770 Isaac Julien, son of Stephen Julien by his first wife, married Susannah Hedges, daughter of Charles Hedges, Sr. and Mary Stilley.[47] Susanna died before her father's will of 1790, but Isaac Julien lived until 1839, having served in the Revolution and lived in both Greene County, Pennsylvania and Miami County, Ohio.

Like the Hedges family, the Stilleys also had origins in New Castle County, Delaware. **Jacob Stilley,** yeoman of Christiana Hundred, New Castle County, and his wife Rebecca Springer had a sizable family, most of whom are named in his will of September 14, 1771.[48] Although he did not leave New Castle County himself, several of his children did. Reference has already been made to Mary Stilley, born June 22, 1715 as Maria, daughter of Jacob Stelle and wife Rebecca.[49] She married Charles Hedges in 1736 and came to the Hedges area north of today's city of Frederick. Her brother Peter Stilley, born March 8, 1717,[50] also came. He had "Saplin Ridge" surveyed for 100 acres on January 15, 1742 .[51] It lay "near Chidley Matthews' land" just north of Rock Creek and today's forks of U.S. Highways 40 and 40-Alternate by the golf course. On May 20, 1749 Peter Stilley resurveyed his tract to increase its size to 295 acres,[52] and in 1793 his son Peter Stilley, Jr. added 65 acres more, calling the whole "Neighbor's Agreement."[53]

According to the Moravian missionary August Spangenberg,[54] Peter Stilley in 1748 was a vestryman and "Vorsteher" in the English church who, because of his friendship with neighboring Moravians, had been called to account. He was was Constable of Middle Monocacy Hundred in 1751 and 1752 and a member of the Grand Jury in 1759. His son John Stilley followed him as Constable for Middle Monocacy Hundred in 1778. In his will of July 25, 1765 Peter Stilley devised his plantation to his son Jacob, but also provided for sons Peter and John.[55] His wife Mary also left a will, dated September 30, 1784, which named daughters Estelle, wife of John Kennedy, and Rebecca, wife of Benjamin Ogle.[56]

---

[47] Ibid., p. 111.
[48] *Delaware Calendar of Wills, New Castle County, 1682-1800*, abstracted by the Historical Research Committee of the Colonial Dames of Delaware (New York, 1911), p. 74.
[49] Burr, *op. cit.*, p. 223.
[50] Ibid., p. 240.
[51] C/S: LG E:286. See map, p. 155.
[52] C/S: BC & GS 5:602.
[53] C/S: IC I:272.
[54] See below, p. 148.
[55] Frederick County Wills, A1:244.
[56] Ibid., GM 2:137.

DULANY'S LOT

In the early period before church and other records began, often a land survey filed at the Colony's Land Office affords the first indication that a new settler had appeared upon the scene. Conversely, for those settlers who did not survey their own land, the history of initial settlement sometimes proves either difficult or impossible. This is particularly true of large areas surveyed as single parcels but subsequently subdivided into a number of smaller tracts or lots which were then rented or sold by the absentee land owner. The recording of such transactions was made at the local County level, if it was made at all, and was the responsibility of the new settler. Often he was ignorant of proper and necessary procedures. Some deeds were entered into County land records immediately, while others may have appeared only after a lapse of considerable time following the new settler's arrival. Leases may never have been recorded.

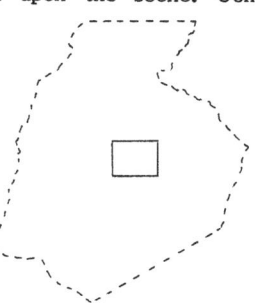

One such tract was "Dulany's Lot," located in the area northeast of today's city of Frederick. To demonstrate the magnitude of the uncertainty concerning its early settlement, one may focus first on those early settlers who are known to have lived there and then define the residue area where information is almost wholly lacking.

"Dulany's Lot" was originally surveyed for Daniel Dulany of Annapolis on May 28, 1724.[1] It was laid out for 3,850 acres extending from the mouth of Glade Creek south along the Monocacy River's east bank to the mouth of Addison Run and from the River eastward a distance of up to five miles. The actual survey seemingly was made contemporaneously with the surveys for his Lordship's "Monocacy Manor" to the north and for "Addison's Choice" to the south, even though their indicated dates were not in the same sequence as the surveys themselves.[2]

Although individual sales of lots within this whole parcel were initially made by Dulany beginning in 1732, eight years after the

---
[1] C/S: EI 5:244.

[2] The survey for "Monocacy Manor" was dated one day later than that for "Dulany's Lot," but the latter marked its beginning at the beginning point of "Monocacy Manor" which thus obviously had to have been surveyed first. Seemingly certificates were sometimes dated more nearly in relation to their dates of recording than to the actual survey work on the ground itself.

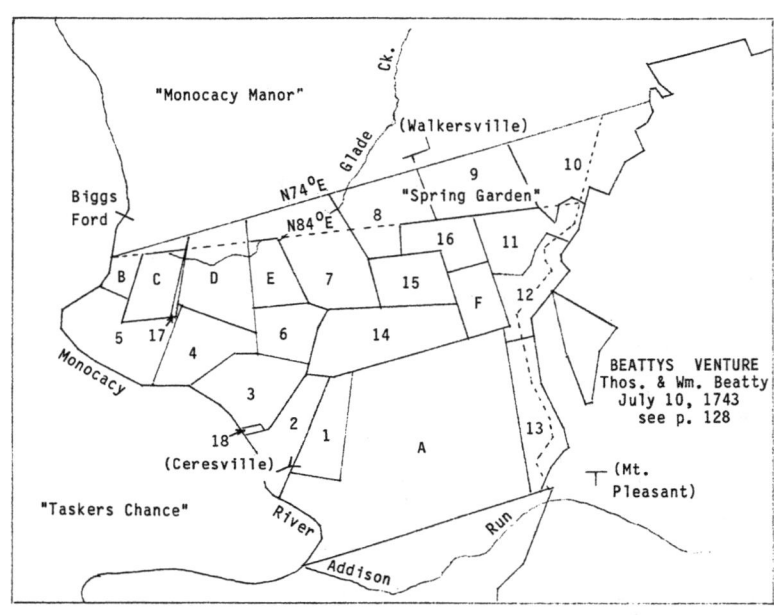

DULANYS LOT
Surveyed May 28, 1724
Patented Apr. 7, 1737

Owners, Pre-confiscation

	ac.		
A	1000	Susanna Beatty	July 17, 1732
B	50	John Biggs	Oct. 1758*
C	100	Allen Farquhar	June 19, 1733
D	200	William Dern	Oct. 29, 1781*
E	100	John Bell	Sept 20, 1781*
F	100	John Martin	Feb. 15, 1732
	1550		

* Prior ownership corroborated by Daniel Dulany, Jr.

** Land Office, Sale Book of Confiscated British Properties

Purchasers, October 10, 1781**

	ac.	
1	135	David Poe
2	137	Geo. Adams (Abraham Haff, lessee)
3	170	John Crabs
4	140	Andrew Baughman
5	189	Joseph Sim (William Rice, lessee)
6	115	John Ramsburg
7	268	Richard Potts
8	169	Thomas Beatty
9	210	Jacob Schley
10	288	Isaac Weyne
11	164	Henry Right
12	116	William Snider
13	149	Abraham Haff
14	257	Caleb Dorsey
15	120	Jacob Schley
16	103	Thomas Beatty
17	3	John Ramsburg
18	2	William Beatty (graveyard)
	2735	

parcel's date of survey, it is interesting to note that title to the land was not actually Dulany's until it was patented to him on April 7, 1737.[3] The reason for this 13-year delay or the validity of title to the lots sold before 1737 is not clear. Avoidance of quitrents during the period when the Proprietor's personal land records were being reestablished may have been a factor.

Far more curious because of the unanswered questions it poses is the observation that on the certificate of survey were plotted not only the outlines of the tract itself, but also within those outlines an indicated area of 1,000 acres which either had been sold to Susanna Beatty of New York or had at least been designated for her.[4] The Beatty tract is still fairly well defined today as the area bounded by State Highway 26 and by Stauffer and Crum Roads. Although we know something about Susanna Beatty, the questions do remain: How and when did she come to know Dulany? Why, as a widow in New York with a family of 10 children, some of them married and all quite well established, would she and they venture into this relatively unsettled frontier region? And exactly when did she and her family actually settle on "Dulany's Lot?"

Her husband John Beatty had come as a young man from Ireland to Ulster County in New York Colony some time before 1691. In that year, on November 7th at Esopus (Kingston), he married Susanna Asfordby, the daughter of well-to-do William Asfordby. Like his father-in-law, John Beatty moved from Kingston to Marblehead, where he was a large landholder and where with his wife he inherited additional land from William Asfordby. He served as trustee of Marblehead in the period 1703-1719 and was overseer of the poor, 1713-1719. In 1714 as surveyor for Robert Livingston, he laid out Livingston's Manor along the Hudson River on both sides of Roelof Johnson's Kill.[5]

Between 1693 and 1711 ten children were born to the Beatty's, namely Robert, William, Charles, Agnes, John, Thomas, Edward, Martha, James and Henry. When in 1721 their father died, these children ranged in age from ten to 28. At least Robert had by then married and he remained in New York. Charles also stayed in New York where he died in 1727. He was not yet thirty years of age, but had been married for three years to Jannetje Jans, daughter of Thomas Jansen. By his 1721 will John Beatty gave his wife Susanna all his land except for the land on which Robert was then living. He also devised an interest in a mill and 20 acres to his son John Beatty, Jr.

---

[3] Patent: EI 2:410.

[4] Original Patented Certificate of Survey, Prince George's County No. 3850. The Certificate makes no reference to Susanna Beatty by name and does not spell out specifically the courses and distances of the 1,000-acre portion. But its outline coincides with what we subsequently know about the Beatty land. It is possible that the outline of the 1,000-acre portion may have been added to the Certificate at any time between the dates of survey and of patent.

[5] Cf. Turk, op. cit., and Frank Allaben, *The Ancestry of Leander Howard Crall* (New York 1908), pp. 91-100.

A misreading of the Maryland Rent Rolls once concluded that Susanna Beatty and at least some of her family had come to Maryland and were in possession of land on "Rocky Creek" by the year 1725. The claim is not substantiated by known records, however, and it is doubtful that any of the family lived there that early. Moreover, analysis of known particulars pertaining to each of the Beatty children shows that four of them, William, John, Thomas and Martha, were in New York as late as 1728. Eight of them, all except Robert and Charles, are first seen in Maryland about 1733.[6] Thus the actual move to Maryland must have occurred within that five year period.

This is corroborated by the dates on which Susanna Beatty received title to her land. The 1,000 acres on "Dulany's Lot" were conveyed to her on July 17, 1732, and on May 24, 1733 she purchased from Capt. John Stoddert 939 acres as her half of the "Rocky Creek" tract across the River.[7] Yet even within this time span some of the family undoubtedly lived for a while in New Jersey: Thomas about 1730, Edward after 1733 and at least two of Robert's children who apparently found spouses there. We therefore must discount the inclusion of Susanna Beatty's 1,000 acres on the 1724 survey plat for "Dulany's Lot" as well as reference to her "possession" of "Rocky Creek" in 1725.

On March 20, 1739 Susanna Beatty was placing her landholdings on both "Dulany's Lot" and her 939-acre half of "Rocky Creek" in the names of her children.[8] With Robert, Charles and Henry now dead, she divided "Rocky Creek" between Agnes, then unmarried, who received 300 acres or nearly half, and William, John and James Beatty together with John Middagh who had married their sister Martha Beatty. Each of the latter four received about 85 acres. Thomas and Edward were thus not included. On the other hand, Agnes Beatty received no part of "Dulany's Lot." It went instead to the other six survivors, each of whom received two parcels, a small strip fronting on the Monocacy River, which averaged 15 or 20 acres and a larger parcel farther east from the River. Only John's two parcels on "Dulany's Lot" were contiguous.

Susanna Beatty wrote her will on June 20, 1742. Though probated on Oct. 30, 1745, a copy appears as one of the first wills recorded in the newly formed Frederick County.[9] She called herself

---

[6] William, John, Thomas, Edward, James and Henry appeared on the 1733 list of taxables in Monocosie Hundred, Martha's husband John "Middock" in 1734 didn't burn tobacco according to law and Agnes has been identified as a baptism witness on Pastor Johann Caspar Stöver's 1736 visit (see below, pp. 368-369, 375). Only Thomas and James were not included on the 1734 tobacco burning list.

[7] Prince George's County Land Records, Q:532, 661. The price for the "Dulany Lot" acreage was £200, or four shillings an acre. For "Rocky Creek" see also above, p. 39.

[8] Prince George's County Land Records, Y:148-153.

[9] Prince George's County Will Book 29:209 and Frederick County Will Book A1:12. Frederick County was formed out of Prince George's County in 1748. The will as recorded in Frederick County spells Moraca as Noraea and Jane as Jean.

"of Monocosey" and mentioned all of her children except Charles, who had died in 1727, and Henry, who presumably died between 1733-1742. Although Robert died in New York, she devised 300 acres of "Rocky Creek" and "Providence" on the Linganore, originally granted to Edward Beatty, to Robert's children John, Moraca, Susannah, George, Margaret and Jane. Susanna and Jane married brothers Peter and Abraham Haff, sons of Lawrence Haff from New Jersey.

Susanna Beatty had lived with her eldest surviving son, William Beatty, Sr. on the southeastern portion of her "Dulany Lot" acreage. It was called the "home plantation" in her will and is known today as Glade Valley Farms near the village of Mount Pleasant. This was the portion deeded to William in 1739 and here William continued to reside with his wife Elizabeth Carmack and their children William, Jr., Eleanor, Mary and Ann.

William Beatty appeared in the Prince George's Court records in 1734, having to pay a fine of 50 pounds of tobacco for failure to perform his duty as a constable for Monocacy Hundred. In the same year his name, and those of his brothers Henry, Edward and John Beatty and his brother-in-law Thomas Middagh were on the lengthy list of those who had not burned their tobacco according to law.[10] In October of 1742 he signed the petition seeking to divide Prince George's County.[11] In 1757 William Beatty willed the home place to his son William Beatty Jr.,[12] who married Mary Dorothea Grosch, daughter of John Conrad Grosch. Of the elder William's daughters, Eleanor married Jacob Young, Ann married Caspar Schaaf, and Mary married first Isaac Elting (son of Cornelius Elting and Rebecca van Metre) and second John Cary.[13]

William Beatty, Jr. was active in community affairs,[14] serving frequently on Frederick County grand juries, as Ensign in his brother-in-law Thomas Middagh's Company during the French and Indian War, as Constable for Manor Hundred (1763) and as Judge of the Orphans Court from 1777 to 1784. He and his wife had 12 children, including an eldest son, William Beatty III, who served with the Flying Camp when it marched to New York in 1776. Young William saw other service during the Revolution in both New Jersey and South Carolina, but was mortally wounded near Camden in April 1781.[15] The story is told that word of his death came to his father who was entertaining guests at his home at Mount Pleasant. The text of the message was not mentioned until the next morning in order not to disturb the guests.[16] George Washington is also said to have been a

---

[10] See Appendix, pp. 368-369.

[11] *Maryland State Papers, No. 1, the Black Books,* 3:9; para. 454 in the *Calendar.* See also pp. 368-369.

[12] Frederick County Wills, A1:113. Eli Beatty, son of William Jr., who was living in Hagerstown in 1856, confirmed that his father had inherited Susanna Beatty's homestead.

[13] Turk, *op. cit.*

[14] Cf. Rice, *The Life, op. cit., passim.*

[15] Frederick *Herald,* May 21, 1825, quoting from the *American Biographical Dictionary.* See also Williams, *op. cit.,* p. 125.

[16] Cf. Frederick *News,* July 17, 1962.

guest at the Beatty home.

John Beatty, Jr., the second oldest surviving son of John and Susanna Beatty, was still a freeholder in New York Colony in 1728, having received through his father's 1721 will a tract of 20 acres and an interest in a mill there. But he was in Maryland by 1733 and presumably married there. By occupation he was a tanner. His portion of the 1,000 acres on "Dulany's Lot" was the most westerly one, extending northward from the Monocacy River near present-day Ceresville and lying somewhat east of today's Woodsboro Road, Highway 194. He also held 85 acres of "Rocky Creek" located on the other side of the River west of "Tasker's Chance," some three miles from the mouth of Carroll Creek. John Beatty's wife was Hendricka Biggs, daughter of neighbor John Biggs. She, too, had been born in the Kingston area of New York. John Beatty died in 1761, and Hendricka, with her second husband Jacob Barton, administered his estate.[17] A son, John Beatty III, moved to Cambridge, Ohio, where he became the ancestor of the Beatty family there. Jacob Barton subsequently leased Lot No. 59 on Monocacy Manor, situated on Israel's Creek midway between Daysville and Woodsboro.

Susanna Beatty in 1739 deeded to her son Edward, a blacksmith, the portion of "Dulany's Lot" situated directly north of his brother William's parcel. In addition, Edward made three surveys of his own, all on Linganore Creek. "Well Watered Bottom" was located at the mouth of Ben's Branch about two and a half miles south of today's Mt. Pleasant.[18] He gave this land to his brother Thomas on November 20, 1740.[19] "Poplar Bottom" was situated off Meadow Road about a mile and a half further downstream.[20] "Providence" was on the Linganore, upstream and just south of what is today called the Old Annapolis Road,[21] where the 1873 Atlas shows the home and mills of P. L. Wilson.[22]

Although Edward Beatty made these surveys in 1732, witnessed the transfer of the 1,000 acres from Daniel and Rebecca Dulany to his mother in the same year and appeared on the 1734 Prince George's County list of those not burning their tobacco properly, he nevertheless was back in Reading Township, Hunterdon County, New Jersey in 1735.[23] There he married Susanna Cock. By 1748 he had returned to Frederick County, where as a creditor he signed the inventory of Cornelius Carmack. In 1754 Abraham Crum and his brother Gilbert became indebted to Edward in their purchase of "Palmer's Choice" and "Palmerzanor."[24] Edward Beatty and his wife

---

[17] Frederick County Administrative Accounts, A 1:224.
[18] C/S: EI 3:432.
[19] Prince George County Land Records, Y:242.
[20] C/S: EI 3/431.
[21] C/S: EI 3:432. The present "Old Annapolis Road" should not be confused with the Annapolis Road which in 1743 followed approximately today's Gas House Pike to the south. See map, p. 229.
[22] Lake, op. cit., p. 33. For location of Edward Beatty's three surveys, see map, p. 229.
[23] Kenn Stryker-Rodda, "The Janeway Account Books, 1735-1746," Genealogical Magazine of New Jersey, 23:7.

Susanna had three children, Ezekiel, Ezra, Elijah, and a posthumous fourth, Edward, Jr., who died young. Edward Beatty himself died in February 1755, his wife Susanna the following August. By the terms of his will, Edward Beatty devised his 160-acre portion of "Dulany's Lot" and Lot No. 65 in Frederick town to Ezekial, his "Resurvey of Poplar Bottom" and "Patrick's Colt" to Ezra and his one-third interest in "Metere," "Palmer's Choice" and "Palmerzaner" to Elijah. Three parts of "Rocky Creek" which he bought from George Beatty, John Beatty and John and Agnes Kimball were to go to the posthumous Edward.[25] Susanna Beatty's brother Henry Cock served as her executor and purchased "Providence," which "with the mill" on January 31, 1777 he devised to his son William Cock.[26] Ezekial and Elijah Beatty in 1774 had a resurvey made on "Poplar Bottom" and surrounding tracts which they called "Resurvey on Middle Plantation."[27]

James Beatty, another son of Susanna, was a tanner and lived for about ten years on "Dulany's Lot." In 1736 he and his brother Thomas were discharged on a complaint filed against them for having insulted the sheriff. In 1739 William Farquhar became indebted to the same two brothers for 206 pounds.[28] There is no record of James's marriage, and his estate division suggests that he had no children. No surveys were made for him and he does not appear to have made land purchases. He did, however, receive land on "Rocky Creek" and on "Dulany's Lot" in the division of 1739.[29] His will of November 4, 1742 was dated after his mother's will, but he died before her. "In common form" his will was probated by Thomas Beatty before Robert Baker on January 29, 1742/43. It divided his possessions among his brothers and sisters, allowing one share for the children of his brother Robert. He also gave William Bigrove "his time and a mare bought of Richard Story."[30] Thomas Beatty subsequently purchased James's land.[31]

Susanna Beatty's daughter Agnes married John Kimball,[32] who was named as one of the seven initial County Commissioners at the time Frederick County was formed in 1748.[33] He also served during the French and Indian War as Lieutenant in Capt. Thomas Middagh's Company.[34] He and Agnes after their marriage lived in the vicinity of today's junction of Butterfly Lane and Route 180 just outside the corporate limits of the city of Frederick.[35] In the 1739 property

---

[24] See above, p. 75.
[25] Frederick County Wills, A1:52.
[26] Frederick County Wills, GM 1:155.
[27] C/S: BC & GS 50:234.
[28] Prince George's County Land Records, Y:4.
[29] Ibid., Y:151.
[30] Prince George's County Wills, 22:528, Hall of Records. James Beatty's estate was still being administered in 1756. See Frederick County Administrative Accounts, A1:120.
[31] Frederick County Land Records, B:178, June 2, 1750.
[32] Church Records, All Saints' Church, Frederick.
[33] Proceedings of the Assembly, 1748-1751, *Archives of Maryland*, op. cit., 46:142.
[34] See Appendix, p. 380.
[35] Patent: BY & GS 3:319 for "Dickson's Struggle," surveyed in

division, as noted above, Agnes received nearly half of her mother's half of "Rocky Creek" but no part of "Dulany's Lot" as did her brothers and sister.

Thomas Beatty, Sr. (1703-1769) was Susanna Beatty's sixth child. He was still in New York on October 23, 1729 when he married Maria Jansen at Kingston, but in the following year they baptised their son Charles in Readington, New Jersey.[36] Shortly after that he came to Maryland where, like all his surviving brothers, he appeared in the 1733 Account of Taxables of Monocosie. He was not included on the 1734 list of those failing to burn their tobacco according to law, but on May 22nd of that year was present to witness a bill of sale from George Sweinhart to Botus [Baltis] Fout.[37] Although he received the middle portion of his mother's part of "Dulany's Lot" in 1739, he subsequently moved from this home area to "Beatty's Delight," which he had had surveyed on the lower part of "Linganore Creek near a mile from Monocacy River".[38]

Thomas Beatty was the father of Charles, Thomas Jr., James, Sarah and Susanna Beatty, the latter the wife of Nathan Maynard.[39] Until the time of the Revolution Thomas Beatty and his sons Charles and Thomas Jr. were among the largest landholders in Frederick County. But Thomas Beatty is best remembered for his long service as a Court Justice, from 1739 with the Prince George's County Court and from 1748 until after 1765 in Frederick County. His was the longest continuous service of all the Justices who served during the Colonial period. A highlight came in November 1765 when the Court under his direction repudiated the Stamp Act and began the long train of events which ultimately led to the American Revolution.[40] Thomas Beatty, Sr. died in 1769, having made Daniel Richards and John Carmack overseers of his estate, which he divided among his children.

Susanna Beatty's daughter Martha married at Kingston, New York Nov. 24, 1728 John Middag, a brother of Robert Beatty's wife Bata Middag. They were the children of George and Marietje Middag. John Middagh, as the name came to be spelled, came to Maryland with the Beatty's. He does not appear in the 1733 Account of

---

1748 for James Dickson.
[36] B. V. D. Wyckoff, transl., "Readington Church Baptisms from 1720," *Somerset County Historical Quarterly*, 4:213.
[37] Prince George's County Land Records, T:164.
[38] C/S: IL B:108. See map, p. 229.
[39] "Land of Valleys," a 100-acre parcel west of today's New London, was surveyed (CS: BC & GS 1:364) on January 29, 1752 for William Cummings of Annapolis. He had it resurveyed to 780 acres on April 7, 1757, but assigned the certificate (CS: BC & GS 9:413) to Thomas Mayner [Maynard], who received the patent. In later years Thomas Beatty's son-in-law Nathan Maynard had further resurveys on this land, on which Lake's *Atlas* of 1873 (*op. cit.*, p. 25) shows the homes of H. G. Mayner and N. Mayner. Methodists claim the baptism of Henry Maynard by Robert Strawbridge dates the beginnings of Methodism in America. See above, p. 102.
[40] Rice, *The Life*, *op. cit.*, *passim*, but especially, for the Stamp Act repudiation, pp. 273-277.

Taxables of Monocosie Hundred, but as Johannes Middaugh he was named on John Nelson's list of the 83 individuals who in 1734 had not burned their tobacco according to law.[41] In the 1739 division of Susanna Beatty's lands, John Middagh received the northeast corner of her 1,000 acres on "Dulany's Lot," bounded on the north and east by today's Stauffer and Crum Roads. He also received one of the six smaller parcels touching the Monocacy River near the mouth of Israel's Creek and one of the four 85-acre parcels on "Rocky Creek." John Middaugh served as a Captain during the French and Indian War. The roster of his Company (see p. 380) gives an indication of some of those individuals who had settled on "Dulany's Lot" and its nearby area by 1757.

John and Martha Beatty Middagh were the parents of Martha, John, Mary and Susanna Middagh. Martha, the eldest daughter, married her cousin Charles Beatty, son of Thomas Beatty, Sr., while Mary married William Ritchie. The Ritchie home on Record Street in the city of Frederick was built about the time of the latter marriage. A son, John Ritchie, first married Catherine Beatty, another child of Thomas Beatty, Sr., and then Ann Barnhold. By the latter marriage he had a son Dr. Albert Ritchie, who married Catherine Lackland Davis, a great granddaughter of Meredith Davis, Sr.[42] Dr. Ritchie was born on a part of "Rocky Creek" which he later sold to the Mount Olivet Cemetery in Frederick. His grandson Albert Ritchie was Governor of Maryland, 1920-1935.

The 1873 Atlas shows residing in that year on the original Beatty 1,000 acres Samuel Hoke, E[dward] A. Shriner, J[acob] H. and E[zra] L. Cramer, William McDaniel, C. A. Thomas and M. Jones.[43]

As previously noted, "Dulany's Lot" and his Lordship's "Monocacy Manor" were surveyed at about the same time in May of 1724. The Manor's southern boundary was set at a compass angle of N74°E, as was the southern boundary of "Dulany's Lot." The north boundary of "Dulany's Lot" was undoubtedly intended to coincide with the southern boundary of the Manor and therefore bear the same angle, but through what was undoubtedly an oversight it was actually set at N84°E. Between these two parcels, then, existed a sizable triangular gap, ten degrees in width, which was discovered and surveyed as "Spring Garden" on November 14, 1730 for John Abington.[44] In size the gap amounted to 680 acres, the equivalent of slightly over a square mile!

Obviously Dulany had not discovered the error when he began making "sales" of parts of "Dulany's Lot" other than Susanna Beatty's 1,000 acres. It is fairly clear that in subdividing the remaining three-quarters of his total acreage Dulany worked from this northern boundary southward rather than extending northward from the Beatty land. He seems to have laid out first a series of lots, working from the River eastward. Each was set with the N84°E azimuth as its

---
[41] See pp. 61-62, 368-370.
[42] Ibid., pp. 81-84.
[43] Lake, op. cit., p. 33.
[44] C/S: AM 1:31; Patent: PL 8:8. For other Abington land, see pp. 39-40.

northern boundary. Subsequent alterations erased some of these courses, but the general pattern is clear from deeds and a resurvey made nearly fifty years later.[45]

Daniel Dulany, Sr. did not always give perfect or immediate title. From the nature of subsequent transactions one might deny the oft-repeated allegations that early settlers didn't always bother to have their deeds recorded: Instead, sometimes deeds just didn't exist! After Dulany's death, his son appears in several deed records as his executor, reviewing what his father had allegedly done and then passing on bona fide title in more or less confirmatory proceedings. Some individuals had "paper," some receipts, some merely the word of what the elder Dulany had "sold" them. Consequently we have no way of knowing exactly when the early purchasers of Dulany's Lot" originally came to the area or when they bought their land from Dulany, or worse, even who they really were.

It was not until 1738 that the "Spring Garden" mistake was discovered and Dulany was able on June 9th of that year to purchase the intervening gap from Abbington for 180 pounds.[46] The date is significant, for anyone with a boundary of N84°E would presumably have gotten his property before Dulany discovered his error or could buy back the property he thought was originally his. This category would most certainly have included Allen Farquhar, John Bell, Sr., and the owner or lessor of land which was later termed, in 1781, Lots 11 and 16.[47]

Allen Farquhar had an agreement from Daniel Dulany dated June 19, 1733 for the purchase of 100 acres of land on "Dulany's Lot," provided he would settle there. He did, but he died in 1738, leaving the land to his widow Catherine and sons William and Allen, Jr. On September 28, 1739 Dulany passed formal title to son William Farquer, who was to arrange its subsequent ownership with his mother and brother.[48] This land was situated near the northwestern corner of "Dulany's Lot," not quite on the Monocacy River, but very near to the point where Glade Creek, which passed through Farquhar's land, empties into the Monocacy. The north boundary of the land was set at N 84° E 103 perches which was identified as part of the 22nd line of "Dulany's Lot." Whether William Farquhar occupied this land after his father's death is not known; it had been supposed that he and his

---

[45] See especially the Unpatented Certificate of a Resurvey of part of "Dulany's Lot" by Francis Deakins, dated August 13, 1781.

[46] Prince George's County Land Records, T:597.

[47] A similar wedge was actually discovered as late as 1786 on the south boundary of "Dulany's Lot" between the 1,000 acres granted Susanna Beatty in 1732 and "Addison's Choice." This amounted to 62 acres and was surveyed for James Beatty. (Frederick County Survey Book, HGO 1:135)

[48] Prince George's County Land Records, Y:95. It will be remembered that Dulany himself had not received his patent to the entire "Dulany's Lot" until April 7, 1737. Thomas and John Beatty stood as securities in 1739 for William Farquhar's faithful performance as executor of his father's estate (ibid., Y:4). See also Maryland Calendar of Wills, op. cit., 8:4.

younger brother remained in the Union Bridge area. On November 6, 1736, for example, the elder Allen Farquer had conveyed the 200-acre "Killfadda" on Little Pipe Creek to his son William Farquer, "lately of Pennsylvania but now of Prince George's County," in order to encourage his son's move from Pennsylvania to today's Union Bridge area in Carroll County.[49] In 1757 the Farquhars sold their parcel on "Dulany's Lot" to Peter and John Berg (later Barrick; residents on the Manor to the north). The Bergs did not hold the land long and in August 1758 sold it to Stephen Ramsburg,[50] who was fashioning a larger piece of 150 acres by combining the original Farquhar 100 acres with another 50 acres located due west, on the River.

John Biggs, who had come to Maryland from New York and New Jersey, was the original purchaser of that 50 acres, although he had no proof of ownership. Daniel Dulany, Jr. at last deeded it to him officially in October 1758, "reposing due trust and confidence in the assurances and declarations of John Biggs."[51] This gave Biggs good title with which to pass the land on to Stephen Ramsburg,[52] whose 150 acre consolidation was one of the reasons for Biggs at long last to get his title clearly defined.

The difference between the Biggs and Farquhar pieces is interesting: Even as late as 1758 Farquhar's north boundary ran at N84°E, undoubtedly because title had actually been so described in 1739. The Biggs piece, however, not only included a northern boundary of N74°E, but possessed a "cap" above the Farquhar piece, representing the "Spring Garden" portion which would have belonged to Farquhar had he and Dulany either known of the "Spring Garden" error or, more probably since the error was already discovered in 1730 some three years before their original contract, had Dulany then owned that strip. This leads to the belief that Biggs probably got his 50 acres *after* Dulany got "Spring Garden" in 1738.

Just east of the Farquhar parcel, **William Dern,** who was of German descent but had also come from New Jersey, established residence on a 200-acre parcel, fairly well defined today by Fountain Rock and Retreat Roads. He was last known in the Raritan region of New Jersey in 1731[53] and had come to the Monocacy area sometime before November 30, 1738 when he witnessed the will of his neighbor "Allan Farquer of Manackus."[54] In March of 1739 he sold a negro slave to William Beatty[55] and on June 17, 1739 as Wilhelm Dern had his

---
[49] Prince George's County Land Records, T:424. This land had been surveyed originally for John Tredane and was patented to him in 1734. It adjoined the 174-acre parcel called "Rock Land." In 1771 William Farquhar conveyed "Kilfadda" to Joseph and Mary Wright. See Maryland Rent Rolls (Frederick No. 1), 32:34 and above, p. 88.
[50] Frederick County Land Records, F:566.
[51] *Ibid.,* F:563.
[52] *Ibid.,* F:608.
[53] John P. Dern, ed., Simon and Sibrandina Geertruid Hart, translators, *The Albany Protocol, Wilhelm Christoph Berkenmeyer's Chronicle of Lutheran Affairs in New York Colony, 1731-1750* (Ann Arbor, 1971), pp. 8-15.
[54] *Maryland Calendar of Wills, op. cit.,* 8:4.

daughter Anna Catharina baptised by Pastor Stöver.[56] The northern boundary of Dern's parcel was set at N74°E, but the official record for this dates only from an October 29, 1781 confirmatory deed from Daniel Dulany's son to William Dern's son. The deed makes reference to a contract or agreement in writing between their fathers, signed by Daniel Dulany, Sr., which in 1781 was in the possession of William Dern, Jr.[57] From this we assume that the original purchase agreement was most likely made between June[58] and November in 1738. Still visible today on this property is the mill race leading to a millsite on Ramsburg's 150 acres to the west. Dern and Ramsburg had agreed on its construction in 1762.[59]

John Bell, Sr., was in the Monocacy area by 1742 when he signed a petition for the division of Prince George's County.[60] He obtained 100 acres of land on the east side of William Dern's lot at a date yet unknown. Whether he got it from Dulany is also unknown. At any rate, there was no good title to it, even when his son John Bell, Jr., who had inherited it, transferred it in 1772 to his brother-in-law Jacob Brengle.[61] The latter had to get title confirmed in 1781 at the time when parts of "Dulany's Lot" and other lands were being resurveyed in connection with the confiscation sale of Loyalist property. Francis Deakins made the survey on September 20, 1781 and on the certificate placed the notation, "As it appears by sundry receipts of money and other papers in the hands of Jacob Bringle that he is entitled to a conveyance from Daniel Dulany, Esq. for 100 acres, ... I have therefore surveyed for him part of a tract called "Dulany's Land [sic]," beginning...." The parcel's northern and southern boundaries were set at N84°E, implying that it, too, may originally have come from Dulany before he got "Spring Garden" in 1738.[62]

Thus we have four parcels of land adjacent to each other, lying from west to east or from the natural common starting point at the River for both the Manor and "Dulany's Lot." One would expect that out of these four (Biggs, Farquhar, Dern and Bell) the first or most westerly ones would bear the earlier northern boundary of N84°E. Instead, the second and fourth ones (Farquhar and Bell) do, and we have no way of explaining how or why the gaps filled later by the first and third lots (Biggs and Dern) could have resulted.

Like Farquhar, **John Martin** also had a deed from the elder Daniel Dulany before he died.[63] Theirs were the only two such deeds

---

[55] Prince George's County Land Records, Y:4.
[56] See below, pp. 134-135, 375.
[57] Frederick County Land Records, WR 2:1066.
[58] When Dulany purchased "Spring Garden" and was first able to use the N74°E azimuth.
[59] Frederick County Land Records, H:135.
[60] *Maryland State Papers, No. 1, The Black Books*, para. 454 in the Calendar.
[61] The 1772 deed was not recorded. For the Brengles, see below, p. 263.
[62] Frederick County Land Records, WR 2:1073-1075. The certificate and plat were appended to the deed.

besides the one for Susanna Beatty's 1,000 acres which were granted by Daniel Dulany, Sr. and were recorded in the County Land Records before Dulany's death in 1753. In corroboration, Farquhar and Martin were the only two besides the Beatty family and Dulany himself who appear on a 1750 Debt Book list for "Dulany's Lot."[64] Martin's land, which he received on February 15, 1732, was a rectangle of 100 acres lying adjacent to the northeast corner of the Beatty parcel and hence next to John Middagh's land.[65] Its location placed it near the Monocacy-Annapolis Road[66] which was first mentioned in 1739. Court records show that John Martin was an overseer for this road between 1744-1747. Martin's location was also near the center of the approximately ninety square mile Manor Hundred for which he was appointed Constable by the Frederick County Court of March 1749. The bounds of this Hundred were described as beginning at the mouth of Linganore Creek, up the Monocacy River to the mouth of Pipe Creek, with Pipe Creek to the fork where Big and Little Pipe Creeks join, with Little Pipe Creek to William Farquhar's Ford and then with a straight line to Linganore Main Road Ford.

Also near to John Martin's land was the land of the Rev. Joseph Jennings, Rector of All Saints' Parish "in Manockesey" for whom land was surveyed on January 21, 1743 in today's Daysville area north of the Beatty land.[67] John and Ann Martin baptised their children (Demarius, Zadock, Appiah, Asa and Aseneth) at All Saints Church in Frederick. On May 14, 1759 John Martin deeded his parcel to Adam Link,[68] who was then the second German to settle on "Dulany's Lot." Link was born in 1721 at Gross Gartach in the Kraichgau, just west of Heilbronn. He came to this country in 1733 and had lived at Oley Hill in Berks County, Pennsylvania before coming to Maryland in 1759.

Even after the death of Daniel Dulany, Sr., during the period that "Dulany's Lot" passed to his son Daniel Dulany, Jr., no further land transfers were made and there are few clues to indicate whether the land was even settled. But if, as is most probable, it was, its settlers were there as lessors or renters, not as landowners. Title remained with Dulany.

In 1781 the Maryland government began confiscating British property, including the land of Loyalists. Property on "Monocacy Manor," "Tasker's Chance," and "Dulany's Lot," where title still remained with Lord Baltimore or with the Dulany family, was subject to such confiscation. Preparatory to the sale of parts of "Dulany's Lot," Francis Deakins was ordered by the Commissioners for the Sale

---

[63] Prince George's County Land Records, Y:666.
[64] Calvert Papers, Maryland Historical Society, MS. 174:54, 72, 73, 77, 88.
[65] The relationship, if any, to Benjamin Martin who was a sergeant in Captain Middagh's Company, p. 380 below, is unknown.
[66] C/S: LG C:54 for "Kendrick's Hap." See also above, p. 56, and below, pp. 228-229.
[67] C/S: LG E:296. For Jennings, see below, pp. 350-351.
[68] Frederick County Land Records, F:718. For a genealogy of the Link Family, see Paxson Link, *The Link Family* (n.s., 1951).

of British Property on August 13, 1781 to "resurvey and lay off for sale...three following tracts of land lying...adjacent to each other, the late property of Daniel Dulany, son of Daniel, to wit, part of a tract called 'Dulany's Lot,' part of a tract called 'Spring Garden' and a tract called 'Addition'." Deakins' resulting map showed as separate parcels the lands of Ramsburg (150 acres), Dern (200), Brengle (100), Link (100) and, as a single unit, the Beatty 1,000 acres. All the remainder, some 2,735 acres, was divided into 18 parcels, most of them varying in size from 103 to 228 acres, suitable for individual tenancy or settlement (see map, p. 116). It may be assumed that after his initial grants of title Dulany subsequently leased this remainder much as was done on Lord Baltimore's "Monocacy Manor" to the north. But we have actual knowledge of earlier tenancy on only two of these: by William Rice on Lot No. 5 at the most westerly bend of the Monocacy and by Abraham Haff on Lot No. 2 to the west of the original Beatty land.[69]

But more interesting is the layout of Lot Nos. 16 and 11 whose northern boundaries again reflect the N84°E azimuth and coincide with the southern boundary of "Spring Garden," thus suggesting that they were originally laid out before 1738. Thomas Beatty purchased Lot No. 16 at the October 10, 1781 confiscation sale as well as the adjoining Lot No. 8. William Beatty purchased Lot No. 18, a tiny two-acre parcel on the River which represented a small graveyard, possibly prepared originally for the burial of his mother Susanna Beatty.[70]

Before leaving the subject of "Dulany's Lot," mention should be made of "Beatty's Venture" which was surveyed just to the east on July 10, 1743 for Thomas and William Beatty.[71] Title was transferred in 1753 to Johann Georg Lingenfelter,[72] another German, who had emigrated from Steinweiler in the Palatinate only the year before. This parcel was deeded in 1763 to Lingenfelter's son Bernhard, who in 1770 added 130 more acres with the purchase of "Beatty's Luck" to the west of "Beatty's Venture" and who then had the whole resurveyed

---

[69] Frederick County Land Records, WR 2:37. The Haff parcel was actually a lease for 14-years. Sons of both men married daughters of neighbor William Dern.

[70] Maryland Land Office, Sale Book of Confiscated British Property, 1781-1785. The subsequent history of the graveyard has been studied in interesting detail by Millard M. Rice and John P. Dern. It is listed in Holdcraft, op. cit., p. 19 as the Cock-Grahame Family Cemetery because these family names were the principal ones remaining in 1952. Undoubtedly it was the graveyard referred to in the death notice for Col. William Beatty who died on May 1, 1803 after a two-year illness: "His remains were deposited in the family burying ground near the River Monocasy in a neat vault planned by himself and constructed under his own directions a few months before his death." (Frederick Herald, May 7, 1803). This graveyard presumably served as the basis for James A. Boyd's claims concerning an early Monocacy "village" (see above, p. 47).

[71] C/S: LG E:408.

[72] Frederick County Land Records, E:74.

as 230 acres in 1775.[73] Bernhard Lingenfelter's brother Abraham leased 100 acres on "Dulany's Lot" itself from Joshua Testill, Dulany's agent in 1779. The land was located just north of the Beatty tract, i.e., north of today's Stauffer Road. and west of Israel Creek.[74] Whether Abraham Lingenfelter lived here is unknown: he was a merchant in Frederick and dealt in a great number of land transactions, perhaps as investments. At any rate, he promised as a condition of the purchase to erect a house and farm of given specifications and to plant 100 apple trees. But the land reverted to the Dulanys and was sold as confiscated property (Lot No. 14) with different metes and bounds two years later. Bernard Lingenfelter in 1791 bought from Henry Right the latter's Lot No. 11, purchased at the 1781 confication sale. This expansion of ownership of land on and near "Dulany's Lot by Bernard Lingenfelter ended in the spring of 1796 when he sold Lot No. 11 to Abraham Crum, in whose family it remained for many years. He also conveyed "Venture" and "Luck" to Daniel Stauffort [Stauffer].[75] By November 1796 Bernhard Lingenfelter at the age of 60 was buying land in Fayette County, Kentucky.

The initial settlement of "Dulany's Lot" occurred about the same time that two interesting lists were being prepared which provide us with something of a census of Monocacy inhabitants at that time. Both have been mentioned previously and both concerned Monocacy Hundred, as the area was then known -- the area of Maryland stretching westward from today's Frederick County.[76] One of these lists, prepared in 1734 by Constable John Nelson, purported to show those individuals who "had no tobacco burnt" in connection with the "price support program" of that day. The other was a list of "taxables" in 1733 as summarized by Constable Flower Swift. Taken together, the two lists name some 117 individuals of which 72 names are common to both lists. The lists in combination coincidentally represent 82 different family names. Alphabetized, the two lists are shown in the Appendix, pp. 368-369, where comparisons can be made.

---
[73] C/S: IC F:100. This parcel was not patented until 1790 (Patent: IC E:464).
[74] Frederick County Land Records, WR 2:109.
[75] For Crum and Stauffer Roads, see above p. 117.
[76] The other Hundreds in Prince George's County in 1733 were known as Western Branch, Collington, Patuxent, Mattapany, Upper Piscataway, Mt. Calvert, Eastern Branch, Potowmack, Rock Creek, and New Scotland.

ARRIVAL OF THE GERMANS

A decade had passed since Charles Carroll in 1721 purchased his license from the Indians to take up the first land in what is now Frederick County, Maryland. During those ensuing ten years some eight Monocacy settlements had begun. Situated largely in the southern and eastern halves of today's County, these early settlements were peopled by men and women who for the most part came from within the Maryland colony or from its immediate neighboring border areas. It is important to realize that most of the new settlers had already been established elsewhere and were merely making a change of locale. The geography was new and their frontier life primitive, but their establishment within the early American culture was not. Most of them were of English stock and their style of agriculture frequently resembled what they had known farther east. Their social and personal living patterns, in other words, set the foundation for the future of their Monocacy settlements.

About 1731 the picture began to change. Or at least it was significantly altered. In striking contrast to the first Monocacy families, many newcomers desperately needed a new home. A large portion was foreign-born, uprooted in the aftermath of European wars and economic privations. Others were seeking a place of refuge on religious grounds. Without ties to those who had come before them, they established themselves independently of the earlier settlers of the first decade. Men like Arnold Livers, Thomas Ogle, Stephen Ramsburg, Henry Munday, Nathaniel Wickham and Richard Touchstone, all new to the area, evolved as their leaders and protectors.

By far the most important group of settlers who arrived in the second decade were the Germans. People of this nationality had begun coming to America in sizable numbers only some twenty-one years earlier. In 1710 they were part of a huge mass migration resulting from the War of Spanish Succession in Europe during the reigns of Louis XIV in France and Queen Anne in England. Eleven crowded shiploads of some 2,400 Germans were escorted from England by British naval convoy in a single sailing which arrived in New York during the summer of 1710.[1] Other ships that year carried Germans to

---

[1] Considerable research concerning this migration has been in progress. Klaus Wust is dealing with the background of the exodus from Germany in 1709. Norman C. Wittwer and John P. Dern have concentrated on the Germans' stay in England and on the ocean voyage. Both studies in large measure correct and augment Walter A. Knittle, *Early Eighteenth Century Palatine Emigration* (Philadelphia, 1937). But the monumental, already published treatise dealing with individual immigrants is Henry Z. Jones, *The Palatine Families of New York* (Universal City, Calif., 1985) in which the origins of some 70% of the 1710 Germans have been traced in Germany itself.

Virginia and North Carolina. Seven years later a group of three shiploads reached Philadelphia.[2] Thereafter, in smaller separate quantities usually aboard single vessels, others followed. The floodgates had been opened and throughout the entire eighteenth century masses of Germans reached American shores. Beginning in 1727 fairly detailed lists of Germans landing at the port of Philadelphia were kept, and these have been meticulously transcribed and analyzed by William J. Hinke.[3] Most of these German immigrants went to Pennsylvania, where, since the area in and around Philadelphia was already well inhabited, large numbers filtered into what were then the western reaches of the colony.

By 1731 the flow of German settlement had crossed the Susquehanna River and was pressing toward Maryland. In the settlements which followed, the Germans tended to select sites in and near the hills, which resembled so closely the hills they had known in their Palatinate area of Germany. In marked contrast the English usually chose the rich rolling, well-watered meadowland. The Germans made their surveys along the Monocacy Road, while the English located on land beside the rivers. The Germans preferred to own only the few acres which they could clear and farm themselves. Many English, but by no means all, possessed much larger acreages, especially in the southeastern part of today's Frederick County, where cultivation involved the use of slaves.

One cannot emphasize too strongly the vital cohesive nature of religion for these early Germans. They were a pious people and their common bond cementing them together in this strange and unfamiliar land was the religion they had known and practiced back in Germany. On the wilderness frontier, however, there were no pastors and no pre-existing churches. Leaders in their midst may have conducted Bible readings and led abbreviated forms of worship services, often in individual homes. But there was no one to baptize or marry their children and no one to guide them in their religious instruction, in their communion, even in the organizing of their congregations and the building of their churches.

---
[2] *Minutes of the Provincial Council of Pennsylvania from the Organization to the Termination of the Proprietary Government* (Philadelphia, 1852), 3:29. Often called *Pennsylvania Colonial Records.*

[3] Ralph Beaver Strassburger and William John Hinke, *Pennsylvania German Pioneers* (Norristown, 1934), 3 Vol. In an effort to keep tabs on the growing number of German immigrants, Lt. Governor Patrick Gordon and his Pennsylvania Provincial Council in 1727 began requiring lists of arrivals at Philadelphia. Altogether Hinke transcribed the lists for 323 ships arriving at Philadelphia between 1727 and 1808. The original lists were prepared in triplicate: List A was made by the Captain or his clerk who reproduced what their English ears thought they heard the Germans give as their names. Two other lists contained signatures, if the Germans could write, or, if they could not, their names as spelled by a sympathetic countryman who could more nearly approximate the German name. These latter lists recorded the Germans' oaths of allegiance to the English Crown (List B) and their abjuration of allegiance to their former sovereigns (List C).

Pastors did accompany the migrating Germans. But the circumstances of their coming, their backgrounds and the degree of their acceptance both by the Germans in America and by sponsoring authorities in Europe varied greatly. Charles H. Glatfelter in his superb study of eighteenth century German churches has provided biographical sketches for 250 Lutheran and Reformed pastors serving in or from the Pennsylvania area between 1717 and 1793.[4] These he divided into four groups which clearly demonstrate that variety. Less than a quarter of the total (55 or 22%) had been ordained in Europe and had come with the backing of European religious bodies in answer to calls from America. Another 31 were regular pastors in Europe who came without a specific call, but hoped to find acceptance in America after their arrival. A third group consisted of some 72 individuals who were not ordained but had had some training in Europe and came with the approval of the European church authorities. Interestingly this left by far the largest group, 92 in all, who worked without previous training or ordainment before they came.

When the first Germans moved from Pennsylvania into the Monocacy area, only a handful of pastors had yet arrived in America. Excluding those who served in the New York area with the Dutch and with the 1710 German immigrants,[5] we can account for no more than five Reformed and three Lutherans[6] who ministered to the Germans as early as 1731.

Johann Philipp Boehm, a Reformed schoolmaster who arrived in 1720 from Worms and Lambsheim, was persuaded in 1725 to begin pastoral duties and was ordained by the Dutch in New York in 1729. He organized Reformed congregations at Falckner's Swamp, Skippack and Whitemarsh in today's Montgomery County, Pennsylvania and in 1727 brought communion to the German Reformed in the Conestoga and Tulpehocken areas. Johann Conrad Templemann, a tailor from Weinheim, north of Heidelberg, arrived about 1721, settled in the Conestoga area of today's Lancaster County where he became a schoolmaster and, like Boehm, was persuaded in 1725 to lead religious services. Not until 1732 did he begin performing sacraments. George Michael Weiss, the first Reformed pastor already ordained in Germany before coming to America, arrived in 1727.[7] He was born in 1700 in Eppingen, southeast of Heidelberg, and brought with him a number of other emigrants from the surrounding Kraichgau area. But in America he only preached to the congregations organized by the others and had no congregation of his own. He left for Europe in 1730 to claim funds raised there for the Reformed in America, and shortly after his return from Europe moved to the New York area where he served until 1746. Johann Peter Müller arrived at Philadelphia aboard the

---
[4] Glatfelter, op. cit., pp. 5-6.
[5] Justus Falckner (served 1703-1723), Joshua [Harrsch] Kocherthal (1708-1719), Johann Friedrich Häger (1710-1721), and Wilhelm Christoph Berkenmeyer (1725-1751).
[6] The Reformed Church has now become a part of the United Church of Christ. Maryland and Pennsylvania Lutherans presently belong to the Lutheran Church in America.
[7] Strassburger-Hinke, op. cit., List 1B, p. 9.

Thistle of Glasgow in 1730.[8] He was ordained by the Presbyterians in Philadelphia and served briefly there, in Germantown and at Skippack during Weiss's absence. He then went to New Goshenhoppen in today's upper Montgomery County. By 1735 he had abandoned the Reformed and as a hermit joined the German Baptist Brethren at Ephrata, eventually succeeding Conrad Beissel as its head. The last of these Reformed ministers, Johann Bartholomew Rieger, did not reach Pennsylvania until 1731.[9] He served briefly in Philadelphia and in 1734 went to Amwell, New Jersey.

This recitation demonstrates not only how transitory was the service of these first Reformed pastors, both in time and place, but also how far away from the Maryland frontier they lived and worked. For the Lutherans the story was somewhat different. Anton Jacob Henckel, a Lutheran pastor from the northern Kraichgau area east of Heidelberg, was almost fifty when he arrived in 1717. Although he came on his own volition, he had been ordained in Germany and had served 25 years as a pastor with various congregations in the upper Kraichgau east of Heidelberg. Extant documentation is meagre, but he undoubtedly was responsible for the organization of the first Lutheran congregations in Pennsylvania. He lived at Falckner's Swamp in today's Montgomery County, Pennsylvania and served German Lutherans throughout present-day Philadelphia and Montgomery Counties, perhaps even extending his work to Tulpehocken in Berks County and Conestoga, northeast of today's city of Lancaster. He worked in these areas steadily for almost eleven years until he died in a fall from horseback in August 1728 at the age of sixty.

Less than a month passed, fortuitously, until two Lutheran successors arrived in Philadelphia. They were father and son, both named Johann Caspar Stöver, born respectively in Frankenberg on the Eder and Lüdorf near Remscheid. Neither had university training and neither had been ordained, although as they signed their names at the head of the ship's arrival list, the father added the abbreviation "Miss." and the son "Ss. Theol. Stud."[10] The elder Stöver's early whereabouts in America has not been pinpointed, although he may have been with the Germans at New Bern in North Carolina. In 1733 he received a call from the Hebron church in today's Madison County, Virginia, and in the same year both he and his son were ordained by Johannes Christian Schultz[11] at Providence in Pennsylvania. The father returned to Germany in 1734 to solicit funds for the Virginia church

----

[8] *Ibid.*, Lists 11 ABC, pp. 32-34.
[9] *Ibid.*, Lists 16 ABC, pp. 47, 51, 53. See also below, pp. 207-208.
[10] *Ibid.*, Lists 8 AB, p. 22.
[11] Johannes Christian Schultz was born in 1701 in Schainbach, where he was ordained in April 1732. He arrived at Philadelphia September 25, 1732 on the same ship with Johann Georg Honig and Philipp Ernst Grüber (see below, p. 198). Although without a call, he was named pastor for the Philadelphia, New Hanover, and Providence Lutheran congregations. In the following year he returned to Europe to solicit financial help, was there arrested for an unknown infraction and never returned to America. See Glatfelter, *op. cit.*, p. 126; Strassburger-Hinke, *op. cit.*, Lists 24 ABC, pp. 88, 89, 91.

and then remained there for five years studying theology, at least a portion of the time in Darmstadt. In 1739 he began his return to America, but died at sea on the way.

Johann Caspar Stöver, Jr., stayed on in Pennsylvania. After Schultz returned to Europe in 1733, Stöver for almost a decade was the only Lutheran minister serving in Pennsylvania. He was destined to remain active until his death in 1779, over half a century after his arrival in this country. He began performing baptisms and marriages a year or so after he came but still three and a half years before he was ordained. Where there were no church books, he kept a record of these events in a personal journal which he began well after the events themselves had occurred.[12] Instead of arranging his baptism entries chronologically, he began grouping them by the families concerned. Under the father's name he recorded a geographical place name, not where the baptism took place, but where the family lived. Since families moved, even the place name could represent their locations as Stöver knew them when he compiled his record, not when he performed the baptism sometimes years before. Such an arrangement makes it difficult to determine from the record alone where Stöver's itinerary took him, but the peripatetic nature of his work is manifestly obvious. Significantly he brought religious preaching and the organizing of congregations to an ever expanding area, an area which had not been visited by either Lutheran or Reformed pastors before him.

In 1735 Stöver began crossing the Susquehanna River, and in May of that first year he got as far as the German Opequon settlement in the western reaches of Virginia. For six years, or until 1740, he returned to Virginia each spring. Enroute, he passed through the Monocacy area where, beginning in April 1736, he stopped to minister to the German settlers along the way.[13] Even after his

---

[12] Johann Caspar Stöver, "Ministerial Records," original at the Historical Society of Pennsylvania, Philadelphia (hereafter: Stöver, op. cit.). Although as yet unpublished, these have been retranscribed and translated by John P. Dern in an effort to correct and to return to the original orthography the earlier transcription by Franklin J. F. Schantz, "Rev. John Casper Stoever's Record of Baptisms and Marriages from 1730 to 1779," *Notes and Queries, Historical, Biographical and Genealogical*, Annual Volume 1896, William Henry Egle, ed. (Harrisburg, 1896); reprinted without corrections but consolidated with an index as *Early Lutheran Baptisms and Marriages in Southeastern Pennsylvania* (Baltimore, 1982).

[13] Abdel Ross Wentz, *History of the Evangelical Lutheran Church of Frederick, Maryland, 1738-1938* (Harrisburg, 1938), pp. 35-40, describes a fancied first trip by Stöver through the Monocacy settlement and on to Virginia in June 1734, prior to his father's departure for Europe the following September. But the basis for Wentz's detailed and theorized surmisals describing the trip seems to rest upon a single entry in Stöver's records, a baptism allegedly in the Monocacy area on June 23, 1734. This involved the family of Jacob Mattheis, who, we feel, came later to Monocacy, probably in the following year. See below, p. 205. Stöver's record likewise

journeys to Virginia ceased, he continued coming to Monocacy for a year or two more. There he preached, baptized children and married young couples,[14] all from families whose land records and relationships are described in succeeding chapters. About 1743, however, Stöver moved farther away from Maryland, shifting his own Pennsylvania abode from Mill Creek, southwest of New Holland in the Conestoga area, to the Quitopahilla settlement between Annville and Lebanon in today's Lebanon County.[15] Thereafter we have no more word of Stöver in the Monocacy area.

In the spring of 1743, David Candler suddenly appeared upon the Pennsylvania-Maryland scene. Apparently he had been earlier in the New York-New Jersey area. A son was born in April 1740 at Schlotterdam on the Passaic River,[16] and perhaps as early as 1738 or 1739 the Germans at Schoharie were corresponding with Candler,

---

shows no ministerial acts in Virginia in 1734 with the possible exception of an inferred baptism in the Seltzer family on April 28th at Massanutten. But on that date Stöver is known to have been in Lancaster, Pennsylvania, and between the two dates his entries show him only farther east in Pennsylvania. The erroneous conclusion results from reading too literally Stöver's grouping of baptism entries by their families' later locales, not by the places where the baptisms took place. Apparently Wentz's dates and spellings for Stöver's subsequent ministerial acts in the Monocacy area were taken from Schantz, *loc. cit.*, and not from the original Stöver record.

[14] For the Monocacy area, see, in the original, Stöver, *op. cit.*, baptisms, pp. 15-23, 25, 28-29, 31-33, 39, marriages, pp. 4-7, Nos. 194, 195, 238, 272, 284, 383, 384. See also below, pp. 374-377.

[15] Glatfelter, *op. cit.*, pp. 140-141.

[16] Edward W. Spangler, *The Annals of the Families of Caspar, Henry, Baltzer and George Spengler, Who Settled in York County* (York, 1896), pp. 85-86, quotes from the Bible of son David Contler [Jr.] that he was "born April 28, 1740 in Schlotterdam on Hackensack River." The small Slotterdam settlement was actually located along the east bank of the Passaic River a short distance above present-day Passaic and some four miles west of Hackensack. Kenn Stryker-Rodda, "Baptisms in the Lutheran Church, New York City, from 1725," *The New York Genealogical and Biographical Record*, 99:105, quotes the church book entry: 29 April [1740] baptized at Hakkinsack in the minister's [Michael Christian Knoll's] home, David, born 19 April, [son] of David Kandelaar and Veronica Philippina; sponsors: Hinrich Beer (in his place Thomas van Rijpen [also of Slotterdam]) and Anna Maria Mergerin." Subsequently in the Conewago church book, Pastor Candler showed his son David as born April 28, 1740, baptized May 6, 1740 with George and Anna Maria Thomas as sponsors! See Frederick S. Weiser, transcriber, "Records of St. Matthews Lutheran Church, Hanover, Pennsylvania," typescript at Adams County Historical Society, p. 5. David Contler, Jr. on October 30, 1763 married Maria Catharina Dünckel (1746-1781), a sister of Margaret Salome Dünckel (1736-1813) who married Philip Caspar Spengler. Our thanks to Frederick W. Bogert and Calvin E. Schildknecht for some of these particulars.

possibly in reference to his serving their religious needs.[17] After coming to Pennsylvania, Candler was probably ordained by Valentin Kraft (1680-1752), under whom Stöver had studied in Germany before coming to America,[18] and/or by Stöver himself. At any rate, in April 1743 Candler succeeded Stöver in ministering to the Germans west of the Susquehanna. He lived first at Conewago, but was to serve Codorus[19] and Monocacy as well. At Conewago he began a church book, entering baptisms made by Yost Mohr during the preceding two years as well as a record of his own children.[20]

Although Candler lived initially at Conewago, it seems quite apparent that he intended almost from the outset to make his home in Maryland. On April 15, 1743 he had 100 acres surveyed in the Monocacy area "west of the road from Kens' to Jacob Neff's." This road today is the county road from Bethel through Charlesville connecting with U.S. Highway 15 south of Hansonville. Candler called his land "Swingaback."[21] The parcel, which was patented to him on September 23, 1743, lay immediately northeast of today's village of Bethel on the road to Mountaindale. Significantly, this was a mid-point among the German settlers along the German Monocacy Road. Long after David Candler's death "Swingaback" was conveyed by his son, William Candler, of York County, on July 23, 1759 to Peter Baltzell for 30 pounds.[22] In 1768 Michael Hufner had a resurvey made on the land, which was then called "Peace."[23]

Do we credit Stöver or Candler with having organized the Monocacy Lutherans as a distinct congregation, and from what date may the congregation be said to have begun? Altogether, the names of some sixty Monocacy families appear in Stöver's records up to the

---

[17] Pastor Wilhelm Christoph Berkenmeyer in inventorying a packet of New York correspondence relating to a call from "the Germans in the North" noted such a letter in 1743. Other letters in the same packet were dated in 1738 and 1739. That was a period, however, in which Berkenmeyer for some reason made only the briefest of entries in his Protocol. He did not mention Candler further. See Dern, ed., *The Albany Protocol*, op. cit., p. 307.

[18] Valentin Kraft had only just arrived at Philadelphia on August 25, 1742: Strassburger-Hinke, op. cit., List 92C, p. 322. See also Stöver, op. cit., p. 62, and below, p. 151.

[19] The Conewago settlement, which straddled today's York-Adams County line, included the area of today's Hanover. About 1743 the settlement in the Codorus Valley became known as York, Pennsylvania.

[20] These included John William born 1738, Elisa Barbara 1741 and John Barnhart 1744. Dates for the latter are missing, no doubt because of Pastor Candler's early death.

[21] C/S: LG E:211; Patent EI 6:610. See map, p. 155. For Jacob Neff and Philip Kens/Kinss, see pp. 111, 169.

[22] Frederick County Land Records, F:760. Hans Peter Baltzell was from Klingen, but left Thaleischweiler for America in 1750, arriving as Peter Balsam at Philadelphia on August 18, 1750: Strassburger-Hinke, op. cit., List 150C, p. 435.

[23] C/S: BC & GS 40:127.

year 1742. That quantity and the extended period of his visits in the Monocacy area certainly did much to knit together the early German Lutheran settlers. But with proof positive we are unable categorically to provide a specific and precise date. The Lutheran historian Dr. Abdel Ross Wentz was first to discredit the 1732 date claimed on a stone monument near Creagerstown as well as a 1737 date based on faulty interpretation of the Unselt baptism record.[24] For his part, Wentz argued that Stöver's visit in November 1738 more probably marked the actual formation of a congregation, but he based his opinion solely on (1) Stöver's having tarried in the Monocacy area longer on that visit than was his usual custom and (2) reference in an Anglican petition of 1739 which noted that the German Lutherans already had their own organization.[25]

Stöver has left us no formal record of his having constituted a congregation. There is no record of an election of elders or other church officers. Other than with his personal record of baptisms and marriages, he probably began no separate church book for the Monocacy congregation as he had done at Lancaster, Muddy Creek and Earltown in Pennsylvania. Even references to the actual existence of a church building are subject to debate.

On October 15, 1742 Philip Kince, Titur Laney and Matthew Reisling, natives of Germany, appeared before the Maryland Provincial Court seeking naturalization. The Court found that they had been inhabitants for at least seven years, had not been absent from the Colonies for over two months at any one time and had received "the Lutheran Sacrament *at the church at Monockecey* on October 10, 1742 according to a certificate signed by John Casper Stover, Lutheran Minister."[26] The italics are ours. Taken literally, and presuming the word "church" was not referring to a farmer's barn, they suggest that an actual church building was in existence before Stöver ended his Maryland visits in October 1742 and had been constructed as a result of his encouragement and urging.

But there is a slightly conflicting notation in the congregation's first church book. Written in 1746, some two to four years after the time of both Stöver and Candler, reference is made to the congregation's having "built the Evangelical Lutheran church a short mile northward from Michael Reisner's plantation in the *time of Pastor David Candler* as is reckoned one thousand seven hundred *forty-three* after the gracious birth of our Saviour and Spiritual Maker, Jesus Christ..."[27]

---
[24] Wentz, *op. cit.*, pp. 46-50. See also pp. 47, 182, and Rice, *New Facts*, *op. cit.*, p. 163-164.
[25] Wentz, *op. cit.*, pp. 50-55.
[26] Provincial Judgment Records (1742-1744), EI 7:110. The communion requirement was designed to guard against naturalization of foreign Catholics. For Philip Kince/Kinss again and for Dieter Laney/Lehnich, see below, pp. 169, 217. Reisling (also Reesling, Rössel, etc.) does not appear in the Land Records, but is frequently found in church and other Frederick County documents.
[27] Frederick Lutheran Church Book, p. 414: "...bauete die Evangelische Lutherische Kirch Eine kleine meil Von michael Reisner

Perhaps more interesting than fixing an exact date for this building is the geography of its location. Dr. Wentz and Dr. Arthur Tracey joined forces in tramping the area one mile north of Reisner's plantation, which the latter had located as shown on pp. 186, 195, below, but they discovered no datable remains surviving the passage of nearly two centuries time. Later, additional references to the church's location confirmed the approximate site: 1) Henry Muhlenberg located it ten miles from Frederick.[28] 2) Charles Carroll petitioned the November 1752 Court that a road be laid out "from the waggon road under the South Mountain about a half a mile to the southward of the Meeting House and to the northeast side of the plantation of Michael Reisener...."[29] 3) A notation in a handwritten manuscript history of the Moravian Church at Graceham in 1790 referred to the "Union [sic] Lutheran and Reformed Church then [1746] standing two miles from here," i.e., from Graceham.[30]

These references have been more fully described by Millard M. Rice,[31] who has further observed that Land Records show only one parcel at this time located both one mile north of Reisner's "Green Spring" and two miles from Graceham. That parcel, known as "Smith's Lot," was likewise patented to Reisner! It was surveyed on March 6, 1743,[32] only five weeks before Candler's survey for "Swingaback." The parcel consisted of 50 acres and was located on Hunting Creek, southwest of today's Jimtown crossroads where Hessong Bridge Road meets State Route 550. Today's Kellys Store Road runs midway between Michael Reisner's "Green Spring" and his "Smith's Lot," a half mile from both, just as noted in Carroll's 1752 petition. Assuming that the Lutherans would not have constructed their church on vacant land and also recognizing Reisner as an active Lutheran whose children had been baptized previously by Stöver, it is within the realm of plausibility that the first Frederick Lutheran Church was

---

seiner Plantation, Nort werts zur Zeit des Herrn Pfarrherrns David Candlers, als mann zehlte Ein Tausent sieben Hundert Drey und Vierzig nach der Gnaden reichen geburt unsers Heÿlandes und seeligmachers Jesu Christi..."

[28] *Hallesche Nachrichten von den vereinigten Deutschen Evangelisch-Lutherischen Gemeinen in Nord America, absonderlich in Pensylvanien*, Mann, Schmucker and Germann edition (Allentown, 1886) 1:352. See also Theodore G. Tappert and John W. Doberstein, *The Journals of Henry Melchior Muhlenberg* (Philadelphia, 1942), 1:158.

[29] "....and from thence to Mr. Ogle's Saw Mill and thence to Owen's Creek about two miles below Mr. Ogle's house and a little below the mouth of Beaver dam branch...." Frederick Court Judgment Records, G, pt. 2:471.

[30] "Historical account of the beginning, progress of the work of the Lord among souls in the neighborhood of the Manacusey in Maryland, and of the gathering and planting of the little congregation of Graceham, associated with the Congregation of the Brethren," found by George Zacharias at the Lititz Archives. Concerning the claim that the church was jointly built by the Reformed, see below, p. 144, 145.

[31] Rice, *New Facts, op. cit.*, pp. 175-182.

[32] C/S: E:295.

thus constructed on "Smith's Lot" about 1742 or 1743.[33]

About the time Candler was beginning his association with the Monocacy Lutherans, a record of Lutheran baptisms in the Monocacy area, separate and distinct from those in Stöver's personal journal, was begun. These appear on the first five *numbered* pages of the first Frederick Lutheran Church Book now kept in the archives at the Theological Seminary at Gettysburg. By carefully separating out those entries which were subsequently inserted on these same early pages, it will be noted that the first 29 entries were all written by the same hand and were placed in chronological order, from October 3, 1742 to April 1744.[34] Therefore, even if they were copied at one sitting from some other beginning record, they were undoubtedly originally recorded at the time of the baptisms, and not [as was often the case with initial entries in new church books] "recalled" ex post facto some months or years after the event. Interestingly, the first four predate October 10, 1742, the last date for which we have a record of Stöver at Monocacy. One of these involved a son of Joh. Hendrick Peschof [Bishop] for whom Hermanus Hartman had stood as sponsor: Their roles were reversed in a September 1740 Monocacy entry in Stöver's personal journal, but there is no duplication between the two records. Could Candler have been picking up the final threads of Stöver's era and splicing them into what was being begun for his own?

A list of those German settlers who had "contributed to the best of their ability" toward the purchase of this church book preceded on an unnumbered page the first page of baptism entries. The list included: Hendrich Sinn, Adam Stoll, Mateus Rehssele [Rössel], Adam Spuch, Hans Georg Schweinhart, Philip Kühntz, Baltzer Pfaut, Felte Verdriess, Dieder Lehnick, Hans Georg Hützel, Joh. Verdriess, Jacob Mateus, Peter Appel, Joh. Georg Götz, Jacob Bene, Conradt Kämp, Jost Schmidt, Joh. Peter Appel, Joh. Tafel Meÿer, Georg Honig, Joh. Georg Gump, Jacob Faut and Friedrich Verdriess. The land records of most of these are discussed in succeeding chapters.

In May, June and October of 1743 and again in March and April of 1744 we have record of Candler's baptizing children in the Monocacy area. There were, on average, some five children on each occasion. Sometimes a number of Reformed people served as sponsors. Also in 1743 David Candler signed a certificate, witnessed by John George Bear and Mathias Reislin, that on June 26th of that year John Verdress had received communion in the Lutheran Church of Manaquice preparatory to his naturalization. A similar attestation for a larger group was signed by Candler on September 25, 1743, this

---

[33] A refutation of claims made in prior years concerning alternative sites in the Creagerstown area has been given above, pp. 47-49. The frustrating vagaries of parcel names leaves as yet no clue concerning who "Smith" might have been. No individual with that name is known in the immediate area or as an associate of Reisner.

[34] Glatfelter, *op. cit.*, 1:193, noting that the Frederick and Conewago Lutheran churchbooks were identical in size and construction, dates the Frederick Lutheran Church Book from 1743.

time with Philip Kince and John Shrier as witnesses. The second list included Mateas Ambrose, Martain Wezler, George Sweinhart, John George Huzell, Valentine Verdris, John Verdris, George Scheidler and others.[35]

Then Candler's work stopped. He had not been of robust health, and sometime after his last baptism entries (May 3, 1744 at York, May 17, 1744 at Conewago) he died. Letters of administration were issued on July 26, 1744 to his widow Philippina.[36] Once again the Monocacy Germans were without prospects of having their own resident minister.

Meanwhile, the Reformed had been doing no better. They mixed well with the Lutherans, no doubt attending their religious services and even appearing on occasion as baptism witnesses for the children of their Lutheran friends. But they had no minister nor organized congregation of their own. We may suspect that there were visits from Reformed ministers out of Pennsylvania much like Stöver's early visits for the Lutherans. But there is no extant record to prove it.

Two suggestions, though purely inferential, come from Maryland naturalization proceedings in 1743. On April 10th of that year Johann Barth. Rieger, then a Reformed pastor at Lancaster, certified to the Maryland Provincial Court for their naturalization purposes that Conrad Kampf and John House were "honest Protestants" adhering to the Heidelberg catechism of the Reformed religion. Peter Hoffman witnessed the certificate.[37] Since all three were Monocacy residents, we may infer that Rieger knew them through their religious association at either Lancaster or Frederick. Likewise, it seems safe to conclude that Johann Conrad Templeman, whom we have also met above, was undoubtedly the minister -- although he is not so designated -- whose name was mistakenly spelled as Edward Templeman in the same Provincial Court Judgment Records of October 19, 1743. He had certified then that on October 9, 1743 Adam Stall, Christian Getson Tanner [Getzendanner], Jacob Stern [Sturm], John Hend [Hand], Jacob Staley, Gasper Mire [Joh. Caspar Myer], Henry Boughtall [Bechtel] and Isaac Miller -- all of them known from other evidence as Reformed -- had "received the sacrament." Jacob Runner [Brunner, later a Reformed Church Elder

---

[35] Candler provided a similar certificate for Jacob Fau[t]z, Andreas Herriott and Martin Kinzmiller as having taken communion at "Cannawacke" on October 2, 1743. Maryland Provincial Court Judgment Records, EI 7:295-296.

[36] Glatfelter, op. cit., 1:27, and Calvin E. Schildknecht, from Lancaster County estate papers. Candler was owed three pounds in Maryland money by each of the Manacusy and Cannawacke congregations and four pounds Pennsylvania money by the Catores congregation. But he himself was in debt for nearly 39 pounds, including £3 to Matthew Resel, £10 to Henrik Sexe, 19sh6d to Conrad Kemp and £3/10 to [Pastor] Vallentin Crafft. After expenses, only 34 shillings remained for distribution. [Veronica] Philippina Candler married Michael Laub as her second husband.

[37] Maryland Provincial Court Judgment Records, EI:161.

in Frederick] and John Peter Houghman [Hoffman] were subscribing witnesses.[38] Like Rieger, Templeman has left us no record of his ministering to the Reformed people in the Monocacy area. But given the number of persons who participated in this communion, for which we have no other record, it seems doubtful that they all journeyed to the area in Conestoga where Templeman lived. Instead, it is quite possible that Templeman had come to Maryland in 1743, even though in that year he was presumably establishing himself, like Stöver, even farther away near Cornwall in Lebanon County.[39] Templeman himself had been naturalized only since April 11-13, 1743.[40]

Beginning in 1743 and extending over the following decade, the Monocacy community was occasionally visited by Moravian missionaries who stopped off on their way to visit Germans in Virginia. The early Moravians originated in Bohemia in the fifteenth century but under subsequent persecution their successors had found refuge during the 1720s at Herrnhut on the Berthelsdorf estate of Count Nicholas Ludwig Zinzendorf (1700-1760), a German nobleman with pietistic Lutheran background. Under his influence the Moravian emphasis on church reform turned more to a curious effort at bringing various denominations together in a voluntary association of beliefs. Moravians claimed theirs was not a separate denomination and the fellowship they espoused required no abandonment of one's prior religion. Zinzendorf himself, for example, had been ordained a Lutheran minister, but simultaneously became a Moravian bishop. Colonization was begun in various places abroad, with the first colony in America settling in Georgia in 1735. Later Moravians visited those Germans already settled in Pennsylvania, and in 1741 they established a colony at Bethlehem which was destined to become the focal center of future Moravian activity in America. Zinzendorf himself spent the year 1742 in Pennsylvania, and in the same year a number of young missionaries likewise came to America. Great emphasis was placed on the work of these Moravian missionaries who traveled widely and preached wherever opportunity afforded, both within organized congregations and among the widely scattered and isolated Germans.

Leonard Schnell and Robert Hussey were the first of these missionaries to come to Maryland, and they did so on an ambitious journey carrying them all the way from Bethlehem in Pennsylvania to Savannah, Georgia. They were part of the so-called "First Sea Congregation," a group of Moravians who had come to this country from London on the snow *Catharine*, arriving at Philadelphia on May 28, 1742.[41] Schnell kept a Diary[42] describing their 1743 trek which

---
[38] *Ibid.*, EI 7:296.
[39] Cf. Glatfelter, *op. cit.*, 1:149.
[40] M. S. Giuseppi, *Naturalizations of Foreign Protestants in the American and West Indian Colonies (Pursuant to Statute 13 George II, c. 7)* (Baltimore, 1979), p. 19.
[41] Strassburger-Hinke, *op. cit.*, Lists 91ABC, pp. 320-322. With them came Hussey's wife Martha (Schnell was unmarried), Jacob Lischy, Johann Brandmüller, Paul Daniel Bryzelius and others found later in the history of Moravianism in America.
[42] "Diarium von der Reise der 2 Brüder Schnell u. Hussey, die

lasted from November until the following February. In it he described their walk on November 16, 1743 from Adam Forney's inn at Conewago along the east side of the Monocacy River, which they eventually forded near Abraham Müller's land on "Tasker's Chance." Although Schnell reported seeing no houses for 25 miles after leaving Conewago, their route confirms the existence of the so-called Manor Monocacy Road described earlier.[43]

On the following day Schnell and Hussey visited the "father-in-law of Bro. Klemf of Philadelphia," who, along with his specific location in the Monocacy area, has not been identified.[44] Schnell preached a sermon and reported "very many" Germans, both Lutheran and Reformed, were living in the neighborhood. The Lutherans reputedly had services every three weeks with the preaching of a certain Schulze, also unidentified, "who wanted to be ordained by Brother Ludwig" [Zinzendorf].[45] On November 18th the missionaries crossed over the mountains, finding only two houses in 20 miles and toward nightfall reached the Potomac River which they crossed on the 19th to enter Virginia. They did not pass through Maryland on their return journey, sailing instead by sea to New York.

About this same time Laurentius Thorstonsen Nyberg (1720-1792), a Swedish Lutheran from Västergötland, trained at Uppsala University and ordained in 1742 by Archbishop Jacob Benzelius, came to Pennsylvania in answer to a call from the Lancaster congregation. It was he, not Stöver or Kraft, who preached the funeral sermon for Candler at Conewago. In so doing he came to the attention of the Monocacy Lutherans, who, initially at least, encouraged his visits to Maryland and sought his help in calling a minister from Sweden. But Nyberg had strong Moravian leanings which proved devisive. Instead of turning to Sweden, he attempted to install as minister one George Nieke, a Swedish teacher from Bethlehem.[46] Disenchantment grew in Lancaster as well, and in 1745

---

nach Georgien besuchen gangen, 1743." The original Diary may be found in the Archives of the Moravian Church in Bethlehem. Portions of it in condensed and abbreviated form were translated and published by William J. Hinke and Charles E. Kemper, "Moravian Diaries of Travels through Virginia," *Virginia Magazine of History and Biography*, 11:370-393.

[43] See above, p. 52-54.

[44] Kenneth G. Hamilton, transl. and ed., *The Bethlehem Diary, 1742-1744* (Bethlehem: The Archives of the Moravian Church, 1971), p. 242, identifies a woman named Susanna as the wife of Friedrich Klemm of Philadelphia.

[45] Hinke and Kemper translated "der von Br. Ludwig ordiniert seyn wolte" as "who pretends to have been ordained by..." Schnell made no reference to Pastor Candler.

[46] Nyberg is not mentioned in the Bethlehem Diary, at least through 1744. But Georg and Johanna Elisabeth Niecke were recorded as arriving at Bethlehem on December 7, 1743 and departing for their "place and charge" [Tulpehocken in Pennsylvania] on January 13, 1744 (Hamilton, *op. cit.*, pp. 172, 184). According to W. C. Reichel, *A Register of Members of the Moravian Church and of Persons Attached*

following a complaint to the Upsala Consistory, Nyberg was condemned for his beliefs and activities.[47]

In 1744 Nyberg had crossed swords with Henry Melchior Muhlenberg, a man of broad perspective who was destined to become the early organizer of Lutheranism in this country. An ordained minister with ties to the pietists at Halle, Muhlenberg had arrived in Pennsylvania late in 1742, ostensibly in answer to a call made nine years earlier by the three German congregations at Philadelphia, Providence and New Hanover. Once established in these congregations, he expanded his attention to outlying congregations and helped them with their calls for more Lutheran pastors from Europe. In 1744 he had joined other Lutheran ministers in an early attempt at discussing their mutual problems and exploring differences in their beliefs. The meeting had been arranged by two Lutheran laymen, both merchants in Philadelphia, Peter Hock, a Swede, and Henry Schleydorn, a German. So bitter was the clash between Muhlenberg and Nyberg that it was another four years before an ensuing meeting could be held.[48] That one, arranged by Muhlenberg himself in 1748, is generally considered the beginning of the Pennsylvania Ministerium, the group which gradually assumed powers of ordination and oversight in overall Lutheran affairs in Pennsylvania.

Also present at the 1744 meeting was Gabriel Nasman,[49] the Swedish Lutheran pastor who served from 1743 to 1750 at Gloria Dei at Wicacoa, now in south Philadelphia. We lack adequate biographical details concerning Nasman and cannot with sufficient certainty ascertain whether it was on his own volition or, as has been popularly although probably erroneously believed, at Muhlenberg's urging that he came to Frederick in 1746. Certainly throughout his Journal, Muhlenberg is severely critical of Nasman and his efforts. Further, the Journal contains not one reference to Nasman's journey to Frederick, let alone the claim that he had come at Muhlenberg's direction or urging.[50]

But come he did, and in the Frederick Lutheran Church Book we find record of his visit. On the Church Book's first page under date of 31 Octob. 1746 he wrote in German, "I, Gab. Nasman, Past.

---

to *Said Church in this Country and Abroad, Between 1727 and 1754* (n.s., 1873; copy at the Library of Congress), p. 75, George Nieke was ordained a Deacon in 1744, labored in the Gospel in the rural districts, and was settled in Menakasy, Maryland in 1747.

[47] Tappert and Doberstein, op. cit., 1:115. See also Glatfelter, op. cit., 1:100-101; 2:514. Nyberg was in England from 1750 to 1776 and then returned to Sweden for the remainder of his life.

[48] There is a gap in Muhlenberg's Journal between March 1743 and February 1746. In that period he wrote to the Lutheran authorities in London and Halle of his trials and tribulations in establishing himself in America. In so doing he made only scant reference to this meeting: "A young Swedish pastor from Lancaster publicly denounced me as a Halle Pietist in a Conference that had been called here by Mr. Peter Kock." See Tappert and Doberstein, op. cit., 1:96.

[49] Sometimes rendered "Naesman" as if with a German umlaut.

[50] Tappert and Doberstein, op. cit., 1:153, 169, 186.

at Vicaco in Philad., preached in this new city located in Manachasi." He also noted that he had baptized seven individuals, one of them a youth 19 years of age. He left the entry of their names in the Church Book to the Elders (Vorsteher) and Schoolmaster, directing that the book be divided into three parts, for "children, marriages and deaths." In an ornate hand the record of seven baptisms does appear, but within the chronological sequence noted above, and so not until pages 8 and 9: The fathers were Peter Appel, Zacharias Barth, Balthasar Fauth, Heinrich Bechtold, Henrich Trauth, Thomas Schley and Georg Jacob Koch.

Nasman obviously took back with him to Philadelphia a rather lengthy written testimonial, almost a pledge of allegiance as it were to true Lutheranism and a denial of the innovations being foisted upon the congregation by passing vagabond preachers. The original document was presumably signed by members of the congregation, but its existence today is unknown. Instead, on the back pages of the Frederick Lutheran Churchbook[51] is a copy, without signatures, written as though in the past tense, but as a reminder (Andenken) for the record of what was done during "the Swedish Pastor Nasmann's" visit. Without regard to its religious import,[52] the two pages of German text yield us some interesting historical facts: The reference to the Evangelical Lutheran Church built a short mile [kleine Meil] northward from Michael Reissner's plantation in 1743 in Pastor Candler's time has been noted above. There is no indication, as sometimes claimed, that the church was jointly constructed with the Reformed as a Union church. Although there is no land record suggesting Dulany's transfer of a lot in Frederick town to the Lutherans before 1752, by 1746 the congregation had seemingly also built, in addition to the church in the hills, a church in the "new town of Frederick."[53] The Lutherans obviously felt themselves sufficiently constituted as a congregation that they were now ready for a church name. In the document itself a space was left for that name to be filled in later. It never was. Finally, for what it may be worth, one notes that the text makes reference to the original's being sent to "the reverend gentlemen and to Pastor Bronnholtz[54] at Germantown," but Muhlenberg himself is not mentioned by name.

After Nasman there is passing word, but scant record of more visits in Frederick by Lutheran vagabonds. The ubiquitous gadfly Carl Rudolph, flitting about the universe, came from Georgia via Virginia and Maryland and ended in New Jersey. Another, known only by the

---

[51] Frederick Lutheran Church Book, pp. 414-415.

[52] Or to its inaccuracies in ascribing the Augsburg Confession to Martin Luther, not Philipp Melanchthon. See Rice, *New Facts, op. cit.,* p. 181n.

[53] die oben gemelte Kirch im Gebürge und die Kirch in der Neuen Stadt FriederichsTawn.

[54] Peter Brunnholtz, a pietist from Schleswig, was sent by the authorities at Halle and arrived early in 1745. He took over the Philadelphia Lutheran congregation from Muhlenberg and served it until his death in 1757. Between 1745 and 1751 he also served the congregation at Germantown. Muhlenberg held him in high esteem.

name of Schmidt, tarried briefly on his way to Virginia and offered both his medical and his spiritual services. Because he was untrained in both, Muhlenberg called him the "empiric" Schmidt who had acted earlier in New Hanover.[55]

In 1747 the German Monocacy settlers, both Lutheran and Reformed, at last received encouraging visits for the first time from the men who were emerging as religious leaders destined to bring constructive help in the organization of local congregations including those in Frederick County. These were Michael Schlatter (1718-1790) for the Reformed and Henry Melchior Muhlenberg (1711-1787) for the Lutherans. Both had been sent by their respective church authorities in Europe and both came with a clearer and wider perspective than did their predecessors concerning the overall religious situation in America. They saw the problems and the opportunities, and each set to work on both.

Muhlenberg's 1747 visit was quite possibly prompted by the assurances contained in the document Nasman had brought back the previous year. His journey carried him from New Hanover on June 10th with stops along the way at Tulpehocken, Lancaster, York and Conewago. At each of the latter he witnessed the divisions which had been created by Nyberg and the Moravians. Two men from Monocacy met him in Conewago, and on the afternoon of June 23rd he set out in a heavy rain for a twelve hour ride of some 36 miles to his Maryland destination. This was in the vicinity of the wooden "hills church" whose location we have described above.[56]

Here he found a congregation badly split. Part of it had only recently sent Carl Rudolph on his way. The others were adhering to the Moravian teacher Georg Nieke -- Muhlenberg called him Mr. Nicky -- who had conveniently left for Bethlehem before Muhlenberg arrived. It was evident that the schism had reached such serious proportions that the English authorities were unable to determine which side was more nearly in the right. Muhlenberg correctly observed the Moravian advantage in having enlisted a tolerant attitude among more respected and well-to-do individuals, some of them even English. So he immediately set to work penning a church constitution much on the order of Nasman's document of the previous year, emphasizing the need for Lutherans to have regularly ordained ministers and establishing church wardens for the congregation. Significantly, he wrote the document in English and then explained it orally to the congregation in German.[57] Again, there is no reference to the Reformed people's participation in the construction of the church building in the hills. But Muhlenberg with careful attention to

---

[55] Tappert and Doberstein, *op. cit.*, 1:158, spell the name as Schmied. In the Hallesche Nachrichten, *op. cit.*, 1:355, the name is Schmidt.

[56] The record of Muhlenberg's trip to "Manaquesy" is his own. See Tappert and Doberstein, *op. cit.*, 1:156-161; also Hallesche Nachrichten, *op. cit.*, 1:352-357.

[57] The text appears at the front of the Frederick Lutheran Church Book on two unnumbered pages following Nasman's title page. It contains no reference to Muhlenberg himself.

community politics invited lawful Reformed ministers to use it.[58] On the other hand, there is no suggestion of a separate Lutheran church in Frederick town itself.

Before and after his sermon on June 24th Muhlenberg repeatedly attempted to get both factions to sign his constitution and even came so close that the Moravian faction intimated it would join if he became their pastor. That was manifestly impossible, he said, because he had been called elsewhere. In the end, only the non-Moravians signed, but there were 34 of them, most of them mentioned in the chapters which follow. Included were six church wardens, Hanss Georg Laÿ, Johannes Reitzmann, Johann Michel Römer, Georg Michel Jesserang, Peter Apfel and Henry Sex. In addition we note Jacob Hoff, Martin Wetzel, Georg Schweinhardt, Georg Hutzel, Gabriel Swinehard, Phillip Küntz, Velten Usselmann, Johannes Schryack, Johannes Verdries, Martin Wetzel [a repeat?], Michell Reisner, Heinrich Sechs,[59] Deter Lehny, Johannes Tafelmeyer, Johann Sechs, Christophel Gag, Valentin Verdries, Hanss Georg Soldner, Johann Christoph Schmied, Johannes Vogler, John Davis, Friederich Verdries, Martin Wetzel Junior, Nicholaus Wetzel, Friederich Willheut, Georg Honig, Jerg Götz and Johannes Schmidt.

The services on June 24, 1747 at the hill church included the baptisms of children of Valentine Verdriess and Christoph Gag. On the next day Muhlenberg rode "ten miles farther on to a newly laid out town where several Lutherans lived who belonged to the congregation and could not come hither on the previous day because of the heavy rain."[60] Here he added more of the above signatures to the church book, preached before a large crowd of Germans and English, held communion, married two couples and baptized three children. The marriages were between Friederich Willheit, Jr. and Anna Maria Weimar and between Johannes Hoffmann from Rohrbach in the Chur-Pfaltz and Mathias Riesslie's widow Anna Barbara.[61] The baptisms included children of Georg Hutzel, John James and Georg Michel Jesserang. Georg Schweinhart and his wife were sponsors on both days and therefore in both places.

Muhlenberg left Monocacy without being able to return the Moravian adherents to the fold. He was naturally dejected and

---

[58] Wentz, op. cit., p. 94, from the punctuation and crowding of lines, surmises quite plausibly that the reference to use by the Reformed was added subsequently, perhaps on the second day in town where the Reformed were more heavily concentrated. Reference to the Reformed is lacking in Muhlenberg's Journal.

[59] After this signature, by mark, the word "Null" was added.

[60] *Hallesche Nachrichten*, op. cit., 1:355.

[61] The baptisms appear in the churchbook in their normal chronological sequence, consistent with prior entries for the same families. But the two marriages are inscribed in an ornate hand on a separate p. 141, away from other entries. Anna Maria's maiden name is given as Wismar, although her father is shown, more correctly, as Weimar (see below, p. 191). The name Riesslie appears variously as Risling, Rössel, Rehssele, Reasling, etc. (see above, p. 137n and below, p. 318).

confessed that it was very distressing and heart-rending to see such wretched conditions. Meanwhile, the Moravian missionary Leonard Schnell returned to the Monocacy area twice more, in the summer of 1747 with Vitus Handrup as his companion,[62] and late in 1749 with Johann Brandmüller.[63] In between these two journeys, Matthias Gottlieb Gottschalk, proceeding alone, came to the Monocacy area in March and April of 1748. Born in Arnswalde, Brandenburg in 1715, Gottschalk studied at Lindheim near Frankfurt. He had come to Bethlehem only the year before his Maryland visit and died a few months after his return. With much feeling he not only carried out his missionary work with a zeal which fostered warm receptions from both German and English settlers, but also did much to prepare the way for subsequent Moravian itinerants. Two Monocacy Germans, Matthias Ambrose and Jacob Matthias journeyed over South Mountain all the way to Jonathan Hager's in today's Washington County to hear Gottschalk preach. They parted from him tearfully. Thomas Prather accompanied Gottschalk a considerable distance through the mountains and Col. Thomas Cresap hosted him generously and offered to sell the Brethren some of his land at £35 per 100 acres.[64]

After his return to Pennsylvania Gottschalk set down an interesting report entitled, "Where Our Brethren Have an Open Door."[65] The usual place for preaching in Manakasy, he noted, was at Mr. Weller's,[66] and across the River on Monocacy Manor some ten German families would like to hear a sermon, concerning which a man named [William] Ellrod could advise.[67] Like Weller, Captain [Joseph] Ogle was a dear host of the Brethren.[68] He might even loan his little gray horse.

It was becoming obvious that those Lutherans favoring the Moravians had by 1748 noticeably pulled away from the Lutheran Church itself. They are conspicuously absent from the list of signers of Muhlenberg's 1747 Church constitution. And by the time August Spangenberg came with Matthias Reuz, the Moravian visitors were

---

[62] Hinke and Kemper, *loc. cit.*, 12/55-61. Handrup came to America in 1746, but subsequently returned to Europe.

[63] Leonard Schnell, "Kurze Beschreibung von unserer Reise nach Virginien," Archives of the Moravian Church, Bethlehem. Hinke and Kemper, "Moravian Diaries," *loc. cit.*, 11:115-131, omit the Maryland portion in their condensed translation. Brandmüller was a native of Basle, Switzerland, where he was born in 1704. He came with the First Sea Congregation, as did Schnell, in 1742, was ordained in 1745 and preached at Allemängel, Swatara and Donegal. He also did missionary work with the Walloons in New York and then taught at Friedensthal near Nazareth, Pennsylvania from 1758-1768. Later he also engaged in book printing. He was drowned in a mill race in 1777.

[64] *Ibid.*, 12:62-76: "Moravian Diaries: Extracts from the Diary of Bro. Gottschalk's Journey through Maryland and Virginia, March 5 - April 20, 1748."

[65] *Ibid.*, 12:77-80.
[66] See below, pp. 210-214.
[67] *Ibid.*, p. 315.
[68] *Ibid.*, p. 329.

spending considerable time in the Monocacy area, rather than merely passing through.

Familiarly known to his brethren as Brother Joseph, August Gottlieb Spangenberg (1704-1792) began his studies at the University of Jena in 1722, met Count Nicholas Zinzendorf in 1727 and became his assistant at Herrnhut in 1733. Spangenberg made four missionary trips to America, coming to Pennsylvania first in 1736. In 1744 he was ordained a Moravian Bishop and for twenty years he served as head of the American branch of the Moravian Church. After Zinzendorf's death Spangenberg succeeded him in 1762. Spangenberg then devoted himself to reducing conflicting tendencies within the Church and to creating a compendium of the faith which became the accepted declaration of the United Brethren belief.[69]

Back in August of 1748, however, Spangenberg's visit to Monocacy was doing much to encourage the development of Moravianism in Maryland. Accompanied by Matthias Reuz, he preached several sermons and baptized a number of children, conferred with favorably disposed English residents, and discussed in some detail the gift of ten acres from Daniel Dulany.[70] In the following year when Schnell revisited the area, his Diary records further discussions concerning the building of a schoolhouse.

The Reformed were also visited. In March of 1746 Christian Henry Rauch (1718-1763) had come to Monocacy during his brief period as a Moravian itinerant missionary. Rauch had come to New York in 1740 to work with the Indians, but popular antagonism to such work, believed to be a hostile undercover effort backed by French Jesuits, put an end to this work. Rauch then worked with Jacob Lischy[71] as itinerants in the Reformed area of Pennsylvania and

---

[69] Donald F. Durnbaugh, *The Brethren in Colonial America* (Elgin, Ill., 1967), p. 270.

[70] [August G. Spangenberg,] "Kurze Nachricht von Br. Joseph's und Matth. Reuzen's Besuch und Land Prediger Reise durch Maryland und Virginien," original manuscript at Archives of the Moravian Church, Bethlehem, Pennsylvania. Hinke and Kemper, *loc. cit.*, 11:235-242 translated a portion of this Diary, but omitted the significant section covering the Monocacy visit on August 3-8, 1748. See also below, p. 213. In the discussion of the geographical "location" of Monocacy (see above, pp. 45-47), it is interesting to observe Spangenberg's contemporary 1748 concept in his third person narrative concerning their day's journey to Weller's home: "On August 5th they left Fredericktown and came to Manakesey (Den 5ten August reisten sie von Friederichstown aus und kamen nach Manakesey)." With the establishment of the town of Frederick, Monocacy was beginning to be considered, at least by these missionaries, a term for the northern part of today's County.

[71] Jacob Lischy (1719-1780), a Swiss Reformed, spent two years at Herrnhut, came to Pennsylvania in 1742 and was ordained by the Moravians in early 1743. He served as the Reformed pastor at Muddy Creek and at York, wavering between the Reformed religion and Moravianism and finally breaking with the latter in 1747. He was accepted by Michael Schlatter and the Dutch Reformed authorities in

extended his efforts to Monocacy and Conococheague.[72] In this work he preceded Michael Schlatter. His Diary makes reference to his preaching in the church at Monocacy, thereby substantiating the latter's existence and indicating the presence of a Reformed congregation even before the arrival of Schlatter.

Michael Schlatter was Swiss, born at St. Gall, but educated at Leyden University in Holland. He alternated in his subsequent work, tutoring and preaching, in both Switzerland and Holland. In 1746 he responded to the Holland Synod's search for a Reformed minister to serve in Pennsylvania and sailed immediately for America. There he conferred with Pastors Boehm, Weiss and Rieger, established himself as pastor in the Philadelphia Reformed congregation and almost immediately set out to visit congregations throughout the land.

In May of 1747 his itinerary took him to the Monocacy area. On May 6th he traveled the forty miles from Yorktown on the Codorus to Monocacy, where on the following day he held preparatory services and baptized 26 children. Communion on May 8th was administered to 86 individuals and after the services he secured pledges from 49 heads of families toward the support of a resident minister. From his diary it is apparent that he probably held these services near where Frederick is situated today: Not only would 40 miles carry him farther from York than to the area of "Smith's Lot," but he also made reference to the "7,000 acres of land in that neighborhood where there was none but such as are of the German Reformed faith."[73] The parcel called "Tasker's Chance" (see separate chapter) was surveyed for 7,000 acres.

Exactly one year later, on May 7, 1748, Schlatter visited Monocacy again and on the 8th "at Fredericktown, a newly laid out town, preached a preparatory sermon in the school house." Having journeyed in the interim to Conococheague in today's Washington County, Schlatter returned one week later to "preach at Fredericktown in a new church which is not yet finished." This time he adminstered communion to 97 "members," baptized several aged persons as well as children, married three betrothed couples, and installed new elders and

---

Holland and continued to work as a Reformed Minister until he left the ministry in 1770.

[72] William J. Hinke, *Ministers of the German Reformed Congregations in Pennsylvania and Other Colonies in the Eighteenth Century* (Lancaster, 1951), pp. 354-358. Rauch in 1749 accepted a call to the short-lived Moravian congregation at Warwick, now Lititz, later served the Moravian congregation at Salem in North Carolina, and finally worked among the Blacks in Jamaica from 1756 until his death in 1763.

[73] Henry Harbaugh, *The Life of Rev. Michael Schlatter* (Philadelphia, 1857), pp. 154-155. Schlatter forwarded to Holland his diary for the year 1746. In 1751 when he returned to Europe, he edited his earlier report, added four years to 1750 and published the result in 1751 in Dutch and in 1752 in German. Harbaugh translated from the German edition. The original manuscript was probably among the papers destroyed by the British when they ransacked Schlatter's home at Chestnut Hill during the Revolution.

deacons." He also explained the apparent existing cohesiveness in the congregation by noting, "It is a great advantage to this congregation that they have the best schoolmaster that I have met in America. He spares neither labor nor pains in instructing the young and edifying the congregation, according to his ability, by means of singing and reading the word of God and printed sermons on every Lord's Day."[74]

The man to whom he referred was Johann Thomas Schley (1712e-1790), who prior to his arrival in America in 1745 had been for the previous ten or eleven years a Reformed schoolmaster in Appenhofen south of Landau in Germany.[75] Although Schley did not secure title to lots in Fredericktown until 1753, he was undoubtedly living there from about May 10, 1746 when he began paying Daniel Dulany quitrent on four of these lots.[76] By occupation he became an innkeeper in Frederick,[77] but his past background marked him as a leader among the Reformed community just as Schlatter had described him. With him as Vorsteher or Elders of the congregation, at least in March 1748, were Christian Getzendanner, Jacob and Joseph Brunner, Jacob Storm and Stephen Remensperger. The following September Conrad Kampf and Adam Stoll were also named.[78]

In October of the same year 1748 two of these men, Stephen Remsperger and Jacob Brunner, returned to Germany for a visit. Their trip had special significance, for enroute, at Frankfurt am Main, Brunner purchased a writing book which on his return became the first churchbook for the Frederick Reformed congregation. A review of the original[79] shows that some 37 initial entries were probably based on recollections of the parents, for they either predate 1749 or were not entered in chronological sequence. A Lutheran baptism on October 31, 1746 of Thomas Schley's first child, for example, was repeated in the Reformed Book.[80] But Adam Stoll listed only his daughter baptized in early 1747, not his son whose baptism on May 1,

---
[74] *Ibid.*, pp. 151, 176-177.
[75] No passenger lists have survived for ships arriving at Philadelphia during the 21-month period from December 1744 to September 1746. But Schley's presence at Appenhofen can be documented as late as March 1744, and his first child was born in America on May 17, 1746.
[76] Frederick County Land Records, E:276.
[77] See below, p. 265.
[78] Pennsylvania Collectie, Inv. No. 74I:20-21, Nos. 14, 15, Algemeen Rijksarchief, 's-Gravenhage. These records are not the originals, as indicated by James Ranck, et al., but were copied into the record book with considerable inattention to the spelling of names, for which Schley should not necessarily be blamed. See James B. and Dorothy Ranck, Margaret R. Motter, and Katherine E. Dutrow, *A History of the Evangelical Reformed Church, Frederick, Maryland* (n.s., 1964), pp. 15-16.
[79] Hall of Records (MdHR 16697), Annapolis. Unfortunately William J. Hinke in his typewritten transcription (1941), now at Fackenthal Library, Lancaster, rearranged the baptisms chronologically so that the actual sequence of entries is lost in his transcription.
[80] See above, p. 144.

1743 also appears in the Lutheran record. Contemporaneous entries did not begin in the Brunner Book until June 1750 so that we can probably date the beginning of the book's use from that time. Multiple entries suggest that some sort of services were being held before the arrival in 1752 of Frederick's first resident Reformed pastor. Daughters of both Sebastian Shaub and Caspar Deubelbies, for example, were baptized on October 9, 1747. There are no entries for May 7, 1748 when Schlatter claimed he baptized 26 children. But on May 7, 1749[!] children of Michael Thomas, Gabriel Thomas, Elias Brunner, Friedrich Unselt,[81] Jacob Sley, Caspar Wenerod and Thomas Schley were baptized, as were on November 1, 1749 children of David DeLatere, Conrad Köhler, Johannes Neff, Christoph Michel and Johannes Berg. Four more children were baptized on June 2, 1750 and then a total of 16 on August 11, 1751! On the latter date Michael Schlatter was in Europe seeking additional pastors for service in America. It is a pity that we have no record to suggest who may have been ministering, even on a passing, itinerant basis, to the Reformed people in Frederick on these dates.

Schlatter returned from Germany in mid-1752 and with him brought six young pastors whom he had enlisted for service in America. Among them was Theodore Frankenfeld (1727-1756), native of Herborn in Nassau-Dillenburg, who was assigned initially to Frederick, Conewago and Conococheague. His church book entries began in late 1752. For Frederick alone he recorded over eighty baptisms before his untimely death in June 1756. The Frederick Reformed Church was at last firmly established and on its way. Finding resident pastors was never afterwards a serious problem.

Purely by coincidence, the year 1752 also marked the arrival of the Lutherans' first resident pastor. After Muhlenberg's departure in 1747, the Frederick Lutherans had continued to flounder, until in April 1749 Johann Helfrich Schaum (1721-1778) appeared upon the scene. Born in Giessen and educated at Halle, Schaum came to Philadelphia with Peter Brunnholtz and Nicholas Kurtz in 1745. After first teaching in Philadelphia, he was assigned in 1748 to the congregation at York from where in April 1749 he began making periodic monthly visits to Frederick. The Frederick Church Book attests to the regularity of these salutary visits. Unfortunately, an injury to his leg placed him on crutches and by February of 1751 brought an end to his trips to Frederick. Valentine Kraft (1680-1752) next appeared upon the scene, but he had grown old, poor and ineffective. Matters declined even further with the appearance of Johann Philipp Streiter. For a number of years after his arrival in 1737[82] Streiter had served congregations in Berks County, but his fellowship was rejected by Muhlenberg's Halle group. By 1751 he had drifted down to Frederick where he incurred the hostility of Samuel Hunter, the Anglican minister, for his practice of conducting

---
[81] For confusion concerning the baptism of Unselt's son Abraham, with records in both Lutheran and Reformed church books, see below, pp. 183.
[82] He arrived September 26, 1737 on the same vessel as did Johann Jacob Weller. Cf. below, p. 211.

marriages, especially those of English couples, without proper proof of credentials. The dispute[83] reached the Frederick Court and emphasized even further in English minds the instability within the Lutheran congregation.

In the end it was not Muhlenberg who solved the Lutherans' ministerial problems, but Daniel Dulany in Annapolis. Dulany well knew the situation in Frederick, and when Bernard Michael Hausihl (1727-1799) reached Annapolis in 1752 on his way to Nova Scotia, Dulany persuaded him to go instead to Frederick. This he did in late 1752. He was shortly afterwards accepted by the Pennsylvania ministers, and thus at long last began a stable continuity within the Frederick Lutheran Church just as had commenced for the Reformed in the same year.[84]

The Moravians were not formally organized until October of 1758. Supposedly John Henry Herzer had been sent from Bethlehem in 1745 as a teacher even before the arrival of George Nieke, who was present in 1746-1748. Sven Roseen was named in 1749-1751,[85] followed by Matthew Reuz in 1751-1752.[86] It was during the latter period, on June 4, 1751, that Daniel Dulany assigned the certificate of survey, made on July 3, 1747 for "Gift" to "a certain Jacob Matthews in trust for Matthias Keitz," obviously a clerk's misspelling for Matthias Reuz. The land was a ten-acre rectangle measuring 110 by 440 yards in size, located "on the south side of a spring leading to Captain's [Owens] Creek"[87] at today's Graceham, two miles east of Thurmont and 14 miles north of Frederick.

The Moravian record names Richard Utley 1752-1754, Christian Richter 1755, Valentine Haidt 1757, and Charles Godfrey Rundt 1758 as interim ministers until John Michael Zahm became Graceham's first resident minister, 1758-1762. On October 8, 1758 the congregation was formally organized by Matthew Hehl and Michael Zahm. Jacob "Matthes" then conveyed Dulany's "Gift" to Jacob Weller, and he in

---

[83] The word for "disputant" in German is "Streiter."

[84] Hauseal, as he later spelled his name, did eventually reach his original destination of Nova Scotia. After serving various congregations in Pennsylvania and New Jersey, he attempted to form a second Lutheran congregation in Philadelphia, fell out with the Ministerium as a result, then went to South Carolina and later to New York. He was a Loyalist during the Revolution and therefore moved to Halifax in 1784. Cf. Glatfelter, *op. cit.*, 1:52-53; Wentz, *op. cit.*, pp. 103-110.

[85] Sven Roseen, ordained a Deacon in 1748, and wife Anna Margaret Rieth are named in Reichel, *op. cit.*, p. 75.

[86] A. L. Oerter, *History of Graceham* (Bethlehem, 1913), pp. 11, 20. Matthäus and Magdalena Reuz were first noted as visitors at Bethlehem in December 1743 and again in October 1744 (Hamilton, *op. cit.*, pp. 172, 208, 247). Reuz had accompanied Spangenberg on their visit to Monocacy in August 1748 (cf. above, pp. 18-19). Later he worked among the Swedes in New Jersey.

[87] Patent: BY & GS 4:139, November 5, 1751. The patent makes no reference to the Moravians or to an intended church. Schultz, *op. cit.*, p. 16, mistakenly claimed the gift was from James Carroll, "a large landowner in that vicinity."

turn deeded it on November 16th to Matthew Hehl, Timothy Horsfield, John Okely and George Klein, all of Bethlehem, to be held by them as trustees for the congregation in Monocacy.[88]

Rather arbitrarily the story of the early German settlement at Monocacy can be divided into two geographical sections, a southern area to the west of today's city of Frederick and a northern area reaching southward from present-day Thurmont to the proximity of Lewistown. Both areas stretched along the German Monocacy Road, and neither could be considered totally separate from the other. The nucleus of the southern area included some of the Germans who arrived earliest, if not in Maryland, at least at the port city of Philadelphia. A large portion of them were of the Reformed religious faith, and many were dependent on such large land investors as Daniel Dulany for their initial acquisition of land. Most of the northern Germans came to America somewhat later, at least 14 of them in the single year 1731 with more in 1732. Their religious preferences tended more to Lutheranism and more independently they acquired their land by personal survey rather than through the Annapolis land investors.

Such generalizations should not be construed as mutually exclusive, however, for time of arrival did not neatly correspond entirely to the area of settlement. Moreover, scholars have yet to address the question of a possible redemptionist period in Pennsylvania during which some of the Germans may have worked for others as a means of paying off the cost of their ocean passage. Such work might have varied among the Germans, thereby governing or affecting their subsequent location within Frederick County. But, if only as a convenience in treating so large a subject, this division between Lower or Southern Germans and Upper or Northern Germans has been made in the following two chapters. Subsequent chapters treat with those Germans who located on the single tract known as "Tasker's Chance" and those who rented on his Lordship's "Monocacy Manor."

----
[88] Frederick County Land Records, F:575. See also Oerter, op. cit., p. 21. Oerter's list of ministers was followed closely by Frederick Lewis Weis, *The Colonial Clergy of the Middle Colonies, 1628-1776* (Worcester, Mass., 1957), pp. 232, 236, 239, 297, 298, 301, 304, 331, 349. Weis claimed most of these came through the port of New York rather than via Philadelphia, with four of them (Herzer, Nieke, Reuz and Utley) arriving together on November 26, 1743.

LOWER GERMAN SETTLEMENT

The first official record found to date which shows the beginning of the German settlement in today's Frederick County is an interesting document in Prince George's County Court records. It concerns one **John George Swinehart** and notes that on November 16, 1731 "at Prince George's County aforesaid John George Swinehard of Prince George's County by his certain writing obligatory acknowledged his debt to John Pawling...." The record further shows that Swinehart had first settled in "Frederick Township in ye County of Philadelphia in ye Prophence of Penselvania" where he, a "Iuman" [yeoman[1]], first contracted this debt of "twelve pounds six shillens and fore pence." He appeared by his attorney in Court on June 24, 1746 and had the writing obligatory read to him. George Gabriel stood pledge and manucaptor for Swinehard, should he be convicted. But Pawling appeared by his attorney, saying "he would not further prosecute." The Court awarded Swinehard his costs.[2]

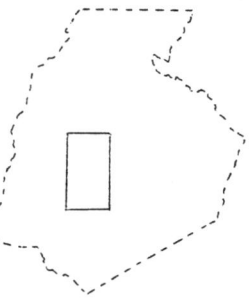

Johann Georg Schweinhart -- as his name was spelled in German -- had arrived in Pennsylvania before January 8, 1725 when his daughter Magdalena was born.[3] He thus does not appear in the Philadelphia arrival lists, which did not begin until 1727. He must have come to the area of today's Frederick County in 1731, for late in 1730 he was still in today's New Hanover Township of Montgomery [then Philadelphia] County, Pennsylvania, where he was associated with other future Monocacy settlers. On November 8, 1730, for example, Dietrich Lehnich, Balthazar Fauth and the latter's wife Susanna were sponsors at the Falckner Swamp Lutheran baptism of Joh. Georg Schweinhardt's son Joh. Peter.[4] I. Daniel Rupp listed Schweinhart as paying quitrent on 100 acres in Frederick Township of today's Montgomery County "prior to" 1734.[5] But in 1734 Schweinhart was

---
[1] A freeholder, generally used to indicate a land owner.
[2] Prince George's County Court Judgment Records, November 1744-June 1746, DD:617-619.
[3] Frederick Lutheran Church Book, Burial Record, 1788, No 5: Born in Pensylvanien January 8, 1725. Her age at death calculates to an implied birth date of December 9, 1724c.
[4] Stöver, op. cit., p. 3.
[5] I. Daniel Rupp, *A Collection of Upwards of Thirty Thousand Names of German, Swiss, Dutch, French and Other Immigrants in Pennsylvania from 1727 to 1776*.... (Philadelphia, 1875), p. 472. Also

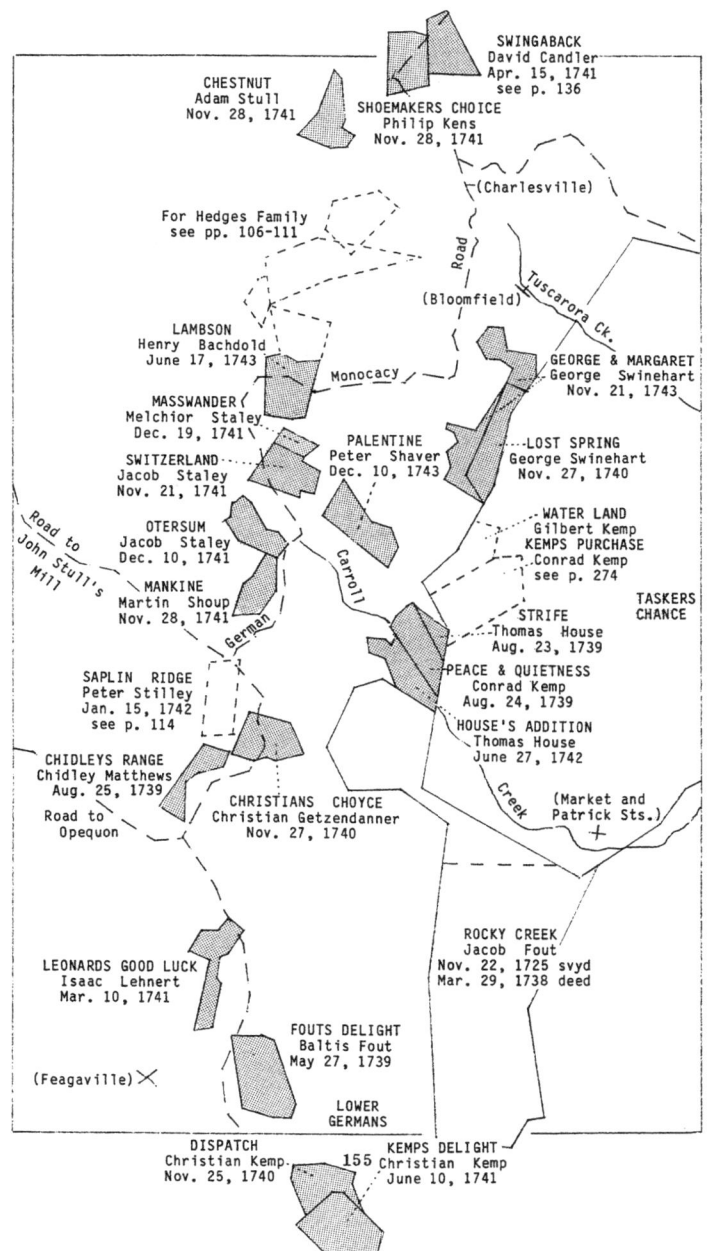

definitely in Prince George's County, selling a wagon to Botus [Baltus] Fout.[6]

We have no knowledge where in the Monocacy area Schweinhardt lived between 1731 and 1740. It is perhaps the more mystifying because on March 2, 1732/33 Charles Calvert, 5th Lord Baltimore, formally offered new settlers, foreign and native alike, free land between the Potomac and Susquehanna Rivers with title in fee simple, merely for the asking. During the ensuing three years families of new settlers could obtain up to 200 acres and single men up to 100 acres without the usual expense of 40 shillings "caution money" per 100 acres. Even the customary annual quitrents of four shillings per 100 acres would not be due until the end of the three years.[7] Why, then, did Schweinhardt and others like him not avail themselves of these terms?[8] Out of ignorance or otherwise, he turned instead to Daniel Dulany, who it can be assumed charged well for his assistance with the survey and the patent which followed.

Schweinhart's 100 acres were surveyed on November 27, 1740 and were known as "Lost Spring."[9] This land abutted the already surveyed "Tasker's Chance" to which Dulany was shortly to acquire title. Quite possibly Schweinhart actually lived on the land before it had been surveyed. In today's terms, "Lost Spring" lay between the northern bounds of Fort Detrick and Tuscarora Creek off Yellow Springs Road. On November 21, 1743 Schweinhardt had this land resurveyed, enlarging it to 235 acres and renaming it "George and Margaret."[10] As a result of this resurvey, a portion of Little Tuscarora Creek was included in Schweinhart's land.

George Swinehart -- as he was henceforth known in English records -- allowed his name to be used as a signatory to the 1742 petition to divide Prince George's Parish.[11] He was naturalized in the Provincial Court on October 19, 1743, having taken communion from David Candler "in the Lutheran Church of Manaquice" on September 25, 1743.[12] On March 17, 1747 he deeded 50 acres of his land to Georg Philipp Klemm[13] at about the time the latter married his

---

on this list were Jacob and Baltus Fauts, Christian Getzendonner and Daniel Frantz.

[6] Prince George's County Land Records, T:240.

[7] Kilty, op. cit., p. 230. "Caution Money" and quitrents have been described above, p. 2, 4.

[8] Schweinhardt was not alone in this regard. Only six surveys were made between 1733 and 1736, none of them for a German. On January 5, 1749/50 Lord Baltimore made a similar offer to foreign Protestants and "such others as shall hereafter come in." This time "Caution money" was payable, but only after five years of settlement.

[9] C/S: LG C:199.

[10] C/S: LG E:355.

[11] See below, p. 371.

[12] Provincial Court Judgment Records, 1742-1744, EI 7:296. For the communion requirement in naturalization proceedings, see above, p. 137n.

[13] Georg Philipp Klemm was born January 28, 1725 at Adersbach near Sinsheim in the Kraichgau area of Germany. He died in

daughter Margaretha Swinehart. The balance of his land was mortgaged to Joseph Mayhew, another son-in-law and an Englishman, who in 1760 released it back to Gabriel, "son and heir of George Swinehart."[14] Soon thereafter Gabriel Swinehard sold the remaining land to Matthias Ringer.[15]

In 1747 both Gabriel and his father -- the former as Swinehard, the latter as Schweinhardt -- signed the Lutheran Church articles prepared by Pastor Henry Melchior Muhlenberg on his visit to Frederick.[16] Together with his sons-in-law George Hutzel, George Clem and Joseph Mayhew, and also with Peter Shaver, Michael Reisner and Jacob Staley, George Swinehart stood as bondsman advancing payment for Nichols Bundrick, merchant, who owed Semple Chevalier £129/4sh. On February 13, 1749, to guarantee payment of his debt, Bundrick mortgaged his lot and building in Fredericktown to these men.[17]

Frederick County August 17, 1771. In his last years he was given to excessive drink. His wife Margaretha Schweinhard was born either on September 29, 1729c (calculated from age at death) or 1734 as given in her burial record. They had nine children including Heinrich who married Catharina Winter in 1783, Anna Maria who married George Winter in the following year, George who married a Barbara, and Michael (Frederick Lutheran Church Book).

[14] Frederick County Land Records, F:918.
[15] Matthias Ringer, the son of Johann Matthias Ringer (1692-1749), was from Bad Rappenau in the Kraichgau. He married in Bonfeld on June 27, 1717 Maria Magdalena "Helena" Nischicker, widow of Johann Jacob Schneider (1692c-1715). These parents emigrated almost immediately after their marriage and settled in New Hanover Township, Philadelphia [now Montgomery] County, Pennsylvania, where the father died in 1749, the mother in 1764 (New Hanover Lutheran Church Book; Muhlenberg Journal). The younger Matthias Ringer appeared frequently in Frederick County Court Judgment Records between 1761 and 1781 as Constable, surety and grand juryman (cf. Rice, *The Life, op. cit.*, pp. 220, 243, 264, 265, 268, 273). For his possible location on or near "Tasker's Chance," see below, p. 261.
[16] See above, p. 146.
[17] Frederick County Land Records, B:139. This is puzzling, since title to only five lots had been granted before 1749 and a Nicholas Bunsell, if this same individual, was not deeded Lot No. 113 (from 2nd to 3rd between Market and Court Streets) until 1751. In June 1750 Bundrick was sued on this mortgage and also on an £11 debt owed George Valentine Matzger. Earlier in 1750 Mary MacKnaul was charged with stealing Bundrick's snuff box for which she was placed in the pillory and sentenced to receive five lashes at the whipping post (Rice, *The Life, op. cit.*, pp. 43-45). Joh. Nicolaus Bundrück was born in Kleinsteinhausen, Germany September 15, 1717 (Hornbach Catholic Church Book), arrived at Philadelphia as Nicholas Bundrigg October 12, 1741 (Strassburger-Hinke, *op. cit.*, Lists 86ABC, pp. 307-309), and as Nicholas Bundrick married April 22, 1744 Anna Maria Müller (Frederick Lutheran Church Book). He was a carpenter in Augusta County, Virginia on April 15, 1754 when he sold two mares to Valentine Husleman of Frederick County, Maryland (Frederick County

George Swinehart petitioned the November 1747 Court of Prince George's County to be made "levy-free" because of his age. To support his claim for such tax exemption, he testified that "it is set down in his Bible that he was born the fourth day of March in the year 1681."[18] His wife, Anna Margreth, was born in July 1691 and died on May 19, 1776, twenty years after his death in 1756. They were married in 1718 and had nine children, of whom five daughters but only the one son Gabriel survived their mother.[19] In addition to Margaretha Klemm [Clem] above, the daughters included Elisabetha who married Joseph Mayhew in Lancaster, Pennsylvania February 1, 1737,[20] Magdalena who married Johann Georg Hutzel on June 14, 1739 at "Manakesen,"[21] Susanna[22] and Anna Maria, baptized by Stöver on April 28, 1736 during his first visit to Monocacy. On November 19, 1745 Gabriel Swinehard married Esther Neff, daughter of Jacob Neff.[23] After George Swinehart's death his widow Anna Margreth Swinehart married Adam Miller in 1759. Miller died in 1767 and she married again in 1771, this time to Philip Grindler.[24]

The first mention of **Joseph Mayhew** was Pastor Stöver's record of his marriage in Lancaster in 1737. At "Manackesen" Stöver baptized the couple's first two children, John William Mayhuw on June 7, 1738 with Georg Swinehardt, Balthasar Fauth and their wives as sponsors and Anna Mayhuw on September 21, 1740 with Gabriel and Susanna Schweinhardt and Anna Margaretha Götzendanner as sponsors.[25] Other than these notations, there is no indication of the Mayhews' religious affiliation except that he was buried in the original All Saints' English Churchyard where his gravestone[26] noted his

---

Land Records, E:417) and then probably went to South Carolina where he was killed as a Loyalist during the Revolution (per research of Max K. Tatum of Albany, Georgia). For Husleman, see also Usselman, p. 146.

[18] His petition was rejected.
[19] Frederick Lutheran Church Book, Burial Record.
[20] Stöver, *op. cit.*, Marriages, p. 3, No. 119. The entry also appears in the Lancaster Lutheran Church Book: See Frederick S. Weiser, "The Earliest Records of Holy Trinity Evangelical Lutheran Church, Lancaster, Pennsylvania, 1730-1744," *Ebbes fer Alle-Eber Ebbes fer Dich* (Pennsylvania German Society Publications, Breinigsville, Pennsylvania, 1980), 14:431.
[21] Frederick Lutheran Church Book, Burial Record, 1788, No. 6. Stöver, *op. cit.*, Marriages, p. 5, No. 238, mistakenly called her Eliesabetha and set the date as June 17th.
[22] A baptism sponsor in May 1743 for her niece Susanna Hutzel (Frederick Lutheran Church Book).
[23] See above, p. 111.
[24] Frederick Lutheran Church Book, Burial Record. The marriage to Adam Müller is also recorded in the Frederick Reformed Church Book, although there the groom's name is not given! At his death, Pastor David Candler owed Adam Miller 9 shillings.
[25] Stöver, *op. cit.*, p. 18.
[26] Copied by Ernest Helfenstein and printed in Brumbaugh, *op. cit.*, 1:267. See also Holdcraft, *op. cit.*, pp. 21-22, 777.

birth "at Hartwell in North Hamptonshire in the Kingdom of Great Britain.[27] Joseph Mayhew did not secure title to his own land until 1752, when "Addition to Chidley's Range" was surveyed for him.[28] It lay to the west of the original "Chidley's Range" which had been surveyed for Chidley Matthews in 1739.[29] The March Court of 1750 questioned Joseph Mayhew about his purchase of a pistol which was reported to have been stolen, and in 1751 the records show that he purchased a slave from Robert Debutts for 80 pounds.[30] In 1757 Joseph Mayhew was a member of Stephen Ramsburg's Militia Company.[31] He signed his will on July 4, 1763 devising his land to his daughter Ann Walling, but with the proviso that if she died without heirs, the land should then go to George Hutzel, Jr., his wife's nephew.[32]

Another of George Swinehart's sons-in-law was **Johann Georg Hutzel**, who was born at Pfaffenhofen, Württemberg, in the Kraichgau near Brackenheim, on October 4, 1711.[33] He is believed to be the Jerg Hertzel who with Ludwig Hertzel arrived at Philadelphia August 29, 1730 on the Scottish ship *Thistle of Glasgow*, which had sailed from Rotterdam by way of Dover.[34] With him came Jean Henri Fortinaux, Caspar Krieger and Christian Thomas, who would also find their way to Frederick County, as well as Peter Müller from Kaiserslautern, for many years a leader of the Brethren at Ephrata in Pennsylvania. A clue to Hutzel's whereabouts after his arrival in America may be found in the records of the Muddy Creek Lutheran congregation in East Cocalico Township, Lancaster County, Pennsylvania. On April 18, 1736 with Elisabetha Linterin he stood as baptism sponsor for a daughter of Peter Trabbinger, presumably of Warwick.[35] In this same record appeared a number of other future Monocacy settlers, both along the northern section of the German Monocacy Road and on "Tasker's Chance." By June 17, 1739 Georg Hutzel was at

---
[27] The village of Hartwell, seven miles south of Northampton, is today separated from its neighboring Salcey Forest by the M-1 Motorway from London to Leeds.
[28] C/S: BC & GS 1:88.
[29] C/S: EI 5:506; see above, p. 84.
[30] Frederick County Land Records, B:449.
[31] See below, p. 379.
[32] Frederick County Wills, A1:191.
[33] Frederick Lutheran Church Book, Burial Record.
[34] Strassburger-Hinke, *op. cit.*, Lists 11ABC, pp. 32-34. He should not be confused with Hans Georg Hertzel (1714-1762), born at Reihen in the Kraichgau who arrived at Philadelphia with his father on September 21, 1727. See Hannah Benner Roach, "Hans Georg Hertzel, Pioneer of Northampton County, and His Family," *Pennsylvania Genealogical Magazine*, 24:159-169.
[35] Frederick S. Weiser, *Record of Pastoral Acts at the Lutheran and Reformed Congregations of the Muddy Creek Church, East Cocalico Township, Lancaster County, Pennsylvania, 1730-1790* (Pennsylvania German Society, Sources and Documents of the Pennsylvania Germans, V, Breinigsville, 1981), p. 21. The transcription of the Reformed entries in this typescript was copied from William J. Hinke's earlier transcription.

"Monakesen" when he married Magdalena Schweinhardt (cf. above). George Hutzel adhered closely to the Lutheran religion in Frederick County, contributing to the purchase of its first church book in 1742, signing Pastor Muhlenberg's "Articles" of 1747 and having his first five children, Susanna, George, Jr., Johannes, Johann Peter and Johann Matthaus, baptized by Lutheran pastors during the period 1743-1753. On October 19, 1743 John George Huzell and his father-in-law George Sweinhart took communion from Pastor Candler preparatory to their naturalization.[36] Hutzel received the patent for "Markley's Purchase" in 1756[37] with its beginning point near the corner of George Swinehart's "George and Margaret." This land lay on the east side of the German Monocacy Road. In 1742, as George Hootsill, he was appointed overseer of the road from the "top of Katoctin to Monocacy Wagon Road ford near Thomas Beatty's," and in 1757 he appeared on the roster of Stephen Ramsburg's Militia Company. George Hutzel died on May 2, 1778 probably of a stroke while enroute to [Matthias] Ringer's house. His widow Magdalena died in June 1788, survived by ten of their twelve children.[38]

Jean Henri Fortinaux, a shipmate of Georg Hutzel, also arrived at Philadelphia on August 29, 1730.[39] He became Heinrich Fortunee in Stöver's German records but **Henry Fortney** in later English documents. He had settled in the Monocacy area sometime before June 7, 1738 when his daughter Susanna Catarina was baptized by Pastor Stöver. She was born the previous October, and Joh. Georg Gump and Susanna Fauth were her sponsors. Leonhardt Lutz and Catarina Geiger were sponsors for a son, Johann Heinrich Fortunee, born December 31, 1739 and baptized September 21, 1740.[40] It was not until 1745, however, that Fortney had his land surveyed. His "Deer Spring" was located on a draft of Rock Creek near Hutzel's parcel.[41] Henry Fortney died in 1754 and his widow Catharine administered his estate.[42] In the following year she purchased from Thomas Taylor for only ten pounds the nearby "Resurvey on Addition to Hazel Thicket" which totaled 436 acres.[43] In 1761 she acquired additional land adjoining "Deer Spring."[44] The latter ultimately passed to their son Henry, Jr. and from him to his brother David Fortney in 1771.[45]

---

[36] Provincial Court Judgment Records, 1742-1744, EI 7:296.
[37] C/S: BC & GS 5:81.
[38] Frederick Lutheran Church Book, Burial Record. This entry's correction of Stöver's marriage record has been noted above, p. 158n.
[39] Annette K. Burgert, *Eighteenth Century Emigrants from German-Speaking Lands to North America: VoL 1, Northern Kraichgau* (Breinigsville, 1983), Vol. 2, Western Palatinate (Birdsboro, Pennsylvania, 1985), 2:121-124, found no tie to the Reformed family of Jonas Fortinet (et var.) of Landstuhl whose members arrived in 1737, 1739 and 1742.
[40] Stöver, *op. cit.,* p. 18.
[41] C/S: LG E:546.
[42] Frederick County Administrative Accounts, A1:34.
[43] Frederick County Land Records, E:817.
[44] *Ibid.,* G:324.
[45] *Ibid.,* O:542.

The early history of the **Fauth family**, whose name evolved eventually into **Fout**,[46] parallels that of the Schweinhardts. Neither appears in the early Philadelphia arrival lists, but both are found "before 1734" in Rupp's early Philadelphia County quitrents. They lived in Frederick Township where Jacob Fouts and Baltus Fouts each had 100 acres of land.[47] Our earliest record is the November 8, 1730 baptism at Falckner's Swamp of Joh. Georg Schweinhardt's son Joh. Peter for whom Balthazar Fauth and his wife Susanna [Bocher] stood as sponsors.[48]

There is record of Baltis Fout in the Monocacy area as early as May 22, 1734, when he, as Botus Fout, purchased a wagon and two horses from the same George Sweinhart.[49] Beginning in 1736, both brothers, if brothers they were, appear frequently in the Lutheran records of Pastor Stöver, whose visits to Manakesen began in that year. Baltasar Fauth's daughter Catharina Barbara was baptized on April 28, 1736. Jacob Fauth and Barbara Teufersbiss [Devilbiss] were the baptism sponsors. At the same time Jacob Fauth's son was baptized and given the name Balthasar. Jacob Fauth on June 16, 1737 was a sponsor for Maria Eliesabetha, the daughter of Joh. Georg Geiger. On January 17, 1738 Baltasar Fauth and his wife stood as sponsors for the baptism of Joseph Mayhew's son John William. Jacob and Anna Maria Fauth were sponsors for the baptism of Balthasar Fauth's son Johann Jacob Fauth, baptized by Gabriel Nasman on October 31, 1746. And on October 11, 1742 Pastor Stöver married Jacob Fauth's daughter Eva Rosina to Joh. Peter Schmidt.

It was not until March 29, 1738 that the Fauths first appear in the Maryland land records. On that date John Stoddard deeded 939 acres, the remaining half of his "Rocky Creek" tract, to Jacob Fout.[50] This land, it will be recalled, was surveyed originally on November 22, 1725 for Thomas Bordley, who shortly before his death in 1726 assigned the certificate of survey to his surveyor James Stoddert. The latter passed ownership to Captain John Stoddard, who then conveyed the northern half of the land to Susanna Beatty on May 21, 1733.[51] Her half of "Rocky Creek" lay along the southern boundary of "Tasker's Chance," also surveyed in 1725, and thus included a portion of today's city of Frederick. Jacob Fout's southern half lay roughly between the northern portions of Ballenger's Creek and New Design Roads just outside the present city limits. A year after Jacob acquired title to

---
[46] Care must be taken to differentiate between the Fout family and that of Hans Michael Pfautz who came from Rohrbach in the Kraichgau area of Germany. Although some of Hans Michael's descendants spell the name "Fouts," the final sibilant usually aids in distinguishing between the two families. See John Scott Davenport, "Earliest Pfautz/Fouts Families in America," *National Genealogical Society Quarterly*, 63:243-263.
[47] Rupp, *op. cit.*, p. 472. Rupp's spelling, unless the genitive was involved, is an exception to the sibilant rule in the preceding note.
[48] Stöver, *op. cit.*, p. 3.
[49] Prince George's County Land Records, T:240.
[50] Prince George's County Land Records, T:576.
[51] See above, p. 39.

his land, Baltis Fout on May 27, 1739 had his own land surveyed and called it "Fout's Delight."[52] His land lay a bit farther west, just east of today's Feagaville.

Both Jacob and Baldus Fout were naturalized on June 4, 1740, Jacob with his children Jacob, Henry, Baldus, Eve, Mary, Margarett and Catherine, Baldus with his children Bauldus, Maria and Catherine.[53] Baltis Fout signed the November 1740 petition for a road from John Pyburn's to John Nelson's and on to Elting's Mill and present-day Beallsville. In 1742, though neither was a member of the Maryland Established Church, both Jacob and Baltis signed the petition to divide Prince George's Parish.[54] They both signed the 1742 petition seeking a division of Prince George's County, and both contributed to the purchase of the first record book for the Gemeine Mannackes [Monocacy Lutheran Congregation]. In 1743 Baltis Fout was overseer of the road "from the top of Katoctin Mountain to the ford of the Monocacy Wagon Road near Thomas Beatty's." And John van Metre, Sr., after leaving the Carroll Creek settlement for Virginia appointed his "well-beloved friend Baltis Foutt .... my true and lawful attorney...." to sell his land "Meadow" to Michael Raymer.[55] Mary Fout in 1748 purchased "Mill Lot" from Henry Ballenger.[56]

Jacob Fout's wife was Anna Maria Zirkel, a daughter of Hans Heinrich Zirkel of Ittlingen, Germany, where she was born on October 9, 1705.[57] The Zirkel family is also not to be found in the Philadelphia port arrival lists. Jacob Fout died between 1746 and 1750, leaving as children, who had been earlier listed in naturalization proceedings on June 4, 1740, Eve, Henry, Jacob, Mary, Baldus, Margaret and Catharine.[58] That descendants remained on the Fout portion of "Rocky Creek" along today's New Design Road seems evident from the 1873 Atlas, which shows there the homes of G[rafton] Fout, D[aniel] Scholl and the heirs of P[eter] Fout and of L[ewis] Fout.[59]

"Baltish Fought" signed his will on April 29, 1751. It was probated May 23, 1751, and in it he named his wife Susanna, sons Baltish and Jacob and daughters Catharine, Susanna and Margaret, the latter the wife of John Shellman. Baltis devised his dwelling place to his son Baltis, Jr. The will's witnesses were Peter Apfel, Davult Coons and Johannes Kuhn. Christian Kemp and Daniel Matthews were to be executors, but they did not serve, leaving the administration to

---

[52] C/S: EI 5:517.
[53] Commission Book No. 82, Maryland Historical Society. This volume is actually one of the records of the Council of Maryland, covering miscellaneous entries, 1733-1783, for ship registrations, military commissions, minister inductions, licenses to preach, naturalizations, etc. See *Maryland Historical Magazine*, 26:138-158, 244-263, 342-361; 27:29-36.
[54] See below, p. 371. The names were obviously transcribed by another hand, for they appear as Paltis and Jacob Foutch.
[55] Prince George's County Land Records, BB 1:491.
[56] See p. 81.
[57] Burgert, *op. cit.*, 1:415.
[58] Commission Book No. 82, *loc. cit.*, p. 157.
[59] Lake, *op. cit.*, p. 11.

widow Susanna.[60] She, a daughter of Georg and Margreth Bocher, had come in 1713 from Lomersheim on the Enz in Württemberg and had been married to Baltis Fout for 30 years. After his death she married as a second husband Caspar Apple, who also predeceased her. She then remained a widow for nearly 18 years, dying at the age of 69 in February 1773 and leaving 25 grandchildren.[61] Her will named her daughter Catharine Shull and gave two-thirds of her estate and "money that may befall me from Germany, either in my own right or my late husband's, to my son-in-law John Shellman.[62]

A further tie between the Falckner Swamp area of today's Montgomery County in Pennsylvania and the settlers on "Rocky Creek" in Maryland involved the family of **Johann Georg Geiger** (1702-1739e). He was the youngest son of Johann Valentin Geiger and Maria Barbara Bauer of Ittlingen in the Kraichgau area of Germany. His eldest brother, likewise named Johann Valentine Geiger (1685-1762), had come to America in 1717 with his father-in-law Pastor Anton Jacob Henckel, whom we have met above.[63] They settled on adjoining 250-acre tracts in New Hanover Township near the present New Hanover Lutheran church, whose congregation Pastor Henckel undoubtedly organized during the decade before his death in 1728. Johann Georg Geiger either accompanied the Henckels in 1717 or possibly followed in the year 1727.[64] At any rate, he was in New Hanover Township by April 17, 1728 when with his brother and the latter's in-laws he signed a petition to the Governor seeking protection from the Indians.[65]

Sometime before 1732 Johann Georg Geiger married Pastor Henckel's youngest daughter Maria Catharina Henckel, who had been born at Daudenzell May 10, 1711 and at the age of six had come to America with her family. They were still in New Hanover Township in 1735 when the two Geiger brothers signed a petition seeking the establishment of township boundaries,[66] but by June of 1737 George Geiger and his wife were definitely in the Monocacy area. There Stöver baptized their daughter Maria Eliesabetha with Jacob Fauth and his wife as sponsors. On March 4, 1739 their fifth and last child, Johann Jacob Geiger, was likewise baptized by Stöver at

---

[60] Frederick County Wills, A1:10; Administrative Accounts A1:20.
[61] Frederick Lutheran Church Book, Burial Record.
[62] Frederick County Wills, A1:446.
[63] See above, p. 133.
[64] Strassburger-Hinke, *op. cit.*, List 1A, p. 8: Hans Jerick Guyger, Conn[estoga?] 4½ persons. This is the only Georg Geiger found in the Philadelphia arrival lists, and he may be suspect because of the indicated size of the family with him, his intended destination of Conestoga and the presence of other Geigers on board who were not from Ittlingen.
[65] The list of petitioners appeared originally in the Pennsylvania Archives, 6th Series, 14:262, was then corrected in 1930 by W. J. Finck, and was once again transcribed by William J. Hinke. A consolidation of the three versions appeared in *The Henckel Family Records* (New Market, Virginia, 1926-1939) pp. 234-239.
[66] *Ibid.*, pp. 240-241.

Monocacy.[67]

George Geiger does not appear in the Maryland land records. But he was undoubtedly living on "Rocky Creek," no doubt purchasing a part of that land from Jacob Fout: On June 24, 1740, after his premature death a year earlier, his widow Catharine "Kiger" secured title to 150 acres on "Rocky Creek" from Jacob Fout.[68] On August 26th she paid her alienation fine and the next day posted a bond of £80 to insure transfer of title to this land, on which she then lived, to her sons George and Valentine Geiger when they came of age and after they paid £8 each to their brother Jacob and their sisters Catharine and Elisabeth.[69] In late 1740 she then married Johann Peter Apple as her second husband. Their further land dealings are discussed in the next chapter as are those of Jacob Matthews who obtained 250 acres also on "Rocky Creek" from Jacob Fout in 1740.

The earliest ship in the Hinke lists to arrive at Philadelphia with Germans aboard who are known to have settled later in the Frederick County area was the *Mortonhouse*. She reached Philadelphia on August 23, 1728, having sailed from Rotterdam by way of Deal in England on the lengthy 69-day voyage. She carried two hundred German immigrants, some of whom reached the Monocacy area during the second decade of its settlement. These included, among others, Jacob Brunner, Jacob Storm and Martin Schaub [later Shoup].[70] The first two lived on "Tasker's Chance" and are discussed in more detail in a subsequent chapter.[71] Suffice it here to note that Jacob Brunner came in advance of his rather large family whose arrival followed in the next year.

It is impossible to determine from the land records when **Martin Shoup** first arrived in Frederick County. He was there, however, before the December 10, 1741 survey for Jacob Staley's "Otersum," since the beginning point for that survey was located "100 yards from Martin Shoup's branch."[72] Earlier still, Martin Schaub's daughter was married at Manaquesen on May 21, 1740 to Peter Schäffer.[73] The Shoup land began with a parcel called "Mankine" which was surveyed for Daniel Dulany on November 28, 1741. But it was not assigned and patented to Martin Shoup until March 23, 1748. It adjoined "Otersum" to the north and was located on a ridge near the main road."[74] Martin Shoup, son of the immigrant,[75] had "Mankine" enlarged to 231 acres through a resurvey in 1754. A part of present-day

---
[67] Stöver, *op. cit.*, p. 17.
[68] Prince George's County Land Records, Y:181-182.
[69] Prince George's County Land Records, Y:181, 196, 200.
[70] Strassburger-Hinke, *op. cit.*, Lists 6AB, pp. 17-20.
[71] See below, pp. 269, 280.
[72] C/S: LG E:384. Shoup's Branch was probably a branch of Carroll Creek.
[73] Stöver, *op. cit.*, Marriages, p. 6, no. 284. See below, p. 180.
[74] CS: BC & GS 23:363; Patented Survey, Prince George's County, No. 1396.
[75] Frederick County Administrative Accounts, A1:26. Martin Shoub, [Jr.] was executor for the estate of Martin Shoub, [Sr.], January 17, 1753.

Shookstown is built just to the west of "Mankine," and the Shook Family cemetery there contains the grave of Elizabeth Shoup (1786-1853).[76] In the 1743 naturalization proceedings Martain Shope was called a Quaker,[77] a fact not observed elsewhere. He died in 1750, leaving a will dated April 13, 1750 which referred to son Christian Shaub, then living in Conestoga, and daughter Anna, children of his first wife. Children of his surviving second wife Susanna were not named,[78] but sons Martin Shoab and George Shoab were on Stephen Ramsburg's Militia Company roster in 1757 during the French and Indian War.[79] Hans Georg Schaub married about 1756 Anna Maria Staley but died before 1761 when she married Adam Hildebrand. The other son, Martin Shoup, Jr., signed his own will on September 10, 1783. In that will he named his wife Soffia [daughter of Conrad Kemp], a nephew Peter Kemp [son of Frederick Kemp] and his own children George, Christian, Peter, Samuel, Catharine Staley, Soffia and Mary Shoup.

A year after Martin Shoup and Jacob Brunner reached Philadelphia, the latter's brother-in-law **Christian Getzendanner** also arrived. He came with the rest of the Brunner family, which included his wife Anna Barbara Brunner,[80] and reached Philadelphia on September 11, 1729. The party had sailed from Rotterdam aboard the ship *Allen* which cleared the English port of Cowes on the Isle of Wight July 7th. Their voyage from England thus lasted 66 days, a lengthy but not unusual time for the crossing.[81] Also on board were Alexander Mack (1680-1735), the first Dunker minister of the German Baptist Brethren, and a number of his followers. The Getzendanners and the Brunners, however, continued to adhere to their Reformed religion. When they reached the Monocacy area, they became the first Reformed church elders and were largely responsible for the establishment of that Church in Maryland.[82]

Christian Getzendanner's father Johann Jacob Gitzendanner was Swiss, although his origins in Switzerland have not to date been found. He had come down the Rhine River sometime before 1694 to settle in the Palatinate between Speyer and Ludwigshafen in the tiny village of Klein Schifferstadt. Undoubtedly there he married

---

[76] Holdcraft, *op. cit.*, p. 1025.
[77] Provincial Court Judgment Records, 1742-1744, EI 7:297.
[78] Frederick County Original Wills, Box 1, folder 27, Maryland Archives, Hall of Records. Conrad Kemp, Jacob Brunner and David Delater witnessed this will. Although indexed as Martin Strob in Frederick County Wills, A1:39, the will itself was not recorded there no doubt because it was written in German.
[79] See below, p. 379.
[80] For the Brunners, see below, pp. 269-273.
[81] Strassburger-Hinke, *op. cit.*, Lists 10ABC, pp. 27-30. The name on these lists is spelled Kitsintander or Kitsenlander depending upon the crossing of the "t". The Brunners signed their name as Bruner, although the Captain's list "heard" it as Prunder. In America German scribes sometimes spelled the Getzendanner name with an umlaut, Götzendanner.
[82] See pp. 150, 270.

Christian's mother Anna Otilia Riester, and there Christian was born about 1694e.[83] Christian Götzendanner and Anna Barbara Brunner were married April 20, 1723 and had as children before they left for America, Susanna Margareta and Gabriel. Along the way, perhaps as they were crossing the English Channel, a son Jacob was born. Their children Catharina, Balthasar, Anna Maria and Adam were born in America.

Again, information is lacking concerning the actual arrival date of this family in today's Frederick County. Christian Getzendanner was paying quitrent in Frederick Township, today's Montgomery County, Pennsylvania, before 1734.[84] He got his Monocacy land, "Christian's Choyce," from Daniel Dulany although the latter did not have it surveyed out of his September 26, 1740 warrant for 412 acres until November 27, 1740.[85] Dulany assigned the survey to Christian Getsetoner on August 13, 1741, and it was patented on November 11, 1742.[86] The original "Christian's Choyce" contained 100 acres and lay near the forks of today's U.S. Highways 40 and 40-Alt, formerly the site of Philip Wertheimer's "Elmwood" home on Rock Creek, now occupied by the Fredericktown Mall Shopping Center. His subsequent land holdings also included today's Country Club and its golf course. In October 1742 Getzendanner's name, albeit mangled into "Christian Citchadaner," appeared on the petition to divide Prince George's Parish.[87] As Christian Getson Tanner on October 9, 1743, he received the sacrament from the Reformed pastor Edward [Conrad] Templeman preparatory to his naturalization.[88]

In 1744, somewhat southwest of "Christian's Choyce," Christian Getzendanner tried his own hand at having land surveyed. The beginning point for the resulting "Allamangle" was "south of the great road just above the head of a hollow that leads to Chidley Matthews' on a draft of Carroll Creek." This description puts the beginning point immediately west of Fulmer's Station which may be identified today as the junction of Mount Phillip Road and Butterfly Lane. The "great road" refers to the German Monocacy Road and should not be construed as meaning an east-west route from "Forrest" [Middletown] along today's Butterfly Lane and the Jefferson Pike leading into downtown Frederick or along the subsequent parallel National Pike and U.S. Highway 40. Instead, in Getzendanner's day the main German Monocacy Road from today's Middletown to Fulmer's Station was shortly to be connected to a new road following approximately today's Mt. Phillip and Willis Derr Roads to Buckeystown and on to the mouth of the Monocacy River. This road was sought by petition in 1745 and was called the road from "Isaac Leonard's to Baltis Fout's to the main

---

[83] Neither marriage nor birth entry appears in the Klein Schifferstadt records, which were kept in the neighboring Iggelheim [Reformed] Church Book. There were several gaps in this record at about this time.
[84] Rupp, op. cit., p. 472.
[85] C/S: LG E:91.
[86] Patent: LG B:533.
[87] See p. 371.
[88] Provincial Court Judgment Records, 1742-1744, EI 7:296.

Monocacy Road at the Quaker Meeting House." The junction with the German Monocacy Road is mentioned in the 1745 certificate of survey for "Addition to New Germany."[89]

In 1748 Christian Getzendanner's name appeared on the list of those being overtaxed by the Sheriff.[90] Then on May 10, 1749 he purchased "Frankford" for 25 pounds from Jacob Smith (1719-1805),[91] who had had these 50 acres surveyed in 1744 "about a mile to the northward of Isaac Leonard's, just above the great road."[92] Getzendanner increased the size of this parcel to 200 acres with a resurvey in 1751.[93] Its site may be identified in the 1873 Atlas as the home of S[olomon] J[oseph] Zimmerman, south of the present junction of Mt. Phillip Road and Butterfly Lane.[94]

"Christian's Choyce" was enlarged to 930 acres with a Resurvey by Christian Getzendanner in 1752.[95] In 1758 he deeded 11 acres to John Medah [Middagh], 241 acres to Joseph Hardman and 60 acres to Valentine Schriver.[96] On April 7, 1764 from "Allamangle" and "Resurvey on Frankford" he conveyed 125 acres to his eldest son Gabriel and a like 125 acres from "Resurvey on Frankford" plus 17 acres from the "Resurvey on Christian's Choyce" to his son Jacob.[97] By his will of December 21, 1766, he devised the remainder of his land "where I now live," called "Resurvey on Christian's Choice" to his youngest son Adam Getzendanner. The will did not mention sons Gabriel and Jacob, who had thus been already provided for, but did name his wife Barbara, his son Baltis (husband of Anna Stoner and later Philippena Stähley Stull), and his daughters Margaret [wife of Gilbert Kemp], Catharine [wife of John Thomas] and Anna Maria [wife of Thomas Schley, Jr.], each of whom was to receive monetary payments from Adam.[98] In 1770 Adam Getzendanner had a resurvey made which included the original "Christian's Choyce" and this he named "Adam's Content."[99] By his will of August 8, 1783, Adam gave his "house and plantation on Content" to his son John.[100]

On September 21, 1731, two years after the Brunners,

---

[89] See above, p. 54.
[90] See below, p. 292.
[91] Frederick County Land Records, B:36.
[92] C/S: LG E:286. Millard M. Rice has done extensive research concerning Jacob Smith and his brother John Smith (1721-1802). Since they are not known in land records before 1743, they are not otherwise included herein, except for Stephen Ramsburg's notation in 1748: See below, p. 292.
[93] C/S: Y & S 7:177.
[94] Lake, op. cit., p. 11. See above, p. 52. The junction may be identified in this Atlas as the road intersection near the home of E. Smith.
[95] C/S: BC & GS 1:129.
[96] Maryland Rent Rolls (Frederick No. 1), 32:85; ibid. (Frederick No. 2), 33:85.
[97] Frederick County Land Records, J:273.
[98] Frederick County Wills, A1:276, probated January 20, 1767.
[99] C/S: BC & GS 41:358.
[100] Frederick County Wills, GM 2:1.

Getzendanners and Sturms arrived in Philadelphia, another party of future Marylanders also reached these shores. These Germans included the Devilbiss family which found its way to Monocacy Manor[101] and the family of Hans Martin Wetzel. The latter settled along the German Monocacy Road but at some distance north of the area described here.[102]

The next vessel to reach Philadelphia with more German immigrants was the little two-masted snow, the *Lowther*, whose home port was at Whitehaven on Solway Firth in northern England. On this voyage, however, she had come from Rotterdam by way of Dover and carried only 78 persons, 33 men and 45 women and children. These came ashore at Philadelphia on October 14, 1731. Among their number were two unmarried men, Anton Bannkauf and Philip Kinss.[103]

Anton Bannkauf first appears in the company of Thomas Cresap and the Germans who had attempted to settle west of the Susquehanna River in the disputed area along the Pennsylvania-Maryland border. That border had been set originally at the 40° parallel of latitude, but under frontier conditions it was not clear where the line actually lay. Twenty years later, for example, Governor Horatio Sharpe was still seeking to learn whether the then "temporary line" lay north of the Potomac River's most northerly bend. If not, much of Maryland's western region was in severe jeopardy.[104] Conflicts in land titles claimed and granted by both Colonies were inevitable. These conflicts were aggravated by the arrival, a year after Bannkauf reached Philadelphia, of a number of other Germans, including Michael Reisner, Jacob Matthias Manshaw, Bernard Weymar and Philip Ernst Grüber, who attempted to settle in the disputed area. The conflicts grew and often took the form of physical violence. On one such occasion, in 1734, Bannkauf and Reisner were among the eight men arrested by a Pennsylvania sheriff. In this particular incident they were soon released, but the arguments and altercations grew.[105]

It was perhaps inevitable that some of these settlers would move on to the more secure areas of today's Maryland. Bannkauf did so, but he seems to have owned no land. Nor are there suggestions in which part of the County he resided. His presence is indicated, however, by references in the 1736 Prince George's County Court records to the grand jury's presenting Robert Debutts on several charges, including one of drawing a cutlass on the Constable and of "making three strokes at Anthony Bancuff, one of which went through Bancuff's westcot and lining."[106] In that same year, on May 17th, Bannkauf was a Lutheran baptism sponsor at "Monockesen" with

---

[101] See below, p. 317.
[102] *Ibid.*, p. 207.
[103] Strassburger-Hinke, *op. cit.*, Lists 127ABC, pp. 54-57. Joseph Fisher, the vessel's master, recorded the future Marylanders' names as Anthony Bankaulf and Philip Kitchin.
[104] See Correspondence of Gov. Sharpe, *Archives of Maryland, op. cit.*, 6:5, 72, 91.
[105] See above, pp. 16-19.
[106] Cf. above, p. 77.

Magdalena Lein for the daughter of Georg Lathly.[107]

Though a relationship is not known, the name is uncommon enough to warrant noting that in 1741 Michael Tablepense [Devilbiss] was the estate administrator for a Magdalene Bancalf or Pongoffen.[108] Conceivably she may have been the Magdalena Debelbesin, age 18, who arrived at Philadelphia with her brothers in 1731 on the ship immediately preceding that which brought Anton Bannkauf. And if she had married Anton Bannkauf, her estate papers suggest that they may have lived near Biggs Ford and that he predeceased her at a relatively young age.[109]

Philip Kinss, as he signed his name in 1731 to the Philadelphia oaths of allegiance and abjuration, was undoubtedly the same individual known subsequently in Maryland as **Philip Küntz**. He was one of the 18 Germans[110] who did not survey their land directly but instead leased it from Daniel Dulany until they could pay for it in full. It was not until April 24, 1752 that **Philip Kens** got title to his land, but he had been in the area at least since 1740 and was well enough established for roads to be designated in relation to his dwelling place. His parcel, "Shoemaker's Choice," was located on the German Monocacy Road at today's Bethel. It had been surveyed initially for Dulany on November 28, 1741 and had its beginning point "on a glade that falls into Tuscarora Creek." The certificate of survey also noted that already "on this land is two small log houses and a small wheat patch."[111] When Pastor Candler had his adjoining land surveyed in 1743, it was identified as lying west of the road from Kins' to Jacob Naff's,[112] presumably the equivalent of today's Sundays Lane from Bethel to the Emmitsburg Pike (or U. S. Highway 15), and then on to Biggs Ford.

On May 10, 1748 Philip Kins for £40 conveyed "Shewmaker's Choice" to Stephen Ransburg,[113] who combined it with his "Stoney Hill" in a Resurvey on September 10, 1750.[114] On May 21, 1740 Joh. Philipp Kuntz and his wife were sponsors at the baptism of Philipp Christoph, son of Georg Henckel of "Manackesen."[115] Philip Kince, Titur Laney and Matthew Reisling took Lutheran communion from "John Caspar Stover at the Church at Monockecey" on October 14, 1742. Five days later they appeared in Provincial Court, took the oaths and were

---

[107] Stöver, op. cit., p. 16. Rachel Lathly was born March 16, 1730. Such delayed baptisms were unusual, but are often explained by the absence of ministers in the frontier area at the time. Georg Lathly does not otherwise appear in Frederick County church or land records.
[108] Prince George's County Administrative Bonds, Nov. 23, 1741 (Box 11, folder 66) and Inventories (Box 13, folder 2), both at Maryland Archives, Hall of Records.
[109] See below, p. 318.
[110] See above, p. 33n.
[111] C/S: LG E:81.
[112] C/S: LG E:211.
[113] Prince George's County Land Records, EE:457.
[114] C/S: BC & GS 1:140.
[115] Frederick Lutheran Church Book, p. 32.

naturalized.[116] The same three, as Philip Kühntz, Dieder Lehnick and Mateus Rehssele, contributed about that time to the purchase of the first Lutheran Church Book. In the following year Philip Kince and John Schrier certified that Pastor David Candler had administered communion in the Lutheran Church of Manaquice on September 25, 1743 to some six other Germans preparatory to their naturalization on October 19th.[117] Philip Küntz signed Muhlenberg's Articles of June 24, 1747. As Philip Kintz, he stood as baptism sponsor on April 2, 1749 for a son of Philipp Angelberger. In September of 1754 Philip Kunz and his wife were sponsors at the baptism of Heinrich Gernhard's son. At the same time their own son Jacob Küntz was baptized with Andreas Berger and Christina Fourtne as sponsors.[118] In 1773 Philip Knewell, not otherwise identified, made bequests to Philip Kuns, as well as to Jacob and John Weller.[119]

Close by "Shoemaker's Choice" and surveyed on the same day, November 28, 1741, again for Daniel Dulany, was **Adam Stull's** tract "Chestnut." It was situated between today's Yellow Springs and Bethel and was obviously being purchased on time. Like the notation on the survey for "Shoemaker's Choice," this survey also carried a hint of prior settlement well before 1741: "On this land is a large log house, one old one and two large wheat fields well fenced."[120] Stull acquired title on October 18, 1744 when "Chestnut" was finally patented to him. In 1746 he resurveyed his parcel to increase its acreage and called the Resurvey "Chestnut Hill."[121] One of the baptisms performed by his Lutheran neighbor Pastor David Candler during the latter's short tenure in the Monocacy area was that of Christoffel Stoll, son of Adam Stoll, on May 1, 1743. Christian Getzendanner and his wife Anna Barbara were the sponsors -- ostensibly an example of Reformed people standing for their Lutheran friends. Adam Stoll was second on the list of those contributing to the purchase of the Frederick Lutheran Church Book, but he did not sign Muhlenberg's Articles of 1747. Instead, Adam Stull and his wife Barbara then begin to appear more frequently in the Reformed Church records. A number of Reformed people, including Adam Stall received the sacrament from Edward [Conrad] Templeman on October 9, 1743 before their naturalization.[122]

The first entry in the new Reformed Church Book, under date of February 6, 1747, was for Elisabeth, daughter of Adam and Barbara

---

[116] Provincial Court Judgment Records, 1742-1744, EI 7:110. Naturalizations required, in addition to the church communion, seven years of residence in the Colonies and no absence exceeding two months at any one time.
[117] Ibid., EI 7:296.
[118] Frederick Lutheran Church Book, p. 32.
[119] Frederick County Wills, A1:476.
[120] C/S: LG E:385.
[121] C/S: BY & GS 1:199.
[122] Provincial Court Judgment Records, 1742-1744, EI 7:296. The others were Christian Getson Tanner, Jacob Stern [Storm], John Hend, Jacob Staley, Gasper Mire [Caspar Myer], Henry Boughtall [Bachdold] and Isaac Miller.

Stoll.[123] Other entries show Adam and Barbara Stull as baptism sponsors in 1746 and 1751 and Adam as a communicant in 1758, 1767 and 1770. In the latter year Adam Stull signed his will, which was probated on July 17, 1772. It named his wife Barbara, his children John, Elisabeth, Christopher (who in 1761 married Philippina Staley, daughter of Jacob Staley[124]), Adam and his deceased children Peter Stull and Catharine Devilbiss. Adam Stull's relationship to John Stull, the miller at Antietam,[125] has not been established. That John Stull wrote his will in 1749, naming his wife Martha, sons Daniel, John, Isaac and Jacob and daughters Mary Greathouse, Elizabeth Johnson, Catharina Swearingham, Margaret Stull and Susanna Stull.[126]

Thomas House lived in the area at the south end of the German Monocacy Road near where it turned west to go over the mountain. Here, "on the side of Carroll Creek, a draft of Monocacy," he had "Strife" surveyed on August 23, 1739. The certificate of survey was assigned to John House, who received the patent.[127] In 1742 John House had additional land surveyed adjoining "Strife," and this he called "House's Addition."[128] By 1808 this land was in the hands of the Murdocks,[129] and in 1815 Eleanor Potts, Mary Murdock, George William Murdock, Harriett Tyler and Ann L. Potts had a resurvey made on both "Strife" and "House's Addition" which they then called "Murdock's Fancy."[130]

The November 1739 Prince George's County Court appointed John House overseer of the road from the "top of Katoctin to the wagon road ford near Thomas Beatty's." The Reformed pastor Johann Bartholomew Rieger, probably then in Lancaster, certified on April 10, 1743 that Thomas House and Conrad Kemp were honest Protestants of the Reformed Heidelberg catechism, thereby making possible their naturalization at Annapolis.[131] By 1744, however, House was beginning to have land surveyed for himself near the mouth of Antietam Creek in present-day Washington County, and here he also purchased a part of Israel Friend's "Antietam Bottom." His son Andrew House did remove to the Antietam area, for his home was identified in a 1768 Court record appointing an overseer for the road "from the fork of Antietam Creek where Andrew House now lives to Sharpsburg." John House purchased the farm animals belonging to

---
[123] Frederick Reformed Church Book, p. 1. This book was purchased in Frankfurt am Main by Johann Jacob Bruner on April 16, 1749. Its first several pages include ex post facto entries from the year 1746, not all of them in chronological order. Unfortunately William J. Hinke rearranged them into chronological order in his typescript transcription now located at the Philip Schaff Library, Lancaster Theological Seminary.
[124] Frederick Reformed Church Book.
[125] See above, pp. 55-56.
[126] Frederick County Wills, A 1:23.
[127] C/S: EI 5:517.
[128] C/S: LG E:570.
[129] Varlé, loc. cit.
[130] C/S: JB D:387.
[131] Provincial Court Judgment Records, 1742-1744, EI 7:161.

Solomon and Rebecca Hedges before they left for Virginia.[132] The Court of 1749 indicted John House for assault on Mary Devilbiss. By 1753, however, he had died. The March Court of that year made reference to John House's suit against Barnet Waymour which it marked "abated by death of plaintiff."[133] He had written his will on February 19, 1752, naming his wife Susanna, a daughter Susanna and four sons, Andrew, George, William and Valentine House.[134] In November of 1753 William and Andrew House were suing Michael Reisner on a debt due John House's estate.[135] Peter Apple in his 1779 will named a daughter Eva House, presumably a daughter-in-law of John House.

Both George and William House were sued by Henry Touchstone, the former in the November Court of 1749 on a debt of £50, his brother in the March Court of 1752. William House made his home in the Catoctin Valley where he owned considerable acreage, some of which he had obtained by surveys.[136] In the 1750s he had served as overseer of the so-called Touchstone Road, and in 1757 his name appeared on the muster roll of Captain Peter Butler's Militia Company.

Conrad Kemp was 48 years of age when on August 17, 1733 he arrived at Philadelphia with his wife Anna Maria Feuerbach, age 38. They brought a growing family consisting of sons Christian 18, Gilbert 16, Frederick 8, Hans Peter 6 and a daughter Catharina 2.[137] Also on board their ship were Joh. Jacob Mattheis, Joh. Jacob Hoff and other future Monocacy settlers. The Kemp family is said to have been originally Swiss from St. Gallen Canton,[138] but their departure was from Untergimpern in the German Kraichgau area between Sinsheim and Bad Wimpfen, where they had lived at least the preceding eight years.[139] They did not come to Maryland directly, but remained for some years in the vicinity of New Holland in Lancaster County, Pennsylvania. There a last daughter was born in 1734, and various members of the family appear in the church records as late as 1738 and 1744. On May 1, 1739 Johann Conrad Kaempf and his daughter-in-law Elisabeth Kemp, wife of Christian Kemp, were witnesses in Lancaster for the marriage of her brother Daniel Ferree.[140] Also in that year and still in Lancaster, Johan Conrad Kemp and his wife Anna Maria were sponsors for a daughter of Johannes Reisman and his wife Barbara Weber. They appeared again for the baptism of their son

---

[132] See above, p. 108.
[133] Rice, *The Life*, *op. cit.*, pp. 98.
[134] Frederick County Wills, A 1:75.
[135] Rice, *The Life*, *op. cit.*, p. 130., See also Frederick County Administrative Accouts, A 1:42, of Andrew and William House.
[136] Including "House's New Design," "Long Bottom," " Upper End of Long Bottom," "Creager's Oversight," "Mill Race," "More Bad Than Good," "Batchelor's Hall" and "Resurvey on Anchor and Hope."
[137] Strassburger-Hinke, *op. cit.*, Lists 29 ABC, pp. 106-113.
[138] From the research of Harry Howard Kemp.
[139] Burgert, *op. cit.*, 1:195.
[140] D. F. Magee, "Emanuel Carpenter, the Lawgiver," Lancaster County Historical Society *Papers* 24:148.

Christian's daughter Anna Maria Kemp, born December 4, 1739.[141]

On August 24, 1739 Conrad Kemp was in the Monocacy area having 50 acres surveyed in the vicinity of John House's "Strife," which had been surveyed the day before. Kemp's parcel, which he called "Peace and Quietness,"[142] was located along Carroll Creek just outside the western boundary of "Tasker's Chance" and very close to the land he and his son Gilbert would later possess on that large tract.[143] Today his "Peace and Quietness" would lie wholly within the western portion of Fort Detrick. On March 12, 1745 Conrad Kemp had another 30 acres surveyed between Frederick and Rocky Springs. This he called "Wilbersign,"[144] and in 1750 he assigned parts of both tracts to his sons Gilbert and Frederick Kemp.[145] Also in 1750 Conrad Kemp had the small 10-acre "Kemp's Lot" surveyed in the area just east of Shookstown at Kemp's Lane on present-day Fort Detrick. Thus Conrad Kemp, the father, most emphatically did not settle anywhere near, as Edward T. Schultz claimed, "the neighborhood of the present town of New Market where he subsequently laid out the village of Kemptown in that vicinity."[146]

The Kemp family had been associated with the Lutherans in Germany and with both Lutherans and Reformed in Pennsylvania. About 1742 Conradt Kemp's name appears among those helping to purchase the first Frederick Lutheran Church Book. He did not, however, sign Muhlenberg's Lutheran Articles in 1747. Instead, when the Reformed Church Book records began, about 1746, the Kemps appeared more and more frequently among those entries. In 1743 the Reformed pastor Johann Bartholomew Rieger had certified concerning Kemp's Reformed religion.[147] In 1748 Stephen Ramsburg listed Conrad Kemp as one of the Germans being overtaxed by the sheriff.[148] In the same year Conrad Kämpf and Frantz Weiss witnessed the will of Hans Peter Hoffman. In its probate both witnesses were listed as Protestant Dissenters, affirming, but not swearing, that they saw Hoffman sign his will.[149] In 1755 Johann Conradt Kämpf and three of

---
[141] First Reformed Church Book, Lancaster.
[142] C/S: TI 1:445.
[143] See below, p. 274.
[144] C/S: LG E:587.
[145] Frederick County Land Records, B:239-241.
[146] Schultz, op. cit., p. 41.
[147] See above, p. 171. Christian and Gilbert Kemp were naturalized on September 27, 1746, Frederick Kemp on September 16, 1751: Provincial Court Records, EI 10:228, EI 13:801.
[148] See below, p. 292.
[149] Frederick County Wills, A1:15; Frederick County Original Wills, Box 1, folder 10, Maryland Archives, Hall of Records. Both Weiss and Hoffman had arrived at Philadelphia in 1733 on the next ship, just ten days after the Kemps. The term Protestant Dissenter at this time referred strictly to a member of a religious body which had separated from the Church of England, but it was also being used to refer to people of the Reformed faith. For these Germans, however, the distinction relating to affirming rather than swearing is more important, pointing to their possibly being Mennonites or, probably less

his sons witnessed the will of Friderich Unselt.[150]

The sons of Conrad Kemp had a number of land surveys made. **Christian Kemp** (1715-1790) began with "Dispatch" (230 acres) and "Kemp's Delight" (100 acres), both surveyed originally for Dr. George Steuart. Steuart assigned the certificates to Christian Kemp, and patents were issued to him in February 1743/44.[151] The two tracts were contiguous and were located southeast of today's Feagaville astride Ballenger Creek Pike on the northeast side of Elmer (formerly Willis) Derr Road where it meets New Design Road. Here, on Ballenger Creek, the original Kemp's Mill was erected.[152] In September 1745 Christian Kemp sought to re-establish the boundaries of the two tracts,[153] and on March 27, 1747 had a resurvey made of "Kemp's Delight."[154] Over a rather wide area other land was surveyed for Christian Kemp, including "Good Luck" (150 acres in the Middletown Valley, August 30, 1745), "Resurvey on Good Luck" (639 acres, January 15, 1752), "Kemp's Long Meadow" (600 acres northeast of present-day Burkittsville, August 4, 1752), "Great Desire" (82 acres east of Middletown, June 20, 1753), "Resurvey on Hunter's Delight" (148 acres about three miles south of today's Middletown, October 31, 1754), "Resurvey on Great Desire" (105 acres, April 26, 1765) and "Addition to Father's Lecture" (near present-day Limekiln).

Christian Kemp's children were born over a forty-year period, the first three in Lancaster County, Pennsylvania to his first wife Elisabeth Feree, widow of her first cousin Abraham LeFevre. Christian Kemp signed the March 1748 petition for a road from Point of Rocks to Frederick, which incidentally would pass through his land and be known today as the Ballenger Creek Pike. He and Daniel Matthews were named as executors of the April 29, 1751 will of Baltis Fout, but they renounced the executorship in favor of Fout's widow Susanna.[155] In 1759 Christian Kemp was named overseer of the road from the top of Katoctin Mountain via George Matthews' place to Ballenger Branch.

Gilbert Kemp (1717-1794) received title to "Water Land," 100 acres at the western tip of "Tasker's Chance," from Daniel Dulany on July 28, 1746.[156] His other land included "Kemp's Discovery" (50 acres east of Indian Springs, July 30, 1750), "Above House" (150 acres, May 17, 1751), "Home House" (150 acres, November 10, 1752), "Below House," "Middle House" and "Hard Bargain" (all near Rocky Springs).

---

likely here, Moravians or Quakers.
[150] Frederick County Original Wills, Box 1, folder 67, Maryland Archives Hall of Records. Unselt came to America on the same ship with Hoffman and Weiss. See below, p. 182.
[151] C/S: LG E:271, 273; Patents: EI 6:684-686.
[152] A photograph of the six-story Kemp's mill appears in Williams, op. cit., opposite p. 40. There it is dated 1785, although reference to Kemp's Mill had already been made in the November 1768 Frederick Court records.
[153] Prince George's County Land Records, EE:6.
[154] C/S: BY & GS 1:611.
[155] Frederick County Wills, A1:10.
[156] Prince George's County Land Records, BB:431. See pp. 259, 274.

Gilbert Kemp's wife was Susanna Margaret Getzendanner, a daughter of Christian Getzendanner. They were sponsors for the first baptism to be entered in the Frederick Lutheran Church Book, that of Isaac Lehnert's son on October 3, 1742.

Frederick Kemp (1725-1804) served in Stephen Ramsburg's Militia Company of 1757. Like his brothers, he also held land over a wide area. His surveys included "Low Kemper" and "Country Seat" (near his father's land), but also "Kemp's Discovery" (near present-day Mount St. Mary's), "Cary's Good Will" (near High Nob), "Rocky Springs" and "Peace and Plenty" (both in today's Emmitsburg District) and "Kemp's Bottom" (55 acres, August 14, 1754). At his home near Rocky Springs, Reformed conferences were held under the leadership of Pastor Philip William Otterbein. Out of these gatherings grew the United Brethren in Christ, whose organizational meeting in 1800 was held at Frederick Kemp's home. Christian Newcomer, Bishop of the United Brethren Church from 1813 until his death in 1830, was a frequent visitor, and Frederick Kemp's son Peter Kemp likewise became a U.B. minister.[157]

The youngest son **Hans Peter Kemp** (1727-1808) also served with Stephen Ramsburg's Militia Company in 1757. Initially he had land surveyed near Indian Springs, including "Finley's Last Chance" and "Rich Bottom." When he wrote his will on December 3, 1807, however, Peter Kemp was devising to his wife his house and two half lots in New Market.[158] About 1750 he had married Anna Catharina Schaub, daughter of Martin Schaub, Sr. Her brother Martin Schaub, Jr., a short while later married Peter's sister Maria Sophia Kemp.

Jacob and **Melchior Staley**, presumably brothers, also lived along the German Monocacy Road in the southern area. With them later was a third namesake called **Jacob Staley the Younger** who very likely was a similarly named third brother. Their anglicized surname was used in offical records, but in church records and wills they continued for a long while to call themselves **Stehli** or a variant thereof. They were Swiss and were the sons of Heinrich Stehli and Maria Steinbrüchel who lived at Maschwanden, southwest of Zürich. A definite tie has not been established to similar namesakes found on the Philadelphia arrival lists, for their particulars are not entirely consistent with what we know both in Switzerland and in Maryland. Jacob Staley, for example, was naturalized on October 19, 1743.[159] Since one of the requirements for such naturalization was residence in the Colonies for at least seven years, he presumably came before 1736. The Swiss records show Jacob Stehli baptized in 1698, his brother Hans Jacob in 1703 and the third brother Melchior in 1719. In the Philadelphia port arrival lists, however, a Jacob Steli arrived on September 25, 1732 who said he was born in 1707c. He came with Philipp Ernst Grüber and Johann Georg Honig, both of whom we shall

---

[157] Hinke, *Reformed Ministers, op. cit.*, pp. 71-79. Charles R. Miller and William L. Raker, *The Histories of the Pennsylvania and Central Pennsylvania Conferences of the Evangelical United Brethren Church* (n.s., 1968), p. 37, includes a photograph of the Kemp home.
[158] Frederick County Wills, GMRB 1:398.
[159] Provincial Court Records, 1742-1744, EI 7:296.

meet shortly in the Monocacy area. But a Jacob Stelly (born 1715c) who arrived on August 26, 1735 is also a possibility.[160] Johann Jacob Stahl, born 1708c, arrived at Philadelphia on September 5, 1738, and with him came Melcher or Melichor Stall (he could not write his name), born 1717c.[161] The latter date looks reasonably close.

In any event, they were in Maryland before 1741 when unique names given to the parcels of land they were buying on time from Daniel Dulany signaled the specific tie to their origins in Switzerland. Their first tract, "Switzerland," consisting of 150 acres, was surveyed for Dulany on November 21, 1741 and was patented to Jacob Staley on September 29, 1744. It was located "on a little hill above a spring that falls into a meadow on the east side of Catoctin Mountain and at the foot thereof."[162] In present-day terms this was between Rocky Springs and Indian Springs. Jacob Staley made this his home plantation and devised it by his 1760 will to his sons.[163] On December 10, 1741 Dulany had tracts surveyed for both men, "Otersum" for Jacob Staley[164] and "Masswander" for Melchior Staley.[165] The latter parcel gave the clue to the church records at Maschwanden where a birth date for Melchior Steheli was discovered which matched his birth record found in Frederick.[166]

The tendency to infer English cognates when viewing German proper names was a failing among early English scribes just as it may be for present-day historians. But, having discovered the true origin of "Masswander" as Maschwanden, one is encouraged to look for a German or Swiss place name in relation to "Otersum." The village of Ottersheim just east of Landau in the Palatinate[167] immediately comes

---

[160] Strassburger-Hinke, op. cit., Lists 24ABC, pp. 87-91; Lists 40ABC, pp. 143-154.

[161] Ibid., Lists 52ABC, pp. 198-203. After 1741 a Melcher Steheli arrived August 30, 1743 (Lists 96ABC), Hans Jacob Ställy August 30, 1749 (List 125C), Jacob Stehli September 11, 1749 (List 129C), Jacob Steli October 4, 1751 (List 174C), Jacob Steeli October 20, 1752, etc. See ibid., passim. Some eleven different Jacob Stehlis and ten different Hans Jacob Stehlis appear about this time in the Maschwanden marriage records alone! The practice of naming sons Jacob and Hans Jacob within the same family was common in Maschwanden.

[162] C/S: LG E:377; Patent: PT 2:166.

[163] Frederick County Wills, A1:218.

[164] C/S: LG E:384; Patent: PT 2:195.

[165] C/S: LG E:589; Patent: LG C:539, April 26, 1746.

[166] Credit for this discovery should be given Gary Myers-Bruggey, who has generously made available the results of his Staley family research. The record in Frederick of Melchior Staley's birth may be derived from his age at death as given in E. W. Reinecke's transcription of the Frederick Reformed Church Book. Reinecke added a record of burials not found in the original Schlatter or Brunner Church Books which he reportedly found on loose scraps of paper written in German by the Rev. William Runckel, Reformed pastor in Frederick from 1784 to 1801.

[167] Credit for this suggestion should again go to Gary Myer-

to mind. In the Reformed Church Book there, no Stehli's are to be found. But married in Ottersheim in 1730 were Johann Theobald Traut from Impflingen and Anna Margaretha Rebstock, who arrived at Philadelphia on August 27, 1733 with a host of other future Marylanders.[168] Also from Ottersheim were Wilhelm Humbert and his wife Anna Barbara Deg who reached Philadelphia on September 29, 1750.[169] As William Umphart, a German Protestant, he applied for a land warrant in Maryland on December 23, 1751 and had 150 acres surveyed on April 25, 1752 as "Umphart's Delight."[170] Wilhelm and Barbara Humbert next appear on August 16, 1754 at the baptism of their daughter Catharina Humbert.[171] Sponsors at the baptism were Henrich Funck and Cathar[ina] Trautin. Two years later Henry Funck was marrying Jacob Staley's step-daughter Catharina. The circle is complete: After Theobald Traut's early death about 1738, his widow Anna Margaretha Rebstock Traut from Ottersheim married as her second husband Jacob Staley from Maschwanden. Jacob Staley's "Otersum" was thus named for his wife's village, not his own.

The certificate of survey for "Otersum" indicated that the beginning point for its 100 acres lay 100 yards from Martain Shoup's Spring Branch and on its east side. Only twelve days before, on November 28, 1741, Dulany had had "Mankine" surveyed for Martin Shoup [Schaub], and the two parcels were thus laid out contiguously. Actually the land on which "Otersum" was to lie had been previously surveyed for Philemon Lloyd and Dr. Charles Carroll[172] who assigned rights to Jacob Staley. It was patented to Staley on December 24, 1744. On May 10, 1750 Jacob Staley enlarged this tract to 423 acres,[173] which ultimately he devised to his sons. After 1743 Jacob Staley acquired additional parcels of land. In 1749 he received the patent for "Craime's Quietness" at Hawbottom in the Middletown Valley, having purchased it from Daniel Dulany for whom it had been originally surveyed on November 22, 1741,[174] the day after the survey

---

Bruggey. The Ottersheim in question bears the German postal number 6741. Another Ottersheim, 6719, situated west of Worms and north of Grünstadt, was a Lutheran community.
[168] Strassburger-Hinke, op. cit., Lists 30AA'BC, pp. 113-115, 765-767. With them were Hans Beter Hoffman, Georg Friederich Unseldt, Frantz Weiss, Hans Jurigh Ley and others.
[169] Strassburger-Hinke, op. cit., List 157C, p. 445.
[170] C/S: BC & GS 12:109 was assigned to Catherine Toms who in 1759 received the Patent: BC & GS 8:626. William Humbert held other land in Frederick County, including "Peru," a part of the "Resurvey on Mistaken Friend" (Frederick County Land Records, H:516), a part of "Second Choice (ibid., M:92) and "Humberts Resurvey" (C/S: BC & GS 47:294), all in today's Myersville area of Jackson District.
[171] Frederick Reformed Church Book, p. 33.
[172] See above, pp 3-8. Since the land had been cultivated but no rights were made good, a special warrant was required.
[173] C/S: Y & S 7:208; Patent: BC & GS 4:223. Here the tract's name was spelled "Othersam" and "Othersum."
[174] C/S: BY & GS 1:628.

for "Switzerland." A parcel known as "The Good Wife," consisting of 87 acres, was surveyed for Jacob Staley himself and was patented to him in 1753.[175] Other surveys included "Jacob's Contrivance," "Second Chance" and "Staley's New Addition." Jacob Staley in 1749 was one of Nicholas Bundrick's creditors.[176] In 1754 he was appointed overseer of the road "from Fredericktown to Jacob Peck's Mill," a road which approximated today's State Route 73 from Frederick to Yellow Springs. Staley's Gap, where U.S. Highway 40 crosses Catoctin Mountain south of High Knob, was named for this family.

On November 21, 1760 Jacob Staley deeded "The Good Wife" to Henry Funk, husband of his stepdaughter Catharina [Traut].[177] As Jacob Steyley he signed his will on December 12, 1760, and a month later in January 1761 it was probated. In it he named his wife Margaretha, daughters Anna Maria Shorb and Phillibinah Steyley and sons Jacob, Henry and Joseph.[178] In February his daughter Anna Maria, who had been married to Hans Georg Schaub, married Adam Hildebrand. In April his widow Margaretha Staley signed her will, which was probated eleven days later. And finally in September, to cap an eventful year, his daughter Philippina married Christoph Stoll.[179] After the death of the latter, Philippina Stoll in 1794 married Balthasar Getzendanner as his second wife.

An interesting provision in Margaretha Staley's will directed that their son Joseph be educated in an "English" school. Thereafter in a number of successive deeds involving all three sons, Jacob and Henry always signed in German script, while Joseph signed in English. A series of these deeds, dated November 19, 1772 after all three sons had reached their majority, divided between them "Switzerland," the "Resurvey on Othersum" and "Scythe."[180] The latter was a small parcel of just over 11 acres received from Charles Beatty in an exchange to even out property lines. "Craime's Quietness" had been conveyed during the elder Jacob Staley's lifetime to a "Jacob Staley the Younger," but the deed had not been recorded. The latter's son Henry Staley finally received title from the same three brothers on June 4, 1796.[181]

Melchior Staley, according to Frederick Reformed Church records which spelled his name as Steheli, was born June 5, 1719c and died March 21, 1791. The indicated birth date compares with a like date found in the Maschwanden Reformed Church records in Switzerland. His wife Anna Barbara was born December 26, 1726c and died April 3, 1790. They located their "Masswander" property along the German Monocacy Road directly adjacent to Jacob Staley's "Switzerland." Much later, Melchior Staley acquired a number of other parcels of land, including first in 1752 a small 7-acre tract in

---
[175] C/S: BC & GS 1:135.
[176] Cf. above, p. 157.
[177] Frederick County Land Records, F:1236. Funk also received land on March 21, 1761 from Nicholas Shaffer, et al. (ibid., F:1308).
[178] Frederick County Wills, A1:150.
[179] Frederick Reformed Church Book.
[180] Frederick County Land Records, P:457-462.
[181] Frederick County Land Records, WR 14:282-285.

Middletown Valley called "Onondrandy."[182] This was increased to 93 acres by his "Resurvey on Onondrandy" in 1764.[183] "Hat Wheel," which had been surveyed for Daniel Dulany in 1744 was finally patented in 1761 to Melchior Staley.[184] And his "Staley's Good Luck" was surveyed for 168 acres in 1772.[185]

In 1757 both Melchior and Jacob Staley were on the muster roll of Stephen Ramsburg's Militia Company.[186] Significantly, Jacob Staley and his wife Margaretha were sponsors at the baptism of Melchior Staley's son Jacob in 1751. There is also record of Melchior Staley's daughter Susanna Barbara for whom in 1747 Henrich Bechdolt and wife stood as baptism sponsors. A 1775 membership list for the Frederick Reformed Church included the names of Melchior Stähly, Barbara Stählin and two Jacob Stähli's in addition to the deceased Jacob Stähli's daughter Philippina Stoll and her husband Christophel Stoll. By the terms of his 1791 will, Melchior Staley left all his land to his son Jacob, who was to make compensating payments to six other unnamed children.[187] Melchior Staley signed his will by mark. The Melchior Staley who arrived at Philadelphia in 1738 signed the oaths there also by mark, thereby lending credence to the probability that they were one and the same individual.

Henry Bachdold by survey of July 17, 1743 located his land slightly north of the Staleys and adjacent to "Charles and Mary" which was surveyed the following November for Charles Hedges.[188] Bachdold called his land "Lambson." Its beginning was "on the waters of the Little Tuscarora to the westward of his plantation," thus implying his presence in the area some time before 1743.[189] Presumably he had been in the country at least since 1736 for his naturalization on October 19, 1743 supposedly required seven years presence in the Colonies.[190] Today Bachdold's land touches the Yellow Springs Road (State Route 73), and through its midst lies present-day Indian Springs Road. On October 31, 1746 during Pastor Gabriel Nasman's historic visit, Johann Friedrich, son of Heinrich Bechtold, was baptized in the Lutheran Church with Johann Friedrich Kämpf as sponsor.[191] Henry Backdolt was listed as one of the overtaxed Germans having to pay a fee to the sheriff whom Stephen Ramsburg mentioned in his complaint to the Maryland Assembly in 1748.[192] In 1749 Henry and Susanna Bachdold (or

---

[182] C/S: Y & S 7:163; Patent: Y & S 6:67.
[183] C/S: BC & GS 27:183; Patent: BC & GS 29:121.
[184] C/S: BC & GS 14:583; Patent: BC & GS 16:561.
[185] C/S: BC & GS 47:207.
[186] See below, p. 379.
[187] Frederick County Wills, GM 2:372.
[188] See above, p. 110.
[189] C/S: LG E:569.
[190] Provincial Court Judgment Records, 1742-1744, EI 7:296. As Henry Baughtall, he had taken the sacrament from Edward [Conrad] Templeman.
[191] Frederick County Lutheran Church Book, p. 9. See also above, p. 144.
[192] See below, p. 292. The printed version, *Archives of Maryland*, op. cit., 28:423, gives Backdolt's first name as Ken.

Bechtel as the name was recorded) sold their land to Jacob Peck, who operated a fulling mill on the Creek there.[193] The November Court of 1750 received a petition from "the inhabitants on the east side of the mountain on the Tuscarora, having no road into Fredericktown that can be passed over with a wagon or with loads on horseback." They asked "that a road be laid out from Fredericktown to Jacob Peck's fulling mill on the Tuscarora." This resulted in the road from Frederick to Yellow Springs. In 1753 John George Loy purchased "Lambson" from Jacob Peck for 160 pounds[194] and later devised it to his son-in-law Peter Shaver.

Isaac Miller had his "Mallingah" surveyed near present-day Bethel on March 5, 1742. It was located "on a level eastward of Isaac Miller's dwelling house and on the side of Tuscarora Creek that runs into Monocacy" — another example suggesting occupancy for some time before the survey itself was actually made.[195] Miller was another of the Germans who were naturalized in 1743 after first receiving the sacrament from Edward [Conrad] Templeman.[196] He was cited by Stephen Ramsburg in 1748 as being overtaxed by the sheriff.[197] On June 10, 1751 Isaac Miller and his wife Ursha conveyed this land to Patrick Matthews,[198] and a few months later Matthews mortgaged it to George Gordon.[199] In 1789 Adam Reass had the land resurveyed as 101 acres and in so doing spelled its name "Mellingah."[200] Isaac Miller also possessed "Stoney Hill" which he conveyed to Ramsburg on June 28, 1748.[201]

The surname of **Peter Shaver** or Schäffer is troublesome, and relationships, if any, to others with similar names have not been adequately resolved.[202] The last land entry made in 1743 was prepared for Peter Shaver. Yet as Peter Schaffer he was already present in "Manaquesen" on May 21, 1740 when Pastor Stöver married him to Anna Schaubin,[203] a daughter of Martin Schaub [Shoup]. Shoup was an Anabaptist and it was not until her wedding day that Anna Schaub, born in 1724, was baptized in the Lutheran Church.[204] She survived her husband and as Ann Shaver served as executrix in 1762 for the estate of Peter Shaver.[205]

---

[193] Frederick County Land Records, B:72; Maryland Rent Rolls (Frederick No. 1), 32:153.
[194] Frederick County Land Records, E:105.
[195] C/S: LG E:212.
[196] Provincial Court Judgment Records, 1742-1744, EI 7:296.
[197] See below, p. 292.
[198] Frederick County Land Records, B:399.
[199] *Ibid.*, B:443.
[200] C/S: IC F:98; Patent: IC E:343.
[201] Prince George's County Land Records, EE:456.
[202] Contrast especially the contemporary Peter Shafer (1728-1792), who married Rosina Loy, daughter of Johann Georg Loy. The latter in 1765 devised "Lambsheim" ["Lambson"] to his son-in-law Peter "Shaver"!
[203] Stöver, *op. cit.*, Marriages p. 6, No. 284.
[204] Stöver, *op. cit.*, Baptisms, p. 22. See below, p. 376.
[205] Frederick County Administrative Accounts, A1:267.

Peter Shaver's survey was called "Palentine." It was dated December 10, 1743 and began "one mile west from the dwelling house of Peter Kemp," i.e., in the area of present-day Rocky Springs.[206] Shaver had other parcels, however, which were surveyed for him after 1743. Such land included "Wolf's Home," "Cross to Night" and "Paul's Boorock." He died in 1761 leaving a will which named his wife Ann and children Henry, Peter, Christian, Martin, Jacob, David, Moses and Catharine. He devised "Palentine" and "Wolf's Home" to his sons Henry and Peter and "Cross to Night" and "Paul's Burgh[!]" to his other five sons.[207] In 1774 Henry Shaver resurveyed "Palentine" along with other parcels which had come into his possession and called the whole "Shaver's Bad Luck."[208]

In the southern portion of the Lower German Settlement, just north of "Fout's Delight," lay the land of **Isaac Leonard,** or so his name was spelled in the land and court records. But as **Isaac Lehnert** he appears as the father of the very first child listed in the Lutheran Church baptism record in October 1742. His land was "Leonard's Good Luck," surveyed on March 10, 1741 immediately south of the "main road" which is now Butterfly Lane at its intersection with Mount Phillip Road.[209] Here the German Monocacy Road turned west to climb over the Catoctin Mountain on its way to Opequon in Virginia. Until 1745 there was no connection farther south toward the mouth of the Monocacy and the Potomac River, but a petition for just such a road was submitted to the March 1745 Court of Prince George's County. Its beginning junction point was to be "above Isaac Leonard's."[210]

Sponsors for the two baptisms recorded in the Frederick Lutheran Church Book clearly indicate Lehnert's ties to the Monocacy Germans. On October 3, 1742 Johann Gilbert Kämpf and his wife [Susanna Margaret Getzendanner] stood as sponsors for Isaac's son Johann Gilbert Lehnert. On February 3, 1745 Conrad Kempff and his wife stood for Jacob Lachmann[211] and his wife as sponsors for Isaac's son Johann Jacob Lehnert.[212] Also in 1745 Van Swearingen and Isaac Leonard appeared before the Court pledging security for a "John Grist, Indian trader of Conococheague."[213] Robert Evans was fined in the same Court, on the information of Henry Touchstone, for assault on Isaac Leonard. And Leonard himself was sued for the £22 he owed John Hepburn.

---
[206] C/S: LG E:394. The reference to Peter Kemp, who was only 16 years of age in 1743, must be in error and must have referred to his father Conrad Kemp, q.v.
[207] Frederick County Wills, A1:158. The will as recorded refers to "Valentine" not "Palentine."
[208] C/S: BC & GS 51:208.
[209] C/S: BY & GS 1:204.
[210] For a further description of this road, see above, p. 54.
[211] For Lochman, see pp. 11-12, 191.
[212] Frederick Lutheran Church Book, p. 1.
[213] Grist's name appeared on the 1718 tax list in Conestoga Township along with that of Martin Chartier, John and Edmund Cartledge and others who came early to western Maryland.

Georg Friederich Unselt (1709c-1756), who does not appear in the Frederick County land records until after the period of this study, should nevertheless be mentioned at least in passing. As a 24-year old unmarried weaver, he arrived at Philadelphia on August 27, 1733 with Hans Peter Hoffman, Frantz Weiss, Johann Georg Loy, Johann Theobald Traut and others destined for future settlement in the Monocacy area.[214] But he did not accompany these shipmates there directly. Instead, he seems to have gone first to the Raritan region of New Jersey. There he associated with a small group of German Lutherans who had come to this country many years before as part of the large German migration of 1709/1710.[215] His name is found in the Janeway store accounts in Somerset County as early as December 1735 and as late as June 1741.[216] In between, the Raritan Lutheran Church records refer to him in October 1737 and September 1739 during the period when the congregation was torn by strife with its pastor Johann Augustus Wolf.[217] That we are dealing with the same man in the Monocacy area is evident from a series of baptism entries in the Frederick Lutheran Church Book. The first of these entries recorded the baptism of Unselt's eldest son Georg Friederich on August 22, 1737, with "Pastor Wolff in Yersey and his wife" as sponsors.[218]

These entries in the Frederick Lutheran Church Book were all made in 1752 by Frederick's first resident minister Pastor Bernard Michael Hausihl well after the dates of the baptisms themselves. Unmindful of their ex post facto nature, early historians erroneously inferred that the congregation was therefore formed at least by 1737. In the same vein, one would err in using these baptism dates to place the Unselt family in the Monocacy area by any given date. Analysis suggests, however, that the family moved from New Jersey to the Cocalico area of the Conestoga settlement in the summer of 1741, for Stöver recorded the baptism of their third child, Johannes, in the Muddy Creek or Cocalico Church Book on November 22, 1741.[219] He included the same entry also in his personal Journal,[220] but there Stöver indicated Ohnselt was at or from Opecken in Virginia. This would appear highly unlikely since one day earlier Stöver had married a couple at or from Swatara, some 17 miles northwest of Cocalico. Still, it could have represented an intention to move to Virginia, for

---
[214] Strassburger-Hinke, op. cit., Lists 30ABC, pp. 113-115, 765. The Captain spelled Unselt's name as Oneself.
[215] The beginnings of the New Jersey Raritan settlement are described by Norman C. Wittwer, The Faithful and the Bold (Oldwick, New Jersey, 1984).
[216] Stryker-Rodda, "Janeway Store Accounts," loc. cit., 34:81 [transcribed as Frederd Onfitt] and 35:191 [Frederick Unsalt].
[217] Simon Hart and Harry J. Kreider, Lutheran Church in New York and New Jersey, 1722-1760 (Ann Arbor, 1962), pp. 134, 152. Seemingly Unselt sided with Pastor Wolf, who claimed that he was holding services in Unselt's home.
[218] Frederick Lutheran Church Book, p. 24.
[219] Muddy Creek Lutheran Church Book, op. cit., p. 57.
[220] Stöver, op. cit., p. 42.

the child's baptism sponsors were Johannes Herr and his wife: John Herr is mentioned in Unseld's will as having land next to his in Virginia. To our knowledge, Unselt did not acquire land in Virginia until 1750 by which time he was definitely in Maryland. His whereabouts between 1742 and 1748 (either in Pennsylvania or in Virginia) therefore remains unknown. Within this period also occurred the baptism on January 13, 1744 of a fourth child, Henricus, for whom, interestingly, Unselt's 1733 shipmate Simon Lindere and his wife stood as sponsors. The baptism locale for their last child, Abraham Unselt, February 10, 1746, is likewise unknown as is the possible relationship of the sponsor, Joh. Hoffman, to Unselt's 1733 shipmate Hans Peter Hoffman.

Unselt's interest in land in the Northern Neck of Virginia can be documented. On March 27, 1750 some 248 acres were surveyed for Frederick Unsult on Tilhance Creek, a branch of Back Creek, now in Berkeley County, West Virginia. Jacob Hood assigned him another 163 acres on Back Creek at North Mountain on November 19, 1750, the same day that Frederick Unsult was a chain carrier for Israel Foulson's survey next door.[221] Unselt devised the former parcel, less 66 acres sold before his death, to his son Frederick. The other parcel, next to John Herr's land, went to Unselt's son John.

Although Unselt did not possess land on "Tasker's Chance," he obviously maintained friendship with his 1733 shipmates who did settle there.[222] One of these was Hans Peter Hoffman whose will named Frantz Weiss, another shipmate, as an executor. When Weiss later wrote his own will, he named Unselt and Johann Georg Loy, a fourth shipmate, as his executors. Unselt also named Loy as one of the executors for his own will. Sometime after 1746 Unselt's wife apparently died. Between May 21, 1748 and the following March 11th Hans Peter Hoffman also died. Then, on April 2, 1749 in a Lutheran service, Friederich Unseld married Hoffman's widow Maria Apollonia Hoffmann.[223] One month later, on May 7, 1749 in a Reformed Church service, Friedrich Unselt and Maria Apolonia had a child Abraham baptized.[224] Alternative hypotheses are possible, but most likely this was the same Abraham Unselt noted in the 1752 Lutheran baptism record as born in 1746.

The marriage to Hans Peter Hoffman's widow undoubtedly explains Unselt's appearance on "Tasker's Chance" in the Debt Book which postdates 1750,[225] although there is no other record of his owning property there. The Moravian missionaries Leonard Schnell and John Brandmüller have left us a description of their journey on October 26, 1749 from Jacob Weller's place (near present-day Jimtown

---

[221] Peggy Shomo Joyner, *Abstracts of Virginia's Northern Neck Warrants and Surveys, Frederick County, 1747-1780* (Portsmouth, 1985), pp. 56, 158.
[222] See below, pp. 262, 277, 294.
[223] Frederick Lutheran Church Book, p. 356.
[224] Frederick Reformed Church Book.
[225] Document #906, MS.174, Maryland Historical Society. He is listed as Mr. Unsold, but will be found in the modern Index under "Land, Unsold."

crossroads) to Frederick, a distance, they said, of 15 miles. On the way, meaning north of town, toward noon they met Friedrich Ohnsell, "who has love for us although he has no association with the Brethren."[226] This would seem to place Unselt on "Tasker's Chance," no doubt on the former Hoffman parcel. He would have lived there, if he did, only temporarily, since Hoffman's parcel under the terms of his will was to be sold or divided for the benefit of the Hoffman children when his wife remarried.

Friedrich Unselt did acquire land west of "Tasker's Chance." His parcel was called "Beauty" and was located "near the side of Little Rock Creek, a draft of Ballenger Creek" in today's Feagaville area. The land had been surveyed for Daniel Dulany on August 16, 1745. Unselt may have been purchasing it on time after that date, but it was not until July 16, 1752 that the land was patented to him.[227] In that same year 1752 Unselt was definitely living in Frederick County, serving with Conrad Grosch as Lutheran Church trustees active in arranging for the installation of the Church's first resident pastor, Bernard Michael Hausihl.[228] On January 15, 1753 "Beauty" was resurveyed. Only 90 of its original 100 acres were found to be clear of other surveys. But three pieces of adjoining vacant land were added, bringing the resurveyed total to 274 acres. It was so patented on April 25, 1754.[229] Unselt wrote his will on December 1, 1755. In it he mentioned his Virginia land noted above and his land in "West Monokesey." The latter was obviously the "Resurvey on Beauty" for it adjoined the lands of Conrad Grosch and the English minister Samuel Hunter ("Doran's Choice").[230] This Maryland land, obviously his home, was devised to his youngest sons Henry and Abraham Unselt with the house itself going to the latter.[231]

---
[226] Schnell, "Kurze Beschreibung," *loc. cit.* See above, p. 147.
[227] C/S: Y & S 7:115.
[228] Wentz, *op. cit.*, pp. 104, 113. For Hausihl, see above, p. 152.
[229] C/S: BC & GS 1:158.
[230] See below, p. 354.
[231] Frederick County Wills, A1:102, probated July 16, 1759. See also Administrative Accounts, A1:175.

UPPER GERMAN SETTLEMENT

For those early Frederick County German settlers whose arrival dates in this country have been determined, the year 1732 marked the highest level of such immigration. Up until 1738 it was likewise the year in which the largest number of ships carrying German immigrants had thus far arrived at Philadelphia, and their number was not to be exceeded again until the period 1749-1754. In these later years, however, the flow of newcomers to American shores did not extend on to Maryland as noticeably as it did in 1732. Altogether, eleven ships reached Philadelphia in 1732, eight of them at the peak of the season in a little over a month's time. This was an average of one ship every four days. Six of these ships carried passengers destined eventually to come to Maryland. Moreover, in all but one instance the future Marylanders arrived together rather than singly. If a ship carried a family found later in Frederick County, it carried one or more other families who later appeared there, too.

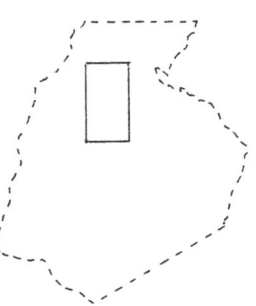

In total, some sixteen future Maryland families are known to have arrived at Philadelphia in the fall of 1732. Coincidentally or otherwise, most of these families tended eventually to settle in the northern part of today's Frederick County, generally along the German Monocacy Road in the area between today's Thurmont and Lewistown. In general they seem not to have purchased their land on time from Daniel Dulany, but instead had their own parcels surveyed directly. Their religion was for the most part Lutheran, as opposed to the more concentrated settlement of the Reformed people farther south. As with other German immigrants, there is a maddening gap of some years after their arrival in this country during which time their whereabouts has not in all cases been established. Still, at least six of them are known to have settled just west of the Susquehanna River near today's Canadochly Creek and to have been engaged in the border dispute with the Pennsylvanian authorities as late as 1736.[1] Moreover, over half of the sixteen can be found in the Lancaster Lutheran Church records of Pastor Stöver.

The town of Lancaster was established in 1730 and Stöver probably began a Lutheran Church Book there some three years later.[2]

---
[1] Michael Reisner, Anton Bannkauf, Philipp Ernst Grüber, Bernard Weymer, Lenhart Firohr, Joh. Georg Baer, and Jacob Matthias Manser. See also above, pp. 17-19.

[2] Glatfelter, op. cit., especially pp. 139-140, 316-318. For

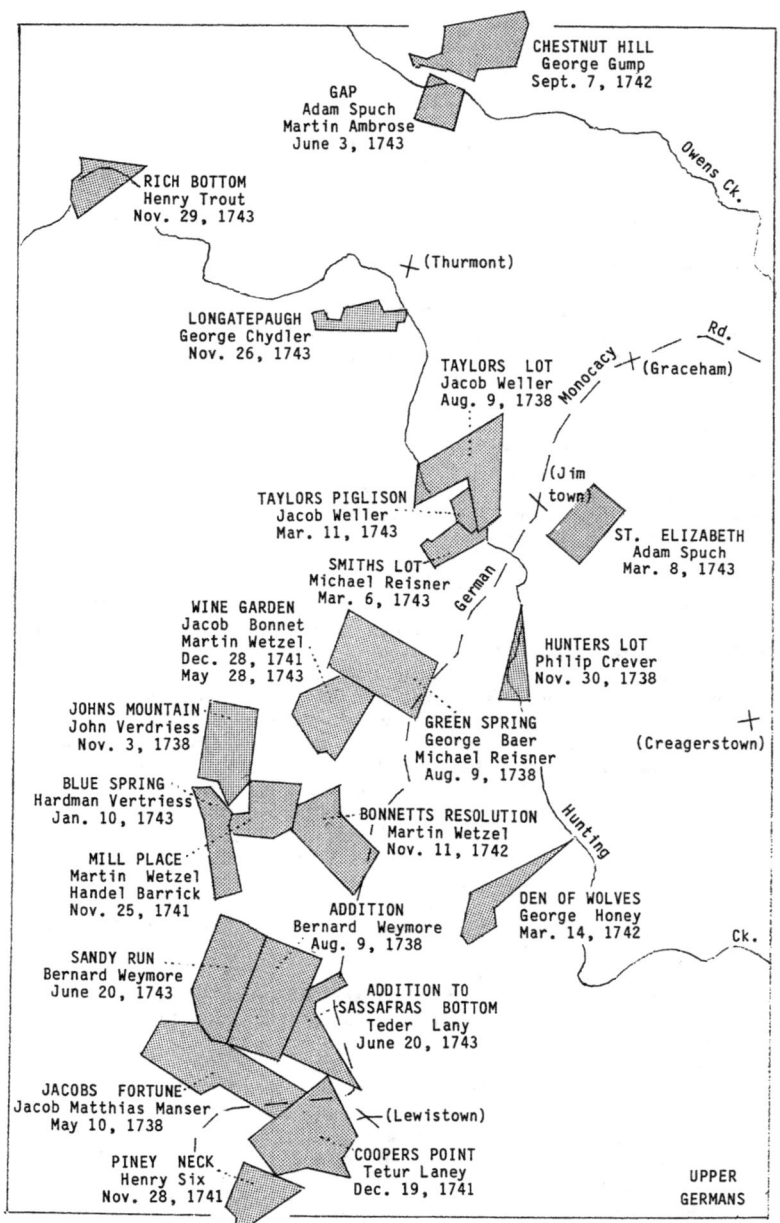

At the time, congregations had not been organized farther west so that his ministerial acts which appear in the Lancaster Church Book may be considered as encompassing Lancaster and all the area beyond, i.e., even across the Susquehanna River to the west. Finding a name in the Lancaster Church Book therefore does not categorically locate the individual within today's Lancaster County. But it does account for the person's presence in today's Pennsylvania and helps to fill the time gap until he can be definitely located in Maryland.

It is most interesting to note that of all those Germans named in the Lancaster Lutheran Church Book who later appear in Frederick County, Maryland, only a scattered one or two had later ties to "Tasker's Chance," "Monocacy Manor" or the Lower German Settlement described in the previous chapter. All the others -- Sinn (at least initially), Schmidt, Reisner, Gruber, Honig, Mattheis, Weller and Miller -- appear in the Upper German area. Although there is danger in over-generalization, one might also observe that while there is duplication of Maryland *names* between the Lancaster Lutheran Church Book and Stöver's personal Journal, only a few of their respective *entries* duplicate one another in the two records.

Farther east in the Conestoga area of Lancaster County, also about 1733, Pastor Stöver began a church book for the fledgling Lutheran congregation at Muddy Creek in today's East Cocalico Township.[3] From these records the earlier whereabouts of three more future residents in the Upper German area may be added, namely Gump, Ambrose and Verdriess. Still farther east, in today's western Montgomery County, Pennsylvania, we encounter Dieter Lehnich.

While we are thus able to account for a number of the 1732 arrivals in Pennsylvania before they came to Maryland, it does seem probable that they were living on Maryland land some time before title to that land was actually theirs. None of them appeared on the 1733 list of Monocosie Taxables.[4] Likewise, though one should hardly expect recently arrived Germans to be growing such an unfamiliar crop so soon, none appeared on the 1734 list of those individuals failing to burn their tobacco properly.[5] By 1736, however, Johann Georg Gump was definitely in present-day Frederick County, and by 1738 we have word also of Philip Ernst Grüber, George Baer, Bernard Weymar, Matthias Mansser, Matthias Ambrose and Valentin Müller. Then Heinrich Sinn, Hans Michael Reisner and Johann Georg Honig followed sometime before 1739. This leaves, from out of the list of 1732 arrivals, only Peter Apple, Johann Peter Schmidt, Hans Michael Werffle, Leonard Moser and Johannes Taffelmeyer who do not make their appearances in Maryland documents or evidence known to us until the 1740s.

Johann Georg Gump was one of the first of this group to reach Philadelphia. He arrived on September 18, 1732 aboard the *Johnson Galley* of London, and with him came Henrich Sinn and

---
bibliographic reference to a transcription of the Lancaster Lutheran Church Book, see above, p. 158n.
[3] Cf. above, p. 159n.
[4] See below, pp. 368-369.
[5] Cf. above, pp. 61-62.

Johann Peter Schmitt. Gump went first to Conestoga in the Muddy Creek area in today's East Calico Township of northeastern Lancaster County, where in the Lutheran Church Book Stöver listed four baptism entries for his children between 1733 and 1739. These entries are not repeated in Stöver's personal Journal, leading to the suspicion that Gump may have remained in Pennsylvania until at least 1739. But only the first child (Johann Georg Gump, Jr., 1733) had a sponsor who continued in the Muddy Creek area. Sponsors for the other children were recognizably from Monocacy, including for Andreas Gump in 1736 Johann Jacob and Margaretha Mattheis, for Catharina Barbara Gump in 1737 Anna Barbara Teuffelsbissin and for Johannes Gump in 1739 Mattheis and Anna Barbara Rössel.

By 1736 Gump was well enough established in Maryland for the Prince George's County Court to name him Constable of the area. It was a distinct honor for a German and one that was seldom repeated in later years. Gump sensed the difficulties and petitioned the March Court to be excused from duty because he was "a new settler and could not read or write or speak English." The records show that Thomas Gittings was appointed in his place.[6] Although Gump was later to become a Moravian, he served as a Lutheran baptism sponsor on June 7, 1738 for the daughter of Heinrich Fortunee[7] and contributed to the purchase of the first Lutheran Church Book about 1742. Also in 1742 he signed the petition to divide Prince George's Parish.[8] Interestingly he took English communion on April 9, 1746 prior to naturalization the following day.[9] This was some three years after the known naturalization proceedings for most other Germans.

It was not until September 7, 1742 that Gump's land records begin. On that date "Chestnut Hill" was surveyed for him, with a beginning point "80 perches from Ambrose's Mill"[10] This placed him in today's Roddy Road area on Owens Creek north of Thurmont, about two miles north of where the German Monocacy Road turned south at present-day Graceham. In 1745 Gump had Thomas Cresap survey adjacent land for him which he called "Four Springs."[11] By 1749, however, Gump had apparently moved to the area southwest of today's city of Frederick. The clue lies in the diaries of the Moravian missionaries Johann Leonhard Schnell[12] and August Gottlieb Spangenberg.[13] On August 3, 1748, bound back to Bethlehem, Pennsylvania from his trip to Virginia, Spangenberg stayed overnight with Georg Gump before traveling north via Frederick town to Manakasie. Schnell and Brandmüller on October 29th of the following year continued their journey from Jacob Weller's place near today's Jimtown crossroads southward a distance of 15 miles to arrive about noon at Friedrich Ohnsell's place,

---
[6] See above, p. 92.
[7] Stöver, op. cit., p. 18. Significantly the Fortunee name, or its variants, does not appear in the Muddy Creek Church Book.
[8] See below, p. 371: Geo. Gomph.
[9] Provincial Court Judgment Records, EI 10:44.
[10] C/S: LG E:102. For Ambrose, see below, p. 202.
[11] C/S: LG E:354.
[12] Schnell, "Kurze Beschreibung," *loc. cit.*
[13] [Spangenberg,] "Kurze Nachricht," *loc. cit.*

the former Hoffman parcel on "Tasker's Chance," north of Frederick.[14] They continued on to Friedrichstawn where they "visited the old Jesrang, who was somewhat friendly."[15] Then, four miles from town and now enroute to Jonathan Hager's in today's Washington County, they came towards evening to the home of Georg Gumpf, where they stayed the night.

Their route suggests that Gump was then occupying land on or near the 167 acres of "Addition to Carrollton" which he later purchased from Charles Carroll in February 1752.[16] This land lay just south of today's Feagaville and west of the land of Christian Kemp. More land was subsequently added with the survey of a parcel called "Hueffianhart" which was patented to Gump in 1753[17] and then sold to George Zimmerman for £900 in 1762.[18] Still more land in the Owens Creek area was surveyed as "Gump's Addition" in 1755, and on this parcel's survey the beginning point was marked "at the foot of Catoctin Mountain at George Gump's resurvey."[19] Also in 1755 George Gump had a survey made for "Germantown" which lay about a mile and a half from Michael Reisner's plantation.[20] Title to the "Chestnut Hill" parcel passed in 1769 to John Gump. In 1772 George Gump, Jr. and his wife Sarah, then living in York County, Pennsylvania, conveyed parts of the Gump land located along the German Monocacy Road to Daniel McCormack.[21]

Gump's ties to the Moravians were further described by Schnell in his Diary entry for October 29, 1749: "John Jacob Weller and Adam Gamb were also there [at the Gump home]. In the evening I conducted a song service at which several newcomers were present. I also at the same time baptized the little daughter of Brother Gumpf, Dorthea. We felt at home in this house...."[22]

Henry Sinn, who came to this country with George Gump, is noted in the chapter pertaining to "Tasker's Chance."[23] A third fellow passenger, **Johann Peter Schmidt**, was naturalized in Maryland on May 3, 1740 with a group probably living on "Tasker's Chance."[24] On October 11, 1742 he married Eva Rosina Faut, eldest daughter of Jacob Fout.[25] Only a few days before, Peter "Smith" joined some 22 other Germans on the petition to divide Prince George's Parish.[26] He and his wife appear frequently in the Frederick County Lutheran Church records as sponsors or as the parents of baptised children, including

---

[14] See pp. 183, 278.
[15] Bartholomäus Jesserang from Thalleischweiler, Germany. He arrived at Philadelphia on September 3, 1739.
[16] Frederick County Land Records, B:515.
[17] C/S: BC & GS 1:152.
[18] Frederick County Land Records, H:9.
[19] C/S: BC & GS 1:318.
[20] C/S: BC & GS 14:422.
[21] Frederick County Land Records, P:320.
[22] Schnell, "Kurze Beschreibung," *loc. cit.*
[23] See also below, p. 190.
[24] See below, p. 260.
[25] Stöver, *op. cit.*, Marriages, p. 7, No. 383.
[26] *Ibid.*, p. 371.

their own Johann Peter Schmidt in 1744 and Maria Margaretha Schmidt in 1750. But the records yield no information concerning their landholdings in Frederick County. It is unlikely, as has been claimed, that Johann Peter Schmidt was the same as the John Smith for whom "Addition to New Germany" was surveyed at today's junction of Butterfly Lane and Mount Phillip Road, west of Frederick.

The earliest date of a land survey for a German in present-day Frederick County was dated May 10, 1738. Called "Jacob's Fortune," the tract's 242 acres were surveyed for Jacob Mathias Minsher. As **Jacob Matthias Manser,** he had arrived at Philadelphia on October 17, 1732 along with Bernard Weymer and Johann Peter Apfel. They had come on the ship *John and William,* the last ship to arrive with immigrants before the 1732 winter season closed the port.[27] Both Manser and Weymer settled first on the west side of the Susquehanna River along with Thomas Cresap, Michael Reisner and the others who were claiming the land as Marylanders. We have previously noted the arrest of Jacob Matthias "Manshaw" in late 1736 and his being carried off to jail in Philadelphia.[28] Obviously his 1738 survey in the German Monocacy area reflected the necessity or the eventual desires of some of the group, Manser included, to live in less disputed territory. Further, it is apparent that even though Jacob Mathias Minsher's survey of "Jacob's Fortune" bore the earliest survey date for a German,[29] others must have come with him at about the same time: His survey had as its beginning point the southwest corner of Bernard Wamar's land, thereby indicating that Weymer was also there then at least as a squatter.

Jacob Mansser witnessed the baptism of Heinrich Sinn's son Jacob Mattheis Sinn on June 17, 1739.[30] Then on September 1, 1740 he made an interesting assignment of his land to the same Henry Sinn. The Provincial Court record notes that "Minsher has inlisted himself in his Majesty's Service in the Expedition against some of the Catholick [Spanish] King's Territories in the West Indies and therefore, in order to settle and improve the parcel of land," Henry Sinn was to have possession of "Jacob's Fortune" and its 242 acres "during the whole term that the said Jacob shall be out of this Province and if it should appear that the said Jacob dye or be killed in the expedition," title to the land was to pass to Henry Sinn during his natural life. After his death it was to go to Jacob Mathias Sinn, youngest son of Henry Sinn, the same child for whom Mansser had been a baptism sponsor just the year before. Should Minsher return, however, "they shall deliver and give up the said tract with all improvements."[31] Presuma-

---

[27] Strassburger-Hinke, *op. cit.,* Lists 28 ABC, pp. 102-106. Jacob Mattheus Manser was unmarried at the time of his arrival.
[28] See above, p. 18.
[29] Patented Survey, Prince George's County, No. 1164. No parcel name appeared on the survey, but as "Jacob's Fortune" the parcel was patented to Jacob Mathias Minsher on August 8, 1738 (Patent: EI 2:719).
[30] Stöver, *op. cit.,* p. 32.
[31] Provincial Court (Land Records), EI 3:193. Curiously, the clerk transcribed, without questioning it, what he thought he saw: he called

bly he did not return, for subsequent land records yield no more word of him as either Manser or Minsher.

Bernard Weymer (later Weymore) likewise arrived at Philadelphia on October 17, 1732 along with his wife Barbara and son Johannes. He, too, lived initially west of the Susquehanna in Cresap's neighborhood and was mentioned in the deposition of October 18, 1735 by Jacob Lochman.[32] The latter described an attack on his home, located two miles south of Little Cadorus Creek within a hundred yards of the main wagon road. During the raid, which was led by Robert Buchanan, High Sheriff for Lancaster County, Lochman's door was forced open, and an attempt was made to carry him off by force, while whipping his wife in the process. Lochman offered security to appear in court, but it was refused. He was carried as a prisoner to the Susquehanna River, enroute to jail in Lancaster, but there the arresting party was met by five "Dutchmen." A fight ensued and Lochman was knocked unconscious. Buchanan himself was taken captive by the Germans who carried him to Cresap's home. The five "Dutchmen" were listed as Barnett Weymour, Michl. Risenar, Feltie Craw, Leonard Feeroar[33] and Francis Clapsaddle.[34]

Like Manser, Bernard Weymore had land surveyed in the German Monocacy area. The survey was dated [if not actually made!] on August 9, 1738, the day after Manser had his "Jacob's
---
Sinn's son Qilathias Sinn! See also Maryland Rent Rolls (Calvert, Prince George's, Frederick No. 2), 4:514-515.

[32] Jacob Lochmann (1709c-1764) married both his wives in Lancaster, i.e., Elisabeth Haffner presumably before 1735 and, in 1750, Maria Catharina Dielforter. The latter was reputedly born at Gernborn [Gersbach?] in the duchy of Zweibrücken March 15, 1715, married first Engelhard Süssmann (who died in Germany), and came to America in 1749 (not found in Strassburger-Hinke, op. cit.) with two of her daughters. Jacob Lochman and his [first?] wife were listed as sponsors on February 3, 1745 for the Lutheran baptism of Isaac Lehnert's son Johann Jacob, although Conrad Kemp and his wife stood in their place. A daughter, Dorothea Lochman (1743-1794) married a Peter Brunner. Jacob Lochman came to Maryland in 1752 with his second wife and was a grand juror in June 1758 (Rice, The Life, op. cit., p. 177). Although his second wife was originally of the Reformed faith, they joined the Moravians in 1757, were probationers in June 1762 and communicants January 1, 1763. He died in his 55th year on February 13, 1764 [1765?], she on January 13, 1788. They were buried in the Moravian cemetery at Graceham. (Graceham Parish Register, transcribed in 1942 by Henry James Young; Frdk. Co. Wills A1:235.)

[33] Lenhart Firohr was 24 when he arrived at Philadelphia on September 21, 1731. He had come on the same ship as the Wetzels and Devilbisses, q.v. With "his bride Maria Barbara Willhautin," he stood, according to Lancaster Lutheran Church Records, as baptism sponsor on September 15, 1734 for a child of John Quickel. He died before Maria Barbara married in 1738 Johann Jacob Weller as her second husband.

[34] Proceedings of Council, 1732-1753, Archives of Maryland, op. cit., 28:82-84.

Fortune" patented. Surveys of "Green Spring" for George Baer and "Taylor's Lot" for Jacob Weller were also dated August 9, 1738. Weymer's survey was for 211 acres and was called "Addition,"[35] a strange name for a parcel which was supposedly Weymore's first. The explanation lies in the difference between dates of actual settlement and dates of the surveys themselves. Clearly Weymore had arrived in Maryland earlier than 1738. For one reason or another he had not surveyed or at least had not dated and presented for recording the survey for land on which he was at first a squatter and which he called "Sandy Run." When the survey for "Sandy Run" was actually made, on June 20, 1743, its certificate noted that already "on this tract are a large log house and a barn and a stable and a dairy and two wheat fields,"[36] certainly indicative of a somewhat lengthy period of settlement before the survey itself. During this prior period of settlement a second parcel (therefore called "Addition") was added to the first parcel ("Sandy Run") and its survey was completed and recorded on August 9, 1738. "Addition" was located next to Manser's "Jacob's Fortune," a little west of the German Monocacy Road and about a mile and a half south of present-day Catoctin Furnace. Since Manser's land began "at a corner of Bernard Wamar's land," we have the suggestion that regardless of survey dates, Weymer actually settled there first! The certificate of survey for the June 20, 1743 survey on "Sandy Run" noted the point of its beginning as "his former tree as he said it is, above his plantation near the foot of Kittoktin Mountain."

In 1739 Pastor Stöver baptised Weymore's son and namesake, entering the name in his Journal as Joh. Bernardt Weinmar. Martin Wetzel and his wife Barbara stood as sponsors. Bernard Weymore signed the 1740 petition for a road to the English church at present-day Beallsville, and in 1747 his son-in-law Friederich Willhaut was one of those signing Pastor Muhlenberg's Articles written in the Frederick Lutheran Church Book. Later Weymore became indebted to Robert Debutts for 155½ pounds of tobacco. Unable to pay, Weymore was sued in the November Court of 1750. The same Court appointed him overseer of the road from Ambrose's Mill to Abraham Miller's Mill, but spelled his name Barnett Waymar. That road in present-day terms extended from Thurmont to Lewistown. The March Court of 1751/52 noted that a suit of John House against Barnet Waymour had been "abated by death of the plaintiff." In subsequent land transactions, Bernard Weymore and his wife Barbara conveyed 50 acres of "Sandy Run" to their son John, who in 1753 deeded it to Valentine Shortacer [Shydacker].[37] Weymore also assigned 100 acres of "Addition" to his son-in-law Frederick Woollyard. A 1769 deed traces the history of Lot 5 on Caspar Myer's "Longacres," now a part of Frederick city.[38] Myer transferred it to John Creager, who left it to his wife Catherine. She married Bernard Weymore (Jr.) and then died

---

[35] C/S: LG E:340.
[36] C.S: LG E:317.
[37] Frederick County Land Records, E:176. The 1873 Atlas shows G. J. Doll's home on the original "Sandy Run" (Lake, op. cit., p. 15).
[38] See below, p. 266.

herself. After her death Myers repossessed the land for non-payment by Creager and then sold it to Charles Beatty.[39]

Georg Baer, Hans Michael Reisner and Hans Georg Soldner crossed the ocean together on the ship *Dragon*, but when they arrived at Philadelphia on September 30, 1732, Baer was too sick to take his oaths at the Philadelphia Court House. Consequently he appears only on the Ship's list prepared by the Captain, who spelled his name as George "Bare."[40] In November 1736 John George Bare was present in the Canadochly area of today's York County, Pennsylvania when the posse from Lancaster attacked Thomas Cresap's home and burned it to the ground. Bare was "seized and carried prisoner with blood running down his face.[41] The Maryland land records further suggest that Baer kept in close touch with one or both of his former shipmates. On August 9, 1738 he had a parcel of land surveyed "in a part of the backland of the border of the [Maryland] Province on the west side of the Monocacy in the forks of Hunting Creek, 160 perches west from the said creek." This was "Green Spring," which without further explanation was patented on February 8, 1738/39, not to Baer, but to Michael Reisner![42] Baer may then have gone to live on "Bear's Den," one of the most easterly parcels carved out of "Tasker's Chance." He was naturalized on May 3, 1740 with a group of other Maryland Germans living on this tract. On September 21, 1740 Joh. Georg Beer had his four-month old daughter Catarina Barbara baptised by Pastor Stöver at "Manackesen" with Joh. Georg Lay and Catarina Barbara Rüssel as sponsors,[43] and in 1742 as George Bare he appeared as one of the petitioners seeking to divide Prince George's Parish. He was a witness, along with Mathias Reislin, certifying that John Verdress had taken Lutheran communion in June of 1743 preparatory to naturalization.[44] Thereafter we hear no more of Baer except for the claim by J. Thomas Scharf that George Baer, Sr., born in Germany, had been buried in the old German Reformed Cemetery in Frederick town, but with a gravestone which was not otherwise legible.[45] "Bear Den" was never conveyed to George Baer, but went instead in 1746 to Jacob Stoner whose son John Stoner deeded it in 1767 to Baltis Getzendanner.[46]

The exploits of **Michael Reisner** with Thomas Cresap and others in the border struggle between Maryland and Pennsylvania have been mentioned above.[47] The evidence is fragmentary, but we do know that

---

[39] Frederick County Land Records, M:57.
[40] Strassburger-Hinke, *op. cit.*, Lists 26 ABC, pp. 96-99.
[41] Affidavit of Sophia Cannon, age 28, December 27, 1736 in Baltimore County, *Maryland Historical Magazine*, *loc. cit.*, 3:44-45.
[42] C/S: LG C:35. Patent: EI 4:540.
[43] Stöver, *op. cit.*, p. 23.
[44] Provincial Court Judgment Records, 1742-1744, EI 7:296.
[45] J. Thomas Scharf, *History of Western Maryland* (Philadelphia, 1882), 1:525. He or his helpers read 15 inscriptions remaining in 1881 at the time the original Reformed Church and Cemetery made way for the present Trinity Chapel on Church Street between Market and Court Streets. See also Holdcraft, *op. cit.*, pp. 24, 1289.
[46] See below, pp. 289-290.

Reisner was one of the eight men arrested for activities with Cresap in 1734 in the Canadochly area west of the Susquehanna River and that two years later he was taken off to the jail in Philadelphia with Cresap, Jacob Mansher and Miles Foy. In the latter fracus the Pennsylvania authorities claimed Reisner mistakenly shot and killed Loughlin Malone, another member of Cresap's group.[48] The impression is gained that Reisner, like Cresap, was perhaps the least likely to be intimidated or pushed too far by the Pennsylvanians. Yet for all his bellicosity he, too, eventually retired to the backwoods above the Monocacy where he and others from Cresap's group formed the nucleus of the German settlement in the northern reaches of present-day Frederick County.

It was Stöver's custom to indicate the father of the children he was baptizing together with a single place name associated with that father. It did not necessarily mean that the baptism occurred at that place or that the family lived at that locale when each of the baptisms took place even though Stöver grouped them under the single family heading. For Michael Reusner, Pastor Stöver marked the locale as Manaquesen and listed two children: 1) Catarina Barbara Reusner, born November 13, 1734, baptized January 1, 1735, sponsor: Anna Catarina Beyerlin, and 2) Anna Eliesabetha Reusner, born January 5, 1739, baptized December 15, 1739 [sic]; sponsors: Michael Rausch and his wife.[49] While Reisner had undoubtedly taken up abode in today's Frederick County by the year 1739, it is incorrect to place him there as early as the year 1734. He and his wife Catarina appear in the Lancaster Lutheran Church Book on April 28, 1734 as sponsors for a child of Sebastian Eberle, who also lived just west of the Susquehanna River.[50]

On August 9, 1738 Reisner had a 200-acre survey made in present-day Carroll County near Silver Run.[51] It was called "Cat-tail Marsh" and was patented to him on February 8, 1738/39, the same day on which he received the patent to Baer's "Green Spring" and just five days before the corrected date of his second daughter's baptism. He conveyed "Cat-tail Marsh" to Peter Youngblood on March 13, 1742

---

[47] Cf. pp. 16-19.

[48] Proceedings of Council, 1732-1753, *Archives of Maryland*, op. cit., pp. 111-114. See p. 18.

[49] Stöver, op. cit., p. 25. This corrects the allegation of three daughters per Schantz, loc. cit. The third daughter claimed by Schantz, Catarina Barbara, born October 29, 1738 (two months before Anna Eliesabetha!) and baptized January 29, 1739 was a daughter of Anastasius Uhler of Lebanon who is listed at the top of the succeeding page in Stöver's original Journal. Stöver also entered the two correct baptism records in the Lancaster Lutheran Church Book, loc. cit., p. 407, adding Anna Elisabetha as the name of Rausch's wife and correcting the error on Anna Eliesabetha Reusner's baptism date to February 13, 1739!

[50] *Ibid.*, p. 404. This entry also appears in the York Lutheran Church Book, but not in Stöver's personal Journal. Eberle arrived at Philadelphia in 1728 on the same ship with Pastor Stöver.

[51] C/S: LG C:32; patent: EI 2:831.

and made "Green Spring" his home plantation. It can be located today a mile and a half east of Catoctin Furnace and a like distance south of Jimtown crossroads. Part of the land is now owned by Mr. Ross Stull. Nearer to "Green Spring" and exceedingly significant in the history of the Lutheran church in Frederick County, as previously discussed, were the fifty acres Reisner had surveyed in 1743 which he called "Smith's Lot."[52] This parcel was located a quarter of a mile north of the northern end of "Green Spring." Reisner kept it for four eventful years until on August 25, 1747 he and his wife Catharine conveyed it to John Bytsel, blacksmith, of Lancaster County, Pennsylvania.[53]

Although they were Germans, Reisner and Bernard Weymore in 1740 signed the petition for a road to the English Church at present-day Beallsville in Montgomery County. In 1742 the March Court fined Reisner for assault upon John Hussey. A daughter, Susanna Margareta Reisner was baptised by Pastor Candler in April 1744. In 1747 Reisner was one of the signers of Pastor Muhlenberg's Articles written into the Lutheran Church Book. The Provincial Court Records show that on May 9, 1747 Reisner mortgaged his property to Daniel Dulany,[54] and on October 20, 1747, with twelve other Germans he was naturalized.[55] In March of the following year he was named as one of the Germans being forced to pay excess quitrents.[56] In 1749 Reisner was one of seven bondsmen of Nicholas Bundrick who, when unable to repay his debt to Semple Chevalier, deeded them a lot and building in Frederick town.[57] A son Johann Martin Reissner was born in April 1750, and Martin Wetzel was the child's Lutheran baptism sponsor. In November 1750 Michael Risener was presented by the Grand Jury for beating John Youngblood. Jacob Barton, Constable of Mannor Hundred, returned Michael Reisner to the same Court for swearing seven oaths, and the Sheriff was ordered to collect fines assessed by the Court.[58]

Through the March Court of 1753 William Beatty demanded the three pounds for which Reisner was indebted to him at the time, and John Row sued Reisner for 6 pounds 11 shillings. In November John House's executors were suing Reisner on a debt due the estate. On March 23, 1753 Reisner gave Daniel Dulany and Samuel Beall, Jr., a two year mortgage due in 1755 on "Green Spring" and on his horses, cows and wagons.[59] William Beatty and John Cook also sued Reisner

---

[52] C/S: LG E:273.

[53] Prince George's County Land Records, EE:281.

[54] Provincial Court (Land Records), 1744-1749, EI 8:296. Dulany had loaned Reisner £36 which were to be repaid by May 9, 1748.

[55] Ibid., EI 10:228. Among the others were Jonathan Hagar, Jacob Miller, Lodowick Miller, Jacob Stull and Joseph Vulgamot.

[56] See below, p. 292. Reisner's given name in this record was erroneously written as Nicholas.

[57] Reisner, through his attorney Henry Darnall, had brought suit against Bundrick in June 1750. See also above, p 157 and Rice, The Life, op. cit., p. 46.

[58] Robert Debutts was accused at the same time, but his charge was for 25 oaths. See Rice, The Life, op. cit., p. 60.

for debts owed them. In 1755 the Grand Jury presented Michael Reisner for "forceable taking out of the possession of Richard Cooke a horse without proving the same," but he was released on grounds of "erroneous charges." Also in 1755 Reisner was charged by John Six, a weaver, and John Ogle for a debt of 40 pounds, but was discharged by the Court. The June Court of 1758 fined Reisner one shilling for "assaulting George Dickson in the execution of his office as under sheriff," and Catherine Honey swore that she had attended Court for eight days "to testify for the Lord Proprietary against Michael Risener." Plagued by debts, Michael Risoner petitioned the Maryland Assembly on June 20, 1761 for release from debtors' prison, where he had "languished for the past three years and four months."[60] In 1762 Reisner conveyed all his properties, with a value of 200 pounds, to Samuel Beall, Jr.,[61] who on November 21, 1764 for 300 pounds sold "Green Spring" with its 200 acres, buildings, orchards, pastures and fences to Conrod Licklighter (Lechlider).[62]

Reisner's friends from Susquehanna days, Joseph Ogle and Henry Munday, had come to Frederick County, but unfortunately both had died before his imprisonment. Reisner and Cresap had long since "parted company" when Cresap sued him in the March Court of 1745. It is doubtful that Reisner's German neighbors had sufficient finances to have been of assistance to him. His final fate is therefore unknown, and further word of him is lacking.

Also aboard the ship *Dragon* when it arrived at Philadelphia on September 30, 1732 was **Hans Georg Soldner**,[63] born about 1702c and hence a couple of years older than Reisner. He claimed to be "of Baltimore County" when on October 25, 1735 he made a deposition concerning events at Thomas Cresap's plantation the previous January or February. He was working then for Cresap when Robert Buchanan appeared with thirty men, including John Wright, Quaker Justice of Lancaster County, lawyer John Emerson, Undersheriff John Powell and others bent on further strife in the Canadochly area. The posse captured Soldner, Philip Crevor, Michael Risnor, Posthan Everly, Leonard Mozar, Enoch Freeland and Emanuel Jones, taking them off to the jail in Lancaster where they were confined for ten days and forced to attend two courts. Michael Rusner, "carpenter of Baltimore County," made similar testimony.[64] After the others had gone on to Maryland, Joh. Georg Soldner, along with Anna Marie Immler, appeared as a baptism sponsor on April 19, 1739 for the son and namesake of Joh. Georg Schreyer, whom Stöver indicated was from Canawacken.[65] Soldner does not appear in the early Frederick County

---

[59] Frederick County Land Records, E:409.
[60] *Maryland State Papers, No. 1, The Black Books*, 4:93 (para. 1161 in the *Calendar)*; Proceedings of the Assembly, 1762-1763, *Archives of Maryland, op. cit.*, 58:585.
[61] Frederick County Land Records, H:254.
[62] *Ibid.*, J:908.
[63] Strassburger-Hinke, *op. cit.*, Lists 26 ABC, pp. 97-99.
[64] Proceedings of Council, 1732-1753, *Archives of Maryland, op. cit.*, 28:85-86.
[65] Stöver, *op. cit.*, p. 19. Conewago, as previously explained, was

land survey or church records until June 24, 1747 when, as Hans Georg Soldner, he signed Muhlenberg's Lutheran church articles. On November 24th of the following year George Saltner and Martin Whetsell for two pounds received title from Daniel Dulany to Lot No. 60 in Frederick town, agreeing to pay quitrent of one shilling per year for 21 years from May 10, 1747 and then two shillings thereafter.[66] The lot was located between Patrick and Church Streets, east of Market Street. On July 10, 1760 George Soltners received from Joseph Chapline the patent for "Widow's Design" near the future Washington County boundary above Locust Valley.[67] As George Sultner he signed his will (by mark) the following February, leaving all his estate to his cousin Catherine Sultner.[68]

    Leonhard Moser was also on hand at the Conojohela confrontation in early 1735. He, too, was one of the 1732 arrivals, having reached Philadelphia along with 14 other Mosers on board the *Adventure* on September 23rd.[69] As Leonard Mozar he was among those jailed by the Lancaster posse in early 1735. Presumably he lived in the Codorus area of today's York County, for as Johann Leonhardt Moser he stood with Philipp Ernst and Charlotta Friderica Gruber as baptism sponsors on July 3, 1736 for a son of Heinrich Stentz.[70] As Lehnert Mosser he first appeared in the Frederick Lutheran Church Book in May of 1743 as a sponsor for the baptism of Georg Hutzel's daughter Susanna. Then as Lehnert Mohsser he was married to Maria Kochher on January 30, 1744.[71] In April of that year he served as sponsor for the Lutheran baptism of Jacob Weller's daughter Elisa Juliyana. Both families later turned to the Moravian religion. In 1758 Moser and his wife Maria were present at the first service in the newly completed Moravian Church at Graceham. Moser was apparently a weaver by trade, for on November 19, 1751 11-year old Michael Coker, obviously a relative of Moser's wife, was apprenticed to Leonard Moser in order to learn that trade.[72] Not until August 3, 1754, did Leonard Moser appear in the survey records. At that time he had "Nolan's Mountain" surveyed in the area where Hunting Creek Reservoir is situated today, some one and a half miles west of Thurmont on the Foxville Road. Later he added "Paradise" and its Resurvey, on Broad (now Muddy) Run where it enters Hunting Creek south of Thurmont.[73] He also had "Stoney Hills" surveyed below

---

the region of German settlement on the South Branch of Conewago Creek including the area along the southern portion of today's Adams-York County border.

  [66] Frederick County Land Records, B:32.
  [67] C/S: BC & GS 14:1. For Chapline, see below, p. 346.
  [68] Frederick County Wills, A1:180; probated August 10, 1762.
  [69] Strassburger-Hinke, *op. cit.*, Lists 23ABC, pp. 83-87. Ages were shown for most of these Moser immigrants, but not for Leonart and Paulus, who were probably at least in their late teens.
  [70] Lancaster Lutheran Church Book, *op. cit.*
  [71] The second marriage recorded in the Frederick Lutheran Church Book.
  [72] Rice, *The Life, op. cit.*, p. 84.
  [73] C/S: BC & GS 30:205.

Emmitsburg, about a half mile south of Motter's.
Another 1732 immigrant was **Philipp Ernst Grüber,** who at the age of 29 arrived in Philadelphia on September 25th with his *Loyal Judith* shipmate Georg Honig.[74] With them came the Lutheran minister Johannes Christian Schultz, who in the following year ordained Johann Caspar Stöver.[75] Grüber also settled early with Cresap and the Canadochly Germans. In January or February of 1735 he was a fourth individual taken prisoner by the Pennsylvanians at Cresap's place. In his deposition the following October he said he was 31 years of age and a planter of Baltimore County.[76] At that time his name was spelled **Philip Crever,** and he alternated thereafter between the two spellings, depending upon the nationality of the scribe making the record. On July 21, 1735 he and his wife Charlotta Friederica, together with Joseph Ogle, stood as sponsors for the baptism at Canashochilie (Conojohela) of children of Thomas Cresap. In August he and his wife were again sponsors, this time for a son of Edward Evans.[77] They likewise appear among Stöver's baptism sponsors in the Lancaster and York Lutheran church books on February 23, 1735 for children of Christian Groll, Nicholas Höltzel and Heinrich Stentz, all probably residents of the Codorus valley. In June and July of 1736 the Grübers were again sponsors, this time for children of Michael Krüger and again of Heinrich Stentz. With them at the latter baptism also stood Joh. Leonhardt Moser.[78] By 1738, however, he was in the Monocacy area, where his own child, Maria Eliesabetha Grüber was baptised by Pastor Stöver on November 25th.[79] Joh. Georg Lay and his wife were sponsors. Five days later, again with his name spelled Philip Crever, he had 100 acres of land surveyed about a half mile north of Michael Reisner's plantation. This he called "Hunter's Lot." Its beginning point was described as "at a spring on the west side of Hunting Creek about two miles from the mountain, the land lying on both sides of the creek."[80] On June 24, 1741 Philip Ernst Grüber and his wife served as sponsors for Catarina and Johannes Verdriess, children of Jacob Verdriess.[81] The Frederick Court on June 28, 1748 awarded Crever 40 pounds in money and 489 pounds of tobacco which Frederick and John Verdress, Jacob Stoner and Abraham Miller acknowledged by confessing judgment.[82] By that year his land

---
[74] Strassburger-Hinke, *op. cit.*, Lists 24 ABC, pp. 88, 90, 92.
[75] Cf. above, p. 133. Schultz returned to Germany in 1734.
[76] Proceedings of Council, 1732-1753, *Archives of Maryland*, op. cit., 28/86-87. See also above.
[77] Stöver, *op. cit.*, pp. 14-15.
[78] Lancaster Lutheran Church Book, *op. cit.* Stöver originally considered the territory west of the Susquehanna River as a part of Lancaster County, which of course it was (provided one ignored Maryland's claims) until the formation of York County in 1749. His initial entries in the York (Codorus) Church Book therefore duplicate and were undoubtedly copied from his earlier entries in the Lancaster Church Book. Cf. Glatfelter, *op. cit.*, p. 477.
[79] Stöver, *op. cit.*, p. 18.
[80] Patent: EI 6:135, December 11, 1738.
[81] Stöver, *op. cit.*, p. 28.

had come into the possession of Joseph Ogle, who had it resurveyed into "Fountain Low."[83]

Because of the associations on the trip across the ocean and similar associations later in Maryland, it seems to be a safe assumption that the **Johann Peter Apfel** who arrived in Philadelphia on October 17, 1732 with Apalonia Apel -- and not the Peter Apple who came with wife Clara a year later on September 29, 1733[84] — was the Peter Apple who appears subsequently in Frederick County records. With them aboard the *John and William* came Bernhard Weymer, Jacob Matthias Manser and Nicklaus Koger. Whether Apalonia was wife or sister is not known, but if she was a wife, she died sometime within the eight years following their arrival. No children are known. Peter Apple first appears in the Monocacy area about 1740 when he married the widow Maria Catharina Geiger.[85] As noted in the previous chapter,[86] she was the youngest daughter of the Pennsylvania Lutheran pastor Anton Jacob Henckel (1668-1728) with whom she had come to America in 1717. About 1736 she and her first husband, Johann Georg Geiger (1702-1739e) arrived in the Monocacy area where two of their five children were baptized by Pastor Stöver. But they had not formally acquired title to land in Maryland until, as a widow, Catharina "Kiger" herself received title from Jacob Fout to 150 acres in the southwestern corner of "Rocky Creek." She recorded the deed on June 24, 1740 and then bound herself for £80 to assure that two-thirds of its acreage would go to her eldest sons George and Valentine Geiger when they came of age.

Peter Apple and his wife were active in Lutheran Church affairs. Joh. Peter Appel was a contributor to the purchase of the first church book in 1742,[87] yet in the same year, along with other Germans, he signed the petition seeking to divide the English Church's Prince George's Parish. Stöver baptised their daughter Eva Rosina also in 1742. Pastor Candler did likewise for a son Johann Peter Apple, Jr. in 1744. Another child, Maria Charlotta, was recorded in 1750. In 1747 Peter Apfel signed Muhlenberg's "Articles" in the new

---

[82] Frederick Land Records, B:59.

[83] C/S: BY & GS 1:658; Patent: BY & GS 2:487. See below, p 326.

[84] Strassburger-Hinke, *op. cit:* Johann Peter Apfel with wife Apalonia, Lists 28ABC, October 17, 1732, pp. 102, 104, 106; Peter Apple with wife Clara, Lists 34ABC, September 29, 1733, pp. 131, 133, 134.

[85] The marriage occurred between September 21, 1740 when Catharine Geiger was a sponsor for a son of Heinrich Fortune, and January 19, 1740/41, when Peter Appel and wife Maria Catharina were sponsors for a daughter of Heinrich Sinn. (Frederick Lutheran Church Book.)

[86] See p. 163.

[87] Not wholly explained is the reason why Appel's name appears twice, once as Joh. Peter Appel, once as Peter Appel. Possibly the contributions were made on different occasions and in different coins. Elsewhere there is no suggestion of two Peter Appels, since Peter Apple's son was born only about the time of the contributions.

Frederick Lutheran Church Book, and he did so as one of the six "church wardens." About 1744 he apparently left "Rocky Creek" for the northern area of German settlement where the German Lutherans were more concentrated.[88] On November 29, 1744 Peter Apell acquired 100 acres from Arnold Livers on the latter's large "Resurvey on Arnold's Delight," located northeast of today's Thurmont.[89] He expanded his holdings there to 295 acres by a Resurvey in 1751,[90] and from that total he was selling lots in 1760 to John Weller, John Young, Matthias Ambrose and others.[91] One of those lots, a one-acre parcel, was given to Matthias Ambrose, Jacob Matthias and Jacob Ambrose on May 15, 1760 that they might "build a school house."[92] About 1765 a log church was built on this site, and in 1769 the above school trustees deeded the property to Martin Dustmain [Deichmann] and Henry Feurure [Firor], trustees respectively of the Lutheran and Reformed congregations there. "They being German have built on said one acre a school house and church."[93] The resulting Union Church was referred to in Matthias Ambrose's 1782 will as "the church at Peter Apple's called Jacob's Church,"[94] but ever afterwards it has been known simply as Apple's Church.[95]

Peter Apple's ties and interests did continue in the "Rocky Creek" area. On November 21, 1750 he purchased from Henry Maynor [Maynard] for £10 a twenty-acre parcel called "Small Hope" which lay adjacent to the Geiger 150 acres.[96] There is reference in the 1751 Court records to an overseer appointed for the road from "Frederick Town to Ballenger's Branch by Peter Apple's Mill." Court road records continue to refer to "Ballenger's Creek by Peter Apple's" in the November terms of 1753, 1754 and 1755.[97] And the Rent Roll prepared for "Rocky Creek" sometime between 1754 and 1759 -- though not considered the most accurately up-to-date of records --

---

[88] One should not emphasize too strongly the apparent geographical separation between Reformed and Lutheran Germans, thereby implying strong differences in their religious beliefs. They were extremely compatible and worked well together, especially in the creation of early union churches. It is interesting to note, however, that about this same time Johann Jacob Matthias, another Lutheran, also moved from "Rocky Creek" to the same area near today's Thurmont.
[89] Prince George's County Land Records, BB:236.
[90] C/S: BC & GS 9:161.
[91] Frederick County Land Records, E:991, 995.
[92] Ibid., F:997.
[93] Ibid., M:31.
[94] Frederick County Wills, GM 2:106.
[95] For further history, see Elizabeth C. Kieffer, *Baptismal Records of Apple's Church, 1773-1848* (Hudson, Wisconsin, 1963), pp. 5-10.
[96] Frederick County Land Records, B:300-301. Henry Maynard was the husband of Thomas Beatty's daughter Susanna. It was the Beatty family which as early as 1733 held title to the half of the original "Rocky Creek" tract which did not go to Jacob Fout, grantor in 1740 of the 150 acres to Apple's wife.
[97] Rice, *The Life, op. cit.*, pp. 132, 151, 176, but these records do not refer to Peter Apple's *mill*.

showed Peter Apple as still "in possession of" the 150 acres.[98] On May 13, 1758 John and George Kisor [Geiger] mortgaged the 150 acres to [their stepfather] Peter Apple and [their brother-in-law] Bernard Renn in order to guarantee their appearance at the next June Court.[99] Finally, Peter and Catharine Apple of Frederick County, Maryland, together with [her son] George Kiger of Loudoun County, Virginia, on December 14, 1763 conveyed the 150 acres on "Rocky Creek" to Michael Miller for £460.[100]

Peter Apple had only one survey made for himself. That was "All Stones" whose 40-plus acres had a beginning point in its 1765 survey "on the east side of the waggon road running from Fredericktown to Marsh Creek [present-day Gettysburg, Pennsylvania]."[101] His son Peter Apple, Jr. predeceased his father, dying in 1775 at the age of only 31.[102] The elder Peter Apple died in 1779, having written his will on March 2nd of that year. In it he named his wife Catharine, four daughters (Eve House, Charlotte Meyer, Mary Matthews and Magdalene Byerly), his deceased son Peter's daughter Susannah Apple and his wife's granddaughter Catharina (Geiger) Coppersmith.[103] The widow, Catharine Henckel Geiger Apple, died in October 1785 at the age of 74.[104]

Johann Georg Honig, known in America as **George Honey,** was born in Germany in 1712. He was 20 years of age and unmarried when he arrived in Philadelphia on September 25, 1732.[105] By October 2, 1737, however, he had a wife Anna Catarina with whom in Lancaster he was a baptism sponsor for the daughter of Gabriel Lämmle. By 1739 Anna Catarina had apparently died, for without her he was a sponsor for John Hill's daughter Anna Maria on August 5th and for Lämmle's son Johann Peter on October 4th. On October 16, 1739 he married Maria Agnes Kretscher.[106] It was not until March 14, 1742 that he had land surveyed in today's Frederick County, Maryland, and even that date preceded notations, in the Lancaster Lutheran Church Book, concerning his carpentry work still in Lancaster in May and June of 1743 on pews below the pulpit and a

---

[98] Maryland Rent Rolls (Frederick County No. 1), 32:29.

[99] Frederick County Land Records, G:264. Though dated May 13, 1758, this was not recorded until November 12, 1761, and possibly only then in order to clear title preparatory to the parcel's ultimate sale.

[100] John Geiger, probably the "Johann" Valentine named in the 1740 bond (p. 199), married Michael Miller's daughter Hannah and quitclaimed his rights to the 150 acres on June 9, 1764. (Frederick County Land Records, J:154, 603.)

[101] C/S: BC & GS 30/171.

[102] Frederick County Wills, A1:536. Here his surname was spelled Appel.

[103] Ibid., GM 1:122. Here the surname was Aple.

[104] Ibid., GM 2:179.

[105] Strassburger-Hinke, op. cit., Lists 24ABC, pp. 88, 90, 92.

[106] Stöver, op. cit., Marriages, p. 5, No. 259. Her maiden name was spelled as Gretscher when they baptized their first child in 1740: First Reformed Church Book, Lancaster.

rail around the altar.[107] His "Den of Wolves" was located "on a draft of Sandy Run" about a mile and a half south of the land of his 1732 shipmate Philip Ernst Grüber.[108] It was one of eight surveys made that year along the German Monocacy Road. Honey did not secure a patent to the land until April 24, 1754, the day before he sold it to Jacob Koller. The latter had a "Resurvey on Den of Wolves" made on November 10, 1761. This amounted to 777 acres and extended from present-day Lewistown to Hunting Creek.[109] In the 1873 Atlas, the homes of James Null and Thomas Staub are shown on Honey's land on Sandy Run.[110] Georg Honig contributed to the purchase of the Lutheran Church Book and in it signed Pastor Muhlenberg's Lutheran Church Articles of 1747. In late 1751 he became security for Adam Spuch's attempted purchase of "St. Elizabeth." In connection with this, Dulany's sons implied that Honey had later gone to Carolina.[111] He was still in Frederick County, however, on September 14, 1753 when he was naturalized.[112]

Matthias Ambrose arrived at Philadelphia on October 11, 1732 aboard the ship *Pleasant* from Rotterdam by way of the English customs port of Deal.[113] Immigrating with him were Valentin Müller and Johannes Tafelmeyer who were also destined ultimately for Maryland. Ambrose settled first in the Conestoga area of Lancaster County. He was 37 years of age. Most likely he was already married or was soon to be, for we have record in the Muddy Creek Church Book of baptisms of four sons born between 1734 and 1741. From the baptism sponsors — Mattheis and Anna Barbara Rössel for son Mattheis in 1739, Johann Friederich Verdriess for son Johann Friederich in 1741 — and from other facts, it is clear that Ambrose had probably moved on to the Monocacy area, even though Stöver's records did not note it, sometime in 1737 or 1738.[114] He would have been nearly 48 when on June 13, 1743 Pastor Candler baptised his daughter Maria Barbara Ambrose. Jacob Weller and his wife Maria Barbara were this child's Lutheran sponsors. Coincidentally Johannes Weller,[115] who arrived in Philadelphia three months later, was shortly thereafter to marry Mattheis Ambrose's older daughter Catharine

---

[107] Lancaster Church Book, *loc. cit.*, pp. 415, 423, 433. Of these entries, only the 1739 marriage record also appeared in Stöver's personal Journal, *op. cit.*, p 5, No. 259.
[108] C/S: LG E:302.
[109] For the history of this land's subsequent disposition, see Rice, *New Facts*, *op. cit.*, pp. 116-117.
[110] Lake, *op. cit.*, p. 15.
[111] See below, p. 210.
[112] Provincial Court Records, EI 15:157.
[113] Strassburger-Hinke, *op. cit.*, Lists 27ABC, pp. 99-101. He signed his name as Matheis Ambrosi. Stöver called him Mattheis Ambrosius.
[114] Muddy Creek Lutheran Church Book transcription, *op. cit.*, p. 27. None of these baptisms appears in Stöver's personal Journal, *op. cit.*, which ordinarily contained Monoacy baptisms regardless of where the family lived first when the record began.
[115] Cf. below, p. 210.

Ambrose. In late September of 1743 Mateas Ambrose received communion from Pastor Candler "in the Lutheran Church of Manaquice" preparatory to his naturalization on October 19th.[116]

Ambrose's Mill was the forerunner of today's town of Thurmont and was used as a reference point in many of the old road records.[117] It was situated a half mile below his parcel called "Gap" which had been initially surveyed June 3, 1743 for Adam Spuch, an early contributor for the purchase of the Frederick Lutheran Church Book. "Gap" was patented to Mattheis Ambrose but not until November 10, 1752.[118] In 1746 Matthias Ambrose had obtained 125 acres of "Arnold's Delight" from Arnold Livers, Sr.,[119] and in 1754 Samuel Collard and his wife Helena Livers, executors for Arnold Livers, deceased, deeded [quitclaimed?] to Matthias Ambrose the same 125 acres.[120] Later, in 1753, Ambrose and his wife Catharine conveyed "Gap" to his son Jacob Ambrose,[121] who had the land resurveyed in 1763.[122] Jacob resurveyed it again in 1773 and at that time changed the name to "Good Neighbor."[123] Mattheis Ambrose had also purchased land in present-day Carroll County, a part of "Arnold's Chance," which he divided among his children Matthias Ambrose, Jr., Henry Ambrose, and the daughter Maria Barbara noted above.[124] In 1762 Henry Ambrose received 168 acres of "Arnold's Delight" from Solomon Harday and his wife Rachel Livers.[125]

In March 1748 Matthias Ambrose and Jacob Matthias journeyed to the area of present-day Hagerstown in Washington County to meet and hear the Moravian missionary Brother Matthias Gottlieb Gottschalk. In his Diary, Gottschalk described his departure after preaching there: "I took leave of my host, Jonathan Häger, who wept and was very sorry that I had to leave him. Ambrosius was also unable to say much because of his emotion."[126] Although some of the Ambrose family in later generations associated with the Moravians, Matthias Ambrose himself stayed with the Lutherans at Apples Church. Together with the same Jacob Matthias and his own son Jacob Ambrose, he was an initial trustee for the Apple school house which later became Apple's Church. In his will, Matthias Ambrose left three pounds to "the church at Peter Apple's called Jacob's Church."[127] He was buried there in 1784 at the age of at least 89.[128] In

---

[116] Provincial Court Judgment Records, 1742-1744, EI 7:296.
[117] Jacob Weller, for example, in 1752 located his "Taylor's Bodkin" survey near the "wagon road that goes from Fredericktown to Ambrose's Mill" (C/S: BC & GS 32:132).
[118] C/S: Y & S 7:210.
[119] Prince George's County Land Records, BB 1:406.
[120] Frederick County Land Records, E:385, March 20, 1754.
[121] Frederick County Land Records, E:330.
[122] Patent: BC & GS 25:226.
[123] C/S: BC & GS 51:326.
[124] Maryland Rent Rolls (Frederick No. 1), 32:60.
[125] Frederick County Land Records, F:801, 803, 806.
[126] See above, p. 147.
[127] Frederick County Wills, GM 2:106.
[128] Holdcraft, op. cit., p. 78. The gravestone shows Ambrose's birth

his will he devised the remainder of his estate to his daughter Catherine Weller and (her husband) John Weller, Sr., adding that "none of the other children shall have claim, I having given them their share."

Valentin Müller, who arrived with Matthias Ambrose in 1732, was married on September 7, 1737 to Eliesabetha Dorothea Lochmann.[129] Although this marriage presumably took place in the Earl Town area of the Conestoga settlement, near today's New Holland in Lancaster County, Müller and his wife were at Manaquesen when their two children were baptized in 1738 and 1740. For Magdalena Müller on November 24, 1738 Magdalena Schweinhardt stood as baptism sponsor. Joh. Jacob Mattheis, his wife Margaretha and the widow Catharina Geiger were sponsors for Anna Eliesabetha Müller on April 27, 1740.[130] Valentin Müller does not appear in the early Maryland land records, but these baptism sponsors suggest the possibility that he may have been living in the Lower German settlement west of today's Frederick.

Between 1744 and 1748 there is brief notice of **Hans Melchior Werffle**, who came to this country on September 21, 1732. Unlike other 1732 arrivals, he was accompanied by no other future settlers in the Monocacy area. Information concerning the mangling of his name into such anglicized variations as Wheyfield and Warfield during his short appearance on "Tasker's Chance" is discussed in that Chapter.[131]

Of **Johannes Tafelmeyer**, who reached Philadelphia with Matthias Ambrose and Valentin Müller, we have even less word. He was one of 23 Germans contributing to the purchase of the first Frederick Church Book about 1742. His presence was also confirmed by Records of the Prince George's County Court which show that in June of 1746 Tafelmeyer was being sued by Abraham Miller for 56 pounds 10 shillings.[132] He has not been found in Stöver's Lutheran records, nor in the Land Records.

Such, then, is the record of the sixteen German immigrants known to have arrived in this country in the Autumn of 1732. It is an observable curiosity, perhaps indicative of their close associations during and immediately after their voyages to America, that they tended for the most part to settle, once they came to Maryland, along the German Monocacy Road in the northern part of today's Frederick County. In counter distinction, as described in the previous chapter, is the story of those German immigrants who are known to have arrived in the following year, 1733. They were in numbers second only to the 1732 arrivals, yet, where their locales are known, most of

---

as February 10, 1690, five years earlier than he claimed on his arrival in this country in 1732. He died August 10, 1784.

[129] Stöver, Marriages, op. cit., p. 3, No. 136. Stöver also recorded this marriage in the Lancaster Lutheran Church Book but there gave no clue to geographic location. For Lochmann, see above, pp. 17-18, 191n.

[130] Stöver, op. cit., p. 18. These baptisms do not appear in the Lancaster Lutheran Church Book as did the parents' marriage record.

[131] See below, p. 288.

[132] Prince George's County Court Records, DD:619.

them pushed farther south in today's Frederick County to "Tasker's Chance" or to the area to its west. Only one or two of them are known to have settled in the northern area.

Seemingly **Johann Jacob Matthias** (1704-1782) was one of these exceptions, but actually he was not. He did arrive in 1733 and he did settle in the northern German area. But his first appearance in Maryland was in the southern German section from where he later moved to the northern. With his wife Margaretha [Jung] he arrived in Philadelphia on August 17, 1733 aboard the ship *Samuel*. He was 29 years of age, she 24. They had been married since 1729, but brought with them no surviving children. Also on this ship were the families of Hans Conrad Kemp, Henrich Roht, Hans Leonhard Wervell, Henrich Bischoff and Jacob Hoff.[133] Although Stöver in his personal *Journal*[134] placed Mattheis (as Stöver consistently spelled his name) in Monocacy from 1734 to 1738, it is apparent that Anna Margaretha, the first of their four children, was baptized June 23, 1734 probably in the Conestoga area of Pennsylvania rather than in Maryland: Stöver made his first trips to Maryland only when he was enroute to Virginia, and he did not get to Virginia in 1734. It is highly unlikely that he would conduct only the one baptism if he *had* gone to Maryland. The witnesses to the baptism are not known to have lived in or had ties to Maryland. And Stöver in succeeding or preceding days was too far away from Maryland to make a visit there even remotely possible. Hence dating his first visit to Maryland solely on the basis of the 1734 Matthias baptism would seem in error.[135]

By April 28, 1736, however, Stöver had begun stopping in the Monocacy area on his trips to Virginia, and on that date he baptized Anna Magdalena Mattheis. Almost annually thereafter Stöver was recording the baptism of succeeding Mattheis children, Anna Magdalena in 1736, Johann Georg in 1737 and Catarina in 1738. In 1736 shipmate Johann Jacob Hoff stood as sponsor for the Mattheis family. Johann Jacob and Margaretha Mattheis returned the favor at the baptism of Anna Maria Hoff on May 16, 1736 when Stöver stopped on his way back from Virginia.[136] Johann Georg Geiger and his

---

[133] Strassburger-Hinke, *op. cit.*, Lists 29ABC, pp. 106-112. Bischoff and Hoff do not appear in Frederick County land records, although both are named in Pastor Stöver's Monocacy baptism Journal, *op. cit.* Henry Bishop is also noted in the records of the March Court of 1745 in a suit against him by John Hepburn. Hoff should not be confused with the family of Abraham Haff of Kingwood Township, New Jersey, who in 1755 received "Providence," inherited from his wife Jane Beatty's grandmother, Susanna Beatty of "Dulany's Lot." Cf. Frederick County Land Records, E:836.

[134] Stöver, *op. cit.*, p. 31.

[135] Wentz, *op. cit.*, p. 39, relying on Schantz, placed this baptism in the Monocacy area. So also did Cunz, *op. cit.*, p. 62, though he seems to have relied on Wentz. William Edward Eisenberg, *This Heritage* (Winchester, Virginia, 1954), pp. 312-321, also followed Schantz.

[136] Stöver, *op. cit.*, pp. 16, 31. One speculates whether it was by chance or otherwise that Stöver first met these couples and how the

wife Catharina Henckel were the sponsors in 1737, while Mattheis Rössel and again Catharina Geiger were the sponsors in 1738. Stöver also recorded all four of these baptisms in the Lancaster Lutheran Church Book. In 1742 and 1744 daughters Anna Maria and Maria Barbara "Mateas" were listed on the first page of the new Frederick Lutheran Church Book toward whose purchase their father, as Jacob Mateus, had contributed. Altogether, 13 children were born to this marriage, 8 sons and 5 daughters.

Like Peter Apple, Johann Jacob Matthias seems to have located first on a part of "Rocky Creek" southwest of today's Frederick. Jacob Fout in 1740 conveyed 250 acres to Jacob "Mattice" from the half of "Rocky Creek" which he had purchased earlier from Captain John Stoddert.[137] Also in 1740, on June 4th, Jacob Matthews, planter, was naturalized along with Jacob and Baldus Fout. So, too, were the Matthews children, George, Margarett, Maudlin and Catherine.[138] Then, about 1743, again like Peter Apple, Matthias moved north. His new land, "Slate Ridge," was located "on the west side of the north fork of Little Captain's Creek near the Mountain." The property lay at the foot of Piney Mountain between present-day Thurmont and Emmitsburg, where now Kelbaugh Road crosses Little Owens Creek. It had been surveyed on May 2, 1739 for Arnold Livers as 123 acres, but was patented on August 26, 1739 to his future son-in-law William Elder.[139] The latter, with his new wife Jacoba Clementina Livers[140] assenting, sold "Slate Ridge" to Matthias on August 19, 1743.[141] Matthias thus became the most northerly of the early German settlers. His land lay north even of the property of Matthias Ambrose and of the first land of George Gump. In 1752 the beginning point of "Worley's Choice" was identified as being near "the road [Cartledge's] that leads from Jacob Matthias' to Antietam and on the west side of a draft of the creek that Ambrose's Mill stands on."[142]

Jacob Matthias was seemingly a friend to all, regardless of religious background. With Jacob Hoff he joined other Germans in signing the 1742 petition to divide Prince George's parish so that the English church could be brought nearer to the people of Monocacy.[143] When the fledgling Moravian congregation was tearing away from its Lutheran neighbors, John Jacob Matthias went with John Jacob Weller to Annapolis in 1747 to seek help from Daniel Dulany. Dulany had ten acres called "Gift" surveyed for what was to become the site of the Graceham Moravian Church, and the certificate was assigned to Jacob Matthias "in trust."[144] In March 1748 Jacob Matthias traveled

---

association was nurtured over the succeeding years. In his records he spelled their names as Mattheis and Hoof.
[137] Prince George's County Land Records, Y:182-183.
[138] Commission Book No. 82, *loc. cit.*, 26:157.
[139] C/S: EI 5:500.
[140] See below, p. 252.
[141] Prince George's County Land Records, BB 1:3.
[142] C/S: Y & S 7:503.
[143] See below, p. 371. Their names were copied here as Jacob Mathews and Jacob Hooff.
[144] See above, p. 152.

over the mountain with his near neighbor Matthias Ambrose to hear the Moravian missionary Brother Gottschalk at Jonathan Hager's place. In October 1749 fellow missionary Leonhard Schnell made his way from Conewago to Jacob Matthias' home, his first stop in the Monocacy area.[145] These men were searching for answers, but probably never contemplated the Moravians as anything other than Lutherans. When it proved otherwise, they withdrew their support. As the Lutheran and Reformed congregations themselves became more centered in the new town of Frederick, the need arose for a school or church in the northern part of the County. Jacob Matthias, Matthias Ambrose and Jacob Ambrose served as initial trustees to receive the May 15, 1760 deed from Peter Apple described above. By 1765 a church building had been added to Apple's one-acre school site and the evolution of today's Apple's Church had begun.

Jacob Matthias surveyed a 30-acre "Addition to Slate Ridge" which was patented to him on September 8, 1762.[146] He then had a "Resurvey on Slate Ridge" made on November 8, 1763, bringing the whole to 579 acres.[147] His land was subsequently known as the Lohr and Zentz Mill properties. As late as April 20, 1774 his name was still being spelled as Jacob Mathias,[148] but ultimately some of the family began anglicizing the name to Matthews. His will is so indexed, but on his wife's gravestone at Apple's Church she was called Margret Mathies. His will of April 2, 1776 named sons Conrad, George, Henry, Philip and John and daughters Margaret Valentine, Magdalena Feeror, Catharina Stull, Mary Flower and Barbara Ambrose.[149] He died May 7, 1782 at the age of 77, but his wife Margaret survived him until October 12, 1788.[150]

Hans Martin Wetzel was another German who settled in the northern area of today's Frederick County. But he reached American shores in 1731, before any of those described above. He was 31 years of age when he arrived in Philadelphia, having been born in Germany about 1700c.[151] He brought with him his wife Maria Barbara, age 33, and three children, Hans Martin, Jr., age 6, Nicholaus age 4 and Katharina age 3.[152] They came with a company of 269 Germans under the leadership of Johann Bartholmew Rieger (1707-1769), a

---
[145] Schnell, "Kurze Beschreibung," *loc. cit.*
[146] C/S: BC & GS 19:315.
[147] C/S: BC & GS 27:116.
[148] Kieffer, *op. cit.*, p. 12. The entry appears on p. 2 of the original church book.
[149] Frederick County Wills, GM 1:249.
[150] Holdcraft, *op. cit.*, p. 774.
[151] Burgert, *op. cit.*, 1:396, has noted a namesake, Johann Martin Wetzel, born at Hasselbach east of Sinsheim in the Kraichgau on November 13, 1719, the son of Johann Jacob Wetzel and Anna Ursula Georg. The family emigrated in 1746 and lived in Lancaster County, Pennsylvania, where Martin Wetzel's sister Susanna married Jacob Oberkirsch. The Frederick [Maryland] Lutheran Church Book records her second marriage to Peter Andrae and her death in Frederick County in 1773 at the age of 44.
[152] Strassburger-Hinke, *op. cit.*, Lists 16ABC, pp. 48, 50-52, 54.

student at Heidelberg University and an early Reformed pastor. Rieger was born in Ober-Ingelheim, where a numerous family of Weitzels also lived. But no connection has been established to the American immigrant or to the Devilbiss family which also came with this group.[153] The immigrant party reached Philadelphia on September 21, 1731 aboard the ship *Brittania* of London, having sailed from Rotterdam by way of Cowes, England.

Almost immediately Rieger was elected pastor of the Reformed congregations in Philadelphia and Germantown, where he served until 1734. He then moved to Amwell, New Jersey and seems to have worked there until 1739. In that year he accepted a call to Lancaster, Pennsylvania, where he remained for the succeeding four years, leaving a sizable record of his baptisms and marriages.[154] At the same time, during the eight years from 1731 to 1739, the Wetzels' whereabouts remains unknown.[155] There is no reason to suspect that they continued their association with Rieger. In fact, when Martin Wetzel first appeared in Maryland, he did so on June 17, 1739 as a Lutheran, not a Reformed, baptism witness for Johann Bernhardt Weinmar.[156] Even though for naturalization purposes Johann Bartholomew Rieger signed a certificate that Conrad Kempf and John House were "honest Protestants of the Reformed Heidelberg Catechism," it was a Lutheran communion from Pastor David Candler which preceded Martain Wezler's own naturalization on October 19, 1743.[157]

In 1740 Martin Wetzel signed the petition for the road from John Pyburn's to John Nelson's "for the benefit of our mill and [Anglican] church."[158] Martin Wetzel first had land surveyed in the area that is now Frederick County on November 25, 1741. He called the 100 acres "Mill Place" and located it on the west side of "Little Hunting Creek near the lower end of a small island."[159] The land lay near the German Monocacy Road some two miles north of present-day Lewistown. It is possible that this had been Wetzel's home before the date of survey, but he assigned the certificate to Handel Barrick who received the patent on October 26, 1742. In 1884 this land was in the possession of George W. Gaver.

On May 28, 1743 Daniel Dulany assigned the certificate of survey for his "Wine Garden"[160] to Martin Wetzel's neighbor Jacob Bonnett,[161] who on the same day reassigned it to Wetzel. Wetzel

---

[153] Rolf Kilian, *Ingelheim am Rhein - Die Familien in Ober-Ingelheim, 1200-1800* (Frankfurt aM, 1961). For the Devilbiss family, see below, pp. 317-319.
[154] Hinke, *Reformed Ministers, op. cit.*, pp. 26-28.
[155] Burgert, *op. cit., passim*, has shown that at least eight immigrant families among the *Brittania's* 1731 passengers came from Waldangelloch, Michelfeld and Kirchardt (villages near Sinsheim in Germany) and then settled in Lancaster County, Pennsylvania.
[156] Stöver, *op. cit.*, p. 21. See also above, p. 192.
[157] Provincial Court Judgment Records, 1742-1744, EI 7:161, 296.
[158] See above, p. 62n.
[159] C/S: LG E:85.
[160] C/S: LG E:208, surveyed December 28, 1741.
[161] See below, p. 214.

received the patent. The parcel's beginning point was "close by Wetzel's Spring branch by the side of a large swamp." It adjoined Michael Reisner's plantation, but was partly absorbed into the later Resurvey which made up "Auburn."[162] In 1743 Wetzel also received the patent for "Bonnett's Resolution," which had been surveyed for Daniel Dulany on November 11, 1742.[163] This he had enlarged in 1752 to 400 acres,[164] and in 1753 he conveyed it to Daniel Lefever. In March 1748 Martin "Wisell" was listed as one of those Germans being overcharged by the Sheriff in his quitrent collections.

Martin Wetzel was a frequent sponsor for Lutheran baptisms of children of his neighbors. In addition to the Weymore child in 1739 cited above, he was also a sponsor between 1745 and 1751 for children of Georg Honig, Georg Kuntz, Zacharias Barth and Michael Reisner. In 1747 father Martin, Sr., and sons Martin, Jr. and Nicolaus Wetzel, all signed Muhlenberg's articles in the Frederick Lutheran church book. Between 1744 and 1749 the same register records the births and baptisms of four Wetzel children, presumably the children of Martin, Jr. These were Johann Jacob,[165] Georg Michael, Joh. Friedrich, and Maria Catharina Wetzel. Their baptism sponsors included Jacob, Georg Michael and Maria Catharina Brunner. Another daughter, Magdalena Elisabetha Wetzel, was baptized in the Frederick Reformed Church in 1751 with Leonhard Hoffman the sponsor. In 1748 Martin Whetsell and George Saltner jointly purchased lot No. 60 in Fredericktown.[166] In 1756 Martin Wetzel, presumably the younger, appeared on Peter Butler's muster roll at the start of the French and Indian War.[167] According to family records no longer available,[168] Martin Wetzel, Jr. married Elizabeth Bonnett, Nicholas Wetzel married Elizabeth Cromerston and John Wetzel married Mary Bonnett, sister of Elizabeth. Other Wetzel children were Catherine and Henry. Further accounts of the exploits of succeeding generations of Wetzels against the Indians in the Ohio Valley may be found in the Draper Papers at the University of Wisconsin. Other descendants remain in the Frederick County area today.[169]

Still to be accounted for are those Germans who settled along

---
[162] C/S: IC Q:497.
[163] C/S: LG E:202.
[164] C/S: GS 1:40.
[165] Germans generally did not use the Old Style dating system. Nevertheless, the indicated February 3, 1744 baptism date for Johann Jacob Wetzel should be a year later. He was born on December 22, 1744.
[166] See above, p. 197.
[167] See below, p. 378. His name is given as Whitsall.
[168] The notes of Prof. J. Clarke Sanders of Keyser, West Virginia, formerly in the possession of the Tracey family, seem not to have been passed on to the Historical Society of Carroll County with the other Tracey papers.
[169] Holdcraft, op. cit., pp. 1217-1218, for example, listed some 88 Wetzel burials. The implication by Daniel Dulany's sons (see below, p. 210) that Martin "Whitesell" had died in Carolina after becoming security for Adam Spuch's 1751 land purchase appears unlikely.

the northern part of the German Monocacy Road before 1743 and who associated closely with the known 1732 group, but whose arrival dates are unknown. These included the Spough, Weller, Bonnett, Vertriess, Laney and Six families.

Adam Spuch, or **Spough** as he was known to English scribes, sought land both by survey and by purchase. His survey of June 3, 1743 for "Gap" was nevertheless patented nearly a decade later to Matthias Ambrose. His attempt to purchase land involved a parcel called "St. Elizabeth" which had been surveyed for Daniel Dulany on March 8, 1742/43.[170] The land comprised 100 acres and was located at the top of a hill immediately east of Jimtown corners on the north side of Jacob's Branch. The latter fed into Hunting Creek about a quarter mile away. Dulany assigned the certificate to Spaugh with the proviso that Spaugh pay Dulany £37 and all the back quitrent owed by Dulany. On November 25, 1751 Spaugh set his obligation in writing, backed by George Honey and Martin Wetzel as securities. Then, before the transaction could be completed, Dulany died. His sons Daniel and Walter Dulany, acting as his executors, sought to have the patent issued in their own names, noting that "Adam Spaugh with both his securities has since run away[171] to Carolina, and Martin Whitesell is also dead." The patent was therefore issued to Dulany's sons on September 29, 1759.[172] Adam Spuch had contributed toward the purchase of the first Lutheran Church Book and appeared with his wife Maria Catrina on its very first page of baptisms as sponsors on October 4, 1742 for Anna Maria, daughter of Jacob Mateas [Matthias]. The name there was spelled "Spach." Adam Spaw was still in Frederick County in 1752 when he registered the marks of a stray horse.[173]

Johann Jacob Weller (1704-1794) and **Johannes Weller** (1716-1792), are both alleged to have come from Diedenshausen near Berleburg in Germany. They did not come together and, if related, were no closer than first cousins.[174] But they did both settle in Frederick County, where Johann Jacob eventually became a mainstay in the Graceham Moravian Church and Johannes associated with the Lutherans at Apple's Church. Johannes Weller's arrival at Philadelphia on September 19, 1743 at the age of 27[175] places him somewhat outside the purview of this study, although occasional references are made to

---

[170] C/S: BC & GS 27:548.
[171] Rather than its modern connotation of absconding or departing clandestinely, the term "run away" merely meant "departed."
[172] Prince George's County Patented Survey No. 1905.
[173] Frederick County Land Records, B:598.
[174] Diedenshausen Church records, at Girkhausen. Johannes Weller's ancestry has been traced back to his great grandfather Hans Georg Weller, but John Jacob's parentage — and birth as claimed by the Graceham parish register -- have not been verified in German Church Books. See Henry James Young, transl., "The Families Belonging to the Moravian Community and Congregation at Graceham in Maryland and Some of Their Neighbors, 1759-1871" [typescript from the Parish Register] (n.s., 1942), p. 120.
[175] Strassburger-Hinke, *op. cit.*, Lists 99ABC, pp. 340-342

his association with the families of earlier arrivals.[176] He lived on a portion of "Arnold's Delight" northeast of present-day Thurmont.

Johann Jacob Weller arrived in this country five years after the majority of his earlier German neighbors, but he came quite soon to their area of Frederick County, where he figured most prominently in its subsequent history. He arrived in Philadelphia aboard the *Saint Andrew Galley* on September 26, 1737.[177] With him came the Lutheran minister Johann Philipp Streiter and the Reformed ministers Johann Hermann von Basten[178] and Peter Henry Dorsius.[179] Supposedly Weller also brought with him a wife, Anna Margaret Koehn, whom he had married in Germany in 1726 and who died of dropsy at Skippack in Pennsylvania after their arrival.[180] But these details have never been verified, nor are there any indications of children born during the decade of their alleged marriage. Supposedly, also, Weller was initially drawn to the Kreutz Creek settlement in today's Hellam Township, York County, Pennsylvania in search of a friend, John Peitzel.[181] The locale is correct, for it was at Hellam (Stöver called it Helm Town) that Johann Jacob Weller was married on April 21, 1738 to Maria Barbara Willheut, the widow of Leonard Vieruhr (1707-1737e).[182]

Maria Barbara was the daughter of Friederich Willheut and a

---
[176] See above, for example, p. 202, Ambrose.
[177] Strassburger-Hinke, *op. cit.*, Lists 47ABC, pp. 179-184.
[178] Van Basten was supposedly Dutch, a 1731 graduate at Duisburg University. He left Pennsylvania in 1738 for New Jersey, Long Island and Fishkill in New York, but eventually disappeared from the records.
[179] Peter Henry Dorsius (1711-1757e) from Moers on the lower Rhine near Düsseldorf studied at the Universities of Groningen and Leyden. He came to America in answer to a call from the Neshaminy congregation in Bucks County, but that congregation became increasingly dissatisfied with him. He was finally dismissed in 1748. Deserting his wife Jane Hoogland in Pennsylvania, he returned to Holland where he sought, but did not gain, dismission from the Holland Deputies so that he could accept a call with the Dutch West India Company on the Gold Coast of Africa. See Hinke, *Reformed Ministers*, *op. cit.*, pp. 318-325 and Glatfelter, *op. cit.*, p. 31.
[180] Young, *loc. cit.*
[181] *Ibid.* Johannes Beitzel and wife Maria Magdalena had children baptised by Jacob Lischy, early Moravian itinerant, in 1746 and 1748 at Kreutz Creek. Their children's sponsors included Lorentz and Elisabeth Krieger. See Henry James Young, *The Private Record of Jacob Lischy, V.D.M., 1743-1769* (typescript, 1934). In 1748, according to Matthias Gottlieb Gottschalk, Mr. Peizel lived in Little Canawage. Cf. also Hinke and Kemper, "Moravian Diaries," *loc. cit.*, 12:278. Johannes Beizel accompanied Schnell and Brandmüller from Canawackes to Jacob Matheus' place, five miles north of Jacob Weller's, on October 20, 1749. Cf. Schnell, "Kurze Beschreibung," *loc. cit.*
[182] Stöver, *op. cit.*, p. 4, No. 166. He recorded the bride's name as Anna Barbara Vieruhr and repeated the entry in the Lancaster Church Book, *loc. cit.*, p. 432.

sister of Anna Magdalena, wife of Martin Frey, and Maria Eliesabetha, wife of Nicolaus Koger. Koger had arrived in Philadelphia on October 17, 1732 along with Bernard Weymer, Mattheus Manser and Peter Apfel. Maria Barbara was also the sister of Friederich Willheut who married Anna Maria Weymar and became the ancestor of the numerous Willhides in Frederick County. Maria Barbara had married Vieruhr in 1734. As Lenhart Firohr he had arrived at Philadelphia at the age of 24 on September 21, 1731. He came on the same ship as the Wetzels and Devilbisses. With "his bride" Maria Barbara Willhautin, he stood as sponsor on September 15, 1734 for a child of Johann Georg Quickel.[183] Nine days later he took part in the attack on the Lancaster County Sheriff who was attempting to jail Jacob Lochman in the Pennsylvania-Maryland border dispute.[184] Maria Barbara had one son by her first marriage, Henry Firor, who in 1757 married Magdalena, daughter of the above Johann Jacob Matthias.

On August 9, 1738, less than four months after the Weller-Willheut marriage, Jacob Willer had his first land surveyed in present-day Frederick County. Called "Taylor's Lot," it had its beginning point "in the backlands of the border of the Province on the west side of Monocacy River on Great Hunting Creek."[185] This placed it about a mile and a half north of Michael Reisner's plantation of "Green Spring" which was surveyed on the same day. In today's terms, Weller's land lay in the general Thurmont area between Blue Mount and Moser Roads, west of Jimtown cross roads. In 1743 Weller had another survey made, which lay between his earlier survey and Reisner's 1743 "Smith's Lot." This he called "Taylor's Piglison."[186] In 1745 he located "Taylor's Shears" midway between present-day Thurmont and Jimtown,[187] and in 1752 he added "Taylor's Bodkin" near the wagon road which is now the Jimtown-Thurmont road. Weller called this the "road that goes from Fredericktown to Ambrose's Mill."[188] Finally, in 1755 he had "Taylor's Needle" surveyed at Jimtown crossroads itself.[189]

Joh. Jacob Weller and his wife Maria Barbara had their first child Johann Jacob baptized on June 15, 1739, probably at Codorus, although Stöver was in the Monocacy area two days later.[190] On September 27, 1741 they were present for the baptism of Maria Barbara's nephew Johann Jacob Koger.[191] When the Frederick Lutheran Church Book was begun, they appear as Lutheran sponsors for

---
[183] Lancaster Lutheran Church Book, loc. cit., p. 405, where his name was spelled Vier Uhr (German, "four o'clock"). The name evolved into Firor.
[184] See above, p. 18.
[185] C/S: LG C:47.
[186] C/S: LG E:214.
[187] C/S: LG E:574.
[188] Patent: BC & GS 32:132.
[189] C/S: BC & GS 1:296.
[190] The entry does not appear in Stöver's personal Journal, op. cit., but is in the Lancaster Lutheran Church Book.
[191] Stöver, op. cit., p. 29. The entry is crossed out as Stöver about this time began the new Codorus or York Church Book.

daughters of Mateus Ambrose on June 13, 1743 and Jacob Mateus on March 29, 1744. The 1744 baptism of their own daughter Elisa Juliyana is also entered in the Frederick Lutheran record. But Weller was not a contributor to the Frederick Lutheran Church Book begun in 1742, and he did not sign the 1747 Articles of Pastor Muhlenberg. Instead, after the arrival of Laurentius Nyberg in 1744 he aligned himself more and more with the faction which eventually split away to form the Moravian congregation at Graceham. Early meetings were held at the Weller home. Following a visit in 1747 by Weller and his friend John Jacob Matthias, Daniel Dulany in Annapolis made provision for the grant of ten acres for the new congregation. The resulting parcel, appropriately named "Gift," was surveyed on July 3, 1747 by Thomas Cresap for Dulany, who then assigned the certificate to Jacob Matthias "in trust for Matthias Keitz [Reuz] and his successors."[192] The lot was patented on November 5, 1751,[193] and its site is occupied today by the Graceham Moravian Church, about a mile and a half northeast of Jimtown crossroads and a similar distance east of the center of Thurmont.

Johann Jacob Weller is frequently mentioned in accounts of the travels of early Moravian missionaries.[194] In 1748, for example, Matthias Gottlieb Gottschalk summarized a list of places where the Moravians would be welcome. "In Manakasy," he wrote, "Are two places where we can preach. The usual place is Mr. Weller's. Across the Manakasy a few German families live, about ten, who would perhaps like to hear a sermon. A man called Ellrod,[195] whom I visited there, will be able to give more information. Captain Ogle and Jacob Weller are both very dear hosts of the Brethren. It would perhaps be a blessing to Mr. Weller's house if Brother Joseph [Spangenberg] would lodge there occasionally."[196] Later, in August 1748, Brother Joseph did visit Weller. In October 1749 the missionaries Schnell and Brandmüller spent nearly a week at the home of Jacob Wöller on their way to Virginia. Schnell reported preaching on the morning of October 22nd, then baptizing Jacob Wöller's daughter Mary Magdalena and his brother [sic] Johann Wöller's son Johannes. Two days were spent visiting people in the surrounding neighborhood. On October 25th a gathering of 34 souls assembled at Wöller's home. Philip Grüber's son Philip Ernst was baptized then, and plans for building a school house were discussed.[197]

---
[192] See above, p. 152.
[193] C/S: BY & GS 5:541; Patent: BY & GS 4:139. There is no mention in either certificate or patent of the Moravians as such. This Gift from "Mr Delany" is noted in August Gottlieb Spangenberg's Diary concerning his visit with Weller on August 7, 1748. See his "Kurze Nachricht," *loc. cit.* Hinke's translation, *Virginia Magazine of History and Biography*, 11:242, omits this notation.
[194] See above, pp. 147, 152.
[195] William Ellrod: see below, p. 315.
[196] Hinke and Kemper, "Moravian Diaries," *loc. cit.*, 12:78.
[197] Schnell, "Kurze Beschreibung," *loc. cit.* The transcription by Hinke and Kemper, Moravian Diaries, *loc. cit.*, 11:116, excludes this portion of the Diary.

It was not until October 8-9, 1758 that the Moravian congregation was formally organized. Among the communicants or probationers at the Sunday service were John Jacob Weller and his new wife Elisabeth Krieger (Maria Barbara had died in 1755), George Gump and his wife Rosina Mack, Lawrence Krieger and his wife Maria Elisabeth Hahn,[198] Leonard Moser and wife Maria Sarah, Caspar Schmidt[199] and wife Christina, George Harbaugh and wife Catharine,[200] Lorentz Protzman and his wife Maria Elisabeth,[201] and Peter Williar and his wife Elisabetha Magdalena Schlim.[202] On Monday, October 9th, George Harbaugh and Lorenz Protzman were elected stewards of the congregation.[203]

The name **Jaques Bonet** would hardly appear to be German, yet that is the spelling given by the 32-year old immigrant who arrived at Philadelphia on August 27, 1733 aboard the ship *Elizabeth*. Perhaps of Huguenot ancestry, he was listed among the 58 "Palatines" who with their families made up the total of 172 passengers on board. Like him, many of these Germans were destined to find their way to Frederick County. Jaques Bonet brought with him his wife Mary, also age 32, and four children who ranged in age from nine months to 8 years. But it was a sad arrival, for daughters Susanna and Christina had died on the way and only Margret, the eldest, and John Simon, the youngest, remained alive.[204]

Jacob Bonnett — so the 1733 ship's captain as well as subsequent Maryland records spelled the name -- first appeared in Maryland land records ten years later. He received from Daniel Dulany on May 28, 1743 the certificate of survey for "Wine Garden" which he then reassigned to Martin Wetzel.[205] Wetzel also received in 1743 the patent for "Bonnett's Resolution," thereby suggesting other dealings between the two men. Bonnett had his own land surveyed the following year and on the May 26, 1744 certificate for "Battleham" noted its location "on the west bank of Hunting Creek below the fork of said creek."[206] His parcel thus lay between present-day Lewistown and Creagerstown, just east of Honey's "Den of Wolves" near where the 1873 Atlas shows the home of G[eorge A.] Graham.[207] By 1753 the land had been resurveyed from 100 to 250 acres for Jacob Bonnett, who assigned it to John Hoofman.[208]

---

[198] Lorentz Krieger in 1744 had "Creager's Delight" surveyed midway between present-day Thurmont and Graceham (C/S: LG E:343) and purchased "Middle Choice" from Joseph Ogle (see p. 326).
[199] See below, p. 330.
[200] George Harbaugh acquired a few acres of "Mount Olivet" near Sabillasville from Schmidt.
[201] The Protzmans later built a home in the village of Graceham.
[202] The Williars also acquired a part of "Mount Olivet" from Caspar Schmidt.
[203] Oerter, *op. cit.*, pp. 23-24. See also above, p. 152.
[204] Strassburger-Hinke, *op. cit.*, Lists 30AA'BC, pp. 113-115, 765-767.
[205] C/S: LG E:208.
[206] C/S: BY & GS 5:542; Patent: BY & GS 4:164.
[207] Lake, *op. cit.*, p. 15.

According to family records, Jacob Bonnett was twice married. Of his children, Catharine married John Six, Mary married John Wetzel, Elizabeth married Martin Wetzel, Jr., and Lewis married Elizabeth Waggoner. Most of the Bonnetts moved on to Rockingham County, Virginia.[209]

John Verdriess, Jr., had "John's Mountain" surveyed for himself on November 3, 1738 in a location somewhat west of the other German settlers.[210] It snuggled up against the foot of Catoctin Mountain and lay immediately south of Catoctin Furnace. Although the name on the patent was recorded as John Nidress, Jr., an unfamiliar surname in the Frederick County area, the mystery was cleared fourteen years later when adjoining vacant land called "Good Will" was surveyed with a beginning point on the west boundary of "John's Mountain" which had been "taken up by John Verdreys."[211] The original beginning point for "John's Mountain" was noted "on the west side of Hunting Creek sixty perches above Mirey Lique," which indicates the probable existence of a salt marsh in Verdriess' day.

At an early date the Verdriess family was probably living near today's Brickerville in what was then known as Warwick, but is now Elizabeth, Township in northern Lancaster County. John Verdriess and his wife stood as baptism sponsors there on March 21, 1730 for a daughter of Johann Georg Bleystein.[212] Likewise Jacob Verdriess and Catharina Euler in February 1736 were baptism sponsors for a child of Friedrich Heinrich Geelwichs[213] and then, a month later, were themselves married at Warwick by Pastor Stöver.[214] Catharina was a daughter of Conrad Eyler (d 1751) of present-day Manheim Township, York County.[215]

By June 24, 1741 Jacob Verdriess was presumably in the Monocacy area when Pastor Stöver baptized his eldest children, Catarina born in 1739 and Johannes born in 1741. Philipp Ernst Grüber, whom we've met above, and Joh. Valentin Verdriess were sponsors for both.[216] An ex post facto entry in the later Frederick

---
[208] C/S: BC & GS 1:166.
[209] From the notes of Professor J. Clarke Sanders of Keyser, West Virginia.
[210] Patent: EI 6:136. No C/S was recorded.
[211] Patent: BC & GS 27:215. "Good Will" was surveyed for 150 acres for Dr. Charles Carroll (1691-1755) on June 29, 1752, but was patented on September 29, 1765 to his son Charles Carroll, Barrister (1723-1783). See chart, p. 26.
[212] Muddy Creek Lutheran Church Book, p. 18, which notes that Bleystein subsequently "became a Dunker." This entry is not included in Stöver's personal Journal, op. cit.
[213] Stöver, op. cit., p. 41, whose spelling and exact date vary slightly from the Muddy Creek Church Book transcription, op. cit., p. 35. Both records place Geelwichs at Conewago.
[214] Stöver, Marriages, op. cit., p. 3, No. 103; Muddy Creek Church Book, op. cit., p. 110.
[215] Cf. York County Land Records, F:511.
[216] Stöver, op. cit., p. 28. Curiously, these baptisms were re-entered in the Frederick Lutheran Church Book, p. 11, without dates

Lutheran Church Book, p. 8, records the birth of Jacob's son Johann Jacob on September 30, 1743. Valentine Verdriess named two of his children similarly, Maria Catrina born in 1743 and Johannes in 1744.[217] Johann Friedrich Verdriess likewise appears in the Monocacy area about this time. On June 24, 1741 he was a baptism sponsor for a son of Matthias Ambrose.[218] John, Valentine and Friedrich Verdriess all contributed to the purchase of the Frederick Lutheran Churchbook about 1742, and each of them signed Muhlenberg's Articles entered in that book in 1747. John Verdress [Sr.?] took Lutheran communion from Pastor Candler on June 26, 1743, followed by John [Jr.?] and Valentine Verdris on September 25, 1743, all preparatory to naturalizations on October 19, 1743.[219] Friedrich Verdriess married Dorothea Buch on November 25, 1746, and the baptisms of their children appear later in the Frederick Lutheran Church Book, Johann Friedrich [Jr.] in 1747 and Johann Jacob in 1749. On March 24, 1769 John Valentine Verdress conveyed "John's Mountain" to Thomas Johnson and Bened[ict] Calvert.[220] But by 1772 Jacob Verdriess had taken his family to Frederick County, Virginia.[221]

Hartman Vertriess (1716-1778) presents a somewhat different picture. His association seems to have been with the Moravians rather than the Lutherans, and he is the only "Verdriess" whose grave has been found in Frederick County.[222] According to the Moravian records,[223] he was born in 6701-Fussengönheim, between Bad Dürkheim and Ludwigshafen in the Palatinate, and with his parents came to America at an early age. He was married to Catharina Bender on February 14, 1744, still at Warwick,[224] then allegedly joined the Moravians at Bethlehem in 1748 but didn't come to Maryland until 1764 when he occupied land given him by his father. Unless his father bore the same given name, this conflicts greatly with the land records. They show Hardman Vertries on October 18, 1753 receiving a patent for "Blue Spring" which had been surveyed initially for Daniel Dulany on January 10, 1742/43. Its beginning point was "at the head of a small branch which descends to the west side of Little Hunting Creek, a branch of Monocacy."[225] The parcel was thus located

---

and with Johannes Verdriess and his wife Catharina as sponsors.
[217] A daughter Maria Magdalena was also baptized in 1747. Frederick Lutheran Church Book, pp. 3, 9, 11.
[218] Muddy Creek Lutheran Church Book, op. cit., p. 27. This entry does not appear in Stöver's personal Journal, though from other records we place Stöver at Monocacy on the day in question. See above, p. 202.
[219] Provincial Court Judgment Records, 1742-1744, EI 7:296.
[220] Frederick County Land Records, M:147; Maryland Rent Rolls (Frederick No. 1), 32:60.
[221] Letter from Dr. J. S. Eilar of Albuquerque, New Mexico, to Dr. Arthur G. Tracey, October 26, 1956.
[222] Holdcraft, op. cit., p. 1173. His gravestone at the Graceham cemetery spells his name Hartman Vertries.
[223] Young, Graceham, op. cit., p. 115.
[224] Stöver, op. cit., No. 442. The entry is missing from the Muddy Creek Church Book transcription.

immediately south of John Verdriess' land. Coincidentally, five days after the January 1743 survey was made, Hartman Verdriess and Catharina Klein were baptism sponsors, still in Lancaster County, for a son of Jacob Heyl, who lived at Warwick.[226]

Dieter Lehnich has not been located among the lists of German immigrants arriving at the port of Philadelphia after 1727. He signed his name with a "TL" mark, but since he could not write his name more fully, any number of phonetic renditions appears in the records for him. Probably nearest correct was Stöver's Dieterich Lehnich, for whose diminutive (Dieter) **Teter Laney** became an anglicized substitute. There is no doubt, however, concerning his German origins. He is first mentioned in the Falckner Swamp area of today's Montgomery County, Pennsylvania, where on November 8, 1730, together with Balthasar and Susanna Fauth, he stood as baptism sponsor for a son of Johann Georg Schweinhart.[227] He did not appear on the Philadelphia County tax lists as owning property in today's Montgomery County before 1734 as did Schweinhardt, Fauts and Getzendonner. But he was named in a 1736 Prince George's County Court case against Robert Debutts, who faced a number of charges, including that of "hitting Tetur Laney on the cheek and causing blood to flow."[228] On May 16, 1736 Lehnich stood as a baptism witness for a daughter of Henry Bray (Prey).[229]

Lehnich presumably lived initially on "Tasker's Chance," probably north of today's city of Frederick, just west of Harmony Grove. His land would have included a portion of present Fort Detrick. In 1737 Benjamin Tasker listed Peter Laney as one of six individuals settled on his "Tasker's Chance" who wanted to purchase the entire tract.[230] By 1741, however, his parcel was probably in the hands of Henry Rhodes[231] and he himself had moved to the area where Lewistown now stands. "Cooper's Point" was surveyed for Tetur Laney on December 19, 1741,[232] and on June 20, 1743 Teder Lany had "Addition to Sassafras Bottom" also surveyed.[233] In 1742 Jno. TeterLany's name was one of the German names which appeared on the petition to divide Prince George's Parish.[234] On October 15, 1742 Titur Laney, Philip Kince and Matthew Reisling were naturalized.[235] As Dieder Lehnick, he contributed to the purchase of the Frederick Lutheran Church Book and in its

---

[225] C/S: BC & GS 1:259.
[226] Muddy Creek Church Book, op. cit., p. 51. The entry is not included in Stöver's personal Journal.
[227] Stöver, op. cit., p. 3. See above, p. 154.
[228] See also above, p. 77.
[229] Stöver, op. cit., p. 16. See below, p. 274.
[230] Maryland Provincial Court Records, EI 8:28. See below, p. 258.
[231] Two corners of Jacob Brunner's "Tasker's Chance" land were nevertheless defined in his deed of 1746 in terms of Tetur Laney's land.
[232] C/S: LG E:86.
[233] C/S: LG E:280.
[234] See below, p. 371.
[235] Provincial Court Judgment Records, 1742-1744, EI 7:110. See also above, p. 169-170.

first pages appears as Peter Lehn among the May 1743 entries when his son Joseph was baptized. In 1747 as Deter (TL) Lehny he "signed" by mark Pastor Muhlenberg's Lutheran "Articles" in that book. In early 1750 a jury acquitted Tetur Laney, charged with stealing two hogs valued at 200 pounds of tobacco from Abraham Miller, another of the 1737 would-be purchasers of "Tasker's Chance."[236] Despite this disagreement, Tetur Lany and his wife Hannah sold the 200 acres of "Cooper's Point" for £80 to Abraham Miller on March 23, 1750.[237] He may already have been meeting severe financial reverses. Indebted to Daniel Dulany on bond, he was "in the custody of the Sheriff" on demand from Silas Enyart and Nicholas Bondrake. To extricate himself on March 26, 1750 he conveyed "Addition to Sassafras Bottom" to Dulany for five shillings.[238]

If one were to divide the early German settlements between those lying to the north of present-day Lewistown and those found south of today's Bethel, the land of **Henry Six** would have been situated in the middle. Located in the vicinity of today's Powell Road southwest of Lewistown, just below Lehnich's land, Hendrick Sicks' "Piney Neck" had been surveyed on November 28, 1741 for Daniel Dulany from whom Six was purchasing it on time. Its beginning point was "on the west side of a glade that falls into Jacob Neff's spring branch," known today as Muddy Run.[239] The added notation on the certificate of survey that "on this land is a logg house, logs round, and a turnip patch" may indicate that someone other than Six had been there for some time previously.[240] Philip Küntz, Adam Stull and Jacob Staley had similar time purchase arrangements with Dulany, all dating from surveys in 1741. But Hendrick Sicks was the last to receive title. His patent was dated August 26, 1746.

Most probably Henry Six arrived in Maryland in 1745. He was the son of Johann Philipp Sixt from the area near Marienfels in the Taunus, northwest of Wiesbaden. Born in 1689, he had come to New York with his parents in the large German emigration of 1709-1710. There on August 3, 1713 he married Anna Christina Theis from Niederbachheim near Gemmerich in the principality of Darmstadt. She also had come with the 1710 migration. Henrich and Christina Six moved to Neu-Ansberg [Hartsmannsdorf[241]] in the Schoharie Valley of upstate New York where most of their children were born. In 1744 Pastor Peter Nicholas Sommer[242] listed his Schoharie Lutheran

---
[236] Rice, *The Life*, op. cit., p. 35. For Abraham Miller, see below, p. 283.
[237] Frederick County Land Records, B:398.
[238] Frederick County Land Records, B:150.
[239] For Neff, see above, p. 111, not to be confused with John Henry Neff, p. 296.
[240] C/S: LG E:588.
[241] See Dern, ed., *Albany Protocol*, op. cit., map p. 99.
[242] Peter Nicholas Sommer (1709-1795) was born in Hamburg where he was ordained by Pastor Johann Georg Palm. In answer to Pastor Wilhelm Christoph Berkenmeyer's appeal and Schoharie's call of 1741, Sommer arrived in New York in 1743 to serve a lifetime in the

parishioners, and in the list included Hinrich Six, his wife Christina and their children Catharina, Christina Elisabetha, Gertraud, Henrich, Johannes, Philip, Conrad, Johannes [sic], and Adam. Anna Maria Dillenbach may also have been a daughter.[243]

The tie to Maryland lies in the 1776 burial record for Catharina Dewis. Born in 1714, she was shown as the daughter of Henrich and Christina Six and the wife of Robert Dewis whom she had married in 1736. The notation further ties to the 1744 Sommer Schoharie list, which also included Robert Dewis [spelled as a German would pronounce "Davis"], wife Cathar. [Six], and children Catharina, Hinrich and Anna Maria Dewis, as well as John and Anna Dewi.

John Davis will be recognized as one of the signers of the Muhlenberg Articles of 1747.[244] Henry Sex, probably the son, though already a church warden, and Henrich Sechs [the father?] also signed, both with an "HS" mark. Three years later, Henry, Henry Jr., Philip and Conrad Six were all listed in the March 1749/50 Frederick County Court records as having sworn evidence to the Grand Jury.[245] Henry Six, the father, born in 1689, petitioned the June Court of 1755 for relief, since he was "upwards of sixty years old and unable to work."[246] On August 19th of that year Henry Six, farmer, obviously his son, purchased 100 acres of "Cat-tail Branch," northeast of Emmitsburg from George and Christina Smith.[247] Presumably he was the Joh. Henrich Sechss who on July 6, 1749 had married Elisabeth Greintsch.[248] He and Elisabeth on May 21, 1752 conveyed "Piney Neck" to Georg Michael Jesserang,[249] the husband of Elisabeth Six, and another signer of Muhlenberg's 1747 Church Articles. Jesserang was born in Pirmasens, Germany in 1719, arrived in Philadelphia with his father Bartholomew Jesserang on December 11, 1739, and married Elisabeth Six on February 5, 1745. He died, less than five years after his father, on

---

Lutheran congregations of the Schoharie and Mohawk valleys. See Dern, ibid., p. 298.

[243] Jones, *Palatine Families, op. cit.*, pp. 959-960, a superb work of detective analysis in both German and New York documents.

[244] See above, p. 146. Since they were still in New York in 1742, neither "Six" signed the 1742 petition to divide Prince George's Parish (see below, p. 371). But John, Peter and John Valentine Presler did, and they also relate to the 1710 German migration. When Andrew Presler was baptized in St. Stephen's Parish, Cecil County, on February 4, 1732/33, he was shown as a son of Andreas Presler and grandson of John Vollintine Presler. The family of Johan Valentyn Bresler (born 1670e) and his wife Anna Christiana, who arrived in New York in 1710 with, among others, son Andreas (born 1700c), has also been traced in New York by Jones, *op. cit.*, pp 102-104, 1159.

[245] Judgment Record, A:397.
[246] Ibid., H:813.
[247] Frederick County Land Records, E:811.
[248] Frederick Lutheran Church Book.
[249] Ibid., B:563. Almost immediately, on November 3, 1752, Jesserang had a Resurvey made (C/S: BC & GS 1:144). In 1766 a part of "Piney Neck" was in the possession of Nicholas Phillips (C/S: BC & GS 30:160).

January 21, 1772, leaving his widow and three daughters.[250] Other Six children appear in the records: Catharina [Six] Davis died on April 23, 1776 at the age of 62 leaving two of five sons and six of seven daughters as survivors.[251] Johannes Sechs married Catharina Barbara Reisner on July 6, 1749. Adam Six was sworn to testify to the Grand Jury in August 1754 and was then discharged.[252]

Two other surveys made in the German area at the very end of the year 1743 should be noted. On November 26, 1743 **George Chydler** had his "Longatepaugh" surveyed "on the north side of a run of Great Hunting Creek at the foot of the mountain."[253] Today this would be located just west of Thurmont. In 1747 Chydler enlarged the acreage by a resurvey.[254] In the Atlas of 1873 the home of Benjamin Firor is shown on Chydler's land.[255]

On November 29, 1743 **Henry Trout** selected "Rich Bottom" for his homestead. It was located "on a rocky hill on the west side of Great Hunting Creek," west of present-day Thurmont on the road to Foxville.[256] But Trout had been in the Monocacy area at least five years before, when on November 24, 1738, as Johann Heinrich Traut, he married Anna Maria Baumin.[257] Two children were baptized in the Lutheran Church, Anna Maria in 1744 and Henrich in 1746.[258] The family then left the Thurmont area when Henry Trout in 1746 purchased "Trout Pond" on "Tasker's Chance" along its northwestern boundary.[259] Later generations moved into the city of Frederick. The Trout family is of special interest for its ties to the families of Hoffman, Ley, Weiss and Unselt, all of whom, having come to America together in 1733, are described in the chapter on "Tasker's Chance."

By way of statistical summary, it may be noted that at the end of 1743 some 40 individual German or Swiss families had settled along the German Monocacy Road between present-day Thurmont and the area west of today's city of Frederick. Of these, no more than five are suspected of being in the area before 1738, the date of the first land record for any of them. But then, almost immediately, ten of the 40 appear in land records in 1738-39 with 14 more by 1743. Two families obtained more than one parcel so that altogether out of 32 total surveys made along the German Monocacy Road between 1738 and 1743 all but six were surveyed for Germans or Swiss.

The delay between actual settlement in Maryland and acquisition of land title is indeterminate at best, but for 17 individuals

---

[250] Frederick Lutheran Church Book, Burials. For Bartholomew Jesserang, see Frederick County Administrative Accounts, A1:424.
[251] Frederick Lutheran Church Book, Burials. Her husband's name is spelled there, again in phonetically perfect German, as Robert Dewiss.
[252] Frederick Court Judgment Record, H2:565, 570.
[253] C/S: LG E:303.
[254] C/S: BY & GS 1:634.
[255] Lake, op. cit., p. 37.
[256] C/S: LG E:305.
[257] Stöver, op. cit., Marriages, p. 4, No. 194.
[258] Frederick Lutheran Church Book, pp. 4, 9.
[259] See also below, p. 299.

whose arrivals in the Monocacy area are known to have preceded their acquisition of land, the average delay in formally acquiring land was six years. This span varied rather markedly between our two arbitrary areas, averaging only four years for those Germans in the upper area, but nine years in the lower section. Eleven of those Germans who were known to have been present before 1743 did not get their land until after that date, some of them not until 1756. For five individuals there is no land record at all. They either were squatters or, more probably, moved on elsewhere. These notations exclude those Germans settled on "Tasker's Chance" or on "Monocacy Manor," whose initial settlements are discussed in subsequent chapters.

CATOCTIN VALLEY

Catoctin Valley stretches from north to south within the hills of western Frederick County. It lies between Catoctin Mountain on the east and South Mountain, the County's western boundary, on the west. Through it flows Catoctin Creek which with its several tributaries traverses a distance of over twenty miles as the crow flies but many more as they meander through the picturesque countryside.

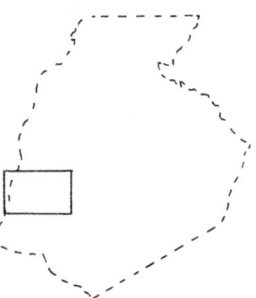

Exactly when **Richard Touchstone** came to the Valley cannot be ascertained, but he did appear on the 1733 list of Monocacie taxables, and on the 1734 list of those "in Monoccosea Hundred that had no tobacco burnt." On March 25, 1734 he leased 100 acres of "Carrollton."[1] His own land, called "Anchor and Hope," was surveyed on March 6, 1739.[2] It lay along Catoctin Creek itself, west and slightly north of present-day Jefferson, and it included what is now known as Lewis' Mill. For long years a bridle path passed his home. It undoubtedly followed an old Indian trail and, although known initially as the road "from Monocacy to Shenandoah Mountain"[3] or the road "from Monocacy to Antietam," it soon became known as the road "via Richard Touchstone's." The road had been made a public road in 1738 with Flayl Payne as its first overseer, but for many years thereafter the Court named Richard Touchstone as its overseer — as early as 1740-1742 and as late as 1745-1749. From Touchstone's place the road crossed South Mountain and entered today's Washington County at Crampton Gap before heading on to Israel Friend's Mill on Antietam Creek.[4] The road was modified in 1745, but continued to be called Touchstone's Road. In the years after 1750 the Court appointed as overseers Flayle Payne who lived near present-day Knoxville, Thomas Hawkins, Michael Creager, William House, Flayle Payne, Jr., Barton Philpot and a younger Thomas Prather, all of whom lived in the area around Jefferson Pike or today's U.S. Highway 340.

Richard Touchstone and his wife Sarah Johnson presumably had sons Richard, Caleb, Daniel, Henry and Stephen Touchstone. In early 1745 Richard Touchstone had a survey made a little south of today's

---

[1] Prince George's County Land Records, T:172, where his name was spelled Tutchston.
[2] C/S: EI 5:509.
[3] Shenandoah Mountain is now known as South Mountain.
[4] See Rice, *New Facts, op. cit.*, pp. 55-59, for an enlightening discussion of this road's subsequent history.

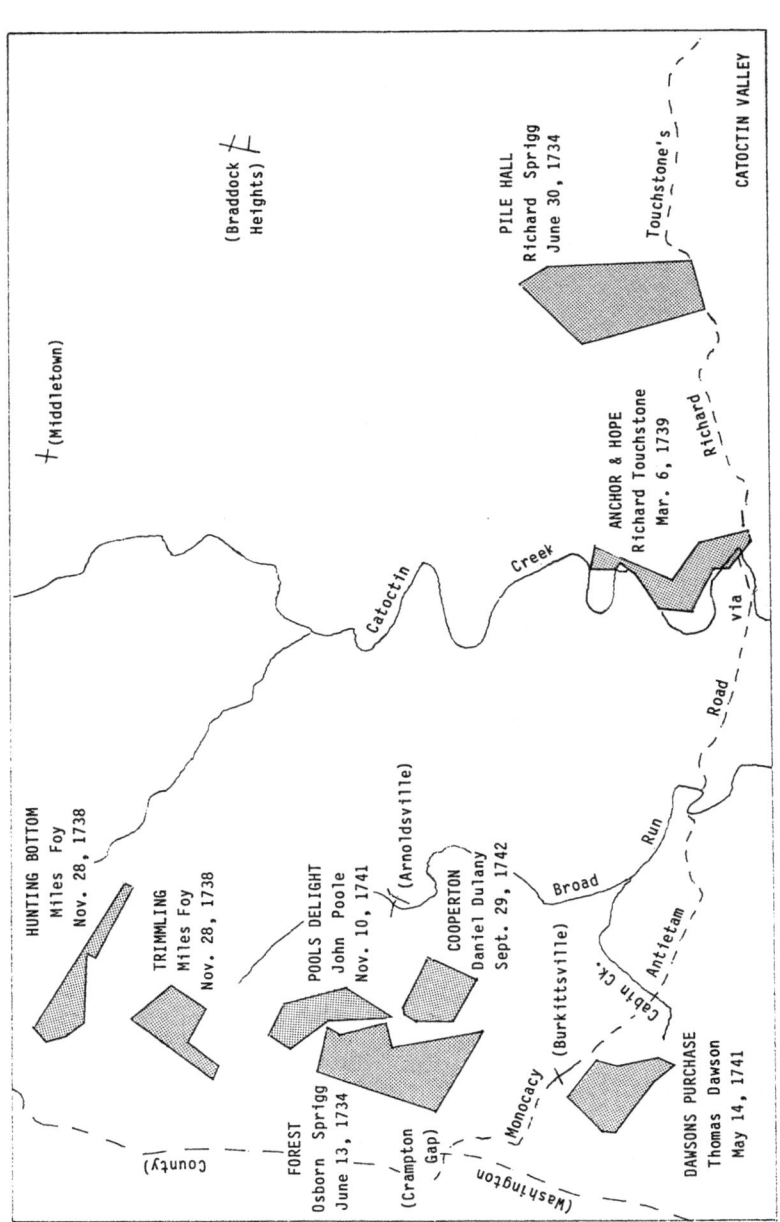

Middletown which he called "Whiskey Alley."[5] He assigned this to his son Caleb Touchstone, who in 1750 sold it to Philip Kiefalpor [Kefauver].[6] Kefauver, with his name next spelled Kanghover, added 500 acres of adjoining vacant land to make a "Resurvey on Whiskey Alley," described in the May 12, 1763 certificate as being "at a place called Tom's Bottom" with its beginning point at "the beginning of the original."[7] The certificate made no mention of any building on the land, which today is occupied by the western portion of Middletown.

"Chancey" was surveyed on February 9, 1744/45 for Richard Touchstone, who assigned the certificate in June to Henry Touchstone.[8] He in turn passed title to Richard Touchstone[9] (father or brother?), who conveyed it to George Moore, Sr.[10] Interestingly, Thomas Cresap and Henry Munday were witnesses to this latter transaction. Additionally, Caleb Touchstone had "Batchelor's Hall" surveyed for himself on July 8, 1746,[11] but conveyed it to Richard Touchstone.[12] In 1746 James Mason had his "Mason's Folly" located "on the east side of Abraham's Creek"[13] between the mountains and about two miles above Richard Touchstone's."[14]

Richard Touchstone appeared in the records of the March 1746 Prince George's County Court along with Joseph Chapline and John Skidmore, standing as pledge for William Hayward, merchant. The Frederick County March Court of 1752 held Richard Touchstone for passing an old Spanish Coin of Eight to James Burgess. But further word is lacking. Seemingly the Touchstones left the Catoctin Valley sometime in the 1750s, for Michael Cregar was then in possession of both "Batchelor's Hall" and "Anchor and Hope."

Richard Touchstone's wife, Sarah Johnson, was the daughter of Daniel and Frances Johnson and the sister of Hannah Johnson, wife of Thomas Cresap. After Daniel Johnson died, his widow Frances married, in succession, Edward Harris, Hugh Grant and **Miles Foy**. The latter in 1736 was a 62-year old woolcomber who claimed he was from Baltimore County though he worked for Elisha Gatchell, Justice of the Peace in Chester County.[15] He and Frances lived near Thomas Cresap's home in the Conojohela [Canadochly] area south of today's Wrightsville on the Susquehanna River. There they experienced the

---
[5] C/S: BC & GS 1:187. [Pat. Ser. 81].
[6] Frederick County Land Records, B:306.
[7] C/S: BC & GS 37:263. Williams, *op. cit.*, p. 500, adds some unsubstantiated claims concerning the use and loss of this land as an early Union Reformed and Lutheran Church.
[8] C/S: TI 1:441.
[9] Frederick County Land Records, B:94.
[10] *Ibid.*, B:101. George, John and William Moore were listed as Monocosie Hundred Taxables in 1733. The same three, along with William Moore, Jr., all signed the 1742 petition to divide Prince George's Parish. See below, p. 369, 371.
[11] C/S: TI 1:34.
[12] Frederick County Land Records, B:367.
[13] I.e., Catoctin Creek.
[14] C/S: TI 1:416.
[15] Proceedings of Council, 1732-1738, *Archives of Maryland*, 28:98.

trials and hostilities of the strife with the Pennsylvanians, including his own arrest in November 1736 at the time Cresap's house was burned.[16] Two years later the Foys, both of them over 60 years of age, came to the foot of South Mountain to settle on Broad Run in Locust Valley, some four miles northwest of the Touchstones' "Anchor and Hope." Two parcels were surveyed for them on November 28, 1738, "Trimm" and "Hunting Bottom."[17] These were the first patents to be placed in the names of both husband and wife. In signing their deed conveying "Trimling" [sic] to James Spurgin on June 24, 1749, Miles Foy stubbornly persisted in claiming his legal residence was his old Susquehanna home "in Baltimore County."[18] But his wife, when she signed "Trimling" over to James Spurgin on Oct. 31, 1752, acknowledged that she was "of Frederick County."[19] Curiously, Francis [sic] Foy appears among the petitioners seeking a division of Prince George's Parish in 1742, but Miles Foy does not.[20] Frances Foy conveyed the remainder of their Locust Valley land on August 7, 1756 to Sarah Hoosman [Hensamer], and then by her will of September 3, 1756 she gave her entire estate to her grandchild, Sarah Hensamer.[21]

On June 13, 1734 **Osborn Sprigg** had 285 acres surveyed on the north side of Conechigany Road near Shenandoah Mountain. He called it "Forest," and it lay, in modern terms, slightly north of Burkittsville.[22] One month later, on June 30, 1734, his nephew Richard Sprigg had "Pile Hall" surveyed for 366 acres along part of this same road, about a mile directly north of today's Jefferson on today's Roy Remsburg Road.[23] The survey called this Israel Friend's Mill Road, but it was also referred to as the Road by Richard Touchstone's and as the Monocacy-Antietam Road. Touchstone's land lay two miles to the west. The Captain Sprigg whose two slaves were listed as Monocacy taxables in 1733 was Richard's father, Edward Sprigg (1697-1761). In the House Journals he was styled as Captain of the Militia in 1730, Major in 1735 and Colonel in 1742. He served for several years as a Justice of Prince George's County Court. In March of 1736 he petitioned the Court for a ferry at the mouth of the Monocacy River,

---

[16] Cf. above, pp. 18-19. As a non-participant observer of this incident, Frances Foy gave detailed eye-witness testimony on December 24, 1736. See especially *Maryland Historical Magazine*, loc. cit., 3:39-41.
[17] C/S: LG C:48-49.
[18] Frederick County Land Records, B:48. James Spurgeon was included on the 1733 tobacco burning list (see p. 369), but he does not appear in the early land survey records. In 1742 he signed the petition to divide Prince George's Parish. So also did William "Spirgin."
[19] *Ibid.*, B:671.
[20] See below, p. 371.
[21] Frederick County Wills, A1:103.
[22] C/S AM 1:375. Care should be taken to distinguish between Sprigg's "Forest" and John Magruder's 1733 C/S: AM 1:365 for "Forrest" near which Middletown was subsequently located. See p. 40, 243.
[23] C/S: EI 3:425; Patent: EI 4:344. Maryland Rent Rolls (Frederick No. 1), 32:50, dated this survey April 13, 1734.

and, thirteen years later, the November 1749 Court of Frederick County contracted with Osborn Sprigg to keep a ferry there. In September 1739 Edward Sprigg purchased "Happy Choice" from William Black.[24]

The Sprigg family was descended from Thomas Sprigg who arrived in this country from England about 1655. He was a Sheriff in Calvert County and died there in 1704. His children included Ann (wife of Philip Gittings), Martha (wife of Thomas Prather), Sarah (wife of John Pearce), Eleanor (wife first of Thomas Hilleary and then of John Nuthall), Elizabeth (wife of Robert Wade), Mary (wife of Thomas Stockett) and Thomas Sprigg, Jr., who married Margaret Mariarte. Thomas, Jr. was a taxable in Collington Hundred in 1719[25] and the father of Eleanor Sprigg (wife of Henry Wright), Margaret (wife of Francis King and Richard King), Priscilla (wife of Ralph Crabb) and Thomas, Edward and Osborn Sprigg. Edward's wife, Elizabeth Pile, was the daughter of Dr. Richard Pile: hence the name "Pile Hall." Osborn Sprigg's grandchildren included Robert Bowie and Samuel Sprigg, Governors of Maryland, another Osborn Sprigg who married a granddaughter of Thomas Cresap, William Sprigg, a Judge in the Northwest Territory, and Ann Sprigg who married Charles Carroll of Belle Vue.[26]

Osborn Sprigg's "Forest" was conveyed in 1745 to Josiah and Absolam Wilson. It is doubtful that Richard Sprigg spent his entire time at "Pile Hall," for he also inherited large tracts of land in southern Maryland from his father-in-law. He also had early surveys made west of South Mountain in Washington County. Nevertheless, "Pile Hall" remained Sprigg property until 1767 when the 360 acres were conveyed to Thomas Taylor for 250 pounds.[27] In 1768 Gabriel Thomas purchased 160 of the original acres,[28] and in the 1873 Atlas a Mrs. Thomas was shown residing there.[29]

Thomas Dawson and John Poole joined the Catoctin Valley settlement in 1741. They both located at the foot of South Mountain, Dawson directly south of present-day Burkittsville and Pool at today's village of Locust Valley. "Dawson's Purchase" was surveyed on May 14, 1741 with its beginning point on the "east side of Blue Ridge and on the south side of Cabin Branch which descends into Catoctin Creek 300 yards below a place called Philip's Cabin."[30] From this description we know that at least a part of today's Broad Run was at one time called Cabin Branch. By reference to the 1873 Atlas, we also know that "Philip's Cabin" was situated between the Ennis home and the Ahalt Mill as shown in that Atlas.[31] In 1750

---

[24] Prince George's County Land Records, Y:92. See above, p. 30.

[25] *Maryland State Papers No. 1, The Black Books*, para. 163 in the Calendar.

[26] Bowie, *op. cit.*, pp. 593-596. Charles Carroll of Belle Vue (1767-1823) was the son of Charles Carroll of Duddington and Carrolsburg: see chart, p. 26.

[27] Frederick County Land Records, K:1086.

[28] Maryland Rent Rolls (Frederick No. 1), 32:50.

[29] Lake, *op. cit.*, p. 35.

[30] C/S: LG C:196.

Thomas Dawson enlarged his tract by a resurvey and then in 1754 conveyed the entire 215-plus acres to Henry Truman.[32] Dawson, or his son, Thomas, Jr., apparently returned to what is now Montgomery County. The name appears with others of that area in a petition to divide All Saints' Parish after the death of the Rev. Samuel Hunter.[33]

John Poole had land which he called "Pool's Delight" surveyed on November 10, 1741.[34] It was located between Osborn Sprigg's "Forest" and the lands of Miles and Frances Foy. On the 1873 Atlas it is marked as the D[aniel] Sigler home.[35] John Poole was another whose name appeared on the 1742 petition to divide Prince George's Parish.

Also shown on our map, page 223, is "Cooperton," one of some two dozen parcels laid out for Daniel Dulany. It was surveyed on September 29, 1742, but the certificate was not filed until the time of patenting in 1763, long after the Dulany's death.[36]

---

[31] Lake, op. cit., p. 31.
[32] Frederick County Land Records, E:467.
[33] Maryland State Papers No. 1, The Black Books, 10:48; para. 864 in the Calendar. See also Scharf, op. cit., p. 504.
[34] C/S: LG E:79.
[35] Lake, op. cit., p. 13.
[36] C/S: BC & GS 19:459

NEW MARKET AREA

The first important roads of present-day Frederick County have been noted as routes running from north to south with some emphasis on the crossing of the Monocacy River at its mouth. It was not until 1733 that a record was made of an east-west route "to Opeckon"[1] and not until 1734 that records report the use of the road to "Israel Friend's mill on Antietam Creek."[2] But these roads were west of the Monocacy and even the Monocacy Manor Road, east of the river, clung closely to it and carried traffic only north and south. The large southeastern area of today's Frederick County was thus left without settlers and roads during these early years.

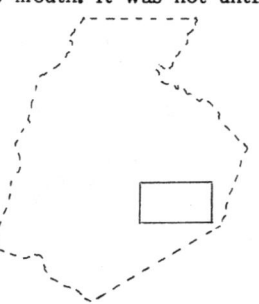

On March 26, 1733 the Maryland Assembly heard a request for a town to be laid out on the Patapsco River at Elk Ridge Landing, now in Howard County, to benefit "the inhabitants of Monocacy and Potowmeck as well as the western end of Baltimore County for their bringing of waggons with grain and other commodities."[3] Thus we have initial word of the interest of tidewater businessmen in procuring produce from the Monocacy area.

The first record of the Monocacy-Annapolis road is found on the certificate of survey for "Kendrick's Hap" in 1739.[4] It was already in sufficient use for the November Court of 1740 to appoint an overseer in the person of John James. James continued to serve until joined by John Martin in 1744 and 1745. Then John Martin and John McKay were overseers for 1746 and 1747, followed by William Turner and William Cummings, Jr. in 1749.

The road began at Monocacy Ford near James Beatty's, then ran south and east from the river to cross Israel Creek and pass the home of William Beatty. It turned southward at what is now the town of Mt. Pleasant toward present-day McKaig, New London and Mount Airy before continuing to Poplar Springs. Thus it traversed a route somewhat south of what is popularly known today as the Old Annapolis Road.[5] Certificates of survey for "Patrick's Colt," "Mackey's Delight," "Pretty Sally" and other parcels mention this important

---

[1] C/S: AM 1:365 for John Magruder's "Forrest." See above, pp. 53, 55, and below, p. 243.
[2] See p. 222.
[3] *Maryland State Papers, No. 1, The Black Books,* 3:108; Proceedings of the Assembly, *Archives of Maryland, op. cit.,* 39:15-16.
[4] C/S: LG C:54.
[5] C/S: LG E:584, 585; Frederick Co. Land Recd. JS 35:518, etc.

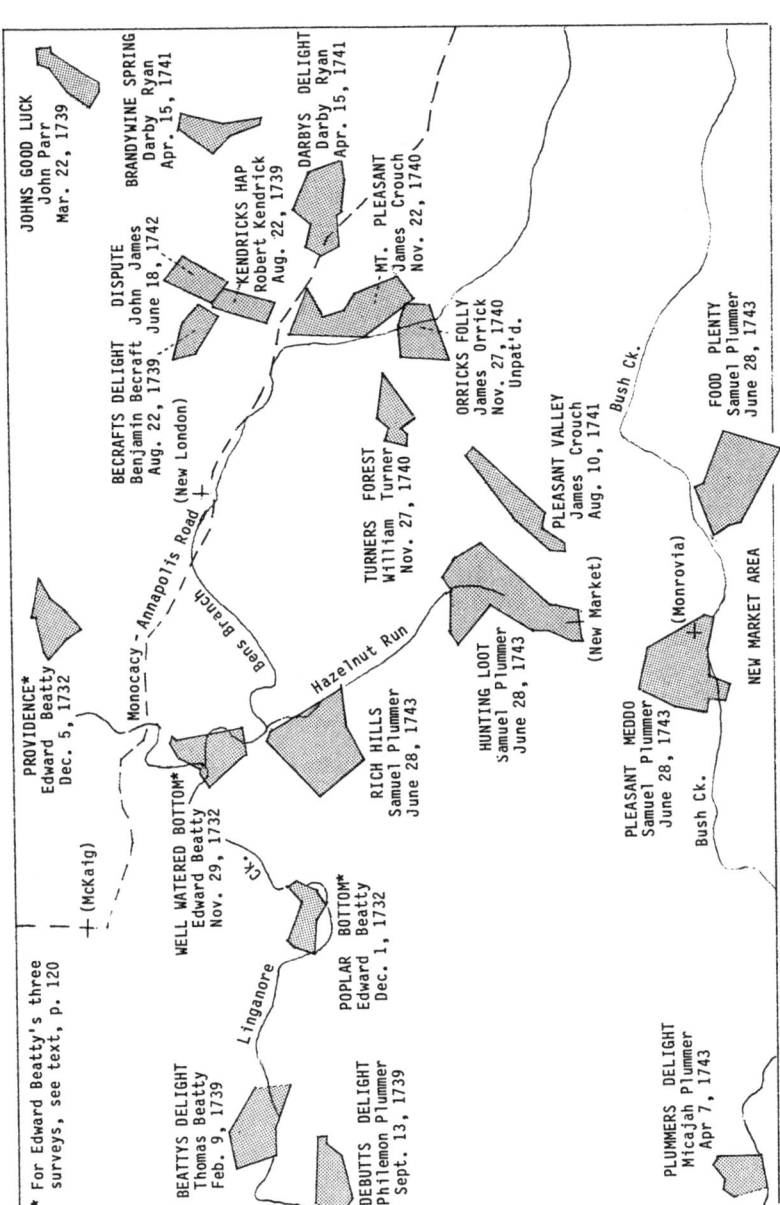

artery of transportation.

"Kendrick's Hap,"[6] lay along Ben's Branch, a tributary of Linganore Creek, one mile east of today's village of New London. **Robert Kendrick** had been living in Monocacy Hundred as early as 1733 when his name appeared on the Taxables list of that year. He was also named on the tobacco burning list of 1734. And the Court of August 1734 excused him from paying taxes because of the illness of his wife and children. It was not until August 22, 1739 that his land was surveyed.

Initially **Darby Ryan** appears to have owned no land of his own, though he too appeared on both the 1733 taxables and the 1734 tobacco burning lists. He was living near the Ballengers in 1737 when he was made overseer of the road "from Mill Branch to the Manor."[7] But subsequently he had moved to the Kendrick neighborhood where on April 15, 1741 he had two surveys made. One of them, "Darby's Delight," had its beginning point on a tributary of "Ben's Branch, a draft of Linganore."[8] It was surveyed for 100 acres. The other, "Brandywine Spring," began its 50 acres "by the side of a great meadow that leads upon a branch of Linganore Creek."[9] Ryan assigned "Darby's Delight" to Edward Dorsey of Anne Arundel County in 1750.[10] Dorsey also acquired "Brandywine Spring" and had a resurvey made on it in 1749 for 427 acres. Its beginning point was described as "on the main [Monocacy-Annapolis] wagon road.[11]

"Mackey's Delight" was surveyed for John Mackey on July 21, 1746. It lay immediately south of present-day Mt. Pleasant, with a beginning point "on the west side of the wagon road leading from Monocacy to Annapolis, near the head of a spring running into the Linganore."[12] In 1749 John Mackey and his wife Margaret conveyed "Mackey's Delight" to Isabella Hussey, seamstress, for 11 pounds in money and 716 pounds of tobacco.[13] Apparently Isabella Hussey then married Darby Ryan, who in 1751 deeded farm animals and household furnishings to his wife Isabella.[14] In 1758, as Isobel Ryan, she willed her entire estate to Darby Ryan,[15] and after her death, he assigned "Mackey's Delight" to James Dickson.[16] Ryan's place was still named in road references at the end of the decade. The Court of 1758, for example, appointed an overseer for the road from "Linganore Chapel to Ryans," and in November of the following year did likewise for the road from "Linganore Chapel to where Darry Ryan lives." This would

---

[6] The word *Hap* derives from happening, meaning chance, fortune, luck, or even "lot."
[7] Mill Branch is now known as Ballenger Creek. Cf. above, p. 81.
[8] C/S: LG E:77, which spells the parcel name "Darry's Delight."
[9] C/S: LG C:190.
[10] Frederick County Land Records, B:199.
[11] C/S: BY & GS 1:147.
[12] C/S: LG E:585.
[13] Frederick County Land Records, B:109.
[14] *Ibid.*, B:415.
[15] Frederick County Wills, A1:117, probated June 12, 1758.
[16] Frederick County Land Records, F:511.

approximate the present Unionville-Woodville Road.

  James Orrick witnessed the will of Allen Farquhar "of Manackus" in 1738.[17] Two years later, Orrick had joined the Kendrick Settlement, having had "Orrick's Folly" surveyed for himself on November 27, 1740. His land was located where Detrick Road crosses Ben's Branch, about a mile and a quarter due south of Kendrick's place. It may be identified in the 1873 Atlas as the home of John Meredith, northeast of New Market.[18] Orrick did not receive the patent,[19] however, and in 1748 the land was incorporated in "Dorsey's Search." The certificate of survey for the latter described Orrick's buildings as "one log house eight feet square and one hut."[20]

  John Parr's survey of March 22, 1739 located "John's Good Luck," on the "east side of a branch of Linganore called Cornwall's Folly."[21] This placed him near today's Unionville-Woodville Road in the vicinity of the Harrisville School Road, two miles northeast of the homes of Robert Kendrick and John James. Through the years the Parr name has been carried down in the Woodville District as a name for a spring, a ridge and a town. In 1748 John Parr, Jr. assigned "John's Good Luck" to John Dorsey, Jr. His parents, John and Mary Parr, Sr., had apparently moved on to the vicinity of Parr Spring, commonly called the uppermost spring of the Patuxent River, which flows into the Chesapeake Bay below the southern tip of Calvert County. Parr Spring is shown on the 1808 map.[22] Quite possibly this may also be the "spring which flows 60 miles from Annapolis" as labeled on Franz Michel's 1707 map,[23] although his sketch suggests closer proximity to Sugar Loaf Mountain than the actual area of Parr's settlement. Near where four counties now come together[24] John Parr in 1744 had two tracts surveyed, "Parr's Range" and "Bush Creek Hill." At Parr's death in 1745, his son Arthur inherited the former, his son Matthew the latter. John Parr's other children were Mark, John, Jr., Theme Ward and Elizabeth. In 1749 Stephen Julien and Darby Ryan petitioned the Frederick County Court for a ruling, "they being bound (as surety) to widow Parr, administratrix of John Parr, deceased; she being dead and the effects of the said Parr being likely to be made away with..."

  Benjamin Becraft joined the area with a survey dated August 22, 1739 which he called "Becraft's Delight." His land lay just east of present-day New London and very close to Kendrick's land.[25] In August 1750 he and George Becraft, farmers, entered into a writing

---

[17] *Maryland Calendar of Wills*, op. cit., 8:4. See pp. 82, 124.
[18] Lake, op. cit., p. 25.
[19] Unpatented Certificate, Prince George's County No. 242.
[20] C/S: BY & GS 1:615.
[21] C/S: BY & GS 1:215.
[22] Varlé, loc. cit. It marked the angle point where the boundaries of Frederick, Montgomery, Anne Arundel and Baltimore Counties then met. These boundaries were altered with the subsequent creation of Howard and Carroll Counties.
[23] See above, p. 8.
[24] Frederick, Montgomery, Howard and Carroll Counties.
[25] C/S: LG C:55. Its precise location has not been pinpointed.

obligatory with John Justice[26] to guarantee the latter's payment to beneficiaries of John James's estate.[27] In that same year George Becraft was named overseer of the road from Linganore Ford to the Anne Arundel County line.[28] George Becraft in 1752 was suing William Slade for slander. Slade had accused Becraft of stealing his beehive, and Becraft was asking £50 in damages. He was awarded £2/10 instead.[29] In 1762 he served on the grand jury, but three years later was convicted, along with Jacob Nicholls, of attempting to obstruct Constable Robert Waller from serving warrants on John Young.[30]

Also close to Kendrick was the land of **James Crouch** for whom "Mount Pleasant" was surveyed on November 22, 1740 "on a branch of Linganore called Ben's Branch."[31] This he enlarged to 176 acres by a Resurvey in 1748.[32] He assigned all of "Mount Pleasant" in 1752 in a deed of gift to his daughter Cloe Mobberly, wife of John Mobberly of Anne Arundel County.[33] But in 1753 he conveyed 36 acres by deed to Benjamin Becraft.[34] On August 10, 1741 James Crouch also had "Pleasant Valley" surveyed, "on the west side of a draft of Bush Creek."[35] He, or his son by the same name, had this acreage increased through a resurvey in 1752, and on the Resurvey's certificate it was noted that there was on this property "an old log dwelling house 20 x 16 feet and three acres of cultivated land."[36] James Crouch's place was still mentioned years later when the November Courts of 1770, 1773 and 1778 appointed overseers for the road from "Rue's Ford [Jug Bridge[37]] to James Crouch's." Today U.S. Highway 40 crosses the "Resurvey on Pleasant Valley" immediately east of the town of New Market.

James Crouch's good friend William Turner, Jr. served as administrator of his estate in 1783. His father, **William Turner, Sr.**, had come to the present-day New Market area somewhat before November 27, 1740 when his "Turner's Forest" was surveyed between Crouch's "Mount Pleasant" and "Pleasant Valley.[38] The Turners were of English origin and may have been related to the Cockey family of Baltimore County, for Thomas Cockey in 1733 bequeathed to "William Turner and heirs the plantation where he now lives, he dying without issue to pass to his brother Solomon."[39] In 1748 William Turner was

---

[26] See above, p. 101.
[27] Rice, *The Life, op. cit.*, p. 52.
[28] *Ibid.*, p. 62.
[29] *Ibid.*, pp. 112-114.
[30] *Ibid.*, pp. 234, 267-268.
[31] C/S: TI 1:407.
[32] C/S: BC & GS 1:146.
[33] Frederick County Land Records, B:635.
[34] *Ibid.*, E:332.
[35] C/S: LG E:80.
[36] C/S: BC & GS 1:169.
[37] A beautiful stone arch bridge built in the early 1800s across the Monocacy River on the old National Pike (U. S. Highway 40) just east of Frederick. It has since been dismantled.
[38] C/S: LG C:188.
[39] *Maryland Calendar of Wills, op. cit.*, 7:226.

made overseer for that part of the Monocacy-Annapolis Road that ran from Linganore Ford (between present-day New London and McKaig) to Anne Arundel County (Poplar Springs). In 1748 and 1750 he had surveys made for "Turner's Promise"[40] and "Turner's Lot,"[41] both near "Turner's Forest." By his will of early 1750 William Turner divided his entire estate between his children, Ann Covell, wife of Jeremiah Covell who was executor of his estate,[42] and Sarah, Mary, Rebecca, William and Rachel Turner.

Solomon Turner joined his brother William in 1748, after our period. He had a considerable number of surveys made, including "Solomon's Flower," a Resurvey on it, "Daniel's Small Tract," a Resurvey on it, "Right and Good Reason" and "Ebony March." His "Solomon's Contrivance and Ned's Study" was resurveyed into "Partnership" with the patent issued to Elizabeth Hall. His "Land of Promise" went to Henry Hall.

John James obtained land in the area on June 18, 1742 with a survey just to the north of Kendrick. He called his parcel "Dispute,"[43] making us wish that we had in addition to the mere names of these tracts an explanation of how the parcels got those names! John James was buried on his own land and his gravestone is still preserved in the private cemetery known today as the James-Kimmel Cemetery. His grave is marked, "The original proprietor, July 11, 1700 - August 1, 1750." As such, it is one of the oldest death records on any of the over 75,000 gravestones still existing in Frederick County today.[44] Inscriptions so early are a rarity, however, and the stone itself, based on its design, was probably erected in the 1800s. John James' son Daniel, born June 9, 1734, died March 9, 1792 and Daniel's wife Lucy, the daughter of Joseph Wood "of Linganore", born November 3, 1733, died January 1, 1827, are also buried in this family cemetery, as are 14 others. The home of [Mrs.] Daniel James is shown along the Monocacy-Annapolis Road on the 1808 Map.[45] Peter Becraft made a "Resurvey on Dispute" in 1754.[46]

In the early settlement of present-day Frederick County almost two decades had passed before members of the Plummer family began their Quaker settlement on Bush Creek near the present town of New Market. Their interests in the Monocacy area were not new, but it was not until the middle of 1743 that surveys set the stage for actual settlement.

The family of Thomas and Elizabeth Smith **Plummer** of Anne Arundel County consisted of ten sons and two daughters: Thomas, Samuel, George, James, John, Jerome, Philemon, Micajah, Yate, Abiezer, Priscilla and Phoebe Plummer.[47] Of these, Micajah, Philemon, Samuel and Thomas had land surveys made in what was to become

---

[40] C/S: BY & GS 1:208.
[41] C/S: Y & S 7:161.
[42] Frederick County Administrative Accounts, A1:96.
[43] C/S: LG E:88.
[44] Holdcraft, op. cit., pp. 2, 29, 50-51, 619.
[45] Varlé, loc. cit.
[46] C/S: BC & GS 1:305.
[47] Bowie, op. cit., p. 576, quoting wills of both parents.

today's Frederick County. They began on September 13, 1739 with two somewhat separated parcels, each 50 acres in size. Philemon Plummer's parcel was located "in the forks of a branch on the south side of Linganore Creek" and was called "Debutts' Delight."[48] Its name suggests a business connection with Robert Debutts, but what such a tie may have been is unknown. Situated near the present Linganore Filtration Plant, this land was included in "Hammond's Request" when the latter was surveyed in 1812.[49] Philemon Plummer died in 1744, leaving a widow Elizabeth, one son (John) who was of age, and eight other children.[50]

For Samuel Plummer a parcel of 50 acres was surveyed "on the west side of Bennett Creek on the east side of Sugar Loaf Mountain." Known as Plummer's Delight," this land was in the area of today's Thurston and Slate Quarry Roads.[51] Its original 50 acres were enlarged in 1760 by Samuel Plummer, Jr.[52]

On June 28, 1743 Samuel Plummer had four surveys filed for himself: "Hunting Loot," "Pleasant Meddo," "Rich Hills" and "Food Plenty."[53] These all lay in the vicinity of today's New Market, just west of the lands of James Crouch and William Turner. "Hunting Loot" was situated immediately north of present-day New Market "at the head of a draft of Linganore Creek." That "draft" flows into Hazelnut Run which in turn joins Ben's Branch a short quarter of a mile before the latter enters Linganore Creek. "Rich Hills" lay to the north with its beginning point "in the forks of Linganore Creek on Ben's Branch." For the most part it was thus situated west of Hazelnut Run and Crickenberg Road. Samuel Plummer's son-in-law Richard Holland resurveyed this parcel in 1761.[54] "Pleasant Meddo" was as far south of "Hunting Loot" as "Rich Hills" was to the north. It lay "in the forks of Bush Creek" and on it part of present-day Monrovia was built. Samuel's son Joseph Plummer increased its size to 412 acres in 1754 and then increased it again to 1,777 acres in 1764. At that time he changed the name of the tract to "Land of Promise."[55] Just to the east lay "Food Plenty" whose beginning point was on the "main branch of Bush Creek."

Samuel Plummer was listed as a taxable in Patuxent Hundred in 1719 and 1733. Apparently he and his wife Sarah Miles continued to maintain their homestead in what is now Montgomery County while his land interests in Frederick County expanded and his sons and sons-in-law settled there. Their son Thomas Plummer, who was named an overseer of roads in 1756, married widow Eleanor Walker Poultney. Son Joseph Plummer and his wife Sarah Sollers had ten children. They

---

[48] C/S: BC & GS 37:221.
[49] C/S: IB B:515.
[50] Prince George's County Bonds, Box 12, folder 63, Inventories, Box 14, folder 26, Hall of Records; Prince George's County Inventories, 30:66.
[51] C/S: EI 5:578. Located east of area shown on p. 90.
[52] C/S: BC & GS 14:57.
[53] C/S: LG E:297, 305, 306, 306.
[54] C/S: BC & GS 14:553.
[55] C/S: BC & GS 24:272.

lived on "Land of Promise," the resurvey of his father's "Pleasant Meddo." Samuel Plummer, Jr. married Mary Tucker and inherited "Plummer's Delight" which he subsequently enlarged. He served on juries in 1750 and 1754 and the grand jury in 1764.[56] In 1760 he was appointed overseer of the road from "Bennett Creek to the west side of Monocacy Ford." Abraham Plummer married Sarah Ward and inherited "Hickory Plains" which had been laid out in 1750. "Supply" was assigned to him in 1767 by his brother-in-law Mahlon Janney.[57]

Samuel and Sarah Plummer's eldest daughter Ruth Plummer married Richard Holland, who, in addition to his resurvey on "Rich Hills," had his own "Bush Creek Mountain" surveyed on September 20, 1755[58] two miles west of New Market near what became the junction of Mussetter Road and the Old National Pike. The latter, now known as State Route 144, near U.S. Highway 40 and Interstate I-70, was referred to in 1753 as the road that "leads from Richard Holland's to Fredericktown."[59] Samuel and Sarah Plummer's daughter Cassandra married William Ballenger, son of the pioneer Henry Ballenger. Daughter Sarah Plummer married Mahlon Janney of the Amos Janney Quaker family who began the settlement of present-day Waterford, Virginia.[60] Rachel Plummer married John Harris. Three daughters were not yet of age when their father died: Elizabeth who later married Moses Harris, Anna who married Joseph Talbert, and Susanna who married Anthony Poultney. Daughter Ursula Plummer never married.

Micajah Plummer, like his brother Samuel Plummer, Sr., named his first survey in today's Frederick County "Plummer's Delight." It was surveyed on April 7, 1743 and it, too, contained 50 acres.[61] Geographically it was not related to the Plummer lands near New Market except that it was located "by a small branch that runs into [the same] Bush Creek" south of today's Frederick Junction. In 1804 it was included in Thomas Johnson's "Alltogether."[62] Micajah Plummer also had "Plummer's Hunting Lot" surveyed for himself. Dated April 8, 1743, one day after his first survey, it began "at the head of Bennett Creek called Piney Branch." In 1754 this land was in the possession of William McLean.[63] In 1745 Micajah Plummer was named overseer of the road from "Monnoccousie near the mouth of Bush Creek to Bennett's Creek," the predecessor for today's Urbana Pike (State Route 355). In 1750 he was presented by the grand jury for stealing a colt belonging to Adam Buttner. Joshua Barton, John Carmack, John Martin, Jr., William Beatty and a host of Buttners stood as his accusers.[64]

Thomas Plummer, a fourth brother, did not begin to acquire land in Frederick County until 1744, but when he did, it was on a

---
[56] Rice, The Life, op. cit., pp. 35, 135, 257.
[57] C/S: Y & S 7:42, 143.
[58] C/S: BC & GS 5:142.
[59] C/S: GS 1:292.
[60] See above, p. 87.
[61] C/S: LG E:298.
[62] C/S: IC Q:507.
[63] C/S: LG E:298; Maryland Rent Rolls (Frederick No. 1), 32:115.
[64] Rice, The Life, op. cit., p. 49.

branch of Bennett Creek and also on Bush Creek farther north. For reasons not recorded, the Plummers did not join with the Quakers at Monocacy Meeting near present-day Buckeystown.[65] Instead, they received permission to hold meetings on First Days in the home of Thomas Plummer on Bush Creek. The congregation became known as the Bush Creek Quakers. Their Meeting House which was erected in 1757 was still being used early in this century. When in 1775 the Monocacy Meeting officially ended, its members joined, not this nearby Bush Creek Meeting, but the Pipe Creek Meeting located at present-day Union Bridge. Even Cassandra Plummer, with her husband William Ballenger, transferred allegiance there and not to the Bush Creek Quakers with whom she had originated.[66] Thomas Plummer died in 1773, leaving his property to his son Thomas Plummer in addition to five pounds in monetary bequests to his son Samuel Plummer and to each of his daughters Dorcus, Priscilla, Phebe, Mary, Susanna and Ruth Plummer.[67]

Rather interestingly, of all the early settlers named in this Chapter, only two, James Dickson and Samuel Plummer, appeared on the 1742 petition to the Maryland General Assembly seeking the division of Prince George's Parish and the creation of All Saints' Parish in the area which was to become Frederick County.[68]

---

[65] See above, pp. 79-88.

[66] Laverne Forbush, "Pipe Creek Friends Monthly Meeting Records," *Western Maryland Genealogy*, 1:19-26, 67-74, 123-130, shows Quaker marriage locales between 1770 and 1861. Half of those recorded took place at the Bush Creek Meeting House, 30% at Pipe Creek and only one (in 1751, outside the above period) at Monocacy. The others were recorded at more distant locales, including those in both Virginia and Pennsylvania. Most entries in this record date from the first decade of the 1800s, more than double those in any other decade.

[67] Frederick County Wills, A1:481. Gale Honeyman of San Francisco has helped immeasurably with his knowledge of the Plummer family.

[68] See below, p. 371.

FLAT RUN (EMMITSBURG)

Robert Wilson located early in the vicinity of present-day Emmitsburg, only a mile and a half from the Pennsylvania border as it was eventually established. He was undoubtedly living there in 1733 when his name appeared on the list of Taxables in Monocosie Hundred. He also appeared on the 1734 list of those inhabitants not burning their tobacco according to law.[1] But it was not until 1742 that his land was surveyed. His tract, called "Wilson's Fancy," was situated on Flat Run in the southeastern portion of today's Emmitsburg. It was surveyed on June 2, 1742, but the patent was not issued until July 12, 1749 and then to his widow Elizabeth Wilson.[2]

Wilson's home was a landmark used in road references.[3] By the time his land was surveyed, a road was in use from the east side of the Monocacy River northward across what is now Stull's Ford to present Loy's Station. It then followed Owen's Creek as a part of Cartledge's Old Road, finally breaking away from that to approximate today's Old Frederick, Dry Bridge and Creamery Roads. Its route may also be defined by reference in the 1873 Atlas to the homes along its way belonging to J[ohn] Walter, Jr., J[oseph] Rosensteel, Mrs. Warthen, T. Manning, Dr. E[dward] Wenschoff and E[li] Horner.[4]

Elizabeth Wilson deeded "Wilson's Fancy" to William Porter on October 9, 1751.[5] A survey made for Porter in 1753 was called "Porter's Addition."[6] It adjoined "Wilson's Fancy," which the certificate acknowledged as belonging to Porter, though it referred to the land as "Wilson's Round About." Obviously there had not been the closest of scrutiny in the early surveys, especially as related to overlaps with the large "Carrollsburg" tract surveyed in 1732.[7] In the 1760s and 1770s several law suits resulted, and the Wilson land proved to be no exception.

---
[1] See below, p. 369.
[2] C/S: BY & GS 1:152; Patent: BY & GS 2:120.
[3] In 1741, for example, the survey for John Digges' "Papan Bottom" on the east side of the Monocacy River referred to the "road leading from Robert Wilson's toward His Lordship's Mannor lying on the said River" (C/S: LG E:62).
[4] Lake, op. cit., p. 17.
[5] Frederick County Land Records, B:455.
[6] C/S: BC & GS 1:332.
[7] See above, p. 30.

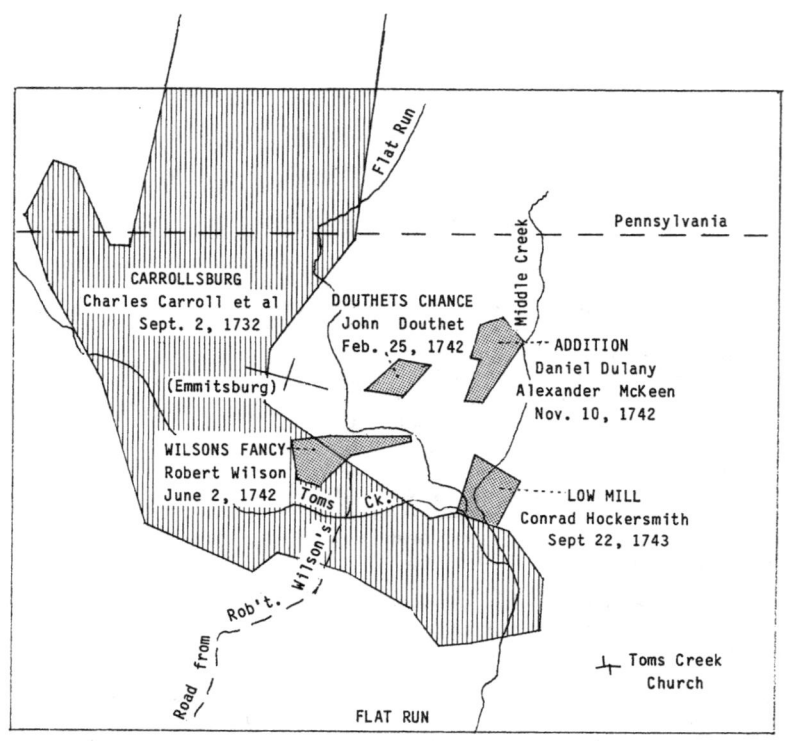

The **Doudith family** had also reached the Monocacy area early. Thomas Douthwhite was listed in 1734 as not burning his tobacco properly and in the following year, as Thomas Doudith, he was named Constable of Monocacy Hundred. He was incapable of serving, however, and was replaced by Solomon Hedges. On May 2, 1740 John Toudith had his daughter Eliesabetha baptised by Pastor Stöver at Manaquesen with Heinrich and Eliesabetha Bischoff standing as sponsors.[8] John Douthet settled just north of Robert Wilson on land he had surveyed on February 25, 1742. His 50 acres, which he called "Douthet's Chance," began "at a white oak standing about 50 perches easterly from Flat Run, a branch of Toms Creek."[9] In 1750 John Douthet conveyed this land to Alexander MacKeen,[10] who had it enlarged by a resurvey[11] and then sold it in 1770 to James Marshall of Lancaster County, Pennsylvania.[12] In passing, we should note a David Doudeth who signed Joseph Wood's 1745 petition for a rerouting of the Monocacy Manor Road.[13]

---

[8] Stöver, *op. cit.*, p. 20. Note especially Stöver's use of the anglicized first name, John.
[9] C/S: LG E:301.
[10] Frederick County Land Records, B:298.
[11] C/S: Y & S 7:175.
[12] Frederick County Land Records, O:1.

The ubiquitous Daniel Dulany was also active in the Flat Run area. He had 80 acres, called "Addition," surveyed on November 10, 1742, beginning "20 perches from a draught of Flat Run, being a draught of Toms Creek."[14] This he assigned in 1750 to **Alexander McKeen** who had it enlarged by means of a resurvey. On March 11, 1764 McKeen conveyed two acres to Samuel Carrick, William Shields, William Porter, William Cochran, Jr. and Alexander McKean, Jr., who had been appointed "by the Presbyterian Congregation at Toms Creek and a committee of the said community." These two acres began "at an oak on the side of a ridge about $N80°E$ 46 perches distant from a natural spring contegous to said McKean's dwelling."[15] Church records indicate that the Presbyterians in the Toms Creek area began services with supply ministers in 1761, three years before this deed and nineteen years before the establishment of the Presbyterian Church in the present city of Frederick. In 1839 the Toms Creek Church was abandoned and the congregation erected a new church in the town of Emmitsburg.[16]

Conrad Hockersmith joined the settlement on Flat Run with a survey on September 22, 1743 for "Low Mill," which was located "between the two branches of Middle Creek of Toms Creek."[17] In today's terms this was about a mile and a half east of the center of Emmitsburg. Five years later Hockersmith had "Long Mile" surveyed, and in 1758 he enlarged his total acreage with a "Resurvey on Long Mile and Low Mill."[18] By 1790 the name was spelled Hockensmith and so it remained in the Emmitsburg area for many generations.

Prior to 1743 the large "Carrollsburg" tract[19] seems to have remained undivided. Its subsequent history, although outside the period of this study, is important as it relates to the establishment of the town of Emmitsburg in 1785. Originally surveyed on September 2, 1732, "Carrollsburg" was first divided on May 6, 1757 when Charles Carroll sold 2,750 acres, mostly in today's state of Pennsylvania, to William Cochran[20] and, on May 13, 1757, 2,260 acres to **Samuel Emmit.**[21] On September 13, 1759 Samuel Emmit conveyed 200 acres of his newly acquired land to Abraham Emmit. This land lay west of the present town of Emmitsburg and had its beginning point near the present Hampton Valley Road.[22] Subsequently Samuel Emmit made further divisions of his land. The parcels so divided included over one

---

[13] See below, p. 311.
[14] C/S: BC & GS 27:581. See also Patented Survey, Prince George's County, No. 21.
[15] Frederick County Land Records, J:188.
[16] James A. Helman, *History of Emmitsburg, Maryland* (Frederick, 1906). See also Williams, op. cit., pp. 448, 467.
[17] C/S: LG E:280.
[18] C/S: BC & GS 12:123.
[19] Not to be confused with the unpatented "Carrollsburg" of 1724, surveyed on a branch of the Linganore. See above, p. 30 for details of their respective surveys and locations.
[20] Frederick County Land Records, F:239
[21] *Ibid.*, F:237.
[22] *Ibid.*, F:839.

hundred acres to William Cochran on February 3, 1763,[23] a portion lying northwest of present-day Emmitsburg to Charles Robinson on April 20, 1773,[24] an area south of today's Emmitsburg to Samuel Fleming in June and October 1777,[25] 106 acres west of Emmitsburg extending south to the present Scott Road to William Shields on September 29, 1787[26] and a portion east of Shields to Samuel Carrick, who renamed his parcel "High Nicking."[27]

By a deed of October 16, 1788 William Emmit, a son of Samuel Emmit, acquired 107 acres of "Carrollsburg" east of Carrick's land and south of today's Emmitsburg.[28] He sold the southern end of this land to Jacob Miscell, a miller, on May 10, 1797.[29] William Emmit also received from his father a portion of "Carrollsburg" (northwest of today's Emmitsburg) which later became known as "Poplar Ridge."[30] Samuel Emmit's son Josiah Emmit received 400 acres of Samuel's land on March 21, 1791. It lay east of St. Joseph's College.[31] Samuel Emmit's homestead with land lying around the forks of Toms Creek, Middle Creek and Flat Run was deeded to Samuel's youngest son, Abraham James Emmit, on August 20, 1793.[32]

The first reference to the town of Emmitsburg appears in the August 12, 1785 deed from Samuel Emmit to his son William. "For consideration of natural love and affection" 35 acres of "Carrollton" were transferred, "wherein the lots of a new town are laid out." Certain lots reserved for members of Samuel Emmit's family were excluded from this transfer, including Lot No. 1 for his wife, Lot No. 17 for Josiah Emmit, Lot No. 16 for daughter Mary, Lot No. 4 for son Abraham James Emmit and Lot No. 10 for a grandson William Porter. Samuel Emmit provided that his son William should "perform the part which the said Samuel Emmit was to perform according to articles of agreement made the fifth day of March last with purchasers."[33] These reserved lots were not recorded except as mentioned in the deed to William Emmit. Twice this deed for 35 acres was revised, on May 29, 1786 upon the discovery that "there is not fully that quantity of land contained within the courses....for the intended use and the said piece of land not beginning at the most convenient places...."[34] and again on June 16, 1787 when notice was made that "the said Samuel by indenture made 1785 made 35 acres of "Carrollsburg" for the use of a town which was then began thereon...."[35]

---

[23] Ibid., J:227.
[24] Ibid., T:260.
[25] Ibid., WR 7:366 and WR 8:268.
[26] Ibid., WR 7:585.
[27] C/S: LG E:290.
[28] Frederick County Land Records, WR 8:268.
[29] Ibid., WR 15:549.
[30] Ibid., WR 11:534.
[31] Ibid., WR 9:688.
[32] Ibid., WR 11:708.
[33] Ibid., WR 6:82.
[34] Ibid., WR 6:454.
[35] Ibid., WR 7:348.

On December 1, 1785 the following lots were sold in the newly laid-out town of Emmitsburg:[36]

2	Michael Row	26	Michael Hockersmith
3	Samuel Caldwell	28	James Hughes
5	Jacob Hockersmith	29	David Tanner
6	Conrad Hockersmith	30	James Larkins
7	Christian Smith	31	Jacob Tanner
8	Patrick Reed	33	John Lock
9	John Whitmore	34	John Webb
12	Adam Hoffman	35	Peter Krise
13	Charles Robin	36	Robert Wrench
19	Samuel Carrick	37-41	Adam Hoffman
20	David Kishner	46	John McGorgen
22	Michael Smith	48	Margaret McDonald
23	James Agnew	49-51	Samuel Blair
24	Daniel Gorden		

Subsequently, on May 13, 1786, Richard Jennings purchased "one front lot on the diamond and on the south side of the great road leading to Baltimoretown."[37] On May 20th of the same year John Troxel purchased 3.4 acres, "out lots of ground."[38]

A piece of land known as "Silver Fancy," surveyed on October 15, 1744 for Daniel Dulany, but patented only after his death to his sons Daniel and Walter Dulany on September 29, 1765,[39] lay next to "Carrollsburg." On March 16, 1763 Daniel Dulany the Younger contracted for the sale of "Silver Fancy" to Daniel Keith. Keith mortgaged his purchase to Dulany, then on February 7, 1797 assigned the parcel to William Emmit. Emmit on March 9, 1798 paid the balance of the mortgage to Mrs. Rebecca [Tasker] Dulany, executrix of Daniel Dulany the Younger, now deceased, who had been executor for the estate of his father.[40]

One month after William Emmit came into possession of "Silver Fancy" he began the sale of lots "known and distinguished on the plat or plan of Addition to Emmitsburg."[41] Some of these reflected the confusion resulting from the overlap of Dulany's parcel on the 20th line of "Carrollsburg." The first deed on August 20, 1798 gave John Troxel one acre Lot Nos. 175 and 179, "being a part of 'Silver Fancy'."[42] But Jacob Winter on August 17, 1799 purchased Lot No. 145 on Church Street, "being a part of 'Carrollsburg' or 'Silver Fancy' as the lines of the said 'Carrollsburg' may finally be settled."[43] Seven days later James Hughes came into possession of 22.5 acres, "part of 'Carrollsburg' and part of 'Silver Fancy,' beginning at the side of the road through Emmitsburg toward Carlisle and running along said road

---
[36] Ibid., WR 6:219-224, 233, 268-273, 275-281, 283-284, 289, 318, 336, 363.
[37] Ibid., WR 6:455.
[38] Ibid., WR 6:461.
[39] C/S: BC & GS 27:84.
[40] Frederick County Land Records, WR 16:377.
[41] The plat is not known to have been recorded.
[42] Frederick County Land Records, WR 11:555.
[43] Ibid., WR 19:86.

N53.5°E 64.5 perches, then N10°W 4.5 perches to a stone in the given line of 'Silver Fancy'...."[44] Also, on August 24, 1799, William Emmit conveyed to Conrad Hersh "front Lot Nos. 185, 186, 187 on Church Street and back Lot Nos. 169, 170, 171 according to the plat by William Kenworthy."[45] The same plat was mentioned in the sale of Lot Nos. 180, 182, 183 and part of 181 to John Armstrong.[46] The exact lines and overlap of "Silver Fancy" were defined in a deed of October 2, 1804 from William Emmit to Jacob Tanner.[47]

---

[44] *Ibid.*, WR 19:75.
[45] *Ibid.*, WR 19:19.
[46] *Ibid.*, WR 19:20.
[47] *Ibid.*, WR 26:161.

MIDDLETOWN AREA

Land records for the area in and around Middletown suggest earlier and more extensive settlement activity than was apparently the case. Although the area was remote, by the 1730s traffic over the Opequon trail through Maryland to Virginia made the region accessible. And the land was available. In 1733 John Magruder surveyed a parcel here which he called "Forrest," and by 1743, though each postdated 1740, five other surveys had been made. But these were the surveys of distant land investors, not of individuals intending to live on the land themselves. Two of the investors, Daniel Dulany and Thomas Wilson, actually held more than one parcel in this area.

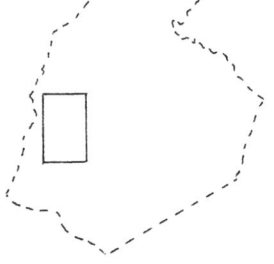

With such land activity, it may not be surprising that early historians, though unmindful of the specific surveys themselves, created the legend that the town of Middletown was established on a tract called "Smithfield" whose name derived from the occupation of Frederick Lauber, an early gunsmith. Lauber had supposedly settled there in 1730, and, so the historians wrote, "a settlement immediately began to form."[1] The land records, however, give no indication of the existence of a Frederick Lauber. There was indeed a "Smithfield," but it dates only from 1750 when it was patented to a Richard Smith.[2] Middletown itself did not begin until Michael Jesserang acquired "Smithfield" in 1766[3] and began laying off lots in that same year.[4]

What then really was the picture near today's Middletown prior to 1743? As far as actual land patents are concerned, **John Magruder's** "Forrest" was surveyed on April 9, 1733 near the junction of Catoctin and Little Catoctin Creeks. It extended southward with a lengthy mile-and-a-quarter "tail" which lay along the western extremity of today's Middletown.[5] To its north lay "Prevention," which was surveyed on May 24, 1740 for **Thomas Wilson.**[6] A few weeks earlier, on April 1, 1740, Wilson had had "Delight" surveyed. It lay in the area of present-day Holter Road and Deer Spring Avenue below

---

[1] Scharf, op. cit., 1:574; Williams, op. cit., p. 500.
[2] C/S: BY & GS 5:616; Patent: BY & GS 3:281.
[3] Frederick County Land Records, B:466. For Michael Jesserang, see p. 189.
[4] For a thorough study of the origins of Middletown, see Rice, New Facts, op. cit., pp. 137-148.
[5] C/S: AM 1:365.
[6] C/S: EI 5:492. For Thomas Wilson, see also p. 43.

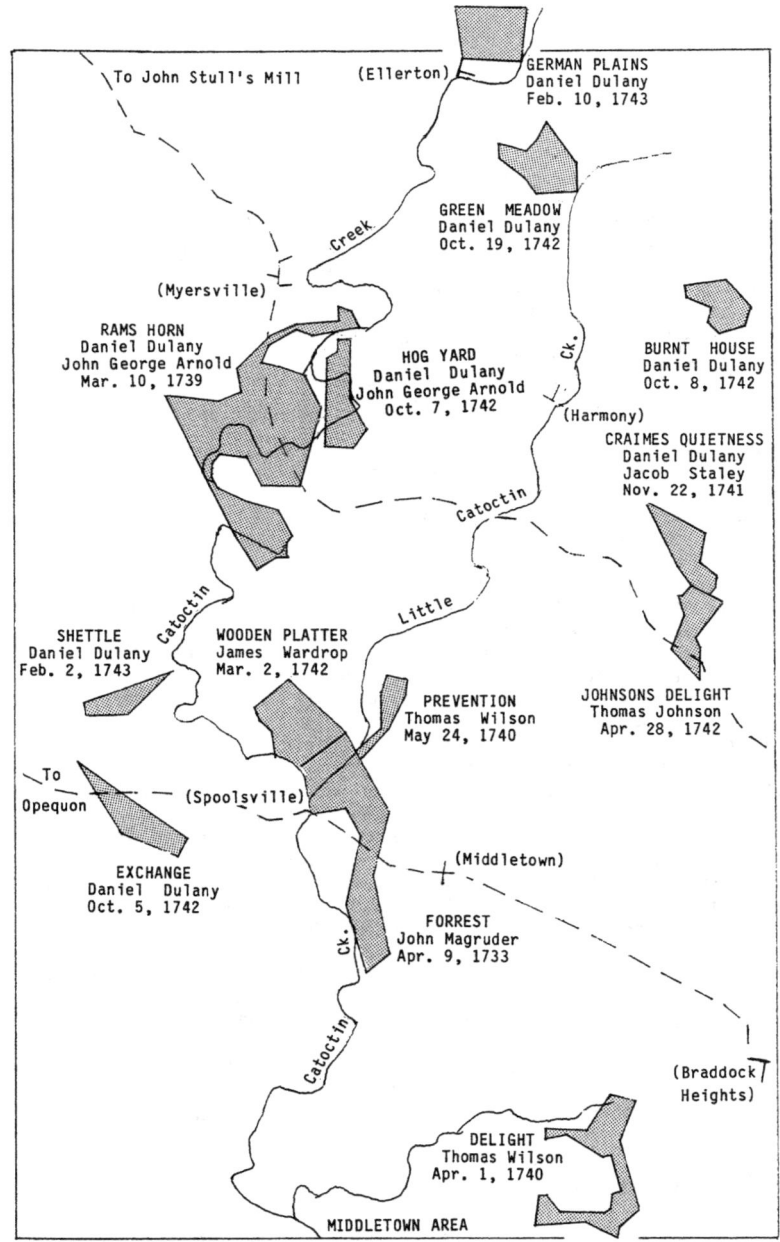

Braddock Heights.[7] **James Wardrop** on March 2, 1742 had "Wooden Platter" surveyed.[8] It adjoined the northwest boundary of "Forrest" and was situated between today's Hagerstown and Palmer Roads. "Exchange," 100 acres located a mile west of Spoolsville, was surveyed on October 5, 1742 for Daniel Dulany,[9] but was not patented until 1765, long after his death, when it went to his sons Daniel Dulany the Younger and Walter Dulany. Dulany's other parcel, "Shettle," was surveyed just east of Bolivar on February 2, 1743. It was patented, also after his death, to Robert Marks in 1755.[10]

Exactly when **Thomas** and **Mark Whitaker** came to the Middletown area has not been ascertained, but Thomas Whitaker does appear on the 1733 list of Monocacy Taxables. He and Mark were associated with the Church of England. Both signed the 1742 petition to divide Prince George's Parish, and Mark Whitaker's marriage on February 6, 1742/43 to Abigail Johnson is recorded in the All Saints Church Book. Beginning in 1741 and for several years thereafter, Mark and Thomas were overseers for the road from "Shenandoah Mountain to Catoctin Mountain." Thomas Whitaker petitioned the March Court of 1745, "Having been appointed overseer of the main road and having marked and distinguished the Patomack Ferry [now Shepherdstown] Road extending to the city of Annapolis and several other remarkable places....to acquaint your honorable worships that a certain Robert Evans hath stopped the said road and will not suffer travellers to pass nor the road to extend through the inclosure as it formerly went but tumbles loggs into the road and hath turned the road where it is mortally impossible to make it good. Pray further instructions..."

By his will of 1744, Thomas Wilson bequeathed his land "Prevention" to Thomas Whitaker.[11] In its initial survey the beginning point had been marked "at the mouth of Mill Run that falls into Catoctin Creek." Mill Run is now called Little Catoctin Creek and a mill situated there became the forerunner of Spoolsville. But the exact location of "Prevention" in relation to John Magruder's "Forrest" and James Wardrop's "Wooden Platter" has not been satisfactorily ascertained. In 1745 Thomas Whitaker himself had 60 acres surveyed, beginning at a white oak "standing on the south side of a creek called the northernmost Bennett's Creek." On May 19, 1750 Thomas Whitaker and his wife Mary conveyed "Prevention" to **Nicholas Fink** for 50 pounds.[12] Fink had it resurveyed in 1752[13] and again in 1764 when he called the resulting 478 acres "Goosebill."[14] Fink had numerous other land dealings, including "Arabia," "Kemp's Discovery," "Schley's Discovery" and "Resurvey on Whiskey Alley," all in this

---
[7] C/S: EI 5:495.
[8] C/S: TI 1:486.
[9] C/S: BY & GS 1:177; Patent: BC & GS 27:528. See also original Patented Survey, Prince George's County, No. 788.
[10] C/S: Y & S 7:105.
[11] *Maryland Calendar of Wills, op. cit.,* 8:266.
[12] Frederick County Land Records, B:172. For Nicholas Fink, see also below, p. 276.
[13] C/S: BC & GS 1:155.
[14] C/S: BC & GS 27:236.

245

same area.[15]

Thomas Wilson's other tract, "Delight," was surveyed in 1788 as "Stoney Land" for Peter Kowellentz (Coblentz)[16] with whose descendant J. Coblentz it remained in 1873.[17] Curiously, another tract, also called "Delight" but located in today's Washington County, was surveyed on June 3, 1740 for John Charlton.[18] In 1753 Mark Whitaker was passing title to half of its 100 acres to Andrew Balus.

One other actual settler in the Middletown area before 1743 was **Thomas Johnson** who had his first survey made on April 28, 1742. His "Johnson's Delight" was located along old U.S. Highway 40 just south of Hawbottom.[19] In 1750 Johnson included this parcel in a resurvey which he then called "Johnson's Lane Between." Its beginning point was on a hill "one quarter mile westward of Catoctin Mountain on the south side of two small branches or draughts of Mill Creek."[20] By his will of 1778 Thomas Johnson gave this land to his daughter Mary, wife of Robert Fuller. It was the "land where they now live."[21] In 1748 Thomas Johnson had had "Johnson's Level" surveyed, beginning "near the head of Tobias' Branch, a draft of Abraham's (Catoctin) Creek, on the north side of Stull's Road near the foot of Catoctin Mountain."[22] This he willed to his son John Johnson as the land where "he now lives." The will also gave his son Joseph Johnson land "surveyed for his father in 1755." Thomas Johnson's other children were Martha, Thomas, Jr., Henry and Robert Johnson.

Toward the end of our period Daniel Dulany had two parcels surveyed in the area north of Myersville. "Green Meadow" on a draft of Abraham's Creek dated from October 19, 1742. It was not patented until twelve years after Dulany's death. Another eight years were to pass before the land was deeded in 1773 to Daniel Gaver (originally Geber, but called Keaver in this deed).[23]

"German Plains," surveyed for Dulany on February 10, 1743, was located northeast of today's Ellerton. It too was not patented until well after Dulany's death when, on May 21, 1762, its 100 acres were assigned to Daniel Leatherman.[24] An early minister with the German Baptist Brethren, Elder Leatherman may well have been in the area earlier than that date. We have record of him in the Conewago area of Pennsylvania in 1738-1741, but cannot verify factually the tradition that he came to Maryland in 1756. His correspondence with Alexander Mack, Jr. in 1785-1794 was dated at Sandbergen,[25] but equating this with Sand Flat east of Wolfsville or with the area near Garfield is unproved.

---

[15] Frdk. Land Recds., F:1260, G:451, H:152, J:432, 1142, P:107.
[16] C/S: IC D:389.
[17] Lake, op. cit., p. 13.
[18] C/S: LG C:189.
[19] C/S: LG E:96.
[20] C/S: Y & S 7:178.
[21] Frederick County Wills, GM 1:28.
[22] C/S: BY & GS 1:172.
[23] C/S: BC & GS 27:552; Frederick County Land Records, T:409.
[24] C/S: BC & GS 14:711. See p. 35.
[25] Durnbaugh, op. cit., pp. 183-184, 243-250. See below, p. 270n.

THE CATHOLIC SETTLEMENT

It is difficult for modern minds to recollect yet alone comprehend the era of English intolerance and suspicion aimed at Roman Catholicism. Catholic King James II had been ousted from the English throne in 1688 during the so-called Glorious Revolution, but the ensuing political and territorial struggles pitting the Protestant government of Queen Anne of England against Catholic King Louis XIV of France fanned anti-Catholic sentiment well into the eighteenth century. By act of Parliament, office holders were required to take the oaths of supremacy of the British Crown and of abjuration and abhorrence aimed against the papacy. This Catholics could not do, and hence they were barred from governmental office. The so-called Catholic menace, real or imagined, provoked the Maryland Assembly in 1718 to disenfranchise all Catholics until they took the oaths.[1] Even by mid-century when hostilities broke into the French and Indian War, the threat of the Catholic French to the Maryland frontier was very real. In 1756 the Lower House of the Maryland Assembly enacted a provision for double taxation of Roman Catholics.[2]

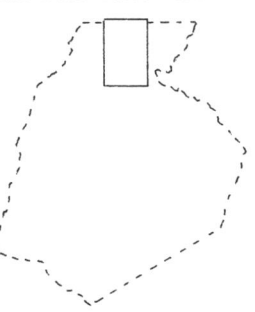

It is at least a possibility that anti-Catholic sentiment encouraged those professing that faith to direct their attention to the northern frontier of the Maryland Colony. We have already noted the land dealings of John Digges, a Catholic from Prince George's County.[3] On October 14, 1727 he had received a Maryland warrant for 10,000 acres[4] against which he had applied 6,822 acres to "Digges' Choice"[5] in the disputed Conewago area around present-day Hanover, Pennsylvania. Digges assigned the right for 500 acres to **Robert Owings** on October 1, 1731. Though a surveyor for the Province of Maryland, Owings was also a Catholic, who had settled at Conewago with the Digges family. He was born in 1692 and had married Hannah Farquhar, daughter of the Quaker Allen Farquhar. Owings made his colonial homestead a sacred place by having the rite of the Catholic Church held in his home until the Conewago Chapel of the

---

[1] Proceedings of the Assembly, 1717-1720, *Archives of Maryland*, op. cit., 33:211, 224.
[2] Charles A. Barker, *The Background of the Revolution in Maryland* (New Haven, 1940), p. 239.
[3] See above, pp. 41-43.
[4] Warant Series, Liber 10, DD:219.
[5] C/S: EI 3:433; Patent: EI 4:332.

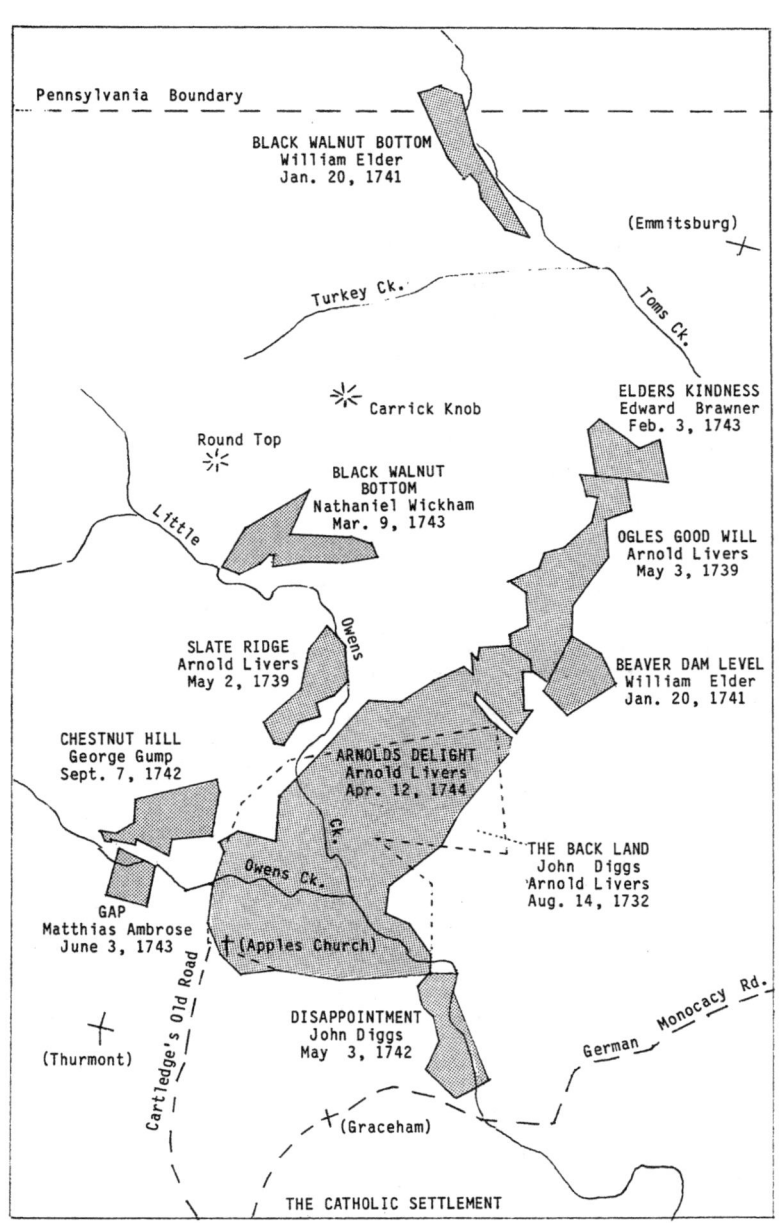

Sacred Heart was built about 1740.

Arnold Livers, a native of Holland, no doubt came to America because of his Catholic religion. He had arrived in Maryland before 1703, when he was a witness to the will of Benjamin Haddock of Prince George's County,[6] and on April 29, 1704 he was naturalized.[7] In 1711 he was buying land from Colonel Henry Darnall. His further land activites in northern Frederick County were most extensive. They began with a tract of 2,578 acres called "The Back Land," which had been surveyed for John Diggs on August 14, 1732, but was patented to Arnold Livers on June 10, 1734.[8] The original survey began "on a small run, one of the forks of Little Captings Creek [Captain's = Owens Creek] which descends to the Monocacy."

In 1739 Arnold Livers stepped up his land acquisition appreciably. In that year alone he had four parcels surveyed, including "Slate Ridge" on May 2nd, "Ogle's Good Will" the next day, "Lubberland" on May 20th, and "Duke's Woods" on June 25th. On April 12, 1744 "The Back Land" parcel was resurveyed into "Arnold's Delight" which then consisted of 1,699 acres.[9] The land covered a fairly wide area northeast of today's Thurmont, lying between U.S. Highway 15 and Apples Church Road and between Little Owens Creek and Ohrndorff Road.

In studying these surveys, one can draw a definite distinction between Digges and Livers in the apparent purposes of their respective acquisitions. The former worked primarily as a speculator, or at least as an investor interested in the pecuniary return to be realized from owning land. Arnold Livers on the other hand acquired his land for the benefit of his family and friends. He was personally interested in what was to become of the Catholic settlement and the protection of its people.

"Slate Ridge" was located a short ways up Eylers Valley, through which flows Little Owens Creek.[10] There the valley is crossed by today's Kelbaugh Road, perhaps a mile northwest of "Arnold's Delight." Adjoining the latter on its northeast was "Ogle's Good Will," extending along today's U.S. Highway 15 as far as College Lane opposite Mount St. Mary's College.[11] Arnold Livers assigned "Slate Ridge" to William Elder, of whom more below. Elder also received a part of "Ogle's Good Will," as did Matthias Riesly, who was deeded 100 acres of that parcel on August 24, 1743.[12] Under the terms of Livers' will, the balance of "Ogle's Good Will" went to his grandchildren.

The other parcels were located somewhat farther afield. "Arnold's Chance" was surveyed on June 17, 1739 near today's Medford

---
[6] *Maryland Calendar of Wills,* op. cit., 3:14, February 24, 1702[/03], probated June 4, 1703. See also Prerogative Court 11:388.
[7] Maryland Laws, LL 2:429.
[8] C/S: EI 3:348; Patent: EI 2:125.
[9] C/S: LG E:562.
[10] C/S: EI 5:500.
[11] C/S: EI 5/500. Despite the name, there is no indication that Joseph Ogle was a party to this parcel's warrant, survey or patent.
[12] Prince George's County Land Records, BB 1:8.

in Carroll County. By 1754, after Arnold Livers' death, 500 of its 600 acres had passed to Matthias Ambrose and his family.[13] "Duke's Woods" marked the site where Libertytown was later built.[14] Slightly over 102 of its 633 acres were sold on November 27, 1742 to Cornelius and William Carmack,[15] but the balance, under the terms of Arnold Livers' will, was sold after his death. After the survey for "Lubberland" was completed in May 1739, its certificate of survey for 99 acres was assigned on August 23, 1739 directly to William Carmack.[16] In 1776 "Lubberland" passed to his sons John and Aquila Carmack.

"Arnold's Delight" was well recognized as a reference point. When "Rich Level," for example, was surveyed for John Digges in 1741, its beginnning point near today's Mumma Ford was identified as being "on the east side of the Monocacy River near a road that leads from Pipe Creek to a place known by the name of The Mountain (alias) Livers' Quarters."[17] Part of "Arnold's Delight" was deeded to others. In 1744 Livers sold 100 acres to John Young[18] and another 100 acres to Peter Apple.[19] In 1746 an additional 125 acres went to Matthias Ambrose.[20] But the residue acreage became the focal point of Livers' Catholic interests.

Arnold Livers' home plantation remained in Mount Calvert Hundred, east of present-day Washington, D.C. It was situated where Western Creek joins the Patuxent River, about three miles from Upper Marlboro, county seat of today's Prince George's County.[21] By the terms of his will, "all that part which was sold me by Colonel Henry Darnall and all that part formerly given to me by Henry Darnall, Esq., in Prince George's County, known or reputed to be the plantation where I now live" was to go to his son Robert Livers. His widow Helena was to have her widowhood in his home.[22] One can only conclude therefore that Arnold Livers, Sr., established a home in the backwoods of present-day Frederick County for the convenience of his religion. The home, it is believed, was that belonging in the 1800s to John A. Roddy and in this century to E. G. Terpenning. The house is situated in a cove made by the mountains near fine cool springs. Although the log buildings have been torn away, the original walls of the main house are preserved on their double stone foundation. The ceilings are of the crown design, and the curved stairway to the second floor shows the wear from feet of many generations. Iron strap hinges of early 1700 design are still used on the low doorways.

---

[13] C/S: LG C:49; Maryland Rent Rolls (Frederick No. 1), 32:60.
[14] C/S: LG C:31.
[15] Frederick County Land Records, Y:571, 572. See above, p. 104.
[16] C/S: LG C:35.
[17] C/S: LG E:63. "Rich Level" was thus located in present-day Carroll County.
[18] Prince George's County Land Records BB 1:234.
[19] Ibid., BB 1:236.
[20] Ibid., BB 1:406. See p. 203.
[21] Information through the courtesy of J. Dudley Digges, Associate Judge, 7th Judicial Circuit Court of Maryland.
[22] Prince George's County Wills, 28:168.

Messages were repeatedly sent to the Maryland Assembly under order of the British Parliament to keep "the strictest watch" on Roman Catholics so that they could not "think themselves more fortunate and easy if their religion was established here." Such official statements directed from the Upper House of the Maryland Assembly to the Lower House added that "we have not a less good opinion than yourselves of the Roman Catholics in the Province and of the many in England in what relates to private life, and even to many actions in public life, yet we dare not answer for the conduct in any affair where the establishment of their religion may come into question."[23] It seems reasonable to assume that under these conditions the Catholic priests and laymen needed comfortable quarters and privacy for worship. Arnold Livers obviously was supplying these needs, probably during the period from 1734 to 1750. Catholics were forbidden to erect churches, but it was permissible to celebrate Mass in a private dwelling, often in a room or rooms set aside for the purpose, so long as the house was on land belonging to a private individual.

Governor Thomas Bladen on May 13, 1745, about the time of the second Jacobite Rebellion led by the "Young Pretender" Prince Charles Edward, advised that he had received information of the "ill-behavior of one Richard Molyneux, a Roman Catholic Priest living in Charles County, and also one Arnold Livers and Daniel Herne, two Roman Catholics of this Province."[24] Father Molyneaux (1696-1766), born and died in England, came to the Colonies between 1733 and 1749. He was Superior of the Maryland Jesuits in 1736 and by the terms of the June 16, 1737 will of the Reverend George Thorold was bequeathed Thorold's land. Witnesses to this will included the Rev. Arnold Livers, Jr., Rev. Robert Harding and Rev. Vincent Philyps.[25] Thus we have knowledge that Arnold Livers' own son had studied for the priesthood.

In March of 1746 an order was issued to the Captain of Militia to accompany the Sheriff with a warrant on "information of some ammunition or arms being lodged and concealed" on the plantation of Arnold Livers. "An outhouse or chapel is said to be the place."[26] No arms were to be removed and complete secrecy was to be maintained. On March 20th Joseph Ogle, Captain of the Militia in Frederick County, reported to the Assembly that "a search was made that day of Arnold Livers' dwelling house, barn and outhouses, but no

---

[23] Proceedings of the Assembly, 1745-1747, *Archives of Maryland, op. cit.*, 44:456.

[24] Proceedings of Council, 1732-1753, *Archives of Maryland, op. cit.*, 28:355. Livers and Herne were to be brought before Chief Justice Philip Thomas of the Provincial Court, but there is no further record in the Council Proceedings.

[25] *Maryland Calendar of Wills, op. cit.*, 8:190, probated November 22, 1742. Arnold Livers, Jr., was born in Maryland May 11, 1705, entered the Society of Jesus at Watten in Flanders and after completing his studies returned to Maryland.

[26] *Maryland State Papers No. 1, The Black Books*, 3:44; para. 493 in the *Calendar*.

arms or ammunition were found. Concerning the chapel, Ogle's reply stated, "There is no chapel in this neighborhood nearer than Connewagoe."[27]

Nevertheless, Peter Brightwell of Prince George's County testified on March 16, 1745/46 that he had been in the house of one John Nicholls[28] and that Nicholls' wife had told him "she would risque her neck" to burn down the house "of Arnold Livers at Monocacy." When questioned further, she told Brightwell that "they would never for the [past] seven or five years suffer any woman to come into it, [and] even the wife of the master of the house had been known to have been at the plantation a month or five weeks and was never suffer'd to come into it. .... Whenever the said Arnold Livers and his sett or company went into the said house there was always a watch or guard set about it."[29]

Arnold Livers died in 1751. He dated his will in Prince George's County on June 7, 1751, naming his daughter Jacoba Clementina Elder [wife of William Elder] as executrix and Dudley Digges, a brother of John Digges of Conewago, as overseer of his estate. In addition to his wife Helena, he also named his children Robert, Anthony, Arnold, James (deceased), Mary and Rachel Livers and his grandchildren Arnold Elder, Anne Livers and Eliza Elder. "Dukes Wood" on Linganore Creek and "Arnold's Chance" on Little Pipe Creek, each comprising about 500 acres, plus lots in Nottingham and Marlborough in Prince George's County, were all to be sold to settle his debts. His remaining interest in "Arnold's Delight" of some 1,070 acres he devised to his children Anthony, Arnold, Mary and Rachel.[30] After his death his wife married Samuel Collard, and in 1754 they conveyed 125 acres of "Arnold's Delight" to Matthias Ambrose. Arnold Livers [Jr.] deeded 268 acres in 1759 to George Loy. Another 286 acres were transferred or quitclaimed to Arnold Livers in 1760 by Charles Boetler and his wife Mary Livers. And in 1762 Solomon Harday and his wife Rachel Livers conveyed 268 acres to Henry Ambrose.

Thomas Cresap in 1745 surveyed 600 acres in an area midway between present-day Union Bridge and New Windsor, now in Carroll County, for the Reverend **Thomas Digges,** a nephew of John Digges of Conewago and a member of the Society of Jesus. The land was called "Mountain Prospect" and is known today as Priestland Valley. Father Digges had studied in Europe and was at New Town in Saint Mary's County in 1742 and 1745 when Father Arnold Livers was also there. Later Father Digges retired to "Mellwood," the estate of his brother Ignatius Digges, where there was a private chapel for worship. Candlesticks used by Father Digges were placed in one of the chapels at Georgetown University in Washington.[31]

---

[27] Ibid., 6:83; para. 509 in the *Calendar.*
[28] John Nichols had 45 acres surveyed for himself between Libertytown and New Windsor in 1748. In the following year he was indicted by the Frederick County Court for a felony.
[29] Proceedings of the Assembly, 1745-1747, *Archives of Maryland, op. cit.,* 44:692.
[30] Prince George's County Wills, 28:168.

After the death of Arnold Livers, Sr., the Catholic fathers established a residence on "Mountain Prospect" at Pipe Creek.[32] In 1751 Henry Cassell of Frederick County testified before the Maryland Assembly that "many of the Germans are Roman Catholic [as are] many of the English and Irish up that way about Pipe Creek. Most of the German Roman Catholic live up toward the mountains..."[33] In 1753 additional testimony was given from Saint Mary's County that it was "understood from one William Fletcher who lived with one Arnold Livers, a Jesuit in Saint Mary's County, that Molyneux was gone back in the country among the Dutch [Germans] and French."[34] On November 18, 1771 title to "Mountain Prospect" was transferred to the Reverend George Hunter.[35] He was the same Father Hunter to whom John Cary in Frederick in 1765 transferred his private property on which the first Catholic "Church" there had been built. That marked the beginning of Church "ownership" in Frederick.[36]

The will of Father Arnold Livers, Jr. was dated in Saint Mary's County on March 19, 1761. He devised his real estate to the Reverend George Hunter of Charles County and "in case he should not survive me" it was to be given to the Reverend John Lewis of Cecil County. Witnesses to the will were Richard Heard, John Arnold and the Reverend William Neale. Father Arnold Livers' Day Book is preserved at Woodstock College, Woodstock, Maryland.[37]

William Elder, said to have been born in England in 1707, emigrated with his wife Ann Wheeler to Saint Mary's County in Maryland in 1732. In 1739 he received the patent to "Slate Ridge" which had been surveyed for his friend Arnold Livers. In the same year his wife died, leaving him with five small children, William, Jr., Guy, Charles, Mary and Richard. About 1743 he married as his second wife Jacoba Clementina Livers, daughter of the same Arnold Livers. Family tradition suggests that William Elder was a Protestant converted to Catholicism.[38] No doubt a wedding gift was Arnold Livers' transfer to his new son-in-law on August 24, 1743 of a portion of "Ogle's Good Will."[39] Here the Elders built their home in which one room was reserved for religious services. The location in this consecrated ground where the house and altar stood is marked by a simple stone surmounted by a cross erected by William Henry Elder, Archbishop of Cincinnati and great grandson of William Elder. The present Mount Saint Mary's College is built on a part of that land.

William Elder had other land. "Black Walnut Bottom" was surveyed for him on January 20, 1741. It was located along what has

---

[31] Information through the courtesy of the Rev. W. C. Repetti.
[32] Thomas Aloysius Hughes, *History of the Society of Jesus in North America, Colonial and Federal* (London, New York, 1907).
[33] Proceedings of the Assembly, 1752-1754, op. cit., 50:54.
[34] Ibid., 50:201.
[35] Maryland Rent Rolls (Frederick No. 1), 32:129.
[36] Williams op. cit., p. 444.
[37] From the Elder Family records, through the courtesy of the Reverend Hugh Phillips of Mount Saint Mary's College, Emmitsburg.
[38] Ibid.
[39] Prince George's County Land Records, BB 1:9.

since become Riffle Road leading from Saint Mary's College to Pennsylvania.[40] The acreage was enlarged by means of a resurvey in 1751, and in 1767 William Elder transferred a part of it to William Shields, a Presbyterian. Shields in 1775 surveyed the land into 404 acres and called it "Shield's Adventure."[41] "Beaver Dam Level" was surveyed for William Elder on the same day as "Black Walnut Bottom." It was located to the east of "Arnolds Delight" and "Ogle's Good Will" with which it was contigous.[42] By 1774 most of this land was in the possession of Charles Beatty, who called it "Ramsey's Rest."[43] "Content" was surveyed and patented to Elder in 1750[44] next to Joseph Ogle's "Peace." By 1752 it had been resurveyed and had passed into Ogle's possession.[45] William Elder also had "Elder's Choice," surveyed in 1751 and located at the head of Beaver Branch within 40 perches of "Ogle's Good Will."[46] By his will William Elder left "Ogle's Good Will" and "Elder's Choice" to his wife Jacoba.[47]

As noted, William Elder by his first marriage had five children. William Elder, Jr. married a Wickham, probably the daughter of Nathaniel Wickham, Jr. They had a son Nathaniel Elder. Guy Elder was married twice and by his second wife had 13 children. Charles Elder married Julia Ward of Charles County and was the grandfather of the Reverend Alexius Elder. Mary Elder married Richard Lilly, who had a number of land parcels surveyed for himself including "Lilly's Lot," "Resurvey on Lilly's Lot," "Fisherman's Lodge," "Hampton Plains," "Dolphin" and "Hampton Forest." William and Guy Elder and Richard Lilly all appear in the 1790 Frederick County Census.

From his second marriage, William Elder and Jacoba had seven children: Elizabeth, Arnold, Thomas, Ignatius, Ann, Aloysius and Francis. Elizabeth Elder married Richard Brawner, son of Edward Brawner. Arnold Elder married Clotilda Green, who, after Arnold's death, married Roger Brooke. Thomas Elder married Elizabeth Spaulding of Charles County and lived for 28 years in Harbaugh Valley. Their son Basil Elder married Elizabeth Snowden and was the father of William Henry Elder, the Archbishop of Cincinnati referred to above. Ignatius Elder moved to the West. Aloysius Elder was twice married and had seven children by his first wife, five by his second. Francis Elder is believed to have married Catherine Spaulding.[48]

Edward Brawner joined the Catholic settlement with his survey of "Elder's Kindness" on February 3, 1743.[49] Again one would like to know the background story implied in a parcel's name. This land was

---

[40] C/S: LG E:95; Patent: EI 6:491.
[41] C/S: IC K:277.
[42] C/S: LG E/97; Patent: EI 6:518.
[43] C/S: IC B:264.
[44] C/S: BY & GS 5:592; Patent: BY & GS 3:320.
[45] C/S: BC & GS 1:167.
[46] C/S: Y & S 7:125.
[47] Frederick County Wills, A1:573.
[48] Phillips, *loc. cit.*
[49] C/S: LG E:282.

located along Emmitsburg Road, the old U. S. Highway 15. It may be identified in the 1873 Atlas as the home of J[oseph] Brawner opposite Mount St. Mary's College.[50] The Brawners appear to have come from Piscataway Hundred in Prince George's County. Edward Brawner was made overseer of the road from Ambrose's Mill to the temporary Pennsylvania line in 1754 and 1755. In his will of April 7, 1760, he noted that he was a widower and the father of sons Richard, Thomas, Henry, Edward, William and John Brawner.[51] His eldest son, Richard Brawner, served as Constable of Upper Monocacy Hundred in 1759 and 1760 and enlarged his father's land through a resurvey in 1771.[52]

Except for land held by Robert Wilson and John Douthet[53] and the few acres surveyed for Daniel Dulany, all the land surveyed during the second decade of Frederick County's settlement, from one mile north of Thurmont to the Pennsylvania border above Emmitsburg, was owned by Catholics. There appear to have been no settlers on "Carrollsburg" at early dates, but the Catholic settlement begun in the forks of Owens Creek by the Livers, Elder and Brawner families expanded progressively northward toward Emmitsburg until today the area has become nationally known. It was at Emmitsburg in 1809 that Elizabeth Ann Bayley Seton (1774-1821), later known as Mother Seton, founded an academy for young ladies which later became St. Joseph's College. In 1850 its Sisters of Charity affiliated with the Society founded by Saint Vincent de Paul in France, and the American Community thereafter was known as its St. Joseph Province. The College closed in 1973, but two years later, in 1975, St. Elizabeth Ann Seton was canonized by Pope Paul VI. Today the College grounds in Emmitsburg are occupied by the National Fire Academy.

In 1786 a Catholic parish had been formed in Emmitsburg, and in 1793 St. Joseph's Church was erected. Since 1852 this church has been in the charge of the Fathers of the Mission, also founded by St. Vincent de Paul and also engaged in charity work.

John Dubois was born in Paris in 1764, was ordained a Priest before canonical age and assisted at Saint Sulpice parish in Paris in 1787. Armed with a passport and a letter from Lafayette, he fled to the United States at the time of the French Revolution. He was warmly received in both Maryland and Virginia, and Patrick Henry reputedly gave him lessons in English. Although he made his first headquarters in Fredericktown, frequent trips to the Emmitsburg area endeared him to that community, where he eventually became a resident. Four years before Mother Seton arrived in Emmitsburg, Father John Dubois purchased land two miles away in the area of the original Frederick County Catholic settlers.[54] Here in 1808 he founded Mount Saint Mary's College, familiarly known as "The Mountain." Thousands of young men have graduated from this institution, including, within its first century of existence, over 500 priests, several

---
[50] Lake, op. cit., p. 17.
[51] Frederick County Wills, A1:141.
[52] C/S: BC & GS 47:478.
[53] See above, pp. 237-238.
[54] Frederick County Land Records, WR 28:97, conveying from Christian Smith 71-3/4 acres of "Enlargement" at one pound per acre.

Archbishops and a Cardinal. Father Dubois worked with the college and seminary until 1826 when he was made Bishop of New York.[55]

In 1835 the Reverend Thomas Butler, Richard Whelan and Edward Sourin had 1,210 acres resurveyed for Mount Saint Mary's College. The land was called "St. Mary's Increase" and included the original tracts of "Ogle's Good Will," "Elder's Choice," "Elder's Resurvey" and "The Resurvey on Ogle's Good Will," as well as Frederick Kemp's "Rocky Springs" and "Peace and Plenty." Here, on what is now Mount Saint Mary's property, are buried William Elder (1707-1775) and his two wives, Ann Wheeler (1709c-1739) and Jacoba Clementine Livers (1717c-1807).[56] When Jacoba Clementine Livers wrote her will in 1807, she had requested that she be buried at the time and the place designated by her "friend, Reverend Mr. John Dubois."[57]

---

[55] Williams, *op. cit.*, pp. 497-498, 511-518, 521-522; "The Story of the Mountain," Emmitsburg *Weekly Chronicle* (1911).
[56] Holdcraft, *op. cit.*, pp. 33, 372.
[57] Frederick County Wills, GMRB 1:328.

TASKER'S CHANCE

Probably the tract name best remembered today is "Tasker's Chance," the land on which most of the city of Frederick is now located. The parcel was a large one, covering 7,000 acres. It lay immediately west of the Monocacy River and extended some four miles northward from the mouth of Carroll Creek. Westward the land stretched between two and four miles from the River, but still fell roughly a mile and a half short of the German Monocacy Road which paralleled its western boundary nearer to Catoctin Mountain. Along its southern border lay John van Metre's "Meadow" (1725) and his son's "Pipe Meadow" (1727).[1] To the southwest was "Rocky Creek (1725).[2] The location of "Tasker's Chance" was thus central within what was to become Frederick County, and it provided a most suitable site for the ultimate county seat.

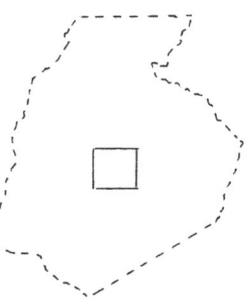

"Tasker's Chance" was surveyed for Benjamin Tasker, a prominent business man in Annapolis who had previously served as the town's mayor and was later to become Commissary General and President of the Maryland Council. It was April 15, 1725 when "Tasker's Chance" was surveyed,[3] but the land was not patented to Tasker until June 9, 1727.[4] The survey was the sixteenth to be made within the confines of present Frederick County -- relatively early in the light of what was to follow.

Exactly when settlement on the tract began cannot be determined. Nor is it known whether Tasker was initially intending to sell or lease his parcel or was forced to some sort of accommodation with early squatters who had merely occupied the land. Those who ultimately settled on "Tasker's Chance" were for the most part Germans, whose pattern of arrival has been discussed in previous chapters. None is known to have been in Maryland before 1736, and in that year only Frantz Weiss, the Brunners and Dieter Lehnich have left us documented traces of their presence.[5]

On June 11, 1737, however, Benjamin Tasker listed six individuals, all Germans, who were settled on his land and wished collectively

---
[1] See above, pp. 69-72.
[2] *Ibid.*, pp. 37, 161.
[3] C/S: IL A:738. See also Original Patented Survey, Prince George's County No. 2113, Hall of Records.
[4] Patent: PL 6:559.
[5] See elsewhere, pp. 217, 263, 273.

to purchase the entire parcel. They were Daniel France [Frantz], Abraham Miller, John George Lye [Loy], Joseph [Joh. Jost] Smith, Peter Laney [Dieter Lehnich] and Jacob Stoner.[6] Four of them lived in a straight line stretching from Stoner's land, where Tuscarora Creek flows into the Monocacy, southwesterly through Miller and France's land to Smith's parcel on which downtown Frederick has since been built. Lehnich and Loy lived away from the River, the former on land where Fort Detrick is now located, the latter farther up Tuscarora Creek, just west of today's U. S. Highway 15. The agreed-upon purchase price was 2,000 pounds plus interest, toward which the six purchasers paid Tasker £841/11 and secured the loan of an additional £941/2. But after seven years and a half attempting to raise the balance they felt constrained to transfer their interest and did so to Daniel Dulany. He paid Tasker £940/11 current money and secured the additional £941/2. Benjamin Tasker thereupon passed title to Dulany on January 13, 1744/45.[7]

One of the provisions in Daniel Dulany's 1745 purchase specified that he was to allow those individuals who were already settled upon "Tasker's Chance" to purchase their land from him. Accordingly, he issued deeds for 21 parcels on July 28, 1746 and for a few more thereafter. These early transfers of title may be summarized thus:

Early Deeds to Parcels on "Tasker's Chance"

Owner	Parcel Name	Acres	Date	Deed*
Weiss, Frantz	"Strife"	206	July 28, 1746	EE:71
Myer, Caspar	"Long Acre"	273	"	BB 1:440
Sinn, Henry	"Loom"	125¼	"	EE:69
Brunner, Henry	"Carroll Creek"	186¼	"	BB 1:441
Brunner, Joseph	"Schiefferstadt"	303	"	BB 1:444
Brunner, John	"What You Will"	232¼	"	BB 1:442
Brunner, Jacob	"Rich Level"	248	"	BB 1:432
Kemp, Conrad	"Kemp's Purchase"	190½	"	BB 1:435
Kemp, Gilbert	"Water Land"	100	"	BB 1:431
Roht, Henry	"Olis"	323	"	BB 1:443
Hoffman, Peter	"Rose Garden"	225	"	EE:73
Fink, Nicolaus		170	"	EE:80
Storm, Jacob	"Indian Field"	202	"	EE:66
Thomas, Christian	"Beaver Den"	209	"	EE:67
Miller, Abraham		294	"	EE:111
Ramsburg, Stephen	"Dear Bought"	307¼	Sep. 25, 1753	E:278
Stoner, Jacob	"Mill Pond"	292	July 28, 1746	BB 1:429
Stoner, Jacob	"Bear Den"	171¾	"	BB 1:429
Ramsburg, Stephen	"Mortality"	473	"	BB 1:436
Neff, John Henry		355½	"	BB 1:439
Loy, John George		213	"	BB 1:438
Smith, James		260	May 17, 1750	B:174
Stoner, Jacob	"The Barrens"	103	July 28, 1746	BB 1:445

* Land Records: Prince George's Co. before 1748, Frederick Co. after 1748.

---

[6] Provincial Court Records, EI 8:28.
[7] Prince George's County Land Records, BB 1:250.

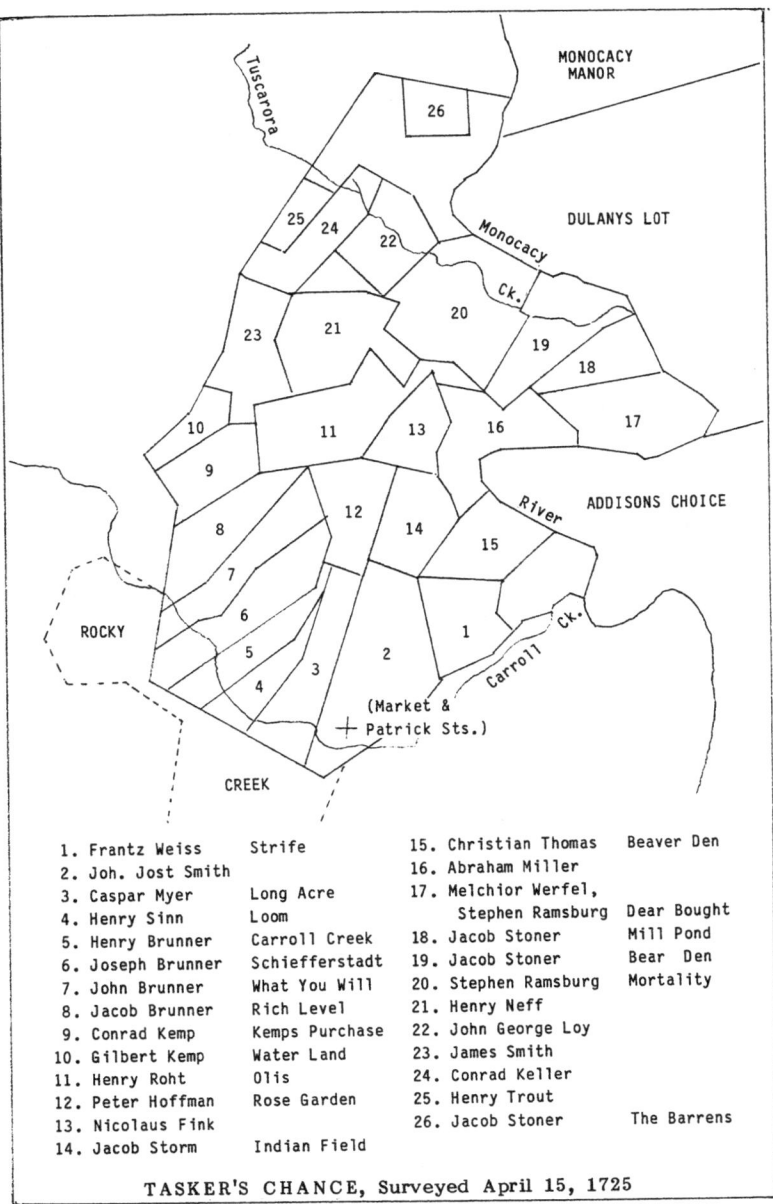

1. Frantz Weiss   Strife
2. Joh. Jost Smith
3. Caspar Myer   Long Acre
4. Henry Sinn   Loom
5. Henry Brunner   Carroll Creek
6. Joseph Brunner   Schiefferstadt
7. John Brunner   What You Will
8. Jacob Brunner   Rich Level
9. Conrad Kemp   Kemps Purchase
10. Gilbert Kemp   Water Land
11. Henry Roht   Olis
12. Peter Hoffman   Rose Garden
13. Nicolaus Fink
14. Jacob Storm   Indian Field
15. Christian Thomas   Beaver Den
16. Abraham Miller
17. Melchior Werfel,
    Stephen Ramsburg   Dear Bought
18. Jacob Stoner   Mill Pond
19. Jacob Stoner   Bear Den
20. Stephen Ramsburg   Mortality
21. Henry Neff
22. John George Loy
23. James Smith
24. Conrad Keller
25. Henry Trout
26. Jacob Stoner   The Barrens

TASKER'S CHANCE, Surveyed April 15, 1725

How many of these individuals had already been living on their land before 1746 or for how long is impossible to determine. We do know, however, that over half of the 23 Germans whose names appeared on the October 1742 petition to the General Assembly seeking a division of Prince George's Parish were at some time connected with "Tasker's Chance." These included all but Johann Georg Loy among the six original 1737 purchasers, as well as Frantz Weiss, Peter Hoffman, Georg Baer, Christian Thomas, Johann Henrich Neff, Joseph Brunner and the latter's three sons Jacob, John and Henry.[8] Moreover, 12 of 14 Germans who were naturalized as a group on May 3, 1740 had ties to "Tasker's Chance" -- Joseph, Jacob, John and Henry Branner [sic], Francis Wise, Hendrick Trout, Joseph Smith, Conrade Keller, John George Bear, Christian Thomas, Abraham Miller and Jacob Stoner.[9]

By 1746 Johann Jost Schmidt had left, and Daniel France's parcel was by then occupied by Jacob Sturm. Abraham Miller and Dieter Lehnich had moved on to the Lewistown area, and their parcels were apparently unoccupied. Of the original six, only John George Loy and Jacob Stoner seemingly remained. About 1753 a new rent roll was drawn up, possibly because the elder Daniel Dulany had just died and the property had passed to his son Daniel Dulany, Jr. The roll named those individuals "in possession" of land on "Tasker's Chance," their acreage, annual quitrents due, and changes in holdings which had occurred after August of 1749.[10] Analysis of the roll shows that since deeds were originally issued in 1746 Abraham Miller, Nicholas Fink and John Henry Neff had deeded their land back to one or the other Daniel Dulany. Melchior Warfield (Werfel) had presumably gotten title to his land, although he was not included among the 1746 grantees. Also in this period Jacob Stoner and Peter Hoffman had died and their land had passed to their heirs. Henry Trout had also died and Frederick Havenor was "in possession" of his parcel. Finally, Joseph Brunner had meanwhile deeded his parcel to his youngest son Elias Brunner.

Subsequent "Tasker's Chance" land transactions down to the time of the Revolution were also noted on this Rent Roll. Thus in 1753 the land of James Smith passed to Christopher Lowndes, and Stephen Ramsburg acquired the Werfel property. The latter then passed to Sebastian Darn [Derr] in 1755. In 1760 Christian Brengle received the Wise parcel from the latter's son Jacob Wise. John George Loy's land was devised to Jacob Loy in 1765. The 103-acre "Barrens" in 1767 went from John to Henry Stoner. Four years later Christopher Myer acquired the original Joseph Brunner property from Elias Brunner, and in 1772 Caspar Myer transferred his original 273 acres to Jacob Pence (Bentz).

Because "Tasker's Chance" was subdivided after its initial patent, we have no certificates of survey to show the outline

---

[8] See below, p. 371.
[9] Commission Book No. 82, *loc. cit.*, pp. 80-81.
[10] Maryland Rent Rolls (Frederick County No. 1), 32:26. This roll is undated, but from its subsequent amended notations can be estimated to have been initially prepared about mid-1753.

boundaries of the various parcels, which in the 1740s comprised about three-quarters of the entire 7,000 acres. A survey made for Daniel Dulany shortly after he took title to "Tasker's Chance" was never filed, nor was there reason to. The next comprehensive survey of any kind was not made for another 35 years. After 1753, with the exception of lots in the town of Frederick, the rent roll records indicate no further transfers of "Tasker's Chance" land. Hence when confiscation of Tory property occurred in 1781 as a means of raising revenue for the Revolution, parts of "Tasker's Chance" still belonged to the Dulany family, and a land resurvey of at least part of "Tasker's Chance" was therefore necessary. By then, however, the picture was vastly changed. The town of Frederick had been built, and numerous alterations in property lines in subsequent deeds and partitions had altered the picture appreciably. The only means of locating the early settlers geographically, therefore, is by a detailed plotting of each parcel from what deed information exists in the land records and then assembling the whole as in a jig-saw puzzle. The result of such an attempt, with observable limitations and uncertainties, is shown on page 259. Even in 1781, as surveyor Francis Deakins wrote, "It appears that a survey was made of the whole tract about 1746 and the lines and courses of the parts then sold and deeded were marked. But the original tract being large and having nothing in the grant to rule it but courses and distances, the variation at this time (1781) throws the parts sold out into the greatest confusion admitting them to be subject to variation."

"Tasker's Chance" had its beginning point near the mouth of Beaver Creek, later called Carroll Creek, where it emptied into the Monocacy River. In 1781 Abraham Faw and Charles Hedges, attempting to ascertain the beginning point, decided it was a tree near a sink hole on the south side of a house "where Matthias Ringer formerly lived."[11] About 1811 another attempt was made to mark this beginning with the erection of a sandstone monument. Jacob Engelbrecht in his *Diary* noted in 1859 that an inscription on the stone was by then nearly obliterated, though he was able to read it as "Beginning of Tasker's Chance, 1725."[12] From this point, somewhat paralleling the Creek, the boundary ran southwesterly for a little over two miles, then turned northwesterly for another mile and a half. Along this southern boundary some seven parcels were defined, those at the western end radiating like lengthy spokes in a wheel.

Title to the first of these lots, tucked within a large bend of the Monocacy River and lying north of Carroll Creek, seemingly remained with Daniel Dulany. Located here near where the Gas House Pike crosses the Monocacy River was Dulany's Mill, which was mentioned in the August 1749 Frederick Court records: The Court ordered that "the overseer appointed to lay out the road from Frederick Town to Mr. Dulany's Mill alter the same and carry it through the back of Francis Wise's plantation and Christian Thomas' land without going through his enclosure, the nighest way to the

---
[11] For Ringer, see also above, p. 151.
[12] Jacob Englebrecht, *The Englebrecht Diary, 1818-1878*, private typescript, without pagination.

mill."[13] The road "from Fredericktown to Dulany's Mill" was frequently mentioned in Court records.[14] Title to this parcel remained with the Dulany family until after the confiscation proceedings of 1781. The work of Faw and Hedges in that year suggests the possibility that Matthias Ringer possibly had lived on this lot, but the 1790 and 1800 censuses placed him in the Emmitsburg District. In 1785 this first parcel on "Tasker's Chance," was sold by the state as confiscated Loyalist property to Col. Baker Johnson (1746-1811). It was known simply as "Lot No. 26" or, after the sale, as "Johnson's Mill."

To the west of "Johnson's Mill" lay "Strife" whose 206 acres had been conveyed to **Francis Wise** by Daniel Dulany on July 28, 1746.[15] It was one of 20 such parcels deeded that day by Dulany to settlers previously located on "Tasker's Chance." The land lay along present-day Gas House Pike, immediately northeast of today's city of Frederick. Christian Thomas was Wise's neighbor to the north. **Frantz Weiss**, son of Jacob Weiss and Anna Margaretha Kessler, was baptized on April 7, 1705 in Mühlhofen, south of Landau in the Palatinate.[16] Over time his brothers Abraham, Hans Peter and David also emigrated. Frantz arrived on the ship *Elizabeth* with his 20-year old bride [Maria] Barbara Traut, whom he had married the previous January. He was listed as a blacksmith. With them traveled several others destined to settle on or near "Tasker's Chance," including Hans Peter Hoffman, Georg Friederich Unselt,[17] Hans Jurigh Ley, Jaques Bonet,[18] Nicholas Sly, Johann Philippus Schmitt and Johan Debalt Trautt. The first three of these married sisters of his wife. They all arrived at Philadelphia on August 27, 1733.[19]

Six weeks later Johann Jacob Weiss was born. Pastor Stöver's baptism entry of December 25, 1733 placed the family at that time in the Muddy Creek area southwest of present-day Adamstown in northeastern Lancaster County, Pennsylvania. There in 1735 a second child Johann Georg Weiss was also born and baptized. The entry for a third child Johannes Weiss, born March 17, 1739 and baptized June 17, 1739, though still included in the Muddy Creek records,[20] was made after the family had moved to Monocacy.

---

[13] Rice, *The Life, op. cit.*, p. 16. See also above, p. 73.
[14] In 1750 John Charlton was overseer of this road, in 1753 Patrick Doran, in 1754 Caspar Sheen, in 1755 Valentine Stickle, in 1759 John Adam Evertt, in 1760 Sampson Lazarus, in 1761 Henry Lazarus, in 1768 Lawrence Prengle [Brengle] and in 1770 Jacob Brengle.
[15] Prince George's County Land Records, EE:71.
[16] Barbelroth Church Book Nr. 2; cf. *born* April 9, 1705 per 1763 property roll (Vermögensverzeichnis): Friedrich Krebs, "Pfälzer Amerika-Auswanderer," *Familie und Volk*, 5:176-177.
[17] See above, pp. 182-184.
[18] *Ibid.*, p. 214.
[19] Strassburger-Hinke, *op. cit.*, Lists 30AA'BC, pp. 113-115, 765-767.
[20] Muddy Creek Church Book, *op. cit.*, p. 27. The three entries do not appear in Stöver's personal Journal as do other Monocacy baptisms on June 17, 1739. Johannes Brunner and his wife Anna Maria were baptism sponsors for the 1739 baptism.

Francis Wise first appears in Maryland records in 1736 as a witness in the trial against Robert Debutts.[21] But he was not one of the 1737 purchasers of "Tasker's Chance." He did appear with other settlers on "Tasker's Chance" in the list of those naturalized in Maryland on May 3, 1740. He also signed the 1742 petition to divide Prince George's Parish. On March 27, 1745 William Downes was suing Francis Wise for trespass. When Downes refused to prosecute further, Wise was awarded his costs.[22] Frantz and Barbara Weiss were Reformed church participants, and their daughter Catharina was baptised in that church in February 1747. In 1748 Francis Wise was named as one of the Germans being overtaxed by the Sheriff,[23] and in the same year Frantz Weiss, together with Johann Conrad Kämpf, witnessed the will of Hans Peter Hoffman, one of his 1733 shipmates.[24] In August 1749 before the same Court which was rerouting the road to Dulany's Mill "through the back of Francis Wise's plantation," Wise was presented by the Grand Jury for "cutting down and destroying the land of John van Metre, an orphan."[25] He was charged again before the June Court of 1751 "for waste committed on the land of John van Metre, an orphan," but the charge was dropped because of Wise's death the previous April. By his will, which was written in German but was not recorded, Wise appointed Frederick Unsellt and Georg Lay as executors and guardians of his eight children. The eldest of these, Mary, Jacob and Elizabeth, were named in the 1740 naturalization proceedings. Wise's will likewise mentioned his brother Peter Weiss and his niece Margaretha, the daughter of his brother Abraham. Both were living with him. From Wise's estate a contribution for benches was made to the Calvinist [Reformed] Church in Frederick.[26]

"Strife" was conveyed by George Loy on March 20, 1760[27] to **Christian Brengel** (1718-1761), the son of Christian and Maria Christina Brengel of Wolfersheim Kreis St. Ingbert on the Blies River near Zweibrücken in the Palatinate. Brengel arrived in America on August 30, 1737 along with Johann Nickel Finck. He lived for some years in today's Lehigh County of Pennsylvania where he married and began his family. In the mid-1750s he moved to Frederick County, but died soon after acquiring the "Tasker's Chance" property.[28]

---

[21] See above, p. 77.
[22] Prince George's County Court Records, DD:44.
[23] See below, p. 292.
[24] Frederick County Wills, A1:14; English translation by Charles H. Wiegel furnished to Clerk of the Court by Ethel Close Buckey.
[25] Rice, *The Life*, op. cit., p. 17. See also above, p. 73.
[26] Original Wills, Frederick County, Box 1, folder 5, Hall of Records, March 30, 1751, probated May 6, 1751. Frederick County Administrative Accounts, A1:105-108, show provision for two coffins, one for himself, the other for his wife.
[27] Frederick County Land Records, F:954. Loy was acting here as executor for Francis Wise. Jacob Wise, heir at law, joined in the deed.
[28] Strassburger-Hinke, op. cit., Lists 44ABC, pp. 169-170, 172; Krebs, loc. cit., 5:179. Nephews Christian, Jacob and George Brengel,

Lawrence J. Brengle (1805-1874) lived on this land in 1873.[29]

All too brief in the story of "Tasker's Chance" was the appearance of **Johann Jost Schmidt**, one of the original six individuals who in 1737 were attempting to purchase "Tasker's Chance" from Benjamin Tasker. Although referred to in Tasker's subsequent deed to Daniel Dulany[30] as Joseph Smith, his proper name may be learned from subsequent references in deeds to property adjoining his.[31] He may have arrived at Philadelphia on August 24, 1728 along with Mardin Schaub, Jacob Sturm, and Jacob Brunner who also settled on or near "Tasker's Chance."[32] Or, born about 1688, he may have come on September 23, 1734 along with a wife Anna Christina and two fairly grown children, Elisabetha Magdelen, age 20, and Peter, age 17.[33] Whichever, he was naturalized in Maryland on May 3, 1740 along with others later found on "Tasker's Chance," and he was present at the time of the 1742 petition to divide Prince George's Parish. But he quickly disappeared from the records after that.

The land Joh. Jost Schmidt was intending to occupy approximated 500 acres in size, by far the largest separate parcel on "Tasker's Chance." It was situated at the most southerly point, a middle point along the southern boundary of "Tasker's Chance." From there it extended northward a mile and a half to Daniel France's land, later known as "Indian Field." After Dulany came into possession of "Tasker's Chance" in 1744, he did not pass title to Schmidt's parcel as he was required to do had the land then been occupied. This further indicates that Schmidt had left the area.

Instead, Dulany kept title in his own name and about the time he began giving title to the other parcels on "Tasker's Chance" he probably had a portion of Schmidt's land laid out as the future site of the town of Frederick. No plat plan was ever filed, and the actual date of the town's beginning cannot be designated specifically. The first reference to the town's "existence" was made by Gabriel Nasman, a visiting Lutheran pastor, who dated a document he wrote on October 31, 1746 in "Friederichs Tawn."[34] In June of the next year

---

who were sons of Christian's brother Kilian, also came to America, the first two in 1754 (*ibid.*, Lists 222ABC, pp. 629, 632, 635), the latter with their sister Anna Catharina about 1764. Jacob married sisters Gertraud and Margaret Bell and in 1772 purchased John Bell's land on "Dulany's Lot." George Brengel married Anna Catharina Beckenbach, while his sister Anna Catharina married, as his second wife, Sebastian Derr, also a resident on "Tasker's Chance." See pp. 126, 289.

[29] Lake, *op. cit.*, p. 11.
[30] Provincial Court Records, EI 8:28.
[31] See, for example, Frederick County Land Records, O:445.
[32] Strassburger-Hinke, *op. cit.*, Lists 6AB, pp. 18-20: Johann Jost Schmidt.
[33] *Ibid.*, Lists 37ABC, pp. 143-146: Signed by mark as Josht Shmidt.
[34] A copy of the document, whose original he took back with him to Philadelphia, was inserted in the Frederick Lutheran Church Book. For its details, see above, p. 144 and also Rice, *New Facts, op cit.*,

the Rev. Henry Melchior Muhlenberg visited the Monocacy area and held Lutheran services near present-day Jimtown crossroads. Then in a report to the Lutheran authorities in Halle, Germany he wrote, "On June 25th (1747) we rode ten miles farther on to a newly laid out town, where several Lutherans lived who belonged to our congregation..."[35] The first road record to name Fredericktown did not do so until the March Court of 1749 appointed an overseer for the road "from Fredericktown to the top of Catoctin Mountain" and from "Fredericktown to John Biggs' Ford." The June Court of that year heard petitions for a road from "Nelson's Ferry (now Point of Rocks) to Fredericktown" and for one from Fredericktown to Dulany's Mill."

Although it was not until 1748 when Dulany granted the first deeds to specific town lots, these initial lots were numbered, obviously in accordance with an existing planned layout of the whole. Since Dulany charged his purchasers an annual quitrent of one shilling per lot, payable on May 10th of each year for the first 21 years, then raised it to two shillings thereafter, it is possible that the difference between initial quitrent dates and dates of the deeds themselves may indicate that many lots were being purchased over a period of time. The deeds for fully three-quarters of the first fifty lots sold had such differences, thus indicating that the town was undoubtedly settled some one to five years earlier than the deeds themselves would indicate:

	Quitrents Began	Deeds Recorded
1746	4	-
1747	-	-
1748	24	5
1749	6	-
1750	7	10
1751	1	13
1752	4	4
1753	3	20

Initially the "town" consisted of 144 long rectangular lots. The first ran along the west side of Chapel Alley [Carroll Street] between present-day All Saints Street and Carroll Creek. From there, six rows of 24 lots each extended west to Record Street and north to Fourth Street. When Daniel Dulany died in 1753, he had conveyed title to only 52 of these lots, including six lots for a Court House and jail as well as two lots for a Lutheran School and Church. Provision had not yet been made for the Reformed Church, the Catholic Church or the Established Church of England.

Although title did not pass until 1753, the four lots with the earliest quitrent dates (1746) went to Thomas Schley, the so-called Reformed schoolmaster who, in Court records at least, appears primarily as a tavern keeper.[36] He came to America in 1745 and on

---
pp. 179, 181.
[35] *Hallesche Nachrichten*, op. cit., p. 352: "Den 25 Junii ritten wir zehen Meilen weiter hinauf zu einer neu angelegten Stadt, wo verschiedene Lutheraner wohneten, welche mit zu der Gemeine gehören...."
[36] Schley, for example, was presented before the November 1749

Lot No. 54 he reputedly built what a hundred years later was called the oldest house in Frederick and two hundred years later the "first" house in Frederick. Its disappearance was described by Jacob Engelbrecht on August 17, 1853: "The oldest house in Frederick, this venerable house at N.E. corner of the Alley (Mrs. Stein's Alley) in Patrick Street is now being torn down to be replaced by a brick house by Mr. William Neidhardt, baker, who now owns it. The old house was built by John Thos. Schley in 1745 or 46 and was always considered the oldest house in our town. The gable end of the house fronted on Patrick Street. Mrs. Catharine Bier, Mr. J. T. Schley's daughter, who died in Baltimore May 26, 1843, aged 95 years, was born in the house and was always considered the first person born in Frederick after it was laid out as a town."[37]

In 1758 John Cary was appointed overseer of "all the streets and lanes in Fredericktown and from the main road to the English Church." The latter was located west of Middle Alley between East All Saints Street and Carroll Creek.[38] Ten years later, in November of 1768, Daniel Dulany the Younger petitioned the Court for an overseer for the streets on his 100 additional lots laid out for Fredericktown. John Adam Pickenpaw was thereupon appointed as that overseer of "all the streets, lanes and alleys in Fredericktown and as far as the end of Caspar Myer's fence that is along the road to Conococheague as well as the new streets lately laid out by Mr. Dulany."

By the time of the 1781 confiscation sale of Tory (Loyalist) property, deeds had not passed for 25 of the original 144 lots. Further additional lots had been laid out extending the town south a block beyond South Street, north to 7th Street, east to East Street and west to Bentz Street, making a total altogether of 351 lots. But this was only a portion of the total parcel envisioned originally by Joh. Jost Schmidt. North and east of the 1781 town of Frederick, 25 additional parcels, each much larger than the city lots, were surveyed on what was to have been Schmidt's 500 acres. These were sold as confiscated property.

West of the Schmidt parcel and now incorporated within the western portion of the city of Frederick lay the land of **Caspar Myer.** He appeared with other Germans in the 1743 naturalization proceedings, having received the Reformed sacrament from Edward [Joh. Conrad] Templeman in August of that year.[39] He called his land "Long Acre," for that was the shape of its 273 acres: just under 100 perches wide over much of its 454 perches length. He received his deed to this land on July 28, 1746[40] and in the 1753 Rent Roll summary is

---

Court for keeping a tippling house, was convicted in March 1750 and was fined 40 shillings.

[37] Engelbrecht Diary, *op. cit.* Mrs. Stein's Alley was later known as Middle Alley and today is called Maxwell Avenue. According to the Frederick Reformed Church Book, Eva Catharina Schley was born March 13, 1749.

[38] See also Varlé's map, *loc. cit.*

[39] Provincial Court Judgment Records, 1742-1744, EI I:296. His name here was spelled Gasper Mire.

[40] Prince George's County Land Records, BB 1:440.

shown "in possession" of the 273 acres.[41] In 1764 he was petitioning the March Court for permission to establish his boundaries, which were "in decay and imperfect." On April 7, 1767 Benedict Assleman, a native of Germany, "being of the Society of Mininists [Mennonites]," identified the beginning point of Myer's land.[42] The Grand Jury in August 1751 presented Caspar Myer, overseer of the road from Frederick, as well as several others for failure to clear the roads. In 1757 Caspar Myer served in Stephen Ramsburg's Militia Company. In that same year he began to sell off portions of his land. The beginning point of two lots which he sold in 1757 to Charles Shell was at a stone on the main road (now Patrick Street) that leads from Frederick Town to Conococheague (Hagerstown area and westward).[43] A description can be found in the surveyor's field book in the office of the Frederick City Engineer. This land lay along Patrick Street west of the line intended to be Record Street between West Church and South Streets.

From 1759 to 1763, Myer sold a series of lots to Henry Wise, Burnet Wren, Jacob Young, Thomas Bowles, Charles Beatty and George Murdock, all of which touched on Carroll Creek.[44] Caspar Myer's "Addition to Frederick Town" was depicted on Samuel Duvall's 1782 plat of Frederick Town.[45] In July of 1771 Caspar Myer gave a deed to Jacob Bentz "for all that tract called 'Long Acre' where the said Caspar Myer now lives, beginning at the beginning of John Jost Smith's land in the 9th line of 'Tasker's Chance' and running .... to Peter Hoffman's land .... except what Caspar Myer laid out in lots adjacent to Fredericktown and sold by him to divers persons...." Bentz paid 1,450 pounds "current money of Pennsylvania" for this remaining part of "Long Acre."[46] Caspar Myer's will was dated December 1, 1771, and by it he bequeathed half a lot with its buildings to his son-in-law Nicholas Hisler. The other half, "where she now lives," went to his wife Barbara. Lot No. 114 in Frederick (the fourth lot west of Market Street, between Second and Third Streets) was devised to his son Henry Myer.[47]

The old city mill, near where the Carillon now stands in Baker

---
[41] Maryland Rent Rolls (Frederick County No. 1), 32:26a.
[42] Frederick County Land Records, L:57. In his testimony Assleman said he lived in Pennsylvania, nine miles from Lancaster. Was he related to Velten Usselmann who signed Muhlenberg's 1747 Articles? The latter also appeared as Valentin Hasleman [Husleman, Usselmann, Wuselman and Whitselman!], having his daughter Maria Margaretha Usselmann baptized in March 1748 (Frederick Reformed Church Book). He bought livestock from Nicholas Bundrick in 1754 (Frederick County Land Records, E:417). But he does not appear in the land records before 1743.
[43] Ibid., F:639.
[44] Ibid., F:642, F:831, G:445, H:235. In each of these Anna Barbara is named as Myer's wife.
[45] George H. Shafer's 1876 copy of this plat hung in the public meeting room of the old City Hall in Frederick.
[46] Frederick County Land Records, O:445.
[47] Frederick County Wills, A 1:462.

Park, was built on "Long Acre" by John Ramsburg in a joint venture with Jacob Bentz.[48] In 1776 a canal was cut through to "Long Acre," then the land of Jacob Bentz, from Philip Sinn's "Loom" to the west.[49] Apparently the canal was constructed out of the old mill race. A number of other historic landmarks on "Long Acre" were designated in an 1844 deed from Abraham Kemp, assigning 53 acres of what was once Caspar Myer's land to William Tyler. That deed mentioned the old Tyler Brick Yard, Eppert's Pailing fence on the south side of Town Creek, an alley (now College Avenue) leading from Bentztown to the Creek, the main road leading from Fredericktown to Brunner's Mill (now Dill Avenue) and the old Reformed graveyard (now Memorial Park).

Heinrich Sinn came to this country from Germany on the *Johnson Galley*, a pink registered in London, which had sailed from Rotterdam by way of Deal in England. He arrived at Philadelphia on September 18, 1732 and qualified with the usual oaths the next day.[50] With him came his wife Katharine and a daughter Anna, as well as Johann Georg Gump, Johann Peder Schmitt[51] and some 325 others. Though Stover indicated in his Journal that Heinrich Sinn was living in "Manaquesen" in 1735, it is probable that the move there came sometime between 1736 and 1739. An entry for the baptism of Sinn's daughter Susanna on March 30, 1735 appears in both his personal Journal and the Lancaster Trinity Lutheran Church Book, but witnesses and other baptisms the same day did not involve Monocacy settlers. Further, in 1736 a son Philip Henry Sinn was baptized at the Lancaster Reformed Church. It was not until June 17, 1739 when a son Jacob Mattheis Sinn was baptized that we can be confident the family had reached Monocacy. This was the last entry Stöver made for "Henrich Sinn of Monoquesen," and all others present that day were from Monocacy. Jacob Mattheis Mansser was the sponsor.

Henrich Sinn's land, called "Loom," was a thin, narrow 125-acre triangle squeezed between the lands of Caspar Myer and Henry Brunner. Sinn received title to the land from Daniel Dulany on July 28, 1746.[52] The 1740 agreement to manage "Jacob's Fortune" while its owner Jacob Manser was off fighting with the King's forces in the West Indies[53] suggests that Sinn might then have been in the area near present-day Lewistown. Nevertheless he was a contributor to the purchase of the Lutheran church book about 1742, and in it are entries recording the baptism of his daughters Maria Catharina in 1741 and Maria Bärbel in 1743.[54] Henry Sinn was still living on "Loom" when he dictated his will on March 7, 1770. In that will, he named his wife Catharine and devised his land on "Tasker's Chance" to his

---
[48] Frederick County Land Records, WR 17:560, December 31, 1798.
[49] *Ibid.*, W:403.
[50] Strassburger-Hinke, *op. cit.*, Lists 21ABC, pp. 71-78. Hinke transcribed his signature as "Sim" while David Crockatt, the ship's Captain, recorded the name as Henrick Saen.
[51] See above, p. 189.
[52] Prince George's County Land Records, EE:69.
[53] See above, p. 190.
[54] Frederick Lutheran Church Book, pp. 1, 3.

son Philip Henry Sinn. The latter was to make compensating payments to his brother Jacob Sinn and his four sisters, Susanna Pickenpaw (wife of Johann Caspar Beckenbach), Barbara Michael, Catharine Fout and Margaret Cronin.[55] It is of interest that Philip Henry Sinn seems to have changed the family's religious affiliation from Lutheran to Reformed, for in 1756 his name appeared on the Frederick Reformed church constitution prepared by Pastor Johann Conrad Steiner.[56]

Four lots located at the southwest corner of "Tasker's Chance" just beyond Henrich Sinn's parcel were the homes of **Joseph Brunner** and his sons **Henry, John** and **Jacob Brunner.** The Brunner family originated in Rothenstein, Switzerland, but before 1679 had migrated to the Palatine village of Klein Schifferstadt, six miles north of the city of Speyer. Only some fifteen families, all adhering to the Reformed religion, lived in this tiny German hamlet.[57] Also known as Schifferstadt auf der Wiesen, or simply Wieser, it was sometimes called das obere Dorf (the upper village) in contradistinction to neighboring Gross Schifferstadt, das untere Dorf or Niederdorf, the lower village. Gross Schifferstadt was truly "gross," a Catholic village of over 1,000 inhabitants, which today has absorbed its little neighbor to the west so that the combination is now known simply as Schifferstadt. The well-known Maryland families of Thomas, Gah, Getzendanner and Storm also came from here.

Johann **Jacob Brunner** was the first to arrive. Baptized at Klein Schifferstadt on February 25, 1703, he had married in 1725 Maria Barbara Sturm, the daughter of Christian Sturm. One son, Johann Peter Brunner, had been born to this couple in 1726. Early in 1728, perhaps as advance agents for the larger emigration which was to follow in the next year, Jacob Brunner and his small family, together with his wife's brother Jacob Sturm, set forth for America. From Rotterdam aboard the ship *Mortonhouse* they sailed to Deal in England and from that place on June 15th left for Philadelphia. Together with Johan Georg Doderer, Mardin Schaub, Johannes Huber, Johann Jost Schmidt, Johann Peter Mölich and other familiar names, they arrived at Philadelphia on August 23, 1728. Their group of 200 souls constituted the sixth list of arrivals in the long array of over 500 such lists which followed over the next eighty years.

Jacob Brunner's land on "Tasker's Chance" was called "Rich Level." Its 248 acres were deeded to him by Daniel Dulany on July 28, 1746, and in the deed a corner of Tetur Laney's land is mentioned.[58] This helps to locate Jacob Brunner's land as lying parallel to and just west of today's U. S. Highway 15 as it passes through the northwestern portion of the city of Frederick. Earlier, on June 29, 1741, Jacob Brunner had had 25 acres surveyed as "Inlett" which was located on a branch of Carroll Creek next to "Beatty's line" on "Rocky Creek." This was patented on September 29, 1743,[59] but by

---

[55] Frederick County Wills, A1:371.
[56] Ranck, *op. cit.*, pp. 29, 190.
[57] Early Reformed Church records were kept in the neighboring Iggelheim parish's Church Book.
[58] Prince George's County Land Records, BB: 1:432.
[59] C/S: LG E:358; Patent: PT 1:179.

1745 it was in the hands of Robert Debutts who sold it to Michael Thomas. In 1751 the 100-acre "Chevy Chase" in Middletown Valley was patented to Jacob Brunner. To this he added 630 acres of vacant land and received a patent for the whole on September 21, 1753.[60] In March of 1755 he sold a portion to Caspar Pickenpaw[61] and conveyed further amounts to his sons Peter and Michael Brunner.[62]

Jacob Brunner was very active in the affairs of the Reformed Church. His name appears frequently in the early Frederick Reformed Church Book, and the Lutheran as well, as baptism sponsor for relatives and friends. He was an initial Elder of the Reformed Church as were his brothers-in-law Christian Getzendanner, Stephen Ramsburg and Jacob Storm, his father Joseph Brunner and the schoolteacher and innkeeper Thomas Schley. Together they "signed" the appeal of March 1, 1748 for a second visit from Pastor Michael Schlatter following his initial trip to the Monocacy area the year before. They were concerned about the inroads being made by the Dunkers through the efforts of Nicolaus Fink and Heinrich Rotts (Rhodes).[63] On October 20, 1748 Jacob Brunner and three others[64] were granted a passport by Governor Samuel Ogle for a return trip to Germany. That the trip was made is shown by the initial entry in the Frederick Reformed Church Book: "Johann Jacob Bruner purchased this writing book for 50 kroner in Frankfurt am Main, April 16, 1749."[65]

In the year 1729, the year following Johann Jacob Brunner's arrival, only two shiploads of German immigrants sailed up the Delaware. The second of these, the ship *Allen*, anchored at Philadelphia on September 11th after a voyage from England lasting 70 days. Among her 126 passengers were Alexander Mack and some thirty families in his colony of German Baptist Brethren.[66] But also on

----

[60] C/S: BY & GS 5:534, GS 1:92; Patent Y & S 6:227.
[61] Frederick County Land Records, E:698. See below, p. 300.
[62] Frederick County Land Records, E:697.
[63] A copy of this letter was discovered in the church archives at The Hague in the Netherlands in 1896-1898 by James. I. Good and William Hinke and again in 1964 by John P. Dern. For a photographic copy and a translation by Miss Elizabeth C. Kieffer, former librarian of the Historical Society of the Evangelical and Reformed Church in Lancaster, see Ranck, *op. cit.*, pp. 15-16. Reference to Hermann for Heinrich Rotts (Henry Rhodes, q.v.) is, of course, a faulty reading. So also are Ranck's interpretations relating to how the individual elders spelled their own names (e.g., Christian Geldtzedaner, Jacob and Joseph Brummer, Stephan Remensperger and Jacob Storm): Schley's letter, whatever its original signatures, was *copied* into the Dutch record by a third hand. See above, p. 150n.
[64] See below, p. 293.
[65] "Johann Jacob Bruner kaufte dieses Schreibuch für 50 Kr. in Frnckfurt am Mayn Anno 1749 d 16 Aprile." The book, rebound in 1824, was used for recording baptisms 1747-1875, marriages 1760-1768 and burials 1829-1874. A smaller book, given the congregation by Pastor Schlatter, contains confirmations 1753-1829, communicants 1758-1843, and marriages 1756-1759 and 1784-1833.
[66] This religious group, sometimes nicknamed Dunkers because of

board was the balance of the Brunner family from Klein Schifferstadt. With the parents Joseph Brunner and wife Catharina Elisabetha Thomas came daughter Anna Barbara Brunner (1701-1766$^+$) and her husband Christian Getzendanner,[67] sons Johannes Brunner (1708-1776) who was sick and therefore could not subscribe to the customary oaths, Johann Henderick Brunner (1715-1775) who was listed as under the age of 15, and daughter Anna Maria Catharina Brunner (1718-1770$^+$).[68] Three sons were thus missing from the list of arrivals at Philadelphia: Gabriel Brunner (born 1706) was confirmed at Klein Schifferstadt in 1719 and would have been old enough to have appeared on the ship's list of adult males, but presumably died either in Germany or enroute to America. Johann Valentin Brunner (born 1711) was not confirmed at Klein Schifferstadt and therefore presumably died there before 1725. Also unaccounted for is Elias Brunner, who would have been six years of age when the family came to America, having been born at Klein Schifferstadt on February 15, 1723. He is well known in later Frederick County history.

Principally because the Brunners were Reformed and Reformed church records did not begin in Lancaster until 1736, no member of this family has been definitely identified in Pennsylvania before the move to Maryland. The Lancaster Lutheran Church Book notes a Maria Catharina Bruner and Leonhardt Lutz, both of them unmarried, who stood as sponsors for the baptism of a child of Johann Frantz Fuchs on December 26, 1733.[69] Were she the daughter of Joseph Brunner, she would have been only 15 years of age. Allegedly Joseph Brunner's daughter Maria Catharina was married on April 13, 1736 in

---

their belief in adult baptism by immersion, was an outgrowth of the Pietistic Movement. In 1708 a small nucleus of eight families at Schwarzenau in Wittgenstein, Germany, under the leadership of Alexander Mack broke away from the formal state religion to establish its own church. Other churches were soon formed at Marienborn and Krefeld. Members of the latter group emigrated to Germantown, Pennsylvania in 1719, the same year the founding group under Mack moved from Schwarzenau to Surhuisterveen in Holland. It was the latter party which came to Pennsylvania in 1729. Cf. also Donald F. Durnbaugh, *European Beginnings of the Brethren* (Elgin, Ill., 1958) and *The Brethren in Colonial America* (Elgin, 1967). See also below, p. 275.

[67] See above, p. 165.

[68] Strassburger-Hinke, *op. cit.*, Lists 10ABC, pp. 27-30. The family name was spelled "Prunder" by the ship's Captain. No surname was shown for the youngest daughter whose complete name Hinke mistakenly transcribed as Anna Maria *Latrine* instead of "Catrine." As Maria Catharina she was born at Klein Schifferstadt on September 29, 1718 and was confirmed there at "age 12" on April 17, 1729 just before the family departed for America.

[69] Lancaster Lutheran Church Book, *loc. cit.*, p. 403 (p. 5 in the original). Stöver, *op. cit.*, does not record this baptism in his personal Journal, but he does (p. 18) place Leonhardt Lutz at Monocacy on September 21, 1740 as a baptism witness, with Catarina Geiger, for a son of Heinrich Fortunee.

Lancaster County by Justice of the Peace Detrick Updegraf to Stephen Ramsburg, and together they settled on "Tasker's Chance." But this has not been verified.[70]

On May 3, 1740 the Brunners swore allegiance to Lord Baltimore, thereby gaining naturalization and the right to possess property. The record is a long one, but serves to identify a number of descendants in this family through the third generation: **Joseph Brunner** and son **Elias**; Jacob Brunner and children Peter, Michael, John, Jacob, Mary and Elizabeth; John Brunner and children John, Jacob, Catharine, Barbara and Mary; Henry Brunner and son John.[71]

On July 28, 1746 Joseph, Henry, John and Jacob Brunner all received deeds from Daniel Dulany for their respective lots on "Tasker's Chance."[72] The four lots lay parallel to each other, stretching in a northeasterly/southwesterly direction and covering much of the western part of today's city of Frederick. From south to north they succeeded one another beginning with Henry Brunner's "Carroll Creek" on the south and extending through father Joseph Brunner's "Schifferstadt" and John Brunner's "What You Will" to Jacob Brunner's "Rich Level," mentioned above, on the north. Carroll Creek flowed through all four parcels. In 1742 Joseph Brunner and his sons Jacob, John and Henry signed the petition to divide Prince George's Parish. In 1748 these four men were named in Stephen Ramsburg's report to the Maryland Assembly concerning the overtaxation of Germans by the Sheriff.[73]

Joseph Brunner lived another five years and wrote his will on January 17, 1753. In it he mentioned no wife, who therefore had presumably died before him. He conveyed his land "Schifferstadt," which he had named for the family's origins in Germany, to his youngest son Elias Brunner. Elias served as a sergeant in his brother-in-law Stephen Ramsburg's militia company in 1757 and is presumed to have constructed part of the large stone house now preserved by the Frederick Landmarks Foundation near the corner of today's Rosemont Avenue and West Second Street at the far end of Baker Park.

Henry Brunner (1715-1775) and his wife Maria Magdalena Sellers appeared frequently as baptism sponsors in the Frederick Reformed Church Book. The Prince George's County Court in 1741 appointed Henry Brunner overseer of the road from the "top of Catoctin Mountain to the Monocacy Waggon Road ford near Thomas Beatty's." In later years he abandoned his 186-acre "Carroll Creek" tract, situated between his father's "Schifferstadt" and neighbor Henry Sinn's "Loom," to live in the town of Frederick. There he wrote his will on December 4, 1775 by which he bequeathed to his wife "our dwelling house in Frederick town where I now live" and a third of his estate. "Carroll Creek" was to go to their sons Henry and Valentine Brunner when the latter (born 1758) was of age. Son Jacob Brunner was to get the

---

[70] The claim has been made by, among others, Schultz, *op. cit.*, p. 41. For Ramsburg, see below, pp. 291-293.
[71] See above, p. 260.
[72] Prince George's County Land Records, BB 1:432, 431, 442, 444.
[73] See below, p. 292. Their surname there was spelled Browner.

town house after his mother's death. Although son John Brunner had already been provided for, he was to get the house adjoining the dwelling house after specified payments to his mother and to Mary Bantz.[74] Henry Brunner's daughters included Barbara (wife of George Bernhard Lingenfelter), Anna Maria (wife of Jacob Cost), Susannah (wife of Jacob Thomas) and Anna Margaretha (wife of John David Jordan).

John Brunner (1708-1776) like his brother Henry was a frequent sponsor for baptisms in the Reformed Church. In 1739 he and his wife Anna Maria had also been sponsors for the Lutheran baptism of a son of Frantz Weiss.[75] His land "What You Will" was situated on the northwest side of his father's "Schifferstadt" between it and his brother Jacob's "Rich Level." By the terms of his February 15, 1776 will, this original land on "Tasker's Chance" was to go to his son John Brunner, Jr., while other land he had purchased, including "Sweed's Folly"[76] and adjoining land gotten from James Hook, was to go to a grandson, the son of his deceased son Jacob. "Good Luck" and "Chestnut Hill" were devised to son Stephen Brunner. The balance of his estate was divided between his four daughters, Catharine Thomas, Anna Barbara Eastin, Elizabeth Ramsberger and Anna Maria Ramsberger.[77]

The above recitation of facts relating to the Brunner families does little to pinpoint their location before they acquired title to land on "Tasker's Chance." They were undoubtedly present at Monocacy, however, by 1736, for Pastor Stöver's Journal noted that Anna Maria Bronnerin and Maria Barbara Bronnerin jointly stood as sponsors for one of the children baptized by Stöver at Manakesen on May 16, 1736. The two Brunners were daughters-in-law of Joseph Brunner, the wives respectively of John Brunner (whom she married in America) and of Jacob Brunner. The maiden name of the former is unknown; the latter was a sister of Johann Jacob Sturm from Schifferstadt. Their presence suggests that all the Brunners, wherever they lived, had probably arrived in the Monocacy area by at least 1736, a fairly early year in the pattern of known German arrivals.

Equally baffling is the family for whom these two ladies served as sponsors. From other records we know that the father of the baptized children was **Henry Bray**, which Stöver recorded as "Henry Prey." The fact that Stöver did not use the customary German "Heinrich" for the father's given name plus his phonetic problems with "B's" and "P's" suggests that at least the father was English while the mother may have been German.[78] Moreover, Henry Bray was no transient, for his name appeared in Court records until the 1750s. He first appeared in the 1733 list of Monocacy taxables and then in the

---
[74] Frederick County Wills, A1:556.
[75] See above, p. 262.
[76] See above, p. 61.
[77] Frederick County Wills, A1:564.
[78] Georg Sturm, *Geschichte meiner Hemiatgemeinde Schifferstadt* (Speyer, 1961), pp. 243-250, lists all documented surnames known to have lived in Schifferstadt from earliest times until 1900. No surname resembling Bray or Prey is included.

1734 list of those not burning their tobacco properly. But no record of his land ownership is known. The March Court of 1736 gave him 40 shillings because of his "loss by fire." And in 1751 he sold his farm animals to Jacob Barr.[79] His children, as listed by Stöver, with baptism sponsors in parentheses, included: Sarah born March 31, 1732 (no sponsors indicated), Anna Maria, born April 15, 1733 (Anna Maria Bronnerin and Maria Barbara Bronnerin, sponsors), Susanna born March 10, 1735 (Dieterich Lehnich and Susanna Fauthin), Catarina born April 16, 1737 (no sponsors), and Eliesabetha born Nov. 3, 1739 (Georg Schweinhardt and wife Maria Eliesabetha).[80]

North of the land of the Brunners lay the land of **Conrad** and **Gilbert Kemp**, whom we have met above.[81] At the westernmost point of "Tasker's Chance" Daniel Dulany on July 28, 1746 deeded two lots to the Kemps, one for 190 acres called "Kemp's Purchase" which went to Conrad Kemp the father, the other for 100 acres known as "Water Land" which went to his second son Gilbert Kemp.[82] These were situated largely within today's Fort Detrick area and were not far distant from other land held by the Kemps in the Rocky Springs area. Conrad Kemp's name appeared among those Germans being overcharged in their 1748 quitrent payments.[83]

Henry Rhodes, as he was called by English scribes, arrived at Philadelphia on August 17, 1733 with his family and that of Johann Conrad Kemp, destined to be next door neighbors on "Tasker's Chance" some thirteen years later. He signed his name as **Henrich Roht**, although the ship's Captain called him Henrick Roodt.[84] He was 45 years of age at the time and brought with him his wife Catharina Roed, 40 years of age, and children Anna Eve 13, William 12 and Catharina Roed 9.[85] The family's subsequent whereabouts is unknown until on July 28, 1746 Daniel Dulany deeded to Henry Roth 323 acres on "Tasker's Chance."[86] Known as "Olis," it was the third largest parcel carved out of the whole tract. It adjoined the Kemps on the west and Jacob Brunner on the south. Apparently this parcel had been occupied earlier by **Dieter Lehnich**,[87] for Henry Rhodes, whatever the spelling of his name, was not listed among the 1737 would-be purchasers of "Tasker's Chance," although Lehnich was. Lehnich was also present in October 1742 when his name appeared on the petition to divide Prince George's Parish. It was shown there as Jno. TeterLany.[88]

At least initially Heinrich and Catharina "Roth" were affiliated

---

[79] Frederick County Land Records, B:585.
[80] Stöver, op. cit., p. 16.
[81] See p. 172.
[82] Prince George's County Land Records, BB 1:431, 435.
[83] See below, p. 292.
[84] The German "oh" and the Dutch "oo" both produce a long "o" vowel, as in Rhode; hence, to English ears, Rhodes or Rhoads. In this short summary, 14 spelling variations may be observed.
[85] Strassburger-Hinke, op. cit., Lists 29ABC, pp. 107-112.
[86] Prince George's County Land Records, BB 1:443.
[87] For Lehnich, see above, p. 217.
[88] See below, p. 371.

with the Reformed Church, and in 1747 they stood as sponsors there for Heinrich, son of Jacob and Margaretha Stahely. But early in the following year the Elders of the Reformed congregation were writing to Michael Schlatter complaining that Heinrich Rotts and his neighbor Nicolaus Fink were then associating with the Dunker Sect and were attempting to convert others as well.[89] In 1748 Henry Roads was listed by Stephen Ramsburg as one of those Germans being overtaxed by the Sheriff.[90] In the following year, perhaps as a result, Henry Rothes deeded "Olis" on "Tasker's Chance" back to Daniel Dulany[91] and went elsewhere. In 1746 Daniel Dulany had had a 50-acre tract called "Round Meadow" surveyed on Hunting Creek in the Hauver's District of northwest Frederick County which was patented to Henry Rothers on September 29, 1750.[92] Described as "near a branch that is noted for the Great Falls through the Mountain and runs to the Monocacy, a draft of the Potomac," it was the second survey in Hauvers District. Until 1753 there were no other surveys there, but on October 28, 1754 Henry Rhodes had 28 acres surveyed just east of today's Foxville which he called "Stones Enough."[93] In 1763 Henry Rhodes resurveyed "Round Meadow" into 375 acres with the certificate noting that on the land were one log cabin, 14 x 14 feet, and 13 acres of cleared land.[94]

We next find Henry Rod in 1749 acquiring 150 acres of "Cockholds Horns"[95] and 102 acres of "Rams Horn." The latter's total 494 acres had been initially surveyed on March 10, 1739 for Daniel Dulany, who assigned the certificate of survey to John George Arnold on February 25, 1743/44.[96] Arnold was a German who had arrived in Philadelphia on October 30, 1738. He was naturalized in Maryland on January 15, 1739 along with his sons John, Daniel, Samuel and Andrew.[97] He sold the 102 acres of "Rams Horn" to Henry Rhods on September 5, 1749[98] and conveyed the remaining 392 acres on January 15, 1753 to his son Daniel Arnold.[99] The 102 acres, subsequently called "Rod's Purchase," were located about a mile south of Myersville. Henry Rod and his wife Catharine held the land until

---
[89] See above, p. 270.
[90] See below, p. 292.
[91] Frederick County Land Records, B:69, August 17, 1749.
[92] C/S: BY & GS 1:628.
[93] C/S: BC & GS 4:332; Patent: BC & GS 3:161..
[94] C/S: BC & GS 21:249.
[95] C/S: BY & GS 1:611; Patent: TI 4:294. The survey of October 14, 1747 was for Robert Evans who assigned it to Henry Rhodes on May 4, 1749.
[96] C/S: PT 2:225. On October 7, 1745 Arnold also acquired the parcel "Hog Yard" (C/S: LG E:397).
[97] Commission Book No. 82, *op. cit.*, p. 78. See also *Maryland Historical Magazine*, 26:155.
[98] Frederick County Land Records, B:133. See also Maryland Rent Rolls (Calvert, Prince George's, Frederick No. 1), 3:211, and (Frederick No. 1), 32:117.
[99] Frederick County Land Records, E:61. Also on January 15, 1753 Arnold conveyed "Hog Yard" to his son Samuel.

February 12, 1750 when they deeded it to Jacob Keller.[100] The latter is believed to have been Jacob Koller, father of the Culler family in Maryland and Virginia.[101] Our last word concerning Henry Rotten was a suit against him by John Trammel for a debt of 2,204 pounds of tobacco. After three continuances, the record of the November Court of 1755 shows the case "abated by death of the plaintiff."[102]

Johann Nicolaus Fink arrived in this country somewhat later than his neighbors, reaching Philadelphia on August 30, 1737, coincidentally on the same ship *Samuel* with the same Captain Hugh Percy who brought Henrich Roht to these shores in 1733.[103] Fink was 33 years of age, born December 15, 1704 at Kusel in the Palatinate, the son of Johann Nickel and Maria Catharina Finck. He had married Charlotta Christina Gervinus in 1733 and with them on their voyage to America also came his brother-in-law Ludwick Becker, the husband of Maria Magdalena Finck. With them also came Christian Brengle, another future resident on "Tasker's Chance." A distinction must be made between the Maryland Fink and another Johann Nickel Fink who arrived one year later on September 9, 1738 at the age of 29.[104] He is generally considered to have been the son of Hans Georg Finck and Anna Maria Hoffmann (and grandson of Henrich Finck and Konrad Hoffmann) who was baptized in Staudernheim, ten miles west of Bad Kreuznach, on February 13, 1707. The record at Staudernheim concerning him is marked: "Anno 1738 Americanus factus" (became an American in the year 1738).[105] Most probably he was the Nicolaus Finck who married a Maria Elisabeth and settled in Hereford Township, Berks County, Pennsylvania.[106] There is, however, confusion, coincidence or possibly a relationship as yet unknown, since traveling with him in 1738 was Johann Henrich Wolter [Walter], another brother-in-law of the Kusel Finck.

The 1737 arrival, then, probably came to the Frederick County area before May 1743 when he and Margreta Schweinhartin stood as Lutheran sponsors for the baptism of Joseph, son of Peter Lehn. Like his neighbor Henry Rhodes, he was not named among the 1737 purchasers of "Tasker's Chance," for he would most probably have arrived after that date. But he was one of the nineteen who received deeds from Daniel Dulany on July 28, 1746.[107] His 170 acres were

---

[100] *Ibid.*, B:341.
[101] Rice, *New Facts, op. cit.*, pp. 81-126. This reference also traces the 1765 "Resurvey on Ram's Horn" and the subsequent disposition of the land.
[102] Rice, *The Life, op. cit.*, p. 164.
[103] Strassburger-Hinke, *op. cit.*, Lists 44ABC, pp. 169-172.
[104] *Ibid.*, Lists 53ABC, pp. 204-208. Sixteen ships arrived with German immigrants in the year 1738, the largest number to date and the largest number until 22 ships arrived in the single year of 1749, forty years after the relatively large and continuing German immigration began.
[105] Michael Tepper, *New World Immigrants* (Baltimore, 1980), 2:127.
[106] Berks County Wills, probated May 9, 1774; information from Miss Lois W. Davidson of Camp Hill, Pennsylvania.
[107] Prince George's County Land Records, EE:80.

located where today's U. S. Highway 15 and State Route 26 join, virtually in the center of "Tasker's Chance." As such, his land was bounded by a ring of parcels belonging to Jacob Storm, Abraham Miller, Stephen Ramsburg, John Henry Neff, Henry Rhodes and Hans Peter Hoffman. Along with Heinrich Rotts, Nicolaus Fink was accused on March 1, 1748 by the Elders of the Reformed Church of turning away from their religion to the Dunker sect and of attempting to convert others within their congregation. Nick. Frisk [obviously Fink] and Henry Roads were listed as being overcharged in the March 1748 quitrent collections. Also like Henry Rhodes, Nicolaus Fink and his wife Charlotte deeded their "Tasker's Chance" land back to Daniel Dulany. They did so on June 22, 1753.[108] Apparently title to this land then remained with the Dulany family, for the parcel was confiscated as Loyalist property at the end of the American Revolution. As noted elsewhere,[109] in 1750 Nicolaus Fink purchased from Thomas and Mary Whitaker 50 acres called "Prevention" in the Middletown Valley[110] which he resurveyed in 1752[111] and again in 1764 when he renamed it "Goosebill."[112] Also in 1750 he had "Arabia" surveyed at the west end of present-day Middletown.[113] By 1772 Nicholas Fink had engaged in over two dozen Frederick County land transactions.

South of the lands of Henry Rhodes and Nicolaus Fink and immediately north and east of the Brunner parcels lay the land of **Hans Peter Hoffman** (1705c-1748), a native of Rohrbach kreis Bergzabern near Steinweiler in the Palatinate area of Germany. An estate inventory there in 1742 noted that Hans Peter Hoffmann, son of Hans Georg Hoffmann and Margaretha, had by then lived in the "new land" for over nine years.[114] This ties him to the Hans Peter Hoffman, age 28, an unmarried farmer, who arrived in Philadelphia on August 27, 1733 aboard the ship *Elizabeth*. With him came the Traut family, Frantz Weiss, Hans Jurigh Ley [Johann George Loy], Georg Friederich Unseldt -- all three of whom married Traut sisters -- Jaques Bonet, Hans Jacob Hoff, Jacob Matthews, Philip Smith and others with whom he would later associate in Maryland.[115] Possibly part of a single group

---
[108] Frederick County Land Records, E:209; Maryland Rent Rolls (Frederick No. 1), 36:26b. Note that Charlotte's name on this deed identifies the Maryland Fink as the one from Kusel and not from Staudernheim.
[109] See above, p. 245.
[110] Frederick County Land Records, B:173, where the grantor's name was spelled Whiteacre.
[111] C/S: BC & GS 1:155.
[112] C/S: BC & GS 27:236.
[113] C/S: Y & S 7:125.
[114] Krebs, *loc. cit.*, 5:178. The inventory in question is at the Staatsarchiv in Speyer.
[115] Strassburger-Hinke, *op. cit.*, Lists 30AA'BC, pp. 113-115, 765-767. The German record of 1742 (see above) and accompanying list of passengers discount the Johann Petter Hofmann who reached Philadelphia on September 30, 1732 along with Hans Michell Reisner, Johann Jacob Beyerle and Felix Brunner (*ibid.*, Lists 26ABC, pp. 96-98) as well as the Johann Petter Hoffman (b. 1711c) who arrived

emigration coming together on more than one ship, Abraham Miller arrived at Philadelphia one day later while the Kemp family had reached the same port only ten days earlier.

Soon after his arrival Hans Peter Hoffman married his shipmate Maria Appolonia Traut. They settled near Muddy Creek in the Conestoga area of Lancaster County along with Frantz Weiss, Johann Georg Ley and other shipmates. When their first child Maria Eliesabetha was baptized on July 7, 1734, Johann Georg Ley and his wife Maria Eliesabetha Traut stood as sponsors. In turn, the Hoffmans were baptism sponsors on March 16, 1735 for Maria Appolonia, daughter of Theobald Traut.[116]

By June 17, 1739 the Hoffmans had moved to Monocacy. On that date they stood as sponsors for the daughter of Johann Georg Ley.[117] In 1742 Peter Hoffman was one of those Germans who, despite their religious preferences and national origin, signed the petition to divide Prince George's Parish. His land on "Tasker's Chance" was one of the original lots granted by Daniel Dulany on July 28, 1746.[118] He called his parcel "Rose Garden," a name which has survived to this day. Together with Daniel France's land to the east, which was mentioned in Hoffman's deed, the two parcels mark the approximate center of "Tasker's Chance." Caspar Myer's "Long Acre" lay to the south of "Rose Garden," the Brunner lots to the west and Henry Rhodes' "Olis" to the north. In today's terms the land includes the U.S. Highway 15 interchange with the Oppossumtown Pike, but it is better known as the home of Governor Thomas Johnson (1732-1819), the first Governor of the state of Maryland and subsequently Associate Justice of the United State Supreme Court. Johnson raised and equipped troops in Frederick during the Revolution and led 1,800 men to join General George Washington in New Jersey in 1776. He had acquired Hoffman's land in 1778[119] and when he conveyed it to his daughter Ann Jennings on January 14, 1788, he referred to it as "Rose Garden, now called Rose Hill."[120]

John Peter Hoffman twice in 1743 witnessed certificates of communion showing that a number of his fellow Germans were of the Reformed religion and could therefore be naturalized.[121] With Gilbert and Christian Kemp, he himself was naturalized on September 27, 1746.[122] He and his wife Maria Apollonia were Reformed baptism

---

with Jerg Hoffman (b. 1701), Adam Hoffman (b. 1715c), and Johann Michael Römer (b. 1715c) on September 5, 1738 (Ibid., Lists 52ABC, pp. 198-203) and the Johann Peter Hoffman who arrived on August 27, 1739 (Ibid., pp. 257, 260, 262).

[116] Muddy Creek Lutheran Church Book transcription, op. cit., pp. 28, 30.

[117] Ibid., though other baptisms on the same day show that the events actually took place in the Monocacy area.

[118] Prince George's County Land Records, EE:73.

[119] Frederick County Land Records, WR 1:2.

[120] Frederick County Land Records, WR 7:665. See also Delaplaine, Edward S., *The Life of Thomas Johnson* (New York, 1927).

[121] Provincial Court Judgment Records, 1742-1744, EI 7:161, 296. On the second of these he was called John Peter Houghman.

witnesses on June 24, 1747 for Maria Apollonia, daughter of Peter and Eva Schumacher.[123] In 1748 Peter Hoffman was included in Stephen Ramsburg's list of Germans being overtaxed by the Sheriff. But on May 21, 1748 Hans Peter Hoffman of Manakesen was ill and with his mark "HPH" signed his will. It was written in German in fairly standard form, placing his liebe Hausfrau in control of his estate until and unless she should remarry. He referred to his children including only one son who was not yet of age, but he named none of them. The will was probated on March 11, 1748[/49] with witnesses Johann Conrad Kämpff and Frantz Weiss, both of them Protestant Dissenters[124] and both residents on "Tasker's Chance," affirming but not swearing that they saw Peter John Hoffman [sic] sign and publish the will.[125] In her administrative accounts, Appolonie Hoffman also declared herself a Protestant Dissenter. Her sureties were Jacob Storm and Christian Thomas, two other landholders on "Tasker's Chance."[126] The Frederick Court Judgment Records for August 1750 name the children of John [Peter] Hufman as Elizabeth, Mary, Appolonia, Barbara, George Peter, Rosina and Mary Magdalene.[127] The first five married, respectively, Daniel Schumacher, Matthias Buckey, Johann Adam Ochs, Johannes Sturm, and widow Maria Dorothea Leu (Loy), In 1749 Maria Apollonia Hoffman remarried, and again there were ties to a 1733 shipmate: Her new husband was Georg Friedrich Unseld.[128]

The lone son of Hans Peter Hoffman was Johann Georg Peter Hoffman, born November 4, 1743. Georg Laÿ (Loy) and his wife Elisabeth, also residents on "Tasker's Chance," were his baptism sponsors. The younger Peter sold "Rose Garden" and removed to Baltimore in 1776. There he affiliated with Philip William Otterbein's United Brethren church, probably having come to know the minister in Frederick County. He became a vestryman and was on the building committee (1785-1786). He was also a member of the first city council and helped to develop a city spring into a park where Mercy Hospital now stands. His business was in importing, and he had a number of stores and warehouses in several cities. He died in 1809 and was buried in the Otterbein churchyard.[129]

Daniel France was on the "Tasker's Chance" stage only briefly. As Daniel Frantz he was in Frederick Township of today's Montgomery County, Pennsylvania, paying quitrents for an undisclosed number of acres sometime before 1734. On the same list were Joh. Georg Schweinhart, Baltus Fauts and Jacob Fauts, each for 100 acres, and Christian Getzendoner.[130] Except for the latter, none of these has been

---
[122] Ibid., EI 10:228.
[123] Frederick Reformed Church Book, p. 4.
[124] For this term, see above, p. 173.
[125] Original Wills, Frederick County, Box 1, folder 10, Hall of Records. On the will's outside cover, Apolonia Hofman was named as Executrix. A copy, translated into English, was inserted in Frederick County Wills, A1, after f. 14.
[126] Testamentary Proceedings, 1746-1749, f. 253.
[127] Rice, The Life, op. cit., p. 52.
[128] Frederick Lutheran Church Book, p 356. For Unselt, see p. 182.
[129] Contributed by Jacob Mehrling Holdcraft.

found on the Philadelphia ship arrival lists at Philadelphia, most likely because they arrived before those lists were begun in 1727. France was one of the six Germans named by Benjamin Tasker as settlers on his land who in 1737 were seeking to purchase the tract as a whole.[131] He signed the 1742 petition to divide Prince George's Parish. But he did not receive a deed to land on "Tasker's Chance." He is also absent from the early Reformed and Lutheran church records and is not found in other land documents. The location of his portion of "Tasker's Chance" is made possible by reference in Daniel Dulany's 1746 deed to Peter Hoffman, France's neighbor to the west.[132] At that time the land became known as "Indian Field" and was deeded to Jacob Storm who was thus settled on France's land. It has not been established whether Daniel France was the father of Johannes and Nicolaus Frantz who do appear in later Frederick County Lutheran church records.

Johann Jacob Sturm (b. 1701) and his sister Maria Barbara Brunner (b. 1702) were early arrivals in America. They were two of the 12 children of Christian Sturm and his second wife Anna Barbara Gah, all natives of Klein Schifferstadt in the Palatinate area of Germany. From this village a number of future Maryland settlers also emigrated, but, unlike the others whose families had been settled at Schifferstadt for less than a generation or so, the Sturm family could trace its history there back to at least 1470. The family is still there, and its current town history was written by a Sturm.[133]

Both Johann Jacob and Maria Barbara were married in Germany, he about 1726e to Anna Benedictina Saur, she on November 25, 1725 to Johann Jacob Brunner as mentioned above. The two couples, each with two children born at Klein Schifferstadt before their departure, emigrated together in the year 1728 and arrived at Philadelphia aboard the ship *Mortonhouse* on August 23rd of that year. With them came Mardin Schaub, Johann Jost Schmidt, Johan Georg Doderer and other individuals whose names are found in subsequent Frederick County history.[134] It was, for the folks from Klein Schifferstadt, something of an advance party, for in the following year the balance of the Brunner family and Christian Getzendanner with his Brunner wife also arrived.

Jacob **Storm**, as he came to be known in America, did not come to Maryland directly but remained in Pennsylvania for over a decade. The Lancaster Reformed Church book records the baptisms in 1739 and 1740 of his eighth and ninth children, Christina and Johann Peter Storm. Then on January 9, 1742 Pastor Stöver recorded the marriage, probably at Earl Town, of Jacob Storm and Maria Saurin.[135] Jacob Sturm was naturalized along with Caspar Myer, Christian Getzendanner and other Marylanders on October 19, 1743, having "received the sacrament" from Edward [Joh. Conrad] Templeman ten

---

[130] Rupp, *op. cit.*, p. 472.
[131] Provincial Court Records, EI 8:28.
[132] Prince George's County Land Records, EE:73.
[133] Georg Sturm, *op. cit.*, 271 pp.
[134] Strassburger-Hinke, *op. cit.*, Lists 6AB, pp. 18-20.
[135] Stöver, *op. cit.*, Marriages, p. 7, No. 345.

days before.[136] Thus his date of arrival in Maryland may be more closely approximated. "Indian Field" on "Tasker's Chance" was conveyed to Jacob Storm by Daniel Dulany on July 28, 1746.[137] The deed is interesting, for in it appears the first reference to a road passing through "Tasker's Chance." The parcel's beginning point was a corner in the parcels of Abraham Miller and Christian Thomas "on the east side of the waggon road." This road lay along the west side of the Monocacy River, between it and the extension of Market Street. It then proceeded somewhat north of today's State Route 26 as the latter curves to the east. There is considerable evidence that this "waggon road" crossed the Monocacy at the mouth of Tuscarora Creek rather than at the present-day crossing near Ceresville. Moreover, this road was the only northern one leading into Fredericktown which was mentioned in the land records before the petitions of 1749 and 1750. It was also not until 1749 that the name Fredericktown itself appeared in the road records.[138]

Jacob Storm was one of the initial elders of the Frederick Reformed Church. His name appears as a signatory on the 1748 appeal to Pastor Michael Schlatter for help in strengthening the congregation against the Dunker sect.[139] But he died at the age of 55 in early 1757, leaving as sons Vandel [Wendell], Jacob the Younger, John, and Peter, as daughters Susanna wife of [Martin] Cuntz, Anna Maria wife of Peter Brunner, Anna Elizabeth wife of Adam Kyle, Maria Barbara wife of Jacob Turner, Christina, Mary, Catharina, Charlotta and a second Anna Maria. In his will of December 27, 1756 he designated Stephen Ransberger [Ramsburg] and John Bruner as executors. Frederick Becker, Samuel Becker and Peter Tofeler were witnesses.[140] In accordance with the provisions of the will, the two executors in 1765 sold "Indian Fields" to Peter Tofler,[141] who on April 17, 1757 had married Anna Maria Sturm.[142] Tofler later conveyed the land to Thomas Johnson. In 1801 Johnson transferred title to his son-in-law John Grahame, for whose benefit, the deed stated, the purchase had been made originally.[143] Earlier, on October 10, 1797,

---
[136] Provincial Court Judgment Records, EI 7:296. The names of these three were recorded as Jacob Stern, Gasper Mire and Christian Getson Tanner.
[137] Prince George's County Land Records, EE:66.
[138] The March Court of 1749 appointed overseers for the roads "from Fredericktown to the top of Catoctin Mountain" and "from Fredericktown to John Biggs' Ford." The June Court heard petitions for a road from "Nelson's Ferry" [present Point of Rocks] to Fredericktown" and for another from "Fredericktown to Dulany's Mill." A 1750 petition was seeking a wagon road from Fredericktown to Jacob Peck's fulling mill on the Tuscarora, approximating today's road from Frederick to Yellow Springs.
[139] See above, p. 270.
[140] Frederick County Wills, A1:105. See also Frederick County Administrative Accounts, A1:189.
[141] Frederick County Land Records, J:1184.
[142] Frederick Reformed Church Book, p. 124.
[143] Frederick County Land Records, WR 20:485.

Johnson had returned 24 acres to Tofler.[144] In later years these 24 acres were in the possession of Margaret Artz, wife of C. Burr Artz for whom the Frederick Library was named. The Artz home across Market Street from today's Governor Johnson School is shown on the map of 1866.[145]

Michael Thomas and **Christian Thomas**, father and son, represented still another family settled on "Tasker's Chance" which had migrated from Klein Schifferstadt in Germany. Like the Brunners, the Thomas family had not been established long in Klein Schifferstadt, but first appeared in the records there in 1679.[146] The origins of Michael's father, Christian Thomas, who died in Klein Schifferstadt in 1708, are as yet unknown. Interestingly, the move from Germany marked the third consecutive year in which emigration to America from this tiny German village had occurred. The moves were not unrelated, for Michael's sister, Catharina Elisabetha Thomas, was the wife of Joseph Brunner who had come to America in 1729, the year before Michael Thomas himself emigrated and the year after their son Jacob Brunner had arrived in 1728. By 1730 Michael Thomas, then in his forties, and his wife Anna Veronica Lang had had eleven children, all born in Klein Schifferstadt. At least three of these died in Germany, but seven of the others are known to have accompanied their father to America. All except the eldest son, Christian Thomas, were under sixteen years of age and so did not appear on the port arrival lists at Philadelphia. But subsequent information shows that sons Philipp Henrich, Hans Michael, Jr., Gabriel, Johann Valentin, Johannes and Christoph Thomas all came, too.

The voyage to America was made on the Scottish ship, *Thistle of Glasgow*, which left Dover on June 19, 1730 and arrived at Philadelphia on August 29th, ten weeks later.[147] Although this was nearly twelve months after the arrival of the balance of the Brunner family in the previous year, it was the next succeeding shipload of immigrants to come from Germany. With the Thomas family also came Jean Henri Fortinaux, Jerg Hertzel and Caspar Krieger. Michael Thomas apparently arrived in a sickened condition and may not have survived. Nothing further is known of him. Our attention is therefore directed instead to Christian Thomas, the eldest son, who was just 16 years of age when he reached Pennsylvania.

It was not until Christian Thomas was 26 years old that we find mention of him in Maryland. He and his brother Hendrick Thomas, but not their father, were naturalized on May 3, 1740. In October of 1742 Christian Thomas signed the petition to divide Prince George's Parish.[148] He alone secured actual title to the parcel on "Tasker's Chance" which henceforth was known as "Beaver Den." It

---

[144] *Ibid.*, WR 15:674.
[145] Bond, *loc. cit.*
[146] Sturm, *op. cit.*, p. 249.
[147] Strassburger-Hinke, *op. cit.*, Lists 11ABC, pp. 31-34; also Fritz Braun, *Auswanderer aus der Umgebung von Ludwigshafen a. Rh. auf dem Schiff "Thistle of Glasgow" 1730*, Schriften zur Wanderungsgeschichte der Pfälzer, Folge 8 (1959).
[148] See below, p. 371.

was conveyed to him by Daniel Dulany on July 28, 1746.[149] In 1748 Stephen Ramsburg named Christian Thomas as one of those Germans who were being taxed excessively by the local sheriff. The Thomas land consisted of just under 210 acres with more than a half mile frontage along the Monocacy River to the northeast. This land, together with that of his neighbor Francis Wise on the south, was mentioned in the August 1749 Court's routing of the road from Fredericktown to Dulany's Mill on today's Gas House Pike.[150] On the 1866 map of Frederick County the home of L[ewis] M[ichael] Thomas (1819-1882) is shown here. Today the land encompasses an area behind the I.O.O.F. home on Jacob Storm's land to the west. It includes Fredericktowne Village. By his will of May 14, 1777 Christian Miller passed this land to his son Christian Thomas, Jr. The will also named son Henry who had left Maryland about 1768, daughters Barbara Stoner and Mary Thomas and a son-in-law Anthony Terrich to whose children Christian Thomas devised the home he had built in the town of Frederick.[151] Christian Thomas' brothers settled for the most part in the area near Adamstown in Buckeystown District. Two near identical gravestones in the family cemetery on Stup Road between the Cap Stein and the Mountville Roads, one for Gabriel Thomas (1721-1794), the other for Valentine Thomas (1724-1796), gave the clues which led earlier genealogists to Klein Schifferstadt.[152]

Directly north of the Thomas land, wrapping around the big bend of the Monocacy River northeast of Frederick, lies the land which originally belonged to **Abraham Miller** (1707?-1754). Unlike most other Germans whose arrival in this country can be determined fairly positively from the ships lists at Philadelphia, Abraham Miller's arrival remains in doubt. Three Abraham Millers appear in the lists before 1743, but there is nothing to deny that the same Abraham Miller made more than one voyage. One Abraham Müller lived in the Great Swamp area of Pennsylvania and frequently visited the Moravians at Bethlehem in 1742-1743.[153]

By near association one would like to think that the future Marylander arrived at Philadelphia aboard the ship *Hope* on August 28, 1733, one day after the ship *Elizabeth* had anchored with a host of other future residents on "Tasker's Chance" including Hans Peter Hoffman, Frantz Weiss and Hans Jurigh Loy. The age of the "Tasker's

---

[149] Prince George's County Land Records, EE:67.

[150] See above, pp. 73, 263. Christian Thomas' younger brother, Christoph Thomas, baptized at Klein Schifferstadt in 1729, married Susanna Margaret Weiss, daughter of Frantz Weiss.

[151] Frederick County Wills, GM 1:19. The name Terrich appears also as Zerrick in subsequent Court records.

[152] George Leicester Thomas, *Genealogy of Thomas Family* (Adamstown, 1954), especially p. 9; Holdcraft, *op. cit.*, pp. 31, 1144-1145. "Valentint Tamas" is the actual spelling inscribed on Valentine's stone. Distinction should be made between this so-called "German" Thomas Family and an "English" Thomas family whose family graveyard is situated only four miles south, near Point of Rocks. The two families were not related except through subsequent intermarriages.

[153] Hamilton, *op. cit.*, pp. 19, 74, 145, 152-154, 172.

Chance" Abraham Miller according to his gravestone (born 1707c[154]) does not match the 22 years (b 1711c) given on his arrival, although from records in Germany the age of his wife Maria Madlena (26) has been found correct.[155] Moreover, there is reason to believe that Frances, widow in 1754 of the "Tasker's Chance" Abraham Müller, was the mother of all his children, including Jacob Miller (1730c-1810). The 1733 arrivals brought no children with them, and therein lies the rub: Abraham Miller's son Jacob had to be born before 1733 if he was of age when he served as his father's executor in 1754. He was born even earlier if he was the mortgagor of "Hazel Thicket" in 1751 and died at the age of 80 in 1810. Alternatively, logic would seem to dictate that Abraham Miller reached Philadelphia on October 7, 1737 aboard the *Charming Nancy* with adults Jacob and Christian Miller, whose names were repeated in Abraham Miller's naming of his own children. But again no son Jacob was listed among the children. Even more negating is the conflict arising from Abraham Miller's presumably being already in Maryland and contracting for land on "Tasker's Chance" four months before this ship arrived! The third possibility, the Abraham Miller who arrived on the *Adventure* on October 16, 1727, is just that, a possibility. We have no indication of his whereabouts for the succeeding decade, and with the exception of John George Swinehart we have record of no other Monocacy German's arrival so early.[156]

Regardless of this uncertainty concerning his arrival in America, Abraham Miller was on hand June 11, 1737 when he and five others agreed to purchase from Benjamin Tasker the entire tract of "Tasker's Chance" for a consideration of £200. But, as related above, the Germans were unable to meet the purchase price and so entered into a subsequent agreement on January 13, 1744 with Daniel Dulany by which Dulany would assume title from Tasker and then sell individual parcels of the whole to settlers when they were able to pay him.[157]

---

[154] A caveat may be in order concerning the reading of Abraham Miller's gravestone by Scharf, *op. cit.*, 1:525. Scharf or his helper made his readings on May 11, 1881 when the old Reformed cemetery was being abandoned. His death date for Abraham Miller agrees with known particulars of Miller's will, but, as Holdcraft, *op. cit.*, p. 791, observes, both birth and death years may be suspect because they are identical to Scharf's readings from a seemingly unrelated Magdalena Schmidt's gravestone in the same cemetery.

[155] Burgert, *Western Palatinate, op. cit.*, 2:239, discovered in the Reformed Church Book at Ulmet that Maria Magdalena Fuhrmann was baptized Aug. 7, 1706 and on July 5, 1730 married Johann Abraham Müller, son of Johannes Müller from Erbach bei Hommburg. The latter locale [not Erdesbach?] has not been identified.

[156] Strassburger-Hinke, *op. cit.*, Lists 5A, p. 16, 31ABC, pp. 116-121, and 49ABC, pp. 188-194. The little man in the rear will please not rise to note the association between Abraham Miller and Dieter Lehnich [Peter Laney], whose name suffered such violent orthographical variations, while observing the presence of a Peter Leman with the 1727 Miller and a Benedict Leman with the 1737 Miller.

[157] Provincial Court Records, EI 8:28.

Miller's presence in 1744 is also confirmed by his serving that year as overseer of the road from "Mill Branch [Ballenger Creek] to the Manor, by his naturalization with other "Tasker's Chance" residents in 1740 and by his signing the 1742 petition to divide Prince George's Parish.

Pinpointing him even further is the account of a visit in 1743 by the Moravian missionaries Leonhard Schnell and Robert Hussey, enroute on their lengthy journey to Georgia from Bethlehem in Pennsylvania. They had traveled by foot on November 16th all the way from Adam Forney's inn at "Canawage"[158] across Big and Little Pipe Creeks. Late in the day they reached the Monocacy River whose crossing Schnell describes in his Diary. The crossing must have occurred near the mouth of Tuscarora Creek, for he wrote: "The third [River] is called Manakes, through which I had to carry my companion because he was very tired, for we had already walked forty miles. A mile farther we found a house, where the people at first objected to taking us in, but were finally persuaded. The host was a Mennonite and his name is Abraham Müller."[159]

By interesting coincidence the crossing of the Monocacy by Schnell and Hussey was undoubtedly made where Joseph Wood in 1749 indicated John Hussey "formerly lived."[160] Such an individual is not mentioned by Schnell, nor do we know his relationship, if any, to his missionary companion Robert Hussey. In the same year 1743, however, John Hussey lived close enough to Miller to accuse him of taking his stray horse. The August Court released Miller after Robert Debutts and Darby Ryan testified in Miller's behalf. In 1748 and again in 1751 Miller is noted as administrator for Hussey's estate![161]

But to return to Abraham Miller's acquisition of title to his "Tasker's Chance" land: It occurred on July 28, 1746 when Miller and eighteen other Germans received their first individual deeds from Dulany.[162] His parcel comprised 294 acres with a beginning point "near the west end of an island [later called Sebastian Derr's Island] in the Monocacy." This refers to the stretch of the River where it flows westerly from its junction with Addison Run. Today's State Route 26 passes through what was the Miller parcel, which also included the old Worman Mill as well as the site of today's city filtration plant.

---
[158] Conewago was the area of German settlement between Littlestown and Hanover in today's Adams County, Pennsylvania.
[159] "1 Meile davon finden wir ein Haus. Sie machten Schwierigkeiten uns zu beherbergen, liesen sich aber endlich bereden. Der Wirth war ein Mennonist u. hies Abrah: Müller." See Schnell, "Diarium," loc. cit., or Hinke-Kemper, "Moravian Diaries," *Virginia Magazine of History and Biography*, loc. cit., 11:372.
[160] See above, p. 54.
[161] Frederick County Administrative Accounts, A1:14. Francis Wise and Stephen Julien were Miller's securities. In the course of the administration, William Cumming sued Miller for money owed him by Hussey. When Cumming failed to appear at the trial, the jury dropped the case and charged Cumming 472½ pounds of tobacco for Miller's costs. Cf. Rice, *The Life, op. cit.*, pp. 52-53.
[162] Prince George's County Land Records, EE:111.

Abraham Miller's name does not appear in the early records of either the Reformed or Lutheran churches.[163] That he was a Mennonite, as noted by Schnell, may give us a clue why he soon left "Tasker's Chance."[164] Nicholas Fink and Heinrich Rotts [Rhodes] as Dunker sect people also left "Tasker's Chance," for they, too, were not adherents to the two principal German religions.[165] Regardless, Abraham Miller and his wife Frances [Frana] deeded their "Tasker's Chance" land back to Dulany on October 26, 1750.[166] On September 1, 1748 "Miller's Chance," 100 acres southwest of today's Lewistown, had been surveyed and patented to Abraham Miller.[167] In March of 1750 he purchased 200 acres of "Cooper's Point" from Teter and Hannah Laney [Lehnich],[168] for whom it had been surveyed December 19, 1741.[169] The Lehnichs were a fourth family who had removed from "Tasker's Chance." Then on October 26, 1751 Miller resurveyed "Miller's Chance," adding two large vacant areas south and east of the original parcel and bringing the total to 1,289 acres.[170] This parcel, which lay to the south of Georg Honig's "Den of Wolves," was patented in 1753 to Edward Dorsey. Finally, on April 19, 1753 Miller purchased for £21 "one certain improvement" called "Dere Spring," which has not been identified. The grantor in 1753 was named in the deed as both Fridrich Ott and Frederick Upe, but signed his name as Fridrich Orr.[171] Altogether Miller operated three mills, and his place became a landmark reference point in the early road records, continuing so until at least 1784.[172]

In the June Court of 1746 Abraham Miller sued Johannes Tafflemeyer for £56/10/-. In 1748 Miller was in turn sued by Hugh Parker for £10/14/6, the cost of several yards of bolting cloth and tails. Parker was a trader, closely associated with Thomas Cresap in exchanges with the Indians in the area of today's Washington County. Also in 1748 Miller and Jacob Stoner joined Frederick and John Verdress in borrowing £40 and 489 pounds of tobacco from Philip Craver [Crever/Grüber].[173] The grand jury of November 1749 presented Abraham Miller for keeping a tippling house, but he was accepted by

---
[163] But his son Christian Miller did appear, in both records, shortly before his father's death in 1754.
[164] In administering his estate, his widow "solemnly affirmed, she being a Protestant Dissenter." (Frederick County Administrative Accounts, A1:169, 1759)
[165] See above, p. 270.
[166] Frederick County Land Records, B:274.
[167] C/S: BY & GS 1:167.
[168] Frederick County Land Records, B:398.
[169] C/S: LG E:86; surveyed again in 1745 for Miller (C/S: TI 1:417).
[170] C/S: BC & GS 1:166.
[171] Frederick County Land Records, E:178.
[172] In 1749, for example, the Court appointed William Elder overseer of the road "from the temporary [Pennsylvania] line to Ambrose's Mill," Martin Wetzel from the latter to Abraham Miller's Mill [thus approximating the present road from Thurmont to Lewistown via Jimtown crossroads] and Jacob Neff for the portion of the road from "Abraham Miller's Mill to the nearest main road to Fredericktown."
[173] Frederick County Land Records, B:59.

the same Court as security for the builders of the new Court House. The March Court of 1750 tried Teter Laney for stealing two hogs from Abraham Miller, but the jury found him not guilty. A year later Abraham Miller and Nathaniel Wickham, Jr. were appointed by the Court to lay out a wagon road to Frederick Town for the benefit of inhabitants along Tuscarora Creek.

Abraham Miller died at his home on September 20, 1754, just two days after dictating his will, which he signed by mark.[174] The will, witnessed by Nathaniel Wickham, Robert MacPherson and Stephen Ramsberger, gave indication of several land transactions then in progress, most of which involved the sale of portions of his "Resurvey on Miller's Chance." Included were 50 acres to son Jacob Miller, 40 acres to Robert Davis, 100 acres to Christian Miller, and 1,000 acres each to Robert MacPherson and Henry Canhart, seemingly considerably more in total area than the 1,289 acres of the Resurvey. A "Resurvey on Cooper's Point" was also underway, and Miller directed it be completed by his son Jacob Miller and by Nathaniel Wickham, Jr.[175] His will also referred to 50 acres of land purchased from Daniel Dulany which was to go to his son Jacob and to 100 acres on which his daughter Elizabeth lived with her husband Christian Peger [Becker?]. Neither tract has been specifically located. The two tracts on which Miller lived, "Cooper's Point" and "Miller's Chance," were to go to his widow Frances and after her death to sons Isaac and Abraham Miller. Also named were the youngest children David and Mary. Not mentioned were Barbara and Louisa, who were named in Abraham Miller's naturalization proceedings in 1740.[176] The will did not specifically call Christian Miller a son, but Frances Miller served with Jacob Miller as executors of a Christian Miller's will in 1756, and David and Abraham Miller were executors for a Christian Miller in 1782. Frances Miller, a Protestant Dissenter who would affirm but not swear, married a Shelhorse as her second husband.[177] There is much required work remaining for the genealogy of this family.

Abraham Miller's former parcel on "Tasker's Chance" remained in the possession of the Dulany Family until October 14, 1783 when the Commissioners for the Sale of Confiscated British Property (Clement Hollyday and Nathaniel Ramsey) conveyed it to John Davidson, an Annapolis merchant.[178] The latter's executors, Samuel Duvall and Thomas Harris, Jr., in 1800 conveyed the land to Hugh Reynolds who then sold part of the land to Dr. Philip Thomas (1747-1815), son-in-law of John Hanson, in turn, under the Articles of Confederation, the first "President of the United States in Congress

---

[174] Frederick County Wills, A1:55. The clerk's rather casual attention to orthography produced some disconcerting spelling variations even within the document itself. A number of these have been adjusted in the light of our other knowledge.
[175] For Wickham, see below, pp. 337 et seq.
[176] See above, p. 260. The children named in 1740 were Jacob, Abraham, Isaac, Barbara and Louisa.
[177] Frederick County Administrative Accounts, A1:169. His given name is not stated.
[178] Frederick County Land Records, WR 4:323.

Assembled." Thomas' deed mentions the mill later known as the Worman mill.[179] Thomas' heirs Ashton and Catherine Hanson Alexander sold the land to Moses Worman in 1820.

East of this land, lying wholly south of today's State Route 26 and tucked within the big bend of the Monocacy River as it flows past Ceresville to the mouth of Addison Run on the opposite bank and then around the curve to Sebastian Derr's Island, lay 307 acres intended for **Johann Melchior Werfel** (1707-1755). Daniel Dulany's 1746 deed for the adjoining land which went to Abraham Miller called him Melchior Wheyfield. As Melchior Warfield[180] this elusive early settler was among those "in possession of" land on "Tasker's Chance" in 1753.[181] And as Melcar Wherfield he was listed by Stephen Ramsburg in 1748 as one of the Germans being overtaxed by the sheriff. If he was therefore German, as most likely he was, he most probably was the young 20-year old Hans Melchior Werffle who arrived at Philadelphia on September 21, 1732 via the pink *Plaisance*.[182] Like Jacob Brunner, he apparently was his family's "advance agent," for one year later, on August 17, 1733, his father Hans [Leonhard] Wervel, age 54, reached Philadelphia on the ship *Samuel*, the same ship which brought Hans Jacob Hoff, Joh. Jacob Matthias, Henrich Roht, the Kemp family and others who settled in the Monocacy region. Accompanying the elder Wervel were his wife Maria Lydia age 52 and children Maria Lydia 26, Hans Jerick [George] 18, Elizabeth 17 and Leonard 8.[183]

The family has been identified as emigrating from Steinsfurt, a village three miles southeast of Sinsheim in the Kraichgau, where the name was spelled Würffel and where Johann Melchior Würffel, son of Hans Leonhard Würffel and Maria Elisabetha Wentz was born on November 10, 1707.[184] But, again like the Brunners and others, the family had earlier come to Germany from Switzerland.[185] Melchor

---

[179] "....from the beginning of Peter Toffler's and Christian Thomas' part of 'Tasker's Chance'....to a stone on the bank of the Monocacy...then up, by and with the meander of Monocacy....to a tree at the mouth of a gut that empties into the Monocacy at the lower end of Sebastian Derr's Island....across the road....reserving the right to clear and repair the tail race into Monocacy from the mill of the said Reynolds [which] stands on the west side of the public road."

[180] No relation to Dr. Joshua Warfield who is mentioned in the March 19, 1750/51 Frederick Court Judgment Records: See Rice, *The Life*, op. cit., p. 67.

[181] Maryland Rent Rolls (Frederick County No. 1), 32:26a.

[182] Strassburger-Hinke, op. cit., Lists 22ABC, pp. 79-83. Unlike other 1732 arrivals (see Chapter on Upper Germans), Werffle seems to have come alone, for no other immigrants on this ship appear in the early Frederick County records.

[183] *Ibid.*, Lists 29ABC, pp. 106-112. The English Captain obviously "heard" Lydia for Lisa: Mother and daughter appear as Maria Elisabeth in the German records, also indicating that, except for the youngest son Leonhardt, the ages given in both 1732 and 1733 lists were understated by three to five years.

[184] Burgert, op. cit., 1:35, 403-404.

[185] From Weinigen near Zürich, per Heinz Schuchmann: See also

Werfel died intestate in Lancaster County, Pennsylvania, possessed of 150 acres in Bart Township and leaving a wife Katharine with seven small children.[186] Whether he had ever occupied the "Tasker's Chance" land is doubtful: In 1745 the Conestoga area was obviously his home, for his daughter Catharina was baptized then in Earl Township (New Holland). Ramsburg's 1748 notation concerning overtaxation remains a mystery, for no deed from Daniel Dulany has been found. Instead, Dulany conveyed the "Wheyfield" parcel on "Tasker's Chance" to Stephen Ramsburg in 1753 who then transferred it to Sebastian Derr in 1755.[187] It became known as "Dearbought," a name by which it is still recognized today.

Jacob Stoner (1713-1748) and his family were mainstays on "Tasker's Chance." With five other Germans -- Abraham Miller, Daniel France [Frantz], John George Loy, Peter Laney [Lehnich] and Joseph [Jost] Smith -- Jacob Stoner sought originally to purchase the entire tract from Benjamin Tasker. For an initial £200 Tasker on June 11, 1737 did assign it to them, but thereafter, as previously related, the Germans were unable to raise the full £2000 purchase price and were forced to agree to Tasker's conveying all 7,000 acres on January 13, 1744 to Daniel Dulany.[188] Of the original six, only Stoner and Abraham Miller remained on July 28, 1746 to receive deeds from Dulany for their individual parcels. When Miller left "Tasker's Chance," only Stoner's heirs were left from the original 1737 group.

But Stoner was unique in another way. Of the nineteen individuals in 1746 who initially received deeds from Dulany, only Stoner received more than one parcel. Two of his three parcels were adjacent to one another and lay just north of the Wheyfield/Werfel parcel. The third, known as "The Barrens," had been surveyed as 103 acres along the north border of "Tasker's Chance" adjacent to "Hedge Hogg."[189] It was thus situated at some distance from the other two, "Bear Den" (172 acres) and "Mill Pond" (292 acres),[190] whose common line approximated today's Liberty Road (State Route 26) as it approaches the Monocacy bridge at Ceresville. Both parcels fronted on the River, opposite "Dulany's Lot" on the east bank. On "Mill Pond," through which flowed Tuscarora Creek, Stoner built his home

---
Karl Diefenbacher, et al., *Schweizer Einwanderer in den Kraichgau nach dem Dreissigjährigen Krieg* (Ladenburg, 1983), pp. 79, 186.
[186] Burgert, *op. cit.*, 1:405, from Lancaster County Orphans Court records.
[187] Maryland Rent Rolls (Frederick No. 1), 32:26b.
[188] Provincial Court Records, EI 8:28.
[189] Prince George's County Land Records, BB:1:445. Not all of Maryland, before the coming of the white man, was blanketed with continuous forest. Stretches of land resembling our western prairies with their grasses or scrubby bushes were frequently mentioned in the early land records and were referred to as Barrens. After Jacob Stoner's death "The Barrens" passed to his son Henry Stoner. The 1873 Atlas (Lake, *op. cit.*, p. 11) shows the home of A. Cramer, south of Hansonville, situated on this parcel. For "Hedge Hogg" see above, pp. 106, 111-113.
[190] Prince George's County Land Records, BB 1:429.

and mill. The wagon road through "Tasker's Chance" passed Stoner's mill and probably continued on to cross the Monocacy, not at today's Ceresville, but a bit farther north near the mouth of the Tuscarora. The ford here, sometimes called Stoner's Ford, was probably the same as was known at other times as Hussey's Ford or Reynold's Ford. "Bear Den" may have been occupied before 1746 by George Baer after he turned "Green Spring" over to Michael Reisner in 1739.[191] But it remained in the Stoner family until title was transferred in 1767 to Baltis Getzendanner, who in 1758 had married Jacob Stoner's daughter Anna.

Jacob Stoner's arrival in America and his early years have not been documented. He may have been the unmarried Jacob Steiner who arrived at Philadelphia on September 10, 1731 with Friedrich Wulheit and Jacob Mumma,[192] but if so and if his gravestone birth date has been read correctly,[193] he was then only 18 years of age. In 1740 Jacob Stoner was naturalized in Maryland, along with his sons John and Jacob. [Jr.]. In October of 1744 he purchased "Isaac's Inheritance," located at the mouth of Linganore Creek, from Isaac van Metre then of Frederick County, Virginia.[194] This land later devolved on Jacob's son Benedict Stoner, who had it resurveyed into "Stoner's Luck."[195] In 1742 Jacob Stoner was one of the Germans who signed the petition to divide Prince George's Parish.[196] On October 16, 1746 Thomas Cresap surveyed 75 additional acres for Jacob Stoner along the north border of "Tasker's Chance" and therefore near "The Barrens."[197] This land, called "Stoner's Chance," also went to son Henry Stoner and later to Baltis Getzendanner. In 1748 Jacob Stoner, Frederick and John Verdress and Abraham Miller borrowed £40 and 489 pounds of tobacco from Philip Crever [Grüber],[198] but before the year was out Jacob Stoner had died. He left no will, and his widow Magdalin became his administratrix. On December 9, 1749 she declared herself a "dissenter"[199] (i.e., Mennonite?) as had Apollonia

---

[191] See above, p. 193.
[192] Strassburger-Hinke, op. cit., Lists 15ABC, pp. 43-46.
[193] Holdcraft, op. cit., p. 1092, repeats a reading (Jacob Steiner, 1713-1748) from Scharf, op. cit., p. 525, made when the stones were being removed from the old Frederick Reformed Cemetery at the time of its abandonment in 1881. The ultimate anglicization of the family name from Steiner to Stoner should remove confusion with the family of Johann Conrad Steiner (1707-1762), native of Winterthur in Switzerland and Reformed minister in Frederick from 1756 to 1759. The latter's son, Jacob Steiner, in 1758 married Maria Anna Schley, daughter of Johann Thomas Schley, but did not accompany his father when the family moved to Philadelphia in 1759. Maryland descendants kept the name as Steiner. See William J. Hinke, Ministers, op. cit., pp. 60-68.
[194] Prince George's County Land Records, BB 1:209.
[195] C/S: BC & GS 45:2.
[196] See below, p. 371.
[197] C/S: TI 1:45.
[198] Frederick County Land Records, B:58.
[199] Loose papers in Administrative Accounts, Hall of Records, 1960.

Hoffman, Abraham Miller and others on "Tasker's Chance." This may explain the absence of the Stoners from the early records of both Reformed and Lutheran Churches and why sons Henry and Benedict were confirmed in 1773 as married adults.

Because at least three of Jacob and Magdalin Stoner's children were minors at the time of their father's death, the March Court of 1754 appointed Benedict Esleman as their guardian.[200] Those children who survived their father included John Stoner (husband of Catharina Elisabetha Ramsburg), Anna (wife of Baltis Getzendanner), Henry (husband of Elisabeth Link) and Benedict Stoner (husband first of Maria Sibylla Loy and then of Anna Barbara Thomas). In another generation, five grandchildren married grandchildren of Jacob Stoner's next door neighbor Stephen Ramsburg. John Stoner had served in his father-in-law Stephen Ramsburg's Militia company in 1757 as had Balzer Getzendanner. In 1767 the elder Stoner's lands were divided among his children, with John Stoner keeping "Mill Pond" where he continued to operate his father's mill on Tuscarora Creek.

Family traditions and allegations to the contrary, the first documented reference to **Stephen Ramsburg** (1711c-1789) appears to be his deed from Daniel Dulany on July 28, 1746 for land on "Tasker's Chance." He was not one of the original six Germans who contracted with Benjamin Tasker in 1737 for purchase of the whole, although with the haziness of men's memories such was claimed a half century later.[201] Likewise his relationship to Johann Georg Riemensberger of southern Frederick County is not borne out by the church records at Walldorf, Germany.[202] Nor should he be confused with the John Steven Regensberger listed as arriving at Philadelphia on August 17, 1729.[203] Nevertheless a plausible but undocumented source places Stephen Remsberg in Lancaster, Pennsylvania on April 13, 1736 when he was reputedly married by Detrick Updegraf, his Majesty's Justice of the Peace for the County of Lancaster, to Cattrina Bruner.[204]

Stephen Ramsburg's land on "Tasker's Chance" was called "Mortality."[205] Of all the parcels carved out of the whole tract,

---

[200] Rice, *The Life*, op. cit., p. 134. Cf. also Assleman, p. 267.

[201] Frederick County Land Records, WR 12:256. This confirmatory deed of April 15, 1794 for "Trout Pond" recited, *inter alliis*, "Whereas Benjamin Tasker with consent of Jacob Stoner, Abraham Miller, Stephen Ramsbarger and others to whom Benjamin Tasker had agreed to sell 'Tasker's Chance'...." But its contention is not substantiated by the contemporary Provincial Court Record, EI 8:28.

[202] Johann Georg Riemensberger (cf. above, p. 41) was born at Walldorf in 1736, the son of Sebastian Henrich Riemensberger and grandson of Jacob Wolfgang Riemensberger. The latter, alleged to have been the father of Stephen in 1711, actually was the father of a daughter Helena Elisabeth Riemensberger, born September 20, 1711.

[203] Strassburger-Hinke, *op. cit.*, List 9A, p. 24. This was the ship Captain's rendition. He himself signed his name as Johann Stephen Rumer or Rümer on Lists 9BC, pp. 25-26.

[204] Daughter of Joseph Brunner and Catharina Elisabetha Thomas of Klein Schifferstadt, later of "Tasker's Chance." Cf. also pp. 271-272. Reformed marriage records in Lancaster did not begin until 1742.

Ramsburg's 473 acres were in size second only to the parcel projected for Johann Jost Schmidt. It stretched from today's Harmony Grove northward to front on the Monocacy River. Through it passed Tuscarora Creek on its way to its mouth on Jacob Stoner's land to the south east. The old Pennsylvania Railroad, enroute to Frederick from the north, also crossed the Ramsburg land[206] as does a portion of today's U.S. Highway 15.

Stephen Ramsburg was nevertheless a trusted friend and leader within the German community and in Frederick County as a whole. He was a frequent witness to his neighbors' wills and was often named as executor of their estates.[207] On numerous occasions he and his wife stood as sponsors for Reformed Church baptisms. He was one of the original elders of that Church, he signed the 1748 appeal to Pastor Michael Schlatter for help in keeping the congregation together and he was one of the trustees in 1764 receiving from Daniel Dulany, Jr., the land on which the Frederick Reformed Church was built.[208] In 1757 during the French and Indian War Stephen Ransberger was named Captain of a militia company. He was one of the few Germans entrusted with such a command and for 42 days of service received seven pounds in pay. The predominance of Germans serving with him is evident from the listing of his Company's roster (see Appendix, page 379).

When wrongs were done, Ramsburg stood up to plead the case of his friends and neighbors. On May 6, 1748, for example, he reported to the Maryland Assembly how the sheriff as tax collector was exacting a 10% surcharge on the annual quitrents plus 15 shillings for his personal use. As examples of those who had so suffered he named Jacob Fout, Peter Apple, Henry Trout, Melcar Wherfield, Christian Thomas, Peter Hoffman, Christian Getson[dann]er, Henry Roads, Conrad Kemp, Francis Wise, Jacob Smith, George Lye [Loy], Isaac Miller, Thomas Johnson, John Smith, John Browner, Jacob Browner, Ken. [Henry] Backdolt, Nicholas [Michael] Reisner, David Delaitre, Martin Wisell [Wetzel], George Windred and Peter Shaffer. Half of these were situated on "Tasker's Chance." He observed that a "great number of the Germans and some others were so much alarmed by the proceedings that several of them have already left the Province and others have disclosed that as soon as they could sell what they possessed, they would go away. Many of the Germans, declaring that being oppressed in their native country induced them to leave it and that they were apprehensive of being equally oppressed here and that therefore they would go away to avoid it."[209]

---

[205] Prince George's County Land Records, BB 1:436.

[206] The railroad bridge crossing the Monocacy at the edge of Ramsburg's land was washed out in the storm of June 1972. Since then today's successor railroad, the Maryland Midland, comes no farther south than the River bank opposite Ramsburg's land.

[207] Cf. Frederick County Wills, A1:105 (Jacob Storm, 1756), A1:152 (John Biggs, 1760), etc.

[208] Frederick County Land Records, J:362. The other trustees at that time were John Brunner, George Hoffman and George Lingenfelter.

Later that same year, on October 20, 1748, Governor Samuel Ogle granted a passport in the form of a certificate to Stephen Remsperger of Frederick County in the said Province, wheelwright, Nicholas Benedick, Jacob Bruner, farmer, and Henry Thomas, waggon maker," all natives of Germany having lived within the said Province for many [eight] years past." They were intending to "visit their native country and their relations and friends there and to return again to their families here.... they are of good reputation and have always been as good and faithful subjects to his Sacred Britannic Majesty.... Please suffer them to pass and repass without hindrance."[210] Apparently the trip was made, for as we have noted Johann Jacob Brunner purchased in Frankfurt on April 16, 1749 a book for the Frederick Reformed Church records.

After his return to Maryland, Stephen Ramsburg had other land transactions. The acquisition on September 25, 1753 of "Dearbought" and its subsequent assignment to Sebastian Derr have been noted above.[211] In 1758 he purchased 150 acres on the east side of the Monocacy River. This land was located at the northwest corner of "Dulany's Lot" near Biggs Ford and included the original Allen Farquhar property on Glade Creek.[212] A three-and-a-half story flour mill was erected which in later years was known as Shank's Mill. In 1910 it was still operating, the last remaining burr mill in Frederick County.[213] Vestiges of the mill race are still clearly visible today. Ramsburg also held "Shoemaker's Choice" and resurveys on both "Stoney Hill" and "Nutt Spring" as well as lots in Frederick town and land in Washington County.[214]

Stephen Ramsburg died on March 7, 1789. His will, signed in German, arranged for manumission of his slaves and provided for disposition of his home plantation "Mortality" as well as a few other miscellaneous parcels of land.[215] His children were Catharina Elisabetha (wife of John Stoner), John (husband of Anna Maria Brunner), Jacob (husband of Elisabeth Devilbiss), Margaret (wife of Henry Myer), Elias (husband of Catharina), Henry (husband of Susanna Devilbiss and later Catharina Stickley), and Christian (husband of Susanna).

Johann Georg Ley (1705c-1765), or **George Loy** as the name

---

[209] Proceedings of Council, 1732-1753, *Archives of Maryland, op. cit.*, 28:423. Joseph Ogle (see below, p. 328) gave a similar deposition. The misspelling of these German names could hardly have been Ramsburg's errors!
[210] Proceedings of the Assembly, *Archives of Maryland, op. cit.*, 44:697-698; *Maryland State Papers No. 1, the Black Books*, 9:23; para. 562 in the *Calendar*. Benedict is not recognized in the early land records. Philipp Henry Thomas, born September 12, 1715 in Klein Schifferstadt, was a brother of Christian Thomas above.
[211] See p. 260 above; Frederick County Land Records, E:278, 764.
[212] Frederick County Land Records, F:352, F:608. See also above, p. 125.
[213] Williams, *op. cit.*, p. 1218.
[214] Frederick County Land Records, G:106, J:1215, L:398, L:628, N:231, etc.
[215] Frederick County Wills, GM 2:304.

came to be known, was Stephen Ramsburg's neighbor to the northwest. He had arrived at Philadelphia on August 27, 1733 aboard the ship *Elizabeth*. With him came Eliza Lee, either a wife or sister, and Johan Henrick Ley, age 13, possibly a younger brother.[216] They were in the company of a number of other future Marylanders, including Hans Peter Hoffman, Frantz Weiss, Georg Friederich Unseldt, Jaques Bonet and the Trout family, most of whom were later to live on or near "Tasker's Chance." It has been claimed that Joh. Georg Ley's wife was Maria Elisabeth Trout, and that is a distinct possibility.[217] For a time after their arrival they lived in the northern part of today's Lancaster County, Pennsylvania, and there their first two children were born, Maria Rosina Ley in 1734 and Joh. Jacob Ley in 1736. Both were baptized by Pastor Stöver, who entered their names in his Muddy Creek Church Book, although he indicated the family was from Warwick in the area near present-day Brickerville.

Although Stöver added a third child to the Muddy Creek record and omitted all three entries from his personal Journal, making no reference to the Leys at Monocacy in either of his books, analysis shows that Anna Eliesabetha Ley, the third child, was born on December 11, 1738 undoubtedly at Monocacy and was definitely there when baptized on June 17, 1739.[218] Most probably the family had come to Maryland about 1737, following their 1733-shipmate Frantz Weiss

---

[216] Strassburger-Hinke, *op. cit.*, Lists 30AA'BC, pp. 113-115, 765-767. Because on his arrival he was too ill to take the oaths of allegiance and abjuration, his name does not appear on Lists B and C. But two Captain's lists A and A' have been discovered, on one of which his name is carried reasonably correctly as "Hans Jurigh Ley, 28, sick." On the other list he has obviously been confused with the younger man and appears as "Johan Henrich Ley, miller, 28." Interestingly, ten days earlier on the ship *Samuel*, which brought Jacob Hoff, Jacob Matthias and the Kemps, were a Matthew Ley (1706-1783), also age 28 [sic], and his wife Anna Maria Ley, age 24. They remained in Pennsylvania, settling in Berks County.

[217] Jennie C. Stewart and Claude Loy Van Dyne, *The Loy Family in America, 1732-1955* (Boulder, Colo., 1955). If this surmisal is correct, since the Trout family arrived on the same vessel but included no unmarried Maria Elisabeth Trout, then the Loys were married before arriving in America and she was the Eliza Lee listed just after the Trout family on List 30A'. Her full name, Maria Elisabetha Laye, is given in a 1747 baptism record in the Frederick Reformed Church Book.

[218] Since Ley's first children were baptized within a month of their birth, as was customary when a pastor was nearby, the six-month delay here underscores the probability of departure from Pennsylvania before 1738. Peter Hoffman and his wife Maria Appolonia were the child's sponsors. Further, although her identity or relationship is unknown, one should not ignore a Magdalena Lein (the name Ley spelled with the German feminine ending) who stood as sponsor at Monocacy on April 28, 1736 for Johann Georg Schweinhardt's daughter Anna Maria and on May 17, 1736 for Georg Lathly's daughter Rachel (Stöver, *op. cit.*, pp. 3, 16).

who was already at Monocacy in 1736. With them also came Peter Hoffman and his wife Maria Appolonia. Both Weiss and Hoffman had also appeared earlier in the Muddy Creek Church Book, and both were present in Monocacy for the 1739 baptism.

On June 11, 1737, according to Benjamin Tasker's report,[219] John George Loy was joining five other Germans in an attempt to purchase the entire "Tasker's Chance" tract. Further, on November 25, 1738 in Pastor Stöver's records Joh. Georg Lay appeared with his wife at Manaquesen as Lutheran baptism sponsors for a daughter of Philipp Ernst Grüber. Stöver named him again at Manaquesen on September 21, 1740, this time as a sponsor for a daughter of Joh. Georg Beer.[220] Baptisms for Loy's own children born in 1746 and later may be found, some in the Frederick Reformed Church Book, some in the Lutheran. Ley's name is not among those who contributed to the purchase of the Lutheran church book about 1742, but as Hans Georg Laẙ he was the first of six wardens to sign the June 24, 1747 church articles prepared by Pastor Muhlenberg. He likewise headed the list of those who made possible the building of the pastor's house in Frederick, having given two days of work and 20 shillings of money.[221]

On July 28, 1746 Daniel Dulany conveyed 213 acres on "Tasker's Chance" to John George Loy.[222] The land was located west of today's U.S. Highway 15 and south of Willow Road. Tuscarora Creek flowed through it. Two years later Stephen Ramsburg was listing Lye as one of the Germans being overtaxed by the sheriff. In March 1753 George Loy and Frederick Unseldt were serving as executors for their shipmate Francis Wise.[223] In that same month Loy purchased Jacob Peck's parcel, called "Lambson," and its mill.[224] The site lay some two miles due west of Loy's "Tasker's Chance" land and was in the Indian Springs area on today's Yellow Springs Road. A petition for the forerunner of that road had been submitted in 1750, only three years earlier.[225] On December 1, 1755 Frederick Unseld named George Lay as one of his executors and guardians for his children. Then, in 1757, although over fifty years of age, George Loy served with his neighbor Stephen Ramsburg's Militia company during the French and Indian War.

Regardless of variations and ultimate evolution in the spelling of Loy's surname, he himself signed his will on August 1, 1765 as Hanns Georg Ley. In the text the name was written as Leih. The will was written in German but to enable its recording it was translated by Thomas Schley. Schley was not overly attentive to exact orthography and the will therefore was filed as that of John George Lyh. But Schley's "translation," though imprecise, was a marked improvement. In the original verbiage Ley dated the will at "Fridrich Gemeinde Phrofentz Marenland" [Frederick County, Province

---
[219] Provincial Court Records, EI 8:28.
[220] Stöver, op. cit., pp. 18, 23.
[221] Frederick Lutheran Church Book, p. 417.
[222] Prince George's County Land Records, BB 1:438.
[223] Rice, The Life, op. cit., p. 119.
[224] Frederick County Land Records, E:105.
[225] See above, p. 178.

of Maryland], and devised to his son Jacob two cows and one bix [pig] in addition to "my blantasche" [plantation] and gristmill on part of "Desgers Shanns" ["Tasker's Chance"]. He gave "Lamsam" ["Lambson" but "Samsheim" per Schley] to his son-in-law Peter Schäffer, the land "where he now lives," and "Arnold's Deleit" to sons Adam and Fridrich Leih.[226] His children included Rosina (wife of Peter Shaver), Jacob, Anna Elisabeth (wife of Sebastian Derr), Apollonia (wife of Frederick Troxell), Maria Sibylla (wife of Benedict Stoner), Adam (husband of Anna Barbara Cassel), Johann Georg (who died young), Frederick (husband of Louisa Gies), and Charlotte Amalie (wife of George Shoup). Son Jacob was named co-executor of his father's will, but died before administration could be completed. Son-in-law Peter Shaver took over as his administrator.[227] Jacob's widow Maria Dorothea Leu then married George Peter Hoffman, son of her father-in-law's shipmates Hans Peter and Maria Apollonia Hoffman.[228]

South of Joh. Georg Ley's land and west of Stephen Ramsburg's "Mortality" lay the land of **John Henry Neff**. His parcel was a rather large 355½-acre tract whose center would be marked today by the junction of Hayward Road and Opossumtown Pike. He seems to have been present on "Tasker's Chance" in October 1742 when, as Henry Knafe, his name appears among the Germans petitioning for the division of Prince George's Parish.[229] Daniel Dulany conveyed the land to Neff in one of the 21 initial deeds to parts of "Tasker's Chance" which were made on July 28, 1746.[230] But Neff's tenure was a short one, and it is questionable whether he lived there long. On August 3, 1750, calling himself "of Frederick County, Virginia," he and his wife Anna conveyed the land back to Dulany.[231] Twenty years later the land was deeded by Daniel Dulany the Younger to his son-in-law Samuel Fleming.[232]

Doctor John Henry Naffe had 470 acres surveyed on March 5, 1749/50 in Virginia at Bushey Bottom on the North Fork of the Shenandoah. He had purchased this land, "where he lived," from Adam Shurel in Jost Hite's grant. On April 20, 1752 he had 200 more acres surveyed "on the side of North Mountain."[233] On June 28, 1749 John Ruddle, Jr. and John Henry Neff worked as chain carriers for Cornelius Ruddle's survey. In the certificate relating to this survey, "John Ruddle was sworn but John Henry Neff would not swore."[234] Such a clue to religious preference directs our attention to the similarity

---

[226] Frederick County Wills, A1:249. Original is at Hall of Records, Box 3, folder 19.
[227] Frederick County Administrative Accounts, A1:385.
[228] Frederick Reformed Church Book marriages.
[229] See below, p. 371.
[230] Prince George's County Land Records, BB 1:439.
[231] Frederick County Land Records, B:243. In both deeds the name is spelled Nave. Also noted in Maryland Rent Rolls (Frederick County No. 1), 32/26a, John Henry Nafe to Dulany, August 23, 1750.
[232] Frederick County Land Records, N:331, March 14, 1770.
[233] Peggy Shomo Joyner, *Abstracts of Virginia's Northern Neck Warrants and Surveys, Orange and Augusta Counties, 1730-1754*, 1:28.
[234] Ibid., p. 31.

of names of Neff's children compared to those listed by Rupp as Mennonites coming from Switzerland to Pennsylvania by way of Germany.[235] John Henry Neff of Shenandoah County wrote his will June 1, 1784 (probated July 29, 1784) naming his wife Anna, sons John, Francis, Jacob, Christley [Christian], and Abram, an "unhealthy" daughter Elizabeth, and son-in-law Jacob Baughman who was married to his daughter Catherine and was to receive one of the two parcels mentioned in the will.[236] Of these children, Jacob, Christian and Abraham Neff signed a Mennonite petition in Shenandoah County in 1785.[237] As with a few others, we question whether religious preference may have been a factor in the Neffs' not staying on "Tasker's Chance."

A relationship, if any, has not been found between John Henry Neff and the Jacob Neff who acquired "Hedge Hogg" near Biggs Ford in 1740.[238] A Margareta Neff of Creutz Creek and Joh. Georg Schaiteler of Manaquesen were married by Pastor Stöver in Lancaster County, Pennsylvania on December 20, 1739,[239] but they lived afterwards in Monocacy: George Scheidler received communion from Pastor Candler "in the Lutheran Church of Manaquice" on September 25, 1743, preparatory to naturalization in October.[240]

James Smith held title only briefly to a 260-acre parcel on "Tasker's Chance" which for £60 was deeded to him by Daniel Dulany on May 17, 1750.[241] It was one of only a very few lots to which Dulany conveyed title *after* his initial deeds of 1746. The lot approximated today's Clover Hill II Subdivision, lying to the south of Poole Jones Road. Smith mortgaged the lot on February 27, 1752 to Christopher Lowndes and Joshua Beall.[242] The former was a prosperous merchant at Bladensburg. Earlier, on March 20, 1750 Smith had given

---

[235] I. Daniel Rupp, *History of Lancaster County, Pennsylvania* (Lancaster, 1844), p. 124: Francis Neff, his sons Francis, Jr., Henry and Daniel and grandsons Henry and Daniel (sons of Daniel), all born in Switzerland, who left there as Mennonites and settled on Neff's Run, a tributary of the Little Conestoga in Lancaster County. C. Henry Smith, "The Mennonite Immigration to Pennsylvania in the Eighteenth Century," *The Pennsylvania-German Society, 1929*, 35:162, n39, adds John Henry Neff, known as the "Old Doctor," as a brother of Francis Neff.

[236] Shenandoah County [Virginia] Wills, B:101. Wills of all his sons except John are also recorded in this County: Francis (1812, H:268), Jacob (1819, L:234), Christian (1814, I:93) and Abraham (1812, H:238). See Amelia C. Gilreath, *Shenandoah County, Virginia, Abstract of Wills, 1772-1850* (n.s., 1980), pp. 158-160.

[237] Miscellaneous Petition, December 10, 1785, 67-48, Virginia State Library, Richmond.

[238] See above, p. 111.

[239] Stöver, *op. cit.*, Marriages, No. 272. Weiser, "Lancaster Lutheran Church," *loc. cit.*, p. 433, shows Stöver's entry repeated in that church register as Joh. Georg Schönteler and Margaretha Nessin.

[240] Provincial Court Judgment Records, 1742-1744, EI 7:296.

[241] Frederick County Land Records, B:174.

[242] *Ibid.*, B:517.

these men a chattel mortgage involving slaves and livestock to indemnify them as sureties or guarantors of Smith's £1,000 debt to James Armstrong, Thomas Ingles and Laurence Debutts, all of St. Mary's County.[243] In 1774 Lowndes and Beall transfered the "Tasker's Chance" lot to Matthias Buckey.[244] Beginning in 1745 and continuing for the following 25 years, Smith was involved in numerous land transactions in today's Washington County. He served on various grand juries, qualified as an attorney and from 1753 on was one of the Justices of the Frederick Court.[245]

Even though no record of a deed to Conrad Keller from Daniel Dulany has been found, there may well have been a survey made which was intended for him. Conrad Keller is believed to have been baptized at Wallisellen, now a part of Zürich, in Switzerland, on March 14, 1706 and as a carpenter to have left for Carolina [i.e., America] in 1734 with wife Barbara Blaar, baptized at Wallisellen on December 9, 1703. They brought with them a son Mattheus, baptized July 25, 1734.[246] Except for their stated ages, the particulars match the Philadelphia port information for Hans Cunrath Keller, who arrived on the ship *Mercury* May 29, 1735 with Barbara and Elisabeth Haller[sic] and Mathias Keller age 1.[247] In 1736 Conrad Keller and his wife were in Lancaster, Pennsylvania, when their son John Caspar was baptized by John Jacob Hock in one of the first recorded Reformed baptisms there.[248] By 1740 they had come to Prince George's County, Maryland where with other residents on "Tasker's Chance" Conrad Keller and his children Mattheus, Gasparus, Susanna and Barbara were naturalized. A further clue to Keller's being on "Tasker's Chance" lies in John George Loy's 1746 deed, whose courses and distances in its property description began "at the end of the third line of John Conrad Keller's land for 159 acres." Apparently Keller's land was intended to be squeezed between, on the one hand, the lands of Loy and Neff to the east and, on the other, Henry Trout's land to the west. Presumably Keller was thought to be still on this land in 1753 when records show him in possession of 159 acres.[249] But by 1781 when Loyalist lands were confiscated during the Revolution, the parcel still belonged to the Dulany family. It was conveyed by the State to Thomas Johnson in 1788.[250] Conrad Keller did remain in Frederick

---
[243] *Ibid.*, B:354.
[244] *Ibid.*, V:461.
[245] Rice, *The Life, op. cit., passim.*
[246] Albert Bernhard Faust, *List of Swiss Immigrants in the Eighteenth Century to the American Colonies* (Washington, 1920-25), 1:92.
[247] Strassburger-Hinke, *op. cit.*, Lists 38ABC, pp. 146-150. Ages do not tally, for Hans Cunrath Käller (Conrad Keller on List 38A) claimed he was 36 years old and Barbara said she was 23. Actually they were 29 and 31, respectively.
[248] First Reformed Church Book, Lancaster. The first baptism in this Church Book took place on June 20, 1736, but marriages were not recorded until 1742. Pastor Hock arrived at Philadelphia on the *Mortonhouse* along with Jacob Brunner, Jacob Sturm and others on August 24, 1728.
[249] Maryland Rent Rolls (Frederick County No. 1), 32:26a.

County, however. On July 18, 1751 in connection with a debt to Daniel Dulany he pledged as security his wagon, livestock, plow and irons for £112 to indemnify his guarantors Conrad Kemp, Jacob Storm, Frederick Unseld, George Laye, Christian Thomas, Joseph Brunner, Christian Smith and Francis Wise, most of them farmers on "Tasker's Chance."[251] On April 23, 1753 "Zura," a parcel of 208 acres adjoining John Biggs' "Good Luck" on the west side of the Monocacy River was surveyed for Conrad Keller.[252] In 1766 Keller conveyed "Zura" on which he lived (208 acres) and "Keepburgh" (50 acres) to his son Adam Keller.[253] These lands were located west of the Monocacy River and east of Fishing Creek near today's Utica. Conrad's son Caspar Keller moved on to Washington County.

We have met **Henry Trout** previously in our discussion concerning the German settlement near Thurmont, where he probably lived from at least 1738 to 1746.[254] In the latter year he purchased from Daniel Dulany for £67/14/3 a lot of 171-3/4 acres called "Trout Pond" located along the northwestern boundary of "Tasker's Chance." It straddled Tuscarora Creek between today's Opposumtown and Poole Jones Roads and thus lay north of the Smith lot and west of the Keller lot described above. Henry Trout was listed by Stephen Ramsburg as being overcharged by the sheriff in the March 1748 quitrent collections.[255] The deed to Trout's land was not recorded, however, for Trout died almost immediately, and it was necessary many years afterwards for his son Jacob Trout to establish ownership anew. This he did in 1794 with a new deed from Daniel Dulany the Younger.[256] The latter, at the age of 72, was thus still rectifying and completing land records from his father's era, which had ended over four decades before.

Henry Trout's widow Anna Maria survived him by 47 years, having remarried in 1747. Her second husband, **Georg Fridrich Haffner** (1716-1794), had come to this country from Fränckischen Saddelhausen in Germany in 1745.[257] He appeared shortly on the Rent Roll as in possession of land on "Tasker's Chance," but there is no record of a deed in his name. While he may have occupied the land in the extreme northwest corner of "Tasker's Chance," it is more likely that he settled on the Trout land after his marriage to Trout's widow and

---

[250] Frederick County Land Records, WR 8:298.
[251] Ibid., B:415-416.
[252] C/S: GS 1:77. Could "Zura" have evolved from "Zürich?"
[253] Frederick County Land Records, K:375.
[254] See above, p. 220. He was naturalized, however, in May 1740 with a group of Germans almost exclusively associated with "Tasker's Chance." See above, p. 260.
[255] Ibid., p. 292.
[256] Frederick County Land Records, WR 12:356. This is the deed, undoubtedly in error so many years after the fact, which indicated Stephen Ramsburg was one of the original 1737 purchasers of "Tasker's Chance." See above, p. 291.
[257] Frederick Lutheran Church Book, Burials. The date of his marriage is obviously an approximation. Cf. the 1748 quitrent notation.

lived there until he died. He was an elder "for many years" with the Lutheran Church, and in the records of that church appear the baptism records of his children. He and Anna Maria had six children and at least 30 grandchildren. His own death notice may be found in the same register, where it is observed that his wife died on Good Friday in 1793, while he died on Good Friday in the following year.

For the extreme northern tier of land on "Tasker's Chance," the equivalent of approximately one square mile in area, we have no definite record of occupants before 1746. Except for "The Barrens" of John Stoner, 103 acres in the center of this area, all of it remained in the Dulany family's possession until 1781. It was then divided into lots numbered 31 and 32, the former along the northeast corner of "Tasker's Chance," the latter in the northwest corner. These were then sold as confiscated Loyalist property.

The Maryland Rent Roll which was prepared for Frederick County about 1753 lists four individuals "in possession of" land on "Tasker's Chance" for whom neither survey nor deed records can be found.[258] Two of them, Peter and Michael Brunner, were sons of Jacob Brunner and therefore might be suspected as having land either near to or possibly even on (as subdivided parts) their father's "Rich Level." But the land records do not bear this out. The other two, **Caspar Beckenbach** [shown as Caspar Pickinpaw] and **Leonard Eberle** [Everly] were brothers-in-law who had come from Eiterbach, near Heiligkreuzsteinach in the Odenwald area of Germany.

Curiously all four do appear elsewhere in the land records, each of them receiving a deed from the same Jacob Brunner, all of them on the same date (March 20, 1755), with all four parcels representing portions of Jacob Brunner's "Resurvey on Chevy Chase."[259] Thomas Cresap had surveyed this land for Daniel Dulany on August 27, 1744. Dulany held the certificate until on April 11, 1751 he assigned it to Jacob Brunner, who then had the land patented in his own name two days later.[260] The land's original 100 acres were subsequently resurveyed into 730 acres, all located in the Middletown District on what was then called "Trap Branch, a draught of Kitoctin Creek." We conclude therefore that the clerk preparing the Rent Roll erred by entering the land granted by Jacob Brunner in the Middletown Valley as though it were located nearby his own home plantation on "Tasker's Chance."

Caspar Beckenbach was born in Eiterbach in 1722, his sister Eva Maria some four years earlier. She married Johann Leonhard Eberle in Eiterbach on February 8, 1740, and between August 1741 and March 1748 four of their children were born there.[261] Although

---

[258] Maryland Rent Rolls (Frederick No. 1), 32:26a. Maryland Debt Books, likewise not always free from error, show Robert Debutts in possession of 217.5 acres on "Taskers Chance" (Debt Book, 1754-1757, Frederick County, 22:42). Such an acreage cannot be identified on this tract.
[259] Frederick County Land Records, E:695-698. The names of the two men from Eiterbach are given in these deeds as Gasper Begabock and Leonard Averlaw!
[260] Original Patented Certificate of Survey, Prince George's County No. 502; C/S: BY & GS 5:534; Patent: BY & GS 3:355.

Leonard Eberle does not appear in the Philadelphia port arrival lists,[262] he and his wife reached Maryland before September 10, 1751 when they stood as baptism sponsors for a daughter of Joh. Georg Kroneiss.[263] That was the same year but a month before October 7, 1751 when Adam, Caspar, Görg Adam, Johann Georg and Georg Leonhardt Beckenbach, all sons of Johann Adam Beckenbach (1657c-1739) of Eiterbach, arrived in Philadelphia.[264]

The story of "Tasker's Chance" can thus be summarized to show that by 1743, the end of the second decade of settlement in the Monocacy region, perhaps a dozen families had settled on its land, but none had yet acquired bona fide title. By 1746 deeds granted to 19 individuals had been confirmed, representing almost three quarters of the tract's total acreage. Of these early purchasers, almost all were German immigrants who as farmers gave their stamp to this central heart of what was to become Frederick County. In religion the great majority of these settlers on "Tasker's Chance" seem to have been Reformed -- Kemp, Storm, Thomas, Stoner, Ramsburg and the Brunners. Only Sinn, Haffner and maybe Frantz were Lutheran, while Loy appears in the records of both churches. This leaves a significant number who presumably were classified as neither -- Roht and Fink as Dunkers, Abraham Miller and Neff as Mennonites, and Weiss and Apollonia Hoffman as Protestant Dissenters "who would not swear." More than half of these latter did not stay long on "Tasker's Chance" but moved elsewhere, some still in Frederick County, others disappearing entirely. As yet by 1743 no town had been laid out on "Tasker's Chance," but the disappearance of John Jost Schmidt, for one, made way soon after in the third decade of Monocacy's history for the ultimate beginnings of the town which would soon be known as Frederick.

---

[261] Edwin T. and Atha Peckenpaugh Brace, *Descendants of Johann Adam and Anna Maria Beckenbach* (Baltimore, 1984), p. 20.

[262] Johann Leonhard Eberle was the son of Johann Adam Eberle. Strassburger-Hinke, *op. cit.*, List 152C, p. 437, does note the arrival at Philadelphia on August 24, 1750 of an Adam Eberle and Conradt Israel Aberle. They came in the company of Johann Adam Franck, Johan Ludwig Rauhzahn, Johannes Blumenschein [John Flowers] and others who figure in later Frederick County history.

[263] Frederick Reformed Church Book, p. 21.

[264] Strassburger-Hinke, *op. cit.*, List 175C, p. 474.

MONOCACY MANOR

Once land was patented to individuals, it was owned by those individuals as freehold property, subject solely to a tiny annual quitrent of a shilling per 100 acres plus an occasional alienation fine levied when and if ownership passed from one individual to another. Therefore, after land had been patented, income accruing to the Proprietor from the land itself was not great. More importantly, increased population, improvements made on the land and development of nearby markets with their accompanying transportation networks all led inevitably to ever increasing land values. Such increases obviously accrued to the freeholders and not to the Proprietor.

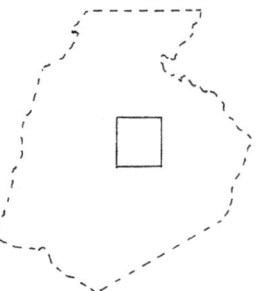

With an eye to the long term future and to their participation in such increased land values, Cecilius Calvert, Second Lord Baltimore and the first Proprietor of Maryland, began in the 1660's setting aside for himself and his heirs land intended for leasing but not for patenting. These lands were called manors. Initially two such manors, each comprising at least 6,000 acres were to be created in every county. By 1684 twenty such manors had been surveyed, all but one of them located on the Eastern Shore or south of present-day Montgomery County on the Western Shore. Three more were added in the succeeding half century with the last manor, Conococheague in present Washington County, set aside in 1734.[1]

As long as alternate land remained relatively cheap, there was little incentive to lease land, and occupancy of the manors therefore proceeded slowly. The "consideration fee" of four pounds sterling over and beyond the annual rent was, in a relatively cashless society, likewise a severe deterrent. It was not eliminated until 1734. On the frontier, manors were not even created until well into the eighteenth century. On May 29, 1724, however, nearly 10,000 acres of land were surveyed and set aside for the Lord Proprietor, his only

---

[1] Susquehanna (New Connaught), Elk River, North East, Kent, Queen Anne's, Nanticoke, Wolcote, Wicomico on the Eastern Shore; West St. Mary's, Snow Hill, Mill, Woolsey, Beaverdam, Chaptico, Pangaiah, Zachiah, Calverton, Anne Arundel, Collington, Gunpowder, My Lady's, Monocacy, and Conococheague on the Western Shore. Gregory A. Stiverson, *Poverty in a Land of Plenty, Tenancy in Eighteenth Century Maryland* (Baltimore and London, 1977) has provided a superb study and analysis of available material pertaining to Maryland's Proprietary Manors.

manor within the bounds of present Frederick County.[2] "Monocacy Manor" was located east of the Monocacy River and north of "Dulany's Lot" and "Spring Garden" with a beginning at their common point, the mouth of Glade Creek. From there the Manor extended north and east to a point one mile beyond present-day Woodsboro. Until September of 1729 this land lay farthest north of all the 28 freehold tracts which had been previously surveyed within the area of today's Frederick County.

Leases were arranged by the Proprietor's agents in Maryland. The absence of surviving manor records concerning their transactions has been explained by the private nature of such records. But how much in the way of detailed information was actually recorded in the first place, let alone transmitted to the Lord Proprietor, is a subject for debate. Indicative of how little was really known in England about these manors and their leaseholds was a communication from Cecilius Calvert, principal secretary appointed by his nephew Frederick Calvert, sixth Lord Baltimore. From London as late as July 9, 1752 he wrote to Benjamin Tasker that "by the ship *Patience*, Captain Steel [commanding], a number of Palatines are embarked for Maryland to settle there, which being notified to me, and a Recomendation to you desired of me, ... I therefore desire you will give such necessary Assistance to these People on their Arrival, to forward them to Manockesy, which I understand is in Frederick County..."[3]

While actual leasing was carried out for Lord Baltimore by his agents Daniel Dulany and Benjamin Tasker, a study of the time table of the land's disposition shows that tracts possessed personally by the Agents themselves in the Frederick County area were sold or leased much faster and earlier than the land on his Lordship's Manor. It was not until August 23, 1741, over seventeen years after the initial survey, that the first parcel on "Monocacy Manor" was leased. By contrast, nearby land on "Dulany's Lot" had been sold as early as 1733. By the end of 1743 some fifteen lots had been leased on Monocacy Manor, an average of five per year. Thereafter, the pace slackened so that by 1760 a total of only 22 more lots had been leased, averaging only a little over one a year.

Initially the term of a lease was designated for a period equal to the natural lifetimes of three individuals selected by the leaseholder. These frequently were for his own life and the lives of perhaps two sons, so arranged with the hopes that one of them would

---

[2] C/S: IL B:198.

[3] Calvert Papers, MS. 174, Document 1147, Maryland Historical Society. We have no further documented suggestions relating to these 1752 arrivals, especially in the Manor's lease records where in the succeeding twelve months only three new leaseholds were created. Captain Hugh Steel and his ship *Patience* made successive voyages to Philadelphia each year, 1749-1753, except in 1752 when he is presumed to have gone to Maryland instead. Theodorus Frid. Haux, grandfather of the diarist Jacob Engelbrecht (see p. 261), arrived on this vessel in 1753. Cf. Strassburger-Hinke, *op. cit.*, Lists 134C, 146C, 164C, 200ABC, pp. 407, 426, 455, 526-529.

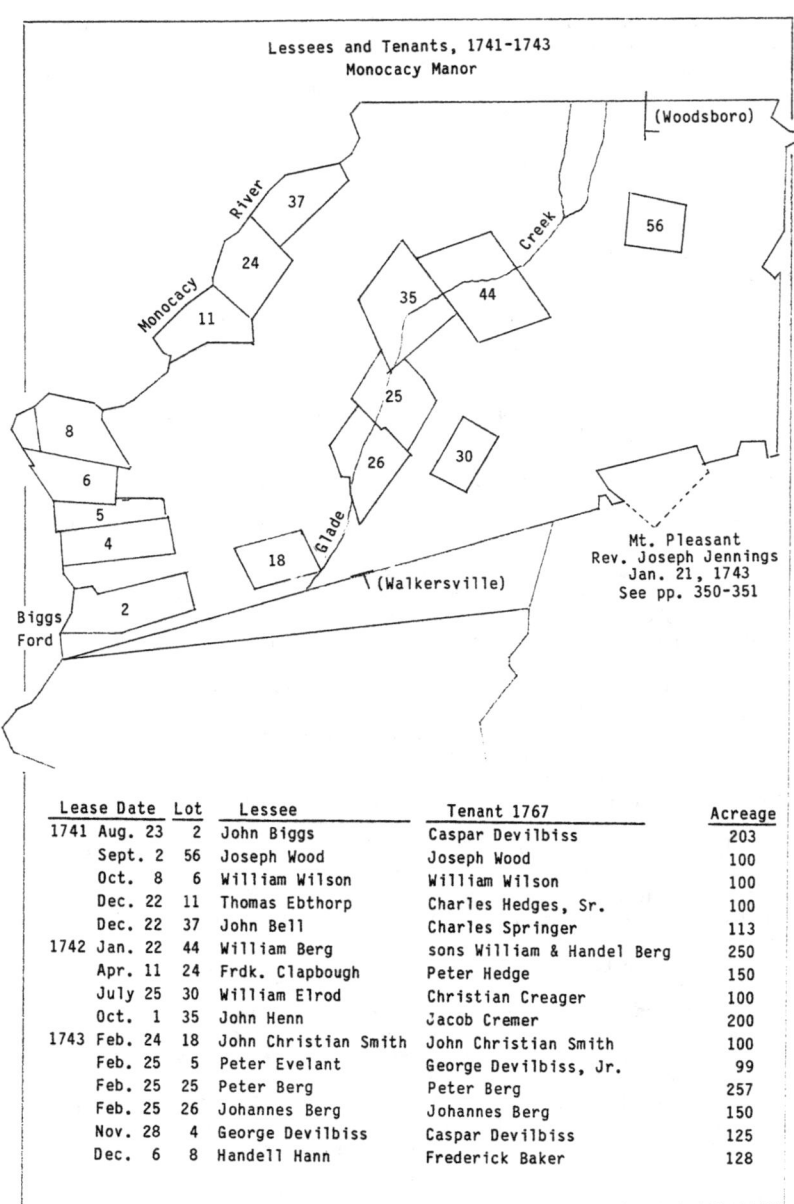

Lessees and Tenants, 1741-1743
Monocacy Manor

Lease Date	Lot	Lessee	Tenant 1767	Acreage
1741 Aug. 23	2	John Biggs	Caspar Devilbiss	203
Sept. 2	56	Joseph Wood	Joseph Wood	100
Oct. 8	6	William Wilson	William Wilson	100
Dec. 22	11	Thomas Ebthorp	Charles Hedges, Sr.	100
Dec. 22	37	John Bell	Charles Springer	113
1742 Jan. 22	44	William Berg	sons William & Handel Berg	250
Apr. 11	24	Frdk. Clapbough	Peter Hedge	150
July 25	30	William Elrod	Christian Creager	100
Oct. 1	35	John Henn	Jacob Cremer	200
1743 Feb. 24	18	John Christian Smith	John Christian Smith	100
Feb. 25	5	Peter Evelant	George Devilbiss, Jr.	99
Feb. 25	25	Peter Berg	Peter Berg	257
Feb. 25	26	Johannes Berg	Johannes Berg	150
Nov. 28	4	George Devilbiss	Caspar Devilbiss	125
Dec. 6	8	Handell Hann	Frederick Baker	128

survive.[4] Rent was set at 10 shillings per 100 acres. Sometime in the late 1750s the rent on new leases was raised to a full pound or 20 shillings per 100 acres, although the old rents continued at their original rates. At the same time alienation fines were doubled from one to two pounds per 100 acres. These applied in the event that a lessee transferred the lease to a third party. After 1760, leases were set for a prescribed length of time, usually for 21 years or slightly less, although one lease ran for only 12 years. These calculated to a termination date for most leases of about 1783-1785. As it turned out, that was not far different from the actual 1781 date when all of "Monocacy Manor" was confiscated and sold as Loyalist property. Leases added after 1760 totaled 33 in number, making a total of 70 individual lots on "Monocacy Manor" in the year 1767.

A typical lease[5] consisted of a printed form into whose blanks specific details were penned, including a property description of the lot itself, names of leaseholders, dates, and annual rental fee (e.g., 12 shillings 6 pence for 125 acres). The typical lease was signed by Governor Thomas Bladen, Benjamin Tasker and the leaseholder. To assure the ground's development with resultant enhancement of future value, it could require, for example, that the leaseholder build "one good substantial dwelling house, thirty feet long and twenty feet wide, with a brick chimney thereto." He was also required within five years to plant 100 apple trees and to maintain that number ever after. Leases often contained a prohibition against excessive cutting of timber, for timber was an existing as opposed to a developable asset of the land. At the expiration of the lease, land and improvements were to revert to the Lord Proprietary.

Gregory A. Stiverson has made a thorough and detailed study of eight selected Maryland manors including "Monocacy Manor."[6] His work shows that "Monocacy Manor," compared to other sample manors, had excellent soil, none of it as yet exhausted through excessive cultivation. The land was classified as poor on only eight out of 69 lots. Virtually all lots were heavily wooded, and over two-thirds of them were self-sufficient in water supply. Poverty was present, just as on the other manors, but more Monocacy tenants were able to accumulate surplus capital for purchase of land elsewhere than

---

[4] Infant mortality made this particularly risky. As late as 1850, Frederick County statistics show, one out of every six deaths was that of a baby who had not yet reached its first birthday, one death in four occurred before the child was two years old and fully half of all deaths involved young people under the age of 20. See Mary F. Hitselberger and John P. Dern, *Bridge in Time: The Complete 1850 Census of Frederick County, Maryland* (Redwood City, Calif., 1978), pp. 484-485, 487.

[5] See, for example, the 1744 lease to John Harlan, whose original is now in the possession of the Maryland Historical Society.

[6] Stiverson, *op. cit.*, pp. 78-81, Tables 3-1 to 3-8, 3-11 to 3-12. This work was based on claims made, after the Loyalist confiscation proceedings, by Henry Harford, natural son of Frederick Calvert (1731-1777), Sixth and last Lord Baltimore. See [Audit Office] AO 12/79:129-142, Public Record Office, Chancery Lane, London.

were tenants on other manors. While houses elsewhere were frame or covered with clapboards or planks, almost all "Monocacy Manor" houses were sturdier, log structures. They averaged 558 square feet in size (20 x 28 feet), considerably larger than those on any of the other manors. Barns were found on 71% of the lots, compared to 17% or less on the other sample manors. Barns averaged 1,022 square feet in size, and one of them measured 2,700 square feet. Eighteen lots had stables, which were almost unknown elsewhere.

Crops grown on "Monocacy Manor" varied considerably from those on the other manors. The latter, located farther south, closer to tidewater and to the established plantations of wealthy English growers, concentrated on the single crop of tobacco. But tobacco was a labor-intensive crop requiring year round work. Not possessing slaves, small leaseholders were limited in the amount of tobacco they could grow. Tobacco was also a luxury crop whose market in far-off England meant dependency on the shipping and trade interests of their wealthier neighbors. Their own consumption needs had to be paid for in cash which in turn was limited by the profits going to these middlemen merchants and shippers. Unable to accumulate capital, these tenants remained in relative poverty.

Tenants on "Monocacy Manor" on the other hand were new to this country, were in large measure of foreign background without the inherent tradition of a tobacco economy and were accustomed to growing a diversity of crops which provided for their personal consumption first. Moreover, the development of domestic markets, first in nearby Pennsylvania, then even closer, meant a significant independence from marketing middlemen. Principal crops on "Monocacy Manor" were thus the relatively more profitable grains such as wheat, corn and rye.[7]

No record remains today which lists leaseholders or tenants on "Monocacy Manor" before 1757. In that year James Dickson, whose responsibility it was to collect the rents, compiled "A list of persons that live on Menococy Mannor Who have pay'd rents."[8] He listed 21 individuals whose lots totaled 3,009 acres. But from other information we can estimate that he failed to collect rents from 17 others whose combined acreage amounted to 1,963 acres. Thus out of approximately £24/17 which he should have collected, he was able to transmit only £15 or 60%. At that, he was one of the conscientious record keepers. Other stewards were quite lax, and Edward Lloyd, who as Lord Baltimore's agent and receiver general was responsible for the management of manor affairs from 1753 to 1768, had failed to settle his accounts with the Proprietor for over two years and seldom spent

---

[7] Crop characteristics in Frederick County in 1850 were similar, with tobacco grown in only the three southeastern Districts of Frederick County and not at all in the Woodsboro District where "Monocacy Manor" had been located (Hitselberger and Dern, op. cit., pp. 502-503). In 1767 a tobacco house was found on only one lot on "Monocacy Manor" (Stiverson, op. cit., p. 66).

[8] [John Thomas] Scharf Papers, MS. 1999, formerly at the Maryland Historical Society, Baltimore, now at the Maryland Archives, Hall of Records, Annapolis.

"A list of persons that live on Monococy Mannor
Who have payd rents to J. Dickson, Collector, Esq.," 1757
(Scharf Papers, MS 1999, Hall of Records, Maryland Archives)

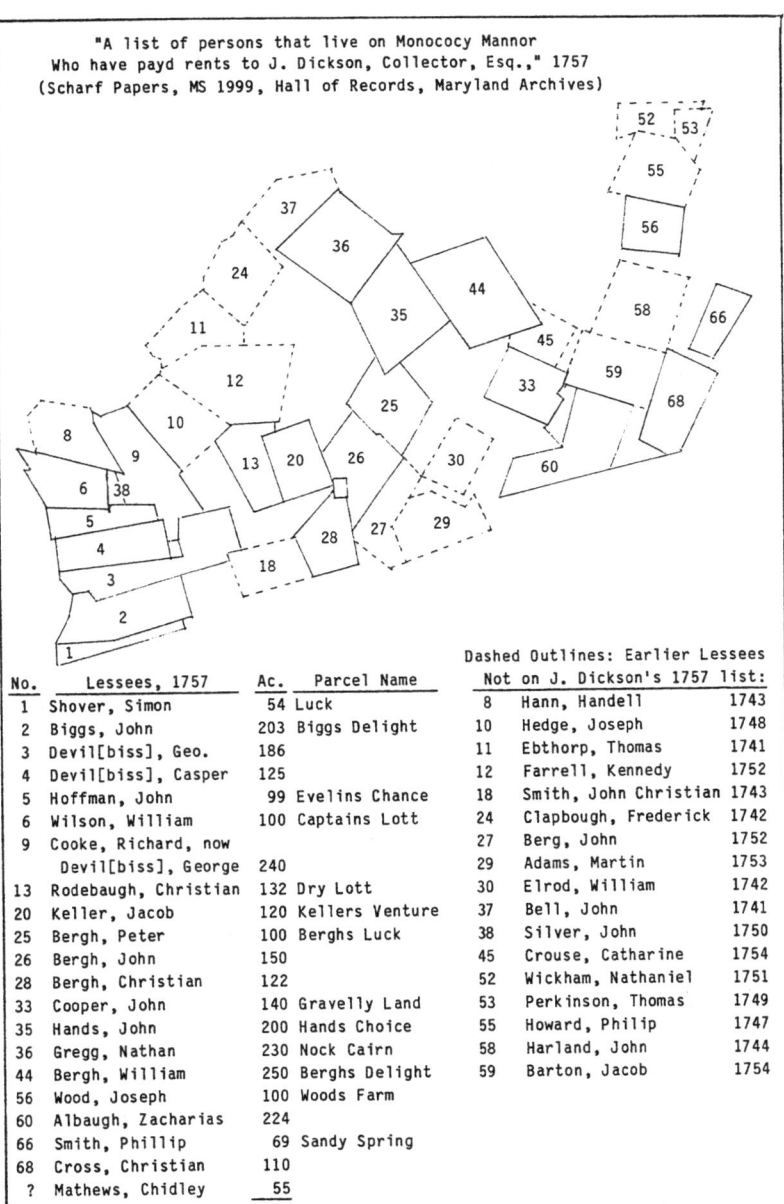

No.	Lessees, 1757	Ac.	Parcel Name
1	Shover, Simon	54	Luck
2	Biggs, John	203	Biggs Delight
3	Devil[biss], Geo.	186	
4	Devil[biss], Casper	125	
5	Hoffman, John	99	Evelins Chance
6	Wilson, William	100	Captains Lott
9	Cooke, Richard, now Devil[biss], George	240	
13	Rodebaugh, Christian	132	Dry Lott
20	Keller, Jacob	120	Kellers Venture
25	Bergh, Peter	100	Berghs Luck
26	Bergh, John	150	
28	Bergh, Christian	122	
33	Cooper, John	140	Gravelly Land
35	Hands, John	200	Hands Choice
36	Gregg, Nathan	230	Nock Cairn
44	Bergh, William	250	Berghs Delight
56	Wood, Joseph	100	Woods Farm
60	Albaugh, Zacharias	224	
66	Smith, Phillip	69	Sandy Spring
68	Cross, Christian	110	
?	Mathews, Chidley	55	
		3009	

Dashed Outlines: Earlier Lessees Not on J. Dickson's 1757 list:

8	Hann, Handell	1743
10	Hedge, Joseph	1748
11	Ebthorp, Thomas	1741
12	Farrell, Kennedy	1752
18	Smith, John Christian	1743
24	Clapbough, Frederick	1742
27	Berg, John	1752
29	Adams, Martin	1753
30	Elrod, William	1742
37	Bell, John	1741
38	Silver, John	1750
45	Crouse, Catharine	1754
52	Wickham, Nathaniel	1751
53	Perkinson, Thomas	1749
55	Howard, Philip	1747
58	Harland, John	1744
59	Barton, Jacob	1754

a day in Annapolis, so engrossed was he in his own affairs.[9]

In 1765 Frederick Calvert, Sixth Lord Baltimore (1731-1777), abandoned his ancestors' policy of holding manor land for its eventual enhancement in value and instead sought to sell all of his manor lands for immediate pecuniary return. To do so, however, necessitated a thorough analysis of all the manors and a summarization of the status of all leases, including some sort of current estimate of the present ages of those whose natural lives governed the terms of the leases. The resulting record, prepared first in 1767 and again in 1768, gives us what information we have concerning the leasing of individual lots on "Monocacy Manor." Names of all leaseholders and their current tenants were indicated for each parcel, as were each parcel's acreage, rental amount and alienation fine.[10] By 1767 it was noted that some of the original leaseholders had died or moved elsewhere. For genealogists beset with the problem of tracing individuals of this era, a notation on one lease (that for Lot No. 29 leased to Martin Adams but set on the life of one Henry Adams) lends a sympathetic note even in that day: "Question if there is such a person."

Apparently the 1768 review indicated that the size of individual lots as previously recorded was incorrect. A survey must then have been made of the entire Manor with acreages recalculated[11] (no record of such a survey is known today). Lot sizes were altered sometimes by as much as 50 acres or 30%, and the size of only five out of 70 lots remained unchanged. In spite of these recalculations, however, the rent rates were not changed, so that it is impossible to derive a common rental rate based solely on the 1768 summation. In total, the 1768 review indicated that the Manor's actual area amounted to just over 9,230 acres of which 7,365 acres, or 80%, were under lease.

Unlike "Tasker's Chance," which was settled almost exclusively by Germans, the land on "Monocacy Manor" was leased to both Germans and English. Lot sizes were smaller than those sold on "Tasker's Chance" and averaged, for those leased during the period of our study, some 134 acres in size, compared to a similar average on "Tasker's Chance" of 240 acres. Initial settlement was made almost exclusively along the Monocacy River, but very shortly the middle of the Manor began to be filled in along today's Glade Road. Thus none of the first parcels was located along present-day Dublin Road, and

---
[9] Stiverson, op. cit., p. 19, quoting from Correspondence of Governor Horatio Sharpe, 1757-1761, *Archives of Maryland*, 9:407. In 1768 Lloyd was succeeded by the Rev. Bennett Allen, for whom see below, p. 355.
[10] Brumbaugh, op. cit., 2:51-60.
[11] The acreages of a great number of lots listed in 1767 appear to be "rounded" as though they had been estimated or approximated initially. Moreover, in almost all instances where the same lot appears on both the 1767 list and on James Dickson's 1757 list (see above, p. 307) the sizes are identical. The 1768 lists, however, appear to be much more precise, as though a more refined surveying technique had been used in the interim. Both 1767 and 1768 lists designated individual lots in numerical sequence. Lot numbers were not shown in the 1757 summary.

only Joseph Wood's land was situated where State Route 194, the Woodsboro Pike, now runs. These observations point to the probability that what was early known as the Manor Monocacy Road must have followed quite closely along the River, where no vestiges have survived today.[12]

Between 1741 and the end of 1743, twelve families had leased fifteen lots on "Monocacy Manor." This number compares with an eventual total of 70 lots as defined in 1767. All but one of the lots leased in the first year were River lots, located on the east bank of the Monocacy between Biggs Ford and today's Links Bridge. In the next two years a number of lots were leased in the center of the Manor, mostly along Glade Creek, so that by the end of 1743 the division between River lots and these more interior ones was about equal. The leasing of lots in the eastern portion of the Manor thus came later. Interestingly, by the time of the 1767 lease reviews two-thirds of the initial fifteen lots were tenanted by someone other than the original leaseholder. A summary of these initial leases appears on page 304.[13]

John Biggs (1687-1761) was the first leaseholder on "Monocacy Manor." He was of English descent, born in Ulster County in New York Colony. There he married Eva Lambertse Brink, and at Kingston eight of his ten children were baptized.[14] About 1726 the family moved to New Jersey, settling in Somerset County in the Raritan River area. Also in this locale were William Dern, his future next door neighbor on "Dulany's Lot," as well as Cornelius Low, Susanna Beatty, the Middaghs and others with whom he would later associate in Maryland. A ninth child was born in New Jersey,[15] and there his wife Eva died. Then, no doubt encouraged by Susanna Beatty, he moved to Maryland sometime after June 1737, when we have the last record of him in New Jersey.[16] In Maryland he married the widow Mary Stilley and on August 23, 1741 leased Lot No. 2 on "Monocacy Manor." His lot, which he called "Biggs Delight," was leased for the natural lives of his sons Benjamin and William Biggs. It was situated near the southwestern corner of the whole tract, just north of the mouth of Glade Creek, two miles west of today's Walkersville. His land fronted along the Monocacy River opposite "Hedge Hogg" on the west bank. Between these parcels the River could be crossed by a ford which today has been replaced by Biggs Ford Bridge.

In addition to his leased land, John Biggs purchased 50 acres on "Dulany's Lot" which in 1758 he sold to Stephen Ramsburg. Ramsburg combined these acres with the former Farquhar parcel on "Dulany's

---

[12] Evidence, however, of its continuation along the River as it crossed "Dulany's Lot" is recalled by residents still living today.

[13] A summary pertaining to all the Manor lots in 1767 appears at the end of this chapter.

[14] Roswell Randall Hoes, *Baptismal and Marriage Registers of the Old Dutch Church of Kingston, 1660-1809* (New York, 1891; reprinted Baltimore, 1980).

[15] Harlingen Dutch Reformed Church Records, *New York Genealogical and Biographical Record*, 40:283.

[16] Stryker-Rodda, "Janeway Store Accounts," *loc. cit.*, 33:7.

Lot" and constructed a mill to serve farmers on the east side of the Monocacy River.[17] Biggs' only land survey was for "Good Luck" in 1751.[18] It represented 100 acres on Fishing Creek in the present Lewistown District which after his death his heirs transferred to Conrad Hockersmith. Further ties to New Jersey were evidenced on July 30, 1754 when John Biggs received a chattel mortgage from George Sexton for underwriting Sexton's loan of £7/5/0 to Malachi Bonham, a Baptist pastor at Kingwood, New Jersey.[19] Also in 1754 John Biggs held a chattel mortgage with Charles Hedges from Robert McPherson to guarantee the latter's appearance in Court the following March.[20] In 1745 John Biggs had witnessed the will of his near neighbor Susanna Beatty. Then in 1760 he wrote his own will, naming his friend and neighbor Stephen Ramsburg as executor.[21] After his death Caspar Devilbiss tenanted his "Monocacy Manor" parcel, since his sons Benjamin and William Biggs had earlier moved to the area of present-day Carroll County north of Detour.

In 1745 Benjamin Biggs (1723-1785) married Henrietta Prudence Deborah Margaretta Munday, daughter of Henry Munday, and in the following year surveyed "Benjamin's Good Luck." This consisted of 214 acres near the present county road from Motters to Six's Bridge over the Monocacy. In 1751 he inherited from his father-in-law a 200-acre portion of "Trura" on the southeastern side of Monocacy" near the mouth of Double Pipe Creek "opposite William Bailey."[22] This he sold to George Shoemaker in 1763. He transferred his other land to his brother William Biggs and about 1769 with his family left Maryland to settle in the Ohio Valley of today's West Virginia panhandle. Joseph Ogle, son of Benjamin Ogle and husband of Benjamin Biggs' daughter Prudence Drusilla Biggs, went with them. Members of the family of Solomon Hedges, who earlier, after leaving Maryland, had settled on the South Branch of the Potomac in Virginia, also came to this panhandle region. Among the Draper Papers at the Wisconsin Historical Society in Madison is much information concerning Benjamin Biggs at Short Creek, near Wheeling, together with accounts of his activities in the Indian Wars, his role with the Continental Army during the Revolution, his return to Fort Pitt in 1779, his command of Fort Henry and Fort McIntosh, and his part in the Whiskey Rebellion of 1793 and the Virginia-Kentucky Resolutions of 1798-1799.[23]

William Biggs (1725-1803) stayed on in Maryland, having initially in 1754 surveyed "Anything" on the Six's Bridge Road to Mumma's

---

[17] See above, pp. 125, 293.
[18] C/S: BC & GS 9:453.
[19] Frederick County Land Records, E:497.
[20] *Ibid.*, E:353.
[21] Frederick County Wills, A1:152.
[22] *Ibid.*, A1:5.
[23] Lyman Copeland Draper (1815-1891), Manuscript Collections, 486 folio volumes, covering mostly the period after the Revolution, with emphasis on interviews with still living early pioneers. See especially Reuben Gold Thwaites, *Descriptive List of Manuscript Collections of the State Historical Society of Wisconsin* (Madison, 1906).

Ford. This was later expanded into a large resurvey called "Six Brothers," so named for William Biggs' six sons: William (married Catherine Furney), John (married Priscilla Wilson), Benjamin (married Elisabeth Ohler), Jacob (married Eva Moon), Frederick (married Mary Wilson) and Joseph (married Mary Kalb). William Biggs also had two daughters, Mary (married Joseph Ogle's son James) and Catherine (married Jacob Cookerly).

Elisabeth, the elder daughter of John Biggs Sr., married Daniel Pittinger in New Jersey, and they also came to Maryland. Pittinger purchased "Royenton Plains" from Henry Munday in 1745[24] and also leased Lot No. 3 on "Monocacy Manor" directly north of John Biggs' lot. Another daughter, Henrietta Biggs, married John Beatty, Jr., a son of Susanna Beatty, and after his death Jacob Barton. A son and namesake of the former, John Beatty [III] (1738-1821), moved to Guernsey County, Ohio. But Henrietta and Jacob Barton remained on "Monocacy Manor," leasing in 1754 Lot No. 59, situated on Israel Creek below Laurel Hill, two miles south of today's Woodsboro. Jacob Barton was Constable of Manor Hundred in 1750.[25] Still another daughter, Mary Biggs, married Joseph Doddridge, who in 1748 had "Antietam Level" surveyed on the present Frederick-Washington County line near the Pennsylvania border.[26] They later moved to Bedford County, Pennsylvania, where she was killed by a runaway horse. Catherine Biggs, the only daughter born in New Jersey, is presumed to have married René Julien and moved to the Carolinas. Sarah Biggs (1750-1822), only daughter of John Biggs' second marriage, married Joseph Hedges, Jr., and went to Bourbon County, Kentucky in 1792.[27]

The second lot on "Monocacy Manor" was leased on September 2, 1741 to **Joseph Wood** (1709e-1782), also of English descent. When, much later, the Manor lots were numbered, Wood's parcel became No. 56. It was leased on the lives of himself and his son Robert, whose ages were estimated in 1767 as 58 and 31 years respectively. Unlike John Biggs and the others who leased Manor land in 1741, Wood settled back away from the River along Israel's Creek, just south of today's Woodsboro. It was a significant location, for it provided the basis for an alternative routing of the so-called Manor Monocacy road running from the present city of Frederick to York County in Pennsylvania. For the first several years this road must have hugged fairly closely to the River, passing by the lots of John Bell, Frederick Clabaugh, Thomas Ebthorp, William Wilson, and John Biggs until it forded the River at a point on "Dulany's Lot" opposite Jacob Stoner's land on "Tasker's Chance" or farther along at today's Hughes Ford. But in November 1745 Joseph Wood petitioned the Prince George's County Court for a road from "Monocacy Crick from where the road crosses the said crick from over the mountain to Annapolis to Pensilvania." The inhabitants of "Monocacy, Israel and both Pipe Cricks," he claimed, were "very seldom warned [ordered] to clear the

---
[24] Prince George's County Land Records, EE:269.
[25] Rice, *The Life, op. cit.*, p. 60.
[26] C/S: BY & GS 1:192.
[27] Much genealogical work on the Biggs family was done during her lifetime by Ethel Close Buckey of Baltimore.

road." The Court made no change, but did make Wood overseer of the existing road. In 1748, by which time more of the central portion of "Monocacy Manor" had been leased, Wood tried again. By petition to the March Court of Frederick County he "humbly sheweth that whereas the road from Monocacy ford where John Hussey formerly lived that leads to Lancaster is very much used by travelers as well as by this inhabitant, and the road being very crooked and stopped up by trees falling across the same, and whereas this road might be laid out a shorter way and do less damage to the settlement that lay near the said road your petitioner therefore humbly prays that there may be a road laid out as aforesaid and three overseers to clear it, from Monocacy Ford crossing my Lord's Manor, crossing Little Pipe Creek and Great Pipe Creek to the temporary line."[28] This time the Court approved and ordered Nathaniel Wickham, Jr., Thomas Beatty and Joseph Wood to lay out such a road.[29] The result became the forerunner of today's Route 194 through Walkersville and Woodsboro, rather than along the Monocacy River farther west. The fact that by 1747 no settlers had surveys within miles of this Manor Monocacy road north of the Manor seems to indicate that at that date most through traffic bound for Pennsylvania used the German Monocacy Road on the opposite side of the Monocacy River.

About this same time it becomes evident that there were two Joseph Woods in the Monocacy area, and they were not father and son. Joseph Wood on "Monocacy Manor" styled himself as "Joseph Wood of Israel Creek," while his namesake who surveyed "Wood's Lot" near Unionville on March 25, 1747 was called "Joseph Wood of Linganore."[30] The latter's wife was named Mary. Joseph Wood of Israel's Creek had two wives, Sarah who died in July 1747 and Catherine Hedges Julien whom he married in September 1747. His son Joseph was born in September 1743. Joseph Wood of Israel's Creek served as foreman of the Grand Jury in 1751 and then became a Justice of the Frederick Court, serving continuously from 1753 through 1763.[31] In the latter year he leased for 21 years some additional land contiguous to his original lot on the Manor. As lot No. 57 it added a few acres to the south and west of his earlier lot, and had the effect of expanding the whole as a single unit. These were the lots which in his will of April 13, 1782 he called "Wood's Farm" and "Addition," leased by him, he said, as a part of "Monocacy Manor." His will named as his ten children Robert, Sarah, Joseph, Mary, Catharine, Abraham, John, Rachel, Rebecca and Ruth.[32]

In the survey made in 1781 when the lots were sold to General Smallwood as confiscated British property, Joseph Wood's son, Major

---

[28] Hussey's Ford was probably the same as what was later called Stoner's Ford. It was located near the mouth of Tuscarora Creek, some little distance north of today's crossing at Ceresville. See above, p. 281.

[29] Frederick County Court Judgment Records, A:18.

[30] Cf. C/S: TI 1:39 and Frederick County Land Records, B:180. See above, p. 103.

[31] Rice, *The Life, op. cit., passim.*

[32] Frederick County Wills, GM 1:272.

(later Colonel) Joseph Wood, [Jr.] was shown as tenant on both lots. The younger Joseph, beginning in 1772, had been surveying land in and around today's Woodsboro, including "Little Worth," "Better Than None," "This or None," "Link Together," "Wood's Chance," "No Whiskey," "Resurvey on Part of Good Neighbor," "Wood's Mill Land," "Worst of All" and "Woodstown Land." The latter was a resurvey made on July 20, 1785 which included Manor Lot No. 52, leased in 1752 to Nathaniel Wickham, but purchased at the 1781 confiscation sale by [then] Captain Wood. The resurvey also included John Digges' "Spring Plain" and some older tracts. On this land Woodsberry Town, now known as Woodsboro, was laid out. Its first lot was sold in 1786.[33] Joseph Wood's eldest son, Robert Wood, also had several surveys made, including "Nothing Ventured Nothing Get," "Addition to First Brother" and "Pleasant Forest." He had also purchased 326 acres of John Digges' "Spring Plain" and had leased "Monocacy Manor" Lots No. 63, west of Woodsboro, and No. 50, a tiny vacancy in the southeastern portion of the Manor.

Toward the end of 1741 three more lots were leased, all of them along the Monocacy River north of John Biggs' Lot No. 2. The first, called "Captains Lot," but designated subsequently as Lot No. 6, was leased to **William Wilson** on the natural lives of John Wilson, age 42 in 1767, William Wilson 37, and Thomas Wilson 26. The latter married Joseph Wood's daughter Elizabeth in 1767. Lot No. 6 was situated near the sharp bend in the Monocacy River opposite Hansonville. In 1767 William Wilson was shown as the tenant in possession, but by 1781, when the Manor was being readied for the confiscation sale, Valentine Mauk was there. Lot No. 11 went to **Thomas Ebthorp**, leased on the life of a Peter Members, age 40. James Dickson had not collected the rent in 1757,[34] and the 1767 review questioned whether Members was still alive, noting that Charles Hedge, Sr.[35] was then the tenant in possession. Hedges was still alive at the time of the confiscation sale, but inexplicably "widow Hedge" was shown as the tenant in 1781. Lot No. 37, west of today's Dublin Road at its intersection with Links Bridge Road, was leased to **John Bell**, on his life, that of his wife Elizabeth and of their son John. In 1767 they were judged to be 60, 50 and 27 years of age, respectively, but obviously had moved on to "Dulany's Lot" just south of the Manor, where we have met them previously[36] and where they could own their own land. In 1767 Charles Springer was the tenant in possession, and in 1781 Mrs. Springer was still there.

Johann Wilhelm Berg, whose descendants later changed the name to **Barrick**, was born in Nordhofen in the Westerwald region of Germany on July 8, 1683, the son of Johann Peter Berg. He married Johanata Maria Andreas there on January 11, 1708 and began a family of ten children.[37] The family is not included in the arrival lists at Philadelphia, but it does appear in New Jersey in 1730 when Johan

---

[33] Frederick County Land Records, WR 6:313.
[34] Scharf Papers, MS 1999, *loc. cit.*
[35] See above, p. 110.
[36] *Ibid.*, p. 126.
[37] From the extensive research of Henry Z. Jones.

William Berg and his three sons, Johannes, Pieter and Johan [Till[38]], were naturalized by act of Assembly.[39] Although Catharina Berg was in the Monocacy area marrying Peter Habach on November 26, 1738,[40] the first Maryland land record for this family dates from January 22, 1742 when William Berg leased a 250-acre lot known as "Berg's Delight." One of the largest lots on "Monocacy Manor," it was situated at the forks of Glade Creek and included the present-day intersection of Glade Road and Links Bridge Road, southwest of Woodsboro. It was subsequently known as Lot No. 44 and was tenanted after his death in 1750 by his sons William and Handel Berg.

This was just the beginning for this rather numerous family. On February 25, 1743 William's son Peter Berg leased Lot No. 25 ("Berg's Luck"), while on the same day his son John Berg leased Lot No. 26 to its south. Peter was 55 years of age in 1767 (born at Nordhoffen on November 27, 1712), his wife Catharine 48 and a son William 27. His brother John Berg, who was two years younger (born May 27, 1714), appeared in the 1767 review with a wife Judith, age 49, and son John, 29. John expanded his holdings on September 29, 1752 by leasing for 21 years[41] the contiguous Lot No. 27. Five months later, on February 24, 1753, the adjoining Lot No. 28 was leased to a cousin Christian Berg, born at Nordhoffen March 16, 1721 as a son of Johann Peter Berg, Jr. and Anna Catharina Schweitzer.[42] Christian later extended his holdings into Lot No. 14 which he held by certificate dated May 12, 1761. Finally, farther north, adjacent to their father's original Lot No. 44 then held by them, William and Handel Berg in October 1762 leased Lots No. 42 and 43, respectively.

By 1767 the family held eight lots totaling together just under a thousand acres. Through this area, from the most northerly Berg lot to the most southerly, flows Glade Creek. Half of the Berg lots were within today's municipal limits of the town of Walkersville. Individual locations may be observed on the map, page 322. Interestingly, the land of John and Christian Berg was surveyed in 1782 so as to exclude on four sides the five acres of land of the Glade Reformed Church north of today's Walkersville. Since the Church's beginnings about 1757[43] presumably postdated the Berg leases, it may be assumed

---
[38] The given names Johann Tillmann were contracted first to Hans Till and then to Handel.
[39] Theodore Freylinghuysen Chambers, *The Early Germans of New Jersey* (n.s., 1893), p. 633.
[40] Stöver, *op. cit.*, Marriages, p. 3, No. 195. Peter Habach and Catharina were back in the Readington and Harlingen areas of New Jersey in 1747. So also was her sister Elisabeth Berg and the latter's husband William Kaes [Case].
[41] This was the only Manor lot leased for a fixed term before the 29 leases made in the period 1759-1765.
[42] Christian Berg's father Johann Peter Berg, Jr. (born 1687) was thus a younger brother of the New Jersey immigrant Johann Wilhelm Berg (1680-1750).
[43] Glatfelter, *op. cit.*, pp. 190-191, observes in Pastor Conrad Steiner's diary the earliest reference to the Glade Church. He reported preaching to "the congregation in the Klet" on ten occasions

that the Bergs had been instrumental in its establishment on their own land. But since no deed had been possible on leasehold land, an Act of the Legislature in 1782 was necessary to prevent confiscation of the Church property. The church book, which was begun in 1769, is quite naturally saturated with entries pertaining to the Bergs and Barricks.[44] Peter Barrick's estate was administered by Catherine and Peter Barrick on June 19, 1775, John Barrick's by his son John on July 28, 1781, and Christian Barrick's on November 2, 1786 by his son Christian.[45] Handeal Barrick left a will dated June 19, 1786 which was probated May 5, 1787. It named his wife Judith and children John, Catherine, Henry, Frederick, and Isaac.[46] William Barrick also left a will. His was dated April 20, 1791, was probated May 19, 1791, and named children William, Susannah, Sarah, Jacob, George, Catherine [Devilbiss], Mary and Michael.[47]

On April 11, 1742 **Frederick Clabaugh** leased Lot No. 24, along the Monocacy River between the lots of Ebthorp and Bell. The term of the lease was based on the lives of his wife Mary, aged 66 in 1767, and son John, 35. But James Dickson was reporting in 1757 that rent was unpaid, and in 1767 Peter Hedge[s] was marked as tenant in possession. Peter Hedges (1717e-1792) was a son of Charles Hedges (1674e-1743) of Newcastle County, now Delaware, and is in turn assumed to have been a brother of the original Joseph Hedges for whom "Hedge Hogg" was surveyed in 1730.[48]

On July 25, 1742 **William Ellrod** leased "Monocacy Manor" Lot No. 30 on the lives of James Read aged 50 (in 1767), Mary 49, and Henry 27. Their relationship, if any, is unknown. The lot lay between today's Maryland Midland Railroad tracks and the Woodsboro Pike (Maryland Route 194) just north of Devilbiss Bridge Road on the outskirts of Walkersville. Ellrod is mentioned in the Moravian Journal kept by Brother Matthias Gottschalk on his journey to Maryland and Virginia in March and April of 1748. In attempting to provide a descriptive guide for subsequent itinerant Moravian preachers, Gottschalk wrote: "The places in Maryland where our brethren have an open door: ...In Manakasy are two places where we can preach. The usual place is at Mr. Weller's. Across the Manakasy a few German

---

in 1757. Since 1896 when the congregation moved into the town of Walkersville proper, the site has remained as the Church's cemetery. Holdcraft, *op. cit.*, in 1954 transcribed 750 of its gravestone inscriptions.

[44] The original of this church book was "rediscovered" by John P. Dern in a closet at the pastor's home in 1958. It was subsequently transferred to the Historical Society of the Evangelical and Reformed Church at Lancaster, Pennsylvania, where Elizabeth Kieffer then made a transcription of the German entries. Although the land survey records of 1781 began spelling the family name as "Barrick," this church record did not make the change from "Berg" until 1826!

[45] Frederick County Administrative Accounts, B 2:362, GM 1:82, GM 1:222, respectively.

[46] Frederick County Wills, GM 2:240.

[47] *Ibid.*, GM 2:378.

[48] See p. 106.

families live, about ten, who would perhaps like to hear a sermon. A man called Ellrod whom I visited there will be able to give more information."[49] This shows that Ellrod was present on "Monocacy Manor" at least from 1742 to 1748 so that Christian Creager, the tenant indicated by the 1767 survey,[50] must have come after those dates. Ellrod was not listed, however, nor was Creager, in James Dickson's 1757 summary of those "who have pay'd rents."[51] On June 14, 1736 Wilhelm Ellrodt was at Warwick (near today's Brickerville in northern Lancaster County, Pennsylvania) when he married Anna Beschell. On the same day, also at Warwick, Eliesabetha Ellrodt married Heinrich Bischoff.[52] As evidence that William Ellrod may have been in the Maryland area somewhat earlier than the initial lease date is the record in Pastor Stöver's Journal, of his baptizing at Manaquesen on June 24, 1741 Eliesabetha, daughter of Jeremias Ellrodt with Deterich Ellrodt and his wife as sponsors. On October 11, 1742, also at Manaquesen Stöver married Anne Catharine Ellrodt to James Conner.[53] The style and spelling of Stöver's marriage entry suggests he did not consider the bride to be a German.

John Hands may have been the German John Hend who took Lutheran communion from Pastor Candler on September 25, 1743 before his naturalization in October.[54] He was listed as having paid his rent in 1757 on "Hands Choice,"[55] the 200-acre lot subsequently known as No. 35, which lay just west of "Berg's Delight." But when the 1767 review was made, it was John Henn who was said to have leased the land on October 1, 1742 on the life of Sarah Henn, then 48, and Elizabeth, 28. Supposedly they had gone to "Caroline" some 16 years earlier, although this conflicts with the 1757 notation. Jacob Cremer was the tenant in possession in 1767.

Of four Manor lots leased in February 1743, Nos. 25 and 26, as mentioned earlier, went to Peter and John Berg. On February 24th **John Christian Smith** obtained Lot No. 18 along what was then thought to be the south border of the whole tract. The 1767 review of Manor leases noted that that lot had been leased on the natural lives of John Christian Smith, then 53 and still listed as tenant in possession, of William Smith 30 and, curiously, of Peter Berg, Jr., 28. In 1781, at the time of the confiscation survey, William Smith, son of Philip Smith, was tenant on this lot. In 1765 a William Smith, perhaps the same individual, leased the adjoining Lot No. 16.

Peter Evelant on February 25, 1743 leased Lot No. 5, fronting on the Monocacy River opposite the mouth of Muddy Run and lying just south of William Wilson's Lot No. 6. By 1757 this lot had been assigned to John Hoffman[56] for a term based on the lives of himself,

---

[49] Hinke and Kemper, "Moravian Missionaries," *Virginia Magazine of History and Biography, loc. cit.*,
[50] Brumbaugh, *op. cit.*, 2:53.
[51] Scharf Papers, MS. 1999, *loc. cit.*
[52] Stöver, *op. cit.*, Marriages, p. 3, Nos. 111 and 112.
[53] Stöver, *op. cit.*, Baptisms, p. 28, Marriages, p. 7, No. 384.
[54] Provincial Court Judgment Records, 1742-1744, EI 7:296.
[55] Scharf Papers, MS. 1999, *loc. cit.*
[56] *Ibid.*

age 55 in 1767, Barbara Hoffman, 56, and George Devilbiss, Jr., 22. By 1767 the latter was indicated as the tenant in possession.

The **Devilbiss Family** arrived early in this country, having come from Germany to reach Philadelphia on September 21, 1731. Presumably the parents had died enroute, for those who did arrive ranged in age from 10 to 22 years. Those listed on the Ship Captain's list included Hans Michel 22, Hans 18, Magdelena 18, Hans Georg 16 and Casper Debelbesin 10. No family name was shown for an Elizabeth Margerita, also age 18, who is presumed by the arrangement of names to have been another member of this family, even though three of the family thus claimed they were of the same age of 18, an adult age for the girls.[57] None was named Barbara, although on six different occasions in Stöver's records where a female "Teufersbiss" stood as a baptism sponsor, he inserted that given name, once simply as Barbara, three times as Anna Barbara, and once each as Catharina Barbara and as Eliesabetha Barbara! The latter may have been the Elizabeth Margerita named in the arrival lists. If the others were Devilbiss wives, they could have been the wife of only the eldest, Hans Michael Devilbiss, for the others at the indicated dates were still too young to be married.

Locating the families for whom these Devilbiss sponsors stood suggests that the Devilbisses possibly came to the Monocacy area about 1736. Anna Barbara Teufersbiss was a sponsor on January 1, 1735 for the eldest child of Joh. Georg Meyer, whom Stöver listed as from Swatara in today's Lebanon County.[58] Michael Reisner, who had not yet come to the Monocacy area, had a daughter baptized on the same day. But all the succeeding baptisms involved Monocacy families. These began on April 28, 1736 when Anna Barbara Teufersbiss was a sponsor for Anna Magdalena, second child of Joh. Jacob Mattheis of Manaquesen,[59] and Barbara Teufersbiss stood for Catarina Barbara, daughter of Baltasar Fauth.[60] Eliesabetha Barbara Teufersbiss (the sister Elisabeth Margareth Devilbiss?) was a sponsor on May 17, 1736 for Eliesabetha, daughter of Adam Backer of Manaquesen.[61] Catharina Barbara Teufersbissen (wife of Hans Michael Devilbiss?) was a sponsor the same day for Catharina Barbara, daughter of Matthias Rössel of Manaquesen.[62] Anna Barbara Teuffelsbissin was a sponsor for Catharina Barbara, daughter of Johann

---

[57] Strassburger-Hinke *op. cit.*, Lists 16ABC, pp. 48-50, 52-53.
[58] Stöver, *op. cit.*, p. 32. This entry also appears in the Lancaster Lutheran Church Book, *loc. cit.*, p. 407 (p. 10 in original).
[59] Stöver, *op. cit.*, p. 31. Joh. Jacob Hoof (Hoff), also of Monocacy (see p. 205n), was the other sponsor. The entry, like the one above, also appears in the Lancaster Church Book, *loc. cit.*, p. 405 (p. 7 in the original). The child's middle name is suggestive of the first named Devilbiss sister.
[60] Stöver, *op. cit.*, p. 15. Jacob Fauth was co-sponsor. This entry was *not* copied into the Lancaster Church Book.
[61] *Ibid.*, p. 16. She was the sole sponsor, the baptism was the only one for this family, and there was again no recopying from Stöver's Journal into later church books elsewhere.
[62] *Ibid.*, p. 15.

Georg Gump on June 16, 1737.[63] Later still, Catharina Divilplease was a witness to the will of Matthias Reasling [Rössel], March 25, 1747.[64] From these notations, assuming that the Devilbisses stayed relatively close together, one can conclude that the brothers and sisters had arrived in the Monocacy area perhaps five years before they are found on "Monocacy Manor."

Hans Michael Devilbiss (1709c-1755), the eldest, served as administrator for the estate of Magdalene Bancalf, who is believed to have been his sister.[65] The inventory, made by William Durrum[Dern] and John Bell on December 11, 1741, names George Devilbees, John Stull (his father-in-law), Mathias Reesling, James Reed,[66] and others known to have been on or near the Devilbiss area of "Monocacy Manor." In 1749 when John House was convicted of assault on the body of Mary Divelbess (her identity has not been satisfactorily established) and fined five shillings, Michael Divelbess, farmer of Frederick County, guaranteed payment of both fine and fees so that House could be dismissed.[67] On December 22, 1755 an administrative bond for the estate of Michael Devilbiss was posted by his brother George Devilbiss, and on the same date Margaretha Devilbiss declared, "I do hereby certify that the administration of my father Michael['s] estate is left to my Uncle George Devilbiss and I will not so administer the same."[68]

George Devilbiss (1715-1785) was the first of the family to appear on "Monocacy Manor." On November 28, 1743, he leased Lot No. 4, adjacent to and south of Peter Evelant's Lot No. 5. The term of the lease was for his natural life and that of his son John. In 1767 they were believed to be 55 and 27, respectively. Like other lots nearby, this lot was largely rectangular in shape with its long length running east and west, its short width fronting on the Monocacy to the west. By contrast, Lot No. 9, a contiguous lot to the northeast, lay in an approximately north and south direction with its short width on the north side also fronting on the Monocacy which here flowed from east to west. The latter lot had been leased originally to Richard Cooke, age 50 in 1767, on the lives of himself, his wife Mary Magdalene, 46, and son Richard Donaldson, 20. By

---

[63] Muddy Creek Church Book, p. 26. Although Stöver repeated all the Gump entries in this Church Book, it is clear that the family had settled in Monocacy as early as 1736.

[64] Frederick County Wills, 25:98 at Hall of Records.

[65] See Prince George's County Administration Bonds, Box 11, folder 66, for Magdalen Pongoffen (November 23, 1741) and Inventories, Box 13, folder 2, for Magdalene Bancalf, Hall of Records. The Inventory also appears in Prince George's County Inventories, ST 4:204 and in Prerogative Court Records, 1741-1742, 26:558, formerly DD 7:558. Michael Devilbiss was called "Tablepence" and "Dinalpost" in these records.

[66] Cf. William Ellrod's lot, above.

[67] Frederick Court Judgments, A:11. See also Rice, *The Life, op. cit.*, p. 13.

[68] Frederick County Administrative Bonds, 36:268; Administrative Accounts, A1:156, Hall of Records, Maryland Archives.

1757, however, this lot had been assigned to George Devilbiss, while Lot No. 4 was then occupied by his brother Caspar Devilbiss.[69] In 1764 George Devilbiss leased an additional 103 acres to the east of Lot No. 9, and this became known as Lot No. 15. These arrangements governed at the time of the 1767 review, but by 1781 Lot No. 5 was tenanted by George Devilbiss, possibly a son of Caspar, and Lot No. 9 was in the hands of John Devilbiss, son of George. After the death of John Biggs in 1761 Caspar Devilbiss also became the tenant on Lot No. 2, first leased by Biggs in 1741. By 1781, however, this lot had passed to William Smith, son of Philip Smith, who also held Lot No. 18, as above. Altogether, well over 700 acres of land, representing most of the western portion of "Monocacy Manor," were under lease to members of the Devilbiss family by the year 1767.

George Devilbiss died in 1785, leaving a will which made no mention of real estate.[70] His children were John, George, Catharina, Adam, Barbara, Rosanna and Frederick Devilbiss. Caspar Devilbiss on the other hand was deeply involved in land transcactions. "Hunting Lot," which had been surveyed in 1741 for Daniel Dulany adjoining Joseph Ogle's homestead near today's Loys Station, was patented in 1751 to Caspar Devilbiss.[71] In 1758 he was made overseer of the road from Major Ogle's [Stull's] Ford to Biggs Ford, virtually connecting, via the Manor Monocacy Road, his two locales. Caspar Devilbiss died in 1777, devising "Hunting Lot" to his son George, "Mill Seat," "Resurvey on Bill's Meadow" and "Deer Park" to his son John, and "Resurvey on Leonard's Range" on the lower German Monocacy Road to son Caspar, Jr.[72] His son George Devilbiss and his wife Elizabeth Ogle, daughter of Alexander Ogle, were buried at Graceham cemetery. Their son Alexander moved to Ohio where he founded the city of Alexandria. His descendants have spelled the name as DeVilbiss. Caspar's son John married Rebecca Ogle, also a daughter of Alexander Ogle, and lived north of the Monocacy River on the old Reverend William Williams homestead purchased by her father. Devilbiss Bridge Road, which now forms the northern limits of Walkersville before the road crosses the Monocacy to meet the Old Frederick Road and U.S. Highway 15, passes John Devilbiss' property. He was buried there in 1826 in a small Devilbiss Cemetery near the mouth of Fishing Creek.[73] Caspar Devilbiss' daughters Anna Elisabeth and Susanna married brothers, Jacob and Henry Ramsburg, sons of Stephen Ramsburg. Daughter Barbara Devilbiss married first Samuel Fleming and then Arnold Hardy. Caspar Devilbiss, Jr. moved to present Carroll County and became Constable of Burnt House Hundred (present-day Taylorsville). He married Maria Susannah Derr.

Handell Hann was the last to lease land on "Monocacy Manor" during the period ending in 1743. He leased Lot 8 on "Monocacy Manor" on December 6, 1743 on his own life and that of his wife

---

[69] Scharf Papers, MS. 1999, *loc. cit.*
[70] Frederick County Wills, GM 2:159.
[71] C/S: BY & GS 5:540.
[72] Frederick County Wills, GM 1:70. William Ballenger was his executor.
[73] Holdcraft, *op. cit.*, pp. 20, 326.

Mary and daughter Catherine. Their ages were stated in the 1767 summary as 45, 40 and 14 respectively, although the anomaly for Catherine, supposedly born ten years *after* the lease date, is apparent. The 1767 summary also noted that they had been gone to Carolina for eight years and that Frederick Baker was then the tenant. This can be substantiated by reference to a deed of December 6, 1753 from Handell Hann, farmer of Frederick County, wife Mary and daughter Catherine transferring the lease on the lot, which he called "Enyarts Folly," to Frederick Becker. The latter was to pay £55 to obtain the lease plus £3 for a year's rent and for arrears due for four years. Permission was granted for this transfer on July 22, 1758 and the deed was recorded four days later.[74]

Such were the beginnings on "Monocacy Manor" during Frederick County's first two decades of settlement. But they were only a beginning, as a comparison with the total number of lots leased by 1767 will show. Twice after 1743 leaseholders and their tenants were subjected to the bitter whims of fate. Despite the unexpired terms of their leases as well as the persevering efforts they had made in developing the land, tenants were twice threatened with sudden, wholesale eviction when the manors were put up for sale. The first of these threats came between 1766 and 1771 when Frederick Calvert, Sixth Lord Baltimore, attempted to sell all his manor lands. The sale was not a great success, however, and while some manors were sold in their entirety or nearly so, not a single lot on "Monocacy Manor" passed hands. The reasons for this failure lay in the high asking price, the scarcity of money itself, the poverty of potential tenant buyers and the fact that sales could not eliminate the unexpired terms of existing tenants.

During the American Revolution, however, the state's need for money and the ground swell against both British subjects and American Loyalists made confiscation inevitable. By this time the lease terms remaining on most manor lots had virtually expired. Payment terms were considerably eased, and prices were determined by auction to the highest bidder rather than by a pre-established asking price. In the case of "Monocacy Manor," payment could even be made by soldiers' pay certificates which were accepted at full face value. A traffic in these pay certificates by army officers and persons of wealth had permitted their concentrated acquisition at considerable discount. The confiscation sale thus permitted their immediate and profitable conversion from paper into valuable real estate.[75]

Tenants, whose meagre capital was vested not in cash but in the improvements they had made on their land, stood little chance against such bidders. Sixty lots on "Monocacy Manor" were sold to army officers with ranks from Captain to General. Fifteen civilians purchased 25 other lots, and one of them, William Bailey, was successful bidder for ten lots. Only two lots on "Monocacy Manor" were sold to a tenant on the land, and he, Joseph Wood, Jr., was also an army officer. It is beyond the scope of our study to follow the

---
[74] Frederick County Land Records, F:505.
[75] Stiverson, *op. cit.*, pp. 117-118.

speculative sale and resale of these lots after the auction. Some were still passing through various hands in the next century before they were finally patented. Likewise, the fate of the displaced tenants remains a study in itself. Theirs could not have been a happy situation.

We have record of further leases which were made after 1743 and up to 1767 when the Manor was considered almost fully tenanted. But without certificates of survey and without deeds to provide detailed lot descriptions we are at a loss to plat the components in map form. As a next best substitute, use may be made of the survey notes made in 1781 at the time of the confiscation sale. Naturally changes had occurred over the preceding four decades and errors discovered in earlier property descriptions served as the basis for creating new lots within the cracks and crannies. Still, a reasonable picture of the early lots can be derived by platting from the 1781 survey notes each of the 85 lots and then assembling the whole as one would work a jig-saw puzzle. This has been done on the maps depicted earlier in this chapter and on the following map on the next page. The latter shows all lots as they were delineated in 1781. In addition, a tabulation is added showing the salient factors concerning each of the lots as of 1768.

Monocacy Manor Leases, 1767-1768
Lots as Surveyed, 1781

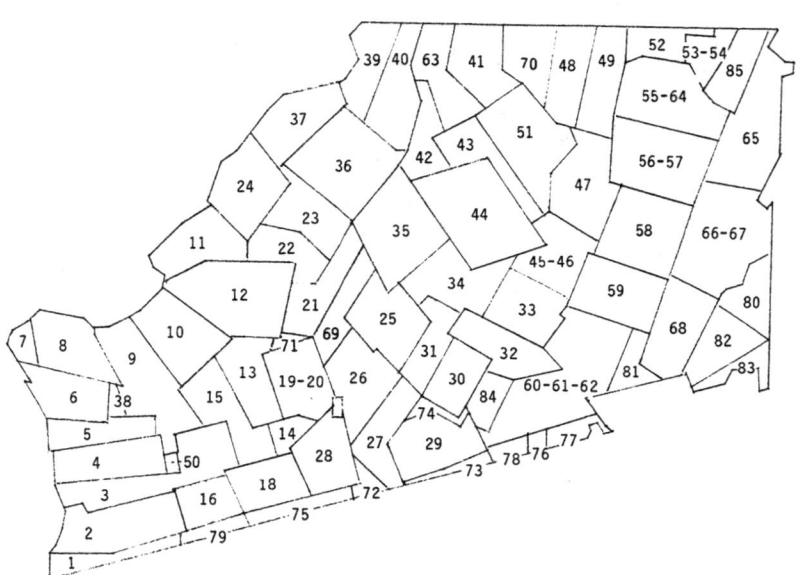

Lot No.	Lessee	Tenant in Possession	Lease Date	Acres 1767	Acres 1768	Term of lease: Years or Lives of:
1	Shover, Simon	Shover, Simon	Nov. 1, 1752	54	49	Simon Shover age 55, Adam s/o Simon 23, Peter Shover 21
2	Biggs, John	Devilbiss, Caspar	Aug. 23, 1741	203	175.5	Benjamin Biggs 43, William Biggs 40
3	Pattinger, Daniel	Miller, Geo, David, & Christian	Mar. 30, 1745	186	173.25	Daniel Pattinger 55, John Pattinger 27, Elizabeth Pattinger 50
4	Devilbiss, George	Devilbiss, Caspar	Nov. 28, 1743	125	138	George Devilbiss 55, John Devilbiss 27
5	Evelant, Peter	Devilbiss, Geo. Jr	Feb. 25, 1743	99	94.75	John Hoffman 55, Barbara Hoffman 56, George Devilbiss s/o George 22
6	Wilson, William	Wilson, William	Oct. 8, 1741	100	100.5	John Wilson 42, William Wilson 37, Thomas Wilson 26
7	Whitnall, Robert	Whitnall, Robert	June 25, 1761	33	29.75	21 years
8	Hann, Handell	Baker, Frederick	Dec. 6, 1743	120	137.25	Handel Hann 45, Mary Hann 40, Catharine Hann 13; all gone to Carolina 8 yrs.
9	Cooke, Richard	Devilbiss, George	Mar. 12, 1754	240	183	Richard Cooke 50, Mary Magdalene 46, Richard Donaldson Cooke 20
10	Hedge, Joseph	Hedge, Charles Jr	Aug. 26, 1748	150	158.5	Solomon Douthet 40; gone to Carolina, 14 yrs. Query if alive?
11	Ebthorp, Thomas	Hedge, Charles Sr	Dec. 22, 1741	100	100.5	Peter Members; query if alive?
12	Farrell, Kennedy	Crum, William	Nov. 8, 1752	250	172	John Farrell 20; query if alive?
13	Rodebaugh, Chrstn.	Cremer, Jacob	Oct. 29, 1751	132	128.75	Christian Rodebaugh 60, Elisabeth Rodebaugh 50, Valentine Wisecup 22; gone to Rays Town 12 yrs. Query if alive?

Monocacy Manor Leases, 1767-1768, cont'd.

Lot No.	Lessee	Tenant in Possession	Lease Date	Acres 1767	Acres 1768	Term of lease: Years or Lives of:
14		Berg, Christian	May 12, 1761*	50	51.75	
15	Devilbiss, George	Devilbiss, George	Oct. 10, 1764	103	103	21 years
16	Smith, William	Smith, William	Sep. 30, 1765	77	85.5	18 years
17	Shover, Simon	Shover, Simon	Sep. 29, 1764	18	22	19 years
18	Smith, John Christn	Smith, John Christn.	Feb. 24, 1743	100	106	John Christian Smith 53, William Smith 30, Peter Berg, Jr. 28
19	Keller, Jacob	Keller, Jacob	Oct. 29, 1764	11.5	11.5	19 years
20	Keller, Jacob	Keller, Jacob	Oct. 29, 1751	120	120	Jacob Keller 38, Mary Keller 17
21	Ritchey, Isaac	Ritchey, Isaac	June 3, 1763	100	100	21 years
22		Beard, John	Nov. 25, 1763*	85	96.25	
23	Shutter, Christian	Shutter, Christian	Feb. 9, 1763	100	85.5	12 years
24	Clapbough, Frdk.	Hedge, Peter	Apr. 11, 1742	150	144	Mary Clapbough 66, John Clapbough 35
25	Berg, Peter	Berg, Peter	May 3, 1753*	257	254.75	Peter Berg 55, Catharine 48, William Berg 27
26	Berg, Johannes	Berg, Johannes	Feb. 25, 1743	150	149	Johannes Berg 53, Judith Berg 49, John 28
27	Berg, John	Berg, John	Sep. 29, 1752	100	100.5	21 years
28	Berg, Christian	Berg, Christian	Feb. 24, 1743	122	119.5	Christian Berg 47, William 35, John 28
29	Adams, Martin	Adams, Andrew	July 22, 1753	136	138.25	Mary Adams 50, Henry Adams: query if there is any such person?
30	Elrod, William	Creger, Christian	July 25, 1742	100	95	James Read 50, Mary Read 49, Henry Read 27
31	Hoover, Henry	Hoover, Henry	May 6, 1761	90	86.25	21 years
32	Creger, Valentin	Creger, Valentine	Oct. 10, 1759	153	124.75	21 years
33	Hooper, Johannes	Hooper, Johannes	June 10, 1749	140	140.5	Johannes Hooper 47, Mary Hooper 37, Charity Hooper 21
34	Abell, Anthony	Cross, John	May 6, 1761	160	142.25	21 years
35	Henn, John	Cremer, Jacob	Oct. 1, 1742	200	203.5	Sarah Henn 48, Elizabeth Henn 28; in Carolina 16 years
36	Gregg, Nathan	Fulton, Robert	Apr. 4, 1745	230	228	William Gregg 40
37	Bell, John	Springer, Charles	Dec. 22, 1741	113	114.25	John Bell 60, Elizabeth Bell 50, John Bell 27
38	Silver, John	Silver, John	June 5, 1750	40	41.5	John Silver 45, Susannah Silver 18
39	Matthews, Samuel	Matthews, Samuel	Oct. 23, 1762	83	84.75	21 years
40	Matthews, John	Humbert, Frederick	Oct. 26, 1762	94	95.75	21 years
41	Humbert, George	Humbert, George	Sep. 29, 1765	200	148.5	18 years
42	Berg, William	Berg, William	Oct. 26, 1762	100	73.75	21 years
43	Berg, Handel	Berg, Handel	Oct. 20, 1762	75	52.75	21 years
44	Berg, William,	Berg sons Wm, Handel	Jan. 22, 1742	250	252	William Berg 40, John Berg s/o Handel 22
45	Crouse, Catharine	Smith, Martin	Mar. 12, 1754	80	64	Catherine Crouse 50, Christian Crouse 22
46	Smith, Martin	Smith, Martin	June 4, 1763	38	34.75	21 years
47	Jarvis, Jabez	Miller, Stephen	Sep. 30, 1763	150	150	18 years
48	Bernard, Luke	Bernard, Luke	Mar. 31, 1763	100	102.75	21 years
49	Bernard, Nathaniel	Hartman, Catharine	Mar. 30, 1763	90	87.5	21 years
50		Wood, Robert	Sep. 29, 1764*	45	45.5	
51	Swan, Robert	Yost, George	Sep. 28, 1762	180	177.25	21 years
52	Wickham, Nathaniel	Carver, John	Dec. 24, 1751	94	88	Nathaniel Wickham 38, Samuel Wickham 32, John Wickham 20
53	Perkinson, Thomas	Miller, Adam	June 20, 1749	47	44.5	Edward Perkinson 30, John Perkinson 27
54	Miller, Adam	Miller, Adam	June 1, 1763	33	32	21 years
55	Howard, Philip	Hufford, Christian	Nov. 12, 1747	150	160	Philip Howard, Sr. 66, Philip Howard, Jr. 41, John Howard 37
56	Wood, Joseph	Wood, Joseph	Sep. 2, 1741	100	101	Joseph Wood 58, Robert Wood 31
57	Wood, Joseph	Wood, Joseph	June 3, 1763	35	35	21 years
58	Harland, John	Harland, John	Feb. 25, 1744	125	135	John Harland 50, Joel Harland 27, John Harland, Jr. 24
59	Barton, Jacob	Crouse, Michael	Sep. 18, 1754	114	115.75	Henrietta Barton 46, Jacob Barton 28
60	Albaugh, Zachariah	Albaugh, Ann	Feb. 28, 1748	224	239.5	John Albaugh 36, Peter Albaugh 28
61	Albaugh, Zachariah	Albaugh, Ann	June 4, 1763	22	28.5	21 years
62	Albaugh, Zachariah	Albaugh, Ann	June 16, 1763	77	70.5	21 years
63	Wood, Robert	Wood, Robert	June 20, 1763	16	16	21 years
64	Hufferd, Christian	Hufferd, Christian	Nov. 4, 1762	10	12	21 years
65	Hertzog, Peter	Hertzog, Margaret	Sep. 29, 1759	100	101	Margaret Hertzog 55, Nicholas Hertzog 32
66	Smith, Philip	Smith, Philip	June 9, 1749	69	70.75	Philip Smith 60, Johannes Smith 23, Peter Smith 21
67	Smith, Philip	Smith, Philip	Sep. 29, 1764	133	133	21 years
68	Gross, Christian	Gross, Christian	June 9, 1749	115	117.5	Christian Gross 55, Mary Gross 45, Jacob Gross 25
69	Creger, Conrad	Creger, Conrad	Sep. 29, 1764	44	44	19 years
70	Miller, Christian	Miller, Christian	Sep. 29, 1764	4	7.5	21 years
				7694	7424	

* Held by certificate from date shown.

ROCKY RIDGE

A small but significant settlement near today's Rocky Ridge opened the way for development of the section of northern Frederick County extending west from Miller's Bridge to Loys Station. The area was near the German Monocacy Road as well as Cartledge's Old Road so that travelers from Pennsylvania bound for Virginia or for Jonathan Hager's place in today's Washington County often encountered here the sole habitation for miles around. The two earliest settlers, Joseph Ogle and Henry Munday, were of English descent, but were born in this country. Both had experienced the rigors of the Conojohelar border "war" and, like Reisner, Bankauf and some of the others, had then sought more peaceful surroundings in the Monocacy area. Both were looked to as leaders. And both eventually had extensive landholdings in the Monocacy area.

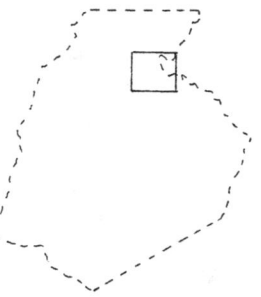

Joseph Ogle (1707-1756) was the grandson of one John Ogle (1649e-1684) who had come from England as a very young man — actually as a boy in his mid-teens. He was a member of the expeditionary force under Colonel Richard Nicolls which in 1664 wrested New Amsterdam from the Dutch and began English history in what we know today as New York.[1] Young John Ogle also participated later that year in the sequel expedition under Captain Robert Carr directed against the Dutch fort at New Amstel on the Delaware. That expedition was likewise successful, and the fort was renamed New Castle. There John Ogle settled to build a family and acquire considerable land in what is now the northern part of Delaware. His grandson Joseph Ogle, son of Thomas Ogle and Mary Crawford, was born in New Castle County and was married there in 1729 to Sarah Winters.[2]

Sometime before 1735 Joseph Ogle joined Thomas Cresap west of the Susquehanna River in what is today Pennsylvania. On June 20, 1735 Pastor Stöver visited the area, perhaps for the first time, and baptized Joseph Ogle's daughter Mary, born April 15, 1735. He indicated in his Journal that the Ogle residence was at Catores,[3] i.e.,

---

[1] The father of John Biggs of "Monocacy Manor" (see above, pp. 125, 309) was also a member of this expedition.
[2] Burr, op. cit., p. 310.
[3] Stöver, op. cit., p. 21. It should be remembered that the place names given in Stöver's Journal were the home locales of the children's parents, not necessarily where the baptism took place.

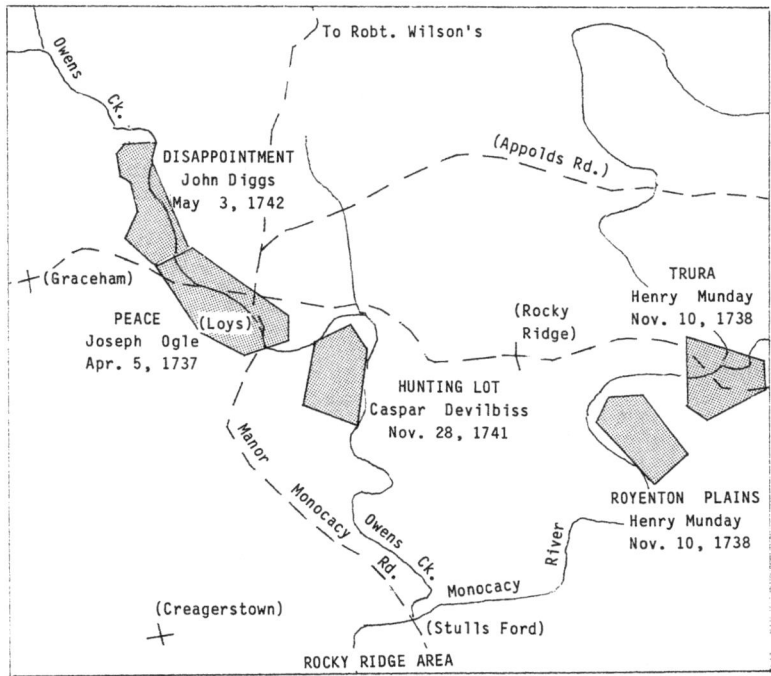

the Codorus Valley in which the city of York was later founded. Andrew and Mary McGuill [Magill], also of Catores, were the child's sponsors, and they, too, had a child baptized that day. Josep and Sarah Ogle were its sponsors. But on the next day, June 21st, Sarah Ogle and Hannah Crysop were sponsors for the baptism of a child of John Low, whose residence was recorded as Canashochele, or Conojohela Creek,[4] some ten miles east of the Codorus Valley, where this Creek flows into the Susquehanna below Wrightsville. Thomas Cresap also lived at Conojohela, and on July 21, 1735, a month later, Josep Ogle, Andrew McGuill, Philipp Ernst Grüber, Charlotta Friederica Grüber, Francis Foy and others, stood as sponsors for four of Cresap's sons.[5]

Although allegedly the Annapolis land records did not show it, Ogle claimed to have purchased his land, a part of "Great Meadow" on the south side of the Codorus, from Magill. There in his buckwheat field on September 23, 1735 the so-called Conojohela War[6] flared up. Andrew Magill, then in his sixties, was attacked by Sheriff Robert Buchanan and others from Lancaster County across the Susquehanna.[7] On November 24, 1736 Ogle witnessed the burning of

---

[4] Ibid., p. 15. As noted, the Creek is called Canadochly today.
[5] Ibid., p. 14.
[6] See above, p. 15-19.

325

Col. Cresap's home by Sheriff Samuel Smith of Lancaster County. Ogle seems not to have been a party to the defense of the house, being ordered from it and staying during the siege in a thicket some 300 yards away. After the house burned down, Cresap, who was wounded in the shoulder, and one or two other men were taken up the River toward Wright's Ferry as captives. One man had been shot to death and another may have escaped. Mrs. Cresap, Rachel Evans, [Frances Cannon] the wife of William Cannon, and John Lowe's daughter survived.[8] Joseph Ogle was still in the area on May 6, 1736 when, accompanied by Thomas Cresap, he was surveying on the west bank of the Susquehanna with Thomas Guin and Thomas Franklin.

Early in the following year Joseph Ogle abandoned the Susquehanna and Codorus Valleys to make his first survey in the Monocacy area. On April 5, 1737 he surveyed 250 acres near the present site of Loys Station, midway between today's town of Thurmont and the Monocacy River at Miller's Bridge. Quite understandably he called the tract "Peace." Its beginning point according to the certificate of survey was on the east side "of Little Captain's [Owens] Creek below Arnold Livers' land."[9] This was one of the most important road junction points in early western Maryland, for here came together Cartledge's Old Road, the German Monocacy Road, a road connecting to the Manor Monocacy Road via Stull's Ford, the road to Robert Wilson's and the road to Pipe Creek and present Carroll County. On January 1, 1745 Ogle enlarged "Peace" to 1,000 acres through a resurvey whose name indicated no doubt his subsequent prosperity. He called it "Peace and Plenty."[10] In his 1756 will Ogle referred to this land as "the plantation where I now live." He devised it to his wife Sarah.[11]

Further land acquisitions of a very sizable nature followed, making Joseph Ogle one of the wealthiest land owners of his day. On June 17, 1745 Thomas Cresap surveyed "Middle Choice" for Joseph Ogle.[12] It was located on Longs Mill Road between Ogle's Ford, now known as Stull's Ford, and Rocky Ridge. Lawrence Creager purchased the land and had it resurveyed in 1750.[13] "Fountain Low" was surveyed on February 16, 1748 as 1,050 acres beginning on the west side of Hunting Creek. It was a resurvey of Philip Crever's "Hunter's Lot"

---

[7] Proceedings of Council, 1732-1753, *Maryland Archives, op. cit.*, 28:81. Andrew and Mary "McGill" were still in the Codorus area in 1740 when they stood as sponsors for a child of Robert Hueston (Stöver, *op. cit.*, p. 15).

[8] "Attack on Cresap's House and Relation of the Case of Thomas Cresap of Baltimore County, Maryland," *Maryland Historical Magazine*, 3:33-47: affidavits by Thomas Cresap, Joseph Ogle, Frances Foy, Rachel Evans, Sophia Cannon, et al.

[9] EI 5:503. Livers' land was "The Back Land," later surveyed into "Arnold's Delight." Ogle's survey was the only one made in the area of today's Frederick County between July 1734 and January 1738.

[10] C/S: TI 1:423.

[11] Frederick County Wills, A1:90.

[12] C/S: LG E:567.

[13] C/S: GS 1:86.

and lay between Michael Reisner's plantation and present-day Creagerstown.[14] Joseph Ogle conveyed parts of this parcel in 1753 to Reverdy Ghiselin, Christopher Edelin and Nathaniel Wickham and by his will devised 50 acres to his son Jehu Ogle, "where his house now stands." Two parcels were surveyed for Ogle in today's Hauvers District, "Hog Hall" in 1749[15] and "Grazing Ground" in the Friends Creek area in 1751.[16] The latter was sold in 1754 to John Miller. "Content," surveyed in 1750 as 210 acres, had the same beginning point as did "Peace."[17] It was enlarged to 685 acres by a survey in 1752,[18] thereby making Ogle's land contiguous with the Moravian Church land at Graceham. Much later, in 1787, "Content" was resurveyed into "Good Fortune."[19] "Farmer's Delight" was surveyed in 1752 near Ogle's Ford.[20] Its subsequent conveyances included 150 acres to Peter Messner, 180 acres in 1769 to Martin Rouzer and 100 acres in 1770 to Christian Koone. Finally, "Ogleton" was surveyed in 1753 as a resurvey of "Samuel Reed's "Creave" and the land surrounding it.[21] "Creave" was described as being "below the ford that leads from the mountain to Pipe Creek."[22] The tract lay on the west side of the Monocacy River from Mumma Ford to near the mouth of Double Pipe Creek. "Ogleton" was patented, after Joseph Ogle's death, to his widow Sarah in 1757. She and her second husband, Adam Henry, conveyed parts of it in 1764 to Henry Neff and to John Griffith.

To the November 1741 Prince George's County Court a petition "of several of the inhabitants about Pipe Creek and Monocacy hereby sheweth that these petitioners being destitute of convenient roads from their several settlements toward the landing of proper places to transmit their goods and apprehend unless your Worships take the inconvenience we labour under into consideration it will remain so too long. Your petitioners hereby humbly pray your Worships that commissions may be issued for one good road from the Mountain near William Elder's through that part of the country most convenient for the inhabitants about Pipe Creek and Monocacy aforesaid, and that John Justice, William Roberts, Neal Poulson and William Elder, or any two of them, be appointed to lay out the same." The resulting road passed Joseph Ogle's homestead. The northwestern end of the road reached William Elder's "Slate Ridge" and was a part of Cartledge's Old Road. The eastern end passed Henry Munday's place,

---

[14] C/S: BY & GS 1:658. Thomas Cresap made the survey. See also Maryland Rent Rolls (Frederick No. 1), 32:221. The 1866 Map of Frederick County (Bond, *loc. cit.*) shows the homes of J. P. Bishop, Mrs. A. Groshon, G. Miller, and S[amuel] Eichelberger on "Fountain Low."
[15] C/S: BY & GS 1:659; patent: TI 4:408.
[16] C/S: Y & S 7:175.
[17] C/S: BY & GS 5:592.
[18] C/S: BC & GS 1:167.
[19] C/S: IC Q:357.
[20] C/S: GS 1:74.
[21] C/S: BC & GS 9:185.
[22] Frederick County Land Records, B:191, Samuel Reed to William Bail[e]y, 1750.

approximating today's State Route 77 through Rocky Ridge and Miller's Bridge.

There were other road descriptions which made reference to Joseph Ogle's place. In 1754 that portion of the German Monocacy Road which passed from Keysville across the Monocacy River at Mumma Ford and continued on toward Ogle's place via today's Appolds Road was known as "Ogle's Wagon Road."[23] What is today called Stull's Ford across the Monocacy between Longs Mill Road on the north and Oak Hill Road on the south, although now no longer used, was for many years known as Ogle's Ford. Road overseers were appointed annually, at least from 1750 to 1763, for the section of the Manor Monocacy Manor road described as running "from Major Ogle's Ford to John Biggs' Ford."[24]

On May 10, 1748 Joseph Ogle joined Stephen Ramsburg in making depositions to the Council of Maryland concerning the practice of forcing German settlers to pay excessive quitrents on their land.[25] When it came time to organize Frederick County and separate it out of the parent Prince George's County, Captain Joseph Ogle, Nathaniel Wickham, Jr., Major Thomas Sheredine, Thomas Franklyne, Thomas Beatty, Daniel Rawlins and Captain John Dorsey were appointed Commissioners to lay out the boundaries.[26] Governor Samuel Ogle's proclamation of December 12, 1748 establishing the Court of Frederick County was addressed to 23 individuals who were constituted as justices to organize the Court. Included were Joseph Ogle and his neighbor Henry Munday.[27] The March Court of 1749 appointed Edward Beatty, Joseph Ogle and Joseph Wood to lay out the road from "Captain" Ogle's Ford to Biggs Ford,[28] and the August Court of 1751 named Nathaniel Wickham, Joseph Ogle, Thomas Stoddart and John Middagh to arrange with a contractor to build a bridge over Israel Creek near Thomas Beatty's place.[29] The same Court appointed John Darnall and Joseph Ogle to serve as referees in a suit between Dr. Richard Cooke and Robert Debutts.[30] Clearly Joseph Ogle was looked to as a leader in the affairs of the fledgling County.

---

[23] C/S: BC & GS 1:359.
[24] Rice, *The Life*, op. cit., pp. 63, 117, 132, 175, 200, 217, 250.
[25] See above, p. 292.
[26] Proceedings of the Assembly, 1748-1751, *Archives of Maryland*, op. cit., 46:11, 142.
[27] Rice, *The Life*, op. cit., pp. 279-284, prints the Proclamation in full. Francis H. Hibbard, *The English Origin of John Ogle, First of the Name in Delaware* (n.s., 1967), claimed Joseph Ogle's father and the Governor were third cousins, descended from Luke Ogle of Eglingham (d. 1604). But the claim is a circumstantial one based solely on an English birth record whose chronology matches the age of Joseph Ogle's immigrant grandfather. Samuel Ogle served as Governor of Maryland from 1731-1732, 1733-1742 and 1747-1752. His wife was Anne Tasker, daughter of Benjamin Tasker, Sr. (1690-1768). See chart, p. 32.
[28] Rice, *The Life*, op. cit., p. 3.
[29] Ibid., p. 80.
[30] Ibid., p. 82.

Joseph Ogle was mentioned by the early Moravian missionaries as a friendly host who helped them with accommodation and transportation on their journeys through Maryland to Virginia. Matthias Gottliieb Gottschalk described his journey of 96 miles from Germantown in Virginia to Captain Ogle's in April 1748. He managed 36 miles on the first day and the remaining 60 miles on the following day, arriving at Captain Ogle's at midnight. In instructions to Brother Joseph[31] he noted that "Captain Ogle and Jacob Weller are both very dear hosts of the Brethren" and that "Kanigetschick[32] was situated 28 miles from Captain Ogle's across the little Blue Mountain toward the northwest where Jonathan Hager is our dear host... If Brother Joseph leaves Captain Ogle's house early Wednesday morning and rests during the hottest part of the day, he can be at Gottfried Mang's house[33] in good time to stay overnight. Captain Ogle might also give Brother Joseph the little gray horse which he had presented to Brother Lighton and which he does not need at all. Thus the journey across the fearfully extended mountains might be made much easier and the night lodging in the valley or on the mountains which are both very unhealthy places, could be avoided."[34] On October 21, 1749 Brothers Schnell and Brandmüller visited the ailing Captain Ogle.[35]

How Ogle himself felt about the Moravians is best revealed in a conversation he had with Pastor Henry Muhlenberg on the latter's visit to Frederick in June of 1747. Muhlenberg's account shows most clearly Ogle's disappointment and dissatisfaction with the English ministers and with Lutheran itinerants such as Carl Rudolph. Quite obviously he preferred the human qualities of his Moravian visitors to the stiff orthodoxy of such as Muhlenberg.[36]

Despite the variety of locales where their children were born, Joseph and Sarah Ogle listed in the records of the All Saint's English Church in Frederick all their births, except that of a last son George whom he named in his will. These children were: Jehu born 1731, Mary 1735, Sarah 1739, Eleanor 1741, Joseph, Jr. 1743, Benjamin 1747, Thomas 1749, William 1751, James 1753 and George.

By 1755 the war clouds were gathering, presaging the coming French and Indian War. On July 9th General Braddock met defeat near Fort Duquesne. But Joseph Ogle did not live to see the threat developing against the outposts of western Maryland. He passed away on April 29, 1756.[37] Leadership was now passing from his generation to the next. Typical of the new leaders was Ogle's own son-in-law Peter

---

[31] August Gottlieb Spangenberg; see above, p. 148.
[32] Conocheague became a German settlement along the Creek of the same name which flows from Pennsylvania through today's Washington County a little west of Hagerstown and empties into the Potomac at Williamsport.
[33] Between today's Smithburg and Leitersburg in Washington County. Mang died in 1754 (Frederick Administrative Accounts, A1:54, 100).
[34] Hinke and Kemper, "Moravian Diaries" *loc. cit.*, 12:75, 78-79.
[35] Schnell, "Kurze Beschreibung," *loc. cit.*
[36] Tappert and Doberstein, *op. cit.*, 1:159.
[37] All Saints Church Book, Frederick. See below, p. 353.

Butler, husband of his daughter Mary Ogle.

On August 30, 1756, Governor Sharpe wrote, "As some advices which I have just received give me great room to fear that a large body of French and Indians will very shortly make a descent on this province and endeavor to break up at once all our settlements in the western parts of Frederick County, and as it is thought expedient and necessary to march a considerable number of the Militia to cover and protect the distant inhabitants...." they will "be supplied with arms and ammunition by Captain Peter Butler of Frederick Town .... the troops are to be put under the command of Colonel Thomas Prather, who lives near Conegocheige."[38]

A week later, on September 5, 1756, John Hall wrote the Governor from Baltimore: "I am also to inform your Excellency that one William Roberts, who is an esteemed man of credit, was with us yesterday and says that he came through South Mountain Thursday last, this side of which he saw houses burnt about four miles from Major Ogle's and that a messenger came to him yesterday morning to give him an account that four men were killed the same day he came through the mountain and at the same gap he passed, which is about sixty-five miles from this place [Baltimore]."

Caspar Schmidt and his wife Christina lived some seven miles from Joseph Ogle's place in the vicinity of present-day Lantz between Sabillasville and Thurmont. They had made a resurvey on Cresap's "Mount Olivet" in 1751.[39] There in 1756, allegedly before her father's eyes, their young daughter Christina was captured by Indians. She was held captive until 1758 when she was released in Philadelphia, but was falsely claimed by a Lancaster resident. Not until a chance meeting in 1769 was she reunited with her family.[40]

We have undated rosters for a number of Maryland Militia Companies which list the names of men who were prepared to serve in the frontier defenses about this time. The lists are included in manuscript form in a book of some 109 pages now kept at the Maryland Historical Society in Baltimore. Interestingly most of these Companies were commanded by men whose earlier land dealings are noted in our pages. Among them, each serving with the rank of Captain, were Elias Delashmutt, John Middaugh, Joseph Chapline, Jonathan Hager, Peter Bainbridge, Stephen Ransberger [Ramsburg] and the aforementioned Peter Butler. Four of these rosters have been included in the Appendix to this work. Since generally the lists provide something of a census of those individuals who were living in the same areas where their Captains resided, it may prove interesting to review the list of names included on the roll for the Company commanded by Joseph Ogle's son-in-law Peter Butler.[41]

Joseph Ogle's 1756 will cryptically noted that "Mary and Peter Butler have parted from each other."[42] Still, when Captain Butler

---

[38] Proceedings of Council, 1753-1761, *Archives of Maryland, op. cit.,* 31:159-160.
[39] C/S: GS 1:94.
[40] Oerter, *op. cit.,* p. 22.
[41] See p. 378; *Maryland Historical Magazine,* 9:260-280, 348-370.
[42] Frederick County Wills, A1:90.

wrote his own will in 1764, he named his wife Mary as executrix.[43] After his death she married Henry Brawner and in 1779 as "Mary Brawner, late widow and relict of Peter Butler," released her rights of dower in the sale of "College Green" to Alexander Ogle.[44] Butler does not appear in early land records before 1743, although in June of 1742 the Prince George's County Court fined him 500 pounds of tobacco, based on testimony from Thomas Cresap that he had neglected his duty as a road overseer. Subsequently his land interests included, in addition to "College Green," other parcels called "Good Will," "Paradise," "Magruder's Thicket," "Locust Thicket," "Paradise Enlarged" and "Butler's Lot." The latter was surveyed near the head of a small draft of Fishing Creek next to "Miller's Chance."[45] This was later resurveyed from 120 to 296 acres.

Joseph Ogle's son William served in the Dunmore War under Thomas Cresap's son Michael Cresap and was present at the signing of the Dunmore Treaty. He also served with Daniel Cresap, Jr. during the Revolution. With his wife Mary Cresap, whom he married in 1777, he had twelve children. Joseph Ogle's daughter Sarah Ogle married her cousin Thomas Ogle in 1756, and their daughter Judith became the wife of Nathaniel Livers.[46] Son Benjamin Ogle married Rebecca Stilley, daughter of Peter Stilley.[47]

Benjamin Ogle (1715-1779) and Alexander Ogle (1730-1783), brothers of Joseph Ogle, also came to Frederick County. Benjamin first appears in 1741, signing the petition for a road from William Elder's to Pipe Creek.[48] Presumably he lived with his brother Joseph Ogle until the latter's death in 1756. He then moved west into today's Washington County where he died in 1777.[49] His sons Joseph, Jacob and Thomas Ogle pushed on into the Ohio Valley, where their exploits on the frontier are recorded in the Draper Papers.[50] Joseph Ogle married Prudence Drusilla Biggs, daughter of Benjamin Biggs and granddaughter of Henry Munday. Their land on Buffalo Creek in today's Brooke County, West Virginia was adjacent to that of Silas and Joseph Hedges. Commissioned a Captain in 1776 by Governor Patrick Henry,[51] Joseph Ogle experienced many bloody encounters and proved himself a fearless frontier fighter. Jacob Ogle, an ensign in his brother's company, met death in Foreman's Massacre. Thomas Ogle, also a Captain, was killed in the Sandusky Expedition. In 1785 Joseph Ogle sold his land on Buffalo Creek[52] and moved on to Illinois Territory. Ogle County in Illinois was named for him, though he never lived within its confines.

---

[43] Frederick County Wills, A1:215.
[44] Frederick County Land Records, A:435.
[45] C/S: Y & S 7:159.
[46] Frederick County Land Records, WR 46:307.
[47] See above, p. 114.
[48] Cf. above, p. 56.
[49] Frederick County Wills, GM 1:126.
[50] See above, p. 310n.
[51] Order Book 1:2, January 7, 1777, Court House, Wheeling, West Virginia.
[52] Ohio County [West Virginia] Land Records, B 21:62.

Alexander Ogle was still a boy when the first two decades of settlement in the Monocacy area ended. Another two decades would pass before he made his appearance in Frederick County. He did so on December 16, 1763 as "Alexander Ogle of New Castle County," grantee of 250 acres of "Williams Project" on the west bank of the Monocacy River near the mouth of Fishing Creek.[53] Later he interested himself in land investments in the panhandle area of today's West Virginia, where his nephews had settled. But he himself never moved west of the Monocacy Valley. On the west side of Devilbiss Bridge he built his residence and mills, whose remains may still be seen today. He was a lifelong miller and supplied flour to the troops during the Revolution. In 1783 he devised his home and mills to his wife Martha, while the land in Ohio County, [West] Virginia went to his daughter Martha, wife of John Wood. His other children included Elizabeth (wife of George Devilbiss), Rebecca (wife of John Devilbiss), Alexander Ogle Jr. (husband of Mary Beatty), Jane (wife of Adam Link) and Mary (wife of Samuel Cock).[54]

Henry Munday (1682c-1751) was somewhat older than his friend and future neighbor Joseph Ogle, but was nevertheless also involved in the land disputes on the west side of the Susquehanna River in today's Pennsylvania. Munday was English and, if the same man, first appears in the records as a witness and devisee named in the 1710 will of William Howard in Baltimore County.[55] He was of London Grove Township, Chester County, when in 1736 a number of individuals asked him to intercede with Governor Samuel Ogle for help in obtaining land in the disputed area west of the Susquehanna. Munday went to Annapolis where he joined with Edward Leet and Charles Higginbotham in obtaining orders for Thomas White as Deputy Surveyor to lay out 200-acre parcels for each of them and for 49 other individuals named by them. Allegedly some or all of the land represented parcels previously taken up on warrants from Maryland by Germans who had subsequently turned to Pennsylvania for support and protection. Munday denied that this was their intent, claiming that they wanted only land which was vacant. In any event it was Cresap who pointed out specific lands available for survey, and supposedly received arms from the Maryland authorities for use in ousting such "defecting" Germans.

This so-called "Chester County Plot" was discovered by the Pennsylvanians and warrants were issued for arrest of its principals, especially Henry Munday. On November 15th he was captured at his home. Papers were found which allegedly incriminated him in the "plot," and detailed the names of the land applicants. Seven of these were members of the Charlton family. Munday was taken to Philadelphia as a prisoner. Edward Leet was also arrested, but Higginbotham escaped.[56]

---
[53] Frederick County Land Records, J:56. See below, p. 345.
[54] Frederick County Wills, GM 2:25.
[55] Maryland Calendar of Wills, *op. cit.*, 4:146; probated March 5, 1717. Aquilla Paca and Thomas Bond were also witnesses.
[56] *Minutes of the Provincial Council of Pennsylvania* (Harrisburg, 1851), 4:100-109. See also Gibson, *op. cit.*, pp. 64-66.

Like his friends at Susquehanna, Henry Munday after his release deserted the disputed area for the peace of Monocacy Valley. There on November 10, 1738, a year and half after Joseph Ogle had arrived, Robert Owings surveyed two tracts of land for Munday. "Trura" had a beginning point at the mouth of a valley, some forty yards from the Monocacy near the mouth of Pipe Creek.[57] It included the mouth of Pipe Creek and lay partly in today's Carroll County. "Royenton Plains" began on the "east side of Monocacy Creek a half mile below where Pipe Creek falls into Monocacy Creek."[58] In 1745 Henry Munday resurveyed "Trura" into 844 acres.[59] "Royenton Plains" was sold to Daniel Pittinger,[60] who had it resurveyed as 119 acres, also in 1745.[61] The two resurveys based on Henry Munday's original land surveys then represented a contiguous whole extending along the Monocacy River almost from Mumma Ford on the north, past Miller's Bridge south to where the Potomac Edison transmission line now crosses the River. This land was connected to Ogle's land to the west by means of a road sought by a petition to the Prince George's County Court in 1741. The resulting road approximated today's Rocky Ridge Road, State Route 77, from Keymar to the west.

On December 13, 1748 Frederick County was organized as a separate entity, distinct from its parent Prince George's County. Henry Munday was chosen as one of the five Justices selected to manage the affairs of the new County. The others were Thomas Beatty, Thomas Prather, William Griffith and Nathaniel Wickham, Jr. The following November Justices Wickham, Munday and Griffith were given the task of arranging the contracts for construction of the new Court House. Through these initial years Munday continued to serve. He remained a Justice until his death in early 1751.[62]

Henry Munday had been a Major in the Maryland Militia and so appeared on a list for the Western Division of Maryland as submitted by Thomas Cresap. In August of 1750 he was listed as *Colonel* Henry Munday when with Thomas Wilson of Toms Creek he entered into a writing obligatory with Mary Sparks, executrix for the estate of Joseph Sparks, thereby assuring payment to Sparks' heirs of legacies due them.[63]

He was especially dear to the early itinerant Moravian

---

[57] C/S: LG C:292.
[58] C/S: LG C:176
[59] C/S: TI 1:456.
[60] Prince George's County Land Records, EE:269. Daniel Pittinger had come from New Jersey where he met and about 1733 married Elizabeth Biggs, daughter of John Biggs (p. 311). On March 30, 1745 he had leased Lot No. 3 on "Monocacy Manor" (just north of the Biggs Lot No. 2) on the lives of himself (age 55 in 1767), Elizabeth (age 50) and son John Pittinger (age 27). By 1767, however, George, David and Christian Miller were tenants on Lot No. 3. No relationship is known between these tenants and Abraham Miller or the later Millers at Miller's Bridge east of Rocky Ridge.
[61] C/S: TI 1:41.
[62] Rice, *The Life*, op. cit., pp. ix, 24 et passim.
[63] Ibid., pp 51-52.

missionaries. Gottschalk in March 1748 noted in his diary a visit at Jonathan Häger's place [near today's Hagerstown] from "Captain and Justice [Thomas] Prather" who "brought greetings from Major Munday and Colonel Crassop." In July of the same year four missionaries arrived in the Monocacy area from Bethlehem, Pennsylvania. Here they separated. Brothers Owen Rice, a Welshman, and John Hopson turned to the southeast toward the lower parts of Maryland and Virginia, while Brothers August Gottlieb Spangenberg[64] and Matthew Reuz[65] headed northwest to Antietam and Conococheague. Major Munday went with the latter pair all the way "from Manakesy to the South Branch of the Potomac." On July 12th they passed over South Mountain and came that same day to "Canigotschik" where they inspected a remarkable cave extending into the earth some three hundred yards and having a capacity at its opening for a thousand people to stand. They stayed the night at the home of Jonathan Hager, baptizing his daughter and the granddaughter of Father Loescher whom they had met on the way. On July 13th they visited several plantations and then came to the home of Captain Baret where they held religious services, preaching to a number of people in English. They stayed the night here and on the following day traveled northwest over the high mountains "called the Blue or North Ridge." On July 16th they came to the home of "Colonel Christopher Grissop,"[66] who owned a fertile piece of land towards the source of the "Potomack" which he had purchased from the "Shawanos."[67] On Sunday July 17th, Spangenberg preached a sermon in English to a number of people and then his party left to cross the North Branch of the Potomac and spend the night with Urbanus Krämer on the South Branch. There on Monday morning Major Munday, "a man of 66 years of age" who had accompanied them "more than a hundred miles," left "with tears in his eyes" to return to "Manakesy."[68]

Henry Munday had other interests far afield from his home. With Thomas Cresap he witnessed a deed transferring "Chancey" from Richard Touchstone to George Moore, Sr.[69] He signed a petition for a road from the mouth of the Conococheague to Harris' Ferry, i.e., from Williamsport to Hagerstown and on to Harrisburg. In 1744 he signed a further petition, along with 60 others from today's Washington County, for a road via Richard Touchstone's.

Henry Munday's will of January 28, 1751 was the fourth to be recorded in the new Frederick County. By it he left 200 acres of "Trura," struck off from the upper end of the original tract opposite William Bailey, to his son-in-law Benjamin Biggs. His daughter Henrietta Biggs and her children were the only descendants

---

[64] See note, p. 148.
[65] For Reuz, see above, pp. 148, 152.
[66] Col. Thomas Cresap!
[67] The Shawnee Indians. See above, p. 14.
[68] Hinke and Kemper, *loc. cit.*, 11:236-237. Interestingly, on that same July 18th the Moravians passed through a district settled by "Hollanders from Sopus," i.e., the van Metres and others from Esopus [Kingston], New York.
[69] Frederick County Land Records, B:104.

mentioned. But he left bequests to a number of godsons and friends, including Thomas Charlton, Michael Cresap (son of Thomas Cresap), John Roberts (son of William Roberts of Pipe Creek), Jonathan Hager, Conrad and Maudlin Hogmire, James Dickson and Arthur Charlton. To Mr. Neighbourg [Lars Nyberg], one of our Moravian ministers, he devised "my saddle and my hair to make him a wig." A tract in Philadelphia County [Pennsylvania] on the Frankfurt Road next to the land of Isaac Norris was to be sold out as building lots. The residue of his estate was then to be paid over to Joseph Ogle, [Jacob?] Matthew and Jacob Weller "for the benefit and encouragement of the [Graceham] school, which is now near said Ogle's land."[70] James Dickson and Jonathan Hager were his executors and in April Joseph Ogle and William Bailey prepared the estate's inventory.[71]

After his death, Henry Munday's executors sold 320 acres of the "Resurvey on Trura" to Nicholas Warner and 324 acres to Jacob Sharrough.[72] John Flower (formerly Johannes Blumenschein) then purchased 77 acres from Sharrough and 50 acres from Warner[73] which he used as the basis for a new resurvey in 1787 called "Pipe Creek Hill."[74] In 1864 Mary Ann Miller, widow of William Miller, Sr., conveyed this land to her eldest son, John William Miller, "it being the same tract patented to John Flower in 1789."[75] In 1829 William Miller used Pittinger's land plus other older tracts for a resurvey which he called "Miller's Fancy."[76] Its beginning point was "at the corner of a graveyard called Pittinger's graveyard."[77]

Not often were road petitions as detailed as the one which included the Rocky Ridge area, as presented to the November Court of 1752 by Dr. Charles Carroll. He asked that "a road be cleared and made a public road from the waggon road under the South Mountain about half a mile to the southward of the Meeting house [the original Monocacy Lutheran church] and to the northeast side of the plantation of Michael Risener [approximating today's Kelly's Store Road] and from thence to Mr. Ogle's sawmill and thence to Owens Creek about two miles below Mr. Ogle's house, and a little below the mouth of Beaver Dam Branch, thence to Monocacy below the plantation of David Baily, thence through Mr. Munday's land to the mouth of Little Pipe Creek and across the said Great Pipe Creek unto the Fork between both and up the said fork to the main waggon road that leads to William Farquers [Union Bridge] as the same has been

---
[70] Frederick County Wills, A1:5.
[71] Frederick County Inventories, A1:181. For William Bailey, see also above, p. 320.
[72] Frederick County Land Records, E:910-911.
[73] Maryland Rent Rolls (Frederick No. 1), 32:180.
[74] C/S: IC D:390, November 4, 1787; patented November 16, 1789. "Pipe Creek Hill" also included a part of the "Resurvey on Sixth Dividend," surveyed for Charles Carroll in 1766.
[75] Frederick County Land Records, JC 6:614, JWLC 2:136.
[76] C/S: GGB 2:119.
[77] Holdcraft, *op. cit.*, p. 30, called this cemetery, his No. 57, the Pittenger Family Cemetery at Millers Bridge. Only three inscriptions remained in 1959.

lately marked by Matthew Sparks at the instance and charge of your petitioner."[78]

Also in the Rocky Ridge-Loys Station area two surveys made for land investors may be mentioned. They are located on the map, page 325. Daniel Dulany had 150 acres surveyed on November 27, 1741 which he called "Hunting Lot." The tract was located on the "south side of a branch of the Monocacy called Little Captains [Owens] Creek within a few perches of Captain Joseph Ogle's land."[79] Ten years later, on November 18, 1751, this land was patented to Caspar Devilbiss, whom we have met above.[80]

Similarly John Diggs had 182 acres surveyed "in the back woods" near "Arnold's Delight." His survey was dated May 3, 1743 and was called "Disappointment."[81] In late 1767 Edward Diggs passed title to this parcel to Jacob Davis.

---

[78] Rice, *The Life, op. cit.*, pp. 108-109.
[79] C/S: BY & GS 5:540.
[80] See p. 319.
[81] C/S: LG E:196.

MID-MONOCACY SETTLEMENTS

Occasionally early settlers came individually, not fitting together in reasonably cohesive neighborhoods and not particularly defining a specific time or place related to other individuals in the early history of the Monocacy Valley. But they were present and should be acknowledged.

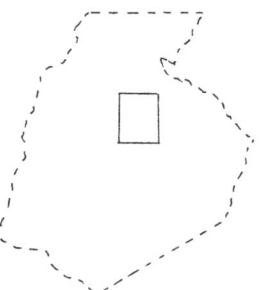

One such individual, **Nathaniel Wickham** by name, played a most significant and influential role in the actual formation of Frederick County itself. He was a man who deserved the gratitude of his contemporaries, yet who was destined to bear the saddest of fates.

For many years he was known as Nathaniel Wickham, Jr., because his father, with the same name, lived to be over ninety years of age.[1] The senior Wickham had married as his second wife Sabina Barnard, widow of Thomas Barnard. The two families undoubtedly had been friends earlier, for Nathaniel Wickham witnessed Thomas Barnard's 1694 will,[2] and Luke Barnard, Thomas' son, named one of his sons for his step-father. Presumably Nathaniel Wickham, Jr. was a son of his father's earlier marriage. The Wickhams owned land in lower Prince George's County, where Nathaniel Sr. was listed as a taxable in Collington Hundred in 1719[3] and both his son and he were taxables in Potomac Hundred in 1733. The two Nathaniels, together with Luke Barnard, contributed toward the erection of Rock Creek Chapel near what is now Rockville in Montgomery County. From all indications in the land records, the older Nathaniel seems to have stayed in present-day Montgomery County.

Nathaniel Wickham, Jr. married Priscilla Tyler, daughter of Robert and Mary Tyler[4] and sister of Elizabeth Tyler who married

---

[1] So he reported to the Prince George's County Court of 1746.

[2] Prince George's County Wills, 7:100. Thomas Barnard named his wife Sabina as executrix. Nathaniel Wickham of Calvert County, now Prince George's County, with wife Sabina Wickham filed her accounts for Barnard's estate (Prince George's Inventories and Accounts, 13 B/67). Sabina inherited land on a branch of the Patuxent River, and her two children, Luke and Mary Barnard, also received land from their father's estate.

[3] *Maryland State Papers No. 1, The Black Books*, op. cit., para. 163 in the *Calendar*.

[4] By his will of 1735 (Prince George's County Wills, 21:911) Robert Tyler devised 200 acres "at the head of the eastern branch of

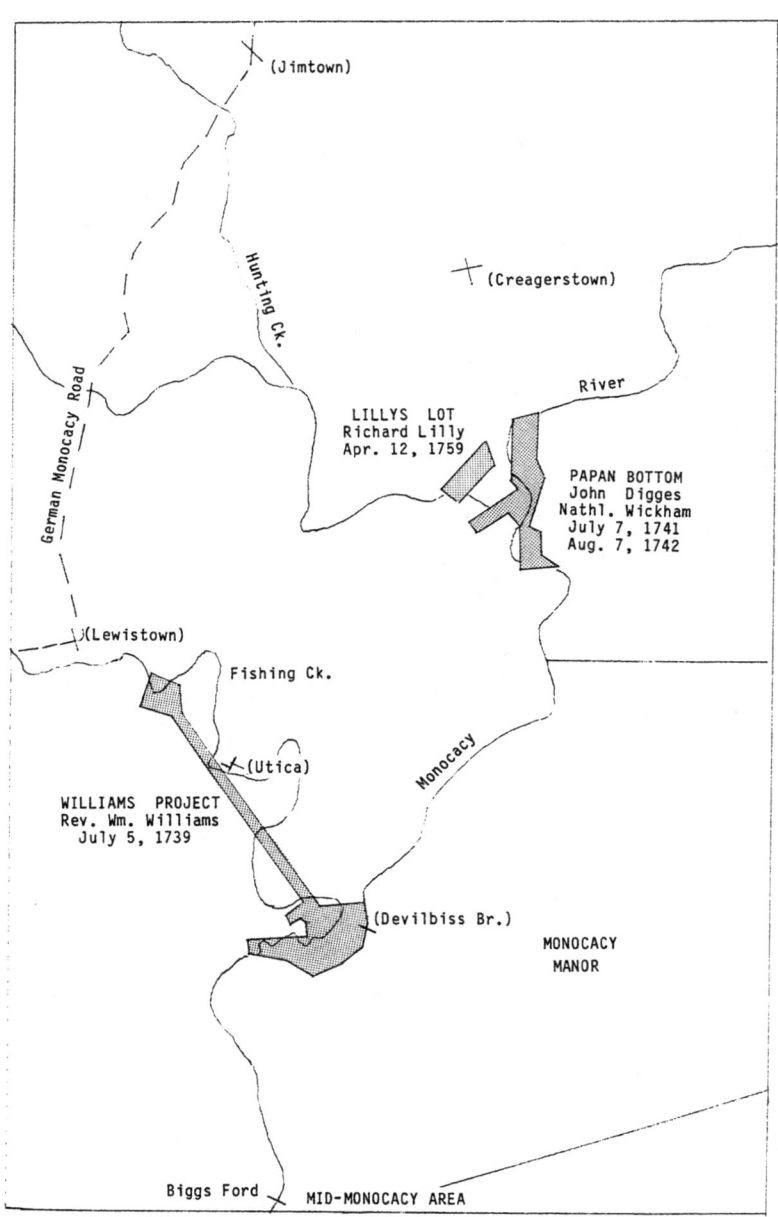

Samuel Pottenger. On January 1, 1721 the two brothers-in-law, Nathaniel Wickham, Jr. and Samuel Pottenger, had a survey made for 1,000 acres in what is now Montgomery County. They called it "Wickham's and Pottenger's Discovery."[5] In March of 1723 they had another 400 acres surveyed in the same locale, and this they called "Fellowship."[6] The 1723 Prince George's County Court appointed Nathaniel Wickham Jr. a ranger for that County and ordered him to lay out a road from his plantation to Sugarland and another to the mouth of Seneca Creek. These appear to be forerunners of today's Maryland State Route 28 from Hunting Hill to Beallsville and Route 112 from Hunting Hill to Seneca. By his will of 1735 Samuel Pottenger gave to each of his sons, Robert and John, 200 acres of "Wickham's and Pottenger's Discovery," the tract "which I bought of Nathaniel Wickham, Jr."[7] Nathaniel Wickham, Jr. had other land in this area, for on March 9, 1748 he sold to William Cummings for five pounds "all that tract of land called 'Hope' near Little Monocacy and near the upper road from Sugarland to Monocacy Ferry."[8]

The first piece of land in the back country which was laid out for Nathaniel Wickham, Jr. was "Clarke's Discovery." An original survey was made on June 14, 1734, but the patent went to John Digges in 1737.[9] "Friends Good Will," on the other hand, was a survey for John Digges, which was patented to Nathaniel Wickham, Jr., in 1742. Its beginning point was "in the back woods of Prince George's County at the junction of Double Pipe Creek and Monocacy. This survey overlapped Henry Munday's "Trura" so that in 1744 the patent had to be "vacated."[10] Both parcels were in today's Carroll County.

On July 7, 1741 John Digges had 160 acres surveyed along the Monocacy River with a beginning point "at a black oak tree on the east side of Monocacy near a road leading from Robert Wilson's towards his Lordship's Manor." This was "Papan [Paw Paw] Bottom," and the road referred to was the early Manor Monocacy Road

---

the Potomac River" to his daughter Priscilla Wickham.

[5] C/S: IL A:437. See also Original Patented Certificate of Survey, Prince George's County, No. 2322. Pottinger assigned his interest to Wickham.

[6] C/S: IL B/20.

[7] Prince George's County County Wills, 22:443.

[8] Frederick County Land Records, B:15. This tract of 50 acres should not be confused with "Hope," the first parcel surveyed in present-day Frederick County. See above, p. 25.

[9] C/S: EI 5/288; Patent: EI 2:607. Wickham assigned his survey to Digges on August 14, 1736. In 1742 Digges was operating a copper mine on this parcel, a mile and a quarter south of today's Middleburg, and was receiving exemption for his "experienced workmen from levies, military service and labor in clearing roads (Proceedings of the Assembly, 1740-1742, *Archives of Maryland, op. cit.*, 42:281, 431). Charles Diehl, a subsequent owner, was able to penetrate the mine's tunnels for some distance, but the entrance is now closed and large funnel-shaped depressions in the woodland above suggest current collapse of these tunnels.

[10] Patent: EI 6:475. See also above, p. 333.

described elsewhere in these pages. Digges assigned "Papan Bottom" to Wickham, who then received the patent on August 7, 1742.[11] The financial arrangements between these two men are unknown, but from July 11, 1735 Wickham owed Digges the sum of fifty pounds on which, rather significantly, he was not paying interest.

"Papan Bottom" extended along the east side of the river, but also crossed to the west side so as to include the mouth of Hunting Creek. Here Nathaniel Wickham made his home, the only land which remained with the family after his death. On June 6, 1749 he had the tract enlarged, calling it henceforth "Resurvey on Paw Paw Bottom." The tract was extended considerably on both sides of the river, thereby including the present-day Creagerstown-Woodsboro Road where it crosses the river as well as almost three miles along the river's course itself. He immediately mortgaged the land to Daniel Dulany, who had discharged Wickham's debt to Osborn Sprigg, and gave Dulany the right to surrender the grant in the Court of Chancery.[12] Wickham never received the patent for "Resurvey on Paw Paw Bottom," nor did Dulany ever claim it. Instead, in 1779 Priscilla Wickham, "daughter and heir of Robert Wickham of Frederick County, deceased, the eldest son and heir of Nathaniel Wickham, also late of Frederick County," conveyed 160 acres of it to Christian Stoner for £500.[13] Apparently granddaughter Priscilla paid into Dulany's estate £75 sterling and £21/19/6 current money "for debts of Nathaniel Wickham paid by Dulany."[14]

The Lower House of the Maryland Assembly on June 9, 1741 ordered its clerk on June 9, 1741 to issue summons for Messrs. Peter Dent, Nathaniel Wickham, Jr., Richard Keene, Thomas Owens, Thomas Cresap, Henry Truman, John Hawkins, Jr. and Joseph Chapline, Justices of Prince George's County, to appear at the "bar of this House" regarding matters of business in Prince George's County.[15] Assembly records also show that on May 14, 1748 Nathaniel Wickham, Jr., Thomas Beattys, Captain Joseph Ogle and others were named Commissioners for Prince George's and Baltimore counties to run boundary lines dividing these counties.[16] The Act to erect Frederick County out of its parent Prince George's County included provision for Nathaniel Wickham, Jr., among others to be responsible for purchasing three acres in an exact square on which to build a Court House and a prison. Nathaniel Wickham had served as a Justice of the Prince George's County Court from 1739 to 1746. When it came time to establish a similar Court for the new Frederick County, it was Nathaniel Wickham who read Governor Samuel Ogle's proclamation

---

[11] C/S: LG E/62. See also above, pp. 43, 49.
[12] C/S: BC & GS 41:15; Patent: BC & GS 36:427.
[13] Frederick County Land Records, WR 1/416.
[14] Later resurveys on the "Resurvey on Paw Paw Bottom" included: "Browning's Inheritance" in 1788 (C/S: IC I:651), "Long Looked For, Come At Last" in 1797 (C/S: IC N:187) and "Ott's Ego" in 1835 (C/S: GGB 4:540).
[15] Proceedings of the Assembly, 1740-1744, *Archives of Maryland*, op. cit., 42:215.
[16] *Ibid.*, 1748-1751, 46:11, 132. See also above, p. 328.

concerning the appointment of new Justices and the establishment of the Court. He was sworn in as one of those first Justices and continued to serve until the November Court of 1755. From 1752 on, he acted as Chief Justice.[17] In 1749 he requested the appointment of three men to lay out a road from Ogle's Ford to Biggs' Ford, and later that year Nathaniel Wickham, Junior, Thomas Beatty and Joseph Wood were appointed to lay out the forerunner of today's State Route 194 from Frederick to Hanover, Pennsylvania.[18]

For construction of the Court House William Griffith, Henry Munday and Nathaniel Wickham were appointed to contract with the builders.[19] In 1750 there was concern about damage being done to the land of the orphan John van Metre, Nathaniel Wickham and Thomas Beatty were assigned to investigate.[20] The same two men were named to arrange for construction of a pillory on the Court House property.[21] Nathaniel Wickham and Abraham Miller in 1751 were given the task of laying out a road to Fredericktown from Jacob Peck's fulling mill.[22] Shortly thereafter Nathaniel Wickham was one of four men charged with seeing that a bridge was constructed across Israel Creek.[23] In 1753 he was named overseer of the road from Ogle's Ford to Biggs' Ford. In the following year he was assigned the responsibility of contracting for ferry service at the Middle Ford on the Monocacy and arranging for the County election for new members of the Maryland Assembly.[24] On July 3, 1755 Governor Horatio Sharpe instructed Wickham, then a Colonel and Commander-in-Chief of the Frederick County Militia, to regulate "the Militia in your county, instantly convening all the Commissioned Officers of the Foot Militia and arranging for periodic musters of the men."[25]

Such were some of the activities of this public-spirited man. Nathaniel Wickham was just as active in land affairs, selecting choice land for his many surveys and patents. But there the story turns. None of this land was destined to remain in his possession free and clear of debt.

On March 9, 1743 he selected 150 acres in what is now Eyler's Valley but was then described as land "near Friend's Mountain." He named this tract "Black Walnut Bottom"[26] and in 1753 used additional vacant land to make a resurvey.[27] But this he conveyed to Joseph Ogle. On April 1, 1746 Thomas Cresap surveyed two pieces of choice land for Wickham. "Turkey Thicket" was located in the crook of Monocacy River "on the top of a high cliff on the west side of the

---
[17] Rice, *The Life, op. cit.,* pp. viii, ix, 285.
[18] *Ibid.,* pp. 3-5.
[19] *Ibid.,* pp. 24, 61.
[20] *Ibid.,* p. 37. See also above, p. 263.
[21] *Ibid.,* p. 45.
[22] *Ibid.,* p. 68.
[23] *Ibid.,* p. 80.
[24] *Ibid.,* pp. 152, 154.
[25] Proceedings of Council, 1753-1761, *Archives of Maryland, op. cit.,* 31:73.
[26] C/S: LG E:271, second of this name. See map, p. 248.
[27] C/S: Y&S 7/176.

Monocacy River opposite the lower end of a bottom taken up by Captain Henry Munday."[28] In later years this location could be identified as the home of George W. Barrick above LeGore Bridge.[29] The other tract, "Locust Thicket,"[30] lay on the east side of the river opposite the mouth of Owen's Creek at what was then called Ogle's Ford, but is known today as Stull's Ford.[31] On April 11, 1751 George Gordon took a mortgage on these two parcels for £108/2/7 and in 1759 Nathaniel and Priscilla Wickham had to convey the tracts to Gordon for the amount of the mortgage and its interest.[32] Subsequently Samuel Chase in 1762 used a part of "Turkey Thicket" for his survey of "Choice"[33] as did Henry and Peter Krise in 1809 for their "Krise's Establishment."[34] Nathaniel Wickham on December 24, 1751 leased Monocacy Manor lot No. 52 (on which the town of Woodsboro is situated today) for the natural lives of his sons Nathaniel, age 38, Samuel, 32, and John, 20.[35] By 1767, however, the lot was tenanted by John Carver. In 1752 Wickham had "Good Luck" surveyed at the south end of his "Resurvey on Paw Paw Bottom."[36] A deed made in 1775 indicates that this land had been lost to mortgagees Samuel, John and Thomas Snowden who "for a valuable consideration made and satisfied by a certain Nathaniel Wickham and in the further consideration of five shillings paid by Henry Wickham" then conveyed the land back to this Henry Wickham.[37]

Nathaniel Wickham's lands in today's Washington and Montgomery Counties fared no better. They carried the same story of mortgages and losses as did his lands in Frederick County. Toward the end of 1755 Nathaniel Wickham suddenly disappears from the records. He is not heard from again until on June 20, 1761 when the Maryland Assembly received his petition, saying that he had been "for five years and eight months languishing prisoner in the goal [sic; jail] of Frederick County for debt and divers sums of tobacco which said debt by reasons of divers losses and misfortunes he was before his confinement unable to pay...." He added further that he had "by dictates of his conscience made all the overtures to satisfy his creditors .... even to make over all his estate both real and personal to them, which they had rejected and still do reject." He had not been guilty, he said, "of fraudulent or decietful practices in or to

---

[28] C/S: LG E:559.
[29] Lake, *op. cit.*, p. 15; Bond, *loc. cit.*
[30] C/S: LG E:580.
[31] C/S: BC & GS 5:547 referred to the "ford that leads from Nathaniel Wickham's to Joseph Ogle's."
[32] Frederick County Land Records, F:940.
[33] C/S: BC & GS 19:398.
[34] C/S: JK U:434. A granddaughter Susan Krise (1824-1893) married George W. Barrick (1816-1895).
[35] In 1763 Luke and Nathaniel Bernard, presumably grandsons of Nathaniel Wickham's mother by her first marriage, leased adjoining Lots Nos. 47 and 48, immediately west of Lot No. 52.
[36] C/S: Y & S 7:497.
[37] Frederick County Land Records, W:552.

cheat or defraud his creditors...." Justices Thomas Beatty, Charles Jones, David Lynn, Thomas Norris, Peter Bainbridge and Moses Chapline recommended clemency.[38]

The children of Nathaniel Wickham and Priscilla Tyler included Robert, Anna, Samuel, Priscilla, John, Henry and Nathaniel (III). Robert Wickham, the eldest son, married Ann Farrell, daughter of Kennedy Farrell. In 1748 Robert purchased Lot No. 37 in Fredericktown on the south side of East Patrick Street near the corner of Market Street. This was sold to George Burckhart in 1789 by Priscilla Wickham, his daughter and heir. Robert Wickham's sister Anna married Samuel Swearingen from whose home, probably on Lot No. 67 east of Court Street between Patrick and Church Streets, the celebration of the Stamp Act repudiation took place in 1765.[39]

Nathaniel Wickham, the third of this name, was assigned crops, farm animals and household goods by his father in 1758 in a bill of sale between father and son.[40] The younger Nathaniel had married in 1755 Sarah Wood, daughter of Joseph Wood of Israel Creek. They may initially have occupied Lot No. 52 on "Monocacy Manor," but that lot was ultimately included in her brother's "Wood's Town Lot." Nathaniel then purchased land adjacent to the northern corner of "Monocacy Manor" which he had resurveyed into "Wickham's Discovery."[41] Part of this was later also included in "Wood's Town Lot." Nathaniel Wickham's will named as children John, Robert, Joseph, a fourth Nathaniel, Elizabeth and Sarah. His brothers Henry and John Wickham, together with his friend Norman Bruce, founder of Bruceville in Carroll County, were his executors.[42]

John Wickham, who died about September 1787 leaving a wife Martha, had on September 19, 1782 assigned a power of attorney to Joseph Wood, Jr., for the purpose of collecting his debts.[43] His brother Samuel Wickham in 1763 purchased a portion of the "Resurvey on Lilly's Lot"[44] which lay along the west and north side of the Monocacy River opposite the "Resurvey on Paw Paw Bottom" on the other bank. He died relatively young, devising his land in 1772 to his sister Priscilla and naming Joseph Wood, Jr. as his executor.[45] The latter transferred his land back to Richard Lilly in 1773.[46]

Like Nathaniel Wickham at the mouth of Hunting Creek,

---

[38] *Maryland State Papers No. 1, the Black Books*, op. cit., 4:93; para. 1161 in the *Calendar*. Proceedings of the Assembly, *Archives of Maryland*, op. cit., 58:586. Michael Risoner and George Baker made similar pleas.
[39] Williams, op. cit., pp. 76-77. Samuel Swearingen had purchased this lot from Kennedy Farrell in 1750 (Frederick County Land Records, E:761).
[40] Frederick County Land Records, F:579.
[41] C/S: BC & GS 47:38.
[42] Frederick County Wills, GM 1:41.
[43] Frederick County Land Records, WR 3:236.
[44] Frederick County Land Records, H:291. See also above, p. 49, 254.
[45] Frederick County Wills, A 1:437.
[46] Frederick County Land Records, U:122.

another individual who fitted into no specific group or area of early settlers was the Reverend **William Williams**. Ubiquitous, peripatetic, litigious and withal most difficult to place in the sequence of Monocacy history, he lived not far from Wickham, just down the river at the mouth of Fishing Creek. First mentioned in 1736 as a Presbyterian missionary, Williams preached initially in the upper Conococheague area which has since become Chambersburg, as well as in the vicinity of today's Greencastle, Mercersburg and Welsh Run, all in Pennsylvania. But the records also show him in the Bullskin and Tuscarora areas of today's West Virginia. In July of 1736 the Orange County Court received a petition from residents stating that the Reverend Mr. Williams, minister of the gospel, had promised to supply them in the administration of his office. The petition asked that meeting places be established, one on Mr. Williams' land near his house and the other on Morgan Bryan's land. This was followed on September 22, 1737 by the notation that "William Williams, a Presbyterian Minister, Gentleman, having taken the oath appointed by Act of Parliament....has certified his intention of holding his meetings at his own plantation and on the plantation of Morgan Bryan."[47]

At this time Bryan's land stretched from Mill Creek to Tuscarora Creek.[48] His home was located southwest of present-day Bunker Hill in southern Berkeley County, West Virginia. Williams was then living on Opequon Creek some eight miles to the southeast, over the ridge from Bullskin Marsh and west of today's Summit Point in Jefferson County. He was deeded this land by Jost Hite in 1738.[49] Like many ministers of his day, in order to provide himself with a material living, Williams was also engaged in trade. It was from these business interests that so many legal suits were heard by the Virginia Courts. For several years Williams seemed to file more cases than any other single individual. His suits were uniformly successful, for judgments almost always came his way. There was other, non-business litigation, too. Justice of the Peace Morgan Morgan presented two men before the February Court of 1738, charging them with robbing the house of Rev. Williams. Then in July, 1738 Williams brought suit himself against more than thirty individuals "for signing a scandalous paper reflecting on ye said Williams." Many of the signers acknowledged their error and begged his pardon.[50] In 1744, a significant date when one contemplates the probable time of his move to Maryland, Williams was fined four pounds and costs for "joyning in bonds of matrimony several persons, he being no orthodox minister.[51] According to Virginia's Frederick Court records, Williams resented the unjust action and was fined 26 shillings for behaving indecently before the Court."

---

[47] Joseph Addison Waddell, *Annals of Augusta County, Virginia: from 1726 to 1791* (Staunton, 1902), p. 132.
[48] This is a third Creek by this name. Cf. above, pp. 13, 46.
[49] Orange County (Virginia) Land Records, April 27, 1738.
[50] One of the defendants was Jonas Hedges (see pp. 108-109).
[51] It should be remembered that, "by law established," only rectors of the Church of England could legally perform marriages. The law was rarely enforced, especially in frontier areas.

The Reverend William Williams' connection with the Monocacy Valley began on July 5, 1739 with his 250-acre survey of "Williams Project."[52] His new land lay on the west bank of the Monocacy River near the mouth of Fishing Creek and stretched two and a half miles northwesterly. It included a lengthy "shank" connecting two enlarged areas much like an elongated dumbbell. One end lay in the vicinity of today's Lewistown, the other along the River opposite Lot Nos. 7-12 on "Monocacy Manor." But only a little over a month later, Williams had a 250-acre tract, "Green Bottom," surveyed "on the west banks of Conococheague Creek."[53] In present-day terms this second tract lay immediately south of the Pennsylvania border in Washington County, Maryland, where the Hagerstown-Mercersburg Road crosses the Conococheague. In 1745 a legal problem arose concerning "Williams Project." Thomas Cresap had surveyed for James Johnson 144 acres "beginning on the west side of the Monocacy 80 perches from the mouth of Fishing Creek." He called the tract "Parson's Delight," but the lands overlapped and so Johnson's survey was declared invalid.

Not entirely resolved is the question whether one or the other of these Maryland surveys was intended as an investment or as a place of residence. We have noted Williams was still in Virginia in 1744. As late as 1755, sixteen years after the two Maryland surveys, Williams' Virginia land was still being mentioned in subsequent survey and patent records in Virginia's Frederick County.[54] Even in a subsequent Maryland survey of 1754 Williams termed himself "of the Colony of Virginia."[55] Inevitably, however, his trail of litigation traces him to the Monocacy area. The Prince George's County Court determined that Evan Shelby, Sr., Evan Shelby, Jr. and Hugh Gilliland should pay Williams ninety pounds sterling and 486 pounds of tobacco on a debt owed Williams. In August of 1750 Williams was in the Frederick County (Maryland) Court suing Hugh Gilliland on a debt of ten pounds. Following a decision in his favor, Williams then sued Gilliland in March 1751 for damages resulting from Gilliland's long failure to pay. A board of inquiry found for Williams in the amount of one shilling, one and a half pence! In August 1751 Williams was in Maryland's Frederick County Court again, this time suing James Fowler for five pounds Virginia money, equivalent to seven and a half pounds Maryland money, the price of a watch he had sold to Fowler.[56] It is not clear whether the William Williams who served on various Frederick County (Maryland) grand juries between 1750 and 1759 was

---

[52] C/S: LG E:593.
[53] C/S: LG C:194.
[54] Frederick County, Virginia, was the parent County of Berkeley and Jefferson Counties, West Virginia. See Joyner, *Frederick County* [Virginia] *Surveys, op. cit.,* concerning the surveys of: John Strode, May 5, 1751 (p. 151); John Keywood, April 5, 1754 (p. 86); Abraham Vanmeter, April 5, 1754 (p. 159); and Moses Keywood, April 17, 1755 (p. 86). The Rev. William Williams of Opequon had also sold land to Francis Fowler, who resurveyed it into a tract of 751 acres on March 29, 1752 (*ibid.,* p. 10).
[55] C/S: BC & GS 5/93.
[56] Rice, *The Life, op. cit.,* pp. 54, 70-71, 83.

the same individual: he is never referred to as a minister.[57] Finally, there is the testimony in 1765 of William Hedges, "about 23 years of age .... that about five years past he and the Reverend William Williams were going together from the said Williams' to Stephen Julien's when the aforesaid William Williams shewed this deponent a bonded white oak standing on the west side of Monocacy Creek about 10 perches from the said creek and said that that tree was the beginning of his land."[58]

It would thus appear that the Reverend William Williams had purchased land in the Monocacy area during the period of our study, but had not moved there to reside until sometime between 1745 and 1750. Although he was referred to in Frederick Court records by his ministerial title, no reference or claim to his serving with a specific Presbyterian congregation in Frederick County has been found.[59] His will, dated September 23, 1759, was probated on October 5, 1759. In it he bequeathed all his estate, real and personal, both in America and in Europe, to the children of his three daughters, Ruhamah Chapline, Sarah Price and Jane Chambers.[60] The reference to an estate in Europe refers to his wife's reputed land holdings in Wales. After Williams' death, his three daughters agreed[61] that "Williams Project" would become the property of the Chapline children, that "Green Bottom" would pass to the Price children and that the other lands would be given to the Chambers children.

Ruhamah Williams' husband **Joseph Chapline** (1707-1768) could trace his ancestry back four generations to the immigrant Isaac Chapline who came to Virginia in 1610. Between them stood three generations of individuals, each named William Chapline.[62] The first of these had brought the family to Maryland to settle in Calvert County. From 1739 to 1747 Joseph Chapline had served as a Justice of the Prince George's County Court, and from 1749 to 1751 he served in the same capacity in the new Frederick County Court. In the County's first election in early 1749 and again in November 1754 and September 1758 he was named a Delegate to the General Assembly in Annapolis.[63] In 1744 he was appointed to help lay out the road via Richard Touchstone's.[64] He, too, became involved in the Gilliland suits including one against Thomas Gilliland in 1753.[65] Joseph Chapline

---
[57] *Ibid.*, pp. 41, 91, 113, 169, 197.
[58] Frederick County Land Records, K:427. From our other knowledge, this testimony undoubtedly occurred at least six, not five, years after the incident in question.
[59] Frederick Lewis Weis in his usually "over-complete" compilations of *The Colonial Clergy, op. cit.*, does not include this William Williams.
[60] Frederick County Wills, A1:130.
[61] Frederick County Land Records, F:1309, 1311.
[62] George N. Mackenzie, *Colonial Families of the United States* (Baltimore, 1914); and Maria Jane Liggett Dare, *Chaplines from Maryland and Virginia* (Franklin Print, Washington, 1902).
[63] Rice, *The Life, op. cit.*, pp. x, 155, 190.
[64] See above, p. 222.
[65] Rice, *The Life, op. cit.*, p. 129.

registered his marriage in the All Saints Parish records as well as the birth dates of their children. Between 1750 and 1764 he took up many tracts of land,[66] but he and Ruhama made their home along the Potomac River about two miles west of present-day Sharpsburg, the town he founded. In 1761 he surveyed "Addition to Williams Project," including vacant land surrounding the original parcel.[67] Then, in 1763, he, Ruhamah and their son William Williams Chapline, conveyed 250 acres of this land for £400 to Alexander Ogle "of New Castle County."[68]

Sarah Williams married **Reese Price** and lived in today's Washington County. As early as 1739 he and his brother-in-law Joseph Chapline had signed a petition asking the Prince George's County Court to erect a court house at Salisbury Plains (present Hagerstown).[69] In 1753 he was named Constable of Conococheague Hundred. He and Sarah had two sons, William and Josiah Price. The latter became an attorney and made his home on "Green Bottom."[70] His son William Price was appointed a United States District Attorney by Abraham Lincoln.

Jane Williams' husband **Benjamin Chambers** is said to have come from Antrim in Ireland in 1726 with three brothers, James, Robert and Joseph Chambers. Benjamin was about 18 years of age at the time. The brothers settled near Harris' Ferry (today's Harrisburg) where they erected a mill. Joseph and Benjamin later moved to the area of today's Chambersburg which the latter is credited with founding. Benjamin Chambers worked with the Pennsylvania authorities during the Conojohelar War at Susquehanna and in later years complained loudly because Thomas Cresap was appointed to important positions in Maryland, while he, Benjamin Chambers, was not equally rewarded by the Pennsylvanians. William Chambers, eldest son of Jane Williams Chambers, attempted to contest the 1763 conveyance of "Williams Project" to Alexander Ogle. But a certificate from Joseph Wood as register of All Saints Parish in Frederick, showed that the birth of William Williams Chapline had occurred on August 28, 1742, thereby making him of age and legally able to sign that deed.

---

[66] Within today's Frederick County: "Mindall," "Watson's Welfare," "Resurvey on Exchange," "Learning," "Nazarite," "Tick Neck," "Policy," "Horse Neck," "Little Good," "Little Left," "Shot Proof," "Tuckett," "Widow's Design," "Black Acorn," "Near the Navel," "Addition to Williams Project," "Barrel" and "Resurvey on Tom's Gift."

[67] Patent: BC & GS 23:225.

[68] See p. 332.

[69] Washington County was not created as a separate county until it was separated from Frederick County in 1776.

[70] Varlé, *loc. cit.*

ALL SAINTS' PARISH

Although they were Catholics, the early Lords Baltimore gave no religious favoritism or official recognition to any one religious group. In this manner they in effect ignored the provision in their Maryland charter which provided for the ascendancy of the Church of England. As a result, no denomination in Maryland could be considered predominant over the others. Anglicans, Catholics, Quakers, Baptists and others were all present. In the aftermath of the anti-Catholic Glorious Revolution, however, the proprietary government in Maryland was replaced by a royal government which continued until 1715. In keeping with attitudes in England, the emphasis against Catholicism intensified, and in 1692 the Maryland Assembly passed the first of a series of Acts for the "Establishment of the Protestant Religion," i.e., the Church of England.[1] The Act provided for the creation of Church of England parishes and levied taxes on all taxable individuals, regardless of their own religious persuasion. The revenue was used to build churches and to support clerics solely of the Church of England.

Unlike our current concept of a parish, comprising members of a given congregation regardless of their place of abode, early Maryland parishes represented distinct geographic areas. County Justices divided their counties into such districts or parishes and arranged for freeholders in each parish to elect six individuals to the parish vestry. The county sheriff then collected the taxes as set by the Justices (initially 40 pounds of tobacco annually per individual) and turned the proceeds over to the vestrymen for the management of the affairs of their parish. This arrangement continued until November, 1776 when disestablishment took place during the American Revolution.

Initially thirty parishes were established in the ten original Maryland counties, but subsequent Acts of Assembly were required as settlements expanded and population grew. The area we know as Frederick County was at first a part of St. John's Parish in Charles, then later Prince George's, County. The Parish's first wooden church, built in 1695, stood near the mouth of Piscataway Creek. Later this became Prince George's Parish, extending territorially as far west as

---

[1] Proceedings of the Assembly, 1684-1692, *Archives of Maryland*, op. cit., 13:425-430. Acts of Assembly were considered in force until and unless the authorities in England objected or disapproved. Three such Acts passed by the Maryland Assembly were overruled in England, principally because they were not deemed liberal enough toward Protestant dissenters. King William, it will be remembered, was a Dutch Calvinist. Thus it was not until 1704 that an Act of Establishment was finally approved. By that time many of the provisions of the earlier Acts had jelled into place.

did Maryland itself. The Rev. John Fraser, whose will named a daughter Susanna, wife of the previously mentioned John Hawkins,[2] was rector for this Parish from 1710 to 1742. In 1719 parish members who were residents of Eastern Branch Hundred met to select a site for a chapel of ease.[3] Colonel John Bradford donated one hundred acres, which his son conveyed by deed of January 3, 1727.[4] The parcel, called "Generosity," lay on Piney Branch and ultimately became the Rock Creek parish church in Washington, D. C. James Hook contributed 200 pounds of tobacco toward the building of this church, and the Thrashers gave ten shillings. We may also note William Ray, John Nelson and Abraham Lakin as taxables in Rock Creek Hundred in 1719.[5]

As population expanded, another chapel of ease was established, this time in 1728 as the Rock Creek Chapel at today's Rockville in Montgomery County. Among the subscribers for the proposed building were a number of individuals or families found later in the Frederick County area. These included John West, Benjamin Thrasher, Samuel Pottenger, Robert Pottenger, Nathaniel Wickham, Jr., Luke Barnard, Arthur Nelson, John Nelson and William Shephard.

Time and the center of population moved ever further. On March 22, 1735 the Maryland Assembly heard a petition from the inhabitants of the "middle part of Prince George's Parish in Prince George's County, praying that an Act may be made to levy a quantity of tobacco on the taxable inhabitants of the Parish to build them a chapel of ease."[6] This petition may have referred to the Monocacy Chapel at present-day Beallsville in Montgomery County, located about four miles south of the mouth of the Monocacy River. Tradition estimates it was built about 1737, and this petition is the only one yet found which tends to approximate that date.

This same structure was also referred to in a November 1740 petition for a road "from John Pyburn's to John Nelson's for the benefit of our mill and *our church* [italics supplied]." The proposed road ran from present-day Beallsville in Montgomery County past Elting's Mill, along a part of Little Monocacy to the mouth of the Monocacy River. A number of those who signed the petition have been noted above.[7]

All this is but a lengthy preamble to the eventual separation out of both Prince George's County and Prince George's Parish of the political and religious divisions we know today. Petitions seeking such divisions were drawn up and sent to the Governor and the Assembly in October 1742. The petition for the division of the Parish included 197 names which are reproduced in the table on page 371. Interest-

---

[2] See above, p. 96.
[3] A place of worship subordinate to the parish church.
[4] Ethel D. Gutridge, "St Paul's Church, Rock Creek Parish, Washington D.C.," *Historical Magazine of the Protestant Episcopal Church*, 19:145.
[5] See above, pp. 61-62, 67, 89.
[6] Proceedings of the Assembly, 1733-1736, *Archives of Maryland*, op. cit., 39:165.
[7] See p. 62n.

ingly, at least 23 of these names belonged to Germans whose religion was not that of the Anglican Church.[8] More than merely assisting their neighbors by signing the petition, they may well have had in mind the potential benefits to be derived from a more local control of the church levies. These, it will be remembered, were assessed against all residents, regardless of their own personal religion.

Separate deliberations concerning the division of County and Parish began in the General Assembly about the same time in October 1742. Although the resulting division of the County did not occur until 1748, the separation of parishes was accomplished before the end of 1742. It was agreed to by the Rev. George Murdock and was passed by the Assembly so that "from and after the 22nd day of November next ensuing, all that part of Prince George's Parish, beginning at Great Senecar Run mouth and running by and with said run to the head thereof, from thence with a due east line to the head of one of the draughts of the Patuxent River and so binding all around as the upper part of said Country is bounded .... is made into a Parish to be called by the name of All Saints' Parish .... giving to the several freeholders thereof full and ample power to elect and make choice of the number of six select Vestrymen and two Church wardens, and also to build and found a church therein...."[9]

Joseph Jennings was appointed on November 23, 1742 as the first rector of the newly formed parish.[10] He may have come directly from England, for no other earlier records concerning him have been found. On October 18, 1743 we do note him at St. Anne's Church in Annapolis providing communion for several Germans seeking naturalization.[11] On January 21, 1743 he had had 150 acres surveyed for himself "on the south side of Back Run, a branch of Israel Creek."[12] Called "Mount Pleasant," this land was located in the present

---

[8] This petition is referred to in Proceedings of the Assembly, 1740-1742, *Archives of Maryland*, op.cit., 42:278. Its original may be found in the Maryland Diocesan Archives at the Maryland Historical Society. Rather inaccurate and incomplete transcriptions have previously appeared in Scharf, *op. cit.*, pp. 503, 500 [sic], and in Ernest Helfenstein, *History of All Saints' Parish* (Frederick, 1932), p. 3. The latter included only 68 individuals. In the original, the Germans' names, obviously written for them, were so badly anglicized as to be in some cases almost unrecognizable. Cf., for example, Citchadaner for Getzendanner and TeterLany for Dietrich Lehnich. In preparing the list on p. 371, we have had the able assistance of F. Garner Ranney, Historiographer of the Maryland Diocese.

[9] Proceedings of the Assembly, 1740-1742, *Archives of Maryland*, op. cit., 42:427-428.

[10] Rightmyer, *Maryland's Established Church*, op. cit., pp. 152, 194.

[11] Provincial Court Judgment Records, 1742-1746, EI 7:296. The Germans were Andrew Shriver, Peter Middlecave, Lutwick Shriver, Michael Will, Conrad Erhard, David Young, George Shrier, Mark Pickler, John Shrier, Jacob Shrier and Nicholas Shrier. At least some of these Germans are recognized as settlers on "Digges Choice" in the Conewago area.

[12] C/S: LG E:296.

Daysville area between Walkersville and Libertytown, north of the Beatty homestead and near the land called "Beatty's Venture." Actually it overlapped a small portion of his Lordship's "Monocacy Manor."[13] On November 13, 1744 Jennings appointed Thomas Cresap his lawful attorney. Then on April 13, 1745, two and a half years after his initial survey, Jennings and his wife Mary made over to Thomas Cresap and John Cook "all the tobacco which shall be taxed and raised by the Justices of Prince George's County in next November's levy, 40 pounds per poll."[14] At the same time he and his wife for £24/16/8 currency and 847½ pounds of tobacco, transferred their land including "the houses and buildings to the same belonging" to Cresap and Cook.[15] They in turn on June 27, 1754 conveyed the land to Caspar Creager for £91/6/-.[16]

Just what became of the Reverend Jennings, how active he was in parish affairs or even whether he ever lived on his "Mount Pleasant" land is not clear. It was after he sold the land, however, that he attempted to lay further claim to the parish revenues. On March 28, 1746 as "clerk rector of All Saints' Parish in Monockesey of Prince George's County" he made an agreement with Robert Debutts and Kennedy Ferrell, empowering them to "collect all the forty pounds of tobacco per pole [sic] to be due and owing to him, the said Joseph Jennings, as Rector of All Saints' Parish .... during the whole time of his residence .... at the rate of 9 shillings currency for each 100 pounds of tobacco .... clear of the sheriff's commission of 5% for collecting and receiving same. Debutts and Farrell posted £500 sterling as bond for this work.[17] The fact that Jennings referred to himself as "of Monockesey" is provocative. Either he was minimizing the importance of the town of Frederick reputedly begun in the previous year or, as is more likely, he was attempting to assert his claims to all of the parish and all of its revenues. In general, a parson held a freehold right to his parish as it was constituted at the time of his induction. Changes could be effected solely by his agreement, resignation or death.[18] That something more was afoot becomes the more apparent in the light of charges by the sheriff, also in 1746, that Jennings had been "absent" for a year and a half. This in turn draws attention to the phrase in the above agreement, "during the whole time of his residence." Had he gone elsewhere and was he now attempting to lay claim, not to current revenues, but to those of an earlier period? But if he had gone elsewhere, he was still a resident of Prince George's County at the time of his death. Robert Debutts filed an inventory of his estate in Prince George's County on May 29, 1748.[19]

Only seven months after the revenue collection agreement, but

---

[13] See map, p. 304.
[14] Prince George's County Land Records, BB 1:296.
[15] *Ibid.*, BNB 1:297.
[16] Frederick County Land Records, E:477.
[17] Prince George's County Land Records, EE:14-15.
[18] Nelson W. Rightmyer, *Parishes of the Diocese of Maryland* (Reisterstown, Md., 1960), p. 4.
[19] Prince George's County Inventories and Accounts, 37:121.

seventeen months before Jennings died, Governor Thomas Bladen on December 11, 1746 appointed the Reverend **Samuel Hunter** as rector of All Saints' Parish! The Parish still had no church, and it is debatable how much actual progress of any sort had been made in the past four years, let alone in the entire period of the region's first twenty-odd years. An appraisal coming from Joseph Ogle, reported by the visiting Lutheran pastor Henry Muhlenberg in June of 1747, was not flattering: "Our former English preacher here [Jennings] was a drunkard. The present parish minister [Hunter] is no better."[20]

While Samuel Hunter's arrival comes after the period of this study, it may nevertheless be enlightening to trace the history of the Established Church in Frederick County a bit further. Hunter had served earlier in Christ Church Parish, Kent Island, where his older brother, the Reverend Henry Hunter, had been incumbent before him. The elder Hunter remained there less than a year before his early death in 1739.[21] He was succeeded by John Bradford, who may not have been in the parish very long at any one time. As evidence of this, on November 8, 1741 Samuel Hunter was appointed "reader." In 1744 he succeeded Bradford as incumbent.

On June 9, 1747 the Vestrymen and Church wardens of All Saints' Parish "in the back parts of Prince George's County" petitioned the Maryland Assembly for monetary help in building a church and two chapels of ease.[22] Later that year the Maryland Assembly authorized a levy of £300 with which to build a church "on Carroll Creek in Fredericktown, a chapel "between Anti Aetam [Antietam] and Connogocheague," and another, "already begun, standing between Monocacy and Seneca Creek."[23] The latter, of course, represents the Beallsville site previously discussed, while the other chapel of ease was to be located near Saint James between present-day Sharpsburg and Hagerstown in Washington County. Two years later a third chapel of ease presumably came into being. There are references to its being built between drafts of the Linganore and Sam's Creeks by inhabitants of that area,[24] but no official record has ever been found to substantiate its existence.

The parish church in Frederick was thus erected sometime after 1747, about the same time that the Lutherans and Reformed were building their first churches in town. While neither Muhlenberg nor Schlatter in accounts relating to their respective visits in Frederick in 1747 indicated in what kind of an edifice they held religious services, the Lutheran minister Gabriel Nasmann in October 1746 did refer to "the church in the new FrederickTown," and Schlatter on his visit in May 1748 wrote that he held Reformed services "in Fredericktown in a church which is not yet finished,"[25] but

---

[20] Tappert and Doberstein, *op. cit.*, 1:159.
[21] Henry Hunter left his entire estate to his brother Samuel (Queen Anne's County Wills, Box 6, folio 32, Hall of Records).
[22] Proceedings of the Assembly, 1745-1747, *Archives of Maryland*, *op. cit.*, 44:463.
[23] Ibid.
[24] See also above, p. 102.
[25] See above, p. 149. Schlatter visited Frederick twice in 1748,

which, with its congregation, "he commended to the Triune God." The Lutheran church apparently did not last long and probably became the school house, for in his 1748 visit Muhlenberg, noting that "the Lutherans did not yet have a church," accepted invitations from the English and the Reformed to preach in their respective churches.[26]

The English church was located between All Saints' Street and Carroll Creek, facing what would be an extension of today's Maxwell Avenue [formerly Middle Alley] to the east.[27] It was a brick structure[28] which with its cemetery occupied Lot Nos. 7 and 8 in the newly laid out town of Frederick. But no deed to either of the original lots appears in the land records. The structure itself survived until 1814 when a new church was constructed on Court Street, using materials from the old building. The cemetery continued in use at the original location until 1854 when Mt. Olivet Cemetery was begun south of town. Many burials were reinterred there, but the old cemetery was not completely abandoned until 1914.[29]

The original of the first Church Book record of baptisms, marriages and burials remains today in the Church vault. Its title page is inscribed as the "Register Book of All Saints Parish, Frederick County, Maryland, Commencing the 4th April 1743." This, of course, is an anachronism: Frederick County did not exist until late 1748. Some people, unmindful of the fact that entries were written well after the events themselves, have even claimed the book was begun in the late 1720s. Because the entries were arranged alphabetically rather than in complete chronological sequence, it is difficult to guess when this book was actually begun, but, pending further study, a date of about 1753 appears most plausible.[30]

---

preaching in the church on his second visit, but in the school house one week earlier.

[26] The Lutherans in 1752 received deeds to Lot Nos. 88 and 89, the former for their church, the latter for a school house, both located north of East Church Street. A provision in the church deed required that the building be constructed within five years. Because progress was halted by the French and Indian War, it became necessary to grant a confirmatory deed in 1758 after which the church was then completed and dedicated in 1762. See Frederick County Land Records, B:570, B:574 and F:535.

[27] See Varlé, *loc. cit.*

[28] See reference to the church in Frederick County Land Records, WR 9:428, Daniel Dulany to Michael Raymer.

[29] For an interesting history of this cemetery and its reinterrals, see Holdcraft, *op. cit.*, pp. 21-22. Lot No. 9, to the west of the original two church lots, was added to the church property sometime after 1764 when it was earlier conveyed by Daniel Dulany the Younger to Jacob Hann. In 1833 the portion of all three lots which lay north of Carroll Creek was conveyed to Stuart Gaither (Frederick County Land Records, JS 45:18, JWLC 1:116), and in November 1915 the Vestry disposed of the remainder south of the Creek to Noah E. Cramer (*ibid.*, 362-515). Our thanks to Millard M. Rice for this added information.

[30] A handwritten transcription made in 1901 by Lucy Harwood

The Reverend Hunter's own land interests began in 1751, with his resurvey on "Leonard's Good Luck," surveyed originally in 1741 for Isaac "Leonard."[31] It stretched north from today's Feagaville toward Butterfly Lane. In this vicinity two years later, on April 9, 1753, Hunter received a patent for "Term Stool" (100 acres) following the assignment on the same day of Daniel Dulany's May 13, 1745 certificate of survey. This land lay "near a mile and a half on the west side of the road [now Butterfly Lane] that goes from John Stull's to the mouth of the Monocacy."[32] In 1754 Hunter had surveys made nearby for 136 acres called "Pleasant Plains"[33] In the same year he purchased 150 acres of the "Resurvey on Johnson's Level" and 50 acres called "Leeds," both north of today's Braddock Heights.[34] In the Lewistown District in 1755 he purchased Thomas Stoddert's "Hogg Park"[35] and then concluded his acquisitions with a survey for "Doran's Choice" with its beginning point "on the side of a hill near Frederick Unsel's land."[36] In 1775 Henry Hunter, a son of the Reverend Samuel Hunter, combined "Resurvey on Leonard's Good Luck," "Term Stool," "Pleasant Plains," "Pleasant Garden" and "Doran's Choice" into a new survey of 644 acres which he called "Castle Henry."[37] This land lay between present-day Feagaville and Mount Phillip Road. It included the upper portion of Ballenger Creek with its several branches and at one place touched the Mount Zion Church Road.

By 1756 the vast territory that was All Saints' Parish had become so populated that the settlers were declaring, "It is impracticable for any one clergyman to discharge his function fully." They therefore petitioned for a division of the Parish "upon the death of Reverend Samuel Hunter, the present incumbent." Among the signers of this petition were Abraham and Gilbert Crum, Nathaniel Wickham, John Carmack, John Justice (Sr. and Jr.), Joseph Justice, Daniel James, George Becraft, Archibald Campbell and the Hickmans and Plummers.[38] Samuel Hunter died shortly thereafter, in October 1758,[39] and was succeeded by the Reverend **Thomas Bacon**. In 1760 sundry inhabitants were petitioning the Assembly for sufficient money to add to the church in Fredericktown and to "rebuild the two chapels of

---

Harrison is at the Maryland Historical Society. Brumbaugh, op. cit., 1:258-262, has printed some of the entries.

[31] C/S: BC & GS 5:140. See also above, p. 181.
[32] C/S: GS 1:126; Patent BY & GS 4:530.
[33] C/S: GS 1:292.
[34] Frederick County Land Records, E:535, 536. Patents had been issued to Thomas Johnson for "Johnson's Level" in 1748 (Patent: TI 4:228) and to William Wilburn for "Leeds" in 1750 (Rent Roll, Frederick No. 1, 32:230). Both were devised in Charles Hedges' 1790 will. See p. 111.
[35] Ibid., E:711.
[36] C/S: BC & GS 5:97. For George Friedrich Unselt, see p. 182.
[37] C/S: BC & GS 51:306.
[38] *Maryland State Papers No. 1, The Black Books,* op. cit., 10:46; para. 862-864 in the *Calendar.*
[39] *The Maryland Gazette,* October 12, 1758: The Reverend Samuel Hunter died "last week."

ease belonging to the said Parish." They described the chapel below Monocacy as "a crazy wooden building [which] hath (upon a view by skillful persons) been judged not worth the repairing." Among others, Thomas Prather signed this petition.[40] In the same year another petition, signed by inhabitants living in present-day Montgomery County, also asked that All Saints' Parish be divided. Notwithstanding Bacon's appointment to succeed Hunter, the 1760 petition noted that the position "has now become vacant by the death of Reverend Samuel Hunter."[41] By Act of April 9-10, 1760 the Parish was divided by creation of All Souls' Parish west of the "Kittockton" Mountains. The Conococheague chapel of ease became the new parish church.[42]

Bacon, known especially for his meticulous collation of Maryland laws, which was published in 1765 and ran to 1,000 folio pages, died in Frederick on May 26, 1768. John Cary's letter to Walter Dulany, written ten minutes after Bacon's death, may be found in the Dulany Papers in Baltimore.[43] Bacon was succeeded by Bennett Allen, a disaster for both the Parish and the authorities in Annapolis. He had been inducted into St. Anne's at Annapolis the year before and just two months prior to Bacon's death had been commissioned Escheator and Receiver General. Since Allen's exploits have been well recorded in detail elsewhere,[44] suffice it here merely to note that the All Saints' parishioners and others in Annapolis objected to him so strongly that he stayed his distance well away from Frederick. He had been forced by deed of October 25, 1768 to agree to the All Saints' Vestry's right to approve or choose three curates to care for various parts of the Parish, and he ceded a portion of the poll tax to support such curates. These were to be located: 1) near where Norman Bruce and Ephraim Howard lived (today's Bruceville), 2) where Thomas Prather and James Smith lived (today's Petersville), and 3) where John Wilson and William Luckett lived (today's Point of Rocks). He also agreed to cede a portion of the same revenue to the Elders of the Fredericktown Reformed Calvinist and Lutheran Churches whose members by law were forced to pay the tax for maintenance of the Church of England.[45] Meanwhile he stayed in Philadelphia or elsewhere until he returned to England in 1775.[46] Frederick County Anglicans thus had no incumbent after 1768 until well after the Revolution.

---

[40] Proceedings of the Assembly, 1758-1761, *Archives of Maryland*, op. cit., 56:502-504, Appendix.

[41] *Maryland State Papers No. 1, The Black Books*, 10:66; para. 997 in the *Calendar*. Similar to the 1756 petition (ibid., 10:46-48) except that Hunter was now deceased.

[42] Ibid., 10:50; para. 1000 in the *Calendar*.

[43] Maryland Historical Society, MS. 1265.

[44] See especially Land, op. cit., pp. 280-285, 328.

[45] Frederick County Land Records, M:39.

[46] Rightmyer, *Maryland's Established Church*, op. cit., p. 157.

EPILOGUE

The preceding chapters have detailed what the records show concerning the first land surveys and their relation to the beginnings of settlement in Old Monocacy. Altogether some 200 surveys in this backwoods area of early Maryland have been described. All of these surveys were made in the relatively short span of only twenty years, and yet they covered, by 1743, virtually all reaches of today's Frederick County.

The people for whom this land was surveyed were a diverse crowd. Not alone did vast differences exist between the absentee land speculators of the established Eastern Shore and those who hewed their dwelling sites out of the wilderness on the land itself. Even among the settlers vast differences have been noted in the cultural, national and religious backgrounds. It was truly a melting pot area, and the first inhabitants inevitably provided a wide and firm foundation for all that was to come. The area's later growth has been important in the history of our Nation.

Although settlements in the first two decades were spread widely throughout the entire County, the parcels we have described were but a beginning. We have really only scratched the surface of the history of land in western Maryland. This fact cannot be emphasized too strongly.

After parcels had been laid out by initial survey, it often became apparent that adjoining land not yet taken up by others could be added to one's individual original parcel. This was done by what were known as Resurveys. A Resurvey was little different from the first surveys themselves except that they encompassed, in whole or in part, areas which had already been previously mapped and patented. Often the Resurvey repeated and showed separately the original survey itself, then indicated what as yet vacant land was being added. Sometimes resurveys discovered and therefore corrected overlaps where earlier surveys impinged upon one another.

Resurveys were patented and recorded in the same manner earlier surveys had been. This involved the problem of naming the succeeding parcel, for names were the means of identifying any particular piece of land. Usually, though not always, the phrase "Resurvey on" was simply added to the old name. But entirely new names were sometimes substituted for the old, and this can make tracing them a bit difficult. More importantly, since resurveys were often also made of other, earlier resurveys, one must be careful in preparing an historical cadastral map to note the exact point in time, like striking a balance sheet, not the period, for which it is intended.

Although a few such resurveys occurred before 1743, countless ones did follow thereafter. To provide a connecting link between the beginning parcels we have described and the existing land as we know it today requires further detailed study beyond the scope of this treatise. But if one wants to trace a parcel through subsequent history, he must delve into the sequence of the succeeding surveys themselves.

That may be the challenge with which we conclude this work: While we have attempted to show a picture of the area by 1743, it would be edifying to see similar pictures for succeeding points in time, say after a second twenty years, at the time Maryland achieved independent statehood, at times coinciding with the Federal censuses, and so on. It would also advance our knowledge to see summations made for the initial surveys in the other western Maryland Counties. The raw data have been gathered in the Tracey files. They only await scholars willing and able to bring the material together.

Hence, rather than entitle these last thoughts as an "Epilogue" to what we have recorded for the beginnings of Monocacy, may we leave them as a challenge to others by calling this a "Prologue" to future studies yet to come? That would be the wish of both Arthur Tracey and Grace Tracey. It is likewise my sincere wish, too.

John P. Dern

APPENDIX

Patent Series: Conversion Table 361
Chronological List of Surveys, 1721-1743 362
Alphabetical List of Surveys, 1721-1743 364
Lists of Inhabitants, 1733-1734 368
Petition to Divide Prince George's County, 1742 . . 370
Petition to Divide Prince George's Parish, 1742 . . 371
Early German Settlement in Frederick County . . . 372
Joh. Caspar Stöver's Records 374
Muster Rolls, 1757 378
Bibliography 381
Index 390

PATENT SERIES
Liber Numbers, 1721-1760

New series	Original Series		
46	PL No. 4	Patents	1715-1721
47	PL No. 5	Patents	1722-1726
48	PL No. 6	Patents	1724-1728
49	PL No. 7	Patents	1727-1730
50	PL No. 8	Patents	1730-1734
51	RY No. 1	Patents	1710-1718
52	CE No. 1	Patents	1714-1722
53	IL No. A	Certificates	1716-1728
54	IL No. B	Certificates	1723-1731
55	AM No. 1	Certificates	1726-1735
56	EI No. 1	Patents	1732-1734
57	EI No. 2	Patents	1734-1739
58	EI No. 3	Certificates	1730-1737
59	EI No. 4	Patents	1734-1740
60	EI No. 5	Certificates	1734-1741
61	EI No. 6	Patents	1737-1744
62	LG No. B	Patents	1739-1744
63	LG No. C	Certificates & Patents	1739-1747
64	LG No. E	Certificates	1741-1746
65	PT No. 1	Patents	1743-1747
66	PT No. 2	Patents	1742-1746
67	BT & BY No. 3	Patents	1745-1748
68	TI No. 1	Certificates & Patents	1743-1748
69	TI No. 3	Patents	1746-1749
70	TI No. 4	Patents	1746-1752
71	BY & GS No. 1	Certificates	1746-1750
72	BY & GS No. 2	Patents	1747-1751
73	BY & GS No. 3	Patents	1748-1762
74	BY & GS No. 4	Patents	1748-1754
75	BY & GS No. 5	Certificates	1748-1752
76	Y & S No. 6	Patents	1752-1755
77	Y & S No. 7	Certificates	1750-1753
78	Y & S No. 8	Patents	1752-1758
79	GS No. 1	Certificates	1748-1753
80	GS No. 2	Patents	1753-1755
81	BC & GS No. 1	Certificates	1751-1756
82	BC & GS No. 2	Patents	1753-1756
83	BC & GS No. 3	Patents	1753-1760
84	BC & GS No. 4	Certificates	1753-1755
85	BC & GS No. 5	Certificates	1754-1757
86	BC & GS No. 6	Patents	1753-1757

Elisabeth Hartsook, *Land Office Records of Colonial Maryland* (Annapolis, 1946), pp. 51-53. Certificate of Survey volumes also include Assignments.

CHRONOLOGICAL LIST OF SURVEYS, 1721-1743
For Alphabetical List and Page References, see pp. 364-367

1721	Nov. 10	Hope
1723	Apr. 20	Carrollton
	Nov. 20	Hope
	Nov. 20	Clovin
1724	Feb. 18	Nelsons Island
	Apr. 21	Metre
	May 1	Black Acre
	May 20	Happy Choice
	May 27	Addisons Choice
	May 28	Dulanys Lot
	May 29	Monocacy Manor
	Nov. 10	Carrollsburg
	Nov. 23	Albins Choice
	Nov. 23	Henry
1725	Mar. 2	Hobsons Choice
	Apr. 15	Taskers Chance
	May 28	Backland
	Nov. 4	Josiah
	Nov. 9	Jones Bottom
	Nov. 18	Meadow
	Nov. 22	Rocky Creek
1726	Jan. 10	Merediths Hunting Qtr.
	Mar. 5	Gunders Delight
1728	Apr. 1	Coxsons Rest
	Apr. 10	Welchs Tract
	Nov. 10	Broken Island
1729	Apr. 15	Abells Lot
	Aug. 1	Pipe Meadow
	Sept 1	Breeches
	Nov. 3	Wett Work
	Dec. 1	Isaacs Inheritance
1730	July 1	Hedge Hogg
	Sept 25	Partnership
	Nov. 2	Pains Delight
	Nov. 14	Merryland
	Nov. 14	Spring Garden
1731	Jan. 4	Kettankin Bottom
	Mar. 27	Good Luck
	Apr. 9	Ivy Church
	May 1	Ramble
	June 25	Gaithers Chance
	Feb. 14	Merryland (Res.)
	Aug. 14	The Back Land
1732	Sept. 2	Carrollsburg
	Sept. 5	Poplar Thicket
	Nov. 29	Well Watered Bottom
	Dec. 1	Poplar Bottom
	Dec 5	Providence
1733	Jan. 12	Chance

1733	Apr. 9	Forrest
	Nov. 16	Hedges Delight
1734	Mar. 26	Two Brothers
	June 13	Forest
	June 18	Sweeds Folly
	June 30	Pile Hall
1737	Apr. 5	Peace
1738	Jan. 7	Thomas
	May 10	Jacobs Fortune
	Aug. 9	Green Spring
	Aug. 9	Taylors Lot
	Aug. 9	Addition
	Nov. 3	Johns Mountain
	Nov. 10	Trura
	Nov. 10	Royenton Plains
	Nov. 28	Hunting Bottom
	Nov. 28	Trimm[ling]
	Nov. 30	Hunters Lot
1739	Feb. 9	Beattys Delight
	Mar. 6	Anchor and Hope
	Mar. 10	Rams Horn
	Mar. 22	Johns Good Luck
	May 2	Slate Ridge
	May 3	Ogles Good Will
	May 20	Lubberland
	May 27	Fouts Delight
	June 25	Dukes Woods
	July 5	Williams Project
	Aug. 22	Becrafts Delight
	Aug. 22	Kendricks Hap
	Aug. 23	Strife
	Aug. 24	Peace and Quietness
	Aug. 25	Chidleys Range
	Sept 13	Debutts Delight
	Sept 13	Plummers Delight
	Oct. 10	Friends Good Will
	Oct. 15	Low Land
	Oct. 20	Hobsons Choice
1740	Feb. 22	Arrow Point
	Feb. 22	Pick Axe
	Apr. 1	Delight
	May 24	Prevention
	Sept 16	Chittam Castle
	Nov. 22	Mount Pleasant
	Nov. 25	Dispatch
	Nov. 27	Christians Choyce
	Nov. 27	Lost Spring
	Nov. 27	Orricks Folly
	Nov. 27	Turners Forest

Date	Name	Date	Name
1741 Jan. 20	Beaver Dam Level	1742 Sept 29	Cooperton
Jan. 20	Black Walnut Bottom	Oct. 5	Exchange
Mar. 10	Leonards Good Luck	Oct. 7	Hog Yard
Mar. 25	Debutts Hunting Ground	Oct. 8	Burnt House
Apr. 7	Sugar Loaf	Oct. 19	Green Meadow
Apr. 15	Darbys Delight	Nov. 6	Bear Den
Apr. 15	Brandywine Spring	Nov. 10	Addition
May 14	Dawsons Purchase	Nov. 11	Bonnetts Resolution
May 23	Dear Bought	1743 Jan. 10	Blue Spring
May 27	Good Luck	Jan. 21	Mount Pleasant
June 1	Refuses	Feb. 2	Shettle
June 10	Kemps Delight	Feb. 3	Elders Kindness
June 29	Inlett	Feb. 10	German Plains
July 3	Justices Delight	Feb. 24	Stoney Hive
July 3	Richards Hunting Ground	Mar. 6	Smiths Lot
July 3	Spring Plain	Mar. 8	Saint Elizabeth
July 3	Williams Intention	Mar. 9	Black Walnut Bottom
July 7	Hazel Valley	Mar. 11	Taylors Piglison
July 7	Papan Bottom	Mar. 14	Den of Wolves
Aug. 10	Pleasant Valley	Apr. 1	Two Brothers
Oct. 21	Matthews Lot	Apr. 7	Plummers Delight
Nov. 10	Pools Delight	Apr. 8	Plummers Hunting Lot
Nov. 21	Palmers Choice	Apr. 15	Swingaback
Nov. 21	Switzerland	May 30	Partnership
Nov. 22	Craimes Quietness	June 3	Gap
Nov. 25	Mill Place	June 3	Digges Lot
Nov. 28	Chestnut	June 12	Boyling Springs
Nov. 28	Hunting Lot	June 17	Lambson
Nov. 28	Mankine	June 18	Jacobs Cowpen
Nov. 28	Shoemakers Choice	June 20	Addn to Sassafras Bottom
Nov. 28	Piney Neck	June 28	Hunting Loot
Dec. 10	Masswander	June 28	Pleasant Meddo
Dec. 10	Otersom	June 28	Rich Hills
Dec. 19	Coopers Point	June 28	Food Plenty
Dec. 28	Wine Garden	July 10	Beattys Venture
1742 Jan. 15	Saplin Ridge	Sept 2	Hooks and Hills
Feb. 1	Abentons Cabin	Sept 22	Low Mill
Feb. 19	William and Elizabeth	Nov. 15	Charles and Mary
Feb 25	Douthets Chance	Nov. 21	George and Margaret
Mar. 2	Wooden Platter	Nov. 26	Longatepaugh
Mar. 5	Mallingah	Nov. 29	Rich Bottom
Mar. 14	Den of Wolves	Dec. 3	Mill Lot
Mar. 15	Jovial Ramble	Dec. 10	Palentine
Apr. 8	Hazzard		
Apr. 12	Black Acre		
Apr. 28	Johnsons Delight		
May 3	Disappointment		
June 2	Wilsons Fancy		
June 15	Partnership (Res.)		
June 18	Dispute		
June 27	Houses Addition		
Sept. 7	Chestnut Hill		

ALPHABETICAL LIST OF SURVEYS, 1721-1743

Name	For	Date	Page Text	Ref. Map	Survey (Patent)
Abells Lot	Parsons, Abel	Apr. 5, 1729	92	90	AM 1:370
Abentons Cabin	*Woodapple, Frederick	Feb. 1, 1742	33n	-	
Addisons Choice	Addison, Thomas	May 27, 1724	31	34	IL B:104
Addition	Weymore, Bernard	Aug. 9, 1738	191	186	LG E:35
Addition	*McKeen, Alexander	Nov. 10, 1742	239	238	BC & GS 27:581
Addn to Sassafras Bottom	Laney, Teter	June 20, 1743	217	186	LG E:280
Albins Choice	Radford, John	Nov. 23, 1724	75	70	IL B:17
Anchor and Hope	Albin, Thomas Touchstone, Richard	Mar. 6, 1739	222	223	EI 5:509
Arrow Point	Hilleary, Thomas	Feb. 22, 1740	91	60	LG C:194
Back Land, The	Digges, John	Aug. 14, 1732	249	248	EI 3:348
Backland	Livers, Arnold (assigned) Bordley, Thomas	May 28, 1725	39	-	Unpat'd.
Bear Den	Chalmers, John	Nov. 6, 1742	105	-	LG E:311
Beattys Delight	Beatty, Thomas	Feb. 9, 1739	122	229	IL B:108
Beattys Venture	Beatty, Thos. & Wm.	July 10, 1743	128	116	LG E:408
Beaver Dam Level	Elder, William	Jan. 20, 1741	254	248	LG E:97
Becrafts Delight	Becraft, Benjamin	Aug. 22, 1739	231	229	LG C:55
Black Acre	Black, William	May 1, 1724	30	-	IL A:464
Black Acre	Griffith, William	Apr. 12, 1742	91	90	GS 1:135
Black Walnut Bottom	Elder, William	Jan. 20, 1741	253	248	LG E:95
Black Walnut Bottom	Wickham, Nathaniel	Mar. 9, 1743	341	248	LG E:271
Blue Spring	*Vertriess, Hardman	Jan. 10, 1743	216	186	BC & GS 1:259
Bonnetts Resolution	*Wetzel, Martin	Nov. 11, 1742	209	186	LG E:202
Boyling Springs	Wells, Joseph	June 12, 1743	85	80	LG E:290
Brandywine Springs	Ryan, Darby	Apr. 15, 1741	230	229	LG C:190
Breeches	Williams, John	Sept. 1, 1729	99	100	IL B:450
Broken Island	Nelson, Arthur	Nov. 10, 1728	59	60	AM 1:27
Burnt House	Dulany, Daniel	Oct. 8, 1742	33	244	BC & GS 1:265
Carrollsburg	Carroll, Chas., et al	Nov. 10, 1724	30	-	IL A:755
Carrollsburg	Carroll, Chas., et al	Sept 2, 1732	239	238	EI 5:89
Carrollton	Carroll, Chas., et al	Apr. 20, 1723	25	29	IL A:405
Chance	Beall, John	Jan. 12, 1733	84	95	EI 5:289
Charles and Mary	Hedges, Charles	Nov. 15, 1743	110	107	LG E:293
Chestnut	*Stull, Adam	Nov. 28, 1741	170	155	LG E:385
Chestnut Hill	Gump, George	Sept 7, 1742	188	186	LG E:102
Chidleys Range	Matthews, Chidley	Aug. 25, 1739	84	155	EI 5:506
Chittam Castle	Digges, Nich. & Ignat	Sept 16, 1740	105	100	LG C:183
Christians Choyce	*Getzendanner, Chrstn	Nov. 27, 1740	166	155	LG B:533
Clovin	Lloyd, Philemon	Nov. 20, 1723	30	-	LG C:43
Coopers Point	Laney, Teter	Dec. 19, 1741	217	186	LG E:86
Cooperton	Dulany, Daniel	Sept 29, 1742	227	223	BC & GS 19:459
Coxsons Rest	Wilcoxson, Thomas	Apr. 1, 1728	94	95	AM 1:303
Craimes Quietness	Pennington, Abraham *Staley, Jacob	Nov. 22, 1741	177	244	BY & GS 1:628
Darbys Delight	Ryan, Darby	Apr. 15, 1741	230	229	LG E:77
Dawsons Purchase	Dawson, Thomas	May 14, 1741	226	223	LG C:196
Dear Bought	Davis, Richard	May 23, 1741	44	100	LG C:184
Debutts Delight	Plummer, Philemon	Sept 13, 1739	234	229	BC & GS 37:221
Debutts Hunting Ground	Debutts, Robert	Mar. 25, 1741	76	-	LG E:78
Delight	Wilson, Thomas	Apr. 1, 1740	245	244	EI 5:495
Den of Wolves	Whitaker, Mark Honey, George	Mar. 14, 1743	202	186	LG E:302

Name	For	Date	Page Text	Ref. Map	Survey (Patent)
Digges Lot	Digges, John	June 3, 1743	43	24	LG E:197, 528
Disappointment	Digges, John	May 3, 1742	43	325	LG E:196
Dispatch	Steuart, Dr. George	Nov. 25, 1740	174	80	LG E:271
	Kemp, Christian (asgnd)				
Dispute	James, John	June 18, 1742	233	229	LG E:88
Douthets Chance	Douthet, John	Feb. 25, 1742	238	238	LG E:301
Dukes Woods	Livers, Arnold	June 25, 1739	250	100	LG C:31
	Carmack, Cornelius & Wm.				
Dulanys Lot	Dulany, Daniel	May 28, 1724	115	116	EI 5:244
Elders Kindness	Brawner, Edward	Feb. 3, 1743	254	248	LG E:282
Exchange	Dulany, Daniel	Oct. 5, 1742	245	244	BY & GS 1:177
Food Plenty	Plummer, Samuel	June 28, 1743	234	229	LG E:306
Forest	Sprigg, Osborn	June 13, 1734	225	223	AM 1:375
Forrest	Magruder, John	Apr. 9, 1733	243	244	AM 1:365
Fouts Delight	Fout, Baltis	May 27, 1739	162	155	EI 5:517
Friends Good Will	Davis, Meredith	Oct. 10, 1739	81	80	LG E:194
Gaithers Chance	Gaither, Benjamin	June 25, 1731	101	100	AM 1:239
Gap	Spuch, Adam	June 3, 1743	203	186, 248	Y & S 7:210
	Ambrose, Martin				
George and Margaret	Swinehart, George	Nov. 21, 1743	156	155	LG E:355
German Plains	*Leatherman, Daniel	Feb. 10, 1743	246	244	BC & GS 14:711
Good Luck	Davis Meredith	Mar. 27, 1731	81	80	(PL 8:649)
Good Luck	Matthews, George	May 27, 1741	85	-	LG E:591
Green Meadow	Dulany, Daniel	Oct. 19, 1742	246	244	BC & GS 27:552
Green Spring	Baer, George	Aug. 9, 1738	193	186	LG C:35
	Reisner, Michael (asgnd)				
Gunders Delight	Erickson, Gunder	Mar. 5, 1726	40	24	IL A:732
Happy Choice	Black, William	May 20, 1724	30	-	IL A:464
Hazel Valley	Digges, John	July 7, 1741	43	-	LG E:62
Hazzard	Thomas, Notley	Apr. 8, 1742	66	60	LG E:192
Hedge Hogg	Hedges, Joseph	July 1, 1730	106	107	AM 1:44
Hedges Delight	Hedges, Solomon	Nov. 16, 1733	108	107	?
Henry	Radford, John	Nov. 23, 1724	40	80	IL B:16
	Ballenger, Henry				
Hobsons Choice	Nelson, Arthur	Mar. 2, 1725	59	60	IL B:131
Hobson's Choice	Nelson, Arthur	Oct. 20, 1739	59	60	LG E:183
Hog Yard	*Arnold, John George	Oct. 7, 1742	275n	244	LG E:397
Hooks and Hills	Hook, James	Sept 2, 1743	65	60	LG E:408
Hope	Fitzredmond, William	Nov. 10, 1721	25	-	FF 7:406
	Bennett, Richard (asgnd)				
Hope (Res.)	Bennett, Richard	Nov. 20, 1723	25	24	IL B:1
Houses Addition	House, Thomas	June 27, 1742	171	155	LG E:570
Hunters Lot	Crever, Philip	Nov. 30, 1738	198	186	(EI 6:135)
Hunting Loot	Plummer, Samuel	June 28, 1743	234	229	LG E:297
Hunting Lot	*Devilbiss, Caspar	Nov. 28, 1741	319	325	BY & GS 5:540
Hunting Bottom	Foy, Miles	Nov. 28, 1738	225	223	LG C:48
Inlett	Brunner, Jacob	June 29, 1741	269	-	LG E:358
Isaacs Inheritance	van Metre, Isaac	Dec. 1, 1729	73	70	AM 1:56
Ivy Church	Williams, John	Apr. 9, 1731	99	100	AM 1:238
Jacobs Cowpen	Williams, William	June 18, 1743	44	-	LG E:278
Jacobs Fortune	Manser, Jac. Matthias	May 10, 1738	190	186	EI 2:719
Johns Good Luck	Parr, John	Mar. 22, 1739	231	229	BY & GS 1:215
Johns Mountain	Verdriess, John	Nov. 3, 1738	215	186	No recd.
Johnsons Delight	Johnson, Thomas	Apr. 28, 1742	246	244	LG E:96
Jones Bottom	Jones, Josiah	Nov. 9, 1725	89	90	IL A:725

Name	For	Date	Page Text	Ref. Map	Survey (Patent)
Josiah	Ballenger, Josiah	Nov. 4, 1725	79	80	IL A:121
Jovial Ramble	Beall, Alexander	Mar. 15, 1742	44	-	LG E:186
Justices Delight	Digges, John Justice, John (asgnd) Becraft, George (asgnd)	July 3, 1741	101	100	LG E:61
Kemps Delight	Steuart, Dr. George Kemp, Christian (asgnd)	June 10, 1741	174	80	LG E:273
Kendricks Hap	Kendrick, Robert	Aug. 22, 1739	228	229	LG C:54
Kettankin Bottom	Magruder, John	Jan. 4, 1731	65	60	EI 2:48
Lambson	Bachdold, Henry	June 17, 1743	179	155	LG E:569
Leonards Good Luck	Lehnert, Isaac	Mar. 10, 1741	181	155	BY & GS 1:204
Longatepaugh	Chydler, George	Nov. 26, 1743	220	186	LG E:303
Lost Spring	*Swinehart, George	Nov. 27, 1740	156	155	LG C:199
Low Land	Low, Daniel Johnson	Oct. 15, 1739	86	60	EI 5:498
Low Mill	Hockersmith, Conrad	Sept 22, 1743	239	238	LG E:280
Lubberland	Carmack, William	May 20, 1739	104	100	LG C:35
Mallingah	Miller, Isaac	Mar. 5, 1742	180	-	LG E:212
Mankine	*Shoup, Martin	Nov. 28, 1741	164	155	BC & GS 23:363
Masswander	*Staley, Melchior	Dec. 10, 1741	176	155	LG E:589
Matthews Lot	Matthews, Thomas	Oct. 21, 1741	85	80	LG E:65
Meadow	van Metre, John	Nov. 18, 1725	69	70	IL B:18
Merediths Hunting Qtr.	Davis, Meredith	Jan. 10, 1726	81	90	IL B:451
Merryland	Tasker, Benjamin Coville, John (asgnd)	Nov. 14, 1730	37	38, 95	IL B:453
Merryland (Res.)	Coville, John	Feb. 14, 1731	37	38	AM 1:345
Metre	van Metre, John	Apr. 21, 1724	69	70	IL B:18
Mill Lot	Ballenger, Henry	Dec. 3, 1743	81	80	LG E:569
Mill Place	Wetzel, Martin	Nov. 25, 1741	208	186	LG E:85
Monocacy Manor	Baltimore, Lord	May 29, 1724	302	322	IL B:198
Mount Pleasant	Crouch, James	Nov. 22, 1740	232	229	TI 1:407
Mount Pleasant	Jennings, Joseph	Jan. 21, 1743	350	304	LG E:296
Nelsons Island	Nelson, Arthur	Feb. 18, 1724	59	60	IL B:132
Ogles Good Will	Livers, Arnold	May 3, 1739	249	248	EI 5:500
Orricks Folly	Orrick, James	Nov. 27, 1740	231	229	Unpatented
Otersom	*Staley, Jacob	Dec. 10, 1741	176	155	LG E:384
Pains Delight	Abington, John Payne, Flayle	Nov. 2, 1730	94	95	AM 1:30
Palentine	Shaver, Peter	Dec. 10, 1743	181	155	LG E:394
Palmers Choice	Palmer, Thomas	Nov. 21, 1741	75	70	?
Papan Bottom	Digges, John Wickham, Nathl. (asgnd)	July 7, 1741	339	338	LG E:62
Partnership	Gittings, Thomas	Sept 25, 1730	92	90	AM 1:372
Partnership	Campbell, John	May 30, 1743	105	100	LG E:576
Partnership (Res.)	Gittings, Thomas Wardrop, James	June 15, 1742	92	90	LG C:654
Peace	Ogle, Joseph	Apr. 5, 1737	326	325	EI 5:503
Peace and Quietness	Kemp, Conrad	Aug. 24, 1739	171	155	TI 1:445
Pick Axe	Hilleary, Thomas	Feb. 22, 1740	91	90	LG C:198
Pile Hall	Sprigg, Richard	June 30, 1734	225	223	EI 3:425
Piney Neck	*Six, Henry	Nov. 28, 1741	218	186	LG E:588
Pipe Meadow	van Metre, John, Jr.	Aug. 1, 1729	72	70	AM 1:56
Pleasant Meddo	Plummer, Samuel	June 28, 1743	234	229	LG E:305
Pleasant Valley	Crouch, James	Aug. 10, 1741	232	229	LG E:80
Plummers Delight	Plummer, Samuel	Sept 13, 1739	234	-	EI 5:57
Plummers Delight	Plummer, Micajah	Apr. 7, 1743	235	229	LG E:298

Name	For	Date	Page Text	Ref. Map	Survey (Patent)
Plummers Hunting Lot	Plummer, Micajah	Apr. 8, 1743	235	-	LG E:298
Pools Delight	Poole, John	Nov. 10, 1741	227	223	LG E:79
Poplar Bottom	Beatty, Edward	Dec. 1, 1732	120	229	EI 3:431
Poplar Thicket	Beal, John, Jr. and Creary, Dr. Thomas	Sept. 5, 1732	40	60	AM 1:321
Prevention	Wilson, Thomas Whitaker, Thomas	May 24, 1740	245	244	EI 5:492
Providence	Beatty, Edward	Dec. 5, 1732	120	229	EI 3:432
Ramble	Prather, Thomas	May 1, 1731	63	60	AM 1:49
Rams Horn	*Arnold, John George	Mar. 10, 1739	275	244	PT 2:225
Refuses	Hawkins, John	June 1, 1741	96	95	LG E:314
Rich Bottom	Trout, Henry	Nov. 29, 1743	220	186	LG E:305
Rich Hills	Plummer, Samuel	June 28, 1743	234	229	LG E:306
Richards Hunting Ground	Digges, John	July 3, 1741	42	100	LG E:64
Rocky Creek	Bordley, Thomas Stoddert, James (asgnd)	Nov. 22, 1725	37 39	155	IL B:108
Royenton Plains	Munday, Henry	Nov. 10, 1738	333	325	LG C:176
Saint Elizabeth	*Spuch, Adam	Mar. 8, 1743	210	186	BC & GS 27:548
Sandy Run	Weymore, Bernard	June 20, 1743	192	186	LG E:317
Saplin Ridge	Stilley, Peter	Jan. 15, 1742	114	155	LG E:286
Shettle	*Marks, Robert	Feb. 2, 1743	245	244	Y & S 7:105
Shoemakers Choice	*Kens, Philip	Nov. 28, 1741	169	155	LG E:81
Slate Ridge	Livers, Arnold Elder, William (asgnd)	May 2, 1739	206	248	EI 5:500
Smiths Lot	Reisner, Michael	Mar. 6, 1743	195	186	LG E:273
Spring Garden	Abington, John	Nov. 14, 1730	123	34	AM 1:31
Spring Plain	Digges, John	July 3, 1741	43	24	LG E:64
Stoney Hive	Pearre, James	Feb. 24, 1743	92	90	LG E:381
Strife	House, Thomas	Aug. 23, 1739	171	155	EI 5:517
Sugar Loaf	Hilleary, Thomas	Apr. 7, 1741	89	90	LG C:181
Sweeds Folly	Nelson, John Sr.	June 18, 1734	61	60	EI 5:294
Swingaback	Candler, Rev. David	Apr. 15, 1743	136	155	LG E:211
Switzerland	*Staley, Jacob	Nov. 21, 1741	176	155	LG E:377
Taskers Chance	Tasker, Benjamin	Apr. 15, 1725	257	259	IL A:738
Taylors Lot	Weller, Jacob	Aug. 9, 1738	212	186	LG C:47
Taylors Piglison	Weller, Jacob	Mar. 11, 1743	212	186	LG E:214
Thomas	Gittings, Thomas	Jan. 7, 1738	93	90	LG C:51
Trimm[ling]	Foy, Miles	Nov. 28, 1738	225	223	LG C:49
Trura	Munday, Henry	Nov. 10, 1738	333	325	LG C:292
Turners Forest	Turner, William	Nov. 27, 1740	232	229	LG C:188
Two Brothers	Fletcher, Thos & John	Mar. 26, 1734	43	-	EI 5:291
Two Brothers	Lakin, Abraham	Apr. 1, 1743	67	60	LG E:379
Welchs Tract	Davis, Meredith	Apr. 10, 1728	81	90	IL B:119
Well Watered Bottom	Beatty, Edward	Nov. 29, 1732	120	229	EI 3:432
Wett Work	Abington, John	Nov. 3, 1729	39	24	AM 1:311
William and Elizabeth	Mears, William	Feb. 19, 1742	91	-	LG E:283
Williams Intention	Digges, John	July 3, 1741	43	100	LG E:59
Williams Project	Williams, Rev. Wm.	July 5, 1739	345	338	LG E:593
Wilsons Fancy	Wilson, Robert	June 2, 1742	237	238	BY & GS 1:152
Wine Garden	*Bonnett, Jacob Wetzel, Martin (asgnd)	Dec. 28, 1741	208	186	LG E:208
Wooden Platter	Wardrop, James	Mar. 2, 1742	245	244	TI 1:486

----

* Surveyed for Daniel Dulany, who assigned certificate as shown.

LISTS OF INHABITANTS, 1733-1734

List of Taxables, 1733 Monocosie Hundred Maryland State Papers No. 1 The Black Books, para. 272 in the Calendar	Those that had no tobacco burnt in Monoccosea Hund. Aug. 1734 Prince George's County Court Records, V:98
Bales, John	Bailes, John
Ballinger, Henry	Ballinger, Henry
Bartlett, John	Bartlett, John
Beatty, Edward	Betty, Edward
Beatty, Henry	Betty, Henry
Beatty, James	
Beatty, John	Betty John
Beatty, Thomas	
Beatty, William	Betty, William
Blavin, Daniel	
Blavin, James	Blevin, James
Backelt, Edward	Bockit, Edward
Bray, Henry	Bray, Henry
Cantrell, Joseph	Cantwell, Joseph
Cannode, Charles	
Cartledge. Edmund	Cartledge. Edmund
Cherry, Thomas	Cherry, Thos.
Clarke, John	
Clarke, William	Clarke, William
Coburn, James	Coburne, James
Cocks, Allen	
Cox, Brewer	Cox, Benj.
Cox, John	Cox, John
Cox, Peter	Coxe, Peter
Davis, John	Davis, John
	Digs' quarter, Mr. Charles two slaves
Dobbin, John Sen	Dobbin, John
Dobbin, John Jun	
Dowthit, John	
Dowthit, Thomas	Douthwhite, Thos.
	Dutchil, William
	Fee, George
Falling, Redmond	
Farquhar, Allen	Forquer, Allen
Friend, Charles	Friend, Charles
Friend, John	
Friend, Nicholas	Friend, Neals
Harland, James	Harling, James
Harland, John	
Hargys, Thomas	Harquis, Thos.
Hedges, Charles	
Hedges, Joshua	
Hedges, Solomon	Hedge, Solomon
Hillyard, John	
Hillyard, Thomas	Hilliard, Thomas
Hives, William	
	Hoops, John
Hugh, John	Hughs, John
Jacks, Jerom	Jacks, Jeremia
Jackson, John	Jackson, John
	Jennings, Will.
John, Capt.	
Johnson, Henry	Johnson, Henry
	Johnson, John
Jones, Evan	Jones, Evan
Jones, Robert	Jones, Robt
Kelley, Bryan	
Kindrick, Robert	Kendrick, Robert
Lyon, Humburston	Lyon, Ambuston

Taxables 1733	"No tobacco Burnt" 1734
Mackee, David	
Matson, James	
Mathews, Chidley	Mahon, James
Mathews, George	Matthews, Chidley
Mathews, William	Matthews, George
Maddock, Johannes	
Myer, John	Middock, Johannes
Moore, George	Miers, John
Moore, John	
Moore, William	Moore, John
Nelson, John	Moore, Will.
Nickolls, Edward	
Nichols, James	Nichols, Edward
Nicholls, John	
Payne, Flayle	Nichols, John
Polson, Richard	
Powell, John	
Pyborn, John	
Ratcliffe, Robert	Pybonn, John
Roberts, John	
Rosson, Charles	
Ryan, Darby	Rien, Darby
Royal, John	Royall, John
Sheppard, William Jr.	Shepherd, William Senr.
Sheppard, William Jr.[sic]	Shepherd, William Junr.
Sherlock, John	
Shoarwell, William	Sherril, Will. Senr.
Scarwill, William Jr.	Sherril, Will. Junr
Southernfield, John	Souterfield, John
Sprigg's quarter, Mr.	Spig's quarter, Capt Ed.
2 slaves	two slaves
Spurgeon, James	Spurgin, James
Spurgeon, William	Spurgin, William
Story, Richard	Story, Richard
Stull, John	Stull, John
Swearingen, Van	Swaningham, Van
Swift, Flower	
Touchstone, Richard	Touchstone, Richard
Tredann, John	Tredan, John
Upton, John	
Vandever, John	Vandever, John
Vametera, Isaac	Vanmater, Isaac
	Vines, Mordecai
	Veach, John
	Vernoy, Cornelius
	Walker, John
Walling, Elisha	Wallen, Elisha
Walling, James	
Walling William	Wallen, William
West, John	West, John
West, Thomas	West, Thomas
Whitaker, Thomas	Whitaker, Thos.
	Willcoxon, John
Wilkinson, Miner	Wilkinson, Minor
Williams, Joseph	Williams, Jos.
Williams, Province	
Willson, John	
Willson, Robert	Willson, Robert
Right, James	Wright, James
106 names	83 names
11 missing	34 missing
117	117

PETITIONERS SEEKING CREATION OF FREDERICK COUNTY, 1742
(Through Division of Prince George's County)

Petition to Governor Thomas Bladen for division of Prince George's County "from the mouth of Rock Creek to a bridge near Kennedy Farell's and then east to the Patuxent River and along the River to Baltimore and Anne Arundel Counties," October 16, 1742. Signed by:

Nath'l. Wickham Jr.	Chas. Higinbotham	Chas. Beavan	Edward Jones
Thomas Marshall	James Wilson	Phillip Mason	Edward Busey
Hen'y Truman	Jonathan Hagar	Leonard Marbury	Joseph Bonner
Richard Keene	John Williams, Sr.	William Ray	Benj. Norris
Jos. Belt	Jeremiah Berry	Benjamin Perry	Meredith Davis
William Beatty	[Thomas] Prather	Humberstone Lyon	Thos. Edmonston
S. Bordley.	[?] Scott	Rig^{tt} Odall	Jonathan Birch
Thos. Brooke, Jr.	George Hardy, Jr.	John Smith	Wm. Beall of Ninian
Jno. Lawrence	Charles Polke	Robt. Evans	Thos. Chittam
John Harvey	T. Sprigg	William Magruder	Thos. Butler
John Lamar	Thos. Brooke	Jno. Wilcoxon, Sr.	Saml. Beall, Jr.
Robt. Pottinger	[?] Boswell	Jno. Wilcoxon, Jr.	Phil. Chittam
Rich^d. Shoves	[?] Beansey	Luke Marbury	Jos. Beall
Jo. [La]nham, Jr.	John Bell	Jas. Craufurd	Thos. Williams, Jr.
James Beall	John Clagett	Danll. Carroll	Wm. Hughes
John McCay	Thom. Mullican	Robt. Bradley	John Adamson
[I]saac Lansdale	James Harvey	Basil Beckwith	Peter Stonestreet
Richd Duckett	Mareen Duvall, Jr.	W. Beanes	Edward Stonestreet
John Wilson	Benj. Duvall	Jno. Hawkins	Thos. Stonestreet
John Wright	Mareen Duvall, Sr.	Richard Brooke	Lawrence Owens
John Orme	The Grand Jury	Robt. Gordon	Edw'd Owen
Phill. Evans	James Magruder	Wm. Thomas	[?] Bell of Robt.
Thos. Gatton	Edward Clag[ett]	Chas. Chartin	Jno. Dawson
Lee Stephen	[?] Dudane	Wm. Luckett	Jno. Lowe, Jr.
Lee Lewis	John Dunn	Richard Lanham	Thos. Williams, Sr.
Middleton Belt	Robert Wade	[?] Rawllings	Thos. Waring
Thos. Kindred	John Philips	Smallwood Coghill	Jno. Contee
John Cramphin	Benjn. Boyd	John Haggerton	Nathan Magruder
James Pollett	Robert Debutt	John Goddard	Thos. Dawson
John Bateman	Henry [M]unday	Paul Talbert	Jno. Lowe, Sr.
William Bright	John Smoote	Jos. Voble	Henry Lowe
Benj^a Belt, Jr.	Jeremiah Jack	Thos. Athey, Sr.	Geo. Dawson
Wm. Magruder Selby	Beanneard Johnson	Walter Athey	Clement Smith
Basil War[ing]	Robert Lamar	James Gibbes	John Orine
E. Sprigg	Charles Clage	Chris. Edelen	John Bowie
Wm. Bowie	George Nicholls	Leonard Wheeler	James Bowie
Jas. Waring	Charles O[dall]	John Cowynn	Jno. Addison
Jno. Levitt	William Potts	Isaac Wells	

Maryland State Papers No. 1, The Black Books, 3:9 (Portfolio); para. 454 in the Calendar.

PETITIONERS SEEKING CREATION OF ALL SAINTS' PARISH, 1742
(Through Division of Prince George's Parish)

Thos. Wilson R.C.	James Veatch	William Watts	Jno Vandewer
Thos Wilson Junr.	Nathan Veatch	John Pyburn	Umberston Lion
Robt Debuts	Matthew Markland	John Pyburn, Jun.	Jacob Fedreck
Willm Ferrill	Soll Stimton	George Calvin	Thos Barnett
Jno Chramphin	William Ellis	Joseph Wells	Benj^a. Osborn
Henry Cramphin	Jer. Hays	Nathan Dawson	Geo Colton
Basill Cramphin	Luke Ray	John Powell	Jno Bell
Jno Owen	William Griffith	Bryan Finican	Jno Fletcher
Thos Jones	Thomas Hulsell	John Valentine Presler	Jno Ward
Flower Swift	Alexander Duvall	John Hutson	Willm Ward
Mark Whiteacar	William Brown	Thos Johnston	Jno Parcons
Thos Whiteacer	Thomas Compton, Jun	Paltis Foutch	Andrew Martin
Benj^a. Williams	John Adams	Jacob Foutch	Geo Ivill
Jos Scidmore	William Jennings	Jacob Mathews	Jno Cabis
Jno Poole	John Presler	Jacob Hooff	Wm Black
Jno Johnson	Peter Presler	Geo Gomph	Hugh Rice
John Veatch	Thomas Prather	Jacob Stoner	Michell Jones
Samuel Elliss	Jo. Nellson	Chid^{ll} Mathew	Jno Fowns
Nathan Maste[rs]	James Hook	Jos. Smith	Robt Howston
Robert Masters	Jno. Hook	Peter Smith	Garatt Golb[?]
John Wilcoxon, Sen	Jno. Delashmett	Fran^{cs} White	Thos Davis
John Wilcoxon, Jun	Elias Delashmett	Dan^{ll} France	Saml Davis
Jas. Dickson	Robt. Owens	Abra^m Miller	James Faun
Francis Foy	Frail. Pain	Chris^n Thomas	Wm Graham
Willam Jones	Thos. Fee	Peter Hoofman	Wm Healer
Wim. Wilcoxon	Jno. Bailey	Christan Citchadaner	Thos Fletcher
Nathaniel Cotman	Geo. Fee	Jos Broner	Gavin Hambleton
Willam. Cotman	Jno. Tumer	Jacob Broner	Thos. Compton
Jos. Hickman	Nathaniel Tucker	Jno Broner	Wm. Morris
John Winsor	Wm. Tucker	Henry Broner	Sam^{ll} MacKinly
James Rimmen	Jno. Tucker	Jno TeterLany	Sam^{ll} Eads
Phillup Taylor	Isaac. Wells	Henry Knafe	Isaac Hardee
Nehemiah Losson	Edward. Mobberley	Jacob Knafe	Jno Mash
Michal Dent Cadel	Wm. Mobberley	Leonard Baker	Wm Pheby
John Shelton	Clement. Mobberley	Geo Swinehart	Thos Wilcason
Richd Losson	Geo. Williams	Geo. Bare	Jno Fryer
Nicolas Elam	Francis Hallbert	Thos. Prather	Rice Ginkins
Charls Shelton	Andrew. Cox	Aron Prather	Charles Bussey
Wm. Hickman	Thos. Morris	Van Swearingan	Wm Norris
Andrew Cottrell	Giles. Williams	Jos Chapline	Sam^{ll} Plummer
John Colliar	William Hunt	Wm. Shepard	Wm. Cook
Francis Colliar	Thomas Hunt	Wm Shepar, Jnr.	Stephan Hamton
Charls Hays	Elezer Hunt	Wm Spirgen	Jno. Wofford
Wm. Hays	John Johnson	James Spurgen	Jno Wats
Thos Chartrd[?]	Willm. Parry	Jno Moore	Benj^a. Warringanf...
William Wheat	Charles Rosson	Wm Moore	Jno Smoot
James Anis	Richard Ransom	Wm Moore, Jnr.	Thos Beall
George Weaver	Robert Evins	Geo Moore	and many more might
Charles Coats	Thomas Gittings	Jno Stull	be added -- if had
William Williams	George Williams	Henry Frieks	time.

The Maryland Diocesan Archives, on deposit in the Maryland Historical Society.

EARLY GERMAN SETTLEMENT IN FREDERICK COUNTY
Individuals Listed by Earliest Documented Appearance

Religion[1] Location[2]		Arrived at Philadelphia	Last Known Elsewhere	First Record in Frdk. Co.	First Land Record
Schweinhart, J. Georg	LG L	pre-1725	Nov. 8, 1730	Nov. 16, 1731	Nov. 27, 1740
Fauth, Jacob & Baltus	LG L		Nov. 8, 1730	May 22, 1734	Mar. 29, 1738
Weiss, Frantz	TC R	Aug. 27, 1733	Aug. 10, 1735	1736	July 28, 1746
Gump, Joh. Georg	UG M	Sept 18, 1732	Dec. 25, 1733	Mar. 1736	Sept 7, 1742
Devilbiss Family	MM L	Sept 21, 1731	Jan. 1, 1735	Apr. 28, 1736	Nov. 28, 1743
Matthias, Joh. Jacob	UG L	Aug. 17, 1733	June 23, 1734	Apr. 28, 1736	Aug. 19, 1743
Hoff, Jacob	L	Aug. 17, 1733	June 23, 1734	Apr. 28, 1736	
Brunner, Jacob	TC R	Aug. 23, 1728	Aug. 28, 1728	May 16, 1736	June 29, 1741
Lehnich, Dieter	UG L	pre-1730	Nov. 8, 1730	May 16, 1736	June 11, 1737
Bannkauf, Anton	LG L	Oct. 14, 1731	1734	May 17, 1736	
Loy, Joh. Georg	TC L	Aug. 27, 1733	Oct. 3, 1736	June 11, 1737	June 11, 1737
Miller, Abraham	TC O			June 11, 1737	June 11, 1737
Stoner, Jacob	TC R?			June 11, 1737	June 11, 1737
Schmidt, Joh. Jost	TC L			June 11, 1737	June 11, 1737
Frantz, Daniel	TC -			June 11, 1737	June 11, 1737
Geiger, Joh. Georg	LG L	pre1728	Dec. 7, 1735	June 16, 1737	(June 24, 1740)
Weymer, Bernard	UG L	Oct. 17, 1732	Oct. 18, 1735	Feb. 8, 1738	Feb. 8, 1738
Manser, Jac Matthias	UG -	Oct. 17, 1732	Nov. 24, 1736	May 10, 1738	May 10, 1738
Fortinaux, Jean Henri	LG L	Aug. 29, 1730	Aug. 29, 1730	June 7, 1738	1745
Baer, Georg	TC -	Sept 3, 1732	Nov. 24, 1736	Aug. 9, 1738	Aug. 9, 1738
Reisner, Michael	UG L	Sept 3, 1732	Oct. 25, 1735	Aug. 9, 1738	Aug. 9, 1738
Weller, Joh. Jacob	UG M	Sept 26, 1737	Apr. 21, 1738	Aug. 9, 1738	Aug. 9, 1738
Verdriess, Joh. et al	UG L	pre-1730	Feb. 5, 1736	Nov. 3, 1738	Nov. 3, 1738
Trout, Henrich	UG L			Nov. 24, 1738	Nov. 29, 1743
Müller, Valentine	LG L	Oct. 11, 1732	Sept. 7, 1737	Nov. 24, 1738	
Grüber, Philipp Ernst	UG L	Sept 25, 1732	July 3, 1736	Nov. 25, 1738	Nov. 30, 1738
Dern, Wilhelm	DL L	NJ pre-1725	Sept 1731	Nov. 30, 1738	pre-1753
Arnold, Joh. Georg		Oct. 30, 1738	Oct. 30, 1738	Jan. 15, 1739	Feb. 25, 1744
Sinn, Heinrich	TC L	Sept 18, 1732	June 12, 1736	June 17, 1739	July 28, 1746
Wetzel, Martin	UG L	Sept 21, 1731	Sept 21, 1731	June 17, 1739	Nov. 25, 1741
Hutzel, Joh. Georg	LG L	Aug. 27, 1733	Apr. 18, 1736	June 17, 1739	July 27, 1746
Ambrose, Matthias	UG L	Oct. 11, 1732	Jan. 6, 1737	June 17, 1739	June 26, 1746
Hoffmann, Joh. Peter	TC R	Aug. 27, 1733	Mar. 16, 1735	June 17, 1739	July 28, 1744
House, Thomas	LG R			Aug. 23, 1739	Aug. 23, 1739
Kemp, Conrad	LG R	Aug. 17, 1733	May 1, 1739	Aug. 24, 1739	Aug. 24, 1739
Brunner, Joseph	TC R	Sept 11, 1729	Sept 11, 1739	May 3, 1740	July 28, 1746
Keller, Conrad	TC R	May 29, 1735	Aug. 25, 1736	May 3, 1740	July 28, 1746
Schmidt, Joh. Peter	UG R	Sept 18, 1732	Sept 18, 1732	May 3, 1740	
Thomas, Christian	TC R	Aug. 29, 1730	Aug. 29, 1730	May 3, 1740	July 28, 1746
Shoup, Martin	LG Q?	Aug. 28, 1728	Aug. 28, 1728	May 21, 1740	Nov. 28, 1741

Name	Religion[1] Location[2]		Arrived at Philadelphia	Last Known Elsewhere	First Record in Frdk. Co.	First Land Record
Küntz, Philipp	LG	L	Oct. 14, 1731	Oct. 14, 1731	May 21, 1740	Apr. 24, 1752
Shaver, Peter	LG	L			May 21, 1740	Dec. 10, 1743
Apple, Peter	UG	L	Oct. 17, 1732	Oct. 17, 1732	late 1740	Nov. 29, 1744
Lehnert, Isaac	LG	L			Mar. 10, 1741	Mar. 10, 1741
Getzendanner, Christ'n	LG	R	Sept 11, 1729	1730	Aug. 13, 1741	Aug. 13, 1741
Stehli/Staley, Jacob	LG	R	Sept 5, 1738?		Nov. 21, 1741	Nov. 21, 1741
Berg, Wilhelm	MM	R		NJ 1730	Jan. 22, 1742	Jan. 22, 1742
Miller, Isaac	LG	R			Mar. 5, 1742	Mar. 5, 1742
Honig, Joh. Georg	UG	L	Sept 25, 1732	Oct. 16, 1739	Mar. 14, 1742	Mar. 14, 1742
Spuch, Adam	UG	L			Oct. 4, 1742	June 3, 1743
Neff, Joh. Henrich	TC	O			Oct. 1742	July 28, 1746
Stull, Adam	LG	R			1742	Oct. 18, 1744
Tafelmeyer, Johannes	UG	L	Oct. 11, 1732	Oct. 11, 1732	1742	
Moser, Leonard	UG	M	Sept 23, 1732	July 3, 1736	May 17, 1743	Aug. 3, 1754
Bonet, Jaques	UG	-	Aug. 27, 1733		May 28, 1743	May 28, 1743
Bachdold, Henrich	LG	L			July 17, 1743	July 17, 1743
Storm, Jacob	TC	R	Aug. 28, 1728	Jan. 9, 1742	Oct. 9, 1743	July 28, 1746
Myer, Joh. Caspar	TC	R			Oct. 9, 1743	July 28, 1746
Werfle, Melchior	TC	R	Sept 21, 1732		pre1746	pre1746
Fink, Nicolaus	TC	O	Aug. 30, 1737	Aug. 30, 1730	July 28, 1746	July 28, 1746
Roht, Henrich	TC	O	Aug. 17, 1733	Aug. 17, 1733	July 28, 1746	July 28, 1746
Ramsburg, Stephen	TC	R			July 28, 1746	July 28, 1746
Soldner, Hans Georg		L	Sept 30, 1732	Apr. 19, 1739	June 24, 1747	Nov. 24, 1748
Unseldt, Geo Friedrich	LG	L	Aug. 27, 1733	Nov. 22, 1741	Apr. 2, 1749	July 16, 1752
Six, Henrich	UG	L	N.Y. 1710	1744	Aug. 26, 1746	Aug. 26, 1746
Vertriess, Hartmann	UG	M		Jan. 15, 1743	Oct. 18, 1753	Oct. 18, 1753

[1] Religion: R = Reformed, L = Lutheran, M = Moravian, Q = Quaker, O = Other
[2] Location: LG = Lower German, UG = Upper German, TC = Taskers Chance, MM = Monocacy Manor, DL = Dulanys Lot.

EXCERPTS FROM JOHANN CASPAR STOVER'S RECORDS
(From his Personal Journal except as noted)

Baptisms

Father	Child's Name	Date of Birth	Sponsors
	Nov. 8, 1730 Falckner Schwamm [Swamp]		
Schweinhardt, Joh. Georg	Joh. Peter	Oct. 30, 1730	Hess, Jeremias, wf & dtr Eva Nelly Lehnich, Dieterich Fauth, Balthazar & wf Susanna
	Dec. 25, 1733 Muddy Creek		
[4]Gump, Joh. Georg	Joh. Georg	Dec. 4, 1733	Brenneisen, Georg Valentin
[4]Weiss, Frantz	Joh. Jacob	Oct. 7, 1733	Simon, Joh. Jacob
	May 12, 1734 Muddy Creek		
[4]Ambrosius, Mattheis	Joh. Philipp	Feb. 6, 1734	Schweickert, Philipp & wf Susanna
	June 23, 1734 [Lancaster?[6]]		
[1]Mattheis, Joh. Jacob	Anna Margaretha	June 11, 1734	Kleeman, Christian & Hoofin, Anna Barbara
	July 7, 1734 Muddy Creek		
[4]Hoffmann, Peter	Maria Eliesabetha	June 24, 1734	Ley, Joh. Georg & wf
	Nov. 24, 1734 [Warwick]		
[4]Ley, Joh. Georg	Maria Rosina	Oct. 31, 1734	Beyerle, Joh. Jacob & wf Maria Rosina
	Jan. 1, 1735 [Lancaster?[7]]		
Meyer, Joh. Georg	Anna Barbara	Oct. 6, 1734	Teufersbissin, Anna Barbara
[1]Reusner, Michael	Catarina Barbara	Nov. 13, 1734	Beyerlin, Anna Catarina
	Mar. 16, 1735 Muddy Creek		
[4]Traut, Theobald	Maria Appolonia	Dec. 6, 1734	Hoffmann, Peter & wf Maria Appolonia
	Mar. 30, 1735 [Lancaster?[8]]		
[1]Sinn, Heinrich	Susanna	Mar. 2, 1735	Rudiessielen, Susanna
	June 20, 1735 Catores [Codorus]		
Ogle, Joseph	Mary	Apr. 15, 1735	McGuill, Andrew & wf Mary
	July 21, 1735 Canashochilie [Conojohela]		
Crysop, Thomas	Daniel	Feb. 28, 1728	Killis, John Parry, Thomas Foy, Francis
Crysop, Thomas	Michael	Aug. 16, 1729	Gruber, Philipp Ernst McGill, Andrew Low, Elizabetha
Crysop, Thomas	Thomas	Feb. 28, 1733	Ogle, Josep Kannely, William McGill, Mary
Crysop, Thomas	Robert	Jan. 17, 1735	Paul, Robert Low, John Grüber, Charlotta Friederica
	Aug. 10, 1735 Muddy Creek		
[4]Weiss, Frantz	Joh. Georg	July 13, 1735	Klein, Joh. Georg & wf Anna

[1] For footnotes, see p. 377.

Father	Child's Name	Date of Birth	Sponsors
		Apr. 18, 1736 Muddy Creek	
[4]Gump, Joh. Georg	Andreas	Oct. 12, 1735	Mattheis, Joh. Jacob & wf Margaretha
		Apr. 28, 1736 Manackesen	
Fauth, Baltasar	Catharina Barbara	Dec. 4, 1735	Fauth, Jacob & Teufersbiss, Barbara
Fauth, Jacob	Balthasar	Mar. 1, 1736	Fauth, Balthasar & wf
[1]Mattheis, Joh. Jacob	Anna Magdalena	Sep. 15, 1735	Hoof, Joh. Jacob & Teufersbissin, Anna Barbara
Schweinhardt, Joh. Georg	Anna Maria	May 15, 1735	Lein, Magdalena
		May 16, 1736 Manackesen	
Hoof, Joh. Jacob	Anna Maria	May 8, 1736	Mattheis, Joh. Jacob & wf Margaretha
Prey, Henry	Anna Maria	Apr. 15, 1733	Bronnerin, Anna Maria & Bronnerin, Maria Barbara
Prey, Henry	Susanna	Mar. 10, 1735	Lehnich, Dieterich & Fauthin, Susanna
		May 17, 1736 Manackesen	
Backer, Adam	Eliesabetha	Jan. 17, 1736	Teufersbiss, Eliesabetha Barbara
Rössel, Matthias	Catharina Barbara	May 1, 1736	Teufersbissen, Catharina Barbara
Mittag, Johannes	Susanna	June 25, 1735	Pattison [Beattys-in!], Agnes
Lathly, Georg	Rachel	Mar. 16, 1730	Banckauf, Anton & Leinin, Magdalena
		Jan. 6, 1737 Muddy Creek	
[4]Ambrosius, Mattheis	Augustus Heinrich	Oct. 13, 1736	Kutschmann, August Heinrich
		June 5, 1737 Manakesen	
Prey, Henry	Sarah	Mar. 31, 1732	---
Prey, Henry	Catarina	Apr. 26, 1737	---
		Oct. 3, 1736 [Warwick]	
[4]Leß, Joh. Georg	Joh. Jacob	Sept. 5, 1736	Beyerle, Joh. Jacob & wf
		June 16, 1737 Manackesen	
Geiger, Joh. Georg	Maria Eliesabetha	Dec. 11, 1736	Fauth, Jacob & wf
[1]Mattheis, Joh. Jacob[10]	Joh. Georg	Mar. 30, 1737	Geiger, Joh. Georg & wife
[4]Gump, Joh. Georg	Catharina Barbara	Apr. 8, 1737	Teuffelsbissin, Anna Barbara
		Aug. 1, 1737 Canashochilie	
Crysop, Thomas	Elizabeth	Jan. 19, 1737	Baselerin, Veronica
		June 7, 1738 Manackesen	
Fortunee, Heinrich	Susanna Catarina	Oct. __, 1737	Gump, Joh. Georg & Fauthin, Susanna
Henckel, Georg	Joh. Balthasar	Dec. 25, 1737	Fauth, Balthasar & wf
[1]Mattheis, Joh. Jacob	Catarina	May 20, 1738	Rössel, Mattheis & Geigerin, Catarina
Mayhuw, Joseph	John William	Dec. 16, 1737	Swinehardt, George & wf, Fauth, Balthasar & wf
		Nov. 24, 1738 Manackesen	
Fauth, Jacob	Catharina	Sep. 30, 1738	Geigerin, Catharina
Hoof, Joh. Jacob	Jacob	Nov. 2, 1738	Bruchel, Samuel & Fauthin, Eva Rosina
Müller, Valentin	Magdalena	Nov. 11, 1738	Schweinhardtin, Magdalena

Father	Child's Name	Date of Birth	Sponsors
		Nov. 25, 1738 Manaquesen	
Gröber, Philipp Ernst	Maria Eliesabetha	June 13, 1738	Lay, Joh. Georg & wf
		Nov. 28, 1738 Manackesen	
Spengel, Georg	Johanna	Sept. 5, 1738	Scherer, Augustus & Schreyerin, Catharina
	Feb. 13, 1739 Manackesen (Lancaster Ch Bk, but see below)		
Reusner, Michael	Anna Eliesabetha	Jan. 5, 1739	Rausch, Michael, wf [Anna Eliesabetha]
		June 15, 1739 [Lancaster, York]	
[5]Weller, Jacob	Joh. Jacob	May 10, 1739	Lochmann, Joh. Jacob & wf Elisabetha
		June 17, 1739 Manackesen	
[4]Leÿ, Joh. Georg	Anna Eliesabetha	Dec. 11, 1738	Hoffman, Peter, wf Maria Appolonia
[1]Sinn, Heinrich	Jacob Mattheis	Jan. 31, 1739	Mansser, Jacob [Mattheis]
Geiger, Joh. Georg	Joh. Jacob	Mar. 4, 1739	Rössel, Mattheis, wf Maria Barbara
[4]Weiss, Frantz	Johannes	Mar. 17, 1739	Brunner, Johannes, wf Anna Maria
[4]Ambrosius, Mattheis	Mattheis	Mar. 20, 1739	Rössel, Mattheis, wf Anna Barbara
[2]Gump, Joh. Georg	Johannes	Apr. 11, 1739	Rössel, Mattheis, wf Anna Barbara
Weinmar, Bernhardt	Joh. Bernhardt	Apr. 15, 1739	Wetzel, Martin, wf Maria Barbara
Dern, Wilhelm	Anna Catharina	May 26, 1739	Rössel, Mattheis, wf Maria Barbara
		Dec. 15, 1739 Manaquesen[9]	
[1]Reusner, Michael	Anna Eliesabetha	Jan. 5, 1739	Rausch, Michael & wf
		Apr. 27, 1740 Manakesen	
Prey, Henry	Eliesabetha	Nov. 3, 1739	Schweinhardt, Georg & wf Maria Eliesabetha
Müller, Valentin	Catharina	Apr. 21, 1740	Mattheis, Joh. Jacob, wf Margaretha, Geigerin, Catharina
		May 2, 1740 Manaquesen	
Toudith, John	Eliesabetha	Apr. 29, 1738	Bischoff, Heinrich, wf Eliesabetha
		May 21, 1740, Manackesen	
Schaub, Martin, an Anabaptist (Wiedertäufer)	Anna	1724	Kintz, Philipp & wf
Henckel, Georg	Philipp Christoph	May 7, 1740	Kuntz, John Philipp & wf
		Sep. 21, 1740, Manackesen	
Fortunee, Heinrich	Joh. Heinrich	Dec. 31, 1739	Lutz, Leonhardt & Geiger, Catarina
Mayhuw, Joseph	Anna	May 1, 1740	Schweinhardt, Gabriel, sister Susanna & Götzdannerin, Anna Margaretha
Beer, Joh. Georg	Catarina Barbara	May 16, 1740	Lay, Joh. Georg & Rösselin, Catarina Barbara
[5]Hartmann, Herman	Eliesabetha	Sept. 5, 1740	Bischof, Heinrich & wf Eliesabetha
		June 24, 1741, Manackesen	
Verdriess, Jacob	Catarina	Mar. --, 1739	Gröber, Philipp Ernst & wf Verdriess, Joh. Valentin
Verdriess, Jacob	Johannes	Apr. 27, 1741	Same sponsors
Ellrodt, Jeremias	Eliesabetha	Apr. 16, 1741	Ellrodt, Dieterich & wf
[4]Ambrosius, Mattheis	Joh. Friederich	June 20, 1741	Verdriess, Joh. Friederich

Father	Child's Name	Date of Birth	Sponsors
		Sep. 27, 1741 [?]	
Koger, Nicolaus	Joh. Jacob	Sept. 4, 1741	Weller, Joh. Jacob, wf Barbara

Entered twice; both crossed out. Neither entry cites nor is near another Manaquesen entry. Three other children, baptized 1736-1740, appear in Lancaster and York Lutheran Church Books.

		Nov. 22, 1741 [Muddy Creek?]	
[3]Ohnselt, Friederich	Johannes	Oct. 22, 1741	Herr, Joh. and Hausahmin, Maria Eliesabetha

		May 20, 1742 Manaquesen	
Appel, Petter	Eva Rosina	May 9, 1742	Pfauthin, Eva Rosina

Marriages

#	Date	Groom	Bride	Location
#136	1737 Sept. 7	Müller, Valentin	Lochmännin, Elisabetha Dorothea	Earl Town
#166	1738 Apr. 21	Weller, Joh. Jacob	Vieruhrin, Anna Barbara	Helm Town [Hellam Tp]
#194	1738 Nov. 24	Traut, Joh. Henrich	Baumin, Anna Maria	Manakesens
#195	1738 Nov. 26	Habach, Peter	Bergin, Catarina	Manakesens
#238	1739 June 17	Hutzel, Georg	[12]Schweinhardtin, Eliesabetha	Monokesen
#272	1739 Dec. 20	Schäiteler,[11] Joh. Georg	Neffin,[11] Margaretha	he Manaquesen, she Creuz Creek
#284	1740 May 21	Schäffer, Peter	Schaubin, Anna	Manaquesen
#383	1742 Oct. 11	Schmidt, Joh. Peter	Fauthin, Eva Rosina	Manaquesen
#384	1742 Oct. 11	Conner, James	Ellrodt, Anne Catharine	Manaquesen

----

[1] Entry duplicated in Lancaster Lutheran Church Book. (No entry appeared solely in Lancaster Church Book.)

[2] Entry duplicated in Muddy Creek Lutheran Church Book.

[3] Entry duplicated in Muddy Creek and Frederick Lutheran Church Books.

[4] Entry appears only in Muddy Creek Lutheran Church Book.

[5] Additional entries in Lancaster Lutheran Church Book.

[6] See text, pp. 134n, 205. Stöver on June 25, 1734 was at Leacock, northeast of Lancaster in the Conestoga area of Pennsylvania.

[7] Stöver was probably in Coventry (west of Spring City in north Chester County) on December 29, 1734, in Cumru Township (southwest of Reading in Berks County) on January 7, 1735 and then back at Coventry on January 10, 1735. He later listed Joh. Georg Meyer, both in his personal Journal, op. cit., and in the Lancaster Lutheran Church Book, as living in Swadara (north Lebanon County between today's Jonestown and Fredericksburg). Anna Catharina Beyerle was the wife of Joh. Michael Beyerle (1698-1781) from Sinsheim with whom she appeared in the Lancaster records as a frequent baptism sponsor between 1733-1739. Therefore, interpretting Stöver's Manaquesen label for Reusner as meaning he was at Monocacy in 1735 would seem in error: See also text, p. 194.

[8] Although Stöver, op. cit., p. 32, showed Sinn as living at Manaquesen, the entry was probably made after Sinn's second child was baptized there on June 17, 1739. Since both entries also appear in the Lancaster Lutheran Church Book and since Susanna Beyerin married Philipp Rudiesielle at "Conestocken" on October 29, 1734 (Stöver, op. cit., No. 65, and the Lancaster Lutheran Church Book), the Lancaster area must have been the probable locale on March 30, 1735.

[9] The Lancaster Lutheran Church Book (Weiser transcription) shows baptism date Feb. 13, 1739 and Rausch's wife's name as Anna Elisabetha.

[10] Ibid. shows baptism date June 10, 1737, although on June 8, 1737 Stöver was still at North Revier [River], Shenandoah, Virginia.

[11] Ibid. shows duplicate entry in Lancaster Lutheran Church Book but for Schönteler and Nessin.

[12] Stöver's error: Her given name was Magdalena. See p. 158n.

FREDERICK COUNTY MUSTER ROLLS, circa 1757*

Captain Peter Butler
34 days' service

Schley, Lieut. Thomas
Grosh, Ensign Conrad
Fergason, [Sgt.] John
Mong, Sgt. Adam
Price, [Sgt.] Thomas
Schaff, Sgt. Casper
Black, Cpl. Valentines
Burnsten, Cpl. Joseph
Hiseler, Cpl. Nicholas
Price. Col. Joseph
Kimble, Wm., drummer
Wood, Robert, clerk
Adams, Valentine
Allen, Michael
Bare, Jacob
Bargar, Christopher
Bargar, Philip
Barger, George
Beatty, Charles
Beatty, George
Bedford, John
Brown, Godfry
Cary, John
Caufman, Henry
Chalten, Arthur
Chalten, John
Chanywolf, Joseph
Combe, Adam
Cook, Francis
Coonce, Philip
Cumper, John
Davis, Daniel
Downey, John
Edelen, Christopher
Engles, Peter

Evartt, Adam
Fox, George
Gardinhover, Jacob
George, Joseph
Crosh, Peter
Hardman, Joseph
Hite, John
Hoffman, George
Hoffman, Jacob
Hoover, Jacob (carp.)
Hoover, Jacob (taylor)
House, William
Isenpeck, George
Jesserang, Michael
Keslar, Bernhard
Kinkley, Frederick
Kinsell, Adam
Kipps, Abraham
Lazaras, Henry
Lazures, Simpson
Lingenfelter, Abraham
Lingenfelter, John
Loybottom, Judah
Luxemberger, Joseph
MacCrory, Daniel
Mance, Casper
Mance, Peter
Martz, Theobald
Missell, Frederick
Orchard, Bastian
Paugh, Balser
Poore, Abraham
Praig, Peter
Queer, Henry
Rhoar, Rudolph

Ripeligh, John
Rule, Clement
Seamer, George
Sharp, Paul
Shell, Charles
Shessler, Adam
Shover, Henry
Shrioner, Matthias
Shrioner, Valentine
Skinn, George
Slim, Simon
Smith, Henry
Snider, Conrad
Snider, George
Snider, Michael
Snowdagle, Jacob
Spangler, Matthias
Stoner, Jacob
Strifler, Valentine
Stumpf, Michael
Summer, John
Sunfrank, Jacob
Tegan, Peter
Turnwolf, Frederick
Waugh, William
Wehaun, Henry
Whitmore, John
Whitsall, Martin
Wise, Henry
Wychel, Adam
Wychel, Bastian
Wortenbaker, Adam
Young, Ludwig
Zerich, Anthony

* See note, p. 380.

Captain Elias Delashmutt
August 13, 1757, 52 days

Hawkins, Lieut. Thomas
Ray, Sgt. Joseph
Fenneley, Cpl. Thomas
Athy, George
Awbry, Francis
Blackburn, Robert
Brown, Benjamin
Brown, James
Brown, John
Butler, Edward
Davis, Daniel
Delashmutt, Elias
Fanchill, Andrew
Fansey, Abraham
Fansey, Edward
Fudar, John
Groddu, William
Hackett, Peter
Hill, John
Jenkins, Ashman
Johnson, John, Jr.
Jones, David
Kemp, Lewis
Miller, Francis
Norwood, Richard
Pack, Thomas
Pickapaw, Peter
Posey, Uzza
Onin, John
Sharp, Mathews
Smith, Daniel
Smoote, John
Terrel, John
Thomas, Christopher
Walling, Delashmutt
Wilson, Joseph

Captain Stephen Ransberger
42 days

Raymer, Lieut Michael
Hedge, Ensign Charles
Brunner, Sgt. Elias
Lany, Sgt. Matthew
Mayhew, Sgt. Joseph
Stilly, Sgt. Peter
Evetts, Cpl. Matthew
Gatsindaner, Cpl. Gabriel
Shawkin, Cpl. Daniel
Sterm, Cpl. John
Beall, Mordecai, clerk
Apple, Peter
Barnes, William
Beall, William
Beller, Christian
Brenner, John
Brenner, John, Jr.
Chrest, Michael
Clark, William
Clemons, Leonard
Coonce, Henry
Coonce, William
Curts, George
Dick, George Peter
Domer, George
Douthit, John
Dufler, George
Dufler, Peter
Fogeler, Anthony
Fout, Henry
Fout, Jacob
Fouts, Balser
Fulweder, Henry
Funk, Henry
Hackadorn, Jacob
Havener, Frederick
Havener, Michael
Hedges, Moses
Hickle, Luderick
Hoff, Jacob
Holts, Benjamin
Hutsell, George
Judey, Winebart
Julian, Stephen
Kemp, Frederick
Kemp, Gilbert
Kemp, Peter
Kernhart, Henry
Ketchindaner, Balser
Kickman, Conrad
Kirtchendaner, Jacob
Laman, Philip Jacob
Leather, John
Loy, George
Miller, Peter
Mire, Casper
Powell, Peter
Ransberger, Adam
Ransberger, George
Road, George
Shaver, Peter
Shoab, George
Shoab, Martin
Shoaf, George
Sim [Sinn?], Henry
Smith, Jacob
Smith, John
Sonpower, Michael
Souder, Philip
Springer, Jacob
Staley, Melchor
Staly, Jacob
Stoner, John
Whelpley, Charles
Whitman, Frederick
Widrick, Martin
Wise, George
Wise, John Peter
Youtchey, Peter

Captain John Middaugh
30 days

Kimball, Lieut. John	Frush, Vandle	Richards, Daniel
Beatty, Ens. Thomas Jr.	Flick, Michael	Richards, Joseph
Black, Sgt. William	Gose, George	Richards, Stephen
Carmack, Sgt. Cornelius	Graves, John	Ridge, Benjamin
Martin, Sgt. Benjamin	Grimes, Martin	Road, Adam
Springer, Sgt. Charles	Halts, Jacob	Ross, Henry
Carmack, Cpl. William	Harlin, Jacob	Roxell, David
Clabough, Cpl. Frederick	Hartsock, George	Shewmaker, Simon
Harlin, Cpl. Isaac	Hartsock, Nicholas	Short, David
Matthews, Cpl. John	Hendrick, John	Shover, Simon
Smith, Philip, drummer	Hildebrand, Heronimus	Sickler, Henry
Whitmall, Robert, clerk	Hinkle, George	Smith, Adam
Allbaugh, Adam	Hoover, Adam	Smith, Andrew
Barrack, Christian	Hoover, Adam	Smith, Christian
Barrack, Handel	Hoover, Petyer	Smith, Mathias
Barrack, John	Huff, Abraham	Smith, William
Barrick, Peter	Huff, Laurence	Snoke, Henry
Barrick, William	Keller, Jacob	Stevens, Jacob
Barton, Jacob	Kiteman, Christopher	Stull, Peter
Beatty, John	Lingenfelter, Barnet	Taxer, Mathias
Bostian, George	Loyd, John	Taylor, Garet
Bowman, Semon	Luts, Jacob	Taylor, Wm of Garret
Burk, David	Lutz, Joseph	Taylor, Wm ditto [sic]
Chance, Henry	Mathews, Samuel	Teal, Philip
Cramer, George	Maxel, Andrew	Teal, Samuel
Cramer, Jacob	Michael, Daniel	Veast, Jacob
Creagar, Conrad	Middaugh, John, Jr.	Walter, Jacob
Creager, Valentine	Pelser, Christian	Wilson, William
Crepell, Peter	Philips, Reubin	Winrod, Jacob
Crosse, John	Prapps, Jacob	Wise, Abraham
Crum, Gilbert, Jr.	Pred, Frederick	Wise, Daniel
Daniel, John	Pringle, Jacob	Wise, Peter
Dayley, Philip	Reed, James	Wise, Valentine
Dorr, Peter	Reynolds, James	Wolfe, Paul
Egleton, John	Reynolds, Thomas, Jr.	

----

* Source: A manuscript of 109 pages showing muster rolls for actual service was prepared for the Committee on Accounts of the General Assembly. Captain Delashmutt's roll, the only one actually dated, suggests the approximate date for the others. Days of service are indicated above for the Captain of each Company, but actual days served by each individual are included in the manuscript. The document, in the possession of the Maryland Historical Society, was transcribed and printed in the <u>Maryland Historical Magazine</u>, 9:260-280, 348-370.

BIBLIOGRAPHY

N.B. Provincial and County records cited in the footnotes are for the most part omitted from the following. For their location and dates see Radoff, Morris L., Skordas, Gust and Jacobsen, Phebe R., *The County Court Houses and Records of Maryland, Part Two: The Records* (Annapolis: The Hall of Records Commission, Publication No. 13, 1963).

Allaben, Frank, *The Ancestry of Leander Crall* (New York, 1908).
Anon, "Historical Account of the Beginning, Progress of the Work of the Lord among Souls in the Neighborhood of the Manacusey in Maryland, and of the Gathering and Planting of the Little Congregation of Graceham, Associated with the Congregation of the Brethren," Lititz Archives.
Baldwin, Jane and Henry, Roberta B., *The Maryland Calendar of Wills, 1635-1743*, 8 vol. (Baltimore, 1904-1928).
Baltimore Museum of Art, *"Anywhere So Long As There Be Freedom," Charles Carroll of Carrollton, His Family and His Maryland* (Baltimore, 1975).
Barker, Charles A., *The Background of the Revolution in Maryland* (New Haven, 1940).
Bibbins, Ruthella Mory, *How Methodism Came, the Beginnings of Methodism in England and America* (Baltimore: The American Methodist Historical Society of the Baltimore Annual Conference, 1945).
Board of Trade Papers, CO/5/1316, Public Record Office, Kew, England.
Bond, Isaac, "Map of Frederick County, Md." (Baltimore: E. Sachse & Co., 1866).
Bowie, Effie Gwynn, *Across the Years in Prince George's County* (Richmond, Virginia, 1947).
Brace, Edwin T. and Atha Peckenpaugh, *Descendants of Johann Adam and Anna Maria Beckenbach* (Baltimore, 1984).
Braun, Fritz, *Auswanderer aus der Umgebung von Ludwigshafen a. Rh. auf dem Schiff* "Thistle of Glasgow," *1730*, Schriften zur Wanderungsgeschichte der Pfälzer, Folge 8 (Kaiserslautern, 1959).
Brumbaugh, Gaius Marcus, *Maryland Records, Colonial, Revolutionary, County and Church from Original Sources* (Baltimore/Lancaster, 1915/1928).
Burgert, Annette Kunselman, *Eighteenth Century Emigrants from German-Speaking Lands to North America*, Vol. 1, *Northern Kraichgau* (Breinigsville, 1983); Vol. 2, *Western Palatinate* (Birdsboro, 1985).
Burr, Horace, translator and transcriber, *The Records of Holy Trinity (Old Swedes) Church, Wilmington, Delaware from 1697-1773* (Wilmington, 1890).

Calendar of Delaware Wills, New Castle County, 1682-1800, abstracted by the Historical Records Committee of the Colonial Dames of Delaware (New York, 1911).

Calendar of Maryland Wills: see Baldwin, Jane and Henry, Roberta B.

Calvert Papers, MS. 174, Maryland Historical Society. Microfilm copies are available, as is a printed Calendar. See especially:
No. 906: Maryland Debt Book, ±1750.
No. 1035: Lloyd, Philemon, Map, Patowmeck Above ye Inhabitants.
No. 1079: Lloyd, Philemon to Co-Partners, July 28, 1732.
No. 1147: Lord Baltimore to Benjamin Tasker, July 9, 1732.

Chambers, Theodore Freylinghuysen, *The Early Germans of New Jersey* (n.s., 1893).

Church Books, Note: The first Frederick Reformed Church Books, both the Schlatter and Brunner volumes, are now housed at the Hall of Records in Annapolis. Frederick's first Lutheran Church Book remains in the Wentz Library at the Lutheran Theological Seminary in Gettysburg. The original All Saints Church Book is kept at the local church in Frederick, but a 1903 transcription by L. H. Garrison may be found at the Maryland Historical Society in Baltimore. For Pennsylvania Lutheran Church Book transcriptions (e.g., Holy Trinity in Lancaster, Muddy Creek in East Cocalico Township, both in Lancaster County) see Weiser, Frederick S., transcriber. German church books cited in the footnotes have been read in the originals at parish churches in Germany or at the Landesarchiv and Staatsarchiv in Speyer.

Colonial Dames of America, *Ancestral Records and Portraits* (Chicago: Grafton Press, 1910).

Commission Book No. 82, Maryland Historical Society. Actually one of the records of the Council of Maryland with miscellaneous entries from 1733-1783. See also *Maryland Historical Magazine*, 26:138-158, 244-263, 342-361; 27:29-36.

Cunz, Dieter, *The Maryland Germans* (Princeton, 1948).

Dare, Maria Jane Liggett, *Chaplines from Maryland and Virginia* (Washington: Franklin Print, 1902).

Davenport, John Scott, "Earliest Pfautz/Fouts Families in America," National Genealogical Society *Quarterly*, 63:243-263.

Deane Papers, The, #65, New-York Historical Society.

Delaplaine, Edward S., *The Life of Thomas Johnson* (New York: The Grafton Press, 1927).

Dern, John P., "The Upper Potomac in 1736," *Western Maryland Genealogist*, 2:86-87.

Dern, John P., ed., Hart, Simon and Sibrandina Geertruid, transls, The *Albany Protocol, Wilhelm Christoph Berkenmeyer's Chronicle of Lutheran Affairs in New York Colony, 1731-1750* (Ann Arbor, 1971)

Dieffenbacher, Karl, *Schweizer Einwanderer in den Kraichgau nach dem Dreissigjährigen Krieg* (Ladenburg, 1983).

Dinwiddie, Robert, Lieutenant Governor of Virginia, 1751-1758, *The Official Records of*, with notes by R. A. Brock (Richmond, 1884).

Draper, Lyman Copeland, Manuscript Collections, 486 folio volumes, State Historical Society of Wisconsin, Madison. Microfilm copies are available at the University of California (Berkeley) and elsewhere.

Dulany Papers, MS. 1265, Maryland Historical Society.
Durnbaugh, Donald F., *The Brethren in Colonial America* (Elgin, Ill., 1967).
Durnbaugh, Donald F., *European Beginnings of the Brethren* (Elgin, 1958).
Englebrecht, Jacob, *The Englebrecht Diary, 1818-1878*. (Private typescript without pagination).
Faust, Albert Bernhard, *List of Swiss Immigrants in the Eighteenth Century to the American Colonies* (Washington, 1920-25).
Fitzpatrick, John C., *George Washington, Colonial Traveler, 1732-1775* (Indianapolis, 1927).
Forbush, Laverne, "Pipe Creek Friends Monthly Meeting Records," *Western Maryland Genealogist*, 1:19-26, 67-74, 123-130.
Gibson, John, *History of York County, Pennsylvania* (Chicago, 1886),
Gilreath, Amelia C., *Shenandoah County, Virginia, Abstract of Wills, 1772-1850* (n.s., 1980).
Giuseppi, M. S., *Naturalizations of Foreign Protestants in the American and West Indian Colonies* (Pursuant to Statute 13 George II, c. 7) (Baltimore, 1979).
Glatfelter, Charles H., *Pastors and People: German Lutheran and Reformed Churches in the Pennsylvania Field, 1717-1793* (Breinigsville: The Pennsylvania German Society, 1980-1981), 2 vol. This superb work deserves a much broader dissemination.
Graffenried, Baron Christoph von, *Account of the Founding of New Bern*, edited with historical introduction and an English translation by Vincent H. Todd ....in cooperation with Julius Goebel.... (Raleigh: Edwards and Broughton Printing Co., State Printers, 1920), pp. 43-52, 88-91, 142-150, 246-254, 347-350.
Gutridge, Ethel D., "St. Paul's Church, Rock Creek Parish, Washington, D.C.," *Historical Magazine of the Protestant Episcopal Church*, 19:145.
Hallesche Nachrichten von den vereinigten Deutschen Evangelisch-Lutherischen Gemeinen in Nord America, absonderlich in Pensylvanien, Mann, Schmucker and Germann edition (Allentown, 1886).
Hamilton, Kenneth G., transl. & ed., *The Bethlehem Diary, 1742-1744* (Bethlehem: Archives of the Moravian Church, 1971)
Hanley, Thomas O'Brien, *Charles Carroll of Carrollton, The Making of a Revolutionary Gentleman* (Chicago: Loyola University Press, 1982).
Hanna, Charles Augustus, *The Wilderness Trail* (New York, 1911).
Harbaugh, Henry, *The Life of Rev. Michael Schlatter* (Philadelphia, 1857).
Harlingen (Reformed Dutch) Baptism Records: See Skillman, William Jones.
Hart, Simon and Kreider, Harry J., *Lutheran Church in New York and New Jersey, 1722-1760* (Ann Arbor, 1962).
Hartsook, Elisabeth and Skordas, Gust, *Land Office and Prerogative Court Records of Colonial Maryland* (Maryland Hall of Records Commission, 1946), pp. 13-77.
Helfenstein, Ernest, *History of All Saints' Parish* (Frederick, 1932).
Helman, James A., *History of Emmitsburg, Maryland* (Frederick, 1906).

Henckel Family Association, *The Henckel Family Records* (New Market, Virginia, 1926-1939).

Hibbard, Francis, *The English Origins of John Ogle, First of the Name in Delaware* (n.s., 1967)

Hinke, William J., "Diary of the Rev. Michael Schlatter, June 1 to December 15, 1746," *Journal of the Presbyterian Historical Society*, (1905) 3:105-121, 158-176.

Hinke, William J., *Ministers of the German Reformed Congregations in Pennsylvania and Other Colonies in the Eighteenth Century* (Lancaster, 1951).

Hinke, William J., transl., "Report of the Journey of Francis Louis Michel from Berne, Switzerland to Virginia, October 2, 1701-December 1, 1702, *Virginia Magazine of History and Biography*, 24:1-43, 113-141, 275-303.

Hinke, William J., Letters Regarding the Second Journey of Michel to America, February 14, 1703 to January 16, 1704 and His Stay in America until 1708," *Ibid.*, 24:289-303.

Hinke, William J. and Kemper, Charles E., "Moravian Diaries: Travels through Virginia" *Virginia Magazine of History and Biography:*

"Extracts from the Diary of Leonhard Schnell and John Brandmueller of their Journey to Virginia, October 12 - December 12, 1749," 11:115-131

"Report and Observations of Brother Gottschalk on his Journey through Maryland and Virginia in March and April, 1748," 11:225-234.

"Extracts from the Diary of the Journey of Brothers Joseph (Spangenberg) and Matthew Reutz through Maryland and Virginia in July and August, 1748," 11:235-242.

"Extracts from the Diary of Leonhard Schnell and Robert Hussey of their Journey to Georgia, November 6, 1743 - April 10, 1844," 11:370-393.

"Diary of the Journey of Rev. L. Schnell and V. Handrup To Maryland and Virginia, May 29 - August 4, 1747," 12:55-61

"Extracts from the Diary of Brother Gottschalk's Journey through Maryland and Virginia, March 5 - April 20, 1748," 12:62-76.

"The Places in Maryland and Virginia Where our Brethren Have an Open Door," 12:77-80.

"Diary of the Journey of the First Colony of Single Brethren to North Carolina, October 8 - November 17, 1753," 12:134-153, 271-181.

Hinshaw, William Wade, *Encyclopedia of American Quaker Genealogy* (Ann Arbor, Mich., 1950), 6:358-359: "Report of the Fairfax Meeting."

Hitselberger, Mary Fitzhugh and Dern, John P., *Bridge in Time: The Complete 1850 Census of Frederick County, Maryland* (Redwood City, Calif., 1978).

Hoes, Roswell Randall, *Baptismal and Marriage Registers of the Old Dutch Church of Kingston, 1660-1809* (New York, 1891; reprinted Baltimore, 1980).

Holdcraft, Jacob Mehrling, *Names in Stone, 75,000 Cemetery Inscriptions from Frederick County, Maryland* (Ann Arbor, 1966; Reprinted 1972 and Baltimore, 1985).

Hook, James William, *Captain James Hook of Greene County, Pennsylvania* (Ann Arbor, 1952).
Hopewell Friends History, 1734-1934, Frederick County, Virginia (Strassburg, Virginia: Shenandoah Publishing Co., 1936), p. 54.
Hughes, Thomas Aloysius, *History of the Society of Jesus in North America, Colonial and Federal* (London, New York, 1907)
Johnson, Christopher, "The Bladen Family," *Maryland Historical Magazine*, 6:298-299.
Jones, Henry Z., *The Palatine Families of New York* (Universal City, Calif., 1985).
Jones, Henry Z., Connor, Ralph and Wust, Klaus, *German Origins of Jost Hite, Virginia Pioneer, 1685-1761* (Edinburg, Virginia, 1979).
Joyner, Peggy Shomo, *Abstracts of Virginia's Northern Neck Warrants and Surveys, Frederick County, 1747-1780* (Portsmouth, Va., 1985).
Ibid., *Orange and Augusta Counties, 1734-1754*. (Portsmouth, 1985).
Kegley, F. B., *Kegley's Virginia Frontier* (Roanoke, 1938).
Keith, Charles P., *Chronicles of Pennsylvania from the English Revolution to the Peace of Aix-la-Chapelle, 1688-1748* (Philadelphia 1917).
Kemper, Charles E., "Documents Relating to Early Projected Swiss Colonies in the Valley of Virginia, 1706-1709" *The Virginia Magazine of History and Biography*, 29:1-17, 180-182.
Kemper, Charles E. "Documents Relating to a Proposed Swiss and German Colony in the Western Part of Virginia, the Petition of Gould, Ochs, Stauber and Harland," *Virginia Magazine of History and Biography*, 29:183-190.
Kenny, Hamill T., *The Origin and Meaning of the Indian Place Names of Maryland* (Baltimore: Waverly Press, 1961).
Kieffer, Elizabeth, *Baptismal Records of Apple's Church, 1773-1848* (Hudson, Wisconsin, 1963).
Kilian, Rolf, *Ingelheim am Rhein - Die Familien in Ober-Ingelheim, 1200-1800* (Frankfurt aM, 1961).
Kilty, John, *The Land-Holder's Assistant and Land-Office Guide* (Baltimore, 1808).
Knittle, Walter A., *Early Eighteenth Century Palatine Emigration* (Philadelphia, 1937).
Krebs, Friedrich, "Pfalzer Amerika-Auswanderer des 18. Jahrhunderts," *Familie und Volk*, 5:176-177.
Lake, D. J., *Atlas of Frederick County, Maryland* (Philadelphia: C. O. Titus & Company, 1873).
Land, Aubrey C., *The Dulanys of Maryland* (Baltimore, 1955).
Link, Paxson, *The Link Family* (n.s., 1951).
Lunt, Dudley, "The Bounds of Delaware," *Delaware History*, 2:1-40.
Mackenzie, George N., *Colonial Families of the United States* (Baltimore, 1914).
Magee, D. F., "Emanuel Carpenter, the Lawgiver," Lancaster County Historical Society, *Papers*, 24:148.
Marye, William B. "The Old Indian Road," *Maryland Historical Magazine*, 15:367-368.
Marye, William B., "Patowmeck Above Ye Inhabitants, a Commentary on the Subject of an Old Map," *Maryland Historical Magazine*, 30:1-11, 114-137.

Maryland, Archives of:
  Correspondence of Governor Horatio Sharpe, 1753-1757 (vol. 6), 1757-1761 (vol. 9).
    Proceedings and Acts of the General Assembly of Maryland, 1684-1692 (vol. 13), 1717-1720 (vol. 33), 1720-1723 (vol. 34), 1724-1726 (vol. 35), 1727-1729 (vol. 36), 1730-1732 (vol. 37), 1733-1736 (vol. 39), 1737-1740 (vol. 40), 1740-1742 (vol. 42), 1745-1747 (vol. 44), 1748-1751 (vol. 46), 1758-1761 (vol. 56).
    Proceedings of the Council of Maryland, 1698-1731 (vol. 25), 1732-1733 (vol. 28), 1753-1761 (vol. 31), 1761-1770 (vol. 32).
Maryland Calendar of Wills: see Baldwin, Jane.
Maryland Department of Natural Resources, Maryland Geological Survey, "Topographic Map of Frederick County" (1982).
Maryland Department of Transportation, State Highway Administration, "General Highway Map of Frederick County, Maryland" (1984).
Maryland Historical Magazine, Miscellaneous Articles, authors not cited:
  "Attack on Cresap's House and Relation of the Case of Thomas Cresap of Baltimore County, Maryland" 3:33-51.
  "French and Indian War" [Muster Rolls], a manuscript prepared for the Committee on Accounts of the General Assembly, ±1757e, 9:260-280, 348-370.
Maryland Rent Rolls at the Hall of Records, Maryland Archives, Annapolis:
  (Calvert, Prince George's, Frederick No. 1) vol. 3.
  (Calvert, Prince George's, Frederick No. 1) vol. 4.
  (Frederick No. 1) vol. 32.
  (Frederick No. 2) vol. 33.
Maryland State Papers No. 1, The Black Books, including printed *Calendar.*
Miller, Charles R. and Raker, William L., *The Histories of the Pennsylvania and Central Pennsylvania Conferences of the Evangelical United Brethren Church* (n.s., 1968).
Nead, Daniel Wunderlich, *The Pennsylvania German in the Settlement of Maryland* (Lancaster, Penna., 1914).
Oerter, A. L., *The History of Graceham, Frederick County, Maryland* (Bethlehem, Penna., 1913).
Owings, Donnell MacClure, *His Lordship's Patronage; Offices of Profit in Colonial Maryland* (Baltimore: Maryland Historical Society, 1953).
Pennsylvania, Minutes of the Provincial Council of, from the Organization to the Termination of the Proprietary Government (Philadelphia, 1851-1853), 10 Volumes.
Pennsylvania Collectie, Inv. No. 74I:20-21, Nos. 14, 15, Algemeen Rijkarchief, 's-Gravenhage.
Phillips, Rev. Hugh, "Elder Family Records," typescript, Mt. St. Mary's College.
Ranck, James B. and Dorothy S., Motter, Margaret R. and Dutrow, Katherine E., *A History of the Evangelical Reformed Church, Frederick, Maryland* (n.s., 1964).
Reichel, W. C., *A Register of Members of the Moravian Church and of Persons Attached to Said Church in this Country and Abroad, Between 1727 and 1754* (n.s., 1873).

Rice, Millard M., *New Facts and Old Families* (Redwood City, Calif. 1976).

Rice, Millard M., *This Was the Life, Excerpts from the Judgment Records of Frederick County, Maryland, 1748-1765* (Redwood City, 1979).

Rightmyer, Nelson Waite, *Maryland's Established Church* (Baltimore, 1956).

Rightmyer, Nelson Waite, *Parishes of the Diocese of Maryland* (Reisterstown, Md., 1960).

Roach, Hannah Benner, "Hans Georg Hertzel, Pioneer of Northampton County and His Family," *Pennsylvania Genealogical Magazine*, 24:159-169.

Rupp, I. Daniel, *A Collection of Upwards of Thirty Thousand Names of German, Swiss, Dutch, French and Other Immigrants in Pennsylvania from 1727 to 1776....* (Philadelphia, 1875).

Rupp, I. Daniel, *History of Lancaster County, Pennsylvania* (Lancaster, 1844).

Schantz, Franklin J. F., "Rev. John Casper Stoever's Record of Baptisms and Marriages from 1730 to 1779," *Notes and Queries, Historical, Biographical and Genealogical*, Annual Volume, William Henry Egle, ed. (Harrisburg, 1896). Reprinted without corrections but consolidated with an index as *Early Lutheran Baptisms and Marriages in Southeastern Pennsylvania* (Baltimore: Genealogical Publishing Company, 1982).

Scharf, John Thomas, *History of Western Maryland* (Philadelphia, 1882).

Scharf Papers, John Thomas, MS. 1999, Hall of Records, Maryland Archives, Annapolis.

Schnell, Leonard, "Diarium von der Reise der 2 Brüder Schnell u. Hussey, die nach Georgien besuchen gangen, 1743." The original Diary may be found in the Archives of the Moravian Church in Bethlehem. Portions of it in condensed and abbreviated form were translated and published by William J. Hinke and Charles E. Kemper, q.v., *Virginia Magazine of History and Biography*, 11:370-393.

Schnell, Leonard, "Kurze Beschreibung von unserer Reise nach Virginien," Archives of the Moravian Church, Bethlehem. See also Hinke and Kemper, *loc. cit.*, 11:115-131,

Schultz, Edward T. "First Settlements of Germans in Maryland" (Frederick, 1896; reprinted 1976).

Skillman, William Jones, "Earliest Baptismal Records of the Church of Harlingen (Reformed Dutch) of New Jersey, 1727-1734," *New York Genealogical and Biographical Record*, 40:281-291.

Smith, C. Henry, "The Mennonite Immigration to Pennsylvania in the Eighteenth Century," The Pennsylvania-German Society (1929) Vol. 35.

Smyth, Samuel Gordon, *Genealogy of the Duke-Shepherd-VanMetre Family* (1909).

Smyth, Samuel Gordon, *The Origin and Descent of an American Van Metre Family* (Lancaster, 1923).

[Spangenberg, August G.], "Kurze Nachricht von Br. Joseph's und Matth. Reuzen's Besuch und Land Prediger Reise durch Maryland und Virginien," original manuscript at Archives of the Moravian Church, Bethlehem, Pennsylvania. Hinke and Kemper, *loc. cit.*, 11:235-242 translated a portion of this Diary, but omitted the significant section covering the Monocacy visit, August 3-8, 1748.

Spangler, Edward W., *The Spengler Families, with Local Historical Sketches* (York, 1896),

Springer, Courtland B. and Ruth L., "Communicant Records, 1713-1756, Holy Trinity (Old Swedes) Church, Part I, 1713-18," *Delaware History*, 5:270-291.

Stewart, Jennie C. and Van Dyne, Claude Loy, *The Loy Family in America, 1732-1955* (Boulder, Colo., 1955).

Stiverson, Gregory A., *Poverty in a Land of Plenty, Tenancy in Eighteenth Century Maryland* (Baltimore and London, 1977). A study of Lord Baltimore's proprietary manors.

Stöver, Johann Caspar, "Ministerial Records," original at the Historical Society of Pennsylvania, Philadelphia. Transcribed by John P. Dern. See also Schantz, Franklin J. F.

Strassburger, Ralph Beaver and Hinke, William John, *Pennsylvania German Pioneers* (Norristown, 1934), 3 vol.

Stryker-Rodda, Kenn, "Baptisms in the Lutheran Church, New York City, from 1725," *The New York Genealogical and Biographical Record*, 99:passim.

Stryker-Rodda, Kenn, "The Janeway Store Account Books, 1735-1746," *Genealogical Magazine of New Jersey*, 33-35: *passim*, especially 35:91-96.

Sturm, Georg, *Geschichte meiner Heimatgemeinde Schifferstadt* (Speyer, 1961).

Tappert, Theodore G. and Doberstein, John W., *The Journals of Henry Melchior Muhlenberg* (Philadelphia, 1942-1945).

Tepper, Michael, *New World Immigrants* (Baltimore, 1980).

Thomas, George Leicester, *Genealogy of Thomas Family* (Adamstown, 1954).

Thwaites, Reuben Gold, *Descriptive List of Manuscript Collections of the State Historical Society of Wisconsin* (Madison, 1906).

Turk, Willie Anne [Cary], *Beatty-Asfordby: The Ancestry of John Beatty and Susanna Asfordby with some of their Descendants* (New York, 1909).

Varlé, Charles, "A Map of Frederick and Washington Counties, State of Maryland" (1808).

Virginia, *Executive Journals of the Council of Colonial, 1721-1739*, McIlwaine, H. R., ed. (Richmond, 1930), Vol. 4.

Virginia State Papers and Other Manuscripts, Calendar of, William P. Fuller, ed. (Richmond 1893) 11:625.

Waddell, Joseph A., *Annals of Augusta County*, Virginia (Staunton, 1902).

Washington, George, *Journals of My Journey over the Mountains, 1747-48*, J. M. Toner, ed. (Albany, N.Y., 1892).

Weis, Frederick Lewis, *The Colonial Clergy of Maryland, Delaware and Georgia* (Lancaster, Massachusetts, 1950).

Weis, Frederick Lewis, *The Colonial Clergy of the Middle Colonies, New York, New Jersey and Pennsylvania, 1628-1776* (Worcester: The American Antiquarian Society, 1957).

Weiser, Frederick S., *Record of Pastoral Acts at the Lutheran and Reformed Congregations of the Muddy Creek Church, East Cocalico Township, Lancaster County, Pennsylvania, 1730-1790: Pennsylvania German Society, Sources and Documents of the Pennsylvania Germans,* V (Breinigsville, 1981).

Weiser, Frederick S., transcriber, "Records of St. Matthews Lutheran Church, Hanover, Pennsylvania," typescript at Adams County Historical Society.

Weiser, Frederick S., "The Earliest Records of Holy Trinity Evangelical Lutheran Church, Lancaster, Pennsylvania, 1730-1744," *Ebbes fer Alle - Ebber Ebbes fer Dich:* Pennsylvania German Society Publications, Vol. 14 (Breinigsville, 1980).

Wentz, Abdel Ross, *History of the Evangelical Lutheran Church of Frederick, Maryland, 1738-1938,* (Harrisburg, 1938).

Williams, Thomas John Chew and McKinsey, Folger, *History of Frederick County, Maryland* (1910).

Winslow, Benjamin, "A Plan of the Upper Part of Patomack River called Cohongorooto, Surveyed in the Year 1736," original at Enoch Pratt Free Library, Baltimore.

Wittwer, Norman C., *The Faithful and the Bold* (Oldwick, N.J., 1984).

Wroth, Lawrence C., "The Story of Thomas Cresap, Maryland Pioneer," *Maryland Historical Magazine,* 9:8.

Wyckoff, B. V. D., transl., "Readington Church Baptisms from 1720," *Somerset County Historical Quarterly,* 4:213.

Young, Henry James, "The Families Belonging to the Moravian Community and Congregation at Graceham in Maryland and Some of Their Neighbors, 1759-1871" (typescript from the Parish Register, 1942).

Young, Henry James, The Private Record of Jacob Lischy, V.D.M., 1743-1769 (typescript, 1934).

INDEX

Because eighteenth century orthography, even in official records, was largely phonetic, an amazing number of spelling variations resulted. This was especially true with German and Indian proper names. We have found, for example, 34 different spellings for the word "Monocacy." One should almost pronounce orally such spellings as Chanandore and Cenantona to obtain "Shenandoah" or to transform Dieterich Lehnich into Tetur Lany. Only close attention to related details permits us to identify Kiefalpor and Kanghover as today's Kefauver. While in our text all spellings as actually recorded have been preserved as closely as possible, to do so in the Index would provide a compiler's nightmare. Hence we appeal to the reader's imagination and ingenuity to bridge the gaps where detailed cross references may be lacking. Punctuation niceties, especially in the use of apostrophes with the genitive, were likewise generally lacking in recorded documents. This will explain their absence in the parcel names indexed below. Parcel names and names of ships are shown in quotation marks. In general, the German feminine ending (-in) with a possible umlaut in the stem has been omitted. Page references in **bold** denote principal references in the text.

Abell, Anthony 323
"Abells Lot" 90 93 362 364
"Abentons Cabin" 15 33 363 364
Aberle, Conradt Israel: see Eberle 301
Abington, Andrew 39
  John 39 40 94 123 124 366 367
  John Beals 62
"Above House" 174
Abraham's (Catoctin) Creek 246
Abrahams Falls 15
Act of Establishment 348
"Adams Content" 167
Adams County, Pa. 50 52 285
  Historical Society 135
Adamson, John 370
Adamstown, Md. 80 283
Adams, Andrew 323
  George 116
  Henry 308 323
  John 28 371
  Martin 307 308 323
  Mary 323
  Valentine 378
Addison, Ann 31
  Anthony
  Eleanor (Smith) 31 32
  Henry 31 49
  John 31 370
  Thomas 31 32 54 364
  Thomas, Jr. 31
Addison Run 31 46 116 285 288
"Addisons Choice" 24 28 34 115 124 362 364
"Addition" (McKeen) 33 238 239 363 364
"Addition" (Weymore) 186 192 362 364
"Addition" (Wood) 312
"Addition to Beaver Dam Level" 20
"Addition to Carrollton" 20 189
"Addition to Chidleys Range" 159
"Addition to Emmitsburg" 241
"Addition to Fathers Lecture" 174
"Addition to First Brother" 313
"Addition to Frederick Town" 267
"Addition to New Germany" 20 54 167 190

"Addition to Saint Elizabeth" 19
"Addition to Sassafras Bottom" 186 217 218 363 364
"Addition to Slate Ridge" 207
"Addition to Spring Garden" 40 128
"Addition to Williams Project" 347
"Addition to Wolf Pit" 19
Adersbach über Sinsheim, Ger. 156
"Adventure," ship 284
Affirming vs. swearing 279 286 287 296
Agnew, James 241
Ahalt Mill 226
Albany Protocol 125 136
Albany, N. Y. 99
Albaugh, Adam 380
  Ann 323
  Zacharias 307, 323
Albin, Thomas 52 53 70 75 364
"Albins Choice" 40 52 53 70 73 75-77 362 364
Alexander, Ashton 288
  Catherine (Hanson) 288
Alexandria, Ohio 319
Algemeen Rijksarchief, s'Gravenhage 150
Algonquian Indians 7
Alienation fine 2 109 164 302 305
All Saints' Parish 47 77 127 348-355
  Baptisms in 127 329
  Cemetery 353
  Church Book 112 245 353
  Churchyard 158
  Petition to form: see Prince George's Parish, Petition to divide
  Petition to divide 227 354 355
  Vestrymen 64
All Souls' Parish 355
"All Stones" 201
"Allamangle" 166-167
Allegany County, Md. 14 20 36
Allemängel (Berks Co., Pa.) 19 147
Allen, Bennett 308, 355
  Michael 378
"Allen," ship 165 270
Alloway Creek, N. J. 69

"Alltogether" 235
Alsenborn, Ger. 41
Ambrose's Mill 188 192 203 206 212 255 286
Ambrose, Augustus Heinrich 375
  Catharina: see Weller 202, 204
  Catharine (w/o Matthias) 203
  Henry 203 252
  Jacob 200
  Johann Friederich 202 376
  Johann Philipp 374
  Maria Barbara 202 203
  Maria Barbara (Matthias) 206-207
  Martin 365
  Matthias 140 147 187 188 200-201 202-204 206-207 209 213 216 248 250 252 372 374-376
  Matthias, Jr. 202 203 207 376
Amwell, N. J. 133 208
Anabaptists 180 376
"Anchor and Hope" 222-225 362 364
Ancrum, Aaron 66
  Elizabeth (w/o Richard) 66
  Elizabeth (d/o John): see Lakin 66
  Elizabeth (d/o Richard): see Thrasher 66
  Jacob 66
  John 66
  Martha (Wells) 66
  Mary: see Delashmutt 66
  Richard 56 66
  Richard, Jr. 66
  Richard (s/o John) 66
  Sarah 85
  Sarah: see Beall 66, 84
  William (s/o John) 66
Anderson, Charles 14 15
  Thomas 87
"Andersons Delight" 19
Andrae, Peter 207
  Susanna (Wetzel) Oberkirsch 207
Andreas, Johanata Maria: see Berg 313
"Andrews Folly and Discontent" 20 97
Angleberger, Philipp 170
Anis, James 371
Annapolis, Md. 9 14 21 23 36 37 41 42 56 77 102 153 171 206 213 231 245 257 287 308 332 355
Anne, Queen of England 2 9 130 247
Anne Arundel County, Md. 44 67 91 230-232 370
"Anne Arundel Manor" 302
Annville, Pa. 135
"Antietam Bottom" 171
Antietam (Ondieta) Creek 12 55-57 67 171 222 228 352
"Antietam Level" 14 311
Antrim, Ireland 347
"Anything" 310
Apple (Apel, Apfel, Appel):
  Apalonia 199
  Caspar 163
  Clara 199
  Eva Rosina (see House): 199 201 377
  Johann Peter 139 144 146 162 164 172 187 190 **199**-201 206 207 212 250 292 373 377 379
  Johann Peter, Jr. 199

Apple (cont'd.):
  Magdalene: see Byerly 201
  Maria Catharina (Henckel) Geiger 160 163 164 199 201
  Maria Charlotta: see Meyer 199 201
  Mary: see Matthews 201
  Peter (h/o Clara) 198
  Susanna (Bocher) Fout 163
  Susanna (d/o Peter, Jr.) 201
Apples Church (Luth. and Refd.) 200 203 207 210 248
Appolds Road 52 325 328
"Arabia (Araby)" 39 245, 277
Archives of Maryland, Annapolis 5
Archives, Moravian Church 142 148
Aris, James 56
Armstrong, James 298
  John 242
Arnold, Andrew 275
  Daniel 33 275
  John 113 253 275
  John George 33 244 275 365 367 372
  Samuel 275
"Arnolds Chance" 203 249 252
"Arnolds Delight" 203 211 248-250 252 254 296 326 336
Arnoldsville 223
Arnswalde, Brandenburg, Ger. 147
Arrival of the Germans:
  In Monocacy 130-153
  Lists at Philadelphia (see also under individual immigrant) 131 154 161-163 175 185 193
"Arrow Point" 60 91 362 364
"Arthurs Island" 61
Articles of Confederation 287
Articles, Muhlenberg's Lutheran Church 145-147 157 160 170 192 195 197 199 202 209 212 216 218 295
Artz, C. Burr 282
  Margaret 282
Asfordby, Susanna: see Beatty 117
  William 117
Assembly, Maryland 22 31 39 42 50 94 96 179 247 251 253 260 292 341 342 346 348 349 352
Assignments 2 3 35 37 39 208 361
Assleman, Benedict 267
Athey (Athy), George 379
  Thomas, Sr. 370
  Walter 370
Attorney General, Proprietary 27 39
  United States 59
"Auburn" 209
Augsburg Confession, Lutheran 144
Augusta, Ga. 65
Augusta County, Va. 157
Averlaw, Leonard: see Eberle, Leonard 300
Awbry, Francis 379

Bachdold (see also Bechtold, etc.):
  Johann Friedrich 179
  Henry 53 140 144 155 170 **179** 292 366 373
  Susanna 179
Back Creek, [W.] Va. 183
"Back Land," The (Digges/Livers) 39 42 248

"Back Land," The (cont'd.):
249 326 362 364
Back Run 350
"Backland" (Bordley) 39 362 364
Backdolt, Ken: see Bachdolt, Henry 292
Backelt (Bockit), Edward 368
Backer, Adam 317 375
　Eliesabetha 317 375
Bacon, Thomas 354-355
Bad Dürkheim, Ger 216
Bad Kreuznach, Ger. 276
Bad Rappenau, Kraichgau, Ger. 157
Bad Wimpfen, Ger. 172
Baer (Bare, Beer), Catarina Barbara 193 376
　Joh. Georg 18 53 139 185-187 192 193-194 260 290 295 365 371 372 376
Bailey, David 85 335
　John 371
　William 310 327 334 335
"Baileys Purchase" 20
Bails (Bailes, Bales), John 368
　Thomas 83
Bainbridge, Peter 33 113 330 343
Baker (see also Becker), Frederick 281 304 320 322
　George 343
　Leonard 371
　Robert 112 121
　Snader 103
　Wilbur 103
"Bakers Lookout" 19
Baldwin, Jane 31
Ballenger Creek (Branch) 46 53 55 57 70 80 81 83 85 109 161 174 184 200 230, 285 354
Ballenger Creek Pike 62 174 267
Ballenger (Bellanger) Families 230
　Cassandra (Plummer) 81 235 236
　Daniel 88
　Hannah (Wright) 79 81 84
　Henry, Sr. of N.J. 81
　Henry 62 79-82 85 87 108 162 235 365 366 368
　James 82
　John 81
　Josiah 45 79-82 366
　Josiah, Jr. 82
　Martha 81
　Mary (Wright) 79 82
　Mary (d/o Henry) 81
　Moses 81
　Rachel 81
　Rebecca 81
　Sarah 82
　William 81 235 236
"Ballengers Endeavor" 19
Balsam, Peter: see Baltzell 136
Baltimore, Lady Martha 32 37
Baltimore, Lords (see also Calvert) 2 16-18 21 23 27 30 32 36 54 127 128 156 272 302 303 306 348 368
Baltimore, Md. 27 102 104 279
Baltimore and Ohio Railroad 56 94 97
Baltimore County, Md. 16 17 85 104 105 196 198 224 228 231 232 255 330 332 370

Balus, Andrew 246
Baltzel (Balsam, Bolsell), Hans Peter 111 136
"Balzell's Content" 111
Bancalf (Bancuff, Bannkauf, Pongoffen):
　Anton 17 77 **168** 169 185 324 372 375
　Magdalene (Devilbiss?) 169 318
Bantz, Mary 273
Baptist ministers 310
Baptists 348
Barbar, Baptist 76
Barbelroth, Ger. 262
Bare (see also Baer), George 193
　Jacob 378
Baret, Capt. 334
Bargar, Christopher 378
　Philip 378
Barger, George 378
Barker, Charles A. 247
Barkett, Dorothy: see Hook 64
Barnard (Bernard), Luke 76 78 337 342 349
　Margaret (Debutts) 78
　Mary 337
　Nathaniel 342
　Sabina: see Wickham 337
　Thomas 337
Barnes, William 379
Barnett, Thomas 371
Barnhold, Ann: see Ritchie 123
Barr, Jacob 274
Barrack, Barrick: see also Berg
Christian 380
　George W. 342
　Handel 186 208 380
　John 380
　Peter 104 380
　Susan (Krise) 342
　William 313-315 380
"Barrel" 347
"Barren Hill" 56
Barrens 289
"Barrens," The 19 258-260 289 290
Bart Twp., Lancaster Co., Pa. 289
Barth, Georg 209
　Zacharias 144
Bartlett, John 368
Barton, Henrietta (Biggs) Beatty 120 311 323
　Jacob 110 120 195 307 311 323 380
　Joshua 235
Baseler, Veronica 375
Basle, Switzerland 147
"Batchelors Hall" 15 20 172 224
Bateman, John 370
"Battleham" 19 214
Baughman, Andrew 116
　Catherin (Neff) 297
　Jacob 297
Baughtall, Henry: see Bachdold 179
Baum, Anna Maria: see Trout 220 377
Bayer, Philip 105
Beall (Beal, Beals), Alexander **44** 366
　Basil 40
　George 21
　James 370
　John 40 **84** 94-96 364 367 370
　Joseph 370

Beall (cont'd.)
 Joshua 297, 298
 Mordecai 379
 Prudence: see Williams 84
 Robert 84 96
 Samuel Jr. 195-196 370
 Sarah (Ancrum) 66 84
 Thomas 66 84 371
 William 379
 William (s/o Nathan) 370
Beallsville, Md. 10 56 62 77 162 192 195 339 349 352
 English chapel near: see Monocacy Chapel
Beanes, W. 370
Beansey, (?) 370
Bear, John George: see Baer 139
"Bear Den" ("Taskers Chance") 193 258 259 289 290
"Bear Den" (Chalmers) 105 363 364
Beard, James 113
 John 323
Beatty Family 116-124
 Agnes: see Kimball 117 118 121 122
 Ann (d/o William): see Schaaf 119
 Bata (Middag) 122
 Catherine (d/o Thomas): see Ritchie 123
 Charles of N.Y. 117-119
 Charles (s/o Thomas) 34 38 122 123 178 193 254 267 378
 Edward 75 102 117-121 229 328 367 368
 Edward, Jr. 121
 Eleanor (d/o William): see Young 119
 Eli 119
 Elijah 75 121
 Elizabeth (Carmack) 119
 Ezekiel 121
 Ezra 121
 George 119 121378
 Henrietta (Biggs): see Barton 120 311
 Henry 117-119 368
 James 56 117 118 121 124 228 368
 James (s/o Thomas) 122
 Jane 118-119
 Jannetje (Jans) 117
 John of N.Y. 104 117
 John, Jr. 117 118 120 121 124 311 368 380
 John III 120 311
 John (s/o Robert) 119
 Margaret 119
 Maria (Jansen) 122
 Martha: see Middagh 117 118 122
 Mary: see Ogle 332
 Mary (d/o William): see Elting, Cary 119
 Mary Dorothea (Grosch) 119
 Moraca 118-119
 Robert of N.Y. 117-119 121 122
 Sarah (d/o Thomas) 122
 Susanna (Asfordby) 31 39 45 104 110 116 117-124 127-128 161 205 309-311
 Susanna (d/o Robert): see Haff 119
 Susanna (d/o Thomas): see Maynard 200
 Susanna (Cock) 120 121
 Thomas 48 53 57 104 116-118 120-124 128 160 162 171 200 229 272 312 328

Beatty, Thomas (cont'd.)
 333 340 341 343 364 368
 Thomas, Jr. 122 380
 William 56 102 104 116-120 125 128 195 228 235 364 368 370
 William, Jr. 119
 William III 119
Beatty Graveyard 47 116 128
"Beattys Delight" 122 229 231 362 364
"Beattys Luck" 128 129
"Beattys Venture" 116 128 129 351 363 364
"Beauty" 19 47 184
Beavan, Charles 370
Beaver Branch 254
Beaver Dam Area 99-105
Beaver Dam Branch (near Ogle) 335
Beaver Dam Brethren Church 99
Beaver Dam Creek 43 99-101 103
"Beaver Dam Level" 254 363 364
"Beaver Den" 258 259 282
Beaver Run (Carroll Creek) 72 261
"Beaverdam Manor" 302
Bechdolt, Bechtel, Bechtold, Boughtall:
 Henrich: see Bachdold 140 144 179
 Susanna 179
Beckenbach (Pickapaw, Pickenpaw), Adam 301
 Anna Catharina: see Brengel 264
 Caspar 271 300-301
 Eva Maria: see Eberle 300
 Görg Adam 301
 Georg Leonhardt 301
 Johann Adam 266 301
 Johann Caspar 269
 Johann Georg 301
 Peter 379
 Susanna (Sinn) 269
Becker[?], Elizabeth (Miller) 287
Becker (See also Baker), Frederick 281 320
 Ludwig 276
 Maria Magdalena (Finck) 276
 Samuel 281
Beckwith, Basil 370
Becraft, Benjamin 101 229 231-232 364
 George 100-101 231 232 354 366
 Peter 233
"Becrafts Delight" 229 231 362 364
Bedford, John 378
Bedford County, Pa. 311
Beer, Catarina Barbara 193
 Hinrich 135
 Joh. Georg: see Baer 295
Beeson, Richard 87
Begabock, Gasper: see Beckenbach, Casper 300
Beissel, Conrad 133
Beitzel, Elisabeth: see Krieger 211
 Johannes 195, 211
 Lorentz 211
 Maria Magdalena 211
Bel's Gap, Mr. 40 55 97
Bell, Elizabeth 313, 323
 Gertraud: see Brengel 264
 John 110 116 124 126 264 304 307 311 313 315 318 323 370 371
 John (Jr.) 126 313 323
 Margaret: see Brengel 264

Bell (cont'd.)
 [?], s/o Robert 370
Beller, Christian 379
"Bellvue" 76
Belmont County, Ohio 111
"Below House" 174
Belt, Ann: see Claggett, Davis & Perry 83
 Benjamin, Jr. 370
 Joseph 61
 Middleton 370
Bender, Catharina: see Vertriess 216
Bene, Jacob 139
Benedick, Nicholas 293
"Benjamins Good Luck" 310
Bennett (Bonnett), Isaiah 59
 Richard 14 15 **25** 31 32 365
Bennett Creek 25 46 89 234-236
Bennett's Creek, "Northernmost" 245
Bens Branch 46 120 229 230 231 232 234
Bentz (Pentz), Jacob 260 267 268
Benzelius, Jacob 142
Berg (see also Barrick):
 Anna Catharina (Schweitzer) 314
 Catharina: see Habach 314 377
 Catharine (w/o Peter) 314 315 323
 Catherine (d/o Handel) 315
 Catherine (d/o William): see Devilbiss 315
 Christian 307 314 315 323
 Christian, Jr. 315
 Elisabeth: see Case 314
 Frederick (s/o Handel) 315
 George (s/o Wm.) 315
 Handel 304 324 325 323
 Henry (s/o Handel) 315
 Isaac (s/o Handel) 315
 Jacob (of William) 315
 Johanata Maria (Andreas) 313
 Johann Peter of Nordhofen, Ger. 313 314
 Johann Tillmann (Hans Till): see Handel 314
 John (Johannes) 125 151 304 307 315 316 323
 John (s/o Handel) 315 323
 John Jr. (s/o John) 314 315 323
 Judith 314 315 323
 Mary (d/o Wm.) 315
 Michael (d/o Wm.) 315
 Peter 125 304 307 315 316 323
 Peter, Jr. 315, 316
 Sarah (d/o Wm.) 315
 Susannah (d/o Wm) 315
 William (John Wilhelm) 304 307 313 322 323 373
 William (Jr.) 304 314 323
 William (III) 315
 William (s/o Peter) 314
"Bergs Delight" 307 314 316
"Bergs Luck" 307 314
Berger, Andreas 170
Bergzabern, Ger. 277
Berkeley County, W. Va. 53 74 87 109 183 344
Berkenmeyer, Wilhelm Christoph 132 136 218
Berks County, Pa. 127 132 151 294

Bernard: see Barnard 342
Berne, Switzerland 8-10
Berry, Jeremiah 370
 Philip 93
Berthelsdorf, Zinzendorf's estate 141
Beschell, Anna: see Ellrodt 316
Bethel, Md. 52, 107 136 169-170
Bethlehem, Pa. 20 141 142 145 147 152 153 188 216 283 285 334
Bethlehem Diary 142
"Betsys Delight" 66
"Better than None" 313
Beyer, Susanna: see Rudiesielle 377
Beyerle (Byerly), Anna Catharina 194 374 377
 Johann Jacob 277 374 375
 Johann Michael 377
 Magdalena (Apple) 201
 Maria Rosina 374
Bibbins, Ruthella Mory 102
Bier, Eva Catharine (Schley) 266
Big Creek, Tenn. 105
Big Pipe Creek 46 52 104 127 285 335
Big Pool, Md. 64
Biggs, Benjamin 309-311 322 331 334
 Catherine (d/o John): see Julien 311
 Catherine (d/o William): see Cookerly 311
 Catherine (Furney) 311
 Elisabeth: see Pittinger 311
 Elisabeth (Ohler) 311
 Eva Lambertse (Brink) 309
 Eva (Moon) 311
 Frederick 311
 Henrietta: see Beatty, Barton 120 311
 Henrietta Prudence Deborah Margaretta (Munday) 310 334
 Jacob 311
 John 110 113 116 120 **125 126** 265 299 304 307 309-312 319 322 324 328 333
 John (s/o William) 311
 Joseph 311
 Mary Stilley 309
 Mary (d/o John): see Doddridge 311
 Mary (d/o Wm.): see Ogle 311
 Mary (Kalb) 311
 Mary (Wilson) 311
 Priscilla (Wilson) 311
 Prudence Drusilla: see Ogle 310 331
 Sarah: see Hedges 311
 William 309-311, 322
 William, Jr. 311
"Biggs Delight" 307 309
Biggs Ford 34 36 42 45 51 52 54-56 106 107 116 169 265 281 297 309 319 328 338 341
Biggs Ford Bridge 31 52 57 309
Bigrove, William 121
Birch, Jonathan 370
Birchfield, Elizabeth (Justice) 101
 Robert 101 103
Bischoff, Bishop:
 Eliesabetha 238 376
 Eliesabetha (Ellrodt) 316
 (Joh.) Heinrich (Peschof) 139 205 238 316 376

Bischoff (cont'd.)
  J. P. 327
Blaar, Barbara: see Keller 298
"Black Acorn" 347
"Black Acre" (Black) 30 91 362 364
"Black Acre" (Griffith) 90-92 363 364
"Black Walnut Bottom" (Elder) 248 253 363 364
"Black Walnut Bottom" (Wickham) 248 341 363 364
Black, Valentines 378
  William 30 91 226 364 365 371 380
Blackburn, Robert 379
Bladen Family 32 37
  Anne (van Swearingen) 32
  Anne: see Tasker 32 37
  Barbara (Janssen) 32 37
  Thomas, Gov. 32 37 77 251 306 351 370
  William 32
Bladensburg, Md. 297
Blair, Capt. 101
  Samuel 241
Blavin, Daniel 368
  James 368
Bleystein, Johann Georg 215
Blies River 263
Bloomfield, Catherine (Hedges?) 109-110
  Isaac 77 110 113
Bloomfield, Md. 155
"Bloomsbury" 44
Blue Mount Road 212
Blue Mountain, Little (South Mountain) 329
Blue or North Ridge Mountains 94 97 226 334
"Blue Spring" 33 186 216 363 364
Blumenschein, Johannes: see Flower, John 301 335
Blunston, Samuel 17
Bocher, Georg 163
  Margreth 163
  Susanna: see Fout, Apple 163
Bockit (Backelt), Edward 368
Boehm, Johann Philipp 132 149
Boetler, Charles 252
  Mary (Livers) 252
Bogert, Frederick W. 135
Bohemia 141
Bolivar, Md. 245
Bolsell, Peter: see Baltzel 111
Bolter, Edward 61
  Elizabeth (Delashmutt) 61
Bond, Issac 97
  Thomas 16 332
Bondrake, Nicholas 218
"Bonds Mannour" 16
Bonet, Jaques (see also Bonnett, Jacob) 214 262 277 294 373
Bonfeld, Kraichgau, Ger. 157
Bonham, Malachi 310
Bonner (Brunner?), Joseph 370
Bonnett (Bonet), Catharine: see Six 215
  Christina 214
  Elizabeth (Waggoner) 215
  Elizabeth: see Wetzel 209 215
  Isaiah: see Bennett 59
  Jacob 33 53 208 214 214-215 367
  John Simon 214

Bonnett (cont'd.)
  Lewis 215
  Margret 214
  Mary (w/o Jacob) 214
  Mary: see Wetzel 209 215
  Susanna 214
"Bonnetts Resolution" 33 186 209 214 363 364
Booker, Bartholomew 113
Booth, John 56
Border Dispute, Pennsylvania/Maryland 16-19 21 42 45 168 185 190 191 193 196 225 324 332
Bordley, Stephen 39 370
  Thomas 37 39 79 161 364 367
Boring, William 17
Bostian, George 380
Boswell, (?) 370
Boughtall, Henry: see Bachdold 170
Bourbon County, Ky. 111 311
Bowie, Effie Gwynn 41
  James 370
  John 370
  Robert (Gov.) 226
  William 370
Bowles, Thomas 267
Bowman, Seman 380
Boyd, Benjamin 370
  James A. 47 128
"Boyling Springs" 79 80 85 363 364
Brace, Atha Peckenpaugh 301
  Edwin T. 301
Brackenburg, William 76
Brackenheim, Ger. 159
Braddock, Gen. Edward 329
Braddock Heights 52 84 111 223 244 245 354
Braddock's Road 21
Bradford, John 349 352
Bradley, Robert 370
Brandmüller, Johann 141 183 213 329
"Brandywine Spring" 229 230 363 364
Branner: see Brunner 260
Branson, Thomas 87
Braun, Fritz 282
Brawner, Edward 248 254 365
  Edward, Jr. 255
  Elizabeth (Elder) 254
  Henry 255 331
  John 255
  Joseph 255
  Mary (Ogle) Butler 331
  Richard 254, 255
  Thomas 255
  William 255
Bray (Prey), Anna Maria 274 375
  Catarina 274 375
  Eliesabetha 274 376
  Henry 217 273 368 375
  Sarah 274 375
  Susanna 274 375
"Breeches" 100 362 364
Brengel (Brengle, Pringle):
  Anna Catharina: see Derr 264
  Anna Catharina (Beckenbach) 264
  Christian of Wolfersheim, Ger. 263
  Christian (Jr.) 260 263 276

Brengel (cont'd.)
  Christian (of Kilian) 263-264
  George 263-264
  Gertraud (Bell) 264
  Jacob 126 128 262-264 380
  Kilian 264
  Lawrence 262
  Lawrence J. 264
  Margaret (Bell) 264
  Maria Christina 263
Brenneisen, Georg Valentin 374
"Brentford" 44
Bresler: see Pressler 219
Brethren, Church of the: known prior to 1908 as the German Baptist Brethren, q.v.
Brickerville, Pa. 215 294 316
Brightwell, John 103 105
  Peter 252
  Sarah (Carmack) 103 105
  William 370
Brink, Eva Lambertse: see Biggs 309
"Britannia" ship 208
British Library, London 9
Broad (Muddy) Run 92 197 223 225 226
"Broken Island" 13 52 59 60 362 364
Bronner: see Brunner 375
Brooke, Clotilda (Green) Elder 254
  Lucy (Smith) 31
  Richard 370
  Brooke, Roger 254
  Thomas 31 370
Brooke Co., W. Va. 331
Brooklyn Heights, Battle of 101
"Brother Try All" 43
"Brothers Agreement" 43
Brown, Benjamin 379
  Godfry 378
  James 103 379
  Jeremiah 82
  John 379
  William 371
Browner (Brunner), Jacob 292
  John 292
"Brownings Inheritance" 340
"Browns Choice" 19
"Browns Delight" 103
Bruce, Norman 39 343 355
  Upton 39
Bruceville 343 355
Bruchel, Samuel 375
Brumbaugh, Gaius Marcus 112
Bruner: see Brunner 165
Brunner Family 257 269-273 280 301
  Anna Barbara (d/o John): see Eastin 273
  Anna Barbara (d/o Joseph): see Getzendanner 165 271
  Anna Margaretha (d/o Hen): see Jordan 273
  Anna Maria (Storm) 281
  Anna Maria (d/o Henry): see Cost 273
  Anna Maria (d/o John): see Ramsburg, John 273, 293
  Anna Maria (w/o John) 262 273 274 375 376
  Anna Maria Catrin (d/o Joseph): see Maria Catharina 271

Brunner (cont'd.)
  Barbara (d/o Henry): see Lingenfelter 273
  Barbara (d/o John) 272
  Catharina Elisabetha (Thomas) 271 282 291
  Catharine (d/o John): see Thomas 272 273
  Dorothea (Lochman) 191
  Elias (s/o Joseph) 151 260 271 **272** 379
  Elizabeth (d/o Jacob) 272
  Elizabeth (d/o John): see Ramsberger 273
  Felix 277
  Gabriel 271
  Georg Michael (s/o Jacob) 209
  Henry (s/o Henry) 272
  Henry (s/o Joseph) 258-260 268-269 271 **272-273** 371
  Jacob (s/o Henry) 272
  Jacob (s/o Jacob) 272
  Jacob (s/o John) 272, 273
  Jacob (s/o Joseph) 77 96 140 150 164 165 171 209 217 258-260 264 **269**-270 272-274 288 292 293 298 300 365 371 372
  Johann Jacob (see Jacob s/o Joseph) 171
  Johann Valentin (s/o Joseph) 271
  John (s/o Henry) 272 273
  John (s/o Jacob) 272
  John, Jr. (s/o John) 272 273 379
  John (s/o Joseph) 78 258 259 262 269 271 **273** 281 292 371 376 179
  Joseph 150 258-260 269-**272** 282 291 299 371 372 379
  Maria Barbara (Sturm) (w/o Jacob) 269 273 274 280 375
  Maria Catharina 209
  Maria Catharina (d/o Joseph): see Ramsburg 271-272 291
  Maria Magdalena (Sellers) 272
  Mary (d/o Jacob) 272
  Mary (d/o John) 272
  Michael (s/o Jacob) 270 272 300
  Peter (s/o George) 191
  Peter (s/o Jacob) 269 270 272 300
  Stephen 273
  Susannah (d/o Henry): see Thomas 273
  Valentine (s/o Henry) 272
Brunnholtz, Peter 144 151
Brunswick 15 37 38 40 94
Bryan, Mary: see Curtis 87
  Morgan 86 87 344
Bryzelius, Paul Daniel 141
"Bubby" 92
Buchanan, Archibald 18
  James 191
  Mary (Pearre) 92
  Robert 18 196 325
Buch, Dorothea: see Verdriess 216
"Buck Lodge" 43
Buckey, Ethel (Close) 263 311
  Mary (Hoffman) 279
  Matthias 279, 298
Buckeystown 29 45 79-81 83 87 166 236
Buckeystown District 283
Bucks County, Pa. 87
Buffalo Creek, W. Va. 108 331

"Bulford" 16
Bullkskin area, W. Va. 344
Bundrick, Anna Maria (Müller) 157
   Nicholas 157 178 195 267
Bunker Hill, W. Va. 344
Bunsell (Bundrick?), Nicholas 157
Buren, Gelderland, Holl. 69
Burckhart, George 343
Burgert, Annette K. 160 284 288 289
Burgess, James 224
   Charles 81
   Jo Ann 73
   John 28
   Sarah: see Hook 65
   Ursula: see Davis
   William 81
"Burgess Choice" 20
Burk, David 380
Burkittsville 34 38 55 95 96 174 223 225 226
Burlington, N. J. 79
Burlington County, N. J. 87
Burns, Johanna (van Metre) 72
Burnsten, Joseph 378
"Burnt House" 15 33 363 364
Burnt House Hundred 319
Burnt House Woods 102
Burr, Horace 109
Busey, Edward 370
Bush Creek 46 70 229 232-236
"Bush Creek Hill" 19 231
"Bush Creek Mountain" 235
Bush Creek [Quaker] Meeting 88 236
Bush River 12
Bushey Bottom, Va. 296
Bussey, Charles 371
Butler, Edward 379
   Mary (Ogle): see Brawner 329-331
   Peter 78 172 209 329-331
Butler, Thomas 256 370
"Butlers Lot" 331
Butterfly Lane 52-54 57 121 166-167 181 190 354
Buttner, Adam 235
Byerly, Magdalena (Apple) 201
Bytsel, John: see Beitzel 195

C/S (Certificates of Survey references) 3
Cabin Branch 226
Cabis, John 371
Cadel, Michal Dent 371
Caldwell, Samuel 241
Calvert, Benedict 216
   Benedict Leonard, 4th Lord Baltimore 27 32
   Cecilius, Secy. to Frederick Calvert, Sixth Lord Baltimore 303
   Cecilius, 2nd Lord Baltimore 302
   Charles, 3rd Lord Baltimore 27 41
   Charles II, 5th Lord Baltimore 27 32 36 156
   Charles (Gov. 1720-1727) 14
   Frederick, 6th Lord Baltimore 32 303 305 308 320
   John 87
   Mary (Janssen), Lady Baltimore 32
Calvert County, Md. 63 231 236 237 346
Calvert Papers 5 13 36 127 303
"Calverton Manor" 302
Calvin, George 371
Calvinists, Dutch 348
Campbell, Archibald 354
   John 366
Cambridge, Ohio 120
Camden, S. C. 119
   Battle of 63
Campbell (Cambill), Archibald 103
   John 100 101 105
Canadochly (Conojohela) Creek and area 15-17 185 193-194 198 224 325 374-375
Canashochele: see Canadochly above
Canavest 10 11
Canawage: see Conewago 285
Candler, David 53 135-140 142 144 155-156 158 160 169-170 195 199 202 208 216 297 316 367
   David, Jr. 135
   Elisa Barbara 136
   John Barnhart 136
   John William 136
   Maria Catharina (Dünckel) 135
   Veronica Philippina: see also Laub 135 140
"Canhodah" 16
Canigotschik: see Conococheague 334
Cannawacke: see Conewago 140
Cannode, Charles 368
Cannon, Frances 326
   Robert 16
   Sophia 19 193 326
   William 16 326
Cantrell (Cantwell), Joseph 368
Cap Stein Road 283
Captains Creek: see Owens Creek 152 336
"Captains Lott" 307
Carlisle, Pa. 241
Carmack, Aquila 105 250
   Catherine: see Richards 104
   Cornelius 45 77 100 103 104 120 250 365 380
   Cornelius (s/o William) 105
   Elizabeth: see Beatty 119
   Elizabeth: see Evans 104
   Eunice (Williams) 105
   Evan 105
   Guein 104
   Jane 103 105
   John (s/o Cornelius) 103 104 122 235 250 354
   John (s/o William) 105
   John C. 105
   Levy 105
   Margery 105
   Mary: see Richards 104
   Mary (Wolfe) 105
   Nathan 105
   Rachel C (Richards) 105
   Sarah: see Brightwell 103 105
   Sarah C. (Wolfe) 105
   Susannah (Justice) 105
   William 100 103-105 250 365 366 380
   William, Jr. 105
"Carmacks Choice" 105
Carnhart, Henry 287

Carolina 10 202 209-210 298 311 320 322 323
Carpenter, Emanuel 172
"Carpouch" 20
Carr, Robert 324
Carrick Knob 248
Carrick, Samuel 239 240 241
Carroll, Ann (Sprigg) 226
  Anthony 26
  Anthony, S.J. 26
  Charles of Annapolis 17 25-26 236 28 30 49 77 83 85 105 110 130 138 189 239 364
  Charles of Belle Vue 28 226
  Charles of Carrollton, the Signer 26-28
  Charles of Duddington I 26
  Charles of Duddington II and Carrollsburg 226
  Charles, the Barrister 25-26, 215
  Charles, the Doctor 25-26 177 215 335
  Charles, the Settler 12 13 25-27
  Daniel 370
  Daniel of Duddington 26 28 30
  Daniel of Killieregan 26
  Daniel of Kings County, Ireland 26
  Daniel of Upper Marlboro 26 28
  Daniel of Upper Marlborough II 26 28
  Eleanor (1712-1734) 26 28 30
  Eleanor (Carroll) (1732-1763) 26 28
  Henry 26 28
  James 26 218
  James [sic] 152n
  Keane 26
  Mary (1711-1739?) 26 28 30
  Mary (1730-1785): see Digges 26 28
  Mary (Darnall) 27
Carroll County, Md. 5 14 19 43 45 50 99 103 194 203 231 319 326 333 339
Carroll County, Historical Society of 6
Carroll Creek 46 49 70 71 73 77 84 120 155 164 166 171 173 257 259 261 265 267 269 272 352-353
"Carroll Creek" 258 259 261 272
Carroll Creek Settlement 58 69-78 99
"Carrollsburg" [patd.] 24 30 237-239 241 255 362 364
"Carrollsburg" [unpatd.] 30 239 362 364
"Carrollton" 13 24-29 63 67 79 81 83 91 222 240 362 364
Cartledge, Edmund 13-15 181 368
  John 13 14 181
Cartledges Old Road 13 51 57 206 237 248 324 326 327
Carver, John 323 342
Cary, John 266 355 378
  Mary (Beatty) Elting 119
"Carys Good Will" 175
Case (Kaes), Elisabeth (Berg) 314
  William 314
Cassel, Anna Barbara: see Loy 296
Cassell, Henry 253
"Castle Henry" 354
"Catherine," snow 141
Catholic King 190
Catholic Settlement 58 247-256
Catholicism, Catholics 2 9 27 41 48 137 247 249 251 253 255 269 348

Catoctin Creek 7 10 5 33 35 40 43 46 56 65-67 84 94-98 222-224 226 243-246 300
Catoctin Furnace 192 195 215
Catoctin (Kitoctin, etc.) Mountain 7 10 15 40 54-56 62 65 83 84 92 160 162 171 174 176 178 181 189 215 222 245-246 257 265 272 281 355
Catoctin Valley 5 43 92 172 222 223 226 Settlement 58 222-227
Catores: see Codorus 324 374
"Cat-tail Branch" 219
"Cat-tail Marsh" 194
Caufman, Henry 378
Caution Money 2 35 65 86 156
Cecil County, Md. 14 15 17 103 219 253
Cedar Cliffs 43
Cemeteries and Graveyards:
  Beatty (Cock-Grahame) 47 116 128
  Devilbiss 319
  Frederick Reformed 193 284 290
  James-Kimmel 233
  Pittinger's 335
  Quaker 88
  Shook Family 165
Cennuntua (Shenandoah): see South Mountain 9
Ceresville 34 45 47 116 120 281 288-290 312
Certificates of Survey 1-3 25 37 48 115 231 321
Chalmers, John 105 364
Chalten (see also Charlton), Arthur 378
  John 378
Chambers, Benjamin 347
  James 347
  Jane (Williams) 346 347
  Joseph 347
  Robert 347
  Theodore Freylinghuysen 314
  William 347
Chambersburg, Pa. 344 348
Chance, Henry 380
"Chance" 84 95-97 362 364
"Chancey" 19 224 334
Chanywolf, Joseph 378
Chapel, Linganore & Sams Creek 102
Chapels of ease 349 352 355
Chapline (Chaplain), Elizabeth: see Hedges 109
  Isaac 346
  Joseph 55 97 224 330 340 346-347 371
  Moses 97 343
  Ruhamah (Williams) 346, 347
  William 347
  William Williams 347
"Chaptico Manor" 302
Chapultepec, Mexico 33
Charetier (Chartier), Martin 10 11 181
"Chargeable" 92 93
"Charles and Mary" 107 110 111 179 363 364
"Charles Choice" 103
Charles County, Md. 251 253-254 348
Charles Edward, Prince (The Young Pretender) 251
Charleston, S.C. 63

Charlesville 136 155
Charlton Family 18 332
  Arthur 22 335
  Captain 21
  John 246, 262
"Charming Nancy," ship 284
Chartin, Charles 370
Chartrd(?), Thomas 371
Chase, Samuel 342
Cheneoowquoque (Monocacy) River 7
Cherk, Margaret (Owings) 98
Cherry, Thomas 368
Chesapeake and Ohio Canal 55 56 59 89 94 97
Chesapeake Bay 231
Chester, Pa. 81
Chester County, Pa. 85 87 106 110 224 332
Chester County Plot 332
Chester Quaker Quarterly Meeting 85
"Chestnut" 33 48 155 170 363 364
"Chestnut Hill" (Brunner) 273
"Chestnut Hill" (Gump) 186 188-189 248 363 364
"Chestnut Hill" (Stull) 170
Chestnut Hill, Philadelphia 149
"Chestnut Valley" 85
Chevalier, Semple 157 195
"Chevy Chase" 19 20 270
Chew, Ann Mary: see Paca 30 32
  Henrietta Maria (Lloyd) 30 32
  Samuel 32
"Chidleys Range" 84 155 158 362 364
"Childrens Chance" 61 86
Chittam, Philip 370
  Thomas 370
"Chittam Castle" 43 100 105 362 364
"Choice" 342
Choolmondley, John 86
Christ (Chrest), Michael 379
Christ Church Parish 352
Christiana Hundred, New Castle Co., Del. 114
"Christians Choyce" 33 155 166-167 362 364
Church Books 5 6
  Cocalico: see Muddy Creek
  Conewago: see Hanover, Pa.
  Frederick "All Saints" English 112 113 329 347 353
  Frederick Lutheran 137 139 143-145 151 160 175 182 188 192 195 206 264 280 295 377
    Initial Purchasers: 139 162 170 173 188 199 202-204 206 210 212 216 217 295
  Frederick Reformed:
    Brunner Book 150 151 170 173 176 267 270 272 293 295
    Schlatter Book 175
  Glade Reformed 315
  Hanover (Pa.) St Matthews Lutheran 135 139
  Harlingen (N.J.) Dutch Reformed 309
  Kingston (N.Y.) Dutch Reformed 309
  Lancaster (Pa.) Trinity Lutheran 158 185 186 191 194 198 201 206 268 271 377
  Lancaster (Pa.) Reformed 201 268 271

Church Books (cont'd.)
  Lancaster (Pa.) Muddy Creek Lutheran 137 159 182 187-188 202 262 294 295 377
  Muddy Creek Reformed 159
  New Hanover (Pa.) Lutheran 157
  New York (City) Lutheran 135
  Stöver's Personal Journal 134-136 139 194 262 268 324
  York (Codorus) Lutheran 194 198
Church Elders, Reformed 165
Church Street, Emmitsburg 241 242
Churches and Congregations:
  Baltimore Otterbein United Brethren 279
  Bush Creek Quaker 88 236
  Church of England (see also under individual parishes) 27 48 56 67 79 344 348-355
  Church of the German Baptist Brethren 35 165 246 270-271 275 281 286 301
  Beaver Dam 99
  Conewago Reformed 151
  Frederick Catholic 265
  Frederick English (All Saints') Church Building 265 352 353
  Frederick Lutheran 79 82 144 151 265 352-353 355
  Frederick Reformed 79 149 151 263 265 269 292 298 352-353 355
  Germantown (Pa.) Reformed 308
  Glade Reformed 314
  Hopewell Quaker 82 87
  Lancaster (Pa.) Lutheran 137 142 145
  Lancaster (Pa.) Reformed 208 268
  Monocacy Lutheran ("Hills") 47 48 50 137 144 145 265 335
  Monocacy Quaker (see also under Quaker) 79 82 88 236
  Muddy Creek (Cocalico) Lutheran 159
  Muddy Creek Reformed 148
  Neshaminy (Pa.) Reformed 211
  New Hanover (Pa.) Lutheran 132 133 143 163 374
  Philadelphia (Pa.) Lutheran 133 143
  Pipe Creek Quaker 88 236
  Providence (Pa.) Lutheran 133 143
  Unionville Methodist Chapel 102
  United Brethren in Christ 175
  Wilmington (Del.) Holy Trinity (Old Swedes) 14 109
Churchman, John 82
Chydler, George 186 220 366
Citchadaner: see Getzendanner 166 350
Civil War 39
Clabaugh (Clapbough), Frederick 304 311 315 323 380
  John 315 323
  Mary 315 323
Clage, Charles 370
Clagett, Ann (Belt): see Davis, Perry 83
  Edward 370
  John 370
  Sarah: see Davis 83
  Thomas 83
  W. B. 98
Clapsaddle, Francis 18 191
Clarke, John 368

Clarke (cont'd.)
  William 368 379
"Clarkes Discovery" (Carroll Co.) 339
Cleary, Dr. Thomas 60
Clem: see also Klemm
  George 157
Clemons, Leonard 379
Clemson Branch 100 101
Clemsonville 99-100 102
Clover Hill II Subdivision 297
"Clovin" 30 362 364
Coats, Charles 371
Coblentz (Kowellentz), Peter 246
  J. 246
Coburn, James 74 368
Cocalico area, Pa. (see also Muddy Creek) 159 182
Cochran, William 30 239 240
  William, Jr. 239
Cock, Henry 121
  Mary (Ogle) 332
  Samuel 332
  Susanna: see Beatty 120
  William 121
Cock-Grahame (Beatty) cemetery 47 116 128
Cockerine, Cornelius 87
Cockey, Thomas 232
Cocks, Allen 368
"Cocolds (Cuckolds) Horn" 20 275
Codorus (Catores) area, York Co., Pa. 136 149-150 197 198 212 324-326 374
Coghill, Smallwood 370
Cohongoroota (Potomac) River 55
Coker (Kocher), Michael 197
"Cold Friday" 103
"Cold Spring Manor" 67
Cold Spring Meeting 82
Collard, Helena Livers 203 252
  Samuel 203 252
"College Green" 331
Colliar, Francis 371
  John 371
Collington Hundred 129 226 337
"Collington Manor" 302
Colonial (Colonel!) Island 40
Colton, George 371
Colvin, George 62
Combe, Adam 378
Combs, Richard, Jr. 103
Combs' Woolpit Branch 103
Commissary General 37 39 257
Commission Book No. 82: 162
Communion before naturalization 156 160 169 170 188 193 202 203 208 216 278 297 316 350
Compton, Thomas 371
  Thomas, Jr. 371
Conechigany (Conogocheague) road 55
Conestoga area, Lancaster Co., Pa. 13 52 132 133 141 163 165 181-182 188 202 204 278 289 377
Conestoga Creek 52
Conewago area (York, Adam Counties, Pa.) 41 42 50 52 54 135-136 140 142 145 196 207 211 246 247 252 350
Conewago Chapel 41 247
Conewago Creek, South Branch 197
Conewago-Monocacy Road 50
Confiscation of Loyalist Property 31 116 127-128 261 262 266 277 287 298 300 305 313 320 321
Conly, Enoch 103
Conner, Anne Catharine (Ellrodt) 316 377
  James 316 377
Connor, Ralph 71
Conococheague (Conechigany, Conogocheague, Kanighetschick, etc.) area 96 149 151 329 344 352 181
  Chapel of ease 355
  Creek 12 330 334 345
  Hundred 347
  "Manor" 302
  Reformed 151
  Road to 55 225 266 267
Conojohela (Canadochly) Creek and area 15-17 185 193-194 198 224 325 374 375
Conojohelar "War" 17 324 347
Conoy Indians 7 10
Conoy Island 9 59
Constables 31 61 64 67 71 84 86 91 93 94 105 108 110 114 119 127 157 168 188 195 232 238 255 311 319 347
Constitution, Reformed Church 269
Contee, Catherine: see Harrison 63
  John 370
"Content" 254 327
Contler: see Cantler
Cook, Francis 378
  John 195 351
  William 371
Cooke, Mary Magdalene 322
  Richard 76 196 307 318 322 328
  Richard Donaldson 318 322
Cookerly, Catherine (Biggs) 311
  Jacob 311
"Coomes His Inheritance" 103
Coonce, Henry 379
  Philip 378
  William 379
Coons, Davult 162
Cooper, George 105
  John 307
"Coopers Point" 186 217-218 286 287 363 364
"Cooperton" 15 33 223 227 363 364
Copper mine 102 104 339
Copper Mine Road 101 103
Cornwall, Pa. 141
"Cornwalls Folly" 231
Cost, Anna Maria (Brunner) 273
  Jacob 273
Cotman, Nathaniel 371
  William 371
Cottacken Mountain: see Catoctin 55
Cottrell, Andrew 371
Coturki (Monocacy) River 7 10 11
"Country Seat" 173
Covell, Ann (Turner) 233
  Jeremiah 233
Coventry, Chester Co., Pa. 377
Coville, Francis 37
  John 34 37 38 95 96 366

Coville (cont'd.)
 Thomas 37
Cowes, Isle of Wight 165 208
Cowynn, John 370
Cox, Andrew 56 371
 Brewer (Benjamin?) 368
 Daniel 69
 John 368
 Peter 368
"Coxsons Rest" 15 40 94-97 363 364
Crabb, Captain 21
 Priscilla (Sprigg) 226
 Ralph 226
Crabs, John 21
Crafft, Vallentin: see Kraft 140
"Craimes Quietness" 33 177-178 363 364
Cramer, A. 289
 Ezra L. 123
 George 380
 Jacob 304 316 322 323 380
 Jacob H. 123
 Noah E. 353
Cramphin, Basil 371
 Henry 371
 John 370, 371
Crampton, John 62
Crampton Gap 50 51 55 97 222 223
Craver, Philip: see Crever/Grüber 286
Craw, Valentine (Feltie) 18 191
Crawford (Craufurd), James 370
 Mary: see Ogle 324
Creagar, Cregar: see also Kreager
 Caspar 351
 Catherine: see Weymore 192
 Christian 304 316 323
 Conrad 323 380
 John 192-193
 Lawrence 326
 Michael 222 224
 Valentine 323 380
"Creagers Delight" 19 214
"Creagers Oversight" 172
Creagerstown 47-49 137 139 186 214 327 338
Creagerstown-Woodsboro Road 47 48 340
Creamery Road 237
Creary, Thomas 40 367
"Creave" 327
Cremer, Jacob 304 316 322 323
Crepell, Peter 380
Cresap, Daniel 20 21 374
 Daniel, Jr. 331
 Elizabeth 375
 Hannah (Johnson) 224
 Hannah (w/o Thos) 21 325-326
 Mary: see Ogle 331
 Michael 21 331 335 374
 Robert 374
 Thomas 15-23 35 44 62 64 77 83 86 92 97 147 168 188 190-191 193-194 196 198 213 224 252 286 290 300 324-327 330-334 340 345 347 351 374 375
 Thomas, Jr. 374
Creutz (see also Kreutz) Creek, York Co., Pa. 211 377
Crever (Grüber), Philip Ernst 186 196 198 286 290 326 365

Crickenberg Road 234
Crockatt, David 268
Cromerston, Elizabeth: see Wetzel 209
Cronin, Margaret (Sinn) 269
Cronise: see Kroneiss
Crops 306
Crosh (Grosh?), Peter 378
"Cross Lot" 14
"Cross to Night" 181
Crosse, John 380
Cross (Crosse), John 323 380
Crouch, Cloe: see Mobberly 232
 James 229 **232** 234 366
 Crouse, Catharine 307 323
 Michael 323
Crum, Abraham 75 122 129 354
 Gilbert 120 354
 Gilbert, Jr. 380
 William 75 322
Crum Road 117 123
Crysop: see Cresap
"Cuckholds Horns" 20 275
Culler, Jacob: see also Koller, Keller 276
Cumberland 66
Cumberland Valley 14
Cummings, William 122 285 339
 William, Jr. 228
Cumru Twp., Berks Co., Pa. 377
Cumper, John 378
Cunnatechegue (Conococheague) Creek 12
Cuntz, Martin 281
 Susannah (Storm) 281
Cunz, Dieter 41 205
Curtis, Mary (Bryan) 87
 Thomas 87
Curts, George 379

Daniel, John 380
"Daniels Small Tract" 233
"Darbys Delight" 229 230 363 364
Darcy, Eleanor S. 27
Dare, Maria Jane (Liggett) 346
Darmstadt, Ger. 134
Darn, Sebastian: see Derr 260
Darnall, Henry 27 195 249 250
 John 25 63 83 85 328
 Mary 25
 Mary: see Carroll 28
Daudenzell, Ger. 163
Davenport, John Scott 161
"Davids Choice" 19
Davidson, John 287
 Lois W. 276
Davis (Devi, Dewis), Ann: see Thompson 83
 Ann (Belt) Claggett: see Perry 83
 Anna (Dewi) 219
 Anna Maria 219
 Catherine Lackland: see Ritchie 84 123
 Catharina (Six) 219, 220
 Charles 83 85
 Daniel 378, 379
 Hinrich 219
 Ignatius (1759-1828) 83 88
 Jacob 336
 James 74
 John 146 219 368
 Meredith 62 63 80-81 82-83 85 88 90

401

Davis, Meredith (cont'd)
  365-367 370
  Meredith, Jr. 83
  Richard 44 83 100 364
  Robert 219 287
  Samuel 62
  Sarah 40
  Sarah (Claggett): see Perry 83
  Sarah (van Metre) 74
  Thomas 83 371
  Ursula (Burgess) 81 83
  Ursula (d/o Meredith, Jr.) 83
Davis Mill, Meredith 83
Dawson, Elizabeth 93
  George 370
  John 370
  Nathan 371
  Thomas 223 226-227 364 370
  Thomas, Jr. 227
"Dawsons Purchase" 223 363 364
Dayley, Philip 380
Daysville 120 127 350
Deakins, Francis 126 127 261
Deal, Engl. 164 202 268 269
Deane, Elizabeth 22
  Silas 22
"Dear Bought" (Davis) 44 100 363 364
"Dear Bought" (Ramsburg/Derr) 258 259 289 293
Deaver, Abraham 67
  Nancy (Lakin) 67
Debelbesin, Magdalena: see Devilbiss 169
Debt Books 4
Debtors Prison 196 342 343
Debutts, Abigail: see Ferguson 76 78
  Anna 76
  John Donaldson 76 78
  Lawrence 75 298
  Margaret: see Barnard 78
  Mary-Ann-Christian-Abigal 78
  Robert 21 47 54 62 75-78 110 159 168
    192 195 217 234 263 270 285 300 328
    351 364 370 371
"Debutts Delight" 77 229 234 362 364
"Debutts Hunting Ground" 76 363 364
Declaration of Independence 27 30
"Deep Run" 20
"Deeps" 14
"Deer Park" 319
"Deer Spring" 160
Deer Spring Avenue 243
Deg, Anna Barbara: see Humbert 177
Deichmann, Martin 200
Delaplaine, Edward S. 278
Delashmutt, Ann: see Warfield 61
  Basil 61 64
  Elias 61 62 64 68 86 102 330 371 379
  Elias, Jr. 61 86 379
  Elizabeth: see Bolter 61
  Elizabeth (Nelson) 61
  John 61 62 68 371
  Linsey 61
  Mary (Ancrum) 66
  Nancy 66
  Rachael: see Lemaster 61
  Sarah 66
  Sarah (Nelson) 61

Delater (Delaitre, DeLatere), David 151 165 292
Delaware 16 106 324
Delaware Bay 16
Delaware Indians 15
Delaware River 270
"Delight" 43 243 244 246 362 364
"Delight" (Washington Co.) 246
"Den of Wolves" 186 202 214 286 363 364
Dent, Peter 340
"Dere Spring" 286
Dern, Anna Catharina 126 376
  John P. 6 36 55 125 128 130 134 136
    270 315 357
  William 116 125 126 128 309 318 372 376
  William, Jr. 126
Derr, Anna Catharina (Brengel) 264
  Anna Elisabeth (Loy) 296
  Maria Susannah: see Devilbiss 319
  Sebastian 260 264 285 288 289 293 296
Derr Island 285 288
Derr Road, Elmer 174
Des Moines, Iowa 73
Detour, Md. 5 310
Detrick Road 231
Detrick, Fort 156 173 217 258 274
Devilbiss (DeVilbiss, Dinalpost, Divilbess, Divilplease, Tablepence, Teufersbiss)
  Family 168 191 208 212 317 372
  Adam (s/o George) 319
  Alexander 319
  Anna Barbara 188 317 374 375
  Anna Elisabeth (d/o Caspar): see Ramsburg 319
  Barbara 161 317 375
  Barbara (d/o Caspar): see Fleming, Hardy 319
  Barbara (d/o George) 319
  Caspar 33 151 304 307 310 317 319 322 325 336 365
  Caspar, Jr. (s/o Caspar) 319
  Catharina 318
  Catharina (d/o George) 319
  Catharine (Berg) 315
  Catharine (Devilbiss) 170
  Catharina Barbara 317 375
  Elisabeth: see Ramsburg 293
  Elizabeth (Ogle) 319 332
  Eliesabetha Barbara 317 375
  Elizabeth Margerita 317
  Frederick (s/o George) 319
  George (Hans Georg) 304 307 317-319 322 326
  George (s/o Caspar) 319
  George, Jr. (s/o George) 304 316 322
  John (Hans) 317 322 332
  John (s/o Caspar) 319
  John (s/o George) 318 319
  Magdalena: see Bancalf 169 317
  Margaretha (d/o Michael) 318
  Maria Susannah (Derr) 319
  Mary 172 318
  Michael (Hans Michael) 169 317 318
  Rebecca (Ogle) 319 332
  Rosanna (d/o George) 319
  Susanna (d/o Caspar): see Ramsburg 293

Devilbiss, Susanna (cont'd.) 319
Devilbiss Bridge 332 338
Devilbiss Bridge Road 315 319
Devilbiss Cemetery 319
Devis, Dewis: see Davis
Dick, George Peter 379
Dickeson, Henry 56
Dickson, George 196
  James 62 63 85 122 230 236 306-308
    313 315 317 335 371
"Dicksons Struggle" 20 63 122
Diedenshausen, Ger. 210
Diefenbacher, Karl 289
Diehl, Charles 339
Dielforter, Maria Catharina: see Lochman 19
Diffendal, John 31
Digges (Diggs), Sir Dudley 41
  Dudley (s/o John) 42
  Dudley (br/o John) 252
  Edward (Gov. of Va.) 41
  Edward (s/o John) 42 336
  Elizabeth Sewall Wharton 41
  Henry (s/o John) 42
  Ignatius (br/o Thos.) 252
  Ignatius (s/o William) 26
  Ignatius (neph/o John) 43 100 105 364
  J. Dudley 250
  John (s/o Col. Wm.) 41-43 48 49 100 101
    103 237 247-250 252 313 325 336 338-
    340 364-367
  Mary (Carroll) 26
  Nicholas 43 100 105 364
  Thomas, Rev. 252
  William, Col. 41 94
  William (s/o John) 42
"Digges Choice" 41 247 350
Digges copper works 102 104 339
"Digges Lot" 24 43 363 365
Digs, Charles 368
Dinalpost: see Devilbiss 318
Dinwiddie, Robert 20
Diocesan Archives, Maryland 350 371
"Disappointment" 43 248 325 336 363 365
Disestablishment 348
"Dispatch" 44 52 80 155 174 362 365
"Dispute" 229 233 363 365
Divelbess, Mary: see Devilbiss 318
Divilplease, Catharina: see Devilbiss 318
Dobbin, John, Sr. 368
  John, Jr. 368
Doberstein, John W. 138 140
Doddridge, Joseph 311
  Mary (Biggs) 311
Doderer, Johan Georg 269, 280
Doll, G. J. 192
Dollyhyde (Dolernides) Creek 44 100
"Dolphin" 254
Domer, George 379
Donaldson, John 76
Donegal (Lancaster Co.), Pa. 147
Doran, Patrick 262
"Dorans Choice" 184 354
Dorr, Peter 380
Dorsey, Caleb 116
  Edward 230, 286
  John 328

Dorsey (cont'd.)
  John, Jr 231
"Dorseys Search" 231
Dorsius, Jane (Hoogland) 211
  Peter Henry 211
Double Pipe Creek 5 310 327 339
Doubs 29 60
Doudith (Doudeth, Douthet, Douthwhite, Dowthit, Toudith, etc.), David 238
  Eliesabetha 238 376
  John 255 256 365 368 376 379
  Mary 110
  Solomon 322
  Thomas 108 110 238 368
"Douthets Chance" 238 363 365
Dover, Engl. 159 168 282
Downes, William 263
Downey, John 378
"Dragon" ship 193 195
Draper, Lyman Copeland 310
Draper Papers 209 310 331
Dry Branch 61
"Dry Lott" 307
Dublin Road 308 313
Dubois, Anna Maria 71
  John 255 256
  Sarah: see van Meeteren 69 71
Duckett, Jacob 28
  Richard 370
Dudane, (?) 370
Dudrear, Philemon Cromwell 31
Dufler, George 379
  Peter 379
Duisburg University 211
"Dukes Woods" 100 104 249 250 252 362 365
Dulany, Benjamin Tasker 33
  Daniel, Sr. 14 19 20 25 30 31-33 35-37
    40 44 48 52 54 73 76 111 120 123-
    128 144 148 150 152 156 164-166 169
    170 176 177 184 185 195 206 208-210
    213-214 216 218 223 227 238 239 241
    243-246 255 258 260-262 264 265 268
    269 272 274-277 297 299 303 331 336
    340 353-354 364 365 367
  Daniel, Jr. 31-33 63 116 124 126-128
    210 241 245 260 266 292
  Elizabeth (French) 33
  Henrietta Maria (Lloyd) Chew 30 32
  Rebecca (Smith) 31 32 120
  Rebecca (Tasker) 32 33 37 241
  Walter 32 48 210 241 245 355
  William B. 33
  William Washington 33
Dulany Papers, Maryland Historical Society 355
"Dulanys Lot" 24 31 33 34 36 40 58 82 105
  107 115-129 205 264 289 293 303 309
  311 313 362 365
Dulany's Mill 73 261-263 265 281 283
Dumpling Creek 91
Dünckel, Margaret Salome: see Spengler 135
  Maria Catharina: see Candler 135 316 376
Dunker (Dunkard) sect: see German Baptist Brethren
Dunmore Treaty 331
Dunn, John 370

"Durnah" 111
Durnbaugh, Donald F. 148 271
Durrum, William: see Dern 318
Dustmain, Martin: see Deichmann 200
Dutch 69 132 324 334
Dutchil, William 368
Dutrow, Katherine E. 150
   Robert I. 31
Duvall, Alexander 371
   Benjamin 370
   Comfort: see Griffith 91
   John 90-91
   Mareen, Jr. 370
   Mareen, Sr. 370
   Samuel 267, 287
Düsseldorf, Ger. 211

Eads, Samuel 371
Earl Twp. (New Holland), Pa. 137 204 280 289
East Cocalico Twp. (Lancaster Co.), Pa. 159 187-188
East Nottingham Twp. (Chester Co.), Pa. 87
"Eastern Branch," ship 35
Eastern Branch Hundred 349
Eastern Shore 23 25 302 356
Eastin, Anna Barbara (Brunner) 273
Eberle (Aberle, Everly), Adam 301
   Conradt Israel 301
   Eva Maria (Beckenbach) 300
   Leonard 300-301
   Johann Adam 301
   Sebastian 194
"Ebony March" 233
Ebthorp, Thomas 304 307 311 313 315 322
Edelen, Christopher 327 370, 378
Edinburgh, Scot. 44
Edmonston, Thomas 370
Egle, William Henry 134
Egleton, John 380
Eglingham, Eng. 328
Eichelberger, Samuel 327
Eilar, J. S. 216
Eisenberg, William Edward 205
Eiterbach, Ger. 300-301
Elam, Nicolas 371
Elder, Alexius, Rev. 254
   Aloysius 254
   Ann (d/o William) 254
   Ann (Wheeler) 253 256
   Arnold 252, 254
   Basil 254
   Catherine (Spaulding) 254
   Charles 253 254
   Clotilda (Green): see Brooke 254
   Eliza 252
   Elizabeth (Snowden) 254
   Elizabeth (Spaulding) 254
   Elizabeth: see Brawner 254
   Francis 254
   Frederick Lutheran 300
   Guy 253 254
   Ignatius 254
   Jacoba Clementina (Livers) 206 252 256
   Julia (Ward) 254
   Mary: see Lilly 253, 254

Elder (cont'd.)
   Nathaniel 254
   Richard 253
   Thomas 254
   William 56 206 248 249 252 253-254 256 286 327 331 364 367
   William, Jr. 253 254
   William Henry 253 254
Elders, German: see also Vorsteher
   Frederick Reformed Church 140 270 277 281 282
   German Baptist Brethren (i.e., Bishop) 246
"Elders Choice" 254, 256
"Elders Kindness" 248 254 363 365
"Elders Resurvey" 256
"Elizabeth" ship 214 262 277 283 294
Elk Ridge Landing 105 228
"Elk River Manor" 302
Ellerton 35 246
Ellicott, Andrew 22
Ellis, William 371
Elliss, Samuel 371
Ellrodt (Elrod, Ellrod), Anna (Beschell) 316
   Anne Catharine: see Conner 316 377
   Dieterich 316 376
   Eliesabetha (d/o Jeremias) 316 376
   Eliesabetha: see Bischoff 316
   Jeremias 316 376
   William 147 304 307 315 316 318 323 213
Elmer Derr Road 174
Elmwood 166
Elting, Cornelius 57 73 74 119
   Eleanor: see Hite 74
   Isaac 119
   Jacomyntje: see Thompson 74
   Mary (Beatty) 119
   Rebecca (van Metre) 74 119
   Sarah: see Hite 74
Elting's Mill, Cornelius 57 62 75 162 349
Emelen, Luke 87
Emerson, John 196
Emmit, Abraham 239
   Abraham James 240
   Josiah 240
   Mary 240
   Samuel 30 **239**
   William 240, 241, 242
Emmitsburg 14 30 54 198 206 219 237-242 248 255
Emmitsburg District 175 262
Emmitsburg Pike 169
England 10 143
England, Church of: see Churches and Congregations
England, Joseph 82
Englebrecht, Jacob 261 266 303
   "Diary" 261 266 303
Engles, Peter 378
English in Frederick County 130 152
"Enlargement" 255
Ennis home 226
Ensey, Dennis 103
Enyart, Silas 218
Ephrata Society 133 159

Eppingen, Ger. 132
Erbach bei Homburg, Ger. 284
Erdesbach, Ger. 284
Erhard, Conrad 350
Erickson, Gunder **40** 365
Escheat 2
Esleman, Benedict 291
Esopus (Kingston), N.Y. 117
Established Church: see Church of England 352
Euler (Eyler), Catharina: see Verdriess 215
Evans (Evins), Edward 16 198
  Elizabeth (Carmack) 104
  Phillip 370
  Rachel 16 19 326
  Robert 181 245 275 370 371
Evartt, Adam 378
Evelant, Peter 304, **316**, 318, 322
"Evelins Chance" 307
Everly, Posthan 196
Evertt, John Adam 262
Evetts, Matthew 379
"Exchange" 20 33 244 245 363 365
Explorers 7-12
Eyler, Conrad 215
Eylers Valley 249 341

Fackenthal Library, Lancaster, Pa. 150 151
Fair Grounds, Frederick 69
Fair Island 73
Fairfax, George 20
  George William 73
  Louisa: see Nelson 63
  Thomas 72 87
Falckner, Justus 132
Falckner Swamp (Montgomery Co.), Pa. 132 133 374
  Lutheran congregation 132 133 154 161 163 217
Falling, Redmond 368
Fanchill, Andrew 379
Fansey, Abraham 379
  Edward 379
"Farmers Delight" 327
Farquhar (Farquer), Allen 42 77 82 110 116 **124**-128 231 293 309 368
  Allen, Jr. 88 124
  Catherine 124
  Hannah: see Owings 42 247
  William 88 121 124 125 335
Farrell, Ann: see Wickham 343
  John 322
  Kennedy 77 307 322 343 351
"Fathers Gift and Uncles Good Will" 93
"Fatt Oxen" 19
Faun, James 371
Faust, Albert Bernhard 298
Fauth, Fauts: see also Fout **161** 163
  Balthasar (Baltus) 144 154 156 279 317 372 374 375
  Balthasar (s/o Jacob) 375
  Catarina Barbara 317 375
  Eva Rosina 375
  Jacob 139 140 156 279 317 372 375
  Susanna (Bocher) 154 274 3374 375
Faw, Abraham 261, 262
Fayette County, Ky. 129

Feagaville 83 97 155 162 174 184 189 354
Fedreck, Jacob 371
Fee, Elizabeth: see Lakin 67
  George 56 68 368 371
  John 68
  Mary 68
  Mary Margaret (Hook) 64 68
  Rachel: see Lakin 67
  Ruth 68
  Sarah (Lyeth) 67
  Thomas 56 62 64 65 **67-68** 371
Feeroar, Leonard: see Firor 191
"Fellowship" 339
Fennely, Thomas 379
Ferguson, Abigail (Debutts) 76 78
  John 378
  Robert 89
Ferree, Daniel 172
Ferrell, Kennedy (see Farrell) 351
Ferries, Monocacy 53 63 81 91 225 226 339
Ferrill, William 371
Feuerbach, Anna Maria: see Kemp 172
Feurure, Henry: see Firor 200
Filtration Plant, Linganore 234
Finck (Fink), Anna Maria (Hoffmann) 276
  Charlotta Christina (Gervinus) 276 277
  Hans Georg 276
  Henrich 276
  Johann Nicholas of Kusel 245 263 276 285 258-260 270 **276**-277 301 373
  Johann Nickel of Staudernheim, Ger. 276
  Maria Catharina 276
  Maria Elisabeth 276
  Maria Magdalena: see Becker 276
  W. J. 163
Finican, Bryan 371
"Finleys Last Chance" 175
Firor (Fearoar, Feeror, Feurure, Firohr): see also Vieruhr
  Benjamin 220
  Henry 200, 212
  Lenhart/Leonard 18 185 191 212
  Magdalena (Matthias) 205-207, 212
  Maria Barbara (Willhaut): see Weller 191
First Mountain: see Catoctin Mountain 62
First Sea (Moravian) Congregation 141 147
Fisher, Joseph 168
"Fisherman's Lodge" 254
Fishing Creek 46 107 299 310 319 331 332 338 344 345
Fishkill, N. Y. 211
Fitzpatrick, John C. 20 22 108
Fitzredmond, William **25** 365
Five Nations 13
Flat Run 236 238 239
Flat Run (Emmitsburg) Settlement 58 237-242
Fleming, Barbara (Devilbiss): see Hardy 319
  Samuel 240 296 319
Fletcher, John **43** 367, 371
  Thomas **43** 367, 371
  William 253
Flick, Michael 380
Flint Hill 80 89 90
Flower (Blumenschein), Anna Maria "Mary" (Matthias) 206-207

Flower (cont'd.)
 John 301 335
Flying Camp 119
Fogeler, Anthony 379
"Food Plenty" 229 234 363 365
Forbush, Laverne 236
Fords 50-52
 Biggs 34 36 42 45 51 52 54-56 106 107 116 169 265 281 297 309 319 328 338 341
 Hughes 9 34 46 53 57 70 311
 Hussey's 46 290 312
 Middle (Furnace) 46 51 52 81 91 341
 Mouth of Monocacy 52
 Mumma 46 51 52 250 327 328 333
 Ogle's (Stull's) 46 51 52 54 319 326-328 341 342 366
 Ogle's Wagon Road 52 328
 Reynolds 290
 Rue's 232
 Stoner's 312
 Stull's 46 51 52 54 237 319 325 326 328 342
Foreman's Massacre 331
"Forest" (Sprigg) 40 43 55 223 225 227 362 365
Forney, Adam 41 142 285
"Forrest" (Magruder) 40 53 166 225 228 243-245 362 365
Fort Detrick 156 173 217 258 274
Fort Dulany, Fla. 33
Fort Duquesne 329
Fort Henry 310
Fort McIntosh 310
Fort Myers, Fla. 33
Fort Pitt 310
Fort Pleasant 74
Fort Ritchie 14
Fort Washington 41
Fortinaux (Fortney, Fortunee), Jean Henri 159 160 282 372
Fortney (Fortinaux, Fortune), Catharina 160
 Christina 170
 Henry (Heinrich) 159 **160** 188 199 271 375 376
 Henry, Jr. (Joh. Henrich Fortunee) 160 376
 Susanna Catarina 160 375
Foulson, Israel 183
"Fountain Low" 199 326 327
Fountain Rock Road 125
"Four Springs" 19 188
"Fourth Dividend" 49
Fout (Fauth, Pfauth): see also Fauth
 Anna Maria (Mary) 81 161
 Balthasar (Baldus, Baltis, Botus) 54 57 62 72 80 82 122 139 154-156 **161-163** 166 174 206 217 355 371 379
 Balthasar (s/o Jacob) 161 162
 Baltish, Bauldus, Jr. (s/o Balthasar) 162
 Catharine (d/o Jacob) 162
 Catharine Barbara (d/o Balthasar): see Shull 161-163
 Eva Rosina: see Schmidt 161 162 189 377
 Grafton 162
 Henry 162 379

Fout (cont'd.)
 Jacob 39 139 140 155 **161-162** 164 189 199 200 206 292 371 379
 Jacob, Jr. (s/o Jacob) 162
 Joh. Jacob (s/o Balthasar) 161-162
 Lewis 162
 Margaret (d/o Jacob) 162
 Margaret (d/o Balthasar): see Shellman 162
 Maria (d/o Balthasar) 162
 Maria Catharina (Sinn) 269
 Mary (d/o Jacob) 162
 Peter 162
 Susanna (d/o Balthasar) 162 163
 Susanna (Bocher) 154 160 162 174 217
Foutch: see Fout
Fouts, Hans Michael: see Pfautz 161
"Fouts Delight" 80 155 162 181 362 365
Foutz, Joseph 101
Fowler, Francis 345
 James 345
Fowns, John 371
Fox, George 378
Foxville 220 275
Foxville Road 197
Foy, Frances (Johnson) Harris Grant 19 86 224 225 227 326 371 374
 Miles 18 19 86 194 223 **224** 225 227 365 367
France (see also Frantz), Daniel 258 260 264 278 279-280 289 371 372
Franck, Johann Adam 301
Frankenberg on the Eder, Ger. 133
Frankenfeld, Theodore 151
"Frankford" 167
Frankfurt aM, Ger. 150 171 270
Frankfurt Road (Phila. Co., Pa.) 335
Franklin (Franklyne), Thomas 328
Franklin, W. Va. 15
Frantz (see also France), Daniel 154 258 279 301 371 372
 Johannes 280
 Nicolaus 280
Fraser, George 98
 John 96 349
 Susanna: see Hawkins 96 349
Frazier, J. T. 98
Frederick Airport 53 76
Frederick County, Md. 4 5 15 19-21 25 27 30 33 35 37 47 50 52 54 55 64 66 74 97 104 118 121 154 225 231 257 301 303 328 333 340 356 (see also Prince George's Co.)
Frederick County, Va. 53 72 74 86 108 290 296 345
Frederick County National Bank 101
Frederick Examiner 101
Frederick Junction 235
Frederick (Town) 18 21 22 37 38 47 57 59 67 69 72 78 81 83 102 104 114 121-123 143 144 146 148-150 153 157 166 173 178 180 183 188 189 197 203 207 209 217 220 235 255 257 258 261 262 264-269 272 281 283 286 287 292 293 301 311 330 341 343 351-353 355
 Lots 157 192
Frederick Towne Village 283

Frederick Twp., Philadelphia (Montgomery) Co. Pa. 154 161 166 279
Fredericksburg, Pa. 377
Fredericktown Mall Shopping Center 166
Freeholder 154
Freeland, Enoch 196
French 20 148
French and Indian War 21 61 63 119 121 123 165 209 247 292 295 329-330 353
French, Elizabeth: see Dulany 33
  Thomas 65
Frey, Anna Magdalena (Willheut) 212
  Martin 211
Friedensthal, Pa. 147
Frieks, Henry 371
Friend, Charles 368
  Israel 55 171 222 228
  John 368
  Nicholas 368
Friends, Society of: see Quakers
Friends (Quaker) Burying Ground 88
Friends Creek area 327
"Friends Good Will" 80 81 83 262 365 339
Friend's Mill Road, Israel 51 55 222 225
Friends Mountain 341
"Friendship" 15 20 49
Frigs, H. 56
Frisk, Nick., see Finck 277
Frost, John 87
Frush(our), Vandle (Wendel) 380
Fry Road 66 67
Fryer, John 371
"Frys Habitation" 20
Fuchs, Johann Frantz 271
Fudar, John 379
Fuhrmann, Maria Magdalena 284
Fuller, Mary (Johnson) 246
  Robert 246
  William P. 22
Fulmer's Station 52 166
Fulton, Robert 323
Fulweder, Henry 379
Funk, Catharina (Humbert) 177-178
  Henry 177 178 379
Furnace Branch 90
Furnace Ford 52 91
Furney, Catherine: see Biggs 311
Füssengönheim, Ger. 216

Gabriel, George 154
"Gabriels Choice" 14
Gag, Christophel 146
Gah Family 269
  Anna Barbara: see Sturm 280
Gaither, Ann 101
  Benjamin 100 101 365
  Cassandra 101
  Elizabeth 101
  Henry 101
  Mary 101
  Sarah 101
  Stuart 353
"Gaithers Chance" 100 101 362 365
"Galloway" 103
Gamb, Adam 189
Gambrill State Park 111

"Game Cock" Company 101
"Gaming Alley" 56
Gannt, Fielder 97 98
"Gap" 186 203 210 248 363 365
Gardinhover, Jacob 378
Garfield 246
Garret, Mr. 37
Gas House Pike 31 261 262 283
Gatchell, Elisha 224
Gatton, Thomas 370
Gaver (Geber), Daniel 246
  George W. 208
Geelwicks, Friedrich Heinrich 215
Geiger, Georg (s/o J. Geo.) 164 199 201
  Hannah (Miller) 201
  Johann Georg 161 163-164 199 205 219 280-282 284-285 287-289 291 295-300 298-299 301 372 375 376
  Johann Jacob 163 164 376
  Johann Valentin Sr. 163
  Johann Valentine [Jr.] (1685-1762) 163
  John [Valentine? s/o Joh. Geo.] 164 199 201
  Maria Barbara (Bauer) 163
  Maria Catharina (Henckel): see also Apple 160 163-164 199 204 206 271 375 376
  Maria Eliesabetha 161 163
Gemmerich, Darmstadt 218
"Generosity" 349
Georg, Anna Ursula: see Wetzel 207
"George and Margaret" 155-156 160 363 365
Georgetown University 252
George, Joseph 378
Georgia 141 144 285
Gerhard, Heinrich 170
German Arrivals
  at Philadelphia, 1732: 185-204
  in Monocacy area 130-153
German Baptist Brethren (Dunkers) 35 99 165 270-271 275 277 281 286 301
German emigration of 1709 9 71 130 182 218
  Ephrata Society 133 159
German Monocacy Road 9 36 51-54 57 131 136 153 155 159-160 166-169 181 185-186 189 192 202 208 221 248 257 312 319 324 326 338
"German Plains" 15 33 35 246 363 365
German settlement, Lower 58 153-184
German settlement, Upper 58 153 185-221
Germans 9 18 35 37 41 42 37 48 50 52 53 61 71 72 127 130-221 253 257 260 292 293 301 303 308 332 349 350 372-377
  In Virginia 53 72 134 141
"Germantown" 189
Germantown, Pa. 133 144 271
  Reformed Congregation 308
Germantown, Va. 329
Germany 130
Germany Twp. (Adams Co.), Pa. 41
Gernborn, Ger. 191
Gervinus, Charlotta Christina: see Fink 276
Gettysburg, Pa. 138
Getzendanner Family (Gatsindaner, Götzdanner, Ketchindaner, Kirtchendaner)

Getzendanner (cont'd.) 269
  Adam 166, 167
  Anna Barbara (Brunner) 165-167 170 271
  Anna Margaretha 158 376
  Anna Maria: see Schley 166-167
  Anna Otilia (Riester) 166
  Anna (Stoner) 167 290 291
  Balthasar (Baltis, Balzer) 166-167 193 290 291 379
  Catharina: see Thomas 166-167
  Christian 33 53 140 150 154 156 165-167 170 175 217 270-271 279-281 292 350 371 373
  Gabriel 166 167 379
  Jacob s/o Christian 166 167 379
  Johann Jacob 165
  John (of Adam) 167
  Philippina (Staley) Stull 167 170 178-179
  Susanna Margareta: see Kemp 166 181
Ghiselin, Reverdy 48 327 327
Gibbes, James 370
Gibson, John 17
Gies, Louisa: see Loy 296
Giessen, Ger. 151
Gift of land, Lord Baltimore's 35 156
"Gift" 20 148 152 206 213
Giles, Arabella (Hook) 64
  John 64
Gilliland, Hugh 345
  Thomas 346
Gilreath, Amelia C. 297
Ginkins, Rice 371
Girkhausen, Ger. 210
Gittings, Ann (Sprigg) 226
  Philip 226
  Priscilla: see Sprigg 93
  Thomas 44 90 92 93 188 366 367 371
Giuseppi, M. S. 141
Glade Creek 31 36 46 115 116 124 293 303 309 314
Glade Reformed Church 314
Glade Road 308 314
Glade Valley Farms 119
Glatfelter, Charles H. 47 132 135 139 140 314
"Gleanings" 67
Gloria Dei, Wicacoa 143
Goebel, Julius 10
Goddard, John 370
Golb(?), Garatt 371
Gold Coast, Africa 211
Good, James I. 270
"Good Fortune" 327
"Good Luck" (Biggs) 299 310
"Good Luck" (Brunner) 273
"Good Luck" (Davis) 80-83 85 362 365
"Good Luck" (Kemp) 174
"Good Luck" (Matthews) 20 85 363 365
"Good Luck" (Wickham) 342
"Good Neighbor" 203
"Good Wife" 178
"Good Will" 215 331
"Goosebill" 245, 277
Goranson, Rita 73
Gorden, Daniel 241
Gordon, George 180 342
  Patrick (Gov of Va.) 131

Gordon (cont'd.)
  Robert 370
Gose, George 380
Gottschalk, Matthias Gottlieb 64 147 203 207 211 213 315 329 334
Götz, Joh. Georg (Jerg) 139 146
Governor Johnson School, Frederick 282
Götzendanner: see Getzendanner 165
Graceham 52 138 152 186 188 191 197 206 213 214 248 325 327
  Cemetery 319
  Moravian Church and School 210 335
Graffenried, Christoph von 9-11 89
Graham, George A. 214
  William 97 371
Grahame, John 281
Grant, Frances (Johnson) Harris: see also Foy 224
  Hugh 224
Gratharm, John 71
"Gravelly Land" 307
Graves, John 380
Graveyards: see Cemeteries
"Grazing Ground" 327
"Great Desire" 174
Great Falls of the Potomac 9-11
Great Hunting Creek 212 230
"Great Meadow" 325
Great Pipe Creek: see Big Pipe Creek 335
Great Swamp area, Pa. 283
Greathouse, Mary (Stull) 171
Green, Abraham 91
  Clotilda: see Elder, Brooke 254
"Green Bottom" 345-347
"Green Meadow" 15 33 246 363 365
"Green Spring" 138 186 192-195 212 290 362 365
Greencastle, Pa. 344
Greene County, Pa. 64 66 111 114
"Greenfield" 93
Greenfield Mills 91 92
Greenfield-Mountville Road 57
Gregg, Nathan 307 323
  William 323
Greintsch, Elisabeth: see Six 219
Gretcher (Kretscher), Maria Agnes: see Honig 201
Griffith, Benjamin 92
  Charles 92
  Comfort (Duvall) 91
  Greenbury 92
  Henry 92
  John 327
  Joshua 92
  Lydia 92
  Orlando 92
  Sarah 91
  Thomas 81
  William 21 282 54-56 77 90 91 97 333 341 364 371
  William, Jr. 92
  William (Anne Arundel Co.) 91
Griffith Falls 92
"Griffiths Chance" 92 93
Grimes, Martin 380
Grindler, Anna Margreth Swinehart Miller 158

Grindler (cont'd.)
 Philip 158
Grissop, Christopher: see Cresap, Thomas 334
Grist, John 181
Groddu, William 379
Groll, Christian 198
Groningen University 211
Grosch, Johann Conrad 119 184 378
 Mary Dorothea: see Beatty 119
Grosh? (Crosh), Peter 378
Groshon, A. 327
Gross, Christian 323
 Jacob 323
 Mary 323
Gross Gartach, Ger. 127
Gross Schifferstadt, Ger. 269
Grove Lime Company 75
Grüber (Crever), Charlotta Friderica 197-198 325 374
 Maria Eliesabetha 198 376
 Philip Ernst 17 53 133 168 175 185-187 196-198 202 213 215 286 290 295 325 326 365 372 374 376 377
 Philip Ernst, Jr. 213
Grünstadt, Ger. 177
Guernsey County, Ohio 311
Guin, Thomas 326
Gump, Andreas 188 375
 Georg Peter 139
 Catharina Barbara 188 317 375
 Dorothea 189
 Johann Georg 160 186 187-189 206 214 248 268 318 371 372 374-376
 Johann Georg, Jr. 188 189 374
 John (Johannes) 188-189
 Rosina (Mack) 214
 Sarah 189
"Gumps Addition" 189
"Gunders Delight" 24 40 52 362 365
"Gunpowder Manor" 302
Gunpowder River 12
Gutridge, Ethel D. 349
Guyger, Hans Jerick: see Geiger

Habach, Catharina (Berg) 314 377
 Peter 314 377
Hackadorn, Jacob 379
Hackensack River, N. J. 135
Hackett, Peter 379
Haddock, Benjamin 249
Haff (Huff), Abraham 116 119 128 205 380
 Jane (Beatty) 119 205
 Lawrence 119 380
 Peter 119
 Susanna (Beatty) 119
Haffner (see also Havenor), Elisabeth: see Lochman 191
 Georg Fridrich 260 299 301
Häger, Johann Fridrich 132
Hager, Jonathan 64 147 189 195 203 207 329 330 334 335 370
Hagerstown 56 119 203 267 329 334 347 352
Hagerstown-Mercersburg Road 345
Haggerton, John 370
Hague, The: see 's Gravenhage 150

Hahn, Maria Elisabeth: see Krieger 214
Haidt, Valentine 152
Haines Branch 99-100
Haitt, John, Jr. 87
Halifax, N. S. 152
Hall, Dorothy 25
 Elizabeth 233
 Francis 25
 Henry 233
 John 330
 Rachel: see Smith 31
Hall of Records, Maryland Archives 2 3
Hallbert, Francis 371
Halle, Ger. 143 151 265
Haller, Barbara: see Keller 298
 Elisabeth: see Keller 298
Hallesche Nachrichten 138 145 146
Halts, Jacob 380
Hambleton, Gavin 371
Hamburg, Ger. 218
Hamilton, Kenneth G. 142
Hammond, Col. Thomas 60 101
"Hammonds Request" 234
Hampshire County, W. Va. 108
Hampton, Stephen 371
"Hampton Forest" 254
"Hampton Plains" 254
Hampton Valley Road 239
Hampstead 1 79
Hanbury, John 20
Hand (Hend), Catharine 320 322
 John 140 170 307 316
Handrup, Vitus 147
"Hands Choice" 307, 316
Hanley, Thomas O'Brien 27
Hann, Catharine 320, 322
 Handel 304 307 319 320 322
 Jacob 353
 Mary 320, 322
Hanna, Charles Augustus 14
Hanover, Pa. 412 50 135 247 285 341
Hanson, John 287
Hansonville 45 107 289 313
"Happy Choice" 30 226 362 365
Harbaugh, Catharine 214
 George 22 214
 Henry 149
Harbaugh Valley, 254
"Hard Bargain" 174
Harday, Rachel (Livers) 203 252
 Solomon 203 252
Hardee, Isaac 371
Harding, John 40
 Robert 251
Hardman, Joseph 167 378
Hardy, Arnold 319
 Barbara (Devilbiss) Fleming 319
 George, Jr. 370
Hardy County, W. Va. 74
Harford, Henry 305
Hargys (Harquis), Thomas 368
Harland (Harlan, Harling), John 305 307 323
 James 368
 Joel 323
 John 368
 John, Jr. 323
Harlingen area, N.J. 314

Harlin, Isaac 380
  Jacob 380
Harmony 56
Harmony Grove 292
Harper, Rachel (Owings) 98
Harpers Ferry 38 66 96
Harris, Edward 224
  Elizabeth (Plummer) 235
  Frances (Johnson): see also Grant, Foy 224
  John 235
  Moses 235
  Rachel (Plummer) 235
  Thomas, Jr. 287
"Harris' Delight" 20
Harris' Ferry, Pa. 334 347
Harrisburg, Pa. 334 347
Harrison, Betsy: see Nelson 63
  Catherine (Contee) 63
  John 63
  Lucy Harwood 353
Harrisville School Road 231
Harrsch, Joshua: see Kocherthal 132
"Harrys Grove" 20
Hart, Gov. John 27
  Simon 125 182
Hart-Runeman, Sibrandina Geertruid 125
Hartman, Catharine 323
  Eliesabetha 376
  Herman 139 376
Hartmannsdorf, Schoharie, N.Y. 218
Hartsock, George 380
  Nicholas 380
Hartsook, Elizabeth 3
Hartwell, Engl. 159
Harvey, James 370
  John 370
"Harveysburough" 20
Hasselbach, Ger. 207
"Hat Wheel" 179
Hausahm, Maria Eliesabetha 377
Hausihl (Hauseal), Bernard Michael 152 182 184
Hauvers District 275 327
Haux, Theodorus Frid. 303
Havener (Havenor, Hufner?): see also Haffner
  Frederick 260 **299** 301 379
  Michael 136 379
"Haw Bottom" 97
Hawbottom 56 177 246
Hawkins, Alexander Thomas 98
  Elizabeth Laurence 98
  George Fraser 97 98
  John 55 56 95 **96** 367 370
  John, Jr. 95 97
  John Stone 98
  Priscilla 98
  Susanna (Fraser) 96 98 349
  Thomas 96 98 222
Hawkins County, Tenn. 105
"Hawkins Mary Peep-O-Day" 94 98
"Hawkins Plains" 97
Hays, Charles 371
  Jeremiah 371
  William 371
Hayward, William 224

Hayward Road 296
"Hazel Thicket" 83 284
"Hazel Valley" 43 363 365
Hazelnut Run 229, 234
"Hazzard" 60 67 363 365
Head, James 110
Healer, William 371
Heard, Richard 253
Heaters Island 7 9 13 59 60
Hebron Lutheran Church, Va. 133
Hedges Family 106-114
  Land of 155
Hedges, Absalom 111
  Agnes (Powelson) 109
  Andrew 112
  Ann 112
  Catherine (w/o Joseph) 106
  Catherine (d/o Joseph): see Julien, Wood 107 109 312
  Charles (1674e-1743) 112
  Charles (s/o Joseph) 53 77 107 109 110 112 114 179 261 262 304 310 313 322 354 364 368 379
  Charles, Jr. 109 111 322
  Dorcas (d/o Joseph) 107 109
  Dorcas (d/o Charles) 111
  Elizabeth (Chapline) 109
  Eneas 113
  Hannah 111
  Isaac 111
  Isabella (Wirk) 111
  Jacob (s/o Charles) 111
  Jonas 72-74 107-109 344
  Joseph, Sr. 42 45 72 74 **106**-110 113 315 365
  Joseph, Jr. 45 77 107 109 110 307 322
  Joseph (s/o Charles) 111 311
  Joseph (s/o Solomon) 331
  Joseph (s/o William) 112 113
  Joshua 107-109 368
  Margaret 111
  Mary (Stilley) 109 114
  Mary: see Wilson 109
  Moses 111 379
  Peter 304, 315
  Rachel 111
  Rebecca (d/o Joseph) 109
  Rebecca (van Metre) 73 108 109 172
  Ruth (d/o Charles) 111
  Ruth (d/o Joseph): see van Metre 74 107 109
  Samuel (s/o Charles) 111
  Samuel (s/o Joseph) 107 109
  Sarah (Biggs) 311
  Shadrack 111
  Silas 331
  Solomon 73 74 77 107-109 172 238 310 365 368
  Susannah: see Julien 111 114
  William 110 **112** 113 345
  William Jr. 112 113
"Hedge Hogg" 106-112 289 309 315 362 365
"Hedges Chance" 111
"Hedges Delight" 107-111 362 365
Hedgesville, W. Va. 109
Hehl, Matthew 153
Heidelberg, Ger. 132-133

Heidelberg Catechism, Reformed 140 171 208
Heidelberg Twp. (York. Co.), Pa. 41
Heilbronn, Ger. 127
Heiligkreuzsteinach, Ger. 300
Helfenstein, Ernest 158 350
Hellam (Helm Town), Penna. 211 377
Helman, James A. 239
Hemp Farm, Abram 65
Henckel, Anton Jacob 133 163 199
   Georg 169 375 376 380
   Joh. Balthasar 375
   Maria Catharina: see Geiger, Apple 163 199
   Philipp Christoph 169 376
Hendrick, John 17 380
Hend, John: see Hand 170
Henley, Francis 84
Henn, Elizabeth 316, 323
   John 304, 316, 323
   Sarah 316, 323
Henry, Adam 327
   Patrick 255 331
   Robert B. 31
   Sarah (Winter) Ogle 327
"Henry" 40 80 81 362 365
Hensamer (Hoosman), Sarah 225
Hepburn, John 181 205
Herborn, Nassau-Dillenburg, Ger. 151
Hereford Twp., Berks Co., Pa. 276
Herne, Daniel 251
Herr, Johannes 183 377
Herrington, Jacob 16
Herriott, Andreas 140
Herrnhut 141 148
Hersh, Conrad 242
Hertzel, Hans Georg 159 282
   Jerg: see Hutzel 159
   Ludwig 159
Hertzog, Margaret 323
   Nicholas 323
   Peter 323
Herzer, John Henry 152 153
Hess, Eva Nelly 374
   Jeremias 374
Hessong Bridge Road 138
Heyd (see Hite), Hans Justus 71
Heyl, Jacob 217
Hibbard, Francis H. 328
Hickle (Hinckle?), Luderick 379
Hickman Family 354
   Joseph 371
   Sarah (van Metre) 74
   William 371
"Hickory Plains" 235
Hickory Tavern 14
Higginbotham, Charles 18 332 370
High Knob 175 178
"High Nicking" 240
Hildebrand, Adam 165 178
   Anna Maria (Staley) Shoup 165 178
   Heronimus 380
Hill, Anna Maria 201
   Henry 28
   John 201 379
Hillard (Hilliard), John 107
   Thomas 107

Hilleary, Eleanor (Sprigg): see Nuthall 226
   Eleanor (Young) 91
   Thomas (I) 91
   Thomas (II) 91
   Thomas (III) 60 89-91 226 364 366 367
   William 91
Himes, D. 63
Hinke, William J. 9 64 130 142 147 148 150 159 163 171 270
Hinkle, George: see Henckel 380
Hisler, Nicholas 267
Historical Society of Carroll County, Md. 6 33 209
Historical Society of the Evangelical and Reformed Church 270 315
"Hit or Miss" 104
Hite (Heyd), Abraham 74
   Anna (Merckle) 71
   Eleanor (Elting) 74
   Isaac (s/o Jost) 74
   Jacob 74
   John 378
   John (s/o Jost) 74
   Jost (Hans Justus) 71 72 74 296 344
   Mary (van Metre) 74
   Rebecca (van Metre) 74
   Sarah (Elting) 74
Hitselberger, Mary Fitzhugh 305
Hives, William 368
Hobson, George 87
"Hobsons Choice" 59 60 362 365
Hock, John Jacob 298
   Peter 143
Hockersmith (Hockensmith), Conrad 238 **239** 240 310 366
   Jacob 241
   Michael 241
Hoes, Roswell Randall 309
Hoff (Hoof), Anna Barbara 374
   Anna Maria 205
   Johann Jacob 172 205 206 277 288 294 317 371 375 379
   Jacob, Jr. 376
Hoffman, Adam 241, 278n
   Anna Maria: see Finck 276
   Appolonia (d/o Hans Peter): see Ochs 279
   Barbara (b ±1711e) 317 322
   Barbara (d/o H. Peter): see Storm 279
   Elizabeth (d/o H. Peter): see Schumacher 279
   George 378
   Hans Georg 277
   Hans Peter 45 140 141 173-174 177 182 183 189 220 258-260 262-263 267 277-278-280 283 393 394-396 371 372 374 376
   Jacob 378
   Jerg 278n
   Johann Georg Peter [Jr.] 279 296
   Johann Peter 277n 278n
   Johannes (John) 146 183 214 307 316 322
   Leonard 209
   Margaretha 277
   Maria Appolonia (Traut): see also Unseld 278 279 290 291 294-296 301 374 376
   Maria Dorothea (Loy) 279, 296

Hoffman (cont'd.)
    Maria Eliesabetha 278 374
    Mary Magdalene (d/o Hans Peter) 279
    Mary (d/o Hans Peter): see Buckey 279
    Peter, Jr: see Johann Georg Peter
    Rosina (d/o Hans Peter) 279
Hoffmann, Anna Barbara (wid/o Matthias
    Riesslie): see Rössel 146
    Anna Maria: see Finck 276
    Johannes 146
    Konrad 276
Hoffmeister, Thomas M. 65
"Hog Hall" 327
"Hog Yard" 33 244 275 363 365
Hoge, Hogue: see Hogg
Hogg, George 106
    Thomas 96
    William 87
"Hogg Park" 354
Hogmire, Conrad 335
    Maudlin 335
Hoke, Samuel 123
Holagon/Holigon, Patrick 62 103
Holdcraft, Jacob Mehrling 41 47 67 128
    279 284 290 315 335 353
Holland 149 211
Holland, Richard 234-235
    Ruth (Plummer) 235
Hollingworth, Abraham 87
Hollyday, Clement 287
Holter Road 243
Holts, Benjamin 379
Höltzel, Nicholas 198
Holy Trinity (Old Swedes) Church,
    Wilmington, Del. 14
"Home House" 174
Honey (Honig), Anna Catharina 196 201
    Johann Georg 53 133 139 146 175 186
        187 198 201-202 209-210 214 286 364
        373
    Maria Agnes (Kretscher/Gretscher) 201
Honeyman, Gale 236
Hood, Jacob 183
Hoofman, John: see Hoffman, John 214
Hoogland, Jane: see Dorsius 211
Hook Family **64-68**
    Arabella: see Giles 64
    Daniel 65
    Daniel, Jr., 65
    Dorothy (Barkett) 64
    Elizabeth (Ward) 66
    James (Sr.) 64 349
    James (Jr.) 40 56 60 63-66 68 273 365
        371
    James (s/o John), Capt. 64 66 67
    James Samuel 65
    James William Hook 64 67
    John 56 62-68 371
    John Snowden 66
    Margaret (Thrasher) 64
    Mary (Lyeth) 67
    Mary: see Fee 64
    Mary: see McGill 65
    Rachel: see Owings 64 98
    Samuel 64
    Sarah (Burgess) 65
    Sarah (Snowden) 65-67

Hook (cont'd.)
    Sarah (Thrasher) 65
    Stephen 64 65
    Thomas 64
"Hooks and Hills" 60 65 363 365
"Hooks Conclusion" 65
"Hooks Neglect Recovered by a Hard
    Struggle" 645
Hooper, Charity 323
    Johannes 323
    Mary 323
Hoops, John 368
Hoosman, Sarah: see Hensamer 225
Hoover, Adam 380
    Adam, (Jr?) 380
    Henry 323
    Jacob (carpenter) 378
    Jacob (tailor) 378
    Petyer 380
"Hope" (Bennett) 15 24 25 339 362 365
"Hope" (Wickham) 339
"Hope," ship 283
Hopewell Monthly Meeting, Quaker 82 87
Hopson, John 334
Hornbach, Ger. 157
Horner, Eli 237
"Horse Neck" 347
"Horseshoe" 19 95 98
Horsfeld, Timothy 153
Hortsey, Cornelius 56
House, Andrew 171-172
    Eve (Apple) 172 201
    George 172
    John 53 108 140 171-173 192 195 208
        318
    Susanna (d/o Thos) 172
    Susanna (w/o Thos) 172
    Thomas 155 171 365 367 372
    Valentine 172
    William 172 222 378
"Houses Addition" 155 171 363 365
"Houses New Design" 172
Howard County, Md. 228 231
Howard, Ephraim 355
    Gideon 103
    John 103 323
    Philip 103 307 323
    Philip, Jr. 323
    William 332
"Howards Range" 103
Howston, Robert 371
Huber, Johannes 269
Hudson River 117
"Hueffianhart" 189
Hueston, Robert 326
Hufferd (Hufford), Christian 323
Hufner, Michael 136
Hugh(s), John 368
Hughes, James 241
    Thomas Aloysius 253
    William 370
Hughes Ford 9 34 46 53 57 70 311
Hulsell, Thomas 371
Humbert, Anna Barbara (Deg) 177
    Catharina 177
    Frederick 323
    George 323

Humbert (cont'd.)
　Wilhelm 177
"Humberts Resurvey" 177
Hundreds, Prince George's Co., 1733　129
Hunt, Elezer 371
　Thomas, Sr. 371
　William 371
Hunter, George 253
　Henry (bro/o Samuel) 352
　Henry (s/o Samuel) 354
　Samuel 111 151 184 227 352 354 355
Hunterdon County, N. J. 120
"Hunters Lot" 186 198 326 362 365
"Hunting Bottom" 223 225 362 365
Hunting Creek 9 43 46-48 107 108 138 186 193 198 202 208 210　212 214-216 220 275 326 338 340 343
Hunting Creek Reservoir 197
Hunting Hill 339
"Hunting Loot" (S. Plummer) 229 234 363 365
Hunting Lot" (Devilbiss) 33 319 325 336 363 365
Husleman (Usselman), Valentine 157-158
Hussey, Isabella: see Ryan 230
　John 195 285 312
　Martha 141
　Robert 141 142 285
Hussey's Ford 46 290 312
Hutsell, George: see Hutzel 379
Hutson, John 371
Hutzel, Eliesabetha (Schweinhardt) 377
　George Jr. 159 160
　Johann George 139 146 157-158 **159-160** 197 372 377 379
　Johann Matthias 160
　Johann Peter 160
　Johannes 160
　Magdalena (Swinehart) 158 160
　Susanna 158 160 197
Hyattsville 91
Hyder, Henry 101

I.O.O.F. Home, Frederick 283
Iggelheim, Ger. 166 269
Illinois Territory 331
Immler, Anna Marie 196
Impflingen, Ger. 177
"Indian Field" 258 259 264 280-281
"Indian Seat" 20
Indian Springs 174 176 295
Indian Springs Road 179
Indians 7 10 12-16 20 21 25 36 74 87 110 130 148 163 286 330 334
Ingles, Thomas 298
"Inlett" 77 269 363 365
Investors, Land 23-44 54 72 153
Iowa State Historical Society 71
Ira Sears Road 91
Ireland, 25 31 102 117
"Isaacs Inheritance" 707 73 290 362 365
Isenpeck, George 378
Israel Creek 31 46 56 104 120 123 129 228 311 328 341 350
Israel Friend's Mill Road 51 55 225 228
Ittlingen, Ger. 162 163
Ivill, George 371

"Ivy Church" 99-101 362 365

Jack (Jacks), Jeremiah 368 370
"Jack of the Green" 50
Jackson, John 368
Jackson District 177
Jacob's Church: see Apple's Church 200
Jacobite Rebellion 252
Jacobs, John 62
　Thomas 28
Jacobs Branch 210
"Jacobs Contrivance" 178
"Jacobs Cowpen" 44 363 365
"Jacobs Fortune" 186 190 192 268 362 365
Jamaica 149
James II, King of England 247
James, Daniel 233 354
　John 56 146 228 229 231-**233** 365
　Lucy (Wood) 233
James-Kimmel Cemetery 233
Janeway Store Accounts, N. J. 182 309
Janney, Amos 84 235
　Mahlon 235
　Sarah (Plummer) 235
Jans, Jannetje: see Beatty 117
Jansen, Joost 69
　Maria: see Beatty 122
　Thomas 117
Janssen, Barbara: see Bladen 32
　Mary: see Calvert 32
　Theodore 32
Jarvis, Jabez 323
Jefferson 55 61 67 83 85 86 222 225
Jefferson Co., W. Va. 344
Jefferson Pike 166 222
Jena, University of 148
Jenkins, Ashman 379
Jennings, Ann (Johnson) 278
　Edmund 19
　Joseph, Rev. 47 77 127 304 350-352 366
　Mary 351
　Richard 241
　William 368, 371
Jenny (Janney), Amos 84 235
Jesserang, Batholomäus 189 219 220
　Georg Michael 146 219 243 378
Jesus, Society of (Jesuits) 148 251 252
Jimtown Crossroads 51-53 138 183 186 188 195 210 212 265 286 338
John, Captain 368
"John and Priscilla" 19 95 97 98
"John and Sarah" 20 65 66
"John and William," ship 190
"Johns Delight" 44
"Johns Good Luck" 229 231 362 365
"Johns Mountain" 186 215 362 365
Johnson, Abigail: see Whitaker 245
　Ann: see Jennings 278
　Baker 262
　Beanneard 370
　Christopher 37
　Daniel 224
　Elizabeth (Stull) 171
　Frances: see Foy 86 224
　Hannah: see Cresap 224
　Henry 368
　James 235

Johnson (cont'd.)
  John 28 111 246 368 371
  John, Jr. 379
  Joseph 246
  Martha 246
  Mary: see Fuller 246
  Robert 246
  Sarah: see Touchstone 222, 224
  Thomas 216 235 246 292 298 354 366
  Thomas, Jr. 246
  Thomas (Gov.) 278 281-282
"Johnson Galley," ship 187 268
"Johnsons Delight" 246 363 366
"Johnsons Lane Between" 246
"Johnsons Level" 15 246 354
Johnston, Thomas 371
Johnsville 99-100 104 105
Johnsville District 43
Jones, Charles 343
  David 379
  Edward 370
  Emanuel 196
  Evan 368
  Henry Z., Jr. 71 130 219 313
  Josiah 89-91 365
  M. 123
  Mary (van Metre) 74
  Michell 371
  Robert 565 62 74 108 112 368
  Thomas 371
  William 371
"Jones Bottom" 89 90 362 366
Jonestown, Pa. 377
Jordan, Anna Margaretha (Brunner) 273
  John David 273
Joseph, Brother: see Spangenberg 213 329
"Josiah" 79-83 85 362 366
Journal, Stöver's Personal: see under
   "Church Books" 268
"Jovial Ramble" 363 366
Joyner, Peggy Shomo 183 296 345
Judey, Winebart 379
Jug Bridge 232
Julien, Allatha 113
  Ann (Hedges) 112
  Catherine (Biggs) 311
  Catherine (Hedges): see Wood 109 110
     113 312
  Isaac 113
  Jacob 109 110 113
  Rachel 113
  René 113 311
  Stephen 110 112 113 114 231 285 345
     379
  Susanna (Hedges)
Justice Family 101
  Elizabeth: see Birchfield 101
  Hans 101
  Jacob 101
  John 100-102 232 327 354 366
  John, Jr. 101-103 354
  Joseph 101 354
  Margaret 101
  Moses 103
  Susannah: see Carmack 105
  William 101
Justices, Frederick County Court 312 333

Justices (cont'd.)
  341 343
"Justices Delight" 42 100 101 363 366

Kaes, Elisabeth (Berg): see Case 314
Kaiserslautern, Ger. 159
Kalb, Mary: see Biggs 311
Kämpf, Johann Conrad: see Kemp 263
Kanawha, Camp 59
Kandelaar: see Candler
Kanghover, Philip: see Kefauver 224
Kanigetschick: see Conococheague 329
Kannely, William 374
Katectin/Katoctin Mtn: see Catoctin 57 66
Keaver (see Gaver, Geber), Daniel 246
Keene, Richard 340 370
"Keepburgh" 299
Kefauver (Kanghover, Kiefalpor), Philip 224
Kegley, F. B. 20
Keith, Charles P. 13
  Daniel 241
Keitz: see Reuz 213
Kelbaugh Road 57 206 249
Keller (Haller), Elisabeth 298
Keller, Adam 299
  Barbara (Blaar) 298
  Barbara (d/o Conrad) 298
  Caspar 298
  Hans Conrad 259 260 298-299 372
  Jacob (Culler, Koller) 276
  Jacob 307 323 380
  John Caspar 298
  Mary 323
  Matthias 298
  Susanna 298
"Kellers Venture" 307
Kelley, Bryan 368
Kelly's Store Road 138 335
Kemp Family 288, 294
  Anna Barbara (Brunner) 181
  Anna Catharina (Schaub/Shoup) 175
  Anna Maria (Feuerbach) 172
  Anna Maria (d/o Christian) 173
  Catharina 172
  Christian 44 62 80 155 162 172-174 189
     278 365 366
  (Johann) Conrad 155 165 171-174 181
     191 205 208 258 259 263 274 279 292
     299 301 366 372
  Elisabeth (Ferree) LeFevre 172
  Frederick 165 172-175 256 379
  Gilbert 155 167 172-174 181 258 259 274
     278 379
  Harry Howard 172
  Lewis 379
  Maria Sophia: see Shoup 165
  (Hans) Peter (s/o Conrad) 172 175 181
     379
  Peter (s/o Frederick) 165 175
  Susanna Margaret (Getzendanner) 167 175
     181
Kemper, Charles E 9 64 72 142 147 148
"Kemps Bottom" 175
"Kemps Delight" 444 80 155 174 363 366
"Kemps Discovery" 174-175 245
"Kemps Long Meadow" 174
"Kemps Lot" 173

Kemp's Mill 174
"Kemps Purchase" 155 258 259 274
Kemptown 173
Kendrick (Kindrick), Robert 56 229 230 231 233 366 368
"Kendricks Hap" 56 127 228-230 362 366
Kennedy, Estelle (Stilley) 114
　John 114
Kenny, Hamill T. 36
Kens (Küntz): see also Coonce, Kinss), Philipp 33 53 112 136 155 169 367
Kent, England 41
Kent Island 352
"Kent Manor" 302
Kentucky 31
Kenworthy, William 242
Kernhart, Henry 379
Kersey, William 14
Keslar, Bernhard 378
Kessler, Anna Margaretha: see Weiss 262
Ketchindaner, Balser: see Getzendanner 379
"Kettankin Bottom" 60 64 362 366
Keymar 333
Keyser, W. Va. 108 209
Keysville 52 54 328
Keywood, John 345
　Moses 345
Kichman, Conrad 379
Kiefalpor, Philip: see Kefauver 224
Kieffer, Elizabeth C. 200 270 315
Kiger: see Geiger
"Kilfadda" 17 125
Killian, Rolf 208
Killis, John 374
Kilty, John 35
Kimball, Agnes (Beatty) 121
　John 121
Kince, Philip: see Kinss 169 217
Kindred, Thomas 370
Kingdom of Two Sicilies 59
"Kingsteinstead" 20
Kingston (Esopus), N. Y. 69 74 117 120 122 309 334
Kingwood Twp. (Hunterdon Co.), N. J. 205 310
King, Francis 226
　Margaret (Sprigg) 226
　Richard 226
Kinkley, Frederick 378
Kinsell, Adam 378
Kinss (Kens, Kince, Kintz, Kühntz, etc.), Johann Philip 33 53 112 136 137 155 169 **168-169** 170 217 218 337 367 376
Kinzmiller, Martin 140
Kipps, Abraham 378
Kirchardt, Ger. 208
Kirk, William 82
Kirtchendaner, Jacob: see Getzendanner 379
Kishner, David 241
Kisor: see Geiger 201
Kitchin, Philip: see Kinss 168
Kiteman, Christopher 380
Kitoctin, Kittoktin Mtn. see Catoctin
Kitsintander, Kitsenlander: see Getzendanner
Kleeman, Christian 374
Klein, Anna 374

Klein (cont'd.)
　Catharina 217
　Joh. George 153 374
Klein Schifferstadt, Ger. 165 269 271 280 282-283 293
Kleinsteinhausen, Ger. 157
Klemf of Philadelphia 142
Klemm (Clem), Anna Maria: see Winter 157
　Barbara 157
　Catharina (Winter) 157
　Friedrich 142
　George 157
　Georg Philip 156 157
　Heinrich 157
　Margaretha (Swinehart) 157
　Michael 157
　Susanna 142
Klingen, Ger. 136
Knafe, Kneff, Henry: see Neff
Knewell, Philip 170
Knittle, Walter 130
Knoll, Michael Christian 135
Knoxville, Md. 222
Koch, Georg Jacob 144
Kocher (Coker), Michael 197
Kochher, Maria: see Moser 197
Köhler, Conrad 151
Kocherthal, Joshua (Harrsch) 132
Koehn, Anna Margaret: see Weller 211
Koger, Johann Jacob 212 377
　Maria Eliesabetha (Willheut) 212
　Nicklaus 199 212
　Nicolaus 377
Kolb, David F. 31
Koller (Culler), Jacob 202 276
Koone, Christian 327
Koontz Chapel 91
Kowellentz, Peter: see Coblentz 246
Kraft, Valentin 136 140 142 151
Kraichgau area, Ger. 71 127 132 133 172 207
Krämer, Urbanus 334
Krebs, Friedrich 262
Krefeld, Ger. 271
Kreider, Harry J. 182
Kretscher, Maria Agnes: see Honig 201
Kreutz (see also Creutz) Creek, York Co., Pa. 211 377
Krieger (Krüger): see also Creager
　Caspar 159 282
　Elisabeth (Beitzel) 211
　Lawrence 214
　Maria Elisabeth (Hahn) 214
　Michael 198
Krise, Henry 342
　Peter 241 242
　Susan: see Barrick 342
"Krises Establishment" 342
Kroneiss, Joh. Georg 300
Krüger: see Creager, Krieger
Kuhn Johannes 162
Küntz, Philip: see also Kinss 169 218
　Jacob 170
Kusel, Ger. 276
Kutschmann, August Heinrich 375
Kyle, Adam 281
　Anna Elizabeth (Storm) 281

Lacefield, William 103
Lachman, Jacob: see Lochman 181
Lafarge, Rachel (van Metre) 74
Lafayette, Marquis de 255
"Laffortys Lot" 19 20
Lake, D. J. 31
Lakin, Abraham 60 64 67 349 367
  Abraham, Jr. 67
  Abraham (III) 67
  Ann (Sheckels) 67
  Benjamin 67
  Daniel 67
  Deborah 67
  Deborah (d/o Abraham Jr.) 67
  Eleanor 67
  Elizabeth (d/o Abraham) 67
  Elizabeth (Ancrum) 66
  Elizabeth (Fee) 67
  John 66
  John (s/o Abraham, Jr.) 67
  Joseph 67
  Martha (Lee) 67
  Martha: see Plummer 67
  Mary (Ungles) 67
  Mary: see Hook 67
  Nancy: see Deaver 67
  Rachel (d/o Abraham) 67
  Rachel (Fee) 67
  Ruth 67
  Sarah (Hook) 64 66 67
  Sarah (d/o Abraham): see Wells 67
  Sarah: see Lyeth 67
  William, Capt. 67
Laman, Philip Jacob 379
Lamar, John 370
  Robert, Jr. 86 370
"Lamars Generosity" 15
Lambsheim, Ger. 132
"Lambson" 155 179 180 295 363 366
Lämmle, Gabriel 201
  Johann Peter 201
Lancaster, Pa. 18 52 133 135 158 185 191 193 196 201 233-235 267 270 298 312 315 316 330 374
Lancaster County, Pa. 13 14 18 132 140 174 195 202 207 217 238 278 289 291 294 297 326
Lancaster Theological Seminary 171
Land, Aubrey C. 20 31
Land Office, Maryland 1-3 16 25 27 35 115 116 128
Land Office, Virginia 86
"Land of Valleys" 122
Landau, Ger. 150 176 262
Lander 60
Lander Road 66
"Lanes Bottom and Hills" 14
Laney: see also Lehnich
  Hannah 286
  Peter (see Teter) 258 284 289
  Teter (Tetur = Dieter) 53 77 137 269 286 287 364
  John Teter 371
Lang, Anna Veronica: see Thomas 282
Lanham, Jo., Jr. 370
  Richard 370
Lansdale, Isaac 370

Lantz 330
Lany, Matthew 379
Larkins, James 241
Lathly, Georg 169 294 375
  Rachel 169 294 375
Laub, Michael 140
  Vernoica Philippina Candler 140
Lauber, Frederick 243
Laurel 64
Laurel Hill 311
Lawrence, John 370
Lay (Laye), Joh. Georg (see also Loy) 198 263 299 376
  Maria Elisabetha (Traut?) 294
Lazaras, Henry 262 378
  Sampson 262
Lazures, Simpson 378
Leacock, Pa. 377
"Learning" 347
Leased land 36 115 128
Leases, leasing 302 303 305 306 308 309 320
Leather, John 379
Leatherman, Daniel 33 35 246 365
Lebanon, Pa. 135 194
Lebanon County, Pa. 135 141
Lechlider, Conrod 196
"Leddy" 111
Lee, Ann 67
  Eliza: see Laye (Loy), Maria Elisabetha (Traut?) 294
  Martha: see Lakin 67
  Thomas 20 37 44
  William 67
"Leeds" 354
Leeds, Engl. 159
Leet, Edward
LeFever (LeFevre), Abraham 174
  Daniel 209
  Elisabeth (Ferree): see Kemp 174
LeGore Bridge 342
Lehigh County, Pa. 263
Lehn, Joseph 218 276
  Peter 276
Lehnert (Leonard), Isaac 53 54 77 80 82 155 166-167 181 354 366
  Johann Gilbert 181
  Johann Jacob 181, 191
Lehnich (Laney, Lehny), Dieter (Teter, Tetur) 53 77 137 146 154 169-170 186 217-218 257-260 269 274 284 286 287 289 350 364 371 372 374 375
  Hannah 218 286
Leih (Loy), Adam 296
  Fridrich 296
Lein [Ley?], Magdalena 169 294 365
Leitersburg 329
Leman, Benedict 284
  Peter 284
Lemaster, Rachael (Delashmutt) 61
L'Enfant, Pierre Charles 22
Leonard: see also Lehnert
  Isaac 54 77 82 166 167 181 354
"Leonards Beginning" 67
"Leonards Good Luck" 80 155 181 354 363 366
Leu (Loy), Maria Dorothea: see Hoffman

Leu, Maria Dorothea (cont'd.) 279 296
"Level Bottom" 14
"Level Farm" 105
Levitt, John 370
Lewis, John 253
Lewistown 52 54 153 185 186 192 202 208 214 217-218 260 266 288 338 345 354
Lewistown District 310
Ley: see also Loy
  Anna Eliesabetha 294
  Anna Maria (w/o Matthias) 294
  Hans Georg (Jurigh) 262 277 278 293-296 374-376
  Johan Henrich 294
  Joh. Jacob 294 375
  Maria Eliesabetha (Traut?) 278 294
  Maria Rosina 294 374
  Matthew 294
Leyden University 149 211
Liberty District 42
Liberty Road 102
Libertytown 45 99-100 104 250 252 350
Library, C. Burr Artz 282
Lick Branch 43
Licklighter (Lechlider), Conrod 196
Lighton, Moravian Brother 329
Lilly, Mary (Elder) 254
  Richard 48 49 254 338
"Lillys Lot" 48 49 254 338
Lilypons 25
Limekiln 174
Lincoln, Abraham 347
Lindere, Simon 183
Lindheim, Ger. 147
Linganore Chapel 102 230
Linganore Creek 30 44 46 53 70 77 100 101 103-105 119 120 122 127 229-232 234 290 352
Linganore Ford 232 233
Linganore Hundred 77 110
Linganore Road 31
Lingenfelter, Abraham 129 378
  Barbara (Brunner) 273
  George 292
  George Bernhard (Barnet) 128 129 273 380
  Johann Georg 128
  John 378
Link Family 127
  Adam 127 128 332
  Elisabeth: see Stoner 291
  Jane (Ogle) 332
  Paxson 127
Links Bridge 309
Links Bridge Road 313, 314
Linter, Elisabetha 159
"Linton" 19
Lion, Umberston: see Lyon 371
Lischy, Jacob 141 148 211
Lititz Archives 138
Little Cadores (Codorus) Creek 17 191
Little Captains (Owens) Creek 206 249 326
Little Catoctin Creek (Mill Run) 38 243-245
Little Conestoga Creek 297
"Little Good" 347
Little Hunting Creek 208 216

"Little Left" 347
"Little Meadow" 56
Little Monocacy River 46 62 339 349
Little Owens Creek 13 46 56 248 249 326 336
Little Pipe Creek 5 14 46 51 56 99 125 127 252-254 256 285 312 335
Little Rock Creek 184
Little Tuscarora Creek 156 179
"Little Worth" 313
Littler, John 87
Littlestown, Pa. 50 285
Livers, Anne 252
  Anthony 252
  Arnold, Sr. 39 47 100 104 130 200 203 206 248 249-253 364-367
  Arnold, Jr. 251, 252
  Helena: see Cullard 203 250
  Jacoba Clementina: see Elder 252
  James 252
  Judith (Ogle) 331
  Mary: see Boetler 252
  Nathaniel 331
  Rachel: see Harday 203 252
  Robert 250, 252
Livingston, Robert 117
Livingston Manor, N. Y. 117
Lloyd, Edward 35 306
  Henrietta Maria (Neale) Bennett 32
  Henrietta Maria: see Chew, Dulany 30-32
  Philemon (1646-1685) 32
  Philemon (1672-1732) 12 13 30 32 36 177 364
Lochman, Dorothea: see Brunner 191
  Elisabeth (Haffner) 191 376
  Eliesbaetha Dorothea: see Müller 204
  (Joh.) Jacob 11-12 17 18 171 181 191 376
  Maria Catharina (Dielforter) 191
Lock, John 241
"Locust Level" 20
"Locust Thicket" 331 342
Locust Valley 40 225 226
Loescher, Father 334
Lohr and Zentz Mill 207
Lomersheim on the Enz, Ger. 163
London, Engl. 9 10 20 39 159 309
London Grove Twp. (Chester Co.), Pa. 332
London Tract 106
"Long Acre" 258 259 266-268 278
"Long Bottom" 172
Long Island, N. Y. 211
"Long Looked For, Come At Last" 340
"Long Mile" 239
"Longacres" 192
"Longatepaugh" 19 186 220 363 366
Longs Mill Road 326 328
"Loom" 258 259 268 272
Losson, Nehemiah 371
  Richard 371
"Lost Spring" 33 155 156 362 366
Loudoun County, Va. 201
Louis XIV, King of France 130 247
Low (Lowe), Cornelius 309
  Daniel Johnson 60 86 366
  Elizabetha 374
  Henry 370

Low (cont'd.)
  John 16 17 325 326 370 374
  John, Jr. 370
"Low Kemper" 175
"Low Land" 362, 366
"Low Mill" 238 239 363 366
Lower German settlement 58 153-184 187 204
Lower Monocacy Hundred 64 67 94
"Lowland" 60 86
Lowndes, Christopher 32 260 297 298
  Elizabeth (Tasker) 32
"Lowther," snow 168
Loy (see also Lay, Leih, Ley, Lye):
  Adam 296
  Anna Barbara (Cassel) 296
  Anna Elisabeth 294 296
  Apollonia: see Troxell 296
  Charlotte Amalie: see Shoup 296
  Elisabeth 279
  Frederick (Fridrich) 296
  George (Hans/Johann Georg) 179-180 182-183 193 198 220 252 258 260 262 263 277-279 283 289 292 293-296 299 372 374-376 379
  Johann Georg, Jr. 296
  Johann Jacob 260 294 296 375
  Louisa (Gies) 296
  Maria Dorothea (Leu): see Hoffman 279 296
  Maria Elisabetha (Traut?) 278 294
  Maria Rosina: see Shafer, Shaver 180 294 296
  Maria Sibylla: see Stoner 291 296
"Loyal Judith," ship 198
Loyalists 31 158 261 266 277 298 300 305 320
Loybottom, Judah 378
Loyd, John 380
Loys Station 52 57 237 319 324 325 326 336
"Lubberland" 100 104 105 249 250 362 366
"Luck" 307
Luckett, J. C. 63
  Sally (Nelson) 63
  William 63 83 355 370
  William, Jr. 63
  William Arthur Nelson 63
"Lucketts Merry Midnight" 63
Ludwig, Brother: see Zinzendorf 142
"Ludwigs New Mill" 50
Ludwigshafen, Ger. 165 216 282
Lüdorf, Ger. 133
Luna, Robert 87
Lunt, Dudley 16
Luther, Martin 144
Lutheran Church in America 132
Lutheran Pastors 132-140 160 211
Luts, Jacob 380
Lutz, Joseph 380
  Leonhardt 160 271 376
Luxemberger, Joseph 378
Lye, Lyh (see Loy), John George 258 292 295
Lyeth, Robert 67
  Sarah (Lakin) 67
  Sarah: see Fee 67

Lynes, Jacob 77
Lynn, David 343
Lyon, Humberstone (Ambuston) 368 370 371

McCay, John 370
McCormack, Daniel 189
MacCrory, Daniel 378
McDaniel, William 123
MacDaniels, James 103
McDonald, Margaret 241
McGill (McGuill), Andrew 325 374
  Mary 325 374
  Mary (Hook) 65
  Patrick, Jr. 65
McGill Home 65
McGorgen, John 241
McGrain, John W. 73
Mack, Alexander 165 270 271
  Alexander, Jr. 246
McKaig, Md. 228 233
McKay, John 228
  Robert 71
Mackee, David 369
McKeen, Alexander 238 239 364
  Alexander, Jr. 239
Mackenzie, George N. 346
Mackey, Ann (Pearre) 92
  John 230
  Margaret 230
"Mackeys Delight" 56 228 230
MacKinly, Samuell 371
McKinsey, Folger 47 101 102
McKinstry Family 99
  S. 99
McKinstry's Mill 42 101
MacKnaul, Mary 157
McLean, William 235
McPherson, John 39
MacPherson, Robert 110 287 310
Maddock, Johannes: see Middagh 369
Madison County, Va. 133
Magee, D. F. 172
Magruder, James 370
  John 37 40 53 60 65 98 243 244 365 366
  Nathan 370
  Williams 370
"Magruders Thicket" 331
Mahon (Matson), James 369
Major Landholdings, East of the Monocacy 34
"Mallingah" 180 363 366
Malone, Loughlin 18 194
Mance, Casper 378
  Peter 378
Mang, Gottfried 329
Manheim Twp. (York Co.), Pa. 215
"Mankine" 33 53 155 164 177 363 366
Manor Hundred 105 127 195 311
Manor Monocacy Road 9 36 51-55 57 104 142 228 309 311 312 319 325 326 328 339
Manors, Proprietary 2 36 302-323
Manser (Mansser, Manshaw, Minsher), Jacob
  Matthias 18 19 53 168 185-187 190 192 194 199 212 268 365 372 376
Manwaring, Joanne 6

"Maple Bottom" 15
Maps, Caveat re 6 28
  County Road 28
  U.S. Geological Survey 28
Marblehead, N. Y. 117
Marbury, Leonard 370
  Luke 370
Mariarte, Margaret: see Sprigg 226
Marienborn, Ger. 271
Marienfels, Taunus, Ger. 218
Markland, Matthew 371
"Markleys Purchase" 160
Marks, Robert 33 245 367
Marriot, A. 31
Marsh Creek (Gettysburg), Pa. 201
Marshall, James 39 238
  Mrs. L. C. 97
  Thomas 370
  William 62
Martin, Andrew 371
  Ann 127
  Appiah 127
  Asa 127
  Aseneth 127
  Benjamin 127
  Demarius 127
  John 62 116 126-127 228
  John, Jr. 235
  Mary 110
  Zadock 127
"Martins Field" 20
"Martins Intent" 20
Martinsburg, W. Va. 79
Martz, Theobald 378
Marye, William B. 7 13 14 36 52
Maryland 2 5-7 10 16-18 21-23 35 36 41 89
  118 131 144 148 168 172 176 187 193
  205 216 219 246 255 264 310 315 346
Maryland Archives, Annapolis 5
Maryland Midland Railroad 292 315
Maryland Monster, The 18
Maryland State Routes:
  # 17: 96
  # 26: 102 117 281 285 288 289
  # 28: 52 81 339
  # 31: 101
  # 36: 277
  # 72: 57
  # 73: 178-179
  # 75: 14 99
  # 77: 57 327 333
  # 78: 62
  # 80: 39
  #112: 339
  #144: 235
  #180: 38 96 121
  #194: 120 309 312 315 341
  #355: 39 235
  #550: 138
Maschwanden, Switzerland 175-178
Mash, John 371
Mason, James 224
  Phillip 370
Mason and Dixon Line 21
Mason Island 59 60
"Masons Folly" 15 224
Massanutten German settlement, Va. 135

Massanutten Mountain 9
"Masswander" 33 155 176 178 363 366
Masters, Nathan 371
  Robert 371
Matson (Mahon), James 369
Mattapany Hundred 129
Matthews (see also Matthias, below):
  Chidley 53 62 84 107 114 155 159 166
    307 364 369 371
  Daniel 162 174
  Elizabeth (Wright) 79 84 85
  Elizabeth (d/o William) 85
  George 28 62 79 84 85 174 365 369
  Hannah 85
  Jacob 164 317 335 371
  John 84 323 380
  Mary (w/o Chidley) 84
  Mary (d/o Chidley) 84
  Mary (w/o William) 85
  Mary (d/o William) 85
  Mary (Apple) 201
  Oliver 79 84 85
  Patrick 180
  Samuel 84 323 380
  Thomas 28 80 84 85 366
  William 28 82 83-85 369
  William, Jr. 85
  William (of York Co.) 88
"Matthews Lot" 80 85 363 366
Matthias (Matthews), Anna Magdalena
    (Maudlin): see also Firor 205-207 317
    375
  Anna Margaretha (d/o Joh. Jacob): see
    also Valentine 205-207 374
  Anna Margaretha (w/o Joh. Jacob)
    204-205 207 375 376
  Anna Maria "Mary" see also Flower
    206-207 210
  Catharina: see Stull 205-207
  Conrad 207
  Henry 207
  Johann Georg 205-207
  Johann Jacob 134 147 152 172 187-188
    200 203-204 205-207 211 213 277 288
    294 372 374-376
  John 207
  Margaretha (Jung) 188, 205
  Maria Barbara: see Ambrose 206-207
  Philip 207
Mattice, Jacob 206
Matzger, George Valentine 157
Mauk, Valentine 313
Maulsby, Betsy (Harrison) 63
  Emily Catherine Contee (Nelson) 63
  William Pinkney 63
Maxel, Andrew 380
Mayhew, Anna 158 376
  Elisabetha (Swinehart) 158
  John William 158 161 375
  Joseph 77 157 158-159 161 375 376 379
Maynard (Maynor), Henry 102 200
  John 102
  Nathan 122
  Susanna (Beatty) 122 200
  Thomas 122
Mayner, H. G. 122
  N. 122

Mc: see under Mac
Meadon, Capt. 21
"Meadow" 69 70 72 76 79 162 257 362 366
Meadow Road 120
Mears, Elizabeth 91
　William 91 367
Medford 249
Medley, Eleanor 86
Meeting House, Monocacy: see under
　Quaker
Meetings: see Quakers
Melanchthon, Philipp 144
"Mellingah" see "Mallingah" 180
"Mellwood" 252
Mellwood Park 94
Members, Peter 313 322
Mendenhall, Martha (Wright) 79
Mennonites 173 267 286 290 297 301
Mercersburg, Pa. 344 345
Merckle, Anna Maria: see Hite 71
"Mercury," ship 298
Mercy Hospital, Baltimore 279
Meredith, John 231
"Merediths Hunting Quarter" 81 91 362 366
Mergerin, Anna Maria 135
"Merryland" 15 24 37-38 95-98 362 366
Mesesipi (Mississippi) Country 8 9
Messner, Peter 327
Methodism 92 102 122
"Metre" 15 69 70 75 121 362 366
Metre Branch (Carroll Creek) 15
Miami County, Ohio 114
Michel, Franz Louis 7-10 53 231
Meyer, Anna Barbara 374
　Charlotte (Apple) 201
　Daniel 380
　Joh. Georg 317 374 377
Michael, Daniel 380
　Maria Barbara (Sinn) 268 269
Michelfeld, Ger. 208
Mid-Monocacy Settlement 58 337-347
Middag, Bata: see Beatty 122
　George 122
Middagh (Middaugh) Family 309
George 122
　John 62 112 118 119 121-122 127 167
　　328 330 369 375
　John, Jr. 123 380
　Marietje 122
　Martha (Beatty) 117 118 122-123
　Martha (d/o John) 123
　Mary: see Ritchie 123
　Susanna 123 375
"Middle Choice" 20 214 238 239 326
Middle (Furnace) Ford 46 52 81 91 341
"Middle House" 174
Middle Monocacy Hundred 114
Middleburg 339
Middlecave, Peter 350
Middlepoint 76
Middletown 44 53-54 166 174 223-225 243
　245 277
Middletown District 243-246 300
Middletown Valley 76 111 174 177 270 277
Middock, Johannes: see Middagh 369
Miers (Myer), John 369
Miles, Sarah: see Plummer 234

Militia, Maryland 17 21 77 225 267 292 295
　330 333 341
Mill Branch (Ballenger Creek) 55 81 109
　230 285
Mill Creek (Mdltn area) 246
Mill Creek, Pa. 135
Mill Creek, Va. 87
Mill Creek, W. Va. 344
"Mill Lot" 80 81 162 363 366
"Mill Manor" 302
"Mill Place" 186 208 363 366
"Mill Pond" 258 259 289 291
"Mill Race" 172
Mill Run (Little Catoctin Creek) 245
"Mill Seat" 319
Miller (see also Müller):
　Abraham 54 192 198 204 217-218 258-
　　260 277-278 281 283-291 301 333 341
　　371 372
　Abraham, Jr. 287
　Adam 158 323
　Anna Margreth Swinehart 158
　Barbara 287
　Charles R. 175
　Christian 284 286 287 322 323 333
　David 287 322 333
　Elizabeth: see Peger (Becker?) 287
　Frances (Frana) 284 286 287
　Francis 379
　George 322, 333
　G. 327
　Hannah: see Geiger 201
　Isaac 53 170 180 292 366 373
　Jacob 195 284 287
　John 327
　John William (Jr.) 335
　Louisa 287
　Maria Madlena 284
　Mary 287
　Mary Ann 335
　Michael 201
　Peter 379
　Stephen 323
　Ursha 180
　William, Sr. 335
Millers at Millers Bridge 333
Millers Bridge 324 326 328 333 335
"Millers Chance" 286 287 331
"Millers Fancy" 335
Mills, John, Sr. 87
　John, Jr. 87
Mills: Ahalt 226
　Ambrose's Matthias 188 192 203 206 212
　　255 286
　Anderson's Thomas 87
　Apple's, Peter 200
　Ballenger's Henry 81
　Davis,' Meredith 83
　Dulany's, Daniel 73 261-263 265 281 283
　Elting's, Cornelius 57 62 75 162 349
　Friend's, Israel 55 222 225 228
　Johnson's, Baker 262
　Kemp's 174
　Lohr and Zentz 207
　McKinstry's 42 101
　Miller's, Abraham 192 286
　Ogle's, Alexander 332

Mills (cont'd.)
  Old City 267
  Peck's, Jacob 178 179 281 341
  Ramsburg's, Stephen 126 310
  Reel's 15
  Reynolds, Hugh 288
  Shank's 293
  Stoner's 290 291
  Stull's, John 55
  Wilson's, P. L. 120
  Worman 285 288
"Mindall" 347
Ministerium, Pennsylvania Lutheran 143 152
Minsher, Jacob Mathias: see Manser 190
Mire, Gasper: see Myer, Joh. Caspar 140 170 **266** 281
Miscell, Jacob 240
"Misery" 15
Missell, Frederick 378
Mississippi country 8 9
Mobberley (Mobley), Chloe (Crouch) 232
  Clement. 371
  Edward 55 97 371
  John 232
  William 371
Moers, Ger. 211
Mohawk Valley, N.Y. 219
Mohr, Yost 136
Mohsser, Lehnert: see Moser 197
Mölich, Johann Peter 269
Molyneux, Richard 251 253
Mong, Adam 378
Monocacy, Battle of 39
Monocacy Area 5 7 10 17 22 45-58 74 86 109 134-136 139 147 148 149 163 182 188 202 205 228 273 324 333 368-369 375-377
Monocacy Chapel (Beallsville), Church of England 56 62 64 192 195 349 352 355
Monocacy Ferry 53 63 81 91 225 226 339
Monocacy Fords (see also under "Fords") 228 235
Monocacy Hundred 14 31 61 62 71 74 93 94 108 119 129 230 238 255 368-369
Monocacy Lutheran Church, Original Hills or Old Log 47 48 50 137 144 145 355
"Monocacy Manor" 3 24 34-36 40 45 52 54 58 107 109 110 115 116 120 123 126-128 147 153 168 187 221 230 237 238 285 302-323 338 339 343 345 351 362 366
Monocacy Meeting (Quaker) 45 79-82 87-88 236
Monocacy Meeting House 54 82-83 87-88
Monocacy River 5 7 10 13-15 23-25 28-31 34 36 37 39 40 42-44 46-48 50-54 57 70 73-75 79-81 83-84 105-107 115-116 118-120 122-123 127 128 142 171 181 228 232 237 250 257 258 259 261 275 281 283 285 288-290 292-293 303 308 309 311-313 326-328 332 333 335 338-340 342 345 352
Monocacy Taxables (1733) 84 94 96 108 109 122 123 187 222 225 230 237 245 273 368 369
Monocacy "Village" 45 47-50 128

Monocacy-Annapolis Road 36 51 56 57 102 103 120 127 228-230 233
Monocacy-Antietam Road 51 55 57 94 222 223 225
Monrovia 229 234
Montgomery, Thomas 37
Montgomery County, Md. 19 30 39 50 57 62 73 74 77 90 91 227 231 234 302 337 339 342 349 354
Montgomery (see also Philadelphia) County, Pa. 71 132 133 154 157 163 217
Moon, Eva: see Biggs 311
  Susanna 84
Moore, Asa 88
  George, Sr. 224 334 369 371
  John 224 369 371
  William Sr. 224 369 371
  William, Jr. 224 371
Moravian Brethren 138 141 145-148 152 153 174 184 197 203 207 210-211 213 214 216 283 329
  Church, Graceham 138 152 206 214 327
  Ministers 152 335
  Missionaries 20 114 141-142 147-148 188 191 203 285 315 329 333-334
  Schism at Monocacy 145-147 213
"More Bad Than Good" 172
Morgan, Morgan 344
Morris, Thomas 56 62 371
  William 371
"Mortality" 258 259 291 293 296
Mortality, Infant 305
"Mortonhouse," ship 164 269 280 298
Moser, Johann Leonardt (Lehnert) 187 196-198 214 373
  Maria (Kochher) 197
  Maria Sarah 214
  Paulus 197
Moser Road 212
Motter, Margaret R. 150
Motters 198 310
Mount Airy 56
Mount Calvert Hundred 129 250
"Mount Hope" 83
"Mount Olivet" 22 214 330
Mount Olivet Cemetery, Frederick 123 353
Mount Phillip Road 52-54 57 166 167 181 190 354
Mount Pleasant 34 45 56 102 116 119 120 228 230
"Mount Pleasant" (Crouch) 229 232 362 366
"Mount Pleasant" (Jennings) 304 350 351 363 366
Mount Pleasant District 31
Mount St. Marys 175
Mount St. Mary's College 249 253-256
Mount Vernon, Va. 41
Mount Zion Church Road 354
"Mountain Prospect" 252 253
Mountaindale 136
Mounts, Joseph 71
Mountville 40 57 85
Mountville Road 283
Mowes, Joseph 56
Mozar, Leonard: see Moser 196
Muddy Creek area, Pa. 188 262 278 374 375 377

Muddy Creek, Pa.
  Lutheran Church Book 137 159 182 187
    188 202 262
  Lutheran Congregation 159
  Reformed Church Book 159
  Reformed Congregation 148
Muddy Run 197 218 316
Muhlenberg, Henry Melchior 138 142-146
  151 152 157 195 197 199 202 209 218
  219 265 267 295 329 352-353
Mühlhofen, Ger. 262
Müller (see also Miller)
  Abraham: see Miller 141
  Adam 158
  Anna Eliesabeth 204
  Anna Maria: see Bundrick 157
  Catharina 376
  Eliesabetha Dorothea (Lochman) 204
  Johann Abraham 284
  Johann Peter 132-133 159
  Johannes 284
  Magdalena 204 375
  Maria Magdalena (Fuhrman) 284
  Peter 159
  Valentine 187 202 204 372 375
Mullican, Thomas 370
Mumma, Jacob 290
Mumma Ford 43 46 51 52 250 327 328 333
Munday, Henrietta Prudence Deborah Margaretta: see Biggs 310
  Henry 18 21 130 196 224 310 311 327
    328 331-335 341 367 370
Murdock, George 62 267 350
  George William 171
  Mary 171
  William 49
"Murdocks Fancy" 171
Mussetter Road 235
Muster Rolls 378-380
"My Lady's Manor" 302
Myer (Miers), Barbara 267
  Christopher 260
  Henry 267 293
  Johann Caspar 140 170 192-193 258 259
    266-268 278 280 281 373 379
  John 367 369
  Margaret (Ramsburg) 293
  Zachariah 44
Myersville 177 246 275

Naesman, Gabriel: see Nasman 143
Nafe, Naff, Jacob: see Neff 109 169
Naffe, Dr. John Henry: see Neff 296
"Nanticoke Manor" 302
Nasman, Gabriel 143 161 179 264 352
National Fire Academy 255
National Pike 21 166 232 235
Naturalization of Germans 137 140 141 156
  160 162 165 170 171 173 175 179 180
  188 189 193 202 203 216 263 264 272
  275 278 280 282 287 290 297-299 316
Nave: see Neff
Nazareth, Pa. 147
"Nazarite" 347
Nead, Daniel W. 47
Neale, Henrietta Maria: see Lloyd 32
  William 253

"Near the Navel" 347
Neff (Knafe, Kneff, Nafe, Naff, Nave):
  Abram 297
  Adam 113
  Anna 296 297
  Catharina (w/o Jacob) 111 113
  Catherine (d/o John Henry): see Baughman 297
  Christley (Christian) 297
  Daniel (of Neff's Run) 297
  Daniel, Jr. (of Neff's Run) 297
  Elizabeth 297
  Esther: see Swinehart 113 158
  Francis (s/o Jacob) 113
  Francis (s/o John Henry) 297
  Francis (of Neff's Run) 297
  Francis, Jr. (of Neff's Run) 297
  Henry (s/o Jacob) 113 327
  Henry (of Neff's Run) 297
  Henry (s/o Daniel of Neff's Run) 297
  Jacob 109 111-113 136 158 169 218 286
    297 371
  Jacob, Jr. 112 113
  Jacob (s/o John Henry) 297
  John Henry, Dr. 113 218 258-260 277
    296-298 301 371 373
  John (s/o Jacob) 113 297
  John (s/o John Henry) 297
  Margareta [Ness?] (Creutz Creek): see
    Schaiteler 297 377
  Margaretta (d/o Jacob) 113
Neff's Run, Lancaster County, Pa. 297
Neidhardt, William 266
"Neighbors Agreement" 114
Neighbourg: see Nyberg, Lars 335
Nelson, Arthur 13 59-61 91
  Arthur, Jr. 59 61 63 98 349 364-366
  Betsy (Harrison) 63
  Elizabeth: see Delashmutt 61
  Emily Catherine Contee: see Maulsby 63
  Jane (w/o John, Sr.) 61
  Jane (d/o Arthur, Jr.) 63
  John (s/o Arthur, Jr.) 63
  John (s/o Roger) 59 63
  John, Sr. (s/o Arthur Sr.) 28 55 59-62 64
    68 75 77 97 123 129 162 208 349 367
    369 371
  John, Jr. (s/o John, Sr.) 59
  Louisa (Fairfax) 63
  Lucy (Waters) 63
  Roger, General (s/o Arthur) 59 63
  Sally: see Luckett 63
  Sarah: see Delashmutt 61
  Thomas 20
  Valentine 61
Nelson's Ferry (Point of Rocks) 265 281
"Nelsons Island" 13 59 60 362 366
Nemacolin 21
Nemacolin's Road 21
Neshaminy congregation, Bucks Co., Pa.
  211
Ness [sic; see Neff], Margaretha 297
Neu-Ansberg settlement, N. Y. 218
Neuchatel, Switzerland 9
Neuse Estuary, N. C. 10
New Amstel, Del. 324
New Amsterdam 324

"New Barn" 75
New Bern, N. C. 133
New Castle, Del. 324
New Castle County, Del. 14 106 109 114 315 332 347
New Design Road 28 29 161, 162, 174
New Garden (N.C.) Quakers 66 81 84
"New Germany" 19
New Goshenhoppen, Pa. 133
New Hanover Lutherans 133 143 145 163
New Hanover Twp. (Montgomery, formerly Philadelphia, Co.), Pa. 154 157 163
New Holland (Lancaster Co.), Pa. 135 172 204 289
New Jersey 69 73 74 107 108 119 125 135 152 182 211 278 309 310 313 333
New London 56 230 231 233
New Market 173 175 229 231-235
New Market area 58 228-236
New Town (Jefferson) 86
New Town, St. Mary's Co. 252
New Windsor 14 45 252
New Windsor Road 101
New York, N.Y. 44 130 132 133 256 324
New York Colony 13 15 31 69 74 117-119 122 125 132 135 142 147 148 152 218 219
Newcomer, Christian 175
Nicholas, Edward
 William 56
Nichols, George 370
 Edward 369
 Jacob 232
 James 369
 John 252 369
 Richard, Col. 324
Nidress (Verdriess), John, Jr. 215
Niederbachheim, Ger. 218
Nieke, George 142 143 145 152 153
 Johanna Elisabeth 142
"Nipple" 92
Nischicker, Maria Magdalena "Helena" see Schneider, Ringer 157
"No Whiskey" 313
Noble, George 39 40 42
"Nock Cairn" 307
Noland, Mr. 61
Nolands Island 13 59
"Nolans Mountain" 197
Nordhofen, Ger. 313 314
Norris, Benjamin 370
 Isaac 335
 Thomas 343
 William 371
North Branch, Potomac River 334
North Carolina 10 13 87 131
"North East Manor" 302
North Fork, Shenandoah River 9 296
North Mountain, Va. 183 296
Northampton, Engl. 159
Northern Neck, Va. 183
Norwood, Richard 9
"Nothing Ventured, Nothing Get" 313
Nottingham Monthly Meeting (Quakers) 87
Nova Scotia 152
Null, James 202
Nuthall, Eleanor (Sprigg) Hilleary 226

Nuthall (cont'd.)
 John 226
"Nutt Spring" 293
Nyberg, Laurentius Thorstonsen (Lars) 142 143 145 213 335

Oak Hill Road 328
Oak Orchard 42 92 99 101 195
Oaths of Allegiance and Abjuration 131 169 193 247 294
Ober-Ingelheim, Ger. 208
Oberkirsch, Jacob 207
 Susanna (Wetzel): see Andrae 207
Ochs, Appolonia (Hoffman) 279
 Ochs, Johann Adam 279
Odall, Charles 370
 Rig^{tt} 370
Odenwald, Ger. 300
Oerter, A. L. 152
Ogle, Alexander 331-332, 347
 Alexander, Jr. (s/o Alexander) 332
 Anne (Tasker) 32 328
 Benjamin (br/o Joseph) 310 331
 Benjamin (s/o Joseph) 114 329 331
 Eleanor 329
 Elizabeth: see Devilbiss 319 332
 George 329
 Jacob 331
 James 311 329
 Jane: see Link 332
 Jehu 327 329
 John (1649e-1684) 324
 John 196
 Joseph 17 18 62 130 138 147 196 198-199 213-214 249 251 252 293 311 319 324-331 333 335 336 340 341 352 366 374
 Joseph (s/o Benjamin) 310 331
 Joseph, Jr. (s/o Joseph) 329
 Judith: see Livers 331
 Luke of Eglingham 328
 Martha (d/o Alexander): see Wood 332
 Martha (w/o Alexander) 332
 Mary (Beatty) 332
 Mary (Biggs)
 Mary (Crawford) 324
 Mary (Cresap) 331
 Mary (d/o Alexander): see Cock 332 332
 Mary (d/o Joseph): see Butler, Brawner 324 329-331 374
 Prudence Drusilla (Biggs) 310 331
 Rebecca (Stilley) 114 331
 Rebecca (d/o Alexander): see Devilbiss 319 332
 Samuel, Gov. 18 19 32 270 293 328 340
 Sarah (Ogle) 329 331
 Sarah (Winters): see Henry 324 325 326 327 329
 Thomas of Del. 324
 Thomas (s/o Benj.) 331
 Thomas (s/o Joseph) 329
 William 329
Ogle County, Ill. 331
Ogles Ford 46 51 52 54 319 326-328 341 342 366
"Ogles Good Will" 248 249 253 254 256 362 366

Ogles Wagon Road 52 328
"Ogleton" 327
Ohio Company, The 20 44
Ohio County, W. Va. 108 332
Ohio River 21
Ohio Territory 67
Ohio Valley 20 209 310 331
Ohler, Elisabeth: see Biggs 311
Ohnselt, Friederich: see Unselt 182 377
Ohrndorff Road 249
Okely, John 153
Old Annapolis Road 228
Old Frederick Road 237 319
Old Swedes Church, Wilmington, Del. 109
Oldtown 14 20 36
Oley Hill, Pa. 127
Oliccin (Olacin, Oleakin) 30 36 53
"Olis" 258 259 274 275 278
Ondieta (Antietam) Creek 12
Onin, John 379
Onion, Stephen 16
"Onondrandy" 179
Opequon (Oppeckon), Va. 7 12 53 72 82 87 134 182 228 344
   Road to 51 155 181
Oppossumtown Pike 278, 296, 299
Orange County, Va. 75 108 344
Orchard, Bastian 378
Ordainment 132 141 142
Orme, John 370
Orr, Fridrich 286
Orrick, James 62 229 366
"Orricks Folly" 229 231 362 366
Osborn, Benjamin 371
"Otersom" 33 155 164 176-177 363 366
Otterbein Philip William 175 279
Ottersheim, Ger 176-177
Ott, Fridrich 286
"Otts Ego" 340
Overseers, Quaker 79
Overseers, Road 54-56 62 81 86 92 96 98 104 109 127 160 171 174 192 222 228 230-231 233 235 245 255 261 265-267 281 285 286 312 319 328 331 341
Overtaxation of Germans by Sheriff 272 274 275 277 279 283 288 289 292 299 328
Overton, Tenn. 105
Owen, Edward 370
   John 371
Owens, Lawrence 370
   Robert 371
   Thomas 340
Owens Creek 46 47 138 152 186 188 189 248 255 325 335 336
Owings, David 98
   Donald MacClure 27
   Hannah (Farquhar) 42 247
   James 98
   Jeremiah 98
   John 98
   Lydia: see Pyles 98
   Margaret: see Cherk 98
   Owen 98
   Rachel (Hook) 64 98
   Rachel: see Harper 98
   Robert 42 64 95 98 247 333

Owings (cont'd.)
   Thomas 98
"Oxford" 44

Paca, Ann Mary (Chew) 30 32
   Aquilla 332
   William, Gov. 30 32
Pack, Thomas 379
Pain, Frail: see Payne, Flayle 371
"Pains Delight" 40 94 95 362 366
Palatinate (Pfalz), Ger. 7 9 131
Palatines 303
"Palentine" 155 181 363 366
Palm, Johann Georg 218
Palmer, Joseph 75
   Thomas 70 75 366
Palmer Road 245
"Palmers Choice" 70 75 120 363 366
"Palmerzaner" 75 120
"Pangaiah Manor" 302
"Papan (Papaw, Paw Paw) Bottom" 43 47-49 54 237 338-340 363 366
"Paradise" 197 331
"Paradise Enlarged" 331
Parcons, John 371
Parish 348
Park Mills 80 89 90
Park Mills Road 89
Parker, Hugh 21 286
Parks, William 39
Parr, Arthur 231
   Elizabeth 231
   John 229 **231** 365
   John, Jr. 231
   Mark 231
   Mary 231
   Matthew 231
   Theme Ward 231
Parr Spring 231
"Parrs Range" 231
Parry, Thomas 374
   William 371
Parsons, Abel 90 **92**
"Parsons Delight" 20 345
"Partnership" (Campbell) 100 105 363 366
"Partnership" (Gittings) 90 92 93 362 366
"Partnership" (Gittings, Res.) 363 366
"Partnership" (Turner) 233
Passaic River, N. J. 135
Pastors, German 132
   Lutheran 132-140 160 211
   Reformed 132-133 146 148 149 151 208 211 290
Patapsco River 12 228
Patent Series 3 361
Patents 2 3 25 35
"Patience," ship 303
Paton Island 65
"Patricks Colt" 56 103 121 228
Patterson Creek, W. Va. 108
Patterson Creek Manor, Va. 73
Pattinger (see also Pittinger), Daniel 322
   Elizabeth 322
   John 322
Pattison, James 17
Pattison (Beattys-in), Agnes: see Beatty 375
Patuxent Hundred 129 234

Patuxent River 64 67 231 250 337 350
Paugh, Balser 378
Paul VI, Pope 255
Paul, Robert 374
"Pauls Boorock [Burg]" 181
Pawling, John 154 155
Payne Family 40
   Flayle, Sr. 55 56 94 222 366 369 371
   Flayle, Jr. 96 222
   John 96
   Peter 96
   Thomas 56 94
"Paynes Industry" 94
"Peace" (Ogle) 254 325-327 362 366
"Peace" (Hufner) 136
"Peace and Plenty" 20 175 256 326
"Peace and Quietness" 155 173 362 366
Pearce, John 226 367
   Sarah (Sprigg) 226
Pearre, Ann: see Mackey 92
   James 90 92
   Mary: see Buchanan 92
Peck, Jacob 178 180 295 341
Peck's fulling mill 281
Peger, Elizabeth (Miller) 287
Peitzel: see Beitzel 211
"Pell Mell" 74
Pelser, Christian 380
Penn, William 16
Pennington, Abraham 15 94-96 364
   Lee R. 15
   Mary 15
Pennsylvania 6 10 13-17 21 30 41 42 50 71 86 125 142 152 238 239 271 280 306 324 332
Pennsylvania Railroad 292
Pentz, Jacob: see Bentz 260
Pepinger, Daniel 110
Pequea Creek, Pa. 36
Percy, Hugh 276
Perkins, Isaac 87
Perkinson, Edward 323
   John 323
   Thomas 307 323
Perkiomen region, Pa. 71 74
Perry, Ann (Belt) Claggett Davis 83
   Benjamin 370
   Ignatius 83
   Samuel 83
   Sarah (Claggett) Davis 83
"Peru" 177
Peschof, Johann Hendrick: see Bishop 139
Peteate, John 87
Peters Road 89
Petersville 37 38 95 355
Petersville District 91
Petitions to Divide:
   County: see Prince George's Co. 349 370
   Parishes: see under Parish name
Petition for Road from Pyburn's to Nelson's 56 62 64 77 162 172 195 208 349
Pfaffenhofen, Württemberg 159
Pfauth (see Fout), Baltzer 139
   Eva Rosina 377
Pfautz Family 161
   Hans Michael 161
Pheby, William 371

Philadelphia, Pa. 16 18 19 41 133 142 153 154 185 190 193 194 264 290 330 332 355
   German Arrival Lists 131 154 161-163 175 185 193
   Lutheran congregations 133 143 144 151 152
   Reformed congregation 149 208
Philadelphia County, Pa. 133 217 335
Philip's Cabin 226
Philips, John 370
   Reubin 380
Phillips, Hugh 253
   John 103
   Nicholas 219
Philpot, Barton 37 222
Philyps, Vincent 251
"Pick Axe" 90 91 93 362 366
Pickapaw, Pickenpaw: see also Beckenbach:
   Caspar 270
   John Adam 266
   Peter 379
   Susanna (Sinn) 269
Pickler, Mark 350
Pietism 141-143 271
"Pile Hall" 55 223 225 226 362 366
Pile, Elizabeth: see Sprigg 226
   Richard, Dr. 226
Pillory 157 341
Pincher, Francis 87
Piney Branch 235 349
Piney Mountain 206
"Piney Neck" 33 186 218 219 363 366
Pipe Creek 42 127 250 326 327 331 333 335
"Pipe Creek Hill" 335
Pipe Creek Meeting, Quaker 88 236
"Pipe Meadow" 70 73 76 257 362 366
Piscataway Creek 7 41 348
Piscataway Hundred 255
Piscataway Indian village 7
Pittinger (Pattinger, Pepinger), Daniel 110 311 322 333 335
   Elisabeth (Biggs) 311 322 333
   John 322 333
Pittinger's Graveyard 335
"Plaisance," pink 288
Plater, George 27
"Pleasant Forest" 313
"Pleasant Garden" 16 354
"Pleasant Meddo" 229 234 235 363 366
"Pleasant Mount" 104
"Pleasant Plains" 354
"Pleasant Valley 229 232 363 366
"Pleasant," ship 202
Plummer Family 354
Plummer, Abiezer 233
   Abraham 235
   Anna: see Talbert 235
   Cassandra: see Ballenger 81 235
   Dorcus 236
   Eleanor (Walker) Poultney 234
   Elizabeth (Smith) 233
   Elizabeth (d/o Samuel): see Harris 235
   Elizabeth (w/o Philemon) 234
   George 233
   James 233

Plummer (cont'd.)
  Jerome 233
  John (s/o Thomas I) 233
  John (s/o Philemon) 234
  Joseph 234
  Martha (Lakin) 67
  Mary (d/o Thomas, Sr.) 236
  Mary (Tucker) 235
  Micajah (s/o Thomas I) 229 233 235 366
  Phebe 236
  Philemon (s/o Thomas I) 62 77 229 233 234 364
  Phoebe 233
  Priscilla (d/o Thomas I) 233
  Priscilla (d/o Thomas, Sr.) 236
  Rachel: see Harris 235
  Ruth (d/o Thomas, Sr.) 236
  Ruth (d/o Samuel): see Holland 235
  Samuel (s/o Thomas I) 229 233-236 365-367 371
  Samuel, Jr. 234-235
  Sarah (Miles) 234
  Sarah (Sollers) 234, 235
  Sarah (Ward) 235
  Sarah: see Janney 235
  Susanna (d/o Thomas, Sr.) 236
  Susanna (d/o Samuel): see Poultney 235
  Thomas I (of Anne Arundel Co.) 233
  Thomas, Sr. (s/o Thomas I) 233 235 236
  Thomas, Jr. 236
  Thomas (s/o Samuel) 234
  Yate 233
"Plummers Delight" (Micajah) 229 235 363 367
"Plummers Delight" (Samuel) 234 235 362 367
"Plummers Hunting Lot" 235 363 367
Poe, David 116
Point of Rocks, Md. 7 10 59-61 67 174 265 281 355
Point of Rocks Settlement 42 58-68 89 99
"Policy" 347
Polke, Charles 370
Pollett, James 370
Polson, Richard 369
Pongoffen, Magdalene (Devilbiss?): see Bancalf, Bannkauf 169 318
Poole, John 56 223 226-**227** 367 371
"Pools Delight" 223 227 363 367
Poole Jones Road 297
Poolesville 10
Poore, Abraham 378
"Poplar Bottom" 120 229 362 367
"Poplar Ridge" 240
Poplar Springs 56 233
"Poplar Thicket" 24 40 41 60 362 367
Porter, William 237 239 240
"Porters Addition" 237
Posey, Uzza 379
Potomac (Patowmack) Ferry 245
Potomac Hills 65
Potomac Hundred 129 337
Potomac River 7 9-11 13 14 16 21-23 29 35-38 40 42 46 50 51-57 59-62 73 84 85 89 94-97 105 142 156, 168 181 228 329 339
  North Branch 334

Potomac River (cont'd.)
  South Branch 15 74 310 334
Potomac River Road 56 97
Pottenger (Pottinger), John 339
  Robert 339 370
  Samuel 339 349
Potts, Ann L. 171
  Eleanor 171
  Richard 76 116
  William 370
Poulson, Neal 327
Poultney, Anthony 235
  Eleanor (Walker): see Plummer 234
  Susanna (Plummer) 235
Powell, John 28 196 369 371
  Peter 379
Powell Road 218
Powelson, Agnes: see Hedges 109
Praig, Peter 378
Prapps, Jacob 380
Prather, Aron 371
  Jonathan (Immigrant) 63
  Jonathan 56
  Martha (Sprigg) 63 226
  Thomas (Sr.) 63 226
  Thomas (Jr.) 21 28 42 60 62 **63-64** 66 68 147 222 334 355 367 370 371
Pred, Frederick 380
Prengle, Lawrence: see Brengel 262
Prerogative Court 3 31
Presbyterians 133
  Frederick 239
  Ministers 344
  Toms Creek 239
President of the United States in Congress Assembled 287
Presler (Bresler), Andreas 219
  Andrew (Jr.) 219
  Anna Christiana 219
  John 219 371
  John Valentine 219 371
  Peter 219 371
Pretender, The Young 251
"Pretty Sally" 56 228
"Prevention" 43 243 244 245 277 362 367
Prey: see Bray 375
  Henry 217
Price, Josiah 347
  Reese 347
  Sarah (Williams) 346 347
  Thomas 378
  William 347
Prick Run 66
Priestland Valley 252
Prince George's County 4 5 14 19 41 44 45 62 64 66 72 81 87 97 104 106 112 118 154 250 328 337
  Hundreds 129
  Petition to divide 77 83 119 162 224 370
Prince George's Parish, Church of England 97 348-350
  Petition to divide 28 64 68 77 84 86 91 94 156 162 188 193 199 206 217 219 224 225 227 236 245 260 263 264 272 274 278 280 282 285 350 **371**
Prince William County, Va. 86
Pringle (Brengel), Jacob 380

Proprietary Agent 27
Prospect Hall, Frederick 63
Protestant Dissenters 173 279 286 287 290 301 348
Protzman, Lorentz 214
　Maria Elisabeth 214
"Providence" 205 229 362 367
Providence Lutheran congregation, Pa. 133 143
Providence Meeting House, Quaker 87
Provincial Convention 22
Prunder: see Brunner 165 271
Purchasers of first Frederick Luth. Church Book 139
Purchasers of "Taskers Chance," 1737: 157-258 263 264 268
Pyburn (Pyborn), Benjamin 62
　John 55 62 64 75 76 97 162 208 349 369 371
　John, Jr. 371
Pyle (see also Pile), Major 21
Pyles, Lydia (Owings) 98

Quaker Meetings:
　Bush Creek 88 236
　Chester Quarterly 81 85
　Cold Spring 82
　Fairfax 87
　Hopewell 82 87
　Monocacy 45 54 79-85 87-88 236
　New Garden 66 81 84
　Nottingham 87
　Pipe Creek 88 236
　Providence 87
Quaker Meeting House, Monocacy 54 82 83 85 87 88 166
Quakers 13 45 54 79-88 96 165 174 196 233 235 348
　Monocacy Settlement 58 79-89 99
　Pennsylvania 84 86
　Virginia 82 86-87
Quattaro (Monocacy) River 7 9
"Queen Anne's Manor" 302
Queer, Henry 378
Quickel, John 191
Quitopahilla Settlement, Pa. 135
Quitrents 2 4 16 23 35 117 154 156 161 195 209-210 260 265 279 292 295 299 302 328
Quynn Orchard Road 75

Radford, John 40 75 80 81 364 365
Raker, William L. 175
"Ramble" 60 63 64 66 362 367
"Rams Horn" 15 33 244 275 363 367
Ramsburg (Ramsberger Ransberger):
　Anna Elisabeth (Devilbiss) 319
　Anna Maria (Brunner) 273 293
　Catharina Elisabetha: see Stoner 291, 293
　Catharina (Stickley) 293
　Catharina (w/o Elias) 293
　Elias 293
　Elizabeth (Brunner) 273
　Elisabeth (Devilbiss) 293
　Henry 293 319
　Jacob 293 319

Ramsburg (cont'd.)
　John 268, 293
　Margaret: see Myer 293
　Maria Catharina (Brunner) 271-272 291
　Stephen 125 126 128 130 150 159 160 165 167 169 173 175 179 180 258-260 267 270 272 277 279 281 283 287-289 291-296 299 309 310 328 330 373 379
　Susanna (Devilbiss) 293 319
Ramsey, Nathaniel 287
"Ramseys Rest" 254
Ranck, Dorothy 150
　James 150
Ranney, F. Garner 350
Ransberger: see also Ramsburg
　Adam 379
　George 379
Ransom, Richard 371
Raritan area, N. J. 125 182 309
　Lutheran congregation 182
Ratcliffe, Robert 369
Rauch, Christian Henry 148 149
Rauhzahn (see Routzahn), Johan Ludwig 301
Rausch, Anna Eliesabetha 194 376
　Michael 194 376
Rawlins, Daniel 328
Rawllings, (?) 370
Ray, Joseph 379
　Luke 371
　William 89 349 370
Raymer, Michael 72 162 353 379
Rays Town 322
Read (Reed), Henry 315 323
　Mary 315 323
　James 315, 318, 323
Reader, Church of England 352
Reading, Pa. 377
Reading Twp. (Hunterdon Co.), N. J. 120
Readington, N. J. 122
Reasling: see Rössel Reass, Adam 180
Reass, Adam 180
Rebstock, Anna Marg: see Traut, Staley 177
Receiver General 4 27 35
Red Clay Creek, Del. 106
Redemptionism 153
Reed, James 380
　Patrick 241
　Samuel 327
Reel's Mill 15
Reesling: see Rössel
Reformed Religion, German 185
Reformed Pastors 132-133 146 148 149 151 208 211 290
"Refuses" 95-97 363 367
Regensberger, John Steven 291
Rehssele, Mateus (see Rössel) 170
Reich Family 75
Reichel, W. C. 142 152
Reichs Ford Road 75
Reihen, Kraichgau, Ger. 159
Reinecke, E. W. 176
Reislin (Reisling: see Rössel), Matthew 137 169 179 193 217
Reisman, Barbara (Weber) 172
　Johannes 146 172
Reisner (Reusner, Risenar, Risner, Risoner):

Reisner (cont'd.):
  Anna Eliesabetha 194 376
  Catharina 194
  Catharina Barbara: see Six 194 220 374
  (Hans) Michael 157 168 172 185-187
    189-191 193-196 198 209 212 277 290
    317 324 327 335 343 365 367 372 374
    376
  Johann Martin 195
  Nicholas [sic] 292
  Susanna Margareta 195
Reitzmann, Johannes 146
Religion, Importance of, to Germans 131
"Remainder" 39
Remsberg, George 41
"Remsbergs Lot" 41
Remscheid, Ger. 133
Rent Roll Keeper 4
Rent Rolls 3 4 118 183 260 266 299-300
Repetti, W. C. 253
Repp, C. 99
Resel (see Rössel), Matthew 140
"Resurvey on Addition to Hazel Thicket" 160
"Resurvey on Anchor and Hope" 172
"Resurvey on Arnolds Delight" 200
"Resurvey on Beauty" 184
"Resurvey on Bill's Meadow" 319
"Resurvey on Breeches" 99
"Resurvey on Chevy Chase" 300
"Resurvey on Christians Choyce" 99 167
"Resurvey on Coopers Point" 287
"Resurvey on Den of Wolves" 202
"Resurvey on Dispute" 233
"Resurvey on Exchange" 347
"Resurvey on Frankford" 167
"Resurvey on Good Luck" 174
"Resurvey on Great Desire" 174
"Resurvey on Hunters Delight" 174
"Resurvey on John and Sarah" 66
"Resurvey on Johnsons Level" 354
"Resurvey on Leonards Good Luck" 354
"Resurvey on Leonards Range" 319
"Resurvey on Lillys Lot" 48 49 254 343
"Resurvey on Long Mile and Low Mill" 239
"Resurvey on Meadow" 72
"Resurvey on Middle Plantation" 121
"Resurvey on Millers Chance" 287
"Resurvey on Mistaken Friend" 177
"Resurvey on Ogles Good Will" 256
"Resurvey on Onondrandy" 179
"Resurvey on Othersum" 178
"Resurvey on Part of Good Neighbor" 313
"Resurvey on Partnership" 44
"Resurvey on Paw Paw Bottom" 48 49 340 342 343
"Resurvey on Pleasant Valley" 232
"Resurvey on Poplar Bottom" 121
"Resurvey on Rams Horn" 276
"Resurvey on Sixth Dividend" 335
"Resurvey on Slate Ridge" 207
"Resurvey on Spring Garden" 105
"Resurvey on Teernoch" 48 111
"Resurvey on Toms Gift" 347
"Resurvey on Trura" 335
"Resurvey on Whiskey Alley" 224 245
Resurveys in general 356-357

Retreat Road 125
Reusner: see Reisner 376
Reuz, Magdalena 152
  Matthias (Matthew) 147 148 152 153 334
Revolution, American 15 22 31 62 63 101
  114 119 122 152 158 261 277-278 310
  320 331 332 348
Revolution, English (Glorious) 2 27 247 348
Revolution, French 255
Reynolds, Hugh 287 288
  James 380
  Thomas, Jr. 380
Reynolds Ford 290
Reynolds' Mill, Hugh 288
Rhoar, Rudolph 378
Rhodes (Rhods, Road, Roads, Rod, Roed, Roht, Roodt, Roth, Rothers, Rothes, Rotten, Rotts, etc.),
  Anna Eve (Roed) 274
  Catharina (w/o Henry Roed) 274 275
  Catharina (d/o Henry Roed) 274
  Henry 33 205 258 259 270 274-278 286 288 292 301 373
  William (Roed) 274
Rice, Hugh 371
  Millard M. 6 33 50 65 86 88 102 128 138 167 353
  Owen 334
  William 116 128
"Rich Bottom" 43 175 186 220 363 367
"Rich Hills" 229 234 235 363 367
"Rich Level" (Digges) 250
"Rich Level" (Brunner) 258 259 269 272 273 300
"Rich Thicket" 20
"Richard and Elizabeth" 66
Richards, Catherine (Carmack) 104
  Daniel 122 380
  John 87
  Joseph 380
  Mary (Carmack) 104
  Stephen 103 105 380
  Thomas 28
"Richards Hunting Ground" 42 100 363 367
Richardson, Ann (Davis): see Thompson 83
  Richard 87
  Thomas 89
  William 83
Richter, Christian 152
Ridge, Benjamin 380
Rieger, Johann Bartholomew 133 140 141 149 171 173 207-208
Riemensberger (see Remsberg), Helena Elisabeth 291
  Jacob Wolfgang 291
  Johann Georg 291
  Sebastian Henrich 291
Rien, Darby: see Ryan 369
Riesly (see also Rössel), Matthias 249
Riesslie, Anna Barbara: see Rössel, Hoffman 146
Riester, Anna Otilia: see Getzendanner 166
Rieth, Anna Margaret: see Roseen 152
Right, Henry 116 129
  James: see Wright 369
"Right and Good Reason" 233
Rightmyer, Nelson Waite 76

Rights (Warrants) 2 41
Rimmen, James 371
Rinehart Family 99
Ringer, Johann Matthias 157 160 261 262
   Maria Magdalena "Helena" (Nischicker) Schneider 157
Ripeligh, John 378
Risenar (Risner, Risoner), Michael (see also Reisner) 191 196 343
Risling: see Rössel
Ritchie, Albert, Dr. 84 123
   Albert, Gov. 123
   Ann (Barnhold) 123
   Betsy Harrison (Maulsby) 63
   Catherine Lackland (Davis) 84 123
   John (s/o William) 123
   John, Judge 63
   Mary (Middagh) 123
   William 123
Ritchey, Isaac
Ritter, George 9
River Road 56 97
Rivers and Creeks, Frederick County 46
Roach, Hannah Benner 159
Road (Roads), Adam 380
   John 379
Road Junctions 57
Road Petitions 335
Roads in 1743: 50-57
   Cartledges Old Road 13 51 57 206 237 248 324 326 327
   Conewago-Monocacy 50
   Creagerstown-Woodsboro 47 48 340
   Friend's Mill, To Israel 55 222 225 228
   German Monocacy 9 36 51-55 57 131 136 153 155 159-160 166-169 181 185 186 189 192 202 208 221 248 257 312 319 324 326 338
   Manor Monocacy 9 36 51-55 57 104 142 228 309 311 312 319 325 326 328 339
   Monocacy-Annapolis 36 51 56 57 102 103 120 127 228-230 233
   Monocacy-Antietam 51 55 57 94 222 223 225
   Monocacy-Shenandoah Mtn. 64 86 222
   Monocacy Ferry-Ballengers Branch 53
   Opequon, To 51 155 181
   Potomac River 56
   Stull's Mill, To John 51 55-57 155
   Touchstone's, Via Richard 61 92 172 222-223 225 346
   Wilson's, To/From Robert 54 237 238 325 326 339
Roberts, John 335 369
   William 327 330 335
Robin, Charles 241
Robinson, Charles 240
   George 87
Rock Creek 114 160 370
Rock Creek Chapel 337
Rock Creek Hundred 129 349
Rock Creek Parish 349
Rock Hall 7 59
"Rock Land" 125
Rockingham County, Va. 215
Rockville 337 349
"Rocky Creek" 24 37 39 79 118-121 123

"Rocky Creek" (cont'd.) 155 161 162 164 199-201 206 257 269 362 367
Rocky Ridge 324-326 328
Rocky Ridge Road 333
Rocky Ridge settlement 58 324-336
Rocky Springs 173 174 181
"Rocky Springs" 175 176 256
Rocky Springs area 274
Rod: see Rhodes, Roht
Roddy, John A. 250
Roddy Road 188
Rodebaugh, Christian 307, 322
   Elisabeth 322
"Rods Purchase" 275
Roed: see Rhodes, Roht
Roelof Johnsons Kill, N. Y. 117
Rohrbach, Kraichgau, Ger. 161 277
Roht (see also Rhodes, etc.), Henry 33 205 258 259 270 274-278 286 288 292 301 373
Rolfe, John 71
Römer, Johann Michael 146 278
Roops Branch 14
"Rose Garden" 258 259 278
"Rose Hill" 278
Roseen, Anna Margaret (Rieth) 152
   Sven 152
Rosensteel, Joseph 237
Rosier, M. 10 11
Ross, Alexander 86 87
   Henry 380
   John 17
Rosson, Charles 369 371
Rössel (Reasling, Reesling, Rehssele, Reislin, Reisling, Resel, Riesslie, Risling, Rüssel):
   Anna Barbara (see also Hoffmann) 146 188 202 376
   Catharina Barbara 193 317 376
   Maria Barbara 376
   Matthias (Matthew) 137 139 140 146 169 170 179 188 193 202 206 217 317 318 375 376
Roth (Rothers, Rothes, Rotten, Rotts): see Rhodes, Roht
Rothenstein, Switzerland 269
Rotterdam, Holland 159 164 168 202 208 268 269
"Round Meadow" 20 275
Round Top 248
Routzahn (Rauhzahn), H. 31
   J. L. 31
   Johann Ludwig 301
Rouzer, Martin 327
Row, John 195
   Michael 241
Roxell, David 380
Roy Remsburg Road 55 225
Royal, John 369
Royal Period (1689-1715) 2 27 348
"Royenton Plains" 311 325 333 362 367
Rudiesielle, Philipp 377
   Susanna (Beyer) 374 377
Ruddle, Cornelius 296
   John, Jr. 296
Rudolph, Carl 144 145 329
Rue's Ford 232

Rule, Clement 378
Rümer, Johann Stephen 291
Runckel, William 176
Rundt, Charles Godfrey 152
Runner, Jacob: see Brunner 140
Rupp, I. Daniel 154 161 297
Rusner, Michael: see Reisner 196
Rüssel, Catarina Barbara: see Rössel 193 376
Ryan, Darby 103 229 **230** 231 285 364 369
   Isabella (Hussey) 230

Sabillasville 214 330
Saddelhausen, Fränckischen 299
Saen, Henrick: see Sinn 268
St. Alban's Masonic Lodge 65
"St. Andrew Galley," ship 211
St. Anne's Church, Annapolis 350
St. Anne's Parish 355
St. Anthony's Church 57
"St. Elizabeth" 33 186 202 210 363 367
St. Gallen, Switzerland 149 172
Saint James, Md. 352
St. John's Ev. Luth. Church, Creagerstown 47
St. John's Parish 348
St. Joseph's Church, Emmitsburg 255
St. Joseph's College 240 255
St. Joseph's Province 255
St. Mary Anne Parish 103
St. Mary Newington, London 39
St. Mary's County, Md. 75 253 298
"St. Mary's Increase" 256
St. Paul's Cathedral, London 39
St. Paul's Church, Rock Creek Parish 349
St. Stephen's Parish 219
St. Sulpice Parish, Paris 255
Saint Vincent de Paul 255
Salcey Forest, Engl. 159
Salem, N. C. 149
Salem County, N. J. 69 107
Salion, Md. 71
Salisbury Plains 347
Saltner, George: see Soldner 197 209
Sams Creek 5 46 51 92 99-101 352
   Area 102
"Samuel," ship 205 276 288 294
Sand Flat 236
Sanders, J. Clarke 209, 215
Sandusky Expedition 331
"Sandy Hook" 94
Sandy Run 202
"Sandy Run" 186 192 363 367
"Sandy Spring" 307
"Saplin Ridge" 114 155 363 367
Saur, Anna Benedictina: see Sturm 280
   Maria: see Storm 280
Savannah, Ga. 141
Savannah River, S. C. 36
Sawantaeny 13
Saylor, R. 99
Scarwill, William, Jr: see Sherril 369
Schaaf (Schaff), Ann (Beatty) 119
   Caspar 119 378
Schäffer (see also Shaver), Anna (Schaub) 164 180 377
Schaff Library, Philip, Lancaster 171

Schainbach, Ger. 133
Schaiteler, Schäiteler (see also Scheidler),
   Johann Georg 140 297 377
   Margaretha (Neff) 297 377
Schantz, Franklin J. F. 1234 135 194
Scharf, Johann Thomas 193 284 306
Schaub (see also Shoup),
   Peter 164 296 377
Schaum, Johann Helfrich 151
Scheidler (Schaiteler), George 140 297
Schell, Catherine A. 31
Scherer, Augustus 376
"Schiefferstadt" 258 259 272 273
Schildknecht, Calvin E. 135 140
Schifferstadt, Ger. 165 269 273 280
Schlatter, Michael 145 148-151 176 270 281 292 352
   Diary 149
Schleswig 144
Schley, Anna Maria (Getzendanner) 167
   Eva Catharine: see Bier 266
   Jacob 116 151
   John Thomas 144 150 151 265 266 270 290 295 378
   Maria Anna: see Steiner 290
   Nicholas 262
   Thomas Jr. 167
   Winfield Scott, Adm. 41
Schleydorn, Henry 143
"Schleys Discovery" 245
Schlimm, Elisabetha Magdalena: see Williar 214
Schlotterdam, N. J. 135
Schmidt, Anna Christina (w/o Joh. Jost) 264
   Caspar 22 214 330
   Christina (d/o Caspar) 330
   Christina (w/o Caspar) 214 330
   Elisabetha Magdalen 264
   "Empiric" 145
   Eva Rosina (Fout) 161 190 377
   Johannes 146
   Johann Jost (see also Smith) 264 266 267 269 280 292 301 372
   Johann Peter 161 187-190 372 377
   Johann Peter, Jr. 190
   Magdalena 284
   Maria Margaretha 190
   Peter (s/o Joh. Jost) 264
Schmied, Johann Christoph 146
Schmitt, Johann Peder 268
   Johann Philippus 262
Schneider, Johann Jacob 157
   Maria Magdalena "Helena" (Nischicker): see Ringer 157
Schnell, Johann Leonard 52 54 141 142 147 148 183 188-189 207 211 213 285 286 329
Schoharie, N.Y. 135 218 219
Scholl, Daniel 162
Schönteler [sic; see Schaiteler], Joh. Georg 297
Schreiber, Andreas 41
Schreyer, Catharina 376
   Joh. Georg 196
Schrier, John 170

Schriver, Valentine 167
Schryack, Johannes 146
Schuchmann, Heinz 288
Schultz, Edward T. 47 152 173
Schultz, Johannes Christian 133 134 198
Schulze, Pastor(?) 142
Schumacher, Daniel 279
  Elizabeth (Hoffman) 279
  Eva 279
  Maria Apollonia 279
  Peter 279
Schwarzenau, Wittgenstein, Ger. 271
Schweickert, Philipp 374
  Susanna 374
Schweinhardt: see also Swinehart:
  Anna Margaretha 157 158
  Anna Maria 158 294
  Eliesabetha [sic] 377
  Elisabetha: see Mayhew 158
  Esther (Neff) 158
  Gabriel 113 146 157 158 376
  Johann Georg 33 53 72 122 139 140 146 154-158 160 161 217 274 279 284 294 365 366 371 372 374-376
  Johann Peter 154 161 374
  Magdalena 154 204 375 377
  Margreta 276
  Maria Eliesabetha 274 376
  Susanna 158 376
Schweitzer, Anna Catharina: see Berg 314
Schwenksville, Pa. 71
Scidmore, Joseph 371
Scott Road 240
Scott, (?) 370
"Scythe" 178
Seamer, George 378
Sears Road, Ira 91
Sechs: see also Six:
  Heinrich 146
  Johann 146
"Second Choice" 177-178
Secretary of State, U. S. 59
Selby, William Magruder 370
Sellers, Maria Magdalena: see Brunner 272
Seltzer Family 135
Seminole Wars 33
Senantona (Shenandoah) River 10
Seneca County, Ohio 111
Seneca Creek (Run) 339 350 352
Seneca Indians 7 13
Seton, Elizabeth Ann Bayley 255
Settlements:
  Carroll Creek 58 69-78 99
  Catholics 58 247-256
  Catoctin Valley 58 222-227
  "Dulany's Lot" 58 115-129
  Flat Run (Emmitsburg) 58 237-242
  Hedges Family 58 106-114
  Lower German 58 153-184
  Mid-Monocacy 58 337-347
  Middletown Area 58 243-246
  "Monocacy Manor" 58 302-323
  New Market Area 58 228-236
  Point of Rocks 58-68
  Quaker 58 79-88
  Rocky Ridge 58 324-336
  Sugar Loaf 58 89-93 99

Settlements (cont'd.)
  "Taskers Chance" 58 257-301
  Upper German 58 153 185-221
  Upper Linganore 58 99-105
  Upper Potomac 58 94-98
Settlers, English & German contrasted 131
Sex (Sexe), Henry (Henrik): see Six 140 146
Sexton, George 310
's Gravenhage (The Hague) 150 270
Shacklett, Benjamin 56
Shafer, George H. 267
  Peter (1728-1792) 180
  Rosina (Loy) 180
Shaffer, Nicholas 178
  Peter 292
Shannandow (Shenandoah) River 87
Shank's Mill 293
Sharp, Mathews 379
  Paul 378
Sharpe, Gov. Horatio 21 22 168 308 329 341
  John 21
Sharpsburg 14 171 347 352
Sharrough, Jacob 335
Shaub: see Shoup
Shaver, Anna (Shoup, Schaub) 164 165 180-181 376 377
  Catharine 181
  Christian 181
  David 181
  Henry 181
  Jacob 181
  Martin 181
  Moses 181
  Peter 155 157 164 180-181 296 366 373 377 379
  Peter, Jr. 181
  Rosina (Loy) 296
"Shavers Bad Luck" 181
Shaves, Richard 370
Shawan (Shuano, Shunto) Town 14 20 30 36
Shawkin, Daniel 379
Shawnee Indians 7 36 87 334
Sheckles, Ann: see Lakin
Sheen, Caspar 262
Shelby, Evan, Jr. 345
Shelhorse, Frances Miller 287
Shell, Charles 267 378
Shellman, John 162, 163
  Margaret (Fout) 162
Shelton, Charls 371
  John 371
Shenandoah County, Va. 297
Shenandoah (South) Mountain 9 50 55 56 97 222 225 245
Shenandoah River 9 10 53 87
  North Fork 9 296
  South Fork 9
Shenandoah Valley 14 71
Shephard, William 349
Shepherd, Elizabeth (van Metre) 72 74
  Thomas 74
  William, Sr. 369 371
  William, Jr. 369 371
Shepherdstown, W. Va. 74 245
Sheredine, Thomas 328
Sherlock, John 369

Sherril, William, Sr. 369
   William, Jr. 369
Shessler, Adam 378
"Shettle" 33 244 245 363 367
Shields, William 239 240 254
"Shields Adventure" 254
Ship Arrival Lists 131 150 156
Ships transporting German immigrants:
   "Adventure" 284
   "Allen" 165 270
   "Brittania" 208
   "Catherine" (snow) 141
   "Charming Nancy" 284
   "Dragon" 193 195
   "Eastern Branch" 35
   "Elizabeth" 214 262 277 283 294
   "Hope" 283
   "John and William" 190
   "Johnson Galley" 187 268
   "Lowther" (snow) 168
   "Loyal Judith" 198
   "Mercury" 298
   "Mortonhouse" 164 269 280 298
   "Patience" 303
   "Plaisance" (pink) 288
   "Pleasant" 202
   "St. Andrew Galley" 211
   "Samuel" 205 276 288 2924
   "Thistle of Glasgow" 133 159 282
Shoab (see also Shoup), George 379
   Martin, Jr. 379
Shoaf, George 379
Shoarwell, William: see Sherril 369
Shoemaker (Shewmaker), George 310
   Simon 380
"Shoemakers Choice" 33 155 169 170 293 363 367
Shookstown 56 57 165 173
Shorb, Anna Maria (Staley): see Shoup and/or Hildebrand 178
Short, David 380
Short Creek, W. Va. 310
Shortacer: see Shydacker 192
"Shot Proof" 347
Shoup (Schaub, Shaub, Shoab, Shorb):
   Anna: see Shaver 164 165 180 376 377
   Anna Catharina: see Kemp 175
   Anna Maria (Staley): see Hildebrand 165 178
   Catharine: see Staley 165
   Charlotte Amalie (Loy) 296
   Christian (s/o Martin, Sr.) 165
   Christian (s/o Martin, Jr.) 165
   Elizabeth 165
   George (s/o Martin, Jr.) 165
   Hans Georg (s/o Martin, Sr.) 164 165 379
   Maria Sophia (Kemp) 165 175
   Martin, Sr. 33 54 155 **164** 165 175 177 180 264 280 269 363 366 372 376
   Martin, Jr. 164 165 175 379
   Mary 165
   Peter 165
   Samuel 165
   Sebastian 151
   Soffia (d/o Martin, Jr.) 165
   Susanna 165
Shover, Adam 322

Shover (cont'd.)
   Henry 378
   Peter 322
   Simon 307 322 380
Shrier, George 350
   Jacob 350
   John 140 350
   Nicholas 350
Shriner, Edward A. 123
Shrioner, Matthias 378
   Valentine 378
Shriver, Andrew 350
   Lutwick 350
Shull, Catharine [Barbara] (Fout) 163
Shunto town (see also Shawan) 20
Shurel, Adam 296
Shutter, Christian 323
Shydacker, Valentine 192
Sickler, Henry 380
Sigler, Daniel 227
Silver, John 307 323
   Susannah 323
"Silver Fancy" 30 241 242
Silver Mines 7 10
Silver Run 194
Sim (Sinn?), Henry 379
Sim, Col. Joseph 31 116
Simmons, James H. 89
Simon, Joh. Jacob 374
Simpson, John 98
Sing, Daniel 103
Sinn (Saen), Anna 268
   Catharine 268
   Heinrich (Henry) 139 187 189 190 199 258 259 **268** 269 272 301 372 374 376 377 379
   Jacob Matthais 190 268 376
   Jacob 269
   Margaret: see Cronin 269
   Maria Barbara ("Bärbel"): see Michael 268 269
   Maria Catharina: see Fout 268 269
   Philip Henry 268 269
   Susanna: see Pickenpaw, Beckenbach 268 269 374
Sinsheim, Ger. 156 172 207-208 288 377
Sisters of Charity 255
Six (Sechs, Sex, Sexe), Adam 219, 220
   Anna Christina (Theis) 218
   Catharina: see Davis 219
   Catharine (Bonnett) 215
   Catharina Barbara (Reisner) 220
   Christina Elisabetha: see Jesserang 219
   Conrad 219
   Elisabeth (Greintsch) 219
   Gertraud 219
   Henry (Heinrich) 33 53 140 146 186 **218-220** 366 373
   Henry, Jr. 219
   John (Johann) 146 196 215 219
   Philip 219
"Six Brothers" 311
Six's Bridge 310
Sixt, Johann Philipp 218
Skidmore, John 224
"Skie Thorn" 19
Skinn, George 378

Skippack, Pa. 132 133 211
Skipton, Yorkshire 15
"Skipton on Creaven" 19
Skordas, Gust 3
Slade, William 232
Slate Quarry Road 234
"Slate Ridge" 56 206 248 249 253 327 362 367
Slaves 52 94 293 298
Sley (see also Schley), Jacob 151
Slim, Simon 378
Sly, Nicholas 262
"Small Hope" 19 200
Smallwood, Gen. William 312
Smith, Adam 380
   Andrew 380
   C. Henry 297
   Christian 241 255 299 316 380
   Christina 219
   Clement 370
   Daniel 379
   E. 167
   Eleanor: see Addison 31 32
   Elizabeth: see Plummer 233
   George 219
   Henry 378
   Jacob 167 292 379
   James 258-260 297-298 355
   Johannes 323
   John 54 167 292 370 379
   John Christian 304 307 316 323
   Johann Jost (Joseph) 258-260 264 266 267 269 280 289 292 301 371 372
   Leonard 86
   Lucy: see Brooke 31
   Peter 189 371
   Philip 277 307 316 319 323 380
   Rachel (Hall) 31
   Rebecca: see Dulany 31 32
   Richard 243
   Samuel 326
   Walter 31 32
   William 16 17 323 380
   William (s/o Philip) 316 319
Smiths Branch, Henry 54 104
"Smiths Choice" 16
"Smiths Lot" 138-139 149 186 195 212 363 367
Smithburg 329
"Smithfield" 243
Smoot (Smoote), John 370 371 379
Snider, Conrad 378
   George 378
   John 44
   Michael 378
   William 116
Snoke, Henry 380
"Snow Hill Manor" 302
Snowdagle, Jacob 378
Snowden, Elizabeth: see Elder 254
   John 342
   Ranier 71
   Richard 40
   Samuel 342
   Sarah: see Hook 65 66
   Thomas 342
Soldiers' Pay Certificates 320

Soldner, Hans Georg 146 193 195-197 209 373
Sollers, Sarah: see Plummer 234
"Solomons Flower" 233
"Solomon's Contrivance and Ned's Study" 233
Solway Firth, Engl. 168
Somerset Co., N.J. 182 309
Sommer, Peter Nicholas 218
Sonpower, Michael 379
Sopus: see Kingston (Esopus), N.Y. 117 334
Souder, Philip 379
Sourin, Edward 256
South Branch, Potomac River 15 74 310 334
South Fork, Shenandoah River 9
South Carolina 119 152 158
South Mountain 5 7 9 10 50 54 55 94 95 97 98 147 222 225 226 330 334 335
Southernfield, John 369
Spach: see Spuch 210
Spangenberg, August Gottlieb (Brother Joseph) 114 147 148 152 188 213 329 334
Spangler, Edward W. 135
   Matthias 378
Spanish Succession, War of 130
Sparks, Joseph 333
   Mary 333
   Matthew 336
   Solomon 103
Spaulding, Catherine: see Elder 254
   Elizabeth: see Elder 254
Speculators, Land 23 41-43 72 249
Spengel, Georg 376
   Johanna 376
Spengler Family 135
   Margaret Salome (Dünckel) 135
Speyer, Ger. 165 269
Spirgin, William 371
Spoolsville, Md. 244 245
Spough, Adam: see Spuch 53
Sprigg, Ann: see Carroll 226
   Ann: see Gittings 226
   E. 370
   Edward 30 225, 226
   Edward (s/o Thos., Jr.) 226
   Eleanor: see Hilleary, Nuthall 226
   Eleanor: see Wright 226
   Elizabeth (Pile) 226
   Elizabeth: see Wade 226
   Margaret (Mariarte) 226
   Margaret: see King 226
   Martha: see Prather 63 226
   Mary: see Stockett 226
   Mr. 369
   Osborn 40 43 48 55 93 223 225-227 340 365
   Osborn (s/o Thomas, Jr.) 226
   Priscilla: see Crabb 226
   Priscilla (Gittings) 93
   Richard 55 223 225
   Samuel, Gov. 226
   Sarah: see Pearce 226
   Sprigg, Richard 366
   T. 370
   Thomas 63 226
   Thomas, Jr. 226

Sprigg (cont'd.)
　Thomas III 226
　William (Judge, Northwest Ter.) 226
Spring City, Pa. 377
"Spring Garden" (Abington) 24 34 40 105
　116 123-126 128 303 362 367
"Spring Garden" (Richards) 20 76 103 105
"Spring Plain" 24 43 313 363 367
Springer, Charles 304 313 323 380
　Courtland B. 14
　Jacob 379
　Rebecca: see Stilley 114
　Ruth L. 14
Spuch (Spough), Adam 53 186 202 203 209
　210 365 367 373
　Maria Catrina 210
Spurgeon (Spirgin, Spurgen, Spurgin), James
　225 369 371
　William 225 369
Squatters 5 23 192
Stabler, William 88
Stahely: see Staley
Stahl (Stall), Johann Jacob 176
Stalcop, Catharine 107
　Catharine (Erickson) 107
　John 107
Staley (Stahely, Stähli, Ställy, Steeli,
　Steheli, Stehli, Stehly, Steli, Stelly):
　Anna Barbara 178
　Anna Margaretha (Rebstock) Traut
　　177-179 275
　Anna Maria: see Shoup, Hildebrand 165
　　178
　Catharine (Shoup) 165
　Henry (s/o Hans Jacob the Younger) 178
　Henry (s/o Jacob) 178
　Jacob 33 53 140 155 157 164 170 **175-
　　179** 218 274 275 364 366 367 373
　　379
　(Hans) Jacob the Younger 175 178 179
　Jacob, Jr. (s/o Jacob) 178
　Jacob (s/o Melchior) 179
　Joseph 178
　Melchior 33 53 155 **175-176** 178-179 366
　　379
　Philippena: see Stull, Getzendanner 167
　　170 178-179
　Susanna Barbara 179
Staley's Gap 178
"Staleys Good Luck" 179
"Staleys New Addition" 178
Stall, Adam: see Stull 140 170
Stall (Stahl), Melichor: see Staley, Melchior
　175
Ställy, Hans Jacob 176
Stamp Act, 1765 Repudiation of 122 343
Staub, Thomas 202
Staudernheim, Ger. 276
Stauffer (Stauffort), Daniel 129
Stauffer Road 117 123 129
Steel, Hugh 303
Steeli, Jacob 176
Steelman, John Hance 14 45
Steheli, Melcher 176
Stehli, Jacob 176
Steiner, Conrad (Pfr.) 314
　Jacob (1731 arrival) 290

Steiner (cont'd.)
　Jacob (s/o Joh. Conrad) 290
　Johann Conrad 269 290
　Maria Anna (Schley) 290
Steinsfurt, Ger. 288
Steinweiler, Ger. 128 277
Stein's Alley, Mrs. 266
Steli, Jacob 176
Stelle, Jacob: see Stilley 114
Stelly, Jacob 176
Stentz, Heinrich 197, 198
Stephen, Lee 370
Stern, Jacob: see Storm, Jacob 281
Stevens, Jacob 380
Stevens(on), Edward 42
Stewart (Steuart), Adam 37
　George, Dr. 44 174 365 366
　Jennie C. 294
Stickle, Valentine 262
Stickley, Catharina: see Ramsburg 293
Stilley (Stilly), Estelle: see Kennedy 114
　Mary: see Biggs 309
　Mary: see Hedges 109 114
　Mary (w/o Peter) 114
　Jacob 109 114
　Jacob (s/o Peter) 114
　John 114
　Peter 53 107 110 114 155 331 367 379
　Peter, Jr. 114 155
　Rebecca: see Ogle 114 331
　Rebecca (Springer) 114
Stimton, Soll. 371
Stiverson, Gregory A. 302, 305
Stockett, Mary (Sprigg) 226
　Thomas 226
Stoddard, Capt. John 161
Stoddart, Thomas 328 354
Stoddert, James 39 161 367
　John 39 118 206
Stoll (see also Stull), Adam 139 150
Stoner, Anna: see Getzendanner 167 290
　291
　Anna Barbara (Thomas) 283 291
　Benedict 290 291 296
　Catharina Elisabetha (Ramsburg) 291 293
　Christian 340
　David 99
　Elisabeth (Link) 291
　Henry 260 289-291
　Jacob 73 193 198 258-260 286 **289-292**
　　301 311 371 372 378
　Jacob, Jr. 290
　John 112 193 260 290 291 293 300 379
　Magdalin 290
　Maria Sibylla (Loy) 291, 296
Stoner's Ford 312
"Stoners Luck" 290
"Stones Enough" 275
Stonestreet, Edward 370
　Peter 370
　Thomas 370
"Stoney Hill" 19 169 180 293
"Stoney Hills" (Moser) 197
"Stoney Hive" 90 92 363 367
"Stoney Land" 246
Storm (Sterm); see also Sturm:
　Anna Elizabeth (d/o Jacob): see Kyle 281

Storm (cont'd.)
  Anna Maria I (d/o Jacob): see Brunner
  Anna Maria II (d/o Jacob): see Tofler 281
  Barbara (Hoffman) 279
  Catharina 281
  Charlotta 281
  Christian (Sturm) 280
  Christina 280 281
  Jacob 140 150 165 170 258-260 264 269 270 273 277 279 280-281 283 298 299 301 373
  Jacob Jr. 281
  Johann Peter 280
  John (Johannes) 279 281 379
  Maria (Saur) 280
  Maria Barbara (d/o Christian): see Brunner 269 280
  Maria Barbara (d/o Jacob): see Turner 281
  Mary (d/o Jacob) 281
  Susanna: see Cuntz 281
  Wendel (Vandel) 281
Story, Richard 121 369
Stouder, Christopher 48
Stöver, Johann Caspar, Sr. 133-134
  Johann Caspar, Jr. 15 17 118 126 133-139 142 169 182 185 194 198 199 202 205 238 262 268 273 274 280 294 295 297 316 324
Stöver's Personal Journal: see under "Church Books"
Strangler, Adam 71
"Strawberry Plains" 50 103
Strawbridge, Robert 102 122
Streiter, Johann Philipp 151 211
"Strife" 155 171 173 258 259 263 362 367
Strifler, Valentine 378
Stringer, Dr. Samuel 99
Strob, Martin: see Shoup 165
Strode, John. 345
Stryker-Rodda, Kenn 120 135
Stull (Stall, Stoll), Adam 33 53 112 139 140 150 155 170 171 218 364 373
  Adam, Jr. 171
  Barbara 170-171
  Catharina (Matthias) 205-207
  Catharina: see Swearingham 171
  Catharine: see Devilbiss 171
  Christoph 170-171, 178-179
  Daniel 171
  Elisabeth (d/o Adam) 171
  Elizabeth (d/o John): see Johnson 171
  Isaac 171
  Jacob 171, 195
  John (Antietam Miller) 51 55-57 155 171 369 371
  John (s/o Adam) 171
  John, Jr. (s/o John) 171
  Margaret 171
  Martha w/o John 171
  Mary: see Greathouse 171
  Peter 171 380
  Philippina (Staley): see Getzendanner 167 170-171 178-179
  Ross 195
  Susanna 171

Stulls Ford 46 51 52 54 237 318 325 326 328 342
Stulls Road 246
Stumpf, Michael 378
Stup Road 283
Sturm (see also Storm):
  Anna Barbara (Gah) 280
  Anna Benedictina (Saur) 280
  Christian 280
  Georg 273 280
  [Johann] Jacob 140 269 273 280 298
  Maria Barbara: see Brunner 269 280
"Sugar Loaf" 89-91 363 367
Sugar Loaf Mountain 9-11 30 39 89 90 92 231 234
Sugar Loaf Area Settlement 58 89-93 99
Sugarland 339
Summer, John 378
Summit Point, W. Va. 344
"Sun is Down and Moon is Up" 76
Sundays Lane 169
Sunfrank, Jacob 378
"Supply" 235
Surhuisterveen, Holl. 271
Surveying Inexactitudes 83
Surveyor General 2 27
Surveyors 247 261 267 332
Surveys 16 25 33 35 36 53 308 321-323 333 356 361-367
  Major 23-24 34
Susquehanna Area 17 18 41 196 225 332 347
  River and Valley 12 16-18 35 42 131 134 135 156 168 185 186 190 191 194 224 324-326
"Susquehanna (New Connaught) Manor" 302
Süssmann, Engelhard 191
Swan, Robert 323
Swaningham, Van: see Swearingen 369
Swatara, Lebanon Co., Pa. 147 182 317 377
Swearingen, Anna (Wickham) 343
  Samuel 343
  Swearingen, Van 181 369 371
Swearingham, Catharina (Stull) 171
Sweden 143
Swedish Lutherans 142 143
  Settlers 152
"Sweeds Folly" 60 61 63 64 273 362 367
Sweinhart: see Schweinhart, Swinehart
Swift, Flower 108 152 369 371
Swinehart: see also Schweinhart
  Anna Margaretha 157 158
  Anna Maria 158
  Elisabetha: see Mayhew 158
  Esther (Neff) 158
  Gabriel 113 146 157 158
  Johann Georg 53 72 122 140 154-158 160-161 217 284 365 366 371
  Johann Peter 154 161
  Magdalena 154 204
  Susanna 158
"Swingaback" 136 138 155 363 367
Swiss settlers 9 148 165 175
Switzerland 9 10 33 149 155 297
"Switzerland" 155 176 178 363 367
Symmer, Alexander 44

435

Tablepence, Michael: see Devilbiss 169 318
Taffelmeyer, Johannes 139 146 187 202 204 286 373
Talbert, Anna (Plummer) 235
 Joseph 235
 Paul 370
Talbot Branch 100 103 105
Tamas, Valentint: see Thomas, Valentine 41 283
Taneytown 43 52
Tankerville, Earl of 37
Tanner, Christian Getson: see Getzendanner 166 281
Tanner, David 241
 Jacob 241, 242
Tanneyhill, Mary 84
 William 56
Tappert, Theodore G. 138 143
Tasker, Anne (Bladen) 32
 Anne: see Ogle 32 328
 Benjamin 32-35 **37** 38 95 96 217 257 258 264 291 295 303 305 366 367
 Elizabeth: see Lowndes 32
 Rebecca: see Dulany 32 33 37
"Taskers Chance" 24 37 45 58 78 106 113 116 120 127 141 149 153 155 156 159 161 173-174 183-184 186 188 189 193 205 217-218 220 221 257-301 308 311 362 367
 Purchasers (1737) 274 276 280 284 289 291 295
 Taxables, Monocacy Hundred (1733) 84 94 96 108 109 122 123 187 222 225 230 237 245 273 368-369
Taxer, Mathias 380
Taylor, Garet 380
 Philip 371
 Thomas 160 226
 William 380
"Taylors Bodkin" 203, 212
"Taylors Lot" 186 192 212 362 367
"Taylors Needle" 212
"Taylors Piglison" 186 212 363 367
"Taylors Shears" 20 212
Taylorsville 102 319
Teal, Philip 380
 Samuel 380
"Teernoch" 111
Tegan, Peter 378
Teley's Cabin 66
Templeman, Edward: see Joh. Conrad
 Johann Conrad 132 140 141 166 170 180 266 280
Temporary Line (Maryland/Penna. boundary) 21 42 286 312
Tenants 2 36 128
Tennessee 105
Tepper, Michael 276
"Term Stool" 56 354
Terpenning, E. G. 250
Terrel, John 379
Terrich, Anthony 283
 --?-- (Thomas) 283
Testill, Joshua 129
TeterLany, Jno: see Lehnich, Dieter 274 350
Teufersbiss, Teuffelsbiss: see Devilbiss

Teufersbiss (cont'd.)
 Anna Barbara 188 317 374 375
 Barbara 161 317 375
 Catharina Barbara 317 375
 Eliesabetha Barbara 317 375
Thalleischweiler, Ger. 136 189
Thatcher, James 75
 Mary 75
"The Barrens" 300
The Hague, Netherlands 150 270
"The Mountain" 255
Theis, Anna Christina: see Six 218
Theological Seminary, Gettysburg 139
"Third Addition to the Res. of Fountain Low" 48 49
"This or None" 313
"Thistle of Glasgow," ship 133 159 282
Thomas Family, English 283
Thomas Family, German 269 282-283
Thomas, Anna Barbara: see Stoner 291
 Anna Maria 135
 Anna Veronica (Thomas) 282
 Barbara: see Stoner 283
 C. A. 123
 Catharina (Brunner) 273
 Catharina Elisabetha: see Brunner 271 282 291
 Catharina (Getzendanner) 167
 Christian (d 1708) 282
 Christian 159 258-261 279 281-283 288 290 292-293 371 372
 Christian, Jr. 283
 Christopher 282 379
 Evan 84 87
 Evan, Jr. 87
 Gabriel 40 41 151 226 283
 George 135
 George Leicester 283
 Hans Michael, Jr. 282
 Henry 283 293
 Jacob 273
 Johann Valentin (Valentine) 40 41 282 283
 Johannes (John) 40 41 167 282
 Lewis Michael 283
 Mary 283
 Michael 151 270 282
 Mrs. 226
 Nathaniel 87
 Notley 56 60 62 63 66 67 111 112 365
 Philip, Chief Justice 251
 Philip, Dr. 287-288
 Philipp Henrich 282
 Samuel Skinner 67
 Susanna (Brunner) 273
 Susanna Margaret (Weiss) 283
 William 56 370
"Thomas" 362 367
"Thomas' Profit" 67
Thompson, Ann (Davis) Richardson 83
 Israel 83
Thompson, Jacomyntje (Elting) 74
 John 74
Thorold, George 251
Thrasher Family 349
 Benjamin 34
 Elizabeth (Ancrum) 66

Thrasher (cont'd.)
  Margaret: see Hook 64
  Sarah: see Hook 65
"Three Sisters" 91
Thurmont 39 42 47 152 153 185-186 188
  192 197 200 206 211 212 214 220 248
  249 255 286 299 326 330
Thurmont District 43
Thurston Road 234
"Tick Neck" 347
Tilhance Creek, [W.] Va. 183
Tobacco 4 61 62 306
  Burning 61 62 64 68 74 96 108 118-120
    122 123 129 187 222 230 237 238
    245 274 368-369
Tobias' Branch 246
Todd, Vincent M. 10
Tofler (Tofeler, Tofller), Anna Maria (Storm) 281
  Peter 281-282, 288
Toms, Catherine 177
"Toms Bottom" 224
Toms Creek 30 46 238 239 248 333
Toms Creek Chapel 30
Tories: see Loyalists
Touchstone, Caleb 222 224
  Daniel 222
  Henry 56 62 172 181 222 224
  Richard 28 50 55 56 62 97 130 **222-224**
    334 346 364 369
  Richard, Jr. 62 222 224
  Sarah (Johnson) 222 224
  Stephen 222
Touchstone Road 61 92 172 222 223
Toudith (see also Doudith), Eliesabetha: 238
  John 238 376
Town Branch 100
"Town Tract" 48
Trabbinger, Peter 159
Tracey, Arthur G. 1 138 216 357
  Grace Louise 1 4-6 357
Tracey Records 1 3 5 6 209 357
Traders 13-23 66 181
Trammel, John 276
Trap Branch 300
Traut Family (see also Trout below) 277 294
  Anna Margaretha (Rebstock): see Staley 177
  Anna Maria (Baum) 377
  Catharina: see Funck 177
  John Theobald (Johann Debalt) 177 182
    262 278 374
  Joh. Henrich 144 377
  Maria Apollonia: see Hoffman 278 374
  Maria Apollonia (d/o Theobald) 278 374
  Maria Barbara: see Weiss 262
  Maria Eliesabetha: see Ley 278
Tredane, John 17 45 99 108 125 369
"Trimmling" 223 225 362 367
Trinity Chapel (Reformed), Frederick 193
Trough Syncline, Hardy Co., W. Va. 74
Trout (see also Traut above)
  Anna Maria (d/o Henry) 220
  Anna Maria (Baum) 220 377
  Anna Maria (wid/o Henry) 299 300
  Henry (Joh. Heinrich) 186 **220** 259 260

Trout, Henry (cont'd.)
  292 298 **299** 367 372
  Henry, Jr. 220
  Jacob 299
  Maria Elisabeth: see Ley 278 294
"Trout Pond" 220 291 299
Troxell, Apollonia (Loy) 296
  Frederick 296
  John 241
Truman, Henry 227 370
Trundle, Otho Wilson 61
"Trura" 20 310 325 333 334 339 362 367
Tucker, John 371
  Mary: see Plummer 235
  Nathaniel 371
  William 56 371
"Tuckett" 347
Tulisses Branch, W. Va. 109
Tullis Run, W. Va. 74
Tulpehocken, Pa. 132 133 142 145
Tumer, John 371
Turk, Willie Ann Cary 104
Turkey Creek 248
"Turkey Thicket" 20 341
Turner, Ann: see Covell 233
  Jacob 281
  Maria Barbara (Storm) 281
  Mary 233
  Rachel 233
  Rebecca 233
  Sarah 233
  Solomon 232 233
  William, Sr. 228 229 232 234 367
  William, Jr. 232 233
"Turners Forest" 229 232 233 362 367
Turners Gap 51
"Turners Lot" 233
"Turners Promise" 233
Turnwolf, Frederick 378
Tuscarora Creeks 13 29 46 56 60 67 85 86
  91 94 97 107 155 156 169 180 259 281
  285 287 289-292 295 299 312
Tuscarora Creek, W. Va. 344
Tuscarora Election District 13
Tuscarora Indians 10 12-13
"Two Brothers" (Fletcher) 43 362 367
"Two Brothers" (Lakin) 60 67 363 367
Tyler, Elizabeth: see Pottenger, Samuel 337 339
  Harriet 171
  Mary 337
  Priscilla: see Wickham 337
  Robert 337

Uhler, Anastasius 194
  Catarina Barbara 194
Ulmet, Ger. 284
Ulster County, N.Y. 117 309
Umphart, William: see Humbert 177
"Umpharts Delight" 177
"Uncles Gift" 20
Undietum Creek: see Antietam 55
Ungles, Mary: see Lakin 67
Union Bridge 45 252 335
Union Churches 200 224
  Monocacy? 138 144-145
Unionville 99-100 102 103 105

Unionville Methodist Chapel 102
Unionville-Woodville Road. 231
United Brethren 175 279
United Church of Christ 132
United States Highways:
  I-70: 235
  I-270: 39 56
  #15: 169 249 255 269 277 278 292 295 319
  #40: 21 53 56 84 114 166, 178 232 235 246
  #40-Alt: 166
  #194: 120
  #340: 61 83
Unselt (Unseldt), Abraham 151 183-184
  Georg Friederich 47 151 174 177 182-184 188 220 262-263 277 279 294 295 299 354 373 377
  George Frederick Jr. 182
  Henry 183-184
  Johannes (John) 182 183 377
  Maria Apollonia Hoffman 183 279
Untergimpern, Ger. 172
Updegraf, Detrick 272 291
  Martin 41
Upe, Frederick: see Orr, Ott 286
"Upper End of Long Bottom" 172
Upper German settlement 58 153 185-221
Upper Linganore settlement 58 99-105
Upper Marlboro 44 250
Upper Piscataway Hundred 129
Upper Potomac settlement 58 94-98
Uppsala Consistory 143
Uppsala University 142
Upshur, Abel P. 59
Upton, John 369
Urbana 91
Urbana Pike 235
Urner, Samuel 101
Usselmann (Hasleman, Husleman, Wuselman, Whitselman), Maria Margaretha 267
  Valentine (Veltin) 146 157 267
Utica, Md. 34 298 338
Utley, Richard 152 153

Vagabond Lutheran Preachers 144
Valentine, Anna Margaret (Matthias) 205-207
"Valentine" see "Palentine" 181
van Basten, Johann Hermann
van Dyne, Claude Loy 294
van Meeteren, Joost Jansen 69
  Sarah (Dubois) 69
van Metre Family 334
  Abraham 72 74 109 345
  Alice 73
  Annah 74
  Catherine 74
  Elisabeth: see Shepherd 73 74
  Garet 74
  Hellita 74
  Henry 72 73
  Isaac 69-71 73 74 290 365 369
  Isaac (s/o John) 72
  Jacob 72 73
  Jacob (s/o Isaac) 74

van Metre (cont'd.)
  Johanna: see Burns 72
  John 15 31 **69** 70 71 74 79 108 109 162 257 366
  John, Jr. 72 73 257 366
  John (III) 72 73 263 341
  Magdalena 72
  Mary (d/o Isaac): see Hite 74
  Mary (d/o John): see Jones 72 74
  Rachel: see Lafarge 72 74
  Rebecca (sist. of John): see Elting 74
  Rebecca (d/o Isaac): see Hite 74
  Rebecca (d/o John): see Hedges 72 73 108
  Ruth (Hedges) 74
  Sarah (d/o John): see Davis 72 74
  Sarah (d/o Isaac): see Hickman 74
Vandever, John 369, 371
van Rijpen, Thomas 135
van Swearingen, Anne: see Bladen 32
Varlé, Charles 59 91
Veach, John 369
Veast, Jacob 380
Veatch, James 371
  John 371
  Nathan 371
Verdriess (Verdress, Verdris):
  Catarina (d/o Jacob) 198 215 376
  Catharina (Eyler; w/o Jacob) 215
  Dorothea (Buch) 216
  Jacob 215 376
  Johann Friedrich 139 146 202 216 286 290 376
  Johann Friedrich, Jr. 216
  Johann Jacob (s/o Friedrich) 216
  Johann Jacob (s/o Jacob) 216
  John (Sr.) 53 146 198 216 286 290 365 372 377
  John, Jr. 186-187 193 **215**-217
  Johannes (s/o Jacob) 198 215 376
  Johannes (s/o Valentin) 216
  John Valentin (Felte) 139 146 215 216 376
  Maria Catrina 216
  Maria Magdalena 216
Vermillion, William 22
Vernoy, Cornelius 369
Vertriess, Catharina (Bender) 216
  Hardman 33 53 186 **216**-217 364 373
Vieruhr: see also Firor
  Anna Barbara 377
  Leonard 211-212
  Maria Barbara (Willheut): see Weller 191 211-212
Vines, Mordecai 369
Virginia 9-11 15 16 21 23 38 44 50 53 54 64 69 71-75 82 86 87 108 109 131 134 141 142 144 188 205 213 243 255 296 310 324 345
Virginia-Kentucky Resolutions 310
"Virgins Delight" 19
Voble, Joseph 370
Vogler, Johannes 146
Von Mülinen, Christoph 10
Vorsteher (German Church Elders) 114 144 150
Vulgamot, Joseph 195

Wachenheim, Ger. 41
Wade, Elizabeth (Sprigg) 226
　Robert 226 370
Waggoner, Elizabeth: see Bonnett 215
Waldangelloch, Ger. 208
Wales 81 87 346
Walker, John 369
Walkersville 34 52 54 116 309 312 314 315
　319 350
Walldorf, Ger. 41 291
Waller, Robert 232
Walling, Ann (Mayhew) 159
　Delashmutt 379
　Elisha 369
　James 369
　William 369
Walliseellen, Switz. 298
Walloons 147
"Walnut Bottom" 103
Walter (Wolter), Johann Henrich 276
　Jacob 380
　John, Jr. 237
Wamar, Bernhard: see Weymer 190
Wappotomack River 15
Warburton Manor 41
Ward, Elizabeth: see Hook 66
　John 371
　Julia: see Elder
　Sarah: see Plummer 235
　William 371
Wardens, Frederick Lutheran Church 295
Wardrop, James 19 20 44 90 92 244 245
　366 367
　Lettice 44
Warfield, Ann (Delashmutt) 61
　Joshua, Dr. 288
　Melchior: see Werfel 260, 288
Waring, Basil 370
　James 370
　Thomas 370
Warner, Nicholas 335
Warrants 2 16 25 41 322
　Common 14 19
　Special 14 65 177
Warringanf..., Benjamin 371
Warthen, Mrs. 237
Warwick, Pa. 149 159 215-216 294 316 374
Washington, Augustine 20 44 62
　George 20 22 30 33 37 63 73 108 119
　278
　Lawrence 20 44
Washington County, Md. 5 7 14 15 18-20
　38 54 55 94 97 111 147 149 171 189
　222 223 226 246 286 293 298 302 311
　324 329 331 334 342 347
Washington, D.C. 5 9 22 59 250 252 349
Washington's Road 21
Waters, Lucy: see Nelson 62
"Water Land" 155 174 258 259 274
Waterford, Va. 235
Wats, John 371
"Watsons Welfare" 19 20 347
Watten, Belgium 251
Watts, William 371
Waugh, William 378
Waymar (Waymour): see Weymer
Weaver, George 371

Webb, John 241
Weber, Barbara: see Reisman 172
Wehaun, Henry 378
Weimar (Weimer, Weinmar), Joh. Bernard:
　see Weymer
Weinheim, Ger. 132
Weinigen, Switzerland 288
Weis, Frederick Lewis 153 346
Weiser, Frederick S. 135 158 159 377
Weiss (Wise), Abraham 262 263 380
　Anna Barbara (w/o Frantz) 262 263
　Anna Margaretha (Kessler) 262
　Catharina 263
　Daniel 380
　David 262
　Elizabeth 263
　Frantz (Francis) 73 77 173-174 182-183
　　220 257-263 273 277-279 283 285 292
　　294 295 299 301 371 372 374 376
　George 379
　George Michael 132 133 149
　Henry 267 378
　Jacob of Mühlhofen 262
　Johann Georg 262 375
　Johann Jacob 260 262 263 374
　Johannes 262 376
　Margaretha (d/o Abraham) 263
　Mary 263
　Johann Peter 379
　Peter 262 263 380
　Susanna Margaret: see Thomas 283
　Valentine 380
"Welchs Tract" 81 90 362 367
"Well Watered Bottom" 120 229 362 367
Weller (Wöller), Anna Barbara: see Maria
　Barbara 377
　Anna Margaret (Koehn) 211
　Catharine (Ambrose) 202
　Elisa Juliyana 197, 213
　Elisabeth (Krieger) 214
　Hans Georg 210
　Joh. Jacob 53 147 148 151 152 170 183
　　186-189 191-192 197 200 206 210-214
　　315 329 335 367 372 376 377
　Joh. Jacob, Jr. 212 376
　Johannes (John) 170 202 204 210 213
　Johannes, Jr. 213
　Maria Barbara (Willheut) Vieruhr 211-212
　　214 377
　Mary Magdalena 213
Wells, Duckett 67
　Isaac 56 62 85 86 370 371
　Joseph 79 80 85 86 364 371
　Margaret 79 85
　Martha: see Ancrum 66
　Rachel: see Wright 79
　Samuel 86
　Sarah (Lakin) 67
"Wells Invention" 86
Welsh Run, Pa. 344
Wenerod, Caspar 151
Wenschoff, Dr. Edward 237
Wentz, Abdel Ross 134 135 137 138 146
　205
　Maria Elisabetha: see Wervel 288
Werfel (Warfield, Wherfield, Wheyfield):
　Catharina (d/o Melchior) 289

Werfel (cont'd.)
　Katharine (w/o Melchior) 289
　Johann Melchior 204 259 **288** 292 298
　　373
　Hans Michael 187
Wertheimer, Philip 166
Wervel (Würffel), Elizabeth 288
　Hans Jerick (George) 288
　Hans Leonhard 205 288
　Leonard, Jr. 288
　Maria Elisabetha "Lydia" (Wentz) 288
Wesley, John 102
West, John 96 349 369
　John, Jr. 37
　Thomas 96 369
West Indies, Expedition against the Spanish 190 268
"West St. Mary's Manor" 302
West Virginia Panhandle 111 332
Westchester County, N. Y. 75
Western Branch Hundred 129
Western Creek 250
Western Shore 4 302
Westerwald region, Ger. 313
"Westfailure" 81
Westminster, Md. 33 50
Westmoreland County, Va. 96
"Wett Work" 24 39 362 367
Wetzel, Anna Ursula (Georg) 207
　Catharina 207, 209
　Elizabeth (Bonnett) 215
　Elizabeth (Cromerston) 209
　Elizabeth (Bonnett) 209
　Georg Michael 209
　Hans Martin 33 53 62 146 168 186
　　191-192 195 197 207-210 212 214 292
　　364 366 367 372 376 378
　Hans Martin, Jr. 146 207 209 215
　Henry 209
　Johann Friedrich 209
　Johann Jacob 207 209
　Johann Martin 207
　John 209 215
　Magdalena Elisabetha 209
　Maria Barbara 192 207 376
　Maria Catharina 209
　Mary (Bonnett) 209 215
　Nicolaus 146 207 209
　Susanna: see Oberkirsch, Andrae 207
Weverton 37 94
Weymer (Wamar, Waymar, Weimar, Weimer, Weinmar, Weymar, Weymore, Weymour):
　Anna Maria (Wismar/Weimar): see Willheut 146 212
　Barbara 191 192
　Joh. Bernard (Barnett, Bernhardt) 53 62
　　77 168 172 185-187 190 191-192 199
　　208 209 212 364 367 372 376
　Joh. Bernard, Jr. 192 376
　Johannes 191
　Catherine (Creager) 192
Weyne, Isaac 116
Wharton, Elizabeth Sewall: see Digges 41
"What You Will" 258 259 272-273
Wheat, William 371
Wheeler, Ann: see Elder 253

Wheeler (cont'd.)
　Leonard 370
Wheeling, W. Va 310
Whelan, Richard 256
Whelpley, Charles 379
Wherfield, Wheyfield: see Werfel
"Whiskey" (Hedges 107 110 111
"Whiskey" (Stull) 56
"Whiskey Alley" 224
Whiskey Rebellion 310
Whitaker (Whiteacre, Whitecar), Abigail (Johnson) 245
　Mark 245 246 364 371
　Mary 245 277
　Thomas 43 245 277 367 369 371
White, Capt. 21
　Francis: see Weiss, Frantz
　Henry 19
　Thomas 332
Whitehaven, Engl. 168
Whitemarsh, Pa. 132
Whitesell: see Wetzel 209-210
Whitmall, Robert 380
Whitman, Frederick 379
Whitmore, George A. 47
　John 241 378
Whitnall, Robert 322
Whitsall: see Wetzel
Wicacoa, Pa. 143
Wickham, Ann (Farrell) 343
　Anna: see Swearingen 343
　Elizabeth 343
　Henry 342 343
　John (s/o Nath. Jr.) 323 342 343
　John (s/o Nath. III) 343
　Joseph 343
　Martha 343
　Nathaniel, Sr. 337
　Nathaniel, Jr. 21 48 49 76 248 254 287
　　307 312 313 323 325 327 328 333
　　337-343 349 354 364 366 370
　Nathaniel III 342 343
　Nathaniel IV 343
　Priscilla (Tyler) 337, 339, 343
　Priscilla (d/o Nath. Jr.) 343
　Priscilla (d/o Robt.) 340 342 343
　Robert (s/o Nath. Jr.) 340, 343
　Robert (s/o Nath. III) 343
　Sabina Barnard 337
　Samuel 323 342 343
　Sarah (Wood) 343
　Sarah (d/o Nath. III) 343
"Wickhams and Pottengers Discovery" 339
"Wickhams Discovery" 343
"Wicomico Manor" 302
"Widows Design" 347
"Widows Lot" 104
"Widows Rest" 85
Widrick, Martin 379
Wiegel, Charles H. 263
Wiesbaden, Ger. 218
Wieser, Ger. 269
"Wilbersign" 173
Wilburn, William" 354
Wilcoxon (Wilcoxson), John, Sr. 369-371
　John, Jr. 370 371
　Thomas **40** 94 95 364 371

Wilcoxon (cont'd.)
  William 371
Wilkins, William **14**
Wilkinson, Minor 369
Will, Michael 350
Willard, A. 99
Willer: see Weller
Willheut (Willhaut, Willhide, Woolyard, Wulheit):
  Anna Magdalena: see Frey 212
  Anna Maria (Weymar) 146 212
  Friederich 146 192 211 290
  Friederich (Jr.) 146 212
  Maria Barbara: see Firor/Vieruhr, Weller 191 211 212
  Maria Eliesabetha: see Koger 211
William II, King of England 348
"William and Elizabeth" 91 363 367
Williams, Benjamin 371
  Edward 56
  Eleanor 101
  Esther 101
  Eunice: see Carmack 105
  George 84 371
  Giles 371
  Henry 101
  Jane: see Chambers 346
  Jean 101
  John 99 101 364 365 370
  John H. 101
  Joseph 369
  Margaret 101
  Martha 101
  Province 369
  Mary (d/o John) 101
  Mary (w/o John) 101
  Prudence (Beals) 84
  Richard 84
  Ruhamah: see Chapline 345, 347
  Sarah: see Price 346
  Thomas, Sr. 56 101 370
  Thomas, Jr. 370
  Thomas John Chew 101 102
  William, Sr., planter 44 365 371
  William, Rev. 319 338 344-346 367
"Williams Intention" 43 100 101 363 367
"Williams Project" 329 332 334 338 345-347 362 367
Williamsport 53
Williar, Elisabetha Magdalena (Schlim) 214
  Peter 214
Willis Derr Road 166 174
Wills, First Frederick County 45
Willson, John 369
  Robert 369
Wilmington, Del. 109
Wilson, Absolam 43 226
  Cumberland 37
  Elizabeth (w/o Robert) 237
  Elizabeth (Wood) 313
  James 370
  John 109 313 322 355 370
  Joseph 379
  Josiah 43 **226**
  Mary: see Biggs 311
  Mary (Hedges) 109

Wilson (cont'd.)
  P. L. 120
  Priscilla: see Biggs 43 311
  Robert 54 237 238 255 325 326 339 367
  Thomas 28 43 243-246 313 322 333 364 367
  Thomas, Jr. 371
  Thomas, R.C.
  William 304 307 311 313 316 322 380
"Wilsons Fancy" 237 238 363 367
"Wilsons Round About" 237
Winchester, Va. 53 113
Windred, Casper 292
Windsor, John 371
"Wine Garden" 33 186 208 214 363 367
Wink: see Wirk
Winrod, Jacob 380
Winslow, Benjamin 55
Winter, Anna Maria (Klemm) 157
  Catharina: see Klemm 157
  George 157
  Jacob 241
Winters, Sarah: see Ogle 324
Winterthur, Switzerland 290
Wirk, Isabella: see Hedges 111
Wirtz, Jacob 61
Wisconsin State Historical Society 310
Wise (see also Weiss), Abraham 380
  Daniel 380
  Francis 73 77 260 262 263 285 292 295 299
  George 379
  Henry 267 378
  Johann Jacob 260 262 263
  John Peter 379
  Peter 380
  Valentine 380
Wisecup, Valentine 322
Wisell, Martin: see Wetzel 209 292
Wismar, Anna Maria: see Weymer
Wittwer, Norman C. 130 182
Wofford, John 371
"Wolcote Manor" 302
Wolf, John Augustus 182
Wolfe, Mary: see Carmack 105
  Paul 105 380
  Sarah C: see Carmack 105
Wolfersheim kr. St. Ingbert, Ger. 263
"Wolfs Home" 181
"Wolfs Lot" 20
"Wolfs Purchase" 20
Wolfsville 236
Wolter (see also Walter), Johann Henrich 276
Wood, Abraham 312
  Catherine (d/o Joseph of Israel Ck.) 312
  Catherine (Hedges) Julien 109 113 312
  Charles 103
  Elizabeth: see Wilson 313
  John 312, 332
  Joseph of Israel Creek 54 103 109 110 238 285 304 307 308 311-312 323 328 341 343 347
  Joseph, Jr. (s/o above) 312 313 320 343
  Joseph of Linganore 103 233 312
  Joseph, Capt. (1749) 21
  Lucy: see James 233

Wood (cont'd.)
  Martha (Ogle) 332
  Mary 312
  Nathaniel 56
  Rachel 312
  Rebecca 312
  Robert 311-313, 323
  Ruth 312
  Sarah (d/o Joseph): see Wickham 343
  Sarah (w/o Joseph) 312
  William 88
Woodapple, Frederick 33 364
"Wooden Platter" 19 44 244 245 363 367
"Woods Chance" 313
"Woods Farm" 307, 312
"Woods Lot" 103 312
"Woods Mill Land" 313
"Woods Town Lot" 343
Woodsboro 34 43 54 104 120 303 311-314 342
Woodsboro District 306
Woodsboro Pike 309, 315
Woodstock College 253
"Woodstown Land" 313
Woodville District 103 231
"Woolsey Manor" 302
Woolyard (Willheit), Frederick 192
"Worleys Choice" 206
Worman, Andrew 105
  Moses 288
Worman Mill 285 288
Worms, Ger. 132
"Worst of All" 313
Wortenbaker, Adam 378
Wren, Burnet 267
Wrench, Robert 241
Wright, Ann 79
  Boyater 79
  Charity 79
  Eleanor (Sprigg) 226
  Elizabeth: see Matthews 79
  Hannah: see Ballenger 79 81
  Henry 226
  James 28 79 82 85 87 369
  James, Jr. 79
  John 62 79 196 370
  John, Jr. 79
  John, J.P. (Pa.) 17
  Joseph 79 125
  Lucy 79
  Lydia 79
  Margaret 79
  Martha: see Mendenhall 79
  Mary (d/o James) 79
  Mary (d/o John) 79

Wright (cont'd.), Mary (w/o Joseph) 79
  Micajah 79
  Oliver 79
  Rachel (Wells) 79
  Rachel (d/o John) 79
  Ralph 79
  Sarah 79
  Susanna 79
  William 79
Wrights Ferry, Pa. 326
Wrightsville, Pa. 15 224 325
Wroth, Lawrence C. 17
Wulheit, Friedrich: see Willheut 290
Würffel: see Werfel, Wervel
Wust, Klaus 71 130
Wychel, Adam 378
  Bastian 378
Wyckoff, B. V. D. 122

Yellow Springs 107 110 111 170 178 281
Yellow Springs Road 156 179-180 295
Yeoman 154
York, Pa. 149 325
York County, Pa. 41 50 52 88 136 189 193 197-198 311
York Lutheran Congregation 145 151
York Reformed Congregation 148
Yorkshire, Eng. 37
Yorktown, Va. 63
Yost, George 323
Young, David 350
  Eleanor (Beatty) 119
  Eleanor: see Hilleary 91
  Henry James 191 210
  Jacob 119 267
  John 200 232 250
  Ludwig 378
Youngblood, John 195
  Peter 194
Youtchey, Peter 379
Yverdon, Switz. 9

Zacharias, George 138
"Zachiah Manor" 302
Zahm, John Michael 152
Zerich (Zerrick; see also Terrich):
  Anthony 283 378
Zimmerman, George 189
  Solomon Joseph 167
Zinzendorf, Nicholas Ludwig 141 142 148
Zirkel, Anna Maria: see Fout, Jacob) 162
  Hans Heinrich 162
"Zura" 299
Zürich, Switz. 175 288 298
Zweibrücken, Ger. 191 263

www.ingramcontent.com/pod-product-compliance
Lightning Source LLC
Chambersburg PA
CBHW071224290426
44108CB00013B/1281